Mergers and Corporate Governance

Business Economics

Series Editor: Scott E. Masten

Professor of Business Economics and Public Policy
University of Michigan, USA

1. Mergers and Corporate Governance
   J. Harold Mulherin

Future titles will include:

Antitrust and Competition Policy
Andrew N. Kleit

Retailing, Distribution and Franchising
Francine Lafontaine

Wherever possible, the articles in these volumes have been reproduced as originally published using facsimile reproduction, inclusive of footnotes and pagination to facilitate ease of reference.

For a list of all Edward Elgar published titles visit our site on the World Wide Web at
www.e-elgar.com

Mergers and Corporate Governance

Edited by

J. Harold Mulherin

Don and Lorraine Freeberg Professor of Economics and Finance
Claremont McKenna College, USA

BUSINESS ECONOMICS

An Elgar Reference Collection
Cheltenham, UK • Northampton, MA, USA

Published by
Edward Elgar Publishing Limited
Glensanda House
Montpellier Parade
Cheltenham
Glos GL50 1UA
UK

Edward Elgar Publishing, Inc.
136 West Street
Suite 202
Northampton
Massachusetts 01060
USA

A catalogue record for this book
is available from the British Library

ISBN 1 84376 421 0

Printed and bound in Great Britain by MPG Books Ltd, Bodmin, Cornwall

Contents

Acknowledgements

The editor and publishers wish to thank the authors and the following publishers who have kindly given permission for the use of copyright material.

American Economic Association for article: Gregor Andrade, Mark Mitchell and Erik Stafford (2001), 'New Evidence and Perspectives on Mergers', *Journal of Economic Perspectives*, **15** (2), Spring, 103–20.

Blackwell Publishing Ltd for articles: Vojislav Maksimovic and Gordon Phillips (2001), 'The Market for Corporate Assets: Who Engages in Mergers and Asset Sales and Are There Efficiency Gains?', *Journal of Finance*, **LVI** (6), December, 2019–65; John R. Graham, Michael L. Lemmon and Jack G. Wolf (2002), 'Does Corporate Diversification Destroy Value?', *Journal of Finance*, **LVII** (2), April, 695–720.

Elsevier for articles: Kenneth Lehn, Jeffry Netter and Annette Poulsen (1990), 'Consolidating Corporate Control: Dual-class Recapitalizations versus Leveraged Buyouts', *Journal of Financial Economics*, **27**, 557–80; Gerald T. Garvey and Peter L. Swan (1994), 'The Economics of Corporate Governance: Beyond the Marshallian Firm', *Journal of Corporate Finance*, **1**, 139–74; Robert Comment and G. William Schwert (1995), 'Poison or Placebo? Evidence on the Deterrence and Wealth Effects of Modern Antitakeover Measures', *Journal of Financial Economics*, **39**, 3–43; Mark L. Mitchell and J. Harold Mulherin (1996), 'The Impact of Industry Shocks on Takeover and Restructuring Activity', *Journal of Financial Economics*, **41**, June, 193–229; J. Harold Mulherin and Annette B. Poulsen (1998), 'Proxy Contests and Corporate Change: Implications for Shareholder Wealth', *Journal of Financial Economics*, **47**, March, 279–313; Stacey R. Kole and Kenneth M. Lehn (1999), 'Deregulation and the Adaptation of Governance Structure: The Case of the U.S. Airline Industry', *Journal of Financial Economics*, **52**, April, 79–117; J. Harold Mulherin and Audra L. Boone (2000), 'Comparing Acquisitions and Divestitures', *Journal of Corporate Finance*, **6**, July, 117–39; David A. Becher (2000), 'The Valuation Effects of Bank Mergers', *Journal of Corporate Finance*, **6**, July, 189–214; Joseph P.H. Fan (2000), 'Price Uncertainty and Vertical Integration: An Examination of Petrochemical Firms', *Journal of Corporate Finance*, **6**, December, 345–76.

Oxford University Press for articles: Sandra Betton and B. Espen Eckbo (2000), 'Toeholds, Bid Jumps, and Expected Payoffs in Takeovers', *Review of Financial Studies*, **13** (4), Winter, 841–82; Robert G. Hansen (2001), 'Auctions of Companies', *Economic Inquiry*, **39** (1), January, 30–43.

University of Chicago Press for articles: Richard Roll (1986), 'The Hubris Hypothesis of Corporate Takeovers', *Journal of Business*, **59** (2, Part 1), April, 197–216; Mark L. Mitchell and Kenneth Lehn (1990), 'Do Bad Bidders Become Good Targets?', *Journal of Political Economy*, **98** (2), April, 372–98.

Every effort has been made to trace all the copyright holders but if any have been inadvertently overlooked the publishers will be pleased to make the necessary arrangement at the first opportunity.

In addition the publishers wish to thank the Library of the University of Warwick and the Library of Indiana University at Bloomington, USA for their assistance in obtaining these articles.

Introduction

J. Harold Mulherin

The corporation is a complex organizational form that is used to produce and distribute goods and services throughout the world. Academic research has long studied the governance of the corporate entity, the decision-making of the executives running the corporations, and the growth and strategic change that are accomplished via mergers, divestitures and other forms of corporate restructuring. See Alchian (1965) for an early survey and critique.

The conceptual work that underpins the research on mergers and corporate governance spans fields such as corporate finance, industrial organization, and the theory of the firm. As summarized by Williamson (1988), much of the underlying framework comes from agency theory and transaction cost economics. This work includes Alchian and Demsetz (1972), Coase (1937), Jensen and Meckling (1976), and Klein, Crawford and Alchian (1978). These papers and other relevant theory have been included in volumes of collected readings such as Keasey, Thompson, and Wright (1999).

The papers selected for this volume emphasize recent empirical research on mergers and corporate governance. Many of the papers were chosen for their provocative questions. Mitchell and Lehn (Chapter 5) ask, do bad bidders become good targets? Roll (Chapter 6) conjectures that mergers simply stem from managerial hubris. Graham, Lemmon and Wolf (Chapter 11) ask, does corporate diversification destroy wealth?

The papers in the volume illustrate the different research methods and measures that have been used to analyze mergers and corporate governance. Reflecting the work in the field, many of the selected papers such as Comment and Schwert (Chapter 14) and Betton and Eckbo (Chapter 7) perform event studies and other large sample analysis on stock prices. The events considered range from acquisitions and divestitures, for example, Mulherin and Boone (Chapter 9), to proxy contests as in Mulherin and Poulsen (Chapter 15). As a complement to the stock price analysis, Maksimovic and Phillips (Chapter 10) address the effect of corporate restructuring on productivity and Andrade, Mitchell and Stafford (Chapter 3) more broadly consider the consistency of the various evidence on the effects of merger activity.

While large sample studies enhance confidence in the generality of results, analysis at the industry level is often a useful vehicle to isolate a particular issue related to mergers and corporate governance. Hence, several of the papers in the volume are industry studies. Fan's (Chapter 2) study of the petrochemical industry exploits the influence of OPEC on organizational structure. Becher (Chapter 4) analyzes the effect of deregulation and mergers on firm value in the banking industry. Kole and Lehn (Chapter 16) gain important insights on the dynamics of corporate governance by studying the effects of deregulation in the airline industry.

The papers in the volume also provide guidance for future work. Mitchell and Mulherin's (Chapter 1) analysis of the causes of merger activity in the 1980s suggests a framework to study the impact of industry shocks in prior and future merger waves. Hansen (Chapter 8) models how to apply auction theory to the institutional setting of the sale of all or part of a corporation. Lehn, Netter and Poulsen (Chapter 12) develop techniques for empirically modeling the determinants of the choices made in corporate restructuring. Garvey and Swan (Chapter 13) offer direction for future work on corporate governance.

The volume is arranged around a series of related questions. These include: Why do firms engage in mergers? How are any gains in mergers distributed between bidders and targets? What are the causes and effects of corporate restructuring activity? Such questions frame the design of the extant research. Structuring the analysis of mergers and corporate governance in the form of questions also indicates that there is still much to be learned from ongoing and future research.

A common theme of the papers in the volume is their direct applicability to important policy issues. For example, a central question addressed by the papers in Part IV is, what is corporate governance and does it matter? The research addressing this query is clearly relevant to both internal corporate policies and external government enactments on matters such as the independence of boards of directors and the compensation of corporate executives.

This Introduction summarizes the findings of the specific papers included in the volume. It also positions each paper within the broader literature and suggests avenues for future research on mergers and corporate governance. The discussion is arranged around the four sections of the volume: the causes and effects of merger activity, takeover bidding, corporate restructuring, and corporate governance.

Part I The Causes and Effects of Merger Activity

The Causes of Merger Activity

A fundamental question addressed in the academic research on mergers and corporate governance is, why do mergers occur? Broad economic factors such as technological change, deregulation and input costs are one possible avenue to consider in addressing this query. This line of inquiry is taken by two of the papers in this volume, Mitchell and Mulherin (Chapter 1) and Fan (Chapter 2). Mitchell and Mulherin examine the factors associated with the industry clustering of merger activity during the 1980s. Fan analyzes the cross-sectional and dynamic changes in vertical integration in the petrochemical industry in the time span before, during and after the OPEC oil embargo.

The hypothesis that broad economic forces are the source of merger activity can be traced to Coase's (1937) seminal work on the nature of the firm. Coase argued that technological change such as inventions in communications would tend to lessen the costs of internal production within a firm and would induce an expansion of firm size. By implication, such technological change will often be associated with mergers.

More recently, Jensen (1993) has elaborated on the link between broad economic forces and merger activity. He argued that technological change affects optimal capacity both for an industry and for a representative firm and thereby induces restructuring at the industry level. Jensen also posited that deregulation will have related effects on optimal firm size and will thereby be associated with merger activity. Finally, he highlighted changing input costs as a further inducement to merger activity. He pointed to the OPEC oil embargo of 1973 as an important impetus for subsequent merger activity in the 1980s.

There is a variety of evidence with which to test whether merger activity is indeed related to broad economic forces. The first piece of evidence is that merger activity tends to cluster in time. For example, Weston, Mitchell and Mulherin (2004) discussed five distinct merger waves in the United States in the 1890/1900s, the 1920s, the 1960s, the 1980s, and the 1990s. Golbe and White (1988) reported that the occurrence of merger waves is associated with booms in the stock market, confirming that mergers are pro-cyclical. Jovanovic and Rousseau (2002) found that merger waves are preceded by a rise in the dispersion of Tobin's Q, defined as the ratio of market value to replacement cost.

Another piece of evidence is that merger activity within a given period of time tends to cluster in particular industries. Studying 25 industries in the 1919 to 1930 time period, for example, Eis (1969) found that five industries account for 67.5 per cent of merger activity. Similar evidence of industry clustering of merger activity was found by Gort (1969) for the 1950s, Mitchell and Mulherin (1996) for the 1980s, Mulherin and Boone (2000) for the 1990s, and Andrade and Stafford (2003) for the 1970 to 1994 period.

Mitchell and Mulherin (Chapter 1) provide an in-depth treatment of the clustering of merger activity at the industry level. Using a sample of 1064 firms in 51 industries between 1982 and 1989, they find that half of the firms in the sample were the targets of a takeover attempt during the 1980s, consistent with the depiction of the 1980s as a period experiencing a merger wave. But they also find significant inter-industry differences in the rate of takeover activity. For example, nearly 70 per cent of the firms in the petroleum, broadcasting, and air transport industries experienced takeover activity, while only 30 per cent of the firms in the metal fabricating, paper, and electronics industries experienced takeover activity. Hence, the merger wave of the 1980s had differential effects across the many sectors of the economy.

To grasp the sources of these differential effects, Mitchell and Mulherin's cross-sectional analysis looks at the industry-level factors that are associated with the clustering of merger activity during the 1980s. Their findings that deregulation and energy dependence are important determinants of merger activity are consistent with Jensen's (1993) depiction of the causes of restructuring activity.

As a complement to the multi-industry analysis of restructuring activity, Fan (2000), reprinted here as Chapter 2, studies the petrochemical industry to more deeply understand the effect of broad economic forces on the decision to merge and on the related decision as to the extent of vertical integration. Building on the concepts of Coase (1937) and Jensen (1993), Fan's premise is that the uncertainty created by the OPEC oil shocks of the 1970s induced petrochemical firms to integrate into their petroleum inputs so as to avoid the transaction costs created by market contracts. Using firm- and product-level data, Fan shows that the decision to vertically integrate was systematically related to level of price uncertainty created by OPEC.

To summarize this section, both theory and evidence suggest that broad economic forces are at the heart of merger activity. Factors such as technological change and deregulation appear to be associated with the level and industry clustering of mergers. Such factors, however, do not necessarily have constant effects over time. For example, while deregulation has been shown to affect merger activity in both the 1980s and the 1990s, a comparison of Mitchell and Mulherin (Chapter 1) and Mulherin and Boone (Chapter 9) indicates that the affected industries differ between the two decades.

A useful avenue for future research is to more closely analyze the extent to which deregulation is an observable proxy for technological change. For example, as discussed in Weston, Mitchell and Mulherin (2004), the deregulation and subsequent merger activity in the telecommunications industry arguably has roots in the invention and implementation of cell phones and other novel communication devices that ended the natural monopoly characteristics of land lines. Hence, future work that examines deregulation and merger activity can peel the onion another layer by considering both the underlying causes of deregulation and the effects of such causal factors on merger activity. Both industry studies and inter-industry analysis should prove fruitful in such inquiries.

Research that digs into the relation between mergers and technological change offers insights into the reason for a positive association between the rate of merger activity and the level of the stock market that has been documented by Golbe and White (1988). Authors such as Shleifer and Vishny (2003) argued that high levels of the stock market induce an excess rate of merger activity. Alternatively, the positive association between the stock market and merger activity may be driven by technological change that jointly increases wealth and also alters the optimal organizational design in certain sectors of the economy. One sector that could serve as a laboratory for such analysis is the pharmaceutical industry where advances in biotech offer novel, valuable products that possibly require new scale in research and development that can be facilitated by mergers of the major global drug producers.

The Effects of Merger Activity

A related inquiry to the underlying causes of mergers is, what are the effects of merger activity? The analysis of this query is often couched in terms of shareholder wealth – do mergers increase or reduce the wealth of shareholders? On the one side have been authors such as Bradley, Desai and Kim (1983, 1988), who have viewed mergers as value-enhancing responses to changing economic conditions, and Alchian and Demsetz (1972) and Manne (1965), who have argued for the disciplinary effects that the market for corporate control has on management. On the other side are those who have modeled mergers as a manifestation of managerial discretion, either due to the temptations of free cash flow, see Jensen (1986), or conscious efforts by management toward entrenchment, for example, Shleifer and Vishny (1989).

The papers included here represent a selection from the large body of evidence bearing on the effects of merger activity. Andrade, Mitchell and Stafford (Chapter 3) provide a systematic treatment of a large sample of mergers. Becher (Chapter 4) reports a detailed analysis of the effects within the banking industry.

The primary technique employed in the empirical analysis of mergers is the event study, which gauges the stock market reaction to the initial announcement of a merger. The conceptual basis for event studies is efficient markets theory, described in a series of articles by Fama (1970, 1991, 1998).

Reviews of the early work of the effect of mergers on shareholder wealth have been published in a pair of surveys, Jensen and Ruback (1983) and Jarrell, Brickley and Netter (1988). Summarizing evidence from the 1960s, 1970s and 1980s, the authors of these surveys concluded that, on average, shareholders of target firms gain from mergers, while the shareholders of bidding firms tend to break even. More recent analysis by Mulherin and Boone (Chapter 9) finds similar results for mergers in the 1990s and also estimates that the combined (target plus bidder) wealth creation in the average merger is 3 per cent. Overall, the available evidence using stock market data generally supports the position that mergers are value increasing.

As an alternative and complement to the analysis of shareholder wealth, researchers have also used measures of accounting performance to analyze the effects of mergers. An example is Healy, Palepu and Ruback (1992). Focusing on the 50 largest US mergers in the 1979 to 1984 period, they found that the operating cash flows for the merging firms increase relative to industry peers following the merger. In regression analysis, they further found that the improvements in operating performance are positively and significantly related to the stock returns at the time of the merger announcement. These results indicate that the stock market forecasts the improved performance following the mergers.

Andrade, Mitchell and Stafford (Chapter 3) provide a useful summary of the effects of mergers in their study of the stock price and accounting performance of 3688 mergers from 1973 to 1998. Consistent with prior research, they find that mergers enhance shareholder wealth. They find that target shareholders gain roughly 20 per cent while bidding shareholders tend to break even, resulting in a combined shareholder return that averages 2 per cent. They also find that accounting performance improves after mergers, which bolsters the evidence from the stock market.

In the large sample studies, it is often hard to pinpoint the actual source of the gains attributed to mergers. The additional detail provided by research at the industry level stands to shed further light on the sources of gains. An example is the banking industry, where state and federal deregulation has enabled the creation of regional and nationwide commercial banks, thereby permitting the estimation of the effects of deregulation and mergers on shareholder wealth and on operating performance. The fourth chapter in the volume by Becher (2000) estimates the shareholder wealth effects for a sample of 558 bank mergers from 1980 to 1997. He finds that the mergers improved the shareholder wealth of the combined bidder and target, indicating that the deregulation-induced mergers created value. Related research by Houston, James and Ryngaert (2001) determined that such value creation stems from the cost savings facilitated by the mergers.

In summary, there are a variety of theories as to the effects of merger activity. As a whole, the empirical evidence indicates that mergers create wealth. The combined bidder and target shareholder returns are positive and are on the magnitude of 3 per cent. Measures of accounting performance are directly related to the appreciation in stock prices. Target shareholders appear to garner the better part of the wealth creation in mergers.

Part II Takeover Bidding

One consistent result from the research on the effects of mergers is that the shareholders of the bidding firm tend to only break even. At first glance, this result is somewhat puzzling. Why do bidders engage in a merger if the expected return is not positive? The responses to this query range from managerial motives to the competitiveness of the merger market and are discussed in four papers in this volume: Mitchell and Lehn (Chapter 5), Roll (Chapter 6), Betton and Eckbo (Chapter 7), and Hansen (Chapter 8).

In an intriguing article, Mitchell and Lehn (1990), reprinted in Chapter 5, address the issue of breakeven bidder returns by asking do bad bidders become good targets? Contrasting the free cash flow model of Jensen (1986) and the disciplinary models of Alchian and Demsetz (1972) and Manne (1965), Mitchell and Lehn note that corporate mergers can not only waste resources but can also punish managers that do so. They predict that firms that make wealth-reducing acquisitions are likely to become targets themselves. Analyzing the acquisition performance of 1158 major corporations from 1982 to 1986 and the performance of firms that did and did not become a takeover target during the 1980s, they found that the average acquisition performance of the sample firms was a breakeven investment. Stratifying the sample based on whether firms later became takeover targets themselves, they found that bidding firms that did not become targets had positive stock price returns from their mergers, while firms that eventually became takeover targets themselves had negative returns from prior acquisitions. These results suggest that the overall findings on bidder returns mask the fact that corporate takeovers can be both an outcome of and a solution to poor managerial decisions.

In an equally provocative article, Roll (Chapter 6) argues that one reason for the absence of positive bidder returns is managerial hubris. In his model, the winning bidder in a corporate takeover may simply have an overoptimistic estimate of the target's value and thereby fall prey to the winner's curse. A prediction of the hubris model is that the combined bidder and target return in a merger is zero – any gain borne by the target shareholders is simply a wealth transfer from the bidding firm. While the general empirical evidence does not support this prediction, Berkovitch and Narayanan (1993) found evidence of hubris in a sub-sample of the mergers that they study.

In discussing the winner's curse, Roll (Chapter 6) is one of a number of authors that model a corporate takeover as an auction. Viewing takeovers as an auction suggests that the result of breakeven bidder returns may simply be a result of competition among actual and potential bidders. Representative theory in this area includes Bulow and Klemperer (1996) and Hirshleifer and Png (1989).

Betton and Eckbo (2000), Chapter 7 in the volume, provide a detailed empirical treatment of the effects of bidder competition in corporate takeovers. They study a sample of 1353 tender offers from 1971 to 1990. Their data entails 2335 takeover bids that include both the bids by the winning bidders as well as those by unsuccessful bidders in an acquisition. In this comprehensive framework, Betton and Eckbo find that the expected return to the initial bidder in a tender offer is insignificantly different from zero. They also find that the premium offered in single-bidder tender offers is on average higher than the initial premium offered in tender offers that have multiple bidders, a result that is consistent with models of preemptive bidding such as Fishman (1988).

Betton and Eckbo also examine the incidence and effects of bidder 'toeholds', defined as an accumulation of ownership in the target firm by the bidder prior to the tender offer. The data indicate that obtaining a toehold increases both the return to the bidder and the likelihood that the bidder will be successful. In what they view as a puzzle, Betton and Eckbo find that in spite of such benefits, only half of the bidders in their sample obtain a toehold before commencing the tender offer.

The eighth chapter in the book by Hansen (2001) provides a model of the takeover process that suggests why this might be so. Hansen begins with the fact that the target firm often administers its own sale. With the assistance of an investment bank, the target contacts potential buyers, provides confidential information to interested parties, and eventually solicits formal written offers from a select set of bidders. In this process, the seller restricts both the number of bidders as well as the flow of information to the selected bidders. Hansen argues that these restrictions protect the target firm from revealing competitively advantageous information to rivals. The control of information and bidders by the target may also affect the incentives of a potential bidder to obtain a toehold.

Boone and Mulherin (2003) sifted through SEC merger documents to empirically study the process of the sale of all or part of a firm. They documented a competitive auction process between multiple potential bidders, even in cases where the financial media only reports the winning bidder. This auction process has several noticeable features that resemble the stylized model of Hansen (Chapter 8). First, as a quid pro quo to receiving confidential information from the target, a potential bidder must sign a standstill provision that precludes the acquisition of an ownership stake in the target, offering one reason that not all bidders obtain a toehold. Second, as modeled by Hansen, the target firm limits the number of active bidders in the auction. In addition to lessening the likelihood that the selling firm will hurt its own value by transmitting important non-public information to rivals, French and McCormick (1984) noted that limiting the number of potential bidders economizes on the information costs, and therefore the net gains, of an auction.

A more general implication of the auction process modeled by Hansen is that the corporate takeover environment is more competitive than portrayed in much of the extant empirical analysis of the process. Other research such as Schwert (1996, 2000) classified a takeover as an auction only if there are two or more firms actively making public bids that are reported in the financial media. Yet in the auctions modeled by Hansen, and exemplified by the SEC data presented in Boone and Mulherin (2003), only the winning bidder is mentioned in the financial media, even though the process usually has multiple bidders. Such competition provides a straightforward explanation for the issue of why bidders in takeovers experience breakeven returns.

Part III Corporate Restructuring

The Causes and Effects of Corporate Restructuring

Corporate restructuring occurs whenever management alters the asset mix within a firm. Under this broad definition, corporate restructuring can encompass both mergers that increase the size of the firm and divestitures that decrease the size of the firm. The papers in this volume by Mulherin and Boone (Chapter 9) and Maksimovic and Phillips (Chapter 10) jointly study restructuring via mergers and divestitures.

In studying corporate restructuring, the natural initial question is, what are the causes of restructuring activity? At a fundamental level, we would expect divestitures and mergers to be driven by the same or similar forces. Indeed, although Coase (1937) argued that technological change would tend to increase the size of the firm, he noted that some inventions might lessen the size of the firm by reducing the costs of contracting in markets.

In their work reprinted in Chapter 9, Mulherin and Boone (2000) provide evidence on the causes of restructuring activity during the 1990s. They begin with a sample of 1305 firms from 59 industries as of 1990. They then track the merger and divestiture activity of the sample firms from 1990 to 1999. They find that roughly half of the sample firms were either acquired or engaged in a major divestiture during the 1990s. Moreover, similar to evidence from the 1980s, this restructuring activity tended to cluster in particular industries. For example, the banking, broadcasting and telecommunications industries had a high rate of merger activity, while the chemical, petroleum and telecommunications industries had a high rate of divestiture activity. This clustering of mergers and divestitures in particular industries is consistent with the argument that underlying economic shocks are an important source of restructuring activity.

A related query is what are the effects of restructuring activity? As discussed in Williamson (1988), the analysis of the effects of corporate restructuring is closely related to the transaction cost economics and agency literatures on the optimal boundaries of the firm. Related to the analysis of the effects of mergers discussed in Part I of this volume, most theories of restructuring predict that corporate divestitures increase shareholder wealth. Transaction cost models such as Coase (1937) argued that the wealth creation stems from an efficient reaction to economic change. Disciplinary models such as Alchian and Demsetz (1972) and agency cost models such as Jensen and Meckling (1976) attributed the gains to improved monitoring of the management of the divested assets.

Mulherin and Boone (Chapter 9) report event–study evidence on the effects of corporate divestitures from 1990 to 1999. For a sample of 370 divestitures, the mean improvement in shareholder wealth is 3 per cent. The results are similar across distinct forms of divestitures including corporate spin-offs, equity carve-outs, and asset sales and are also consistent with research on divestitures during the 1960s, 1970s and 1980s.

As a complement to the analysis of shareholder wealth, Maksimovic and Phillips (Chapter 10) use Census data to study the effects of corporate restructuring on plant-level productivity. They study a total of 35 291 plant reallocations from 1974 to 1992. They find that restructuring is pro-cyclical in that the rate of plant reallocations is higher during periods of overall economic expansion. They also find that restructuring improves performance; they report a mean industry-adjusted increase in productivity of 2 per cent. Hence, the results from the Census data are in synchronisation with the event study analysis of shareholder wealth.

Is There a Diversification Discount?

The analysis of the effect of divestitures on shareholder wealth and on plant productivity focuses on *changes* in corporate asset mix. Related analysis considers the effect of the *level* of a firm's asset mix on value. In particular, research considers the effects of the breadth of diversification on firm value. Chapter 11 in this volume by Graham, Lemmon and Wolf (2002) asks the question does corporate diversification destroy wealth?

The analysis of diversification and firm value faces the thorny issue of making a clean comparison of diversified and non-diversified firms. Berger and Ofek (1995) developed a method that relies on industry segment data from Compustat. They estimated ratios, such as market value to sales, for firms operating in a single segment and used such segment ratios to impute a value for each segment of a diversified firm. The imputed value of the segments was then compared with the actual value for the diversified firm. Employing such analysis, Berger and Ofek (1995) estimated that diversification results in a 15 per cent discount in the value of a firm's assets. Lang and Stulz (1994) reached similar conclusions in their comparison of the Tobin's Q of single- and multi-segment firms.

This evidence suggests that corporate managers systematically impinge on value by deciding to diversify. However, the research methods and data sources have been questioned on several dimensions. Whited (2001) provided evidence on the significant measurement error in estimates of Tobin's Q. Villalonga (2003) pointed out the noisiness in Compustat segment data. Boone (2000, 2001) noted that the reliance on SIC codes to measure diversification ignores the efficiencies of vertical integration. Martin and Sayrak (2003) summarized the estimation issues in the research on corporate diversification and shareholder value.

In an effort to address the estimation problems in this research, Graham, Lemmon and Wolf (2002), Chapter 11 in the collection, combine event study analysis and segment data to estimate the return to diversification. Looking at the stock market reaction to the announcement of 356 mergers, they find that the mergers increase combined bidder and target shareholder by 3.56 per cent, indicating that the mergers enhance corporate value. They found a reduction in firm value, however, when they re-estimated using the Berger and Ofek (1995) segment technique. Graham, Lemmon and Wolf attribute this to the fact that the acquired firm was discounted prior to the merger, rather than diversification causing the discount. They suggest a reconsideration of the benchmarking of multi-segment firms with single-segment units.

Restructuring Choice

A related critique of the diversification discount literature is that the segment analysis is a one-size-fits-all approach that fails to account for the variety of governance arrangements available to managers and the heterogeneity of industries and firms. Numerous studies, however, have shown that governance arrangements vary systematically with the nature of transactions. (See, for example, Masten (1984), Monteverde and Teece (1982), and Mulherin (1986).)

Empirical analysis by Lehn, Netter and Poulsen (1990), reprinted as Chapter 12, provides an example of the usefulness of accounting for this heterogeneity in the context of the restructuring decision. The restructuring methods they study – dual-class recapitalizations and leveraged buyouts – are similar in that both increase the voting control of a select group of insiders or investors. The methods differ, however, in that firms employing dual-class recaps remain as publicly traded entities while firms conducting leveraged buyouts are taken private. Examining 97 dual-class recapitalizations between 1976 and 1987 and 283 leveraged buyouts from the interval 1980 to 1987, they find that, compared with the leveraged buyout firms, the firms conducting dual class recapitalizations have greater sales and employment growth, larger R&D/Sales ratios, and higher market to book ratios. The results indicate that, given the desire to consolidate voting control, the decision to remain a publicly traded corporation is a function of growth prospects. Consistent with the transactions cost literature, the choice of organizational form varies cross-sectionally with the underlying attributes of firms. Future research could study other decisions faced by managers such as the choice between a merger and a divestiture and, given the choice to divest, whether to do so via an asset sale, an equity carve-out or a spin-off.

Part IV Corporate Governance

The analysis of mergers and corporate restructuring often begs the question as to why some of the motivating reasons for such transactions could not have been resolved within the firm itself through more effective governance. Research on corporate governance considers the internal rules and external forces that frame the decision-making by the managers of firms. Theoretical papers on the theory of the firm – for example, Alchian and Demsetz (1972), agency costs – for example, Jensen and Meckling (1976) and transaction cost economics such as Williamson (1988) modeled governance as the establishment and enforcement of a nexus of contracts between stockholders, management, debtholders, and other claimants to a corporation. The four papers in this volume that apply this theory are Garvey and Swan (Chapter 13), Comment and Schwert (Chapter 14), Mulherin and Poulsen (Chapter 15), and Kole and Lehn (Chapter 16).

Garvey and Swan's 1994 survey of the literature on corporate governance that is reprinted as Chapter 13 provides a useful synthesis of the conceptual issues and a summary of the empirical research in the area. The internal features of corporations that have been the focus of governance research include executive compensation, insider and block ownership, and the composition of the board of directors. As in the merger and restructuring literature, a fundamental question addressed in the empirical research on corporate governance is whether observed governance arrangements are an efficient response to a firm's attributes or instead represent the efforts of entrenched managers to expropriate wealth. Complicating the analysis is the fact that many governance variables are endogenously determined, for example, Hermalin and Weisbach (1998), and may act as either substitutes or complements to one another – see Agrawal and Knoeber (1996).

One of the first questions that arises is whether corporate governance matters at all. Often the literature attempts to answer that question by simply regressing a performance measure (for example, Tobin's Q or accounting returns) on a governance variable (such as management or insider ownership). An example of this approach is Morck, Shleifer and Vishny's (1988) study that related Tobin's Q to insider ownership. Using piecewise regression, they found that an increase in ownership is initially related to improved performance but that higher levels of ownership were associated with reduced performance. The interpretation they gave to their results is that higher levels of ownership facilitate entrenchment of management. An alternative interpretation, however, is that performance measures such as Tobin's Q vary systematically with the intangible assets within a firm and that management ownership varies cross-sectionally with asset makeup. Evidence supporting this second interpretation includes Demsetz and Lehn (1985) and Demsetz and Villalonga (2001).

An especially interesting aspect of corporate governance is the use of antitakeover provisions by management. As posed by DeAngelo and Rice (1983), the central query is whether such provisions are evidence of management entrenchment or instead are in the interest of shareholders. The poison pill security, for example, is a means for a firm's incumbent management to impede potential buyers from acquiring a large stake in the firm. Such takeover impediments are often viewed as blatant moves by management to escape the pressures of the market for corporate control and thereby detract from shareholder value. However, an alternative argument is that such obstacles to a takeover can actually aid shareholders by increasing a target firm's bargaining power during a takeover battle.

Comment and Schwert (Chapter 14) provide an in-depth analysis of the role of poison pill securities. Using a comprehensive database of corporate takeovers and poison pill adoptions from 1975 to 1991, they consider whether poison pills have lessened the likelihood that a firm would be acquired and the effect that they have on the premium paid in an acquisition. Consistent with the notion that poison pills benefit shareholders, they find that the use of poison pills does not appear to have deterred takeovers and that they appear to have a positive effect on the takeover premium.

The lack of a deterrent effect of takeover impediments is somewhat perplexing. One reason for such a finding may be that related governance mechanisms have evolved to react to the development of innovations such as poison pills. One such mechanism is the proxy contest in which another firm or set of outside investors attempts to gain control of a corporation's board of directors. Among other things, board control enables the outsiders to nullify the obstacles of a poison pill or other takeover impediment.

Mulherin and Poulsen (1998), reprinted as Chapter 15, study the role played by proxy contests in the past two decades. They analyze a sample of 270 proxy contests for board seats from 1979 to 1994. Consistent with models such as Alchian and Demsetz (1972), they find that proxy contests enhance the wealth of target shareholders. Such wealth gains, however, are attained at firms acquired in the course of the proxy contest and/or that remove incumbents in the period during and immediately after the contest. These results indicate that proxy contests are one governance response to the potential negative effects wrought by the impediments developed by incumbent management to inhibit takeovers.

Kole and Lehn (Chapter 16), provide a more general analysis of the evolution of corporate governance in response to changing economic conditions. They rely on the deregulation of the airline industry in 1978 to provide a natural experiment with which to consider the factors that affect governance variables. Their results indicate that the governance at the deregulated airlines gravitates toward the structure at unregulated firms from other industries. In particular, ownership concentration and the use of stock-based forms of compensation increase following deregulation. In related analysis of the banking industry, Crawford, Ezzell and Miles (1995) also found that pay-for-performance sensitivity heightens following deregulation. These results of changes in response to deregulation suggest that governance indeed is a function of a firm's underlying environment.

Conclusion

As noted at the beginning of this Introduction, the research on mergers and corporate governance has a long history. Writing in 1969, for example, Alchian posed the central research question, how can the corporate form, with all of its inherent conflicts of interest, manage to survive?

Posed in this manner, the research on mergers and corporate governance is directed at what Coase (1992) labeled 'the institutional structure of production'. As guidance for future analysis, Coase (1992) stated, 'The process of contracting needs to be studied in a real-world setting. We would then learn of the problems that are encountered and of how they are overcome, and we would certainly become aware of the richness of the institutional alternatives between which we have to choose'. The Electronic Data Gathering, Analysis and Retrieval (EDGAR) system of the US Securities and Exchange Commission (SEC) is one of the many information vehicles that can be tapped to implement Coase's call for institutional research in the study of mergers and governance. For example, the plethora of information in the SEC's EDGAR filings can shed light on the contrasting models of corporate auctions found in Roll (Chapter 6) and Hansen (Chapter 8). Similar databases can be used to study novel contracting arrangements such as joint ventures, strategic alliances, and venture capital arrangements.

Future research aimed at more fully discerning the causes and effects of various features of mergers and corporate governance would be also well-advised to heed Hayek's 1937 admonition, 'before we can explain why people commit mistakes, we must first explain why they should ever be right'. Such advice is certainly pertinent in dealing with the estimation issues in measuring diversification discounts (or premiums). Another area where cautious research would be well applied is in the analysis of long-term performance following corporate restructuring. As discussed by Fama (1998), much of the extant empirical analysis of long-term performance is ad hoc and often quick to argue for either managerial or market irrationality. Where many of the past studies have focused on whether an investment portfolio of merging firms can beat the market, perhaps an alternative research direction would be to ask how subsequent economic conditions affect merger performance.

In general, the topics in mergers and corporate governance provide ripe avenues for continued empirical research. Ongoing changes in the political and business world offer a rich environment in which to conduct future study. The broad privatization movement across the globe enables a variety of new analyses on the response of corporations to changes in the cost-reward system. The innovation in information wrought by the Internet provides new avenues for tests of Coase's 1937 prediction that the size of the firm responds to new inventions. Technological advances in fields ranging from biotech to telecommunications offer specific platforms to examine the dynamic causes and cross-sectional effects of merger and restructuring activity. The material in this volume provides some avenues by which this new research can be conducted.

References

Agrawal, Anup and Charles R. Knoeber (1996), 'Firm Performance and Mechanisms to Control Agency Problems between Managers and Shareholders', *Journal of Financial and Quantitative Analysis*, **31**, September, 377–97.

Alchian, Armen A. (1965), 'The Basis of Some Recent Advances in the Theory of Management of the Firm', *Journal of Industrial Economics*, **14**, November, 30–41.

Alchian, Armen A. (1969), 'Corporate Management and Property Rights', in Henry Manne (ed.), *Economic Policy and the Regulation of Corporate Securities*, Washington: American Enterprise Institute.

Alchian, Armen A. and Harold Demsetz (1972), 'Production, Information Costs, and Economic Organization', *American Economic Review*, **62**, December, 777–95.

Andrade, Gregor, Mark Mitchell and Erik Stafford (2001), 'New Evidence and Perspectives on Mergers', *Journal of Economic Perspectives*, **15**, Spring, 103–20.

Andrade, Gregor and Erik Stafford (2004), 'Investigating the Economic Role of Mergers', *Journal of Corporate Finance*, **10**, January, 1–36.

Becher, David A. (2000), 'The Valuation Effects of Bank Mergers', *Journal of Corporate Finance*, **6**, July, 189–214.

Berger, Philip G. and Eli Ofek (1995), 'Diversification's Effect on Firm Value', *Journal of Financial Economics*, **37**, January, 39–65.

Berkovitch, Elazar and M.P. Narayanan (1993), 'Motives for Takeovers: An Empirical Investigation', *Journal of Financial and Quantitative Analysis*, **28**, September, 347–62.

Betton, Sandra and B. Espen Eckbo (2000), 'Toeholds, Bid Jumps and Expected Payoffs in Takeovers', *Review of Financial Studies*, **13**, Winter, 841–82.

Boone, Audra L. (2000), 'Can Focus Explain Carve-Out Gains?', paper presented at the meeting of the Western Finance Association, Sun Valley Idaho, June.

Boone, Audra L. (2001), 'The Interaction of Ownership, Governance and Product Markets: Evidence from Equity Carve-Outs', paper presented at the meeting of the Western Finance Association, Tucson, Arizona, June.

Boone, Audra L. and J. Harold Mulherin (2003), 'Corporate Restructuring and Corporate Auctions', working paper, College of William and Mary and Claremont McKenna College.

Bradley, Michael, Anand Desai and E. Han Kim (1983), 'The Rationale Behind Interfirm Tender Offers: Information or Synergy?', *Journal of Financial Economics*, **11**, 183–206.
Bradley, M., A. Desai and E. H. Kim (1988), 'Synergistic Gains from Corporate Acquisitions and Their Division Between the Stockholders of Target and Acquiring Firms', *Journal of Financial Economics*, **21**, 3–40.
Bulow, Jeremy and Paul Klemperer (1996), 'Auctions versus Negotiations', *American Economic Review*, **86**, March, 180–94.
Coase, R.H. (1937), 'The Nature of the Firm', *Economica*, **4**, November, 386–405.
Coase, R.H. (1992), 'The Institutional Structure of Production', *American Economic Review*, **82**, September, 713–19.
Comment, Robert and G. William Schwert (1995), 'Poison or Placebo? Evidence on the Deterrence and Wealth Effects of Modern Antitakeover Measures', *Journal of Financial Economics*, **39**, 3–43.
Crawford, Anthony J., John R. Ezzell and James A. Miles (1995), 'Bank CEO Pay–Performance Relations and the Effects of Deregulation', *Journal of Business*, **68**, April, 231–56.
DeAngelo, Harry and Edward M. Rice (1983), 'Antitakeover Charter Amendments and Shareholder Wealth', *Journal of Financial Economics*, **11**, April, 329–59.
Demsetz, Harold and Kenneth Lehn (1985), 'The Structure of Ownership: Causes and Consequences', *Journal of Political Economy*, **93**, December, 1155–77.
Demsetz, Harold and Belen Villalonga (2001), 'Ownership Structure and Corporate Performance', *Journal of Corporate Finance*, **7**, September, 209–33.
Eis, Carl (1969), 'The 1919–1930 Merger Movement in American Industry', *Journal of Law and Economics*, **12**, October, 267–96.
Fama, Eugene F. (1970), 'Efficient Capital Markets: A Review of Theory and Empirical Work', *Journal of Finance*, **25**, 383–417.
Fama, Eugene F. (1991), 'Efficient Capital Markets: II', *Journal of Finance*, **46**, December, 1575–617.
Fama, Eugene F. (1998), 'Market Efficiency, Long-Term Returns, and Behavioral Finance', *Journal of Financial Economics*, **49**, 283–306.
Fan, Joseph P.H. (2000), 'Price Uncertainty and Vertical Integration: An Examination of Petrochemical Firms', *Journal of Corporate Finance*, **6**, December, 345–76.
Fishman, Michael J. (1988), 'A Theory of Preemptive Takeover Bidding', *Rand Journal of Economics*, **19**, 88–101.
French, Kenneth R. and Robert E. McCormick (1984), 'Sealed Bids, Sunk Costs, and the Process of Competition', *Journal of Business*, **57**, 417–41.
Garvey, Gerald T. and Peter L. Swan (1994), 'The Economics of Corporate Governance: Beyond the Marshallian Firm', *Journal of Corporate Finance*, **1**, 139–74.
Golbe, Devra L. and Lawrence J. White, 'A Time-Series Analysis of Mergers and Acquisitions in the U.S. Economy', chapter 9 in Alan J. Auerbach (ed.), *Corporate Takeovers: Causes and Consequences*, Chicago: The University of Chicago Press, pp. 265–309.
Gort, Michael (1969), 'An Economic Disturbance Theory of Mergers', *Quarterly Journal of Economics*, **83**, November, 624–42.
Graham, John R., Michael L. Lemmon and Jack G. Wolf (2002), 'Does Corporate Diversification Destroy Wealth?', *Journal of Finance*, **57**, April, 695–720.
Hansen, Robert G. (2001), 'Auctions of Companies', *Economic Inquiry*, **39**, January, 30–43.
Hayek, F.A. von (1937), 'Economics and Knowledge', *Economica*, **4**, February, 33–54.
Healy, Paul M., Khrishna G. Palepu and Richard S. Ruback (1992), 'Does Corporate Performance Improve After Mergers?', *Journal of Financial Economics*, **31**, 135–75.
Hermalin, Benjamin E. and Michael S. Weisbach (1998), 'Endogenously Chosen Boards of Directors and Their Monitoring of the CEO', *American Economic Review*, **88**, March, 96–118.
Hirshleifer, David, and I.P.L. Png (1989), 'Facilitation of Competing Bids and the Price of a Takeover Target', *Review of Financial Studies*, **2**, 587–606.
Houston, Joel F., Christopher M. James and Michael D. Ryngaert (2001), 'Where do Merger Gains Come from? Bank Mergers from the Perspective of Insiders and Outsiders', *Journal of Financial Economics*, **60**, 285–331.

Jarrell, Gregg A., James A. Brickley and Jeffry M. Netter (1988), 'The Market for Corporate Control: The Empirical Evidence Since 1980', *Journal of Economic Perspectives*, **2**, Winter, 49–68.
Jensen, Michael C. (1986), 'Agency Costs of Free Cash Flow, Corporate Finance and Takeovers', *American Economic Review*, **76**, May, 323–29.
Jensen, Michael C. (1993), 'The Modern Industrial Revolution, Exit, and the Failure of Internal Control Systems', *Journal of Finance*, **48**, July, 831–80.
Jensen, Michael C. and William H. Meckling (1976), 'Theory of the Firm: Managerial Behavior, Agency Costs, and Ownership Structure', *Journal of Financial Economics*, **3**, 305–60.
Jensen, Michael C. and Richard S. Ruback (1983), 'The Market for Corporate Control: The Scientific Evidence', *Journal of Financial Economics*, **11**, 5–50.
Jovanovic, Boyan and Peter L. Rousseau (2002), 'The Q-Theory of Mergers', *American Economic Review*, **92**, May, 198–204.
Keasey, Kevin, Steve Thompson and Mike Wright (1999), *Corporate Governance*, Cheltenham, UK and Northampton, MA, USA: Edward Elgar Publishing.
Klein, Benjamin, Robert G. Crawford and Armen A. Alchian (1978), 'Vertical Integration, Appropriable Rents, and the Competitive Contracting Process', *Journal of Law and Economics*, **21**, October, 297–326.
Kole, Stacey R. and Kenneth Lehn (1999), 'Deregulation and the Adaptation of Governance Structure: The Case of the U.S. Airline Industry', *Journal of Financial Economics*, **52**, April, 79–117.
Lang, Larry H.P. and Rene Stulz (1994), 'Tobin's Q, Corporate Diversification, and Firm Performance', *Journal of Political Economy*, **102**, 1248–80.
Lehn, Kenneth, Jeffry Netter and Annette Poulsen (1990), 'Consolidating Corporate Control: Dual-class Recapitalizations versus Leveraged Buyouts', *Journal of Financial Economics*, **27**, 557–80.
Maksimovic, Vojislav and Gordon Phillips (2001), 'The Market for Corporate Assets: Who Engages in Mergers and Asset Sales and Are There Efficiency Gains?', *Journal of Finance*, **56**, December, 2019–65.
Manne, Henry G. (1965), 'Mergers and the Market for Corporate Control', *Journal of Political Economy*, **73**, April, 110–20.
Martin, John D. and Akin Sayrak (2003), 'Corporate Diversification and Shareholder Value: A Survey of Recent Literature', *Journal of Corporate Finance*, **9**, January, 37–57.
Masten, Scott E. (1984), 'The Organization of Production: Evidence from the Aerospace Industry', *Journal of Law and Economics*, **27**, October, 403–17.
Mitchell, Mark L. and Kenneth Lehn (1990), 'Do Bad Bidders Become Good Targets?', *Journal of Political Economy*, **98**, 372–98.
Mitchell, Mark L. and J. Harold Mulherin (1996), 'The Impact of Industry Shocks on Takeover and Restructuring Activity', *Journal of Financial Economics*, **41**, June, 193–229.
Monteverde, Kirk and David J. Teece (1982), 'Supplier Switching Costs and Vertical Integration in the Automobile Industry', *Bell Journal of Economics*, **13**, Spring, 206–13.
Morck, Randall, Andrei Shleifer and Robert Vishny (1988), 'Management Ownership and Market Valuation: An Empirical Analysis', *Journal of Financial Economics*, **27**, 293–315.
Mulherin, J. Harold (1986), 'Specialized Assets, Governmental Regulation, and Organizational Structure in the Natural Gas Industry', *Journal of Institutional and Theoretical Economics*, **142**, September, 528–41.
Mulherin, J. Harold and Audra L. Boone (2000), 'Comparing Acquisitions and Divestitures', *Journal of Corporate Finance*, **6**, July, 117–39.
Mulherin, J. Harold and Annette B. Poulsen (1998), 'Proxy Contests and Corporate Change: Implications for Shareholder Wealth', *Journal of Financial Economics*, **47**, March, 279–313.
Roll, Richard (1986), 'The Hubris Hypothesis of Corporate Takeovers', *Journal of Business*, **59**, April, 197–216.
Schwert, G. William (1996), 'Markup Pricing in Mergers and Acquisitions', *Journal of Financial Economics*, **41**, 153–92.
Schwert, G. William (2000), 'Hostility in Takeovers: In the Eyes of the Beholder?', *Journal of Finance*, **55**, December, 2599–640.
Shleifer, Andrei and Robert M. Vishny (1989), 'Management Entrenchment: The Case of Manager-Specific Investments', *Journal of Financial Economics*, **25**, 123–39.

Shleifer, Andrei and Robert M. Vishny (2003), 'Stock Market Driven Acquisitions', *Journal of Financial Economics*, **70**, December, 295–311.
Villalonga, Belen (2004), 'Diversification Discount or Premium? New Evidence from BITS Establishment-Level Data', *Journal of Finance*, **59**, April, 479–506.
Weston, J. Fred, Mark L. Mitchell and J. Harold Mulherin (2004), *Takeovers, Restructuring and Corporate Governance* (fourth edition), Prentice Hall: Upper Saddle River, New Jersey.
Whited, Toni M. (2001), 'Is It Inefficient Investment that Causes the Diversification Discount?', *Journal of Finance*, **56**, October, 1667–91.
Williamson, Oliver E. (1975), *Markets and Hierarchies*, New York: Free Press.
Williamson, Oliver E. (1988), 'Corporate Finance and Corporate Governance', *Journal of Finance*, **43**, July, 567–91.

Part I
The Causes and Effects of Merger Activity

[1]

ELSEVIER Journal of Financial Economics 41 (1996) 193–229

JOURNAL OF Financial ECONOMICS

The impact of industry shocks on takeover and restructuring activity

Mark L. Mitchell*,[a], J. Harold Mulherin[b]

[a]*Graduate School of Business, University of Chicago, Chicago, IL 60637, USA*
[b]*Smeal College of Business, Penn State University, University Park, PA 16802, USA*

(Received December 1994; final version received June 1995)

Abstract

We study industry-level patterns in takeover and restructuring activity during the 1982–1989 period. Across 51 industries, we find significant differences in both the rate and time-series clustering of these activities. The interindustry patterns in the rate of takeovers and restructurings are directly related to the economic shocks borne by the sample industries. These results support the argument that much of the takeover activity during the 1980s was driven by broad fundamental factors and have general implications for the stock price spillover effects of takeover announcements, corporate performance following takeovers, and the timing of takeover waves.

Key words: Industry shock; Takeover; Restructuring; Mergers and acquisitions
JEL classification: G34

1. Introduction

The large number of corporate takeovers during the 1980s has been characterized as the fourth takeover wave in the U.S. during the past 100 years. This paper assesses the proposition that industry shocks contribute to the extensive

*Corresponding author.

We acknowledge comments on prior drafts by Eugene Fama, Joseph Fan, Gordon Hanka, David Ikenberry, Mike Maloney, Krishna Palepu (the referee), G. William Schwert (the editor), Dennis Sheehan, Fred Weston, session participants at the NBER Corporate Finance Workshop and the 1994 ASSA Meeting, and seminar participants at the Federal Trade Commission, Northwestern University, and Penn State University. Mark Carhart, Violet Law, and David Schanzer provided research assistance.

SSDI 0304-405X(95)00860-H

takeover and restructuring activity of that decade. Examples of shocks include deregulation, changes in input costs, and innovations in financing technology that induce or enable alterations in industry structure. The hypothesis we maintain in our analysis is that corporate takeovers such as tender offers, mergers, and leveraged buyouts are often the least-cost means for industry structure to respond to the changes brought about by economic shocks. Our central prediction is that the takeover and restructuring activity in the 1980s clusters in the industries that experience shocks of the greatest magnitude.

A number of observers point to factors such as deregulation as being part of the impetus for the 1980s takeover wave. However, little systematic analysis has been performed regarding the importance of such shocks for industry variation in takeover and restructuring activity. The analysis of the 1980s has instead focused on the role of hostile takeovers and leveraged buyouts in restructuring the assets at particular firms. Our analysis of industry shocks broadens the knowledge of the forces at work behind the wave of takeovers during the 1980s.

Our research is motivated by the relatively meager understanding of the dynamics of takeover activity. Prior research finds that takeovers do not occur evenly over time, but instead cluster in distinct waves. Past studies have been less successful, however, in determining the reasons why takeover activity varies over time. As such, the treatment of takeover waves has tended to be ad hoc, with each of the four takeover waves in the past century having its own label: the 1890s for monopoly, the 1920s for oligopoly, the 1960s for conglomerate takeovers, and the 1980s as the decade of hostile bust-up takeovers.

Consistent with this ad hoc characterization, the recent burst of takeover activity that began in 1993 has been viewed as a distinctly new wave that is driven by strategic, synergistic factors. One notable feature of the current takeover activity is that it clusters in a few particular industries. Table 1 reports that seven of the 50 industries tracked by Mergerstat Review account for half of the takeover activity during 1993 and 1994. Moreover, the industries with the greatest activity are sectors that are currently responding to deregulation, technological advancements, and other fundamental factors. Many commentators contrast this response of specific industries to fundamental change with the widespread bust-up takeovers in the 1980s.

In spite of the perceived differences between takeovers in the 1980s and 1990s, our results indicate that the takeover activity in the two decades shares common features. Like the recent patterns displayed in Table 1, our analysis shows that takeover activity in the 1980s clusters disproportionately at the industry level. Moreover, we find that industries experiencing the greatest amount of takeover activity in the 1980s are those exposed to the greatest fundamental shocks. The empirical results support the argument that broad-based fundamental factors play an important role in the takeover and restructuring activity of the 1980s.

The importance of industry shocks for takeover activity in these two decades suggests a direction for future research on the time series of takeovers during the

Table 1
Takeover activity during 1993–94

This table lists seven industries that account for more than half of the takeover activity in the 1993–94 period for the 50 industries tracked by Mergerstat Review. Takeover value is in $ millions. % of total takeover value is the value of takeovers in a particular Mergerstat industry divided by the total value of takeovers in the Mergerstat sample. % of total equity value is the value of the firms in a Mergerstat industry divided by the total equity value at year-end 1992 for all publicly traded firms on CRSP. The matching between CRSP and Mergerstat is done via SIC codes. (Mergerstat Review provides the SIC codes associated with each Mergerstat industry; CRSP provides the primary SIC code for each listed firm.)

Industry	Takeover value	% of total takeover value	% of total equity value
Banking & finance	$ 51,637	12.8%	2.5%
Broadcasting	$ 43,129	10.7	0.8
Communications	$ 27,661	6.9	4.3
Leisure & entertainment	$ 25,339	6.3	1.5
Insurance	$ 22,017	5.5	2.4
Health services	$ 21,896	5.4	1.0
Wholesale & distribution	$ 15,704	3.9	1.5
Sum for 7 industries	$207,383	51.5	14.0
Total takeover value	$403,071		

entire century. Past work on this topic has focused with mixed success on macroeconomic variables as the source of takeover activity; the most robust result from this line of research is that takeover activity is positively related to overall stock market performance. Our results suggest that a fruitful research design would consider the joint effect of macroeconomic and industry-level factors in modeling the behavior of takeovers over time.

Our work is relevant to the recent debate concerning the decline in the takeover market at the end of the 1980s. Linking takeover activity with fundamental shocks is consistent with the analysis of Comment and Schwert (1995), who argue that relatively broad-based economic factors, rather than state laws and firm-specific antitakeover amendments, reduced the number of takeovers.

Our work also has implications for interpreting the effect that a takeover announcement for one firm in an industry has on the equity value of other industry members. Because we find that takeover activity has industry-driven factors, our results imply that one firm's takeover announcement gives information about other industry members that may be tied to economic fundamentals rather than market power, as is often asserted by regulators.

Some observers express concern that takeovers are too often followed by business failures. Because we find that takeovers are driven in part by industry shocks, it is not surprising that many firms exhibit volatile performance following takeovers, with actual failures following some negative shocks. Rather than being the actual source of performance changes, the takeovers are often merely messengers of the underlying economic changes taking place in the industry.

The paper proceeds as follows. Section 2 develops our arguments on the link between industry shocks and takeover activity, and places our approach in the context of prior research. Section 3 describes our data set and reports evidence on the overall magnitude of takeover activity during the 1980s. Section 4 analyzes the extent to which there were interindustry differences in the rate of takeover activity during the 1980s, and Section 5 reports the interindustry variation in the timing of takeovers. Section 6 relates the variation in the rate of takeover activity to measures of industry shocks. The final section summarizes the analysis and discusses the implications of the results.

2. Industry shocks and takeover activity

Our concept of an industry shock is any factor, whether expected or unexpected, that alters industry structure. Similarly, we define takeovers broadly to include tender offers, mergers, and leveraged buyouts. In most of the analysis, we group friendly and hostile takeovers together. Because our analysis focuses at the industry level, the means of, or intent behind, a particular takeover is secondary to the fact that organizational change is taking place.

2.1. Shocks, industry structure, and takeover activity

In linking takeover activity and industry shocks, we assume that the structure of an industry, including the number and size of firms, is a function of factors such as technology, government policy, and demand and supply conditions. Major changes, or shocks, in any of these factors cause shifts in industry structure. This neoclassical framework of the dynamics of industry structure is sufficient for our purposes, especially given the lack of a more detailed dynamic model in the industrial organization literature. Breshnahan (1989), for example, notes that much of the analysis in industrial organization has focused on market power, rather than specifically addressing the response of industry structure to economic shocks.

Firms in an industry can respond to a shock either internally or externally. For example, a technological shock that triggers an increase in firm size can be accomplished either through internal expansion or takeovers. Our maintained hypothesis is that the takeover route is often the least-cost method to alter industry structure.

As a specific example of takeover activity and industry shocks, consider the ongoing changes in the U.S. banking system. Recent federal legislation has removed regulatory hurdles to nationwide banking, and industry members have responded by expanding across state lines and regional boundaries. Analysts predict that the economies of scale brought about by such expansion will lower operating costs by roughly 33% (Standard & Poor's Industry Surveys, June 4, 1992, p. B4). With assets already in place, takeovers are arguably the quickest way to accomplish this expansion, as internal growth would create excess capacity in the relatively mature banking industry. Hence, it is not altogether surprising that the banking industry sits atop the list in Table 1 by having more than $50 billion in takeover activity in the 1993–94 period.

Related arguments can be made that link takeover activity with negative industry shocks. A shock-driven decline in demand can cause the members of an industry to close unprofitable facilities, but it can also pressure firms to merge the remaining facilities in order to react to the post-shock optimal plant size. For example, Dutz (1989) provides theory and case-study evidence that takeovers in the steel industry in the 1980s allowed firms to better accomplish downsizing by eliminating duplicate facilities and matching capacity, thus maintaining economies of scale under the new industry structure of fewer firms. Jensen (1993) suggests that the ongoing consolidation and organizational change in many industries can be traced to the alteration in input costs that stemmed from the oil price shocks of the 1970s.

2.2. Related research on takeovers

A large body of research has studied takeover activity. Much of the analysis of takeovers in the 1980s has been firm-specific in nature, and has shown the role of takeovers in reversing value-decreasing acquisitions (Mitchell and Lehn, 1990), returning assets to their core industries (Bhagat, Shleifer, and Vishny, 1990; Comment and Jarrell, 1995), penalizing poor managerial performance (Morck, Shleifer, and Vishny, 1988, 1989), and improving cash flow and other fundamentals (Kaplan, 1989; Smith, 1990). Another set of analyses considers the effect that macroeconomic variables have had on the level of takeover activity over long periods of time (see, e.g., Becketti, 1986; Golbe and White, 1988; Melicher, Ledolter, and D'Antonio, 1983).

Relative to these firm-specific and macroeconomic analyses of takeover activity, our research design more closely resembles the approach found in papers such as Blair and Schary (1993) and Gort (1969), which study restructuring and takeover activity at the industry level. Blair and Schary (1993) find some evidence of a relation between financial restructuring and free cash flow during the first part of the 1980s, although the findings are not robust to the entire decade. Gort (1969) documents interindustry variation in the rate of takeover activity during the 1950s, and suggests that the patterns are consistent with an economic disturbance model. As part of his analysis of takeovers at the turn of the century, Nelson (1959) also notes industry differences in the rate of takeover activity. McGowan (1971, Table 5) reports international evidence on the industry clustering of takeovers during the 1950s and 60s.

Our research broadens the inquiry into the sources of interindustry variation in takeover and restructuring activity. To some extent, our approach attempts to empirically implement Jensen's (1993) model in which the takeovers and restructurings of the 1980s are linked to widespread technological, regulatory, and economic change. Our approach is also consistent with Weston, Chung, and Hoag's (1990) observation that recent takeover activity has been high in industries undergoing deregulation, experiencing oil price shocks, and otherwise facing structural alteration.

3. Takeover and restructuring activity during the 1980s

This section describes the primary database on takeover and restructuring activity used in this study. In reporting summary statistics, we corroborate two stylized facts: The takeover activity of the 1980s was widespread, and it targeted large firms. The database entails 1,064 firms that were listed in the Value Line Investment Survey at year-end 1981. Our sample is a refinement of that used in Mitchell and Lehn (1990), covering 51 industries for which Value Line followed ten or more firms.[1] The firms in the database comprise more than 60% of the value of the listings on the NYSE, AMEX, and NASDAQ as of year-end 1981.

For each of the sample firms, we search the *Wall Street Journal*, Dow Jones Broadtape, Moody's Industrial Manuals, the Value Line Investment Survey, and related financial publications for evidence of takeover and/or restructuring activity during the 1982–89 period. The starting year for the analysis parallels the initiation of the tolerant antitrust policy of the Reagan administration and the beginning of the 1980s bull market. The ending year coincides with the significant decline in takeover activity at the close of the 1980s, as documented by Comment and Schwert (1995).

The use of Value Line as the source for the sample ensures that the firms are heavily covered by the financial press, thereby enabling the analysis of both successful and unsuccessful bids, not just completed takeovers. Our classification of takeovers includes tender offers, mergers, and leveraged buyouts. Additionally, in the absence of an explicit takeover bid, a firm is classified as having a defensive asset restructuring if it undertakes a significant sale of assets or a major recapitalization that can be traced to implicit takeover pressure, such as a large block purchase by a corporate raider or the growing incidence of acquisitions in the firm's industry.

[1]Heavily regulated industries such as utilities and financial services are excluded from the analysis. Because we restrict the analysis to firms incorporated in the U.S., two industries in our sample – Medical Services and Coal, Uranium, and Geothermal – have only nine firms.

Table 2 reports the frequency of the takeover and restructuring activity for our sample during the 1982–89 period. Twenty-seven percent of the firms experience a friendly bid, while 23% are the object of a hostile acquisition attempt. An additional 7% of the firms undertake a defensive asset restructuring, indicating that 57% of the sample firms experience a takeover attempt or major restructuring during the eight-year period of examination. The value-weighted data tell a similar story: Roughly half the sample shows the footsteps of some form of takeover or restructuring during the 1980s.

The more detailed categories in Table 2 indicate that 41% of the firms in the sample are actually acquired – 25% via a successful friendly takeover, 8% in a successful hostile takeover, and 8% in a friendly acquisition that follows an

Table 2
Frequency of takeover and restructuring activity during 1982–89

This table presents the incidence of takeover and restructuring activity for a sample of 1,064 firms listed in the Value Line Investment Survey at year-end 1981. Takeover and restructuring activity in the 1982–89 period is determined by searching financial periodicals. Takeovers include tender offers, mergers, and leveraged buyouts. Friendly takeovers are those not initially opposed by target management. Hostile takeovers are those initially opposed by target management. Defensive asset restructurings include any major asset restructuring or recapitalization induced by implicit takeover pressure, such as a large block purchase by a corporate raider or the growing occurrence of takeover activity in the firm's industry. The value-weighted % is the total value (market equity plus book debt) of the firms in the respective category divided the total value of the full sample, for which all values are recorded at year-end 1981.

Classification	Number of firms	Equally weighted %	Value-weighted %
Friendly takeover target	286	26.9%	13.6%
Successful	268	25.2	13.0
Unsuccessful	18	1.7	0.6
Hostile takeover target	243	22.8%	23.4%
Successful	85	8.0	7.3
Unsuccessful	35	3.3	2.2
Unsuccessful followed by friendly takeover	87	8.1	7.0
Unsuccessful followed by restructuring	36	3.4	6.9
Defensive asset restructuring	78	7.3%	11.8%
Asset restructuring	64	6.0	9.0
Financial recapitalization	14	1.3	2.8
Remainder of the sample	457	43.0%	51.2%
Total sample	1,064	100.0%	100.0%

In 15 successful friendly takeovers, the bidder gained control without an actual takeover. In four unsuccessful friendly takeovers, the firms subsequently engaged in major asset restructurings.

unsuccessful hostile attempt. On a value-weighted basis, 27% of the sample is actually acquired. The evidence on actual acquisitions affirms the breadth of takeover activity during the 1980s.

Since Value Line covers the more actively traded firms, the description of takeover activity in our primary data base applies to the larger publicly traded firms. As an assessment of the robustness of the summary statistics, we employ the CRSP database to replicate the analysis of actual takeovers. For the 5,294 NYSE, AMEX, and NASDAQ firms listed on the CRSP files at year-end 1981 (total equity value of $1.3 trillion), we impose criteria similar to those used for the data set taken from Value Line. That is, we use the two-digit SIC industry classification and exclude industries with fewer than ten firms, regulated industries such as utilities and financial services, and firms for which a two-digit SIC code is unavailable. The resulting data set consists of 3,660 firms (total equity value of $1.0 trillion) in 46 industries. We then track each firm until the end of 1990 to determine whether CRSP dropped the firm because of a tender offer, merger, or leveraged buyout.[2] This procedure indicates that 31% of the CRSP sample is acquired during the period of study; weighting by equity value, 28% of the CRSP sample is acquired. These percentages compare with 41% and 27%, respectively, for the equally weighted and value-weighted incidence of actual takeovers in the Value Line sample. The comparable size of the value-weighted numbers in the two samples attests to the breadth of takeover activity during the 1980s. The greater fraction of firms actually acquired in the Value Line sample indicates the degree to which the corporate control activity of the 1980s involves large firms.

To further benchmark takeover activity during the 1980s, we construct data sets for takeovers during two earlier decades. For the 2,094 NYSE and AMEX firms that were listed on CRSP as of July 2, 1962, we find that 425 (20%) were acquired by the end of 1972, although on a value-weighted basis, the fraction of takeover activity was only 7% during the 1962–72 period. Similarly, for the 6,277 NYSE, AMEX, and NASDAQ firms listed on CRSP as of January 1, 1973, 1,202 (19%) were acquired by the end of 1981, although, as in the 1960s, the percentage of equity acquired was only 8%. Hence, the rate of actual takeover activity in the 1960s and 70s was not only less than the 1980s, but the activity in the earlier periods was tilted much more toward small firms, as indicated by the noticeably smaller value-weighted numbers for takeover activity in the earlier decades.

[2]We track the firms through 1990 because we only have actual takeover completion dates for the CRSP sample, rather than the announcement dates available for the Value Line sample. Ending the tracking period at earlier dates (such as December 1989 or June 1990) does not alter the results applying to the CRSP sample here or later in the paper.

4. Industry differences in the rate of takeover and restructuring activity

In analyzing whether industry shocks are a source of takeover activity, our first step is to examine whether there is significant variation in the amount of takeover activity across the industries in our sample. Table 3 reports the takeover and restructuring activity for each of the 51 Value Line industries. We report the equally weighted and value-weighted fraction of the 1982–89 activity for five categories: total takeover and restructuring activity, takeover attempts, friendly bids, hostile bids, and actual takeovers. The presentation of the various classifications of takeover activity allows both comparisons with, and extensions of, prior analysis of the 1980s. To a large extent, however, the finer distinctions, such as friendly versus hostile takeovers, are not central to our main question of the impact of industry shocks on takeover activity.

The data in Table 3, presented in descending order of the equally weighted fraction of total takeover and restructuring activity, indicate a wide variation in the rate of takeover and restructuring across the 51 industries during the sample period. In seven industries (Entertainment, Drugstores, Petroleum Producing, Broadcasting, Textiles, Tire and Rubber, and Integrated Steel), three-fourths or more of the firms receive a takeover bid or undertake a major restructuring between 1982 and 1989. At the other extreme, one-third or fewer of the firms in Paper and Paper Products, Specialty Chemicals, and Metal Fabricating experience takeover and restructuring activity. The value-weighted measure of takeover and restructuring activity exhibits even more interindustry variation: The standard deviation of the value-weighted measure is 25% compared to only 15% for the equally weighted frequency. The finer classifications of takeover activity also vary widely across industries. Overall, the data in Table 3 reveal a noticeable interindustry variation in takeover activity during the 1980s, although no industry is fully immune to takeover pressure. Furthermore, both friendly and hostile bids occur in nearly all industries.

We next use chi-square tests to assess whether the variation in takeover and restructuring activity is significant across the 51 Value Line industries. The null hypothesis is that the actual takeover rate in each industry equals its expected takeover rate. (The expected takeover rate is that for the entire Value Line sample.) Table 4 reports the probability values associated with the null hypothesis of equal rates of activity across industries for three measures: total takeover and restructuring activity, takeover attempts, and actual takeovers.[3]

[3]We perform separate analysis for friendly and hostile takeover attempts, and obtain results similar to those reported in Table 4. We do not report the results for the finer categorization of takeover attempts because they are somewhat redundant, given the results for total takeover attempts, and also because the distinction between friendly versus hostile takeovers is not integral to our analysis of industry shocks.

Table 3
Cross-sectional variation in takeover and restructuring activity by Value Line industry during 1982–89

This table presents the takeover and restructuring activity during 1982–89 across 51 industries encompassing 1,064 firms listed in the Value Line Investment Survey at year-end 1981. Takeover and restructuring activity in the 1982–89 period is determined by searching financial periodicals. Industry value is the sum of the total value (book debt plus market equity, in $ millions) of the firms in the industry as of year-end 1981. Total activity is the fraction of firms in an industry that experience a takeover bid or a major restructuring in the 1982–89 period. Takeover attempts is the fraction of firms that receive a takeover bid. Friendly bids and hostile bids respectively segregate the fraction of takeover bids into friendly and hostile categories. Actual takeovers reports the fraction of firms that actually realize a change in control. The 'Equal' columns show the % of firms in an industry that experience activity. The 'Value' columns show the proportion of total value in an industry, based on year-end 1981 values, that experiences activity in the 1982–89 period. The data are presented in descending order of the fraction of firms experiencing takeover or restructuring activity.

Industry	Number of firms	Industry value	Total activity		Takeover attempts		Friendly bids		Hostile bids		Actual takeovers	
			Equal	Value	Equal	Value	Equal	Value	Equal	Value	Equal	Value
Entertainment	17	11,204	82%	88%	71%	83%	47%	22%	24%	61%	59%	61%
Drugstores	10	3,525	80	79	70	67	60	51	10	16	70	67
Petroleum producing	19	17,972	79	91	63	71	26	14	37	57	47	63
Broadcasting	13	8,200	77	83	77	83	38	42	38	41	69	64
Textiles	17	4,248	77	82	76	82	41	22	35	60	71	81
Tire & rubber	12	7,464	75	90	67	75	17	4	50	71	50	31
Integrated steel	12	17,441	75	81	33	44	17	12	17	32	17	9
Air transport	23	18,462	74	70	70	70	39	42	30	28	48	41
Toiletries & cosmetics	15	7,011	73	97	60	91	27	7	33	84	47	47
Metals & mining	11	13,862	73	57	64	43	0	0	64	43	18	16
Natural gas	21	41,647	71	76	67	53	29	17	38	36	57	45
Precision instruments	21	17,811	71	28	62	14	48	8	14	6	43	8
Retail stores, special lines	17	6,810	71	34	65	30	35	15	29	15	47	26
Grocery stores	20	10,662	70	72	70	72	35	19	35	53	65	60
Truck & transport leasing	20	7,118	70	58	45	42	15	5	30	37	45	42
Integrated petroleum	36	2,14,134	69	60	56	41	17	8	39	34	39	28
Hotels & gaming	12	8,000	67	81	42	38	8	6	33	32	17	10
Coal, uranium, geothermal	9	4,620	67	56	44	36	22	4	22	32	22	4
Construction machinery	17	11,740	65	27	65	27	24	9	41	17	53	20

Multiform	40	38,755	63	79	50	40	28	20	23	20	45	38
Building	58	23,195	62	65	52	44	29	19	22	26	40	29
Replacement auto parts	15	5,710	60	48	47	37	27	12	20	25	33	33
Home appliances	10	2,740	60	44	60	44	50	26	10	22	60	44
Original equip. auto parts	10	3,807	60	34	50	23	40	22	10	1	50	23
Packaging & containers	22	9,206	59	70	50	67	23	20	27	47	45	66
Publishing	22	10,778	59	48	59	48	32	16	27	32	50	24
Oilfield services	27	37,193	59	52	41	37	30	32	11	5	30	30
Apparel	26	3,987	58	74	54	68	35	52	19	16	46	63
Fast food & restaurants	16	6,779	56	31	50	28	31	19	19	9	50	28
Medical services	9	9,916	56	59	56	59	.44	47	11	12	56	59
Food processing	54	40,722	56	57	52	51	28	25	24	26	48	50
Machinery	38	16,757	55	48	50	38	37	27	13	12	47	31
Retail stores	38	35,333	55	30	50	28	29	7	22	21	39	19
Industrial services	19	6,713	53	25	53	25	47	23	5	2	47	24
Computer data processing	31	63,916	52	14	45	11	19	2	26	9	45	11
Shoes	12	4,515	50	44	33	35	17	12	17	23	17	12
Mfg. hous. & rec. vehicles	12	890	50	37	42	36	42	36	0	0	42	36
General steel	10	1,725	50	34	40	28	20	14	20	14	40	28
Aerospace & defense	28	24,383	50	34	46	25	25	8	21	17	39	18
Basic chemicals	13	45,656	46	26	38	25	15	7	23	18	23	7
Electrical equipment	34	33,430	44	22	38	8	26	6	12	2	38	8
Diversified chemicals	14	21,212	43	41	21	12	7	7	14	5	21	12
Toys & school supplies	10	1,410	40	29	40	29	30	23	10	6	40	29
Health care & hosp. supply	23	19,965	39	16	35	14	13	3	22	12	35	14
Drugs	13	28,814	38	31	38	31	31	30	8	1	38	31
Office equipment & supplies	13	7,243	38	19	38	19	31	13	8	6	38	19
Machine tool	16	5,378	38	21	38	21	6	1	31	20	31	20
Electronics	41	26,688	37	25	37	25	22	20	15	5	29	23
Paper & paper products	27	32,245	33	24	33	24	7	4	26	20	26	21
Specialty chemicals	22	8,058	27	14	27	14	9	5	18	9	14	8
Metal fabricating	19	4,463	26	21	26	21	16	15	11	6	26	21
All firms	1,064	1,013,512	57%	49%	50%	37%	27%	14%	23%	23%	41%	28%

The first two columns of p-values in Table 4 are based on conventional chi-square statistics: the Pearson chi-square statistic and the likelihood ratio chi-square statistic.[4] For both test statistics, the null hypothesis is rejected for all categories of takeover and restructuring activity.

A drawback of these conventional test statistics is that they are only approximations of the true p-values; statistics research has shown that the approximations may not be valid for cases in which some of the expected frequencies are less than five. For the Value Line sample, there are several industries for which this is the case. For example, in the category of actual takeover occurrences, the expected takeover rate is 41% implying an expected frequency of less than five takeovers for the 13 industries with less than 13 firms. One way of reducing the number of industries with expected frequencies below five is to group related industries, such as those in the different steel sectors. When we do so, the probability values associated with the various takeover categories fall noticeably.

As a more general improvement over the weakness in the conventional tests in the presence of sparse data, we compute exact tests of significance that yield the true p-values regardless of sample size. Specifically, we employ the simulation algorithms developed by Mehta and Patel (1983), which extend the Fisher exact test for a 2×2 table to an $r \times c$ table. Using their algorithm, we simulate probability distributions associated with the takeover and restructuring data, and obtain the likelihood that the observed data exhibit variation across industries.[5] These probability values are presented in the third column of Table 4, and confirm that the variation in takeover activity during the 1982–89 sample period is indeed significant.

To verify the robustness of the results, we analyze the actual takeovers during 1982–90 in the 46 SIC-designated industries taken from the CRSP files. As reported in Table 10 in the Appendix, this larger sample of 3,660 firms also exhibits interindustry variation in takeover activity. For example, 60% of the firms in Food Stores are acquired between 1982 and 1990, compared with only 10% of the firms in Coal Mining over the same interval. Weighting by equity value, the fraction of actual takeovers ranges from 71% in Textile Mill Products

[4]The Pearson chi-square statistic pertains to the difference between the actual and expected proportions of takeover and restructuring activity across industries. It takes the form: $Q_p = \sum_i \sum_j (Actual_{ij} - Expected_{ij})^2 / Expected_{ij}$. The likelihood ratio chi-square statistic pertains to the ratio of the actual and expected proportions across industries: $G_2 = 2 \sum_i \sum_j Actual_{ij} \ln(Actual_{ij}/Expected_{ij})$.

[5]We thank Montse Fuentes and Augustine Kong of the Department of Statistics at the University of Chicago for the simulation work and for helpful discussions on this topic. The SAS statistical package also applies the Mehta and Patel (1983) algorithm, but memory constraints impede execution when the number of control groups (i.e., industries) is high relative to the number of observations, as is the case for our sample.

Table 4
Tests comparing takeover and restructuring frequency across industries

This table reports the probability values from tests assessing the null of no variation in takeover and restructuring activity across 51 Value Line industries during the 1982–89 period, and actual takeovers across 46 CRSP SIC industries during the 1982–90 period. Pearson refers to the Pearson chi-square statistic that pertains to the difference between the actual and the expected proportions of corporate control activity across industires: $Q_p = \sum_i \sum_j (Actual_{ij} - Expected_{ij})^2 / Expected_{ij}$. Likelihood ratio refers to the likelihood ratio chi-square statistic that pertains to the ratio of the actual and expected proportions across industries: $G_2 = 2\sum_i \sum_j Actual_{ij} \ln(Actual_{ij}/Expected_{ij})$. Exact test is based on the simulation of probability distributions using algorithms developed by Mehta and Patel (1983). Degrees of freedom are 50 for the three Value Line categories and 45 for the CRSP sample. A description of the Value Line takeover and restructuring categories is provided in Table 3. The CRSP sample is described in Table 10 in the Appendix.

	Probability value		
Category	Pearson	Likelihood ratio	Exact test
Total activity	0.003	0.002	0.002
Takeover attempts	0.081	0.060	0.064
Actual takeovers	0.069	0.042	0.040
Actual takeovers, CRSP sample	0.001	0.001	0.001

to 3.7% in the Leather industry. As reported in Table 4, the statistical tests indicate that the fraction of actual takeover occurrences varies significantly at the 0.001 level across the 46 SIC industries. These data confirm the results from the Value Line sample, and indicate that the interindustry variation in takeover activity during the 1980s is a broad phenomenon.

5. Industry differences in the timing of takeover and restructuring activity

To complement the prior section, we next examine the extent to which the timing of takeover and restructuring activity during the 1980s varies across industries. Using tests for equality of variance and for equality of means, we find that relative to the entire distribution the takeovers in a given industry tend to cluster in a subsample of years during the 1980s. This evidence is consistent with the argument that industry shocks contribute to the takeover and restructuring activity of the 1980s. The relatively tight distribution of activity in a particular industry suggests that takeovers and restructurings in that industry are driven by a common shock.

Table 5 presents the number of takeovers and restructurings by industry on an annual basis for the 1982–89 period. The data are sorted by the maximum fraction of takeovers and restructurings occurring in an industry in an adjacent two-year period within the eight-year sample period. While the choice

Table 5
Takeover and restructuring activity by year for Value Line industries

This table reports the number of takeovers and restructurings by industry by year for a sample of 1,064 firms from 51 industries listed on Value Line as of fourth quarter 1981. A takeover or restructuring is assigned to the year in which the initial announcement of the event occurs. Maximum cluster % in 2 years is the greatest fraction of takeovers and restructurings occurring in an industry in an adjacent two-year period.

	Number of takeovers and restructurings per year								Maximum cluster % in
Industry	82	83	84	85	86	87	88	89	2 years
Orig. equip. auto parts	0	0	0	2	4	0	0	0	100%
Home appliances	0	0	0	1	4	0	1	0	83
Drugstores	0	0	4	2	1	0	1	0	75
Paper & paper products	0	0	1	3	3	0	1	1	67
Basic chemicals	0	0	0	2	2	0	1	1	67
Specialty chemicals	0	0	0	0	1	1	2	2	67
Air transport	0	2	1	1	6	5	1	1	65
Grocery stores	1	0	2	0	2	5	4	0	64
Construction machinery	1	0	1	0	3	4	1	1	64
Drugs	0	0	0	1	0	1	0	3	60
Broadcasting	0	2	0	4	2	1	0	1	60
Metal fabricating	0	1	0	0	1	0	3	0	60
Replacement auto parts	2	0	0	0	1	1	2	3	56
Tire & rubber	0	1	1	1	1	3	2	0	56
Petroleum producing	2	5	3	3	1	1	0	0	53
Electronics	2	0	0	1	2	2	4	4	53
Oilfield services	1	1	7	1	4	0	0	2	50
Entertainment	4	3	2	2	1	0	0	2	50
Mfg. hous. & rec. vehicle	3	0	0	0	0	1	1	1	50
Aerospace & defense	4	0	1	3	4	1	1	0	50
Metals & mining	1	0	0	2	0	2	2	1	50
Coal, uranium, geothermal	1	1	1	2	0	0	0	1	50
Shoes	0	0	0	1	1	2	1	1	50
Toys & school supplies	1	0	2	0	0	0	1	0	50
Diversified chemicals	0	1	0	0	2	1	2	0	50
Hotels & gaming	0	0	0	2	2	2	1	1	50
Multiform	2	5	7	3	1	4	2	1	48
Precision instruments	1	2	0	0	4	3	3	2	47
Electrical equipment	0	0	2	2	4	3	3	1	47
Fast food & restaurants	1	0	2	0	1	1	2	2	44
Integrated steel	1	3	1	1	3	0	0	0	44
Health care & hosp. supply	3	0	1	3	0	0	2	0	44
Computer data processing	0	3	2	1	4	3	1	2	44
Retail stores	4	1	8	1	4	1	2	0	43
Retail stores, special line	2	0	1	0	4	1	1	3	42
Medical services	0	1	1	0	1	1	1	0	40
General steel	2	0	0	1	1	0	1	0	40
Apparel	1	2	3	3	2	1	2	1	40
Office equip. & supplies	1	1	1	1	1	0	0	0	40

Table 5 (continued)

Industry	Number of takeovers and restructurings per year								Maximum cluster % in 2 years
	82	83	84	85	86	87	88	89	
Publishing	2	1	3	0	1	1	3	2	38
Packaging & containers	0	1	2	3	2	2	1	2	38
Textiles	3	2	2	1	1	2	2	0	38
Truck & transport leasing	1	2	2	2	3	2	2	1	36
Toiletries & cosmetics	0	1	1	2	2	1	1	3	36
Natural gas	2	3	1	3	2	1	1	2	33
Building	3	5	7	3	6	1	6	5	33
Food processing	4	4	3	6	2	2	8	1	33
Machinery	4	3	2	4	3	2	1	2	33
Machine tool	1	1	0	1	1	0	0	2	33
Integrated petroleum	3	4	5	3	4	1	5	0	32
Industrial services	3	0	3	0	3	0	1	0	30
Annual total	67	62	86	78	108	65	83	58	
% of all takeovers & restructurings	11.0	10.2	14.2	12.9	17.8	10.7	13.7	9.6	

of a two-year window is somewhat arbitrary, alternate groupings (e.g., a three-year period) yield similar conclusions.

The data in Table 5 suggest that takeover activity in a given industry tends to cluster within a narrow range of time. In the Original Equipment Auto Parts industry, for example, all six of the takeovers occur within a period of less than two years. Similarly, 83% of the takeovers in the Home Appliance and 75% in the Drugstore industries occur in a two-year period. More generally, we find that 50% of the takeovers in a given industry clusters within a two-year period; in other words, half of the takeovers in an industry tend to occur within one-fourth of the sample period. Similar results hold for value-weighted measures of clustering. This clustering of takeover activity by industry contrasts with the more evenly distributed takeover and restructuring activity for the full sample, which we report at the bottom of Table 5. Here, the maximum two-year cluster, found in the 1985–86 grouping, is 31%. Of course, several of the industries do not exhibit time-series clustering.

To perform a more formal analysis on whether takeover and restructuring activity clusters over time at the industry level, we use conventional procedures that compare the dispersion of an entire pool of data with the dispersion within control groups. First, we employ the chi-square test of the equality of variances, which computes the difference between the natural log of the variance of the entire sample and the weighted average of the variance of the 51 industry subsamples (see, e.g., Johnston, 1984, p. 298).

Table 6
Variation in the timing of takeover and restructuring activity

This table reports tests of the null hypothesis of no variation in the timing of takeover and restructuring activity for three takeover categories across 51 Value Line industries during 1982–89, and for actual takeovers across 46 CRSP SIC industries during 1982–90. Panel A reports results from chi-square tests that compare the variance of the timing of takeover activity for an entire sample with that within control groups (i.e., industries). Panel B reports results from ANOVA F-tests for the equality of mean takeover dates across industries. Degrees of freedom are 50 for the Value Line categories and 45 for the CRSP sample.

Panel A: Chi-square tests for the equality of variance

Category	Chi-square statistic	Probability value
Total activity	98.49	0.0001
Takeover attempts	103.20	0.0001
Actual takeovers	87.44	0.0008
Actual takeovers, CRSP sample	261.00	0.0001

Panel B: ANOVA F-tests for the equality of means

Category	F-statistic	Probability value
Total activity	2.02	0.0001
Takeover attempts	1.77	0.0015
Actual takeovers	1.53	0.0155
Actual takeovers, CRSP sample	1.67	0.0040

As reported in panel A of Table 6, the chi-square tests for the equality of variance indicate significant industry clustering. For each of the Value Line categories, the p-value is 0.0008 or lower. Replication of the analysis using data based on the actual takeover occurrences in two-digit SIC industries also indicates significance at the 0.0001 level. The tighter time distribution of takeover and restructuring at the industry level vis-à-vis the full sample confirms the time-series industry clustering of takeovers and restructurings. It is consistent with the argument that industry shocks are a source of the takeover and restructuring activity of the 1980s.

As a related test of clustering, we examine the interindustry variation in the mean takeover date. For the 607 firms that experience a takeover or restructuring in the Value Line data set, we assign a number based on announcement month that ranges from one if the takeover is announced in January 1982 to 96 if the takeover is announced in December 1989. We then use analysis of variance to test if the mean takeover month is the same across industries. Panel B of Table 6 displays the p-values from the ANOVA F-tests. In all cases, the p-values indicate significant variation in the time-series pattern of takeovers and restructurings by industry during the 1980s.

We perform the same analysis on the 1,133 actual takeover occurrences in the sample of CRSP-listed firms from the 46 industries classified by two-digit SIC codes. The sample dates range from January 1982 to December 1990, which we linearize from 1 to 108. As also reported in Table 6, the *p*-value is 0.004, confirming the significant variation over time in takeover activity by industry.[6]

The interindustry differences in the time-series clustering of takeover activity distinguish the 1980s from the two prior decades. For two samples of takeover occurrences taken from the CRSP files spanning July 1962 to December 1972 and January 1973 to December 1981, we replicate the analysis of variance tests. In contrast to the results from the 1980s, we find no evidence of significant industry clustering in the earlier time periods. These results concur with Palepu (1986), who finds no evidence of acquisition clustering by industry in the 1971–79 period.

6. Industry shocks and industry variation in takeover activity

The existence of interindustry differences in takeover activity reported in the prior two sections is consistent with the argument that industry shocks contribute to the 1980s takeover wave. In this section, we examine more explicitly the relation between industry shocks and takeover activity during the 1980s. We first analyze a broad-based proxy for industry shocks that is based on sales and employment data, and then study the effect of specific shocks, including deregulation, energy dependence, foreign competition, and financing innovations.

6.1. Broad industry shocks

Our concept of a shock is any factor that alters industry structure. Examples of industry shocks range from specific factors, such as deregulation and input price volatility, to broader effects, such as demographic or technological change. Whatever the underlying source, a shock leads to a change in industry structure. Our premise is that takeover and restructuring activity accommodates such change.

One way to gauge the shocks borne by an industry is to directly measure the economic change experienced by the industry's members. To create a proxy for industry shocks, we compute abnormal industry sales growth between 1977 and

[6] We conduct an additional examination of the timing of takeover and restructuring activity across industries, using chi-square tests to determine if takeover activity clusters at annual intervals and at biannual intervals. Consistent with the results reported in Table 6, the tests strongly reject the null of no industry clustering of takeover activity. These tests, however, suffer from the same weaknesses as discussed for the chi-square tests in Section 4. Analyzing, for example, 441 actual takeovers in eight year across 51 industries implies expected values of less than five in all cells of the contingency table.

1981, the five years preceding the sample period of 1982–89. Computing shocks from the same time period for all industries abstracts from the fact that the timing of takeover activity varies across industries. But in focusing on the 1977–81 period, we seek to assess whether the industries undergoing the most change in the period immediately preceding the 1980s takeover boom account for a disproportionate share of that takeover wave. The estimation of industry sales shocks in a period prior to that of the takeover sample also allows us to include data for all 1,064 firms in the sample.

For each of the 51 industries in our Value Line sample, we use Compustat data to first compute industry sales growth between 1977 and 1981. For the measure of the industry sales shock, we then take the absolute value of the difference between a particular industry's sales growth and the average sales g rowth across all 51 industries. This measure corresponds to our concept of a shock, because it emphasizes that shocks can have both positive and negative effects on industry growth. To benchmark the importance of the proxy for shocks, we also analyze the effect that industry sales growth has on takeover activity. As a further means of assessing the robustness of the results, we compute a similar shock variable based on employment data.

Table 11 in the Appendix reports the sales and employment shock measures for the 51 sample industries, with the data sorted by the sales shock measure. Note that the industries with the largest values for sales shocks include Medical Services, whose sales growth of 101% during the 1977–81 period was 83 percentage points greater than the sample average, and Manufactured Housing & Recreation Vehicles, whose sales growth of − 43% was 61 percentage points below the sample average. By construction, both of these industries experienced large sales shocks between 1977 and 1981. Other industries with large values for the sales shock measure include much of the energy sector, which had high sales growth in the late 1970s, and underperformers, such as Textiles and Tire and Rubber. The employment shock measure provides a similar ranking to that for sales, with a correlation coefficient between the two shock measures of 0.81.

Panel A of Table 7 reports regressions of three measures of industry takeover activity on both sales shocks and sales growth. Each regression uses 51 observations, one for each industry in the sample. The results indicate that sales shocks are directly related to industry takeover activity. For example, the coefficient on Sales Shock in the Total Activity regression indicates that a 10-percentage-point deviation in industry sales growth from the sample average leads to a 4.6-percentage-point increase in takeover and restructuring activity in an industry. Similar results hold for the regressions using other measures of takeover activity. Sales shocks are positively and significantly related to the takeover attempts and actual takeovers across industries. By contrast, industry sales growth has no explanatory power for the industry variation in takeover activity during the 1980s.

Table 7
Regressions of takeover activity on broad industry shocks

This table reports regressions of industry measures of takeover activity on measures of industry shocks based on sales and employment data from the 1977–81 period. Panel A regresses takeover activity on industry sales shocks, and also industry sales growth, a proxy for industry performance. Panel B regresses takeover activity on industry employment shocks, and also industry employment growth, a proxy for industry performance. The definitions of the three takeover and restructuring categories are provided in Table 3. Industry sales and employment shocks and growth are defined in Table 11 in the Appendix. Each regression uses 51 observations. *t*-statistics are in parentheses.

Panel A: Takeover activity, sales shocks, and sales growth

	Total activity	Takeover attempts	Actual takeovers
Intercept	44.08	36.39	27.02
	(8.92)	(8.34)	(7.07)
Sales shock	0.46	0.47	0.47
	(2.10)	(2.38)	(2.74)
Sales growth	− 0.04	− 0.11	− 0.11
	(− 0.26)	(− 0.72)	(− 0.82)
Adjusted R^2	0.05	0.07	0.10

Panel B: Takeover activity, employment shocks, and employment growth

	Total activity	Takeover attempts	Actual takeovers
Intercept	46.64	36.81	26.95
	(10.34)	(9.36)	(7.74)
Employment shock	0.45	0.53	0.51
	(1.77)	(2.39)	(2.60)
Employment growth	− 0.22	− 0.21	− 0.14
	(− 1.16)	(− 1.26)	(− 0.93)
Adjusted R^2	0.03	0.07	0.09

These results indicate that takeover and restructuring activity is related to industry change, rather than being restricted to only low-growth or only high-growth industries. Indeed, in results not presented in Table 7, we find identical results from univariate regressions that employ only the sales shock or the sales growth explanatory variable. Takeover and restructuring activity is positively and significantly related to sales shocks, indicating that both high sales growth and large sales declines contribute to above-average takeover activity at the industry level.

Panel B of Table 7 replicates the analysis, using employment shocks and employment growth as the explanatory variables. Similar to the sales shock results, employment shocks are positively related to takeover activity. In contrast, employment growth is not significantly related to takeover activity.

As further evidence of the importance of industry shocks for takeover activity, we re-estimate the regressions, using sales and employment data for the 623 firms that remained independent entities through 1989. More than 73% of the firms, 457 out of 623, neither received a takover bid nor engaged in restructuring activity during the sample period. In results not reported, the evidence from these surviving firms closely resembles that presented in Table 7. The industry sales and employment shocks estimated solely from the surviving firms are positively and significantly related to industry takeover and restructuring activity. Hence, the relation between industry shocks and takeover activity is not merely driven by acquired firms, but actually reflects industry-wide phenomena.

6.2. *Specific industry shocks*

The generic proxies for industry shocks analyzed in the prior section indicate the overall changes borne by the sample industries, rather than directly measuring shocks themselves. To focus the analysis on the sources of industry change that lead to takeover activity, we next examine the relation between takeover activity and specific industry shocks.

To determine the shocks to include in the analysis, we survey analyst reports of the sources of change facing the industries in our sample. As reported in Table 8, for the high-takeover industries these shocks include deregulation, energy price volatility, foreign competition, and financing innovations. Similar factors have been cited by Jensen (1993), Ravenscraft (1987), and Weston, Chung, and Hoag (1990) in their retrospectives on the 1980s takeover wave. We develop the measurement of each of these four shocks in turn.

6.2.1. *Deregulation*

Several industries reported in Table 8 experienced major federal deregulation in the late 1970s and early 1980s. As discussed in analysis of specific industries (e.g., Baltagi, Griffin, and Rich, 1995; Phillips, 1991; Rose, 1985; Whinston and Collins, 1992), deregulation removed artificial constraints on the size of existing firms and induced entry by new firms. The adaptation to these changes in industry organization could be facilitated by takeovers. Our expectation is that the shock of deregulation is positively related to takeover and restructuring activity.

As a measure of deregulation, we employ a dummy variable equal to one for five industries in our sample: Air Transport, Broadcasting, Entertainment, Natural Gas, and Trucking and Transport Leasing. These industries all experienced major federal deregulation; indeed, a search of industry name and the code word 'deregulation' on the Dow Jones News Service produces over 100 stories for each of these industries, more than for any of the other industries in our sample.

Table 8
Sources of change in industry structure

This table reports reasons offered for the changing structure of high-takeover industries during the 1980s. Reference sources for this table include the Value Line Investment Survey, S&P Industry Outlooks, the U.S. Industrial Outlook, the *Wall Street Journal*, and other analyst reports.

Industry	Source of change
Air transport	Airline Deregulation Act of 1978 phased out the government control of airline routes and pricing during the early 1980s. The deregulation facilitated entry, the development of the hub-and-spoke system, and the movement to nationwide route systems.
Apparel, Textiles	A significant increase of imports, induced in part by a shift to an antiprotectionist foreign trade policy, prompted consolidation as a means of streamlining operations to compete effectively.
Broadcasting, Entertainment	FCC policies in the early 1980s eliminated programming and ownership regulations that had limited the number of radio and television stations held by one corporation, and had impeded the sale of radio and television stations. Cable Communications Policy Act of 1984 phased out rate restrictions on cable TV.
Coal, uranium, geothermal	Changes in petroleum prices first induced expansion, and later contraction, in these energy sectors.
Drugstores	Moderate growth prospects and new competition from grocery stores and discounters (such as Walmart) induced consolidation among industry members.
Food processing	Excess capacity in mature industry due to low population growth rate led to consolidation.
Grocery stores	Declining industry growth, relaxed antitrust environment, high tangibility of assets, and ability to use leverage financing led to change in industry structure.
Hotels & gaming	Volatility in real estate and building prices.
Integrated petroleum, Oilfield services, Petroleum producing	1973 OPEC embargo and 1978–79 Iranian oil-export cutoff created price volatility that ultimately caused industry restructuring and consolidation.
Integrated steel	Secular decline in steel demand and subsidized foreign competition resulted in excess capacity and consolidation.
Medical services	The implementation of Medicare's Prospective Payment System in 1983 changed reimbursement from cost-based to a fixed payment per diagnosis. This inducement to curb costs prompted alterations in industry structure and promoted the growth of HMOs.
Metals & mining	Foreign competition, brought on in part by subsidization by foreign governments, resulted in excess capacity and subsequent industry consolidation.

continued over

Table 8 (continued)

Multiform	Conglomerates formed in the 1960s and 1970s restructured in the 1980s.
Natural gas	The Natural Gas Policy Act of 1978 phased in price deregulation and encouraged the combination of pipelines to enable regional and national gas transportation systems.
Packaging & containers	Foreign competition and the realignment from metal and glass led to industry restructuring.
Tire & rubber	Longer-lasting radial tires, rising imports, and the reduced demand for automobiles following energy price increases created excess capacity and subsequent industry consolidation.
Truck & transport leasing	Trucking deregulation of 1980 allowed new entry, resulting in excess capacity that led to consolidation.
Toiletries & cosmetics	Demographic changes slowed industry growth and led to consolidation.

6.2.2. Energy dependence

Jensen (1993) states that one shock driving takeover activity during the 1980s was the oil price volatility stemming from the 1973 OPEC boycott and continuing in the 1979 Iran embargo. He suggests that the shock not only directly affected the oil industry itself, but also was important for the structure of industries in which energy was a major input.

To empirically test the importance of the oil shock for takeover activity, we develop a proxy for energy dependence. Using data compiled every five years by the Department of Commerce, we estimate the fraction of inputs comprised of energy in 1982 for each of the industries in our sample. The data are presented in Table 12 in the Appendix . The qualitative ordering of the data is as one might expect. Energy and transportation industries are at the top of the list. Computations using Department of Commerce data from 1977 and 1987 yield similar orderings for the fraction of energy inputs by industry.

To proxy for energy dependence, we construct a dummy variable equal to one for any industry in which energy comprises 10% or more of input costs, a fraction large enough to induce industry change following rising energy prices. We also assign a dummy variable of one to Oilfield Services and Petroleum Producing. Although energy is not a large direct input in these two cases, the industries are clearly energy-related.

6.2.3. Foreign competition

Prior research (e.g., Clark, Kaserman, and Mayo, 1990; Katics and Petersen, 1994; MacDonald, 1994) documents the growing vulnerability of many U.S.

industries to foreign competition, and has found that changes in foreign competition affect price – cost margins and other measures of industry efficiency. We address the question of whether any industry consolidation induced by changes in foreign competition is accompanied by heightened takeover activity. Table 8 notes some leading examples, such as the Apparel, Textiles, Steel, and Tire and Rubber industries. Our analysis examines whether these cases generalize across the 51 sample industries.

To create a proxy for shocks stemming from foreign competition, we use data from the Department of Commerce to estimate the change in the import penetration ratio (imports/industry supply) in the 1980s for the 51 industries in our sample. Specifically, we compute the average import penetration for the five years prior to our sample, 1977–81, and for the sample period, 1982–89. We then compute the change in the import penetration ratio between these two time intervals.

The import data are reported in Table 13 in the Appendix . The data affirm the notion that import penetration increases in many industries during the 1980s. As a proxy for a foreign competition shock, we assign a dummy variable equal to one for the top third of the sample (17 industries) experiencing the greatest increase in import penetration during the 1980s. Designation of this subsample includes industries such as Textiles and Steel within those classified as experiencing a foreign competition shock. The results reported below are not affected by the specification of this variable.

6.2.4. Financing innovations

Another shock during the 1980s is the significant increase in high-yield debt financing. The enhanced ability to use leveraged financing removes obstacles to takeovers, especially at larger firms. Indeed, our comparison of takeover targets in the 1980s vis-à-vis the two prior decades indicates that one distinguishing feature of the 1980s merger wave is the relatively large size of takeover targets.

The increased accessibility of leveraged financing in the 1980s can be expected to have differential effects across industries. Jensen and Meckling (1976) and Myers (1977) point out the limitations of debt financing in the presence of asset substitutability and intangible assets. Empirical papers by Bradley, Jarrell, and Kim (1984) and Long and Malitz (1985) document that the fraction of debt in capital structure is inversely related to R&D/sales at the industry level. The basic notion is that a higher degree of project substitution can take place in R&D expenditures compared to those for plant and equipment. Correspondingly, we expect takeover activity in the 1980s to be greater in industries having low R&D/sales ratios. Hence, to capture the effect of financing innovations across industries, we estimate R&D/sales in 1981 for each industry in our sample.

In developing this empirical proxy, we chose 1981 so as to incorporate all firms in the analysis. Our results are not sensitive to this particular year, as R&D/sales at the industry level is very stable over time. For example, the correlation coefficient between 1977 R&D/sales and 1989 R&D/sales

is 0.97 for the 51 Value Line industries. Other measures of asset tangibility, such as capital expenditures, are not as stable over time. Moreover, capital expenditures mimic cash flows more so than R&D, and thereby pick up performance effects in addition to asset tangibility. Additionally, due to investment-related tax shields, capital expenditures work against the tax advantages of debt financing.

6.3. Regression analysis of takeover activity and specific industry shocks

Table 9 reports the regression analysis of takeover activity and specific industry shocks. Univariate regressions correspond to each of the four shocks and each of the three measures of takeover activity. Multiple regressions incorporate all four shocks.

Panel A of Table 9 reports the results where the dependent variable is the total takeover and restructuring activity in an industry. In the univariate regressions, both deregulation and energy dependence have a positive effect on takeover and restructuring activity: The coefficients are more than two standard deviations different than zero. These results are consistent with the notion that the reorganization prompted by relaxed regulation and volatile oil prices contributes to the takeover wave of the 1980s. Foreign competition, however, does not have a significant effect on takeover and restructuring activity. Although import penetration increases in high-takeover industries such as Textiles and Steel, which are experiencing a general decline in the world market, foreign competition also heightens in low-takeover industries such as Computer Data Processing and Electronics, for which the world market is rapidly expanding. Industry R&D/sales is negatively and significantly related to takeover and restructuring activity, supporting the notion that innovations in financing techniques were important for the takeover and restructuring activity of the 1980s. In the multiple regression, R&D/sales is the only explanatory variable with a coefficient more than two standard deviations different from zero. This is due in part to the fact that some of the deregulated and energy-dependent industries with heavy takeover and restructuring activity also have low levels of R&D/Sales.

Panel B of Table 9 repeats the analysis of specific industry shocks, using takeover attempts as the dependent variable. The results resemble those for total takeover and restructuring activity. In the univariate specifications, both deregulation and R&D/Sales have a significant effect on takeover attempts. The coefficient on energy dependence, however, is no longer more than two standard deviations different from zero. This is because energy-dependent industries such as Oilfield Services and Trucking and Transport Leasing responded to the oil shocks by employing major restructurings and joint ventures, rather than takeovers. As in the prior analysis, foreign competition has no significant effect on takeover attempts. In the multiple regression, both deregulation and R&D/sales have a significant effect on takeover attempts.

Table 9
Regressions of takeover activity on specific industry shocks

This table reports regressions of industry measures of takeover activity on specific measures of industry shocks, including deregulation, energy dependence, foreign competition, and ability to debt-finance. Panel A reports regressions for total takeover and restructuring activity. Panel B reports regressions for takeover attempts. Panel C reports regressions for actual takeovers. Deregulation is a dummy variable for five industries experiencing major federal deregulation: Air transport, Broadcasting, Entertainment, Natural gas, and Trucking & transport leasing. Energy dependence is a dummy variable for energy-related industries and any industry in which energy accounts for 10% or more of input costs as described in Table 12 in the Appendix. Import vulnerability is a dummy variable equal to one for the top third of the industries described in Table 13 that experience the greatest increase in import penetration in the 1980s. R&D/sales (for 1981) proxies for debt-financing ability and is taken from Compustat. Each regression uses 51 observations. *t*-statistics are in parentheses.

Panel A: *Total takeover and restructuring activity*

	(1)	(2)	(3)	(4)	(5)
Intercept	46.76 (13.82)	46.89 (13.21)	51.18 (12.24)	59.42 (15.81)	54.92 (11.32)
Deregulation	28.24 (2.61)	—	—	—	17.90 (1.61)
Energy dependence	—	19.26 (2.01)	—	—	4.82 (0.49)
Import vulnerability	—	—	– 4.94 (– 0.68)	—	2.60 (0.40)
R&D/sales	—	—	—	– 6.77 (– 4.22)	– 5.94 (– 3.55)
Adjusted R^2	0.10	0.06	– 0.01	0.25	0.27

Panel B: Takeover attempts

	(1)	(2)	(3)	(4)	(5)
Intercept	37.96 (12.79)	39.25 (12.09)	42.71 (11.49)	48.96 (14.25)	46.58 (10.70)
Deregulation	28.24 (2.98)	—	—	—	23.59 (2.37)
Energy dependence	—	10.75 (1.23)	—	—	– 5.62 (– 0.64)
Import vulnerability	—	—	– 5.94 (– 0.92)	—	– 0.34 (– 0.06)
R&D/sales	—	—	—	– 5.64 (– 3.84)	– 4.98 (– 3.32)
Adjusted R^2	0.14	0.01	– 0.003	0.22	0.26

Table 9 (continued)

Panel C: Actual takeovers

	(1)	(2)	(3)	(4)	(5)
Intercept	29.33	30.66	32.59	37.40	35.82
	(10.82)	(10.49)	(9.79)	(11.65)	(8.67)
Deregulation	21.37	—	—	—	19.59
	(2.46)				(2.08)
Energy dependence	—	5.48	—	—	− 7.28
		(0.70)			(− 0.88)
Import vulnerability	—	—	− 3.53	—	0.30
			(− 0.61)		(0.06)
R&D/sales	—	—	—	− 4.10	− 3.72
				(− 2.99)	(− 2.61)
Adjusted R^2	0.09	− 0.01	− 0.01	0.14	0.16

The analysis of actual takeovers in panel C of Table 9 is nearly identical to the results for takeover attempts. In both the univariate and multiple regressions, deregulation and R&D/sales are significantly related to takeover activity. Energy dependence and foreign competition have no explanatory power for the interindustry variation in actual takeovers.

The regression analysis is consistent with the proposition that takeover activity is affected by industry shocks. The analyses of broad-based shocks to sales and employment and of more explicit proxies for shocks find a significant relation between industry shocks and the takeover and restructuring activity of the 1980s.

Of course, the evidence on industry shocks far from fully explains the interindustry variation in takeover activity during the 1980s. One reason is that the explanatory variables used in the regression analysis are imperfect measures of industry shocks. A case in point is the foreign competition variable. While the variable captures the supply-side effects of imports, it does not account for the overall world demand conditions facing an industry. Hence, the foreign competition proxy used in the regression analysis has no significant relation with industry takeover activity.

Another limitation of the analysis is the absence of a model of the heterogeneous timing of the response to shocks across industries. The 1980s are instead treated as a uniform block of time. We do not attempt to discern why, for example, the broadcasting industry undergoes takeover activity more immediately after deregulation than does the air transport industry. We have sacrificed a finer understanding of the dynamics of the response to a single shock in a particular industry so that we can empirically examine the shock-takeover relation across a broad set of industries.

Finally, the imperfect nature of our proxies for industry shocks questions whether we have accurately depicted the effect of shocks on takeover activity. A case in point is whether the R&D/sales variable, which provides the greatest explanatory power in our regressions, is a suitable proxy for innovations in junk-bond financing. To address this issue, we study the relation between takeover activity and industry measures of R&D/sales during the 1970s.[7] A univariate regression yields an insignificant coefficient on the R&D/sales variable and an R-square of only 0.02. The contrast between the strong relation of R&D/sales and takeover activity during the 1980s with the weak relation in the prior decade, together with our related findings on the breadth of takeover activity at large firms in the 1980s, suggests that R&D/sales is capturing the effect of innovations in junk-bond financing.

7. Summary and implications of the empirical results

This paper studies the takeover and restructuring activity at the industry level during the 1980s takeover wave. We find that the takeover and restructuring activity in a particular industry tends to cluster within a narrow range during the sample period. On average, half of the takeovers and restructurings in an industry take place in one-fourth of the sample period, suggesting that common factors influence the takeovers occurring in an industry. We also document a significant interindustry variation in the rate of takeover and restructuring activity that is directly related to the magnitude of economic shocks borne by industries in the late 1970s and early 1980s, indicating a link between industry shocks and subsequent takeover and restructuring activity. The link is maintained for all surviving firms in an industry, affirming that the relation between industry shocks and takeover activity stems from industry-wide phenomena, rather than being due solely to target firms. We also report evidence that specific shocks such as deregulation and financing innovations contribute to the magnitude of the takeovers and restructurings during the 1980s. Overall, the empirical results suggest that the takeover wave of the 1980s entails an adaptation of industry structure to a changing economy. In the remainder of this section, we discuss some additional implications of the results.

[7]To analyze R&D/sales and takeover activity during the 1970s, we start with the intersection of (1) the 6,278 firms listed in the CRSP files as of December 31, 1972, and (2) the 1,855 firms from Compustat for which R&D/sales data are available as of December 1972. Adding the further requirement of 10 firms per industry obtains a data set of 1,431 firms in 31 industries; these firms account for 50% of the equity value of the overall CRSP data set. We then regress the value-weighted fraction of industry takeover activity in the 1973–79 period on the industry measures of R&D/sales.

7.1. Spillover effects of takeover announcements

Linking industry shocks with takeover activity suggests that the announcement of a takeover at one firm in an industry should be accompanied by a positive revaluation of other industry members. To test this implication, we take the announcement month for each of the 607 firms subject to a takeover or restructuring, and compute the abnormal return for the value-weighted portfolio of firms in the same industry. We employ the standard market model with an estimation period of 60 months, and compute *t*-statistics from the cross-sectional variances of abnormal returns. We find that the value-weighted abnormal return of the other firms in an industry is 0.5% (*t*-statistic = 3.18) in the month of the announcement. The Fama and French (1993) three-factor model yields similar findings. These results concur with Eckbo's (1983) finding of a positive and significant reaction at industry rivals to the announcement of 150 horizontal mergers, and Slovin, Sushka, and Bendeck's (1991) documentation of a positive industry stock price reaction to the announcement of 128 going-private transactions.

These spillover effects of merger announcements are often interpreted by antitrust regulators as evidence of anticipated market power. Our analysis points to a more benign explanation. Since we find that takeovers and restructurings are driven by industry shocks, the positive response to takeover announcements by industry members could represent the anticipation of ongoing restructuring throughout the industry.

7.2. Performance following takeovers

The standard textbook model holds that takeovers should increase value through improved cash flows from factors such as synergy and economies of scale. Empirically, however, the performance effects of takeovers are subject to considerable debate. Compare, for example, Healy, Palepu, and Ruback (1992) with Ravenscraft and Scherer (1987).

If industry shocks are a source of takeover and restructuring activity, then post-takeover performance should not necessarily be expected to improve, especially compared to a pre-shock benchmark or to industry cohorts. For example, the shock of deregulation to an industry such as Air Transport would not have a positive effect on the profits of incumbent firms if compared to the rents in a cartelized environment. Similarly, the shock of foreign competition has not been beneficial to the Apparel industry if compared to a period of heavy trade barriers. Firms consolidating via takeovers in the Apparel industry should not necessarily be expected to improve cash flows, especially since the consolidation takes place soon after the shock of foreign competition.

To measure the change in performance due to merger, researchers benchmark to the corresponding change in industry performance. For mergers driven by industry shocks, our empirical analysis, however, implies that the benchmark firms are also undertaking mergers, restructurings, and other value improvements in response to the industry shocks. In the Home Appliance industry for example, six of the ten firms were acquired in less than a two-year period. Consequently, while a merger will in fact create value, the industry-adjusted change in performance may indicate otherwise.

Many commentators have linked business failures in the 1990s to prior takeover activity. Although some takeovers are clearly the result of poor management decisions, post-takeover failure can stem from underlying industry shocks. Takeovers induced by negative or even positive shocks cannot be considered the primary cause of the changes in a firm's fortunes. Instead, takeovers and related restructuring activity are the message bearers of the more fundamental changes facing an industry. In such cases, more business failures may occur if takeovers are inhibited. However, conducting such counterfactual analysis suffers from ambiguous benchmarks.

7.3. The timing of takeover waves

The 1980s stand out as one of the most active takeover periods during the past century. Our analysis links the takeover and restructuring activity of that decade to industry shocks. This is consistent with Comment and Schwert's (1995) emphasis on general economic factors, rather than particular state laws and firm-specific poison pills, as being the source of the decline in takeovers at the beginning of the 1990s. Indeed, the recent return of takeover activity documented in Table 1 indicates that the corporate control market is not dead, and that takeovers will continue to cluster in industries that bear shocks of significant magnitude.

Whereas hundreds of takeover studies during the past 20 years have shed light on the role of takeovers in redirecting the investments of specific firms, these studies have been less successful in discerning why takeovers happen in waves. Indeed, Brealey and Myers (1991, p. 923) propose that takeover waves are one of the 10 unexplained puzzles in the field of financial economics. Most prior analyses, in posing macroeconomic variables as the source of takeover waves, have had mixed explanatory success. Our results indicate that future efforts should incorporate industry-level data. Various evidence suggests the fruitfulness of such an approach. Both Nelson (1959) for the turn of the century and Gort (1969) for the 1950s document interindustry differences in the rate of takeover activity. Taggart (1988) points to similar sectoral factors at play during the takeovers of the 1920s. A systematic analysis of the relation between industry shocks and takeover activity during the past century may shed light on the less-than-fully understood phenomenon of takeover waves.

222 M.L. Mitchell, J.H. Mulherin/Journal of Financial Economics 41 (1996) 193–229

Appendix

Table 10
Cross-sectional frequency of actual takeover occurrences during 1982–90 for CRSP-listed firms

This table reports the occurrence of actual takeovers across a sample of 46 two-digit SIC industries encompassing 3,660 firms taken from the CRSP tapes. Equal reports the fraction of takeover occurrences. Equity reports the fraction of the equity of an industry that was acquired.

				% takeovers	
Industry	SIC code	Number of firms	Number of takeovers	Equal	Equity
Food stores	54	53	32	60.4	56.2
Railroad transportation	40	15	9	60.0	52.8
Textile mill products	22	53	28	52.8	71.3
General merchandise	53	56	27	48.2	23.6
Miscellaneous retail	59	56	26	46.4	65.8
Stone, clay, glass, concrete	32	62	28	45.2	41.5
Hotels	7	35	15	42.9	44.9
Motor freight transportation	42	31	13	41.9	21.8
Non-building construction	16	17	7	41.2	27.1
Apparel	23	69	28	40.6	60.7
Furniture & home furnishings	57	15	6	40.0	6.4
Food products	20	122	48	39.3	29.6
Paper products	26	54	21	38.9	21.4
Transportation services	47	13	5	38.5	7.9
Transportation equipment	37	95	36	37.9	15.5
Personal services	72	16	6	37.5	12.3
Eating & drinking places	58	64	24	37.5	22.5
Building materials	52	16	6	37.5	52.4
Apparel & accessory stores	56	32	12	37.5	35.9
Air transportation	45	40	15	37.5	30.0
Primary metal	33	91	34	37.4	19.0
Rubber & plastic products	30	62	23	37.1	23.8
Health services	80	45	16	35.6	53.3
Motion pictures & video	78	30	10	33.3	56.3
Miscellaneous manufacturing	39	65	21	32.3	50.9
Medical & photographic equipment	38	214	69	32.2	16.5
Fabricated metal products	34	156	50	32.1	38.0
Building construction	15	25	8	32.0	16.3
Amusement & recreation services	79	22	7	31.8	49.5
Furniture & fixtures	25	33	10	30.3	17.6
Machinery, except electrical	35	328	96	29.3	20.5
Chemicals	28	182	51	28.0	19.2
Wholesale trade, durables	50	119	33	27.7	13.7
Communications	48	58	16	27.6	13.3
Printing & publishing	27	77	21	27.3	10.1
Business services	73	219	59	26.9	30.9

Table 10 (continued)

Industry	SIC code	Number of firms	Number of takeovers	% takeovers Equal	% takeovers Equity
Wholesale trade, nondurables	51	54	13	24.1	15.8
Electrical machinery	36	339	81	23.9	14.4
Lumber & wood products	24	44	10	22.7	17.3
Petroleum refining	29	45	10	22.2	28.7
Leather	31	24	5	20.8	3.7
Oil & gas extraction	13	389	82	20.6	35.3
Metal mining	10	67	10	14.9	18.4
Engineering & misc. services	89	34	5	14.7	44.2
Special-trades construction	17	14	2	14.3	39.0
Coal mining	12	10	1	10.0	6.8
All firms		3,660	1,133	31.0%	27.7%

Table 11
Industry sales and employment shocks, 1977–81

This table reports values for sales and employment growth and sales and employment shocks over the 1977–81 period for 51 Value Line industries. The data are sorted based on the sales shock variable. Sales growth is the real growth in sales between 1977 and 1981 for each industry, computed as ln(*Sales 1981/Sales 1977*), where sales values are put in real terms using the GNP deflator. Sales shock is the absolute value of the difference between an industry's sales growth and the average industry sales growth of 18.12% for the full sample of 51 industries. Employment growth is the growth in the number of employees between 1977 and 1981 for each industry, computed as ln (*Employment 1981/Employment 1977*). Employment shock is the absolute value of the difference between an industry's employment growth and the average industry employment growth of 10.40% for the full sample of 51 industries. Industry members are taken from firms listed on Value Line in the fourth quarter of 1981. Sales and employment data are taken from Compustat.

Industry	Sales growth	Sales shock	Employment growth	Employment shock
Medical services	100.70%	82.58%	99.03%	88.63%
Mfg. housing & rec. vehicles	– 42.52	60.64	– 29.26	39.66
Petroleum producing	64.54	46.42	– 6.25	16.65
Tire & rubber	– 15.84	33.96	– 26.59	36.99
Natural gas	50.98	32.85	16.77	6.37
Textiles	– 11.40	29.52	– 16.51	26.92
Oilfield services	42.30	24.18	23.24	12.83
Integrated petroleum	41.47	23.35	18.15	7.74
Original equipment auto parts	– 4.88	23.01	– 3.74	14.14
Coal, uranium, geothermal	41.01	22.88	5.30	5.11

Table 11 (continued)

Industry	Sales growth	Sales shock	Employment growth	Employment shock
Apparel	– 1.77	19.90	– 7.93	18.34
Home appliances	– 0.65	18.77	– 14.39	24.79
Replacement auto parts	1.61	16.52	8.06	2.35
Hotels & gaming	34.62	16.50	30.35	19.94
Paper & paper products	3.45	14.68	– 4.66	15.07
Packaging & containers	4.18	13.94	– 4.49	14.90
Construction machinery	4.45	13.67	– 1.66	12.06
Air transport	30.88	12.75	18.23	7.82
Toys & school supplies	30.55	12.43	15.54	5.13
Integrated steel	5.71	12.42	– 5.70	16.11
Industrial services	30.13	12.01	22.01	11.60
Publishing	29.37	11.24	16.50	6.09
Broadcasting	8.25	9.88	15.17	4.76
Metals & mining	8.33	9.80	– 0.41	10.82
Food processing	8.57	9.55	15.03	4.63
Grocery stores	9.18	8.94	17.60	7.20
Basic chemicals	26.79	8.67	12.17	1.76
Diversified chemicals	9.58	8.55	12.33	1.93
Entertainment	10.43	7.69	4.22	6.18
Retail stores	11.27	6.85	5.20	5.20
Trucking & transport leasing	12.38	5.74	7.04	3.36
Machine tool	23.71	5.58	12.83	2.42
Health care & hosp. supply	23.47	5.35	15.59	5.19
Machinery	13.45	4.68	5.49	4.92
Metal fabricating	22.40	4.28	12.69	2.28
Electrical equipment	13.59	4.17	7.43	2.97
Computer data processing	22.23	4.11	23.49	13.09
Retail stores, special lines	22.03	3.91	24.66	14.25
Fast food & restaurants	21.97	3.84	29.78	19.38
Multiform	15.30	2.82	9.68	0.72
Drugstores	20.75	2.62	25.71	15.31
Precision instruments	20.60	2.48	10.60	0.20
Specially chemicals	15.95	2.17	10.56	0.16
Drugs	16.29	1.83	6.28	4.13
General steel	19.92	1.79	– 2.89	13.30
Aerospace & defense	19.64	1.52	12.61	2.21
Building	16.66	1.47	8.46	1.94
Electronics	19.53	1.41	20.82	10.42
Shoes	16.85	1.27	23.43	13.03
Toiletries & cosmetics	17.89	0.23	18.07	7.67
Office equipment & supplies	18.04	0.08	14.99	4.58
Average	18.12%	13.44%	10.40%	11.63%

Table 12

Energy dependence by industry

This table reports the dependence of an industry on energy inputs for the 51 Value Line industries. Energy fraction is the fraction of an industry's inputs comprised of energy inputs. Data are for 1982, and are taken from the *1982 Benchmark Input–Output Accounts of the United States*, U.S. Department of Commerce, December 1991, and 'Benchmark Input–Output Accounts for the U.S. Economy, 1982', *Survey of Current Business*, Volume 71, July 1991. Energy inputs are defined as those coming from Coal (industry #7), Crude petroleum (industry #8), and Petroleum refining (industry #31). The Value Line industries are matched with the industries used in the input–output tables via primary and secondary SIC codes.

Value Line industry	Input–output industry	Energy fraction
Integrated petroleum	Petroleum refining	73.92%
Natural gas	Gas production & distribution (utilities)	35.33
Air transport	Air transportation	25.26
Coal, uranium, geothermal	Coal	15.78
Trucking & transport leasing	Motor freight transportation & warehousing	10.07
Metals & mining	Iron & ferroalloy ores	7.08
Basic chemicals	Chemicals & selected chemical products	5.73
Diversified chemicals	Chemicals & selected chemical products	5.73
Specialty chemicals	Chemicals & selected chemical products	5.73
General steel	Primary iron & steel manufacturing	4.74
Integrated steel	Primary iron & steel manufacturing	4.74
Paper & paper products	Paper & allied products	3.74
Oilfield services	Crude petroleum & natural gas	3.63
Petroleum producing	Crude petroleum & natural gas	3.63
Building	New construction	3.41
Drugstores	Retail trade	2.26
Grocery stores	Retail trade	2.26
Retail stores, special lines	Retail trade	2.26
Retail stores	Retail trade	2.26
Hotels & gaming	Hotels & lodging places	1.57
Textiles	Broad & narrow fabrics, yarn & thread mill	1.42
Drugs	Drugs	1.31
Publishing	Printing & publishing	1.31
Tire & rubber	Tire & inner tubes	1.22
Machine tool	Metalworking machinery & equipment	1.20
Toys & school supplies	Games, toys & children's vehicles	1.16
Electrical equipment	Electrical industrial equipment	1.10
Metal fabricating	Fabricated structural metal	1.09
Toiletries & cosmetics	Toilet preparations	1.08
Health care & hosp. supply	Surgical & medical instruments	1.08
Apparel	Apparel	1.00
Packaging & containers	Glass containers	0.98
Precision instruments	Scientific & controlling instruments	0.95
Original equipment auto parts	Motor vehicle parts & accessories	0.74
Replacement auto parts	Motor vehicle parts & accessories	0.74
Multiform	Miscellaneous machinery	0.72

226 M.L. Mitchell, J.H. Mulherin/Journal of Financial Economics 41 (1996) 193–229

Table 12 (continued)

Value Line industry	Input–output industry	Energy fraction
Mfg. housing & rec. vehicles	Mobile homes	0.72
Medical services	Hospitals	0.71
Computer data processing	Electronic computing equipment	0.69
Office equipment & supplies	Office, computing & accounting machines	0.66
Industrial services	Other business services	0.65
Machinery	General industrial machinery & equipment	0.63
Entertainment	Motion pictures	0.57
Food processing	Food & kindred products	0.50
Aerospace & defense	Aircraft	0.48
Electronics	Electronic components & accessories	0.43
Construction machinery	Construction machinery & equipment	0.43
Fast food & restaurants	Eating & drinking places	0.36
Home appliances	Household appliances	0.25
Shoes	Shoes, except rubber	0.21
Broadcasting	Radio & TV broadcasting	0.11

Table 13
Change in the import penetration ratio

This table reports the interindustry variation of the change in the import penetration ratio between the 1977–81 and 1982–89 periods for the 51 Value Line industries. The import penetration ratio is the ratio of imports divided by new supply. Import avg. 1977–81 is the average of the import penetration ratio for the 1977–81 period. Import avg. 1982–89 is the average of the import penetration ratio for the 1982–89 period. Change is the difference between the import penetration ratios in the 1982–89 and 1977–81 periods. Import data are taken from SIC industries found in various editions of the *U.S. Industrial Outlook* and *U.S. Commodity Exports and Imports as Related to Output*, both compiled by the U.S. Department of Commerce. Value Line and SIC industries are matched using primary and secondary SIC codes.

Value Line industry	SIC industry	Import avg. 1977–81	Import avg. 1982–89	Change
Shoes	Footwear, except rubber	31.18%	55.84%	24.66%
Machine tool	Machine tool, metal cutting	18.04	34.94	16.90
Apparel	Apparel	15.40	29.71	14.31
Construction machinery	Construction machinery	4.90	14.48	9.57
Office equipment & supplies	Office equipment	18.02	26.38	8.35
Computer data processing	Electronic computing	4.70	12.63	7.93
Orig. equip. auto parts	Motor vehicle parts	8.80	14.96	6.16
Replacement auto parts	Motor vehicle parts	8.80	14.96	6.16
Home appliances	Household appliances	8.56	14.11	5.55
Electronics	Electronic components	13.90	19.35	5.45

Table 13 (continued)

Value Line industry	SIC industry	Import avg. 1977–81	Import avg. 1982–89	Change
Tire & rubber	Tire & inner tubes	11.40	16.55	5.15
Machinery	General industrial machinery	4.24	8.80	4.56
Multiform	General industrial machinery	4.24	8.80	4.56
General steel	Steel mill products	11.50	15.80	4.30
Integrated steel	Steel mill products	11.50	15.80	4.30
Electrical equipment	Electrical equipment	5.88	10.00	4.12
Textiles	Textile mill products	4.50	7.28	2.78
Basic chemicals	Chemicals & allied products	4.30	6.53	2.23
Diversified chemicals	Chemicals & allied products	4.30	6.53	2.23
Specialty chemicals	Chemicals & allied products	4.30	6.53	2.23
Precision instruments	Measuring & controlling devices	3.78	5.80	2.02
Toys & school supplies	Games, toys & children's vehicles	19.84	21.80	1.96
Packaging & containers	Glass containers	0.92	2.60	1.68
Drugs	Drugs	4.86	6.50	1.64
Toiletries & cosmetics	Toilet preparations	0.92	2.55	1.63
Aerospace & defense	Aircraft	3.80	5.43	1.63
Integrated petroleum	Petroleum refining	7.40	8.91	1.51
Metal fabricating	Fabricated structural metal	0.68	1.86	1.18
Food processing	Food & kindred products	3.86	4.73	0.87
Paper & paper products	Paper & allied products	7.20	7.95	0.75
Health care & hosp. supply	Surgical & medical instruments	5.60	6.34	0.74
Air transport	Air transportation	0.00	0.00	0.00
Broadcasting	Communication	0.00	0.00	0.00
Building	Building construction	0.00	0.00	0.00
Drugstores	Miscellaneous retail	0.00	0.00	0.00
Entertainment	Motion pictures	0.00	0.00	0.00
Fast food & restaurants	Eating & drinking places	0.00	0.00	0.00
Grocery stores	Food stores	0.00	0.00	0.00
Hotels & gaming	Hotels & lodging places	0.00	0.00	0.00
Industrial services	Business services	0.00	0.00	0.00
Medical services	Health services	0.00	0.00	0.00
Mfg. housing & rec. vehicles	Mobile homes	0.00	0.00	0.00
Natural gas	Electrical, gas & sanitary services	0.00	0.00	0.00
Retail stores	General merchandise	0.00	0.00	0.00
Retail stores, special lines	Miscellaneous retail	0.00	0.00	0.00
Trucking & transport leasing	Motor freight transport & warehouse	0.00	0.00	0.00
Coal, uranium, geothermal	Coal	0.28	0.28	– 0.01
Oilfield services	Oil & gas field machinery	1.02	0.98	– 0.04
Publishing	Printing & publishing	0.84	0.56	– 0.28
Metals & mining	Metal & mining	15.84	12.31	– 3.53
Petroleum producing	Crude petroleum & natural gas	41.18	26.91	– 14.27

References

Baltagi, Badi H., James M. Griffin, and Daniel P. Rich, 1995, Airline deregulation: The cost pieces of the puzzle, International Economic Review 36, 245–258.

Becketti, Sean, 1986, Corporate mergers and the business cycle, Federal Reserve Bank of Kansas City Economic Review, 13–26.

Bhagat, Sanjai, Andrei Shleifer, and Robert Vishny, 1990, Hostile takeovers in the 1980s: The return to corporate specialization, Brookings papers in microeconomics (Brookings Institution, Washington, DC).

Blair, Margaret M. and Martha A. Schary, 1993, Industry-level pressures to restructure, in: Margaret M. Blair, ed., The deal decade (Brookings Institution, Washington, DC).

Bradley, Michael, Gregg A. Jarrell, and E. Han Kim, 1984, On the existence of an optimal capital structure: Theory and evidence, Journal of Finance 34, 857–880.

Brealey, Richard A. and Stewart C. Myers, 1991, Principles of corporate finance, 4th ed. (McGraw-Hill, New York, NY).

Breshnahan, Timothy F., 1989, Empirical studies of industries with market power, in: Richard Schmalensee and Robert D. Willig, eds., Handbook of industrial organization (North-Holland, Amsterdam).

Clark, Don P., David L. Kaserman, and John W. Mayo, 1990, Barriers to trade and the import vulnerability of U.S. manufacturing industries, Journal of Industrial Economics 38, 433–447.

Comment, Robert and Gregg A. Jarrell, 1995, Corporate focus and stock returns, Journal of Financial Economics 37, 67–87.

Comment, Robert and G. William Schwert, 1995, Poison or placebo? Evidence on the deterrent and wealth effects of modern antitakeover measures, Journal of Financial Economics 39, 3–43.

Dutz, Mark A., 1989, Horizontal mergers in declining industries: Theory and evidence, International Journal of Industrial Organization 7, 11–33.

Eckbo, B. Espen, 1983, Horizontal mergers, collusion and stockholder wealth, Journal of Financial Economics 11, 241–273.

Fama, Eugene F. and Kenneth R. French, 1993, Common risk factors in the returns on stocks and bonds, Journal of Financial Economics 33, 3–56.

Golbe, Devra and Lawrence J. White, 1988, A time-series analysis of mergers and acquisitions in the U.S. economy, in: Alan J. Auerbach, ed., Corporate takeovers: Causes and consequences (University of Chicago Press/NBER, Chicago, IL).

Gort, Michael, 1969, An economic disturbance theory of mergers, Quarterly Journal of Economics 83, 624–642.

Healy, Paul M., Krishna G. Palepu, and Richard S. Ruback, 1992, Does corporate performance improve after mergers?, Journal of Financial Economics 31, 135–175.

Jensen, Michael C., 1993, The modern industrial revolution and the challenge to internal control systems, Journal of Finance 48, 831–880.

Jensen, Michael C. and William H. Meckling, 1976, Theory of the firm: Managerial behavior, agency costs and ownership structure, Journal of Financial Economics 3, 305–360.

Johnston, J., 1984, Econometric methods, 3rd ed. (McGraw-Hill, New York, NY).

Kaplan, Steven N., 1989, The effects of management buyouts on operating performance and value, Journal of Financial Economics 24, 581–618.

Katics, Michelle M. and Bruce C. Petersen, 1994, The effect of rising import competition on market power: A panel data study of U.S. manufacturing, Journal of Industrial Economics 42, 277–286.

Long, Michael S. and Ileen B. Malitz, 1985, Investment patterns and financial leverage, in: B.M. Friedman, ed., Corporate capital structures in the United States (University of Chicago Press/NBER, Chicago, IL).

MacDonald, James M., 1994, Does import competition force efficient production?, Review of Economics and Statistics 76, 721–727.

McGowan, John J., 1971, International comparisons of merger activity, Journal of Law and Economics 14, 233–250.

Mehta, Cyrus R. and Nitin R. Patel, 1983, A network algorithm for performing Fisher's exact test in $r \times c$ contingency tables, Journal of the American Statistical Association 78, 427–433.

Melicher, Ronald W., Johannes Ledolter, and Louis J. D'Antonio, 1983, A time series analysis of aggregate merger activity, Review of Economics and Statistics 65, 423–430.

Mitchell, Mark L. and Kenneth Lehn, 1990, Do bad bidders become good targets?, Journal of Political Economy 98, 372–398.

Morck, Randall, Andrei Shleifer, and Robert W. Vishny, 1988, Characteristics of targets of hostile and friendly takeovers, in: Alan J. Auerbach, ed., Corporate takeovers: Causes and consequences (University of Chicago Press/NBER, Chicago, IL).

Morck, Randall, Andrei Shleifer, and Robert W. Vishny, 1989, Alternative mechanisms for corporate control, American Economic Review 79, 842–852.

Myers, Stewart, 1977, Determinants of corporate borrowing, Journal of Financial Economics 5, 147–175.

Nelson, Ralph L., 1959, Merger movements in American industry, 1895–1956 (Princeton University Press/NBER, Princeton, NJ).

Palepu, Krishna G., 1986, Predicting takeover targets: A methodological and empirical analysis, Journal of Accounting and Economics 8, 3–35.

Phillips, Laurence T., 1991, Contractual relationships in the deregulated transportation marketplace, Journal of Law and Economics 34, 535–564.

Ravenscraft, David J., 1987, The 1980s merger wave: An industrial organization perspective, in: Lynn E. Brown and Eric S. Rosengren, eds., The merger boom (Federal Reserve Bank of Boston, Boston, MA).

Ravenscraft, David J. and F.M. Scherer, 1987, Life after takeover, Journal of Industrial Economics 36, 147–156.

Rose, Nancy L., 1985, The incidence of regulatory rents in the motor carrier industry, Rand Journal of Economics 16, 299–318.

Slovin, Myron B., Marie E. Sushka, and Yvette M. Bendeck, 1991, The intra-industry effects of going private transactions, Journal of Finance 46, 1537–1550.

Smith, Abbie J., 1990, Corporate ownership structure and performance: The case of management buyouts, Journal of Financial Economics 27, 143–164.

Taggart, Robert A., 1988, Comment, in: Alan J. Auerbach, ed., Corporate takeovers: Causes and consequences (University of Chicago Press/NBER, Chicago, IL).

Weston, J. Fred, Kwang S. Chung, and Susan E. Hoag, 1990, Mergers, restructuring, and corporate control (Prentice Hall, Englewood Cliffs, NJ).

Whinston, Michael D. and Scott C. Collins, 1992, Entry and competitive structure in deregulated airline markets: An event study analysis of People Express, Rand Journal of Economics 23, 445–462.

[2]

ELSEVIER

Journal of Corporate Finance 6 (2000) 345–376

Journal of
CORPORATE
FINANCE

www.elsevier.com/locate/econbase

Price uncertainty and vertical integration: an examination of petrochemical firms

Joseph P.H. Fan *

School of Business and Management, Hong Kong University of Science and Technology, Clear Water Bay, Kowloon, Hong Kong People's Republic of China

Accepted 21 April 2000

Abstract

The petrochemical industry employs assets subject to temporal and site specificity. The OPEC oil price shocks of the 1970s made it difficult to write contracts covering business dealings in the industry. I use this production and economic setting as a natural experiment to test transaction cost theory. In support of the theory, I find that input price uncertainty in the 1970s positively affected the extent of vertical integration by firms into input stages. Moreover, the positive reaction of vertical integration to price uncertainty mainly occurs in transactions subject to asset specificity. I also examine price controls and market power as alternative explanations for vertical integration in the industry, but fail to find support for these hypotheses. © 2000 Elsevier Science B.V. All rights reserved.

JEL classification: L22; D23
Keywords: Vertical integration; Price uncertainty; The petrochemical industry

1. Introduction

In his presidential address to the American Finance Association, Jensen (1993) asserts that the OPEC oil price shocks in the 1970s and the associated ten-fold increase in oil prices have had far-reaching implications on corporate structure. He further pinpoints that the wave of mergers and restructuring in the 1980s actually began in 1973, the year of the first oil price shock. In support of the Jensen's thesis, Mitchell and

* Tel.: +852-2358-8016; fax: +852-2358-1749.
E-mail address: pjfan@ust.hk (J.P.H. Fan).

PII: S0929-1199(00)00006-7

Mulherin (1996) find that industry shocks affect merger and restructuring activities. In this paper, I provide further refinement of this argument through a microanalytic treatment of Jensen's insights within a particular industry. I analyze and empirically test several hypotheses pertaining to the causes of vertical integration in the petrochemical industry. The period of study is the 1970s during which two oil price shocks induced high input price uncertainty in the industry. I examine how increased price uncertainty affects the extents of input self-sufficiency by petrochemical firms. Within the petrochemical industry, abundant prior evidence suggests that major operational restructuring took place subsequent to the oil price shocks.[1] The time period and the industry together provide a natural experiment to test how an organization adapts its structure to economic changes.

The transaction cost theory of Williamson (1971, 1975, 1979) and Klein et al. (1978) maintains that vertical integration is a response to asset specificity caused by specialized investment that has lower value outside a given transaction. If a contract is drawn to govern the transaction, the specialized investment creates an ex post bilateral bargaining situation in which opportunistic rent seeking, or holdup, by the transactors may occur. Vertical integration is proposed as a solution to the holdup problem, because the possibility of holdup is suppressed under the common ownership. The theory also emphasizes that uncertainty is a necessary condition for asset specificity to influence organizational structure. Without uncertainty, a perfect contract can be written to safeguard the transaction; hence, there is no need for vertical integration. By the same token, given the existence of asset specificity, vertical integration will react positively to an increase in uncertainty.

Prior empirical tests of the transaction cost theory have focused on asset specificity. Consistent with the theory, these studies generally find that vertical integration increases with asset specificity. Relatively less evidence is available on the role of uncertainty. Relevant to the current paper, several studies examine the effects of the oil price shocks on contract provisions (Goldberg and Erickson, 1987; Crocker and Masten, 1988, 1991). These studies document decreases in contract length, more frequent price adjustment and renegotiation for long-term contracts in the petroleum coke and natural gas industries after 1973.

As a complement to prior research, I compare the relative advantage between vertical integration and contract governance in the petrochemical industry during the 1970s. The industry is marked by substantial asset specificity. I examine whether firms embark on vertical integration to avoid holdup problems in supply contracts, which are exacerbated by high price uncertainty. I also test the hypothesis that the degree of the impact of price uncertainty on a firm's extent of vertical integration varies systematically with the degree of asset specificity. To capture asset specificity in the industry, proxy variables are constructed for the input substance and industry agglomeration. Lastly, I examine two alternative explanations for vertical integration in the industry. One possibility is

[1] See Bower (1986), Spitz (1988), Stobaugh (1988), Chapman (1991), Lane (1993), and Arora and Gambardella (1998).

that firms integrate vertically to circumvent price controls. Another possibility is that the firms integrate vertically to exercise market power.

The findings in this paper are generally consistent with the predictions of the transaction cost theory. I find strong evidence from the 1970s that input price uncertainty and asset specificity jointly affect vertical integration in the industry. In contrast to this general consistency with transaction cost theory, my evidence fails to support the price control or the market power hypotheses.

The remainder of the paper is organized as follows. Section 2 discusses the theory and related prior evidence. Section 3 provides an overview of the industry, including sources of asset specificity, contracting problems in the 1970s, and cases of organizational responses. Section 4 reports empirical results. And Section 5 concludes the study.

2. Theory and related prior evidence

There are many potential explanations for vertical integration, including risk aversion (Blair and Kaserman, 1978),[2] price inflexibility (Carlton, 1979),[3] price controls (Stigler, 1951), and market power.[4] In his early work on the nature of the firm, Coase (1937) focuses on transaction costs: vertical integration is used when the costs of market transactions exceed the costs of internal organization. This section discusses the transaction cost theory and evidence. The applicability of the theory to the petrochemical industry will subsequently be examined and compared with alternative explanations in the section on empirical analysis.

2.1. The transaction cost theory

Much of transaction cost analysis emphasizes asset specificity. Specialized assets, because of their limited exchange opportunities outside a given transaction, create quasi-rents that are subject to expropriation by parties in the transaction. The higher the degree of asset specificity, the larger the quasi-rents at stake, and hence the higher the holdup incentive. As the holdup problem becomes severe, a contract may not be sufficient to safeguard the transaction. Williamson (1971, 1975, 1979) and Klein et al. (1978) posit that vertical integration is one solution to the holdup problem, because

[2] Producers at two stages of production may merge their operations to reduce total risk, providing that returns at the two stages are negatively correlated. The application of the risk aversion hypothesis is limited, as it relies on the assumption that capital markets are imperfect in that stockholders can not fully diversify away the risk by forming portfolios.

[3] The cited study by Carlton shows that quantity risk caused by inflexible prices can induce vertical integration. Firms with relatively stable input requirements may integrate into input production to avoid paying a premium for the input that is induced by the fluctuating demand by other buyers. Lieberman (1991) finds support for this hypothesis in the chemical industry.

[4] There are a number of ways that a firm may gain market power through vertical integration. Several widely discussed sources of market power include foreclosure, price discrimination, and entry barriers. See Perry (1989) for a survey.

unified ownership suppresses the holdup possibility.[5] Several types of asset specificity have been discussed in the literature: site specificity, physical asset specificity, human capital specificity, and dedicated assets (Williamson, 1985). In addition, temporal specificity refers to transactions whose performance depends on timing, while the technology and the assets involved are quite common in nature (Masten et al., 1991; Pirrong, 1993).

Although asset specificity is important, the transaction cost theory stresses that uncertainty is a necessary condition for asset specificity to induce vertical integration. The idea is simple. Without uncertainty, a perfect contract covering full contingencies can be written. There is no possibility of holdup, hence no need for vertical integration. In an analysis of contract choices, Klein (1992, 1996) shows that, in the face of uncertainty, a contract will be designed to reduce holdup probability as well as the potential gain from the holdup. Two recent studies elaborate on that idea (Klein and Murphy, 1997; Baker et al., 1997). Both predict that vertical integration will be used when markets are highly uncertain. High price uncertainty implies a high possibility that a market price will fall outside a contract's self-enforcement range in its own terms along with the transactors' reputation capital, resulting in holdup and costly renegotiation. Because vertical integration eliminates the holdup possibility, a positive reaction of vertical integration to price uncertainty is expected.

The self-enforcement analysis also predicts the direction of vertical integration, i.e., who will be the owner and who will be the non-owner. In vertical integration, the party with more reputation capital is more likely to be the owner while the party with less reputation capital is more likely to be the non-owner. By giving the residual rights to the party with better reputation, the expected gains from holdup are reallocated from the party with poorer reputation to the other party with better reputation. This arrangement reduces the probability of holdup, as each party's expected gains from holdup now more closely coincide with his/her reputation capital.

2.2. Prior evidence

Prior empirical research[6] on vertical integration focuses on the cross-sectional analysis of asset specificity. Various types of asset specificity have been reported to increase vertical integration in a variety of industries[7] as well as in several cross-industry studies.[8] Evidence on the role of uncertainty is less extensive and mostly based on

[5] Grossman and Hart (1986) emphasize that asset ownership in vertical integration is the primary reason that the holdup problem is solved. The owner of the asset is entitled to all contractually unspecified residual rights, which means the holdup problem and the associated investment inefficiencies can be minimized.

[6] See Shelanski and Klein (1995) for a survey of the empirical literature.

[7] A partial list of the industries includes automobile (Monteverde and Teece, 1982), aluminum (Stuckey, 1983), aerospace (Masten, 1984), electricity generation (Joskow, 1985), natural gas (Mulherin, 1986b), chemical (Lieberman, 1991), and pulp and paper (Ohanian, 1994).

[8] See Levy (1985) and Cave and Bradburd (1988). See also Spiller (1985) and Weiss (1992) in the context of vertical mergers.

survey data.[9] Worth noting are several papers examining the effects of the oil price shocks on contract provisions. Goldberg and Erickson (1987) study petroleum coke contracts and report that the sudden increase in price volatility after 1973 resulted in contracts of shorter duration and easier termination. Crocker and Masten (1988, 1991) study natural gas contracts and find that the duration of these contracts decreased following 1973. None of these papers studies vertical integration. However, Goldberg and Erickson conjecture that price shocks increased the advantage of vertical integration relative to long-term contracts. The premise is that shortening the contract length is not necessarily a remedy for transactions involving asset specificity, because frequent bargaining at contract renewal time incurs deadweight losses.

Another potential contractual response to price shocks is the use of price indices. To reduce the probability of holdup due to price changes, contract prices can be indexed to input prices, labor costs, or demand factors. However, price indices are not attractive when their relations with the values of the underlying products are variable. Goldberg (1985) studies the court dispute between Alcoa and Essex on their long-term contract on aluminum in the 1970s. He finds that the main problem is that the price indices in the contract did not track changing production costs and demand for aluminum, which were both soaring after 1973. Mulherin (1986a) reports that only 2% of natural gas contracts written during the 1940s and 1950s had price escalators based on a general index; the price adjustment of the remaining contracts was based on renegotiation. He explains that the general index was not used because the price of natural gas did not have a defined correlation with the general economy. Goldberg and Erickson document more extensive uses of price indices in post-1973 petroleum coke contracts, compared with pre-1973 contracts. However, it is pointed out that the price indices were not meant to ensure automatic price adjustment for the life of the contracts but only to provide a reference point for renegotiation. In a study of coal contracts, Joskow (1988) finds that it is difficult for indices to track large short-term changes in coal prices associated with demand or supply shocks. The celebrated case of Fisher Body versus General Motors (Klein et al., 1978; Klein, 1988) also demonstrates this point. General Motors could not avoid the opportunistic behavior of Fisher even though a sophisticated price-indexed contract had been designed to avoid the problem.

In summary, the literature documents that substantial contractual changes took place after the first oil price shock of 1973. The evidence indicates that in the face of high price uncertainty, contracts may not be optimal in governing transactions subject to asset

[9] Walker and Weber (1984, 1987) study the make-or-buy decision of automobile components. They find greater uncertainty about production volume increases the likelihood that a component is produced in-house. In the second paper, they find that the uncertainty only affects the make-or-buy decision when the market is thin. This interactive effect between uncertainty and asset specificity supports the transaction cost prediction. Several studies focus on the relations between downstream demand uncertainty and firms' decisions to forward integrate into sales or distribution. Anderson and Schmittlein (1984) and Anderson (1985) do not find demand uncertainty important in explaining forward integration into sales and distribution by electronic component manufacturers. The latter study does find that integration is positively affected by the interactive effect of asset specificity and demand uncertainty. John and Weitz (1988) find that downstream demand uncertainty positively affects the decision to maintain in-house sales forces in a sample of industrial manufacturers.

specificity. The transaction cost theory suggests a possibility for vertical integration been increasingly used in place of contracts to govern these transactions. This hypothesis will be examined with data from the petrochemical industry in the following analysis.

3. Overview of the industry

Petrochemical production proceeds in stages from original energy inputs to primary petrochemicals to intermediate products. The intermediate products are supplied to chemical processing industries for the manufacturing of detergents, fertilizers, pharmaceuticals, plastics, solvents, synthetic fibers, and synthetic rubbers. Fig. 1 provides an example of petrochemical production stages.

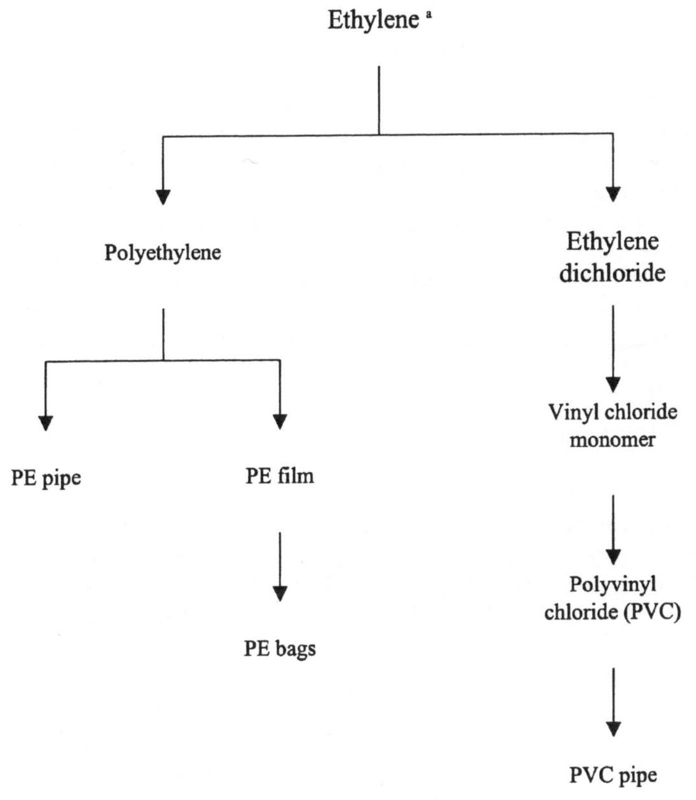

[a] Ethylene is derived from naphtha or natural gas. It is an input of a wider variety of petrochemicals than the ones illustrated here. The figure, meant to be illustrative, only shows two streams of ethylene derivatives.

Fig. 1. Example of petrochemical production stages.

3.1. Sources of asset specificity

The petrochemical industry has substantial temporal and site specificity. The temporal specificity is caused by technology and cost factors. Many processes require continuous flows of inputs to production plants. Disruptions of input flows cause lower production yields or even plant idling. Temporarily shutting down a plant is costly due to high fixed costs and substantial clean-up costs required before the plant can be put to on use again. The high costs associated with production interruption imply that non-performance in quantity, such as delaying delivery, can be an effective holdup strategy, even if the technology and the assets involved are quite common in nature.

Site specificity is also prevalent in the industry. Many petrochemical inputs are difficult to handle, transport, or store as inventories. This is particularly relevant for inputs that are of gaseous substances. They need to be stored in expensive, heavy, thick-walled tanks at very low temperatures and/or high pressures. For typical operating plants, the gaseous inputs can be stored for only a few hours or a few days before production. The inputs are transported over short distances by specialized trucks, trains, or barges equipped with storage tanks. These methods are not suitable for transportation over long distances, because the quality of the inputs deteriorates with time and travel distance. Transportation and storage concerns motivate suppliers and users of the gaseous petrochemical inputs to build plants in close proximity. As the plants are immobile, the users and the suppliers are locked into bilateral relationships that are subject to potential hold-up problems. The holdup problems related to storage and transportation costs have been found to affect the governance structures in the natural gas industry (Mulherin, 1986a). Likewise, site specificity in the petrochemical industry is expected to affect its firms' vertical integration decisions.[10]

3.2. Contracting problems after 1973

Supply contracts in the petrochemical industry typically have 1- to 3-year durations and are automatically renewed. Termination is permitted provided there is 3- to 6-month advanced notice. These contracts are intended to maintain long-term relationships between transactors while preserving flexibility for adaptation. Some contracts have very long terms, i.e., 10 to 20 years. These long-term contracts tend to be drawn for gaseous inputs produced and sold in remote locations.[11] Most contracts have price protection provisions allowing prices to be periodically adjusted within the contract duration. The

[10] The effects of site specificity on vertical integration are documented in several other studies. Joskow (1985) reports that while 85% of the coal used to generate electricity is supplied by the market mechanism, virtually all of the mine-mouth coal mines are owned by utilities. Spiller (1985) finds that combined excess stock returns of vertically merging firms upon their merger announcements are positively related to their geographic proximity.

[11] Dow Chemical has two 20-year contracts with Alberta Gas Ethylene agreeing to take substantial percentages of two ethylene plants' output (Dow Chemical 1996 Annual Report). Union Carbide has a 20-year ethylene contract to purchase part of the output of a Canadian ethylene plant (Union Carbide 1996 Annual Report).

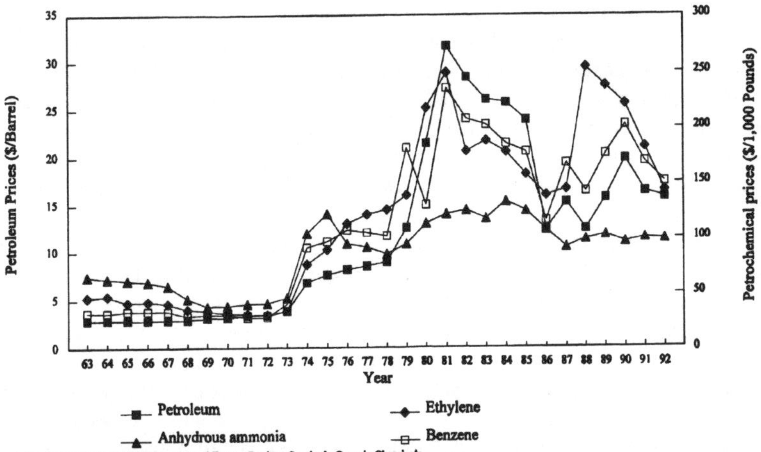

Data sources: Agricultural Prices, Annual Energy Review, Synthetic Organic Chemicals

Fig. 2. Annual Petroleum and Selected Primary Petrochemicals Prices.

price adjustments are made by renegotiation or by predetermined formulas. In a typical price formula, the contract price is indexed to oil prices, wholesales prices, and other suppliers' cost factors. These price adjustment mechanisms are also observed in other industries such as natural gas (Mulherin, 1986a), petroleum coke (Goldberg and Erickson, 1987), and coal (Joskow, 1988).

Non-availability of historical data limits an investigation of how petrochemical contracts have evolved over time. However, public disclosures reveal that significant changes in contracting practices took place during the 1970s, especially shortly after the first oil price shock of 1973. It was reported that the frequency of price adjustments changed from quarterly to monthly.[12] Contract lengths became shorter for some petrochemical materials.[13] However, there was hardly a universal pattern of contractual changes across transactions, as some transactors responded to the oil price shocks by entering into long-term agreements.[14] What, then, has made 1973 a watershed of contractual changes? The clue is provided in the patterns of petrochemical input prices (Fig. 2). Before 1973, the input prices were generally stable with few fluctuations. After 1973, the levels and the volatility of the input prices increased dramatically. The sudden increase in price volatility created immense pressures for price adjustments in contracts.

[12] Chemical Marketing Reporter, 1974, 'Contract Terms Are Changing; Quarterly Importance Fading', 206, September 30, page 13.

[13] Chemical Marketing Reporter, 1973, 'Shorter Contracts and Curbs on Force Majeure Are Urged at EPCA Meeting in Venice', 204, October 8, page 4.

[14] Dow Chemical and Du Pont reported in their 1974 Annual Reports that they had entered into long-term arrangements to secure adequate quantities of petrochemical raw materials. In 1980, shortly after the second oil shock, Du Pont entered into a long-term arrangement with Shell Chemical to 'ensure' a supply of about one-third of its purchased domestic olefin feedstock needs over the following 10 years.

Prior to 1973, input price changes in the industry were infrequent.[15] The infrequent price changes in part reflected the stable price pattern during that period and in part reflected the transactors' unwillingness to haggle over prices.[16] Haggling increases the possibility of input disruptions that are costly to transactions subject to temporal specificity. To avoid haggling, the transactors would implicitly agree not to change prices often. That is, they would tolerate temporary small dispersions between the prices determined in their contracts and prices determined in other contracts or in spot markets.[17]

When the input prices were stable, the implicit agreements supported by the transactors' reputations were self-enforcing (Klein and Murphy, 1997; Baker et al., 1997). However, when the prices turned volatile after 1973, such contracts became difficult to maintain. During the period of price escalations, holdups by suppliers took the form of threats not to deliver the requested amounts unless buyers paid much higher prices than required by contract. Still other suppliers declared *force majeure*, due to their own procurement problems. In this case, the limited quantity of inputs would be rationed among existing customers.[18] There were strong incentives for suppliers to deviate from pro rata allocation. Suppliers were tempted to allocate more to customers paying higher prices while shorting others who paid lower prices. In his survey of the chemical industry's contracting practices in the 1970s, White (1982) reports that in the case of rationing, allocation was hardly on the pro-rata basis. He provides some explanation on why the deviation from pro rata allocation is possible. The conventional practice in the chemical industry was to specify a minimum and maximum quantity provision in contracts.[19] The intention of the suppliers was to urge the buyers to take as much as they could but not to insist that they take the minimum amount. As a result, the

[15] Carlton (1985) examines transaction prices of supply contracts during 1957–1966. He documents that the average duration between price changes for 658 chemical contracts was 12.8 months. This duration is long compared to the time between price changes for nonferrous metals (4.3), petroleum (5.9), plywood (4.7), and truck motors (5.4); and it is comparable to the durations for steel (13.0), cement (13.2), and glass (10.2). See also Mulherin (1986a), Goldberg and Erickson (1987), Joskow (1988), and Crocker and Masten (1988, 1991).

[16] The avoidance of frequent haggling became evident during my interviews with several petrochemical executives who were formally engaged in raw material purchasing during the 1970s.

[17] There has not been an organized spot exchange for petrochemical inputs. Some inputs are bought and sold for agreeable prices through spot networks where brokers or traders bring together buyers and sellers by telephone. Suppliers mainly use the spot markets to digest their excess supplies. Buyers access the spot markets either for their urgent needs or for low prices (Ching, 1986). The traders' roles in searching for information and facilitating transactions are similar to those of middlemen in the petroleum coke industry, as described by Goldberg and Erickson (1987). However, differences exist between the two. The coke middlemen are usually also coke producers. They enter contractual arrangements with other coke producers before reselling the coke to end users. On the other hand, traders of petrochemicals simply line up suppliers and buyers. They typically do not produce or consume the petrochemicals nor do they enter contracts with any parties.

[18] Rationing or allocating goods by quantity is not an uncommon practice in the industry. Suppliers occasionally use it when their products are on unexpected low supply due to a plant accident or a temporary surge in demand. See Barzel (1974) for an early discussion of rationing. See also Carlton (1991) for a more recent analysis.

[19] According to White (1982), the convention is deeply rooted in the industry, but the reason of it is unclear.

quantities specified in the contracts did not necessarily bear relationship with the quantities actually taken by the buyers historically. Most suppliers therefore allocated not by contract amounts but by historical take. The allocation by historical take provided the suppliers plenty of discretion, as it was hard for the buyers or the courts to monitor the historical take of individual buyers. In sum, the suppliers' incentives of deviating from pro rata allocation and the actual possibility of it created uncertainty in the buyers about being held up by their suppliers.

One potential solution to the ex post bargaining problems created by price uncertainty might have been the use of price indices. Unfortunately, price indices could not be relied on to indicate changes in petrochemical prices after 1973. Due to the high price volatility, the relations between the petrochemical prices and the price indices were unstable over time. The weakened price correlations thwarted index-based price adjustment mechanisms in supply contracts.[20] Price indices were therefore not sufficient to solve the contracting problems in the industry during the 1970s.

3.3. Organizational responses

The contracting problems in the petrochemical industry during the 1970s created wide spread holdup problems in inter-firm contracts, which could not be easily alleviated by alternative contractual solutions. Were firms in the industry induced to integrate vertically into input production? Before an empirical investigation of this question, I describe how several organizations responded to the contracting problems.

3.3.1. Du Pont

Shortly after the first oil price shock, Du Pont, a leader of the petrochemical industry, experienced difficulties in procuring adequate raw materials for the production of numerous products. The raw material problem was caused primarily by the inability of certain suppliers to fulfill contract commitments. The problem was severe enough for Du Pont to embark on backward integration through a series of acquisitions. During 1975, Du Pont agreed to a joint venture with National Distillers and Chemical for the production and sale of synthetic gas and carbon monoxide to provide feedstock for production of methanol by Du Pont and acetic acid by National Distillers. Also, Du Pont and Atlantic Richfield entered into a joint venture for the production of petrochemical raw materials used in the manufacture of fibers, plastics, and elastomers. In 1976, Du Pont unsuccessfully attempted to acquire Shenandoah Oil, which was engaged in exploring for and producing oil and natural gas. In 1980, shortly after the second oil price shock, Du Pont entered into a joint natural gas exploration program with Conoco, Du Pont eventually acquired the entire natural resource concern in 1981.

3.3.2. Hercules

By 1975, Du Pont was the single largest consumer of Hercules' product, dimethyl terephthalate (DMT), which is used to produce polyester. Hercules, in response to Du

[20] See Goldberg (1985), Goldberg and Erickson (1987), and Joskow (1988).

Pont's earlier request to increase the supply, doubled its DMT capacity. Shortly after the first oil price shock, Du Pont unexpectedly announced its decision to become a self-sufficient producer of polyester intermediates. The reversal came as an enormous surprise to Hercules. Construction of a new production plant was halted immediately, resulting in a write-off of about $14 million.[21] The reaction of Hercules to Du Pont's contractual breach was to exit gradually from the DMT business.

3.3.3. PPG

PPG is a leading producer of glass and coating materials. In the late 1960s, the company decided to begin producing primary petrochemicals. It entered a 50–50 joint venture with Commonwealth Oil Refining (CORCO) to construct, at that time, one of the world's largest olefin plants at Penuelas, Puerto Rico. The plant made primary petrochemicals from petroleum feedstock purchased from CORCO. PPG also built a wholly owned complex at Guayanilla, Puerto Rico, which used the ethylene from the olefin plant to produce a variety of petrochemical intermediates. PPG's total investment in Puerto Rico was $150 million.

The Puerto Rican operations began in 1971. In 1973, shortly after the first oil shock, "CORCO experienced difficulty in supplying sufficient feedstock to keep the olefin plant operating and refused to supply any feedstock except at substantially higher prices than had been contracted for".[22] CORCO and PPG filed suit against each other; the dispute was settled in 1975. However, CORCO later filed a petition for bankruptcy protection in 1978, and it asked the Court for authority to reject the PPG–CORCO joint venture and integration agreements.[23] The Court granted CORCO's request. PPG took over the joint venture and was later forced to shut down the olefin plant and its wholly owned downstream operations in Puerto Rico. The Puerto Rican operations contributed to operating losses of more than $140 million between 1971 and 1978. PPG eventually abandoned its involvement in the primary petrochemical sector.

The above anecdotal evidence indicates that contracting problems in the 1970s were sufficiently severe to affect firms' organizational choices. In particular, the Du Pont's response to its contracting problems suggests that vertical integration could be optimal for some firms in the face of high price uncertainty. I investigate this hypothesis in the following empirical analysis.

---

[21] Hercules' CEO, in an interview with Dyer and Sicilia (1990, p 390), recalled that "Du Pont arrived at this decision after one of its suppliers in another product line suddenly raised prices. Because Du Pont relied heavily on the supplier, it had little choice but to pay. To avoid what they regarded as extortion — or the threat of it — Du Pont's top executives resolved that the company would no longer tolerate dependence upon any single supplier... We (Hercules) talked seriously about suing the Du Pont company for leading us on in this manner but decided there was no profit in attempting to sue one of our most important customers. We already had a penalty clause in our contract, and indeed, Du Pont paid a modest penalty for materials it did not take".

[22] PPG, 1974 Annual Report.

[23] PPG, 1978 Special Letter to Shareholders.

4. Empirical analysis

In this section, I report on a large-sample empirical investigation into the questions of whether and under what conditions firms embark upon vertical integration in the face of price uncertainty. In the process, the transaction cost hypotheses as well as several rival hypotheses will be tested.

4.1. Data sample

The sampling years include 1972, 1982, and 1992. The three samples facilitate the comparison of vertical integration before, during, and after the period of the oil price shocks. I primarily employ two data sources identified by Lieberman (1991): *Directory of Chemical Producers* (SRI International, various years) and *Synthetic Organic Chemicals* (US International Trade Commission, various years). The former source provides exhaustive information on annual plant capacity, location, and ownership for approximately 200 chemical products in the domestic US market. The latter contains annual production, sales, and unit values of a wide variety of chemicals. Additional data including annual prices and production quantities of ammonium products are secured from the Agricultural Prices (US Department of Agriculture, various years) and Current Business Statistics, (US Department of Commerce, various years) respectively.

From these data sources, a list of products and their primary inputs is prepared. For a product to be included, the following criteria must be met to enable the construction of empirical measures. First, the product must have an identifiable primary input and not be a by-product. Second, domestic plant capacity and ownership data for the product and its primary input must be available in the three sampling years. Lastly, annual prices of the primary input must be available between 1963 and 1992. The sampling criteria result in a list of 49 products. Table 1 presents the sample products, their producers in number, their primary inputs, and input substances. As reported, the 49 products are each derived from one of 24 primary inputs. There are totally 490, 409 and 347 product-firms in 1972, 1982, and 1992, respectively. The number of producers of a given product ranges from several to more than 40. The average number of producers across the products is 10, 8, and 7 in the three samples, respectively. The decreased average number of producers over time reflects the trend of producers exiting from the industry since the 1970s.

Table 2 presents a list of the top 50 producers ranked by the total number of observations for each producer over the three years. The observations are diversely distributed across the producers, as no single producer accounts for more than 5% of the total observations. For the three sampling years as a whole, the top 50 producers account for 64% of the observations. Among the top 50 producers, 23 are chemical companies, 19 are oil-and-gas companies, and the remaining 8 are diversified companies with significant businesses outside the chemical and the oil-and-gas industries.

4.2. Measurement

4.2.1. Vertical integration

Vertical integration is measured by the input self-sufficiency ratio (ISR): a firm's in-house input capacity divided by the required input capacity to support completely the

Table 1
Sample petrochemical products, their producers in number, their primary inputs, and input substances

No.	Product	Number of Producers			Primary input	Input is gaseous
		1972	1982	1992		
1	ABS resins	7	3	3	Styrene	No
2	Acetic acid	6	5	4	Methanol	No
3	Acetone	4	4	1	Isopropyl alcohol	No
4	Acrylic acid	1	4	4	Propylene	Yes
5	Acrylonitrile	4	4	5	Propylene	Yes
6	Adipic acid	5	2	2	Cyclohexanone	No
7	Ammonium nitrate	38	32	25	Ammonia	Yes
8	Ammonium phosphate	28	24	14	Ammonia	Yes
9	Ammonium sulfate	8	6	5	Ammonia	Yes
10	Benzoid acid	5	3	2	Toluene	No
11	Benzyl chloride	4	3	2	Toluene	No
12	Bisphenol A	4	5	4	Phenol	No
13	Caprolactam	2	2	2	Cyclohexane	No
14	Cumene	12	12	10	Benzene	No
15	Cyclohexane	9	8	4	Benzene	No
16	Cyclohexanone	8	4	4	Cyclohexane	No
17	Dimethylterephthalate	5	3	3	*p*-Xylene	No
18	Ethanolamines	5	4	4	Ethyl oxide	Yes
19	Ethyl acetate	5	4	2	Ethyl alcohol	No
20	Ethyl chloride	6	4	1	Ethylene	Yes
21	Ethylbenzene	14	12	12	Ethylene	Yes
22	Ethylene dichloride	12	12	11	Ethylene	Yes
23	Ethylene glycol	13	11	10	Ethylene	Yes
24	Ethylene oxide	13	12	10	Ethylene	Yes
25	Formaldehyde	19	13	16	Methanol	No
26	Fumaric acid	5	4	3	Maleic anhydride	No
27	Hexamethylene Tetramine, TECH	7	6	2	Formaldehyde	No
28	Isopropyl alcohol	4	4	3	Propylene	Yes
29	Maleic anhydride	6	2	4	Benzene	No
30	Methyl Isobutyl ketone	4	4	3	Acetone	No
31	Methyl mecrylate	3	3	3	Acetone	No
32	*n*-Butyl acetate	4	3	3	*n*-Butyl alcohol	No
33	*n*-Butyl alcohol	7	7	5	Propylene	Yes
34	Nitric acid	46	38	34	Ammonia	Yes
35	Nitrobenzene	7	5	5	Benzene	No
36	Pentaerythritol, MONO	5	4	3	Formaldehyde	No
37	Phthalic anhydride	8	5	4	*o*-Xylene	No
38	Polyethylene-HD	13	13	10	Ethylene	Yes
39	Polyethylene-LD	14	12	10	Ethylene	Yes
40	Polypropylene	9	11	16	Propylene	Yes
41	Polystyrene	18	16	16	Styrene	No
42	Polyvinyl alcohol	4	3	3	Vinyl acetate	No
43	Polyvinyl chloride resins	21	15	13	Vinyl chloride	No
44	Propylene oxide	6	1	2	propylene	Yes

Table 1 (*continued*)

No.	Product	Number of Producers			Primary input	Input is gaseous
		1972	1982	1992		
45	SBR rubber	10	7	4	1,3-Butadiene	Yes
46	Styrene	10	9	8	Ethylbenzene	Yes
47	Urea	31	28	19	Ammonia	Yes
48	Vinyl acetate	3	4	4	Ethylene	Yes
49	Vinyl chloride	8	9	10	Ethylene dichloride	No
Total number of producers	490	409	347			
Average number of producers	10.00	8.35	7.08			

manufacturing of its product. The denominator of ISR, the required input capacity, is estimated from multiplying the product capacity with the input–output conversion ratio — the quantity of the input required for producing a one-unit quantity of the output. When the firm uses the input to produce multiple products, its in-house input capacity is prorated by the individual products' input requirements. By construction, ISR is bounded below by zero but not bounded above.

Panel A of Table 3 reports summary statistics of ISR. The mean ISR is 2.00, 1.44, and 1.30 in the 1972, 1982, and 1992 samples, respectively. The values suggest that the average firm is more than self sufficient in its input requirement. However, substantial differences in the value of ISR exist across products and firms, as indicated by the large standard errors, 5.18, 2.89, and 2.44, in the three respective years. The medians of ISR are 0.99, 0.82, and 0.77, substantially smaller than the mean statistics. The differences suggest that extreme values cause the reported large mean statistics. The existence of the extreme values is also indicated by the maximum statistics, 70.83, 41.78, and 21.13, in the three respective years. Both the mean and median statistics display a decreasing pattern over time, suggesting that the overall degree of input self-sufficiency has been declining.

Panel B of Table 3 reports the sample distribution across different levels of input self-sufficiency. There exists a wide dispersion of organizational choices across the firms and product sectors. Some producers rely solely on external markets for inputs. In the three respective years, 30%, 31%, and 40% of the sample firms do not produce any input in-house. Some producers are partially integrated: 19%, 24%, and 23% of the firms in the three respective years produce some but less than sufficient inputs in-house. There are also fully integrated producers: 50%, 44%, and 35% of the sample firms are fully or more than fully self-sufficient in their input requirements.

4.2.2. Independent variables

In Section 2, the transaction cost theory makes predictions regarding how vertical integration is affected by price uncertainty and asset specificity. To test these predictions, several proxy variables are selected based on the industry characteristics discussed

Table 2
Top-50 petrochemical producers

Rank[a]	Firm[b]	Number of product-firms				Cum%[c]	Type[d]
		1972	1982	1992	Total		
1	Union Carbide	24	16	13	53	4.25	Chemical
2	Monsanto	22	19	10	51	8.35	Chemical
3	Du Pont	14	19	11	44	11.88	Chemical
4	Dow Chemical	16	14	13	43	15.33	Chemical
5	Royal Dutch/Shell (Netherlands/UK)	13	12	8	33	17.98	Oil and gas
6	Eastman Kodak	11	10	10	31	20.47	Diversified
7	Celanese	14	10	0	24	22.39	Chemical
8	BASF (Germany)	5	9	8	22	24.16	Chemical
9	AMOCO (Standard Oil of IN)	7	6	6	19	25.68	Oil and gas
10	Exxon (Standard Oil of NJ)	7	7	5	19	27.21	Oil and gas
11	Phillips Petroleum	8	7	3	18	28.65	Oil and gas
12	Allied Chemical	13	4	0	17	30.02	Chemical
13	Chevron (Standard Oil of CA)	5	3	9	17	31.38	Oil and gas
14	Gulf Oil	9	8	0	17	32.74	Oil and gas
15	Hercules	9	5	3	17	34.11	Chemical
16	Occidental Petroleum	6	3	8	17	35.47	Oil and gas
17	USX (US Steel)	7	10	0	17	36.84	Diversified
18	Borden	7	7	2	16	38.12	Diversified
19	Air Products and Chemicals	5	6	4	15	39.33	Chemical
20	Olin	9	5	1	15	40.53	Chemical
21	Atlantic Richfield	2	7	4	13	41.57	Oil and gas
22	PPG	5	5	3	13	42.62	Diversified
23	BF Goodrich	5	4	3	12	43.58	Diversified
24	CF Industries	4	4	4	12	44.54	Chemical
25	Mississippi Chemical	4	4	4	12	45.51	Chemical
26	Quantum Chemical (Nat'l Distillers and Chem.)	2	3	7	12	46.47	Chemical
27	Texaco	2	5	5	12	47.43	Oil and gas
28	American Cyanamid	6	5	0	11	48.31	Chemical
29	Hoechst Celanese (Germany)	0	0	11	11	49.20	Chemical
30	J.R. Simplot	2	5	4	11	50.08	Chemical
31	ICI (UK)	4	4	2	10	50.88	Chemical
32	Reichhold Chemical	6	4	0	10	51.69	Chemical
33	Coastal Corp	1	4	4	9	52.41	Oil and gas
34	El Paso Natural Gas	5	4	0	9	53.13	Oil and gas
35	Ethyl	4	5	0	9	53.85	Chemical
36	Farmland Industries	1	4	4	9	54.57	Chemical
37	Getty Oil	4	5	0	9	55.30	Oil and gas
38	Mobil Oil	4	3	2	9	56.02	Oil and gas
39	Tenneco	8	1	0	9	56.74	Diversified
40	Terra Chemical International	3	3	3	9	57.46	Chemical
41	Union Oil of CA	5	4	0	9	58.19	Oil and gas
42	W.R. Grace	4	5	0	9	58.91	Diversified
43	Fina (American Petrofina, Belgium)	3	2	3	8	59.55	Oil and gas

Table 2 (*continued*)

Rank[a]	Firm[b]	Number of product-firms				Cum%[c]	Type[d]
		1972	1982	1992	Total		
44	Cominco American	2	3	3	8	60.19	Chemical
45	Standard Oil of OH	4	4	0	8	60.83	Oil and gas
46	Williams	4	4	0	8	61.48	Oil and gas
47	Georgia-Pacific	1	5	1	7	62.04	Diversified
48	Koch	3	2	2	7	62.60	Oil and gas
49	Rohm and Hass	3	2	2	7	63.16	Chemical
50	Sun Oil	4	1	2	7	63.72	Oil and gas
Sub-total	316	291	187	794	63.72		
All others	174	118	160	452	36.28		
Total	490	409	347	1246	100.00		

[a]The producers are ranked by the total number of observations (product-firms) in the three sampling years.

[b]Prior names and foreign ownership are indicated in parentheses.

[c]The numbers indicate cumulative percentages of product-firms over the full sample.

[d]The producers are each classified into the chemical, oil-and-gas, or diversified type according to their main business involvement.

in Section 3. I describe the proxies and their predicted relations with vertical integration as follows.

Table 3
Input self-sufficiency ratios[a] (ISR) of petrochemical firms

	1972	1982	1992
Panel A: Summary statistics			
Mean	2.00	1.44	1.30
Standard error	5.18	2.89	2.44
Median	0.99	0.82	0.77
Maximum	70.83	41.78	21.13
Minimum	0.00	0.00	0.00
Panel B: Distribution of firms by levels of input self-sufficiency			
ISR = 0	151 (30.8%)	128 (31.3%)	141 (40.6%)
0 < ISR < 0.5	26 (5.3%)	37 (9.0%)	9 (2.6%)
0.5 < = ISR < 1	68 (13.9%)	61 (15.0%)	73 (21.1%)
ISR > = 1	245 (50.0%)	183 (44.7%)	124 (35.7%)
Total product-firms	490	409	347

[a]The input self-sufficiency ratio (ISR) is the firm's in-house input capacity divided by the required input capacity to fully support the manufacturing of its product. The denominator of the ISR, the required input capacity, is estimated from multiplying the product capacity with the input-output conversion ratio — the quantity of the input required for producing a one-unit quantity of the product. When the firm uses the input to produce more than one product, its in-house input capacity is prorated by the individual products' input requirements.

The first variable is input price uncertainty (*Pu*), measured as the standard deviation of residuals from the following de-trending regression:

$$\log(P_{it}) = a_i + b_i t + u_{it},$$

where P_{it} is the average price of the ith input in year t. The regression is run for each of the inputs and each decade ending in 1972, 1982, and 1992, using annual prices of the 10 prior-and-inclusive years. The theory predicts a positive relation between *Pu* and vertical integration, particularly during the 1970s.

The second variable is asset specificity. To capture asset specifity, I use a dummy variable, *Gas*, as in Lieberman (1991). *Gas* equals one if the input in question is a gas, or else it equals zero. Many petrochemical processes involve gaseous inputs. As reported earlier in Table 1, 6 of the 24 inputs in the sample are gaseous. The same table shows that 22 of the 49 products in the sample require gaseous inputs. Gaseous inputs are associated with greater temporal and site specificity than non-gaseous inputs. I expect a positive relation between *Gas* and vertical integration.

The transaction cost theory emphasizes the interactive effects of uncertainty and asset specificity. That is, the larger the asset specificity, the greater the organizational response to uncertainty. It can therefore be expected that, in the face of high price uncertainty, gaseous input users will maintain a higher degree of input self-sufficiency than will users of non-gaseous inputs. This hypothesis will be tested in regression analysis where *Gas* interacts with *Pu*. A significant positive estimated coefficient of the interaction term will be consistent with the hypothesis.

Several control variables are considered in the analysis. The first control variable is the producer's scale (*Scale*) measured as a producer's total capacity divided (normalized) by the average capacity of all producers of the same product. The producer's scale can affect vertical integration through a reputation effect or a production cost effect. The cited studies of Klein and Murphy (1997) and Baker et al. (1997) predict a positive relation between a firm's degree of vertical integration and the size of its reputation capital. Assuming a firm with a larger production scale also has more reputation capital, one expects a positive relation between *Scale* and the extent that the firm integrates into the input stage. Alternatively, the producer's scale can affect input production costs. Riordan and Williamson (1985) predict that vertical integration is positively related to firm size. They reason that as the size of a firm increases, its input requirement increases, and hence the production cost of in-house production of the input becomes lower through the scale effect. Using *Scale* as a proxy for firm size, one expects a positive relation between *Scale* and the extent of the firm's input self-sufficiency. Both of the reputation and the production cost effects reach the same prediction: a positive relation between *Scale* and vertical integration.

Another control factor is capacity balance. Balancing capacity between production stages has been shown to be important in the aluminum industry. Stuckey (1983) reports that integrated firms on average have balanced capacity across the mining, smelting, and fabricating stages of the industry. He argues that, in so doing, the firms are able to circumvent thin intermediate markets. Consider the following example that is typical in the petrochemical industry. The efficient scale of a downstream plant is small while the efficient scale of its corresponding upstream (input) plant is large. A firm producing at the efficient scale will face a capacity-balancing problem when it integrates into the input stage. It will have to produce either the input at a less-than-efficient scale to maintain capacity balance or build an efficient input plant and sell excess input to the market. Both of the options may be overly costly and hence discourage the firm's vertical integration. I construct a proxy, *Bcap*, to capture the capacity balance effect. For a given product, *Bcap* is the average capacity of input plants divided by the average capacity of product plants. One expects a negative relation between *Bcap* and input self-sufficiency.

Table 4 provides a summary of the independent variables, their predicted relations with vertical integration, and their empirical measures. As indicated, the transaction cost theory predicts that the input self-sufficiency in the industry increases with the use of gaseous inputs, the degree of input price variability, and the joint effect of the two. The literature also predicts that the input self-sufficiency is positively affected by producer's scale and the size of the input plant relative to that of the product plant.

4.2.3. Basic statistics

Table 5 presents mean statistics of the independent variables. The table also compares means of the variables between producers that own input plants and those that do not. Of the 490, 409, and 347 product-firms, 339, 281, and 206 owned at least one input plant in 1972, 1982, and 1992, respectively. Several observations are worth noting from the table. First, the highest input price uncertainty occurred in the decade of the oil price shocks, followed by the more recent decade, then by the decade prior to 1973. Consistent with the prediction, the firms that owned input plants in 1982 on average experienced larger input price uncertainty in the 1970s than the firms without input plant ownership; the difference is statistically significant at the 1% level. But the difference is not significant in the 1972 and the 1992 samples. Second, the majority of the firms in the sample use gaseous inputs: 58%, 61%, and 59% of the firms in the three respective samples. Moreover, firms are more likely to own input plants if their inputs are gaseous,

Table 4
The independent variables, their predicted relations with vertical integration, and their empirical measures

Variable	Predicted relation with vertical integration	Empirical measure
Input price uncertainty (*Pu*)	Positive	Standard deviation of residuals from the input price de-trending regression[a]
Asset specificity (*Gas*)	Positive	Dummy variable equal to one if the input is gaseous, or zero if otherwise
$Pu * Gas$	Positive	Product of the input price uncertainty and the asset specificity measures
Producer's scale (*Scale*)	Positive	Producer's capacity normalized by the average capacity of all producers
Capacity balance (*Bcap*)	Negative	Average input plant capacity divided by average product plant capacity

[a]The de-trending regression is $\log(P_{it}) = a_i + b_i t + u_{it}$, where P_{it} is the average price of the ith input in year t. The regression is run for each of the inputs and each decade ending in 1972, 1982, and 1992, using annual prices of the 10 prior-and-inclusive years.

Table 5
Mean statistics of the independent variables and comparison of the mean variables between producers' that own input plants and others that do not[a]

Variable[b]	Year	All producers	Producers with input plant ownership	Producers without input plant ownership	*T*-statistic for diffirence in means
Pu,	1972	0.0828	0.0812	0.0864	−0.81
input price uncertainty	1982	0.2518	0.2554	0.2439	2.97***
	1992	0.1735	0.1746	0.1718	0.33
Gas,	1972	0.58	0.65	0.41	5.17***
asset specificity	1982	0.61	0.67	0.47	3.73***
	1992	0.59	0.65	0.51	2.46***
Scale,	1972	1.42	1.56	1.08	4.47***
producer's scale	1982	1.52	1.71	1.12	4.64***
	1992	1.48	1.63	1.26	2.53***
Bcap,	1972	4.75	4.55	5.18	−1.3
capacity balance	1982	4.15	3.96	4.56	−1.43
	1992	4.41	3.71	5.42	−3.53***

* Significant at the 0.10 level; ** Significant at the 0.05 level.
*** Significant at the 0.01 level.

[a]Of the 490, 409, and 347 observations (product-firms), 339, 281, and 206 owned at least one input plant in 1972, 1982, and 1992, respectively.

[b]*Pu* is the standard deviation of residuals from the de-trending regression: $\log(P_{it}) = a_i + b_i t + u_{it}$, where P_{it} is the price of the ith input in year t. The regression is run for each of the inputs and each decade ending in 1972, 1982, and 1992, using annual prices of the 10 prior-and-inclusive years. *Gas* is a dummy variable equal to one if the input is gaseous, or zero if not. *Scale* is the producer's capacity normalized by the average capacity of all producers. *Bcap* is the average capacity of input plants divided by the average capacity of product plants.

consistent with the predicted effect of asset specificity. In 1982, 67% of the firms owning input plants used gaseous inputs, whereas only 47% of the firms not owning input plants used gaseous inputs. The difference is statistically significant at the 1% level. Similar differences are also registered for the 1972 and the 1992 samples. Third, the average value of *Scale* is significantly greater for the firms with input plant ownership than the firms without input plant ownership in each of the three sampling years. The evidence is consistent with the reputation and the production cost effects. Fourth, as the mean statistics of *Bcap* indicate, the average capacity of petrochemical input plants is more than four times larger than the average capacity of downstream product plants. Consistent with the capacity balance effect, *Bcap* is generally smaller for product-firms owning input plants than other firms not owning input plants, though the difference is significant only in the 1992 sample.

In summary, the results of the univariate comparisons in Table 5 are generally consistent with the predicted effects of price uncertainty and asset specificity. The results also suggest that the reputation, production cost, and capacity balance effects are relevant to vertical integration in the industry and should be controlled in regression analysis.

4.3. Regression analysis

This section reports on multivariate regression analysis to examine the transaction cost hypotheses. I examine individual effects of price uncertainty and asset specificity, joint effects of the two, and effects of industry agglomeration.

4.3.1. Individual effects

For each of the three sampling years, separate Tobit regressions are performed to determine the effects of input price uncertainty, asset specificity, and the control variables on the input self-sufficiency of the producers. To mitigate the bias resulting from some extraordinarily large values of ISR, the dependent variable is re-defined as $VI = \log(\text{ISR} * 100)$, where each of the zero-value ISR*s* is replaced by 1 before taking the natural logarithm.

Equations (1), (2), and (4) of Table 6 report the coefficients estimated separately from the 1972, the 1982, and the 1992 samples. An overview across the equations reveals several results. First, the estimated coefficients of *Gas* are all positive and significant at the 1% level. Given that gaseous inputs are associated with higher degrees of asset specificity than non-gaseous inputs, the evidence is consistent with the transaction cost

Table 6
Tobit regressions of vertical integration on input price uncertainty, asset specificity, and control variables[a]

Independent variable[b]	1972	1982		1992
	(1)	(2)	(3)	(4)
Intercept	1.77***	−1.63	−3.90***	1.35*
	(4.31)	(−1.33)	(−3.93)	−1.63
VI_{72}			1.05***	
			(15.21)	
Gas	1.39***	1.54***	0.49*	1.22***
	(4.34)	(4.40)	(1.81)	(2.54)
Pu	−1.64	12.66***	10.03***	0.66
	(−0.64)	(2.77)	−2.85	(0.13)
Scale	0.37***	0.44***	0.08	0.45***
	(3.36)	(4.00)	(1.00)	(2.81)
Bcap	−0.01	−1.00**	−0.04	−0.22***
	(−0.12)	(−2.22)	(−1.14)	(−4.40)
Log likelihood	−1042	−848	−490	−688
Observations	490	409	285	347

Asymptotic *t*-statistics are in parentheses.

* Significant at the 0.10 level.

** Significant at the 0.05 level.

*** Significant at the 0.01 level.

[a]The dependent variable is $VI = \log(\text{ISR} * 100)$, where ISR is the input self-sufficiency ratio. If ISR = 0, it is set to 1 before taking log.

[b]VI_{72} is *VI* measured in 1972. *Gas* is a dummy variable equal to one if the input is gaseous, or zero if not. *Pu* is the standard error of residuals from the de-trending regression: $\log(P_{it}) = a_i + b_i t + u_{it}$, where P_{it} is the average price of the *i*th input in year *t*. The regression is run for each of the inputs and each decade ending in 1972, 1982 and 1992, using annual prices of the 10 prior-and-inclusive years. *Scale* is the produce's capacity normalized by the average capacity of all producers. *Bcap* is the average capacity of input plants divided by the average capacity of product plants.

view that vertical integration increases with asset specificity. Second, the estimated coefficient of *Pu* is positive and statistically significant at the 1% level in the 1982 sample but not significant in the 1972 and 1992 samples. The evidence is consistent with the view that the holdup problems unique to the high price uncertainty in the 1970s are not mitigated by alternative contractual mechanisms, forcing firms to increase their degrees of vertical integration. Third, vertical integration increases with *Scale*, as the estimated coefficients are positive and significant at the 1% level across the equations. *Scale* used as a proxy for the size of the producer's reputation capital provides evidence for the argument that vertical integration facilitates self-enforcement by giving ownership rights to the more reputable parties in transactions (Klein and Murphy, 1997; Baker et al., 1997). Alternatively, using *Scale* as a proxy for firm size, the evidence is consistent with the argument that large firms face smaller production cost disadvantage relative to markets when they integrate into input stages (Riordan and Williamson, 1985). Lastly, the estimated coefficients of *Bcap* are generally negative and are statistically significant in the 1982 and 1992 samples. The evidence is consistent with the capacity balance effect of Stuckey (1983).

As a test of robustness, a partial adjustment model is performed on 285 product firms that survived through the decade between 1973 and 1982. The dependent variable is the 1982 *VI*. The model includes *VI* measured in 1972 as one additional independent variable. The equation used for (3) in Table 6 reports the estimated coefficients. As one would expect, the estimated coefficient of the lagged *VI* is positive and highly significant. The effect of *Pu* remains positive and significant at the 1% level. The coefficients of *Gas, Scale, and Bcap* maintain their previous signs but their explanatory power becomes weaker.

One condition to contemplate is the high inflation during the decade after 1973, particularly in 1982. Might the inflation cause a spurious relation between the price uncertainty and the vertical integration measures, as reported in Table 6 and earlier in Table 5? Two reasons suggest that it does not. First, price trends have been removed from the price uncertainty measure through the de-trending regressions. Second, the vertical integration measure is constructed from the 1982 plant capacity data. If the 1982 inflation had affected vertical integration, any effects would show up in the capacity data of later years because altering plant capacity typically requires a lead time of 1 to 2 years.

In summary, the results from the multiple regressions in Table 6 are generally consistent with the predictions of the transaction cost theory. The firms' vertical integration into input production is positively affected by asset specificity and the price uncertainty provoked by the oil price shocks. The evidence from the control variables indicates that the reputation, production cost, and capacity balance factors systematically affect the firms' extents of input self-sufficiency.

4.3.2. Joint effects

It has been predicted that the impact of input price uncertainty on vertical integration increases with asset specificity. To examine this hypothesis, the regression models of Table 6 are amended with an interaction term, $Pu * Gas$, and then re-estimated. Table 7 presents the results of this analysis. Equations (1), (2), and (4) in Table 7 report the

Table 7
Tobit regressions of the interactive effects of input price uncertainty and asset specificity on vertical integration[a]

Independent variable[b]	1972	1982		1992
	(1)	(2)	(3)	(4)
Intercept	2.00***	−0.03	−2.95***	1.35
	(4.65)	(−0.02)	(−2.63)	(1.28)
VI_{72}			1.04***	
			(15.07)	
Gas	0.17	−5.49*	−3.04	1.21
	(0.24)	(−1.90)	(−1.42)	(0.95)
Pu	−3.40	6.7	6.60*	0.64
	(−1.26)	(1.30)	(1.64)	(0.13)
Pu ∗ *Gas*	16.01**	28.10***	14.18*	0.05
	(1.96)	(2.45)	(1.67)	(0.00)
Scale	0.36***	0.45***	0.09	0.45***
	(3.27)	(4.09)	(1.12)	(2.81)
Bcap	−0.01	−0.11***	−0.05	−0.22***
	(−0.33)	(−2.75)	(−1.38)	(−3.66)
Log likelihood	−1040	−845	−488	−688
Observations	490	409	285	347

Asymptotic *t*-statistics are in parentheses.

* Significant at the 0.10 level.

** Significant at the 0.05 level.

*** Significant at the 0.01 level.

[a]The dependent variable is $VI = \log(\text{ISR} * 100)$, where ISR is the input self-sufficiency ratio. If ISR = 0, it is set to 1 before taking log.

[b]VI_{72} is *VI* measured in 1972. *Gas* is a dummy variable equal to one if the input is gaseous, or zero if not. *Pu* is the standard error of residuals from the de-trending regression: $\log(P_{it}) = a_i + b_i t + u_{it}$, where P_{it} is the average price of the *i*th input in year *t*. The regression is run for each of the inputs and each decade ending in 1972, 1982 and 1992, using annual prices of the 10 prior-and-inclusive years. *Scale* is the produce's capacity normalized by the average capacity of all producers. *Bcap* is the average capacity of input plants divided by the average capacity of product plants.

estimated coefficients from the Tobit regressions for the three sampling years. Different from the previous results in Table 6, the effect of *Pu* is no longer significant in 1982 while the interactive effect of *Pu* and *Gas* is positive and significant in 1972 and 1982, but not significant in 1992. Also worth noting, after including the interaction term, the coefficient of *Gas* becomes insignificant to weakly negative across the regression models. The evidence suggests that the joint effects of price uncertainty and asset specificity dominate the individual effects in explaining vertical integration. The estimated coefficients of *Scale* and *Bcap* maintain their previous signs and levels of significance. As in equation (3), the partial adjustment model run on the 1982 sample yields similar, albeit weaker, results, compared with the results in equation (2).

The evidence suggests that the positive reaction of vertical integration to input price uncertainty is attributed to producers requiring gaseous inputs. The gaseous input users are subject to a higher degree of asset specificity than are the non-gaseous input users, because their transaction possibilities are contrived by the high transportation and

Table 8
Mean fractions of producers' capacity located in the Gulf Coast States of Texas and Louisiana

Year	Number of producers	All producers	Producers using gaseous inputs	Producers using non-gaseous inputs	T-statistic for diffirence in means
1972	490	0.40	0.47	0.30	4.11***
1982	409	0.47	0.50	0.40	2.23**
1992	347	0.52	0.56	0.44	2.29**

* Significant at the 0.10 level.
** Significant at the 0.05 level.
*** Significant at the 0.01 level.

storage costs of the gas (Mulherin, 1986a). The expected high costs of supply disruption motivate the gaseous input users to adopt high degrees of input self-sufficiency in response to price uncertainty. The evidence is therefore consistent with the transaction cost prediction.

Vertical integration in the 1992 sample cannot be related to price uncertainty, as none of the coefficients of *Pu* and the interaction terms in Tables 6 and 7 is statistically significant. Several market developments may have reduced the need for using vertical integration to deal with price uncertainty in the more recent period. Middlemen may have increased their roles in aligning buyers and sellers and in collecting and aggregating pricing information (Ching, 1986; Goldberg and Erickson, 1987). Globalization and increasing openness of markets may have served the same purpose of reducing the costs of arm's length transactions. The introduction of modern risk management instruments and techniques[24] may have enhanced firms' ability to mitigate the costs of price fluctuations (Sykuta, 1996). These hypotheses are left for future research.

4.3.3. Effects of industry agglomeration

The Gulf of Mexico in the US region has a high concentration of petrochemical plants. This is illustrated in Table 8, where I report mean percentages of producers' capacity located in the Gulf Coast states of Texas and Louisiana. In 1972, petrochemical producers on average had 40% of their production capacity located in the Gulf region. Over time, the capacity share increased to 47% in 1982 and then to 52% in 1992. The pattern of capacity concentration is particularly significant for producers requiring gaseous inputs. For these producers, their average Gulf region capacity shares are 47%, 50%, and 56% in the three respective years. In contrast, for producers using non-gaseous inputs, the figures are much lower: 30%, 40%, and 44%, respectively. The differences in the Gulf region output capacity shares between the two groups of producers are statistically significant in all sampling years.

Industry infrastructures in the region play an important role in the capacity concentration. The region has integrated pipeline systems connecting users and suppliers of

[24] With proper risk management tools, companies can enter into independent supply contracts without having to worry about price risk. See Chang and Joseph, 1997, "Shell Launches Firm to Help Manage Risk in Price Fluctuation", *Chemical Marketing Reporter*, July 28.

several gaseous inputs. Commercial storage facilities are also abundant.[25] These infrastructures make possible transportation over longer distances and storage of larger amounts, which in turn facilitate transaction possibilities for producers and suppliers. Transactions carried out in the Gulf region are expected to have lower degrees of asset specificity relative to transactions in other regions.

To examine the effects of the industry agglomeration on producers' vertical *NGulf*, are created. *Gulf* equals one if a producer has plant(s) in the Gulf Coast states of Texas and Louisiana; if not, it equals zero. *NGulf* equals one if the producer does not have any plant located in the two Gulf Coast states; if not, it equals zero. The regression models of Table 7 are revised to allow the *Gulf* and the *NGulf* variables to interact separately with $Pu * Gas$.

The regression results are presented in Table 9. The estimated coefficients of *Gas*, *Pu*, *Scale*, and *Bcap* are of similar magnitudes and significance levels as those reported in Table 7. The focus here is the pair of the interaction terms. In the 1972 regression, the estimated coefficient of $Pu * Gas * Gulf$ is not significant while the coefficient of $Pu * Gas * NGulf$ is positive and significant, (1). The evidence suggests that, prior to 1973, if gaseous input users are located in the Gulf region, it is not necessary to change their degrees of vertical integration in response to price uncertainty. Increasing vertical integration is necessary only for producers in the non-Gulf region. In the 1982 regressions, both the coefficients of $Pu * Gas * Gulf$ and $Pu * Gas * NGulf$ are significantly positive ((2) and (3)). The results suggest that, after the oil price shocks, price uncertainty increases the vertical integration of the firms requiring gaseous inputs, regardless of their geographic locations. Lastly, vertical integration in the 1992 sample cannot be related to input price uncertainty, as none of the coefficients of *Pu* and the interaction terms is significant, (4).

The overall evidence suggests that industry agglomeration facilitates transaction possibility, reduces the degree of asset specificity in transactions, and therefore weakens the effect of price uncertainty on vertical integration. However, if price uncertainty is high, merely concentrating in one region is not sufficient to solve contracting problems.

4.4. Alternative explanations for organizational change

In this section, I examine two alternative hypotheses to explain vertical integration in the petrochemical industry: price controls and market power.

4.4.1. Price controls

A short-term but potentially important factor that hampered price adjustment in the petrochemical input markets is the general price control instituted by the Nixon Administration during 1971 to 1974. Between 1973 and 1974, the price control coupled with the oil embargo created a severe scarcity of petrochemical inputs. During that period, many suppliers could not produce sufficient amounts to meet their contract

[25] Large quantity storage is made by cylindrical tanks with large capacities, underground caverns, or jugs leached out of underground salt domes.

Table 9
Tobit regressions of the effects of industry agglomeration on vertical integration[a]

Independent variable[b]	1972	1982		1992
	(1)	(2)	(3)	(4)
Intercept	1.98***	−0.01	−2.95***	1.35
	(4.60)	(−0.00)	(−2.63)	(1.28)
VI_{72}			1.04***	
			(14.85)	
Gas	0.46	−5.31*	−3.12	1.14
	(0.63)	(−1.83)	(−1.46)	(0.82)
Pu	−3.43	6.64	6.66*	0.63
	(−1.27)	(1.30)	(1.65)	(0.13)
*Pu * Gas * Gulf*	7.54	26.58**	14.84*	0.3
	(0.73)	(2.30)	(1.74)	(0.04)
*Pu * Gas * NGulf*	15.39**	28.38***	14.00*	0.97
	(1.89)	(2.48)	(1.65)	(0.09)
Scale	0.39***	0.46***	0.08	0.45***
	(3.54)	(4.18)	(1.00)	(2.81)
Bcap	−0.02	−0.12***	−0.05	−0.22***
	(−0.66)	(−3.00)	(−1.38)	(−3.66)
Log likelihood	−1039	−844	−488	−688
Observations	490	409	285	347

Asymptotic t-statistics are in parentheses.
* Significant at the 0.10 level.
** Significant at the 0.05 level.
*** Significant at the 0.01 level.
[a]The dependent variable is $VI =$ log(ISR * 100), where ISR is the input self-sufficiency ratio. If ISR = 0, it is set to 1 before taking log.
[b]VI_{72} is VI measured in 1972. *Gas* is a dummy variable equal to one if the input is gaseous, or zero if not. *Pu* is the standard error of residuals from the de-trending regression: $\log(P_{it}) = a_i + b_i t + u_{it}$, where P_{it} is the average price of the ith input in year t. The regression is run for each of the inputs and each decade ending in 1972, 1982, and 1992, using annual prices of the 10 prior-and-inclusive years. *Gulf* (*Ngulf*) is a dummy variable equal to one if a firm has (does not has) plant(s) in the Gulf-Coast states of Texas and Louisiana, or zero if not. *Scale* is the produce's capacity normalized by the average capacity of all producers. *Bcap* is the average capacity of input plants divided by the average capacity of product plants.

obligations because of not being able to pass their input costs on to their customers by sufficiently raising contract prices. They instead invoked allocation programs to distribute the limited quantities among their customers. The allocation scheme could be quite ambiguous and create buyers' uncertainty about been unfairly rationed. An aggravating factor of the allocation uncertainty is related to spot markets. During the price control period, the spot markets became active gray markets where inputs were bought and sold at prices much higher than the controlled contract prices. The large price dispersions might have tempted suppliers to long spot buyers while shorting their contract buyers, hence damaging the effectiveness of contract governance before the control was lifted in 1974. As Stigler's (1951) theory suggests, the firms might have integrated into input stages to circumvent the input markets distorted by the price control. Price controls have been found to affect governance choices in other industries.

Similar to the petrochemical industry, the regulation of wellhead prices in the natural gas industry led to a scarcity condition in the early 1970s (MacAvoy and Pindyck, 1973). Hubbard and Weiner (1986) study the effects of the price control on provisions of contracts between natural gas producers and pipelines. They find that the price control increased the use of the take-or-pay provision, due to non-price competition among pipelines. In particular, they report that the use of the take-or-pay provision increased sharply after 1973, because the non-price competition was intensified by the increased demand for gas and the expectation of decontrol in the near future.[26]

To evaluate the effects of the price control on vertical integration in the petrochemical industry, I study input price jumps around the two oil price shocks. The regression model of Table 6 is amended with two additional independent variables, *Jump73* and *Jump79*, then re-estimated using the 1982 sample. For a given input, *Jump73* is defined as the natural logarithm of the ratio of the 1974 average price to the 1973 average price. *Jump79* is similarly defined as the natural logarithm of the ratio of the 1980 average price to the 1979 average price. My focus is *Jump73*. If the price control was binding, one expects to observe jumps in the input prices immediately after the price control was alleviated in early 1974. Furthermore, the more binding the price control was, the greater the extent of the price jump should be. To be consistent with the predicted effects of the price control, one should observe a positive reaction of the firms' vertical integration to *Jump73*.

Table 10 presents the regression results. The estimated coefficients of *Gas*, *Scale*, and *Bcap* are of similar magnitudes and significance levels as in Table 6. Here I focus on the price jump variables. As in equation (1), vertical integration is unrelated to the price jumps: the coefficients of *Jump73* and *Jump74* are insignificant. Equation (2) jointly considers the effects of *Pu* and the price-jump variables. The coefficient of *Pu* remains positive and significant at the 1% level. The coefficient of *Jump73* turns negative and significant. The coefficient of *Jump79* stays insignificant. In sum, the positive effect of input price uncertainty observed in the 1982 sample cannot be explained by the price jumps immediately after the two oil price shocks. In particular, the insignificant-to-negative coefficients of *Jump73* do not support the view that vertical integration of the firms was uniquely induced by the allocation uncertainty created by the price control and the input price hikes during 1973 to 1974. The evidence is more consistent with the view that the firms' vertical integration was affected by the general input price uncertainty in the decade after 1973.

4.4.2. Market power

One rationale for petrochemical firms to engage in input production is that the firms can extend their market power to the input markets, for example through foreclosing competitors' access to the inputs. To investigate this hypothesis, I study the concentration of input markets. The ability of a firm using vertical integration to extend market power is positively affected by the concentration of the market in question. A Herfindahl index is constructed to capture input market concentration. The index is measured as the

[26] The National Gas Policy Act of 1978 deregulated wellhead prices.

Table 10
Tobit regressions of the effects of the input price jumps in 1973 and 1979 on vertical integration[a]

Independent variable[b]	(1)	(2)
Intercept	1.52	−0.91
	(1.44)	(−0.73)
Gas	1.28***	1.65***
	(3.04)	(3.83)
Pu		21.87***
		(3.62)
Jump73	0.06	−3.93**
	(0.04)	(−2.36)
Jump79	0.51	0.60
	(0.54)	(90.65)
Scale	0.46***	0.43***
	(4.18)	(3.90)
Bcap	−0.10**	−0.11***
	(−2.17)	(−2.44)
Log likelihood	−852	−845
Observations	409	409

Asymptotic t-statistics are in parentheses.

*Significant at the 0.10 level.

**Significant at the 0.05 level.

***Significant at the 0.01 level.

[a]The 1982 sample is used in the regressions. The dependent variable is $VI = \log(\text{ISR} * 100)$, where ISR is the input self-sufficiency ratio. If $ISR = 0$, it is set to 1 before taking log.

[b]*Gas* is a dummy variable equal to one if the input is gaseous, or zero if not. *Pu* is the standard error of residuals from the de-trending regression: $\log(P_{it}) = a_i + b_i t + u_{it}$, where P_{it} is the average price of the ith input in year t. The regression is run for each of the inputs and each decade ending in 1972, 1982, and 1992, using annual prices of the 10 prior-and-inclusive years. *Gulf* (*Ngulf*) is a dummy variable equal to one if a firm has (does not has) plant(s) in the Gulf-Coast states of Texas and Louisiana, or zero if not. *Jump73* (*Jump79*) is the natural logarithm of the ration of the 1974 (1980) average price to the 1973 (1979) average price. *Scale* is the produce's capacity normalized by the average capacity of all producers. *Bcap* is the average capacity of input plants divided by the average capacity of product plants.

sum of the squared capacity shares of firms producing the input. The value of the index ranges between 0 and 1 and increases with the market concentration level. Panel A of Table 11 reports summary statistics of the index. From the mean and median statistics, petrochemical input markets generally have low levels of concentration. The mean is only 0.09, 0.10, and 0.09 in 1972, 1982, and 1992, respectively. The median is 0.08, 0.07, and 0.07 in the three respective years. Even at the maximum, the concentration level is not high: 0.32, 0.33, and 0.35, respectively. The low input market concentration casts doubt on market power as an explanation for the vertical integration in the industry.

To further investigate the market power hypothesis, I compare the mean input concentration between integrated producers (with input plant ownership) and other non-integrated producers (without input plant ownership). The market power hypothesis predicts that a producer is more likely to integrate vertically (own input plants) when the input market is more concentrated. It turns out that vertical integration and market

Table 11
Statistics of the Herfindahl index of petrochemical input market concentration[a]

	1972	1982	1992
Panel A: Overall summary statistics			
Mean	0.09	0.10	0.09
Standard error	0.06	0.06	0.06
Median	0.08	0.08	0.07
Maximum	0.32	0.33	0.35
Minimum	0.03	0.05	0.06
Panel B: Mean statistics by producers' input plant ownership			
Producers that own input plants	0.08	0.09	0.09
Producers that do not own input plants	0.11	0.12	0.11
T-statistic for difference in means	−4.68***	−4.01***	−3.02***
Panel C: Mean statistics by input substance			
Producers that use gaseous inputs	0.05	0.07	0.06
Producers that use non-gaseous input	0.13	0.14	0.14
T-statistic for difference in means	−16.54***	−13.97***	−12.36***

* Significant at the 0.10 level.
** Significant at the 0.05 level.
*** Significant at the 0.01 level.
[a]The Herfindahl index of an input market is the sum of the squared capacity shares of individual input firms. The sample includes 490, 409, and 347 firms producing 49 products derived from 24 inputs in 1972, 1982, and 1992.

concentration are related, but in a direction opposite to what is predicted by the hypothesis. As reported in Panel B of Table 11, producers facing less concentrated input markets are more likely to own input plants than producers facing more concentrated markets. The differences in the mean concentration index between the integrated and non-integrated firms are negative and statistically significant in all of the three sampling years.[27] The evidence from this analysis suggests that market power cannot explain the vertical integration of petrochemical producers into input stages.

5. Conclusion

I study vertical integration in the petrochemical industry with a focus on the 1970s, the period of the oil price shocks. I find that producers' degrees of input self-sufficiency

[27] The negative relation between market concentration and vertical integration is likely a spurious relation caused by gaseous inputs. As shown in the regression analysis (Tables 6 and 7), producers of gaseous inputs are more likely to integrate vertically. At the same time, the markets for gaseous inputs are also less concentrated. This is shown in Panel C of Table 11, where I compare the market structure between gaseous and non-gaseous inputs in 1972, 1982, and 1992. The number of gaseous input producers is over twice as many as the number of non-gaseous input producers. The Herfindahl concentration index of the gaseous inputs is two-times lower than that of the non-gaseous inputs.

are positively related to the price uncertainty during that period. The positive reaction of vertical integration to the input price uncertainty mainly occur among producers requiring gaseous inputs that are subject to high degrees of asset specificity. Vertical integration in the industry is also related to industry agglomeration. I report that, prior to the first oil price shock, the extents of vertical integration of firms located along the US Gulf Coast were less affected by price uncertainty than firms located in other areas. However, after the price shock, the firms' extents of vertical integration were positively affected by input price uncertainty, regardless of their geographic locations.

The findings generally support the transaction cost view that uncertainty provoked by dramatic events reduces the advantage of contracts relative to vertical integration in governing relationship-specific transactions. The paper also provides evidence consistent with the reputation, production cost, and capacity balance effects articulated in the literature. In contrast, several rival hypotheses of transaction cost are rejected in the paper. Vertical integration in the industry is not motivated by price controls, nor is by market power.

This paper has demonstrated the value of industry study in analyzing organizational changes and issues in financial economics. Related examples are Mulherin's (1986b) analysis of vertical integration and contracting in the natural gas industry, Zingales' (1998) analysis of exit and financing in the trucking industry, and Kole and Lehn's (1999) paper on the adaptation of governance structure in the airline industry. These studies have used exogenous shocks to form natural experiments in one industry, which allow empirical tests of theories in great detail and precision.

There are abundant opportunities for applying industry research on topics in finance and organizational economics. Future industry studies might include analysis of deregulation and the electric utility industry, technological change and the telecommunications industry, and the end of the Cold War and restructuring in the defense industry. More efforts toward this direction are warranted.

Acknowledgements

This paper is from Chapter 2 of my PhD dissertation. I thank my committee members, Kenneth Lehn (chair), Esther Gal-Or, Harold Mulherin, and Michael Spiro for their guidance. This paper also has benefited from comments by Denis Carlton, Keith Crocker, Hao Li, Marvin Lieberman, Scott Masten, Nick Palmer, Janet Smith, Michael Sykuta, three anonymous referees, and the session participants of the 1996 WEA and the 1999 AEA Meetings, as well as editorial assistance by Virginia Unkefer. Research support from the Center for Research on Contracts and the Structure of Enterprise at the Katz Graduate School of Business of the University of Pittsburgh and the Hong Kong Research Grant Council is gratefully acknowledged.

References

Anderson, E., 1985. The salesperson as outside agent or employee: a transaction cost analysis. Marketing Science 4, 234–254.

Anderson, E., Schmitten, D.C., 1984. Integration of the sales force: an empirical examination. Rand Journal of Economics 15, 385–395.

Arora, A., Gambardella, A., 1998. Evolution of industry structure in the chemical industry. In: Arora, A., Landau, R., Rosenberg, N. (Eds.), Chemicals and Long-term Economic Growth: Insights from the Chemical Industry. Wiley, New York, NY.

Baker, G., Gibbons, R.S., Murphy, K.J., 1997, Relational contracts and the theory of the firm, NBER Working Paper 6177.

Barzel, Y., 1974. A theory of rationing by waiting. Journal of Law and Economics 17, 73–95.

Blair, R.D., Kaserman, D.L., 1978. Vertical integration, tying, and antitrust policy. American Economic Review 68, 397–402.

Bower, J.L., 1986. When Markets Quake. Harvard Business School Press, Boston.

Carlton, D.W., 1979. Vertical integration in competitive markets under uncertainty. Journal of Industrial Economics 27, 189–209.

Carlton, D.W., 1985. The rigidity of prices. American Economic Review 76, 637–658.

Carlton, D.W., 1991. The theory of allocation and its implications for marketing and industrial structure: why rationing is efficient. Journal of Law and Economics 34, 231–262.

Cave, R.E., Bradburd, R.M., 1988. The empirical determinants of vertical integration. Journal of Economic Behavior and Organization 9, 265–279.

Chapman, K., 1991. The International Petrochemical Industry: Evolution and Location. Basil Blackwell, Cambridge.

Ching, D.R., 1986. Two price systems: alternative models of spot/contract procurement in the US chemical industry, PhD dissertation, Harvard University.

Coase, R.H., 1937. The nature of the firm. Economica 4, 386–405.

Crocker, K.J., Masten, S.E., 1988. Mitigating contractual hazards: unilateral options and contract length. Rand Journal of Economics 19, 327–343.

Crocker, K.J., Masten, S.E., 1991. Pretia ex machina? Prices and process in long-term contracts. Journal of Law and Economics 34, 69–99.

Dyer, D., Sicilia, D.B., 1990. Labors of a Modern Hercules: The Evolution of a Chemical Company. Harvard Business School Press, Boston.

Goldberg, V.P., 1985. Price adjustment in long-term contracts. Wisconsin Law Review, 527–543.

Goldberg, V.P., Erickson, J.R., 1987. Quantity and price adjustment in long-term contracts: a case study of petroleum coke. Journal of Law and Economics 30, 369–398.

Grossman, S., Hart, O., 1986. The costs and benefits of ownership: a theory of vertical and lateral integration. Journal of Political Economy 94, 691–719.

Hubbard, R.G., Weiner, R.J., 1986. Regulation and long-term contracting in US natural gas markets. Journal of Industrial Economics 35, 71–79.

Jensen, M.C., 1993. The modern industrial revolution, exit, and the failure of internal control systems. Journal of Finance 48, 831–880.

John, G., Weitz, B.A., 1988. Forward integration into distribution: an empirical test of transaction cost analysis. Journal of Law, Economics, and Organization 4, 337–355.

Joskow, P.L., 1985. Vertical integration and long-term contracts: the case of coal-burning electric generating plants. Journal of Law, Economics, and Organization 1, 33–80.

Joskow, P.L., 1988. Price adjustment in long-term contracts: the case of coal. Journal of Law and Economics 31, 47–83.

Klein, B., 1988. Vertical integration as organizational ownership: the fisher body-general motors relationship revisited. Journal of Law, Economics, and Organization 4, 199–213.

Klein, B., 1992. Contracts and incentives: the role of contract terms in assuring performance. In: Werin, L., Wijkander, H. (Eds.), Contract Economics. Basil Blackwell, Oxford.

Klein, B., 1996. Why hold-ups occur: the self-enforcing range of contractual relationships. Economic Inquiry 34, 444–463.

Klein, B., Crawford, R.A., Alchian, A.A., 1978. Vertical integration, appropriable rents, and the competitive contracting process. Journal of Law and Economics 21, 297–326.

Klein, B., Murphy, K.J., 1997. Vertical integration as a self-enforcing contractual arrangement. American Economics Review 87, 415–420.

Kole, S.R., Lehn, K.M., 1999. Deregulation and the adaptation of governance structure: the case of the US airline industry. Journal of Financial Economics 52, 79–117.

Lane, S.J., 1993. Corporate restructuring in the chemical industry. In: Blair, M.M. (Ed.), The Deal Decade: What Takeovers and Leveraged Buyouts Mean for Corporate Governance. The Brookings Institution, Washington, DC.

Levy, D.T., 1985. The transactions cost approach to vertical integration: an empirical examination. Review of Economics and Statistics 67, 438–445.

Lieberman, M.B., 1991. Determinants of vertical integration: an empirical test. Journal of Industrial Economics 39, 451–466.

MacAvoy, P.W., Pindyck, R.S., 1973. Alternative regulatory policies for dealing with the natural gas shortage. Bell Journal of Economics and Management Science 4, 454–498.

Masten, S.E., 1984. The organization of production: evidence from the aerospace industry. Journal of Law and Economics 27, 403–418.

Masten, S.E., Meehan Jr., J.W., Snyder, E.A., 1991. The cost of organization. Journal of Law, Economic, and Organization 7, 1–25.

Monteverde, K., Teece, D., 1982. Supplier switching costs and vertical integration in the automobile industry. Bell Journal of Economics 13, 206–213.

Mitchell, M.L., Mulherin, J.H., 1996. The impact of industry shocks on takeover and restructuring activity. Journal of Financial Economics 41, 193–229.

Mulherin, J.H., 1986a. Complexity in long-term contracts: an analysis of natural gas contractual provisions. Journal of Law, Economics, and Organization 2, 105–177.

Mulherin, J.H., 1986b. Specialized assets, governmental regulation, and organizational structure in the natural gas industry. Journal of Institutional and Theoretical Economics 142, 528–541.

Ohanian, N.K., 1994. Vertical integration in the US pulp and paper industry, 1900-1940. Review of Economics and Statistics 76, 202–207.

Perry, M.K., 1989. Vertical integration: determinants and effects. In: Schmalensee, R., Willig, R.D. (Eds.), Handbook of Industrial Organization vol. I. Elsevier Science Publishers, Amsterdam, Netherlands.

Pirrong, S.C., 1993. Contracting practices in bulk shipping markets: a transactions cost explanation. Journal of Law and Economics 36, 937–976.

Riordan, M.H., Williamson, O.E., 1985. Asset specificity and economic organization. International Journal of Industrial Organization 3, 365–378.

Shelanski, H.A., Klein, P.G., 1995. Empirical research in transaction cost economics: a review and assessment. Journal of Law, Economics, and Organization 11, 335–361.

Spiller, P.T., 1985. On vertical mergers. Journal of Law, Economics, and Organizations 1, 285–312.

Spitz, P.H., 1988. Petrochemicals: The Rise of an Industry. Wiley, New York, NY.

SRI International, various years, Directory of Chemical Producers (Stanford Research Institute, Menlo Park, CA).

Stigler, G., 1951. The division of labor is limited by the extent of the market. Journal of Political Economy 59, 185–193.

Stobaugh, R.B., 1988. Innovation and Competition: The Global Management of Petrochemical Products. Harvard Business School Press, Boston.

Stuckey, J., 1983. Vertical Integration and Joint Ventures in the Aluminum Industry. Harvard University Press, Cambridge.

Sykuta, M.E., 1996. Futures trading and supply contracting in the oil refining industry. Journal of Corporate Finance: Contracting Governance, and Organization 2, 317–334.

US Department of Agriculture, National Agricultural Statistics Service, various years, Agricultural Prices (Government Printing Office, Washington DC).

US Department of Commerce, Bureau of Economic Analysis, various years, Current Business Statistics (Government Printing Office, Washington DC).

US International Trade Commission, various years, Synthetic Organic Chemicals (Government Printing Office, Washington DC).

Walker, G., Weber, D., 1984. A transaction cost approach to make-or-buy decisions. Administrative Science Quarterly 29, 373–391.

Walker, G., 1987. Supplier competition, uncertainty, and make-or-buy decisions. Academy of Management Journal 30, 589–596.

Weiss, A., 1992. The role of firm specific capital in vertical mergers. Journal of Law and Economics 35, 71–88.

White, J.J., 1982. Contract law in modern commercial transactions, an artifact of twentieth century business life? Washburn Law Journal 22, 1–22.

Williamson, O.E., 1971. The vertical integration of production: market failure consideration. American Economic Review 61, 112–123.

Williamson, O.E., 1975. Markets and Hierarchies: Analysis and Antitrust Implications. Free Press, New York.

Williamson, O.E., 1979. Transaction cost economies: the governance of contractual relations. Journal of Law and Economics 22, 233–261.

Williamson, O.E., 1985. The Economic Institutions of Capitalism. Free Press, New York.

Zingales, L., 1998. Survival of the fittest or the fattest? Exit and financing in the trucking industry. Journal of Finance 53, 905–938.

[3]

Journal of Economic Perspectives—Volume 15, Number 2—Spring 2001—Pages 103–120

New Evidence and Perspectives on Mergers

Gregor Andrade, Mark Mitchell, and Erik Stafford

Empirical research on mergers and acquisitions has revealed a great deal about their trends and characteristics over the last century. For example, a profusion of event studies has demonstrated that mergers seem to create shareholder value, with most of the gains accruing to the target company. This paper will provide further evidence on these questions, updating our database of facts for the 1990s.

But on the issue of why mergers occur, research success has been more limited. Economic theory has provided many possible reasons for why mergers might occur: efficiency-related reasons that often involve economies of scale or other "synergies"; attempts to create market power, perhaps by forming monopolies or oligopolies; market discipline, as in the case of the removal of incompetent target management; self-serving attempts by acquirer management to "over-expand" and other agency costs; and to take advantage of opportunities for diversification, like by exploiting internal capital markets and managing risk for undiversified managers.

Most of these theories have been found to explain some of the mergers over the last century, and thus are clearly relevant to a comprehensive understanding of what drives acquisitions. In addition, some of these reasons for mergers appear to be more relevant in certain time periods. For example, antitrust laws and active enforcement have made merger for market power difficult to achieve since the 1940s. The heyday of diversification mergers was in the 1960s, and there is evidence to suggest many of those mergers were ultimately failures. Mergers as instruments

■ *Gregor Andrade is Assistant Professor of Business Administration, Mark Mitchell is Associate Professor of Business Administration, and Erik Stafford is Assistant Professor of Business Administration, all at Harvard Business School, Harvard University, Boston, Massachusetts. Their e-mail addresses are ⟨gandrade@hbs.edu⟩, ⟨mmitchell@hbs.edu⟩ and ⟨estafford@hbs.edu⟩, respectively.*

for market discipline do not seem to appear on the radar until the 1980s, but although it is customary to label the 1980s as the era of hostile takeovers, only 14 percent of deals in that decade involved hostile parties.

A recent strand of the literature, exemplified by Mitchell and Mulherin (1996), has tried to address the issue of why mergers occur by building up from the two most consistent empirical features of merger activity over the last century: 1) mergers occur in waves; and 2) within a wave, mergers strongly cluster by industry. These features suggest that mergers might occur as a reaction to unexpected shocks to industry structure. We believe this arena is a potentially fruitful one to explore from both a theoretical and empirical point of view. It also seems to correspond to the intuition of practitioners and analysts that industries tend to restructure and consolidate in concentrated periods of time, that these changes occur suddenly, and that they are hard to predict. However, identifying industry shocks and documenting their effect is challenging.

In this paper, we provide evidence that merger activity in the 1990s, as in previous decades, strongly clusters by industry. Furthermore, we show that one particular kind of industry shock, deregulation, while important in previous periods, becomes a dominant factor in merger and acquisition activity after the late 1980s and accounts for nearly half of the merger activity since then. In fact, we can say without exaggeration or hyperbole that in explaining the causes of mergers and acquisitions, the 1990s were the "decade of deregulation."

Of course, in the end, knowing that industry shocks can explain a large portion of merger activity does not really help clarify the mechanism involved, which brings us to the issues we know least about: namely, what are the long-term effects of mergers, and what makes some successful and others not. Here, empirical economists, and we include ourselves in this group, have had very little to say. We hope that over the next decade merger research will move beyond the basic issue of measuring and assigning gains and losses to tackle the more fundamental question of how mergers actually create or destroy value.

Mergers in the 1990s: What's New?

Many of the results discussed here have been reported by other authors, using different samples, and over various time periods. In this paper, we document merger activity using the stock database from the Center for Research in Security Prices (CRSP) at the University of Chicago. This database contains pricing information for all firms listed in the New York Stock Exchange (NYSE), American Stock Exchange (AMEX), and Nasdaq. We focus on mergers where both the acquirer and the target are publicly traded U.S.-based firms.

Figure 1 displays two different measures of annual merger activity. The dotted line represents the number of firms acquired during the year expressed as a fraction of the beginning-of-year number of firms in CRSP. The solid line gives a sense for the values involved, obtained by dividing the aggregate dollar value of

Figure 1
Aggregate Merger Activity

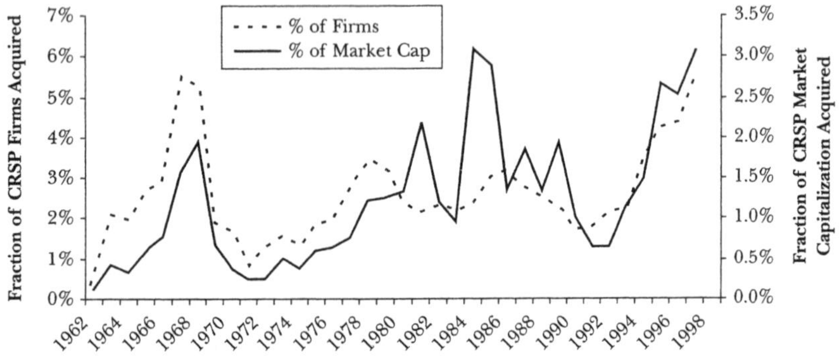

mergers over the year by the total beginning-of-year market capitalization of the firms listed on CRSP.[1] The evidence is entirely consistent with the well-known view that there have been three major waves of takeover activity since the early 1960s. Interestingly, the 1960s wave contained many more deals, relative to the number of publicly available targets, than the 1980s. However in dollar terms, the 1980s were far more important, as large multi-billion dollar deals became common. On a value-weighted basis, the 1980s were truly a period of massive asset reallocation via merger, and as reported by Mitchell and Mulherin (1996), nearly half of all major U.S. corporations received a takeover offer. It is astounding that the merger and acquisition activity in the 1990s seems to be even more dramatic and widespread, with number of deals comparable to the 1960s, and values similar to the 1980s.[2]

For the remainder of the paper, we will focus on the 26 years beginning in 1973, since that is the period during which Nasdaq firms are fully incorporated into CRSP, an event which drastically altered the size and composition of the sample. This results in about 4,300 completed deals. Table 1 reports key descriptive statistics and characteristics for our merger sample, broken down by decade.[3]

The evidence in Table 1 suggests that mergers in the 1980s and 1990s are different in many ways. The first key distinction is the overwhelming use of stock as a method of payment during the latter decade. About 70 percent of all deals in the 1990s involved stock compensation, with 58 percent entirely stock financed. These numbers are approximately 50 percent more than in the 1980s.

Perhaps related to the predominance of stock financing, note the virtual

[1] Both measures are expressed as percentages of total CRSP firms, to control for the overall growth in the number of firms listed over the sample period.
[2] Our data only goes to 1998. However, the wave has continued, and in fact, 1999 is reported to be the largest year ever for U.S. mergers, on a total dollar value basis.
[3] See Schwert (2000) for similar descriptive statistics and characteristics for mergers during 1975-1996 involving exchange-listed (NYSE and AMEX) targets.

Table 1
Characteristics and Descriptive Statistics by Decade, 1973–1998

	1973–1979	*1980–1989*	*1990–1998*	*1973–1998*
N	789	1,427	2,040	4,256
All Cash	38.3%	45.3%	27.4%	35.4%
All Stock	37.0%	32.9%	57.8%	45.6%
Any Stock	45.1%	45.6%	70.9%	57.6%
Hostile Bid at Any Point	8.4%	14.3%	4.0%	8.3%
Hostile Bid Successful	4.1%	7.1%	2.6%	4.4%
Bidders/Deal	1.1	1.2	1.0	1.1
Bids/Deal	1.6	1.6	1.2	1.4
Own Industry	29.9%	40.1%	47.8%	42.1%
Premium (Median)	47.2%	37.7%	34.5%	37.9%
Acquirer Leverage > Target Leverage	68.3%	61.6%	61.8%	62.9%
Acquirer Q > Target Q	68.4%	61.3%	68.3%	66.0%
Relative Size (Median)	10.0%	13.3%	11.2%	11.7%
Fraction of Acquirer Announcement Returns < −5%	14.9%	17.0%	19.4%	17.5%
Fraction of Acquirer Announcement Returns > 5%	9.6%	11.3%	10.7%	11.1%

disappearance of hostility in the takeover market. We define a bid as hostile if the target company publicly rejects it, or if the acquirer describes it as unsolicited and unfriendly. Only 4 percent of transactions in the 1990s involved a hostile bid at any point, compared to 14 percent in the 1980s, and a hostile bidder acquired less than 3 percent of targets.[4] Consistent with this more "friendly" atmosphere, the average transaction in the 1990s involved only one bidder, and 1.2 rounds of bidding, far less than during the 1980s.

The evidence for the 1980s by itself is interesting, because it suggests that the hostility of takeover activity during that time was less severe than generally believed. Mitchell and Mulherin (1996) report that 23 percent of the firms in their sample receive a hostile bid at some point during the 1980s; however, their sample only includes firms listed in the Value Line Investment Survey, which are generally larger, better-known companies. During the same period, only 14 percent of the firms in our sample receive a hostile offer. Since we include all publicly traded firms, the contrast in these two results suggests that hostile activity was practically nonexistent among the smaller, lesser-known companies.

Finally, the 1990s continue a trend, begun in the 1970s, of an ever-increasing percentage of mergers where both parties are in the same industry (defined at the

[4] Schwert (2000) questions the bifurcation of mergers into friendly and hostile categories. He performs numerous analyses to show that hostile deals, as described in the press, are no different from friendly deals in economic terms, that is, based on accounting and stock performance data.

Table 2
Top Five Industries Based on Average Annual Merger Activity

1970s	*1980s*	*1990s*
Metal Mining	Oil & Gas	Metal Mining
Real Estate	Textile	Media & Telecom.
Oil & Gas	Misc. Manufacturing	Banking
Apparel	Non-Depository Credit	Real Estate
Machinery	Food	Hotels

2-digit SIC code level), now nearly half. The picture of mergers in the 1990s that emerges is one where merging parties, often in closely related industries, negotiate a friendly stock swap.

Of the recent empirical findings highlighted in the literature, one of the most interesting is the presence of industry clustering in merger activity. Mitchell and Mulherin (1996) document industry clustering by target firms for the 1980s and Andrade and Stafford (1999) document industry clustering by acquiring firms during the 1970-1994 period.[5] Although merger and acquisition activity, as discussed above, occurs in readily identifiable waves over time, these waves are not alike. In fact, the identity of the industries that make up each merger boom varies tremendously. A simple way to see that is to compare the level of merger activity in each industry over time. If we rank industries in each decade by the market values of all acquired firms, and then correlate these ranking across decades, we find that the correlations are negligible—that is, industries that exhibit high levels of merger activity in one decade, are no more likely to do so in other decades. As Table 2 illustrates, there is no overlap between the top five industries, ranked by merger values, of the 1980s and 1990s.

If mergers come in waves, but each wave is different in terms of industry composition, then a significant portion of merger activity might be due to industry-level shocks. Industries react to these shocks by restructuring, often via merger. These shocks are unexpected, which explains why industry-level takeover activity is concentrated in time, and is different over time, which accounts for the variation in industry composition for each wave. Examples of shocks include: technological innovations, which can create excess capacity and the need for industry consolidation; supply shocks, such as oil prices; and deregulation.[6]

[5] There is also evidence of clustering in earlier periods. See Nelson (1959) for evidence on the first half of the twentieth century, and Gort (1969) for the 1950s.

[6] Another potential explanation for why mergers occur in waves and cluster by industry might be that mergers are examples of "information cascades" (Bikchandani et al., 1992). The basic idea is that an action, in this case a merger, informs agents in similar circumstances about the profitability of similar actions, in this case other mergers. Hence, once there is a first merger in an industry, the likelihood of other similar mergers occurring goes up, which would explain clustering. However, the theory says nothing about what precipitates that first "triggering" merger in an industry. As discussed later, there is strong evidence, both in this paper and others, that merger activity is related to specific industry shocks,

The view that merger activity is the result of industry-level shocks is not new. Among others, Gort (1969), Jensen (1986), Morck, Shleifer and Vishny (1988), and Jensen (1993) all hypothesize as much. However, recently there has been evidence successfully tying mergers to specific shocks. Mitchell and Mulherin (1996) show that deregulation, oil price shocks, foreign competition, and financial innovations can explain a significant portion of takeover activity in the 1980s. In the introduction to *Mergers and Productivity*, a collection of in-depth case studies of mergers, editor Steven Kaplan (2000) concludes, "a general pattern emerges from these studies. It is striking that most of the mergers and acquisitions were associated with technological or regulatory shocks."

Of the shocks listed above, deregulation is an ideal candidate for analysis. First, it creates new investment opportunities for the industry. Second, it potentially removes long-standing barriers to merging and consolidating, which might have kept the industry artificially dispersed. Finally, it is fairly well-defined in time and in terms of parties affected, so empirically we know where and when to look.

We classify the following industries as having undergone substantial deregulation since 1973: airlines (1978), broadcasting (1984 and 1996), entertainment (1984), natural gas (1978), trucking (1980), banks and thrifts (1994), utilities (1992) and telecommunications (1996). We define a ten-year period around each of these events (three years before to six years after) as a "deregulation window." Figure 2 displays, for each year, the percentage of total merger activity represented by mergers in industries in the deregulation window. During most of the 1980s, this percentage hovers around 10–15 percent. After 1988, however, deregulated industries account for nearly half of all annual deal volume, on average.[7] This is consistent with the evidence in Table 2 that banking and media/telecommunications are two of the most active industries in the 1990s.

It is clear that deregulation was a key driver of merger activity over the last ten years. Whether rightly or wrongly—and the jury is still out on the efficiency benefits and value enhancements brought about in these industries—the fact is that deregulation precipitated widespread consolidation and restructuring of a few industries in the 1990s, frequently accomplished through merger.

In our view, the industry shock explanation for mergers has added substantially to our understanding of mergers, not so much how mergers create value, but rather why and when they occur. The results presented here update and expand the evidence on industry shocks with specific emphasis on deregulatory events.[8] Future empirical research on mergers should attempt to control for industry shocks.

---

such as deregulation. We therefore believe that the industry shocks better account for the fundamental forces behind merger activity.

[7] Per our readings of industry analyst reports, deregulation shocks often extend well beyond the direct industries targeted. We did not, however, attempt to measure the indirect impact of deregulation shocks on related industries.

[8] Also, see Mulherin and Boone (2000) for an analysis of industry shocks and mergers in the 1990s.

Figure 2
Annual Value of Mergers in Deregulated Industries as a Percent of Total Merger Value

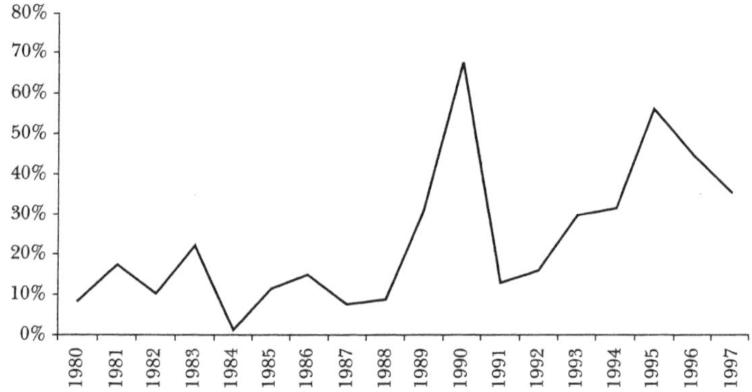

Winners and Losers in the Merger Game

Mergers represent massive reallocations of resources within the economy, both within and across industries. In 1995, the value of mergers and acquisitions equaled 5 percent of GDP and was equivalent to 48 percent of nonresidential gross investment. From the firm's perspective, mergers represent quite extraordinary events, often enabling a firm to double its size in a matter of months. Consequently, measuring value creation (or destruction) resulting from mergers and determining how this incremental value is distributed among merger participants are two of the central objectives in finance and industrial organization merger research.

Stock Market Reaction to Merger Announcements

The most statistically reliable evidence on whether mergers create value for shareholders comes from traditional short-window event studies, where the average abnormal stock market reaction at merger announcement is used as a gauge of value creation or destruction. In a capital market that is efficient with respect to public information, stock prices quickly adjust following a merger announcement, incorporating any expected value changes. Moreover, the entire wealth effect of the merger should be incorporated into stock prices by the time uncertainty is resolved, namely, by merger completion. Therefore, two commonly used event windows are the three days immediately surrounding the merger announcement—that is, from one day before to one day after the announcement—and a longer window beginning several days prior to the announcement and ending at the close of the merger.

Table 3 displays announcement period abnormal returns for both acquirers and targets, as well as for the acquirer and target combined. The average announcement period abnormal returns over the three-day event window for the target and

Table 3
Announcement Period Abnormal Returns by Decade, 1973–1998

	1973–79	*1980–89*	*1990–98*	*1973–98*
Combined				
[−1, +1]	1.5%	2.6%[a]	1.4%[a]	1.8%[a]
[−20, Close]	0.1%	3.2%	1.6%	1.9%
Target				
[−1, +1]	16.0%[a]	16.0%[a]	15.9%[a]	16.0%[a]
[−20, Close]	24.8%[a]	23.9%[a]	23.3%[a]	23.8%[a]
Acquirer				
[−1, +1]	−0.3%	−0.4%	−1.0%	−0.7%
[−20, Close]	−4.5%	−3.1%	−3.9%	−3.8%
No. Obs.	598	1,226	1,864	3,688

Note: Statistical significance at the 5 percent level is denoted by [a].

acquirer combined are fairly similar across decades, ranging from 1.4 percent to 2.6 percent, and averaging 1.8 percent overall for 3,688 completed mergers. In addition, the combined average abnormal returns over this event window are reliably positive, suggesting that mergers do create shareholder value on average. When the event window is expanded to begin 20 days prior to the merger announcement and end on the merger closing date, the combined average announcement period abnormal return is essentially identical at 1.9 percent. However, statistical precision is considerably reduced as the event window is lengthened to an average of 142 days, and this estimate cannot be reliably distinguished from zero.

Target firm shareholders are clearly winners in merger transactions. The average three-day abnormal return for target firms is 16 percent, which rises to 24 percent over the longer event window. Both of these estimates are statistically significant at the 1 percent level. In 1998, the median equity market value for target firms was $230 million, such that a 16 percent announcement period abnormal return corresponds to $37 million for target firm shareholders over a three-day period. Another benchmark to gauge the magnitude of this return is the average annual return for all publicly traded firms, which is around 12 percent. In other words, over a three-day period, target firm shareholders realize a return equivalent to what a shareholder would normally expect to receive over a 16-month period.

The average announcement period abnormal return estimate for target firms is remarkably stable across decades. This is interesting in the light of the evidence on clustering of merger activity. Each decade is associated with merger activity concentrated in different industries, but the target firms consistently have abnormal returns of 16 percent in the announcement period. Together, these two observations suggest that merger premia are fairly similar across different types of merger transactions.

The evidence on value creation for acquiring firm shareholders is not so clear cut. The average three-day abnormal return for acquirers is −0.7 percent, and over the longer event window, the average acquiring firm abnormal return is −3.8 percent, neither of which is statistically significant at conventional levels. Although the estimates are negative, they are not reliably so. Thus, it is difficult to claim that acquiring firm shareholders are losers in merger transactions, but they clearly are not big winners like the target firm shareholders.

The results in Table 3 are consistent with results presented in earlier summary papers by Jensen and Ruback (1983) and Jarrell, Brickley and Netter (1988). Mergers seem to create value for shareholders overall, but the announcement-period gains from mergers accrue entirely to the target firm shareholders. In fact, acquiring firm shareholders appear to come dangerously close to actually subsidizing these transactions. However, the picture is not quite complete. The full sample results hide an important distinction based on the financing of these transactions. In particular, mergers financed with stock, at least partially, have different value effects from mergers that are financed without any stock.

From the acquiring firm's perspective, stock-financed mergers can be viewed as two simultaneous transactions: a merger and an equity issue. On average, equity issues are associated with reliably negative abnormal returns of around −2 to −3 percent during the few days surrounding the announcement. Many models have been developed to explain this finding, mostly focusing on information differences between managers and outside investors (Myers and Majluf, 1984). The basic idea is that managers are more likely to issue equity when they perceive that it is overvalued by the stock market than when undervalued. Consequently, investors observing an equity issue bid down the stock price. Therefore, it is important to separate the stock-financed mergers from the others before making final judgement on the value effects for shareholders, especially for the acquiring firms.

Table 4 displays average announcement period abnormal returns for subsamples split on the basis of whether any stock was used to finance the merger transaction. Interestingly, the negative announcement period stock market reaction for acquiring firms is limited to those that finance the merger with stock. Acquiring firms that use at least some stock to finance their acquisition have reliably negative three-day average abnormal returns of −1.5 percent, while acquirers that abstain from equity financing have average abnormal returns of 0.4 percent which are indistinguishable from zero. These findings are consistent with the notion that the announcement period reaction for the acquirer to a stock-financed merger represents a combination of a merger announcement and an equity issue announcement.

Target firm shareholders also do better when there is no equity financing. The three-day average abnormal return for target firms is 13 percent for stock-financed mergers and just over 20 percent for mergers financed without stock. Interestingly, this is not merely a manifestation of larger deals having smaller premia and a greater tendency to be stock-financed. After controlling for deal size, this difference remains (11.3 percent for large stock deals and 17.8 percent for large non-stock deals). Financing also has a significant impact on inferences about overall value creation from mergers. The combined average abnormal returns for

Table 4
Announcement Period Abnormal Returns for Sub-Samples, 1973–1998

	Stock	*No Stock*	*Large Targets*
Combined			
[−1, +1]	0.6%	3.6%[a]	3.0%[a]
[−20, Close]	−0.6%	5.3%	6.3%
Target			
[−1, +1]	13.0%[a]	20.1%[a]	13.5%[a]
[−20, Close]	20.8%[a]	27.8%[a]	21.6%[a]
Acquirer			
[−1, +1]	−1.5%[a]	0.4%	−1.5%
[−20, Close]	−6.3%	−0.2%	−3.2%
No. Obs.	2,194	1,494	511

Note: Statistical significance at the 5 percent level is denoted by [a].

stock-financed mergers are zero, suggesting that this subset of mergers do not increase overall shareholder value. On the other hand, the combined three-day abnormal returns for mergers financed without any stock are reliably positive at 3.6 percent.

Based on the announcement-period stock market response, we conclude that mergers create value on behalf of the shareholders of the combined firms.

Long-Term Abnormal Returns

For many years, the traditional wisdom was that the announcement-period stock price reaction fully impounds the information effects of mergers. However, several recent long-term event studies measuring negative abnormal returns over the three to five years following merger completion cast doubt on the interpretation of traditional short-window event study findings. According to these studies, investors systematically fail to assess quickly the full impact of corporate announcements, with the implication that inferences based on announcement-period event windows are flawed, particularly those attempting to document the wealth effect of the event. In fact, some authors find that the long-term negative drift in acquiring firm stock prices overwhelms the positive combined stock price reaction at announcement, making the net wealth effect negative.

The most dramatic long-term abnormal performance comes from certain subsamples of acquiring firms. For example, Loughran and Vijh (1997) separately calculate long-term abnormal returns for acquiring firms using stock financing and those paying with cash over the period 1970-1989. They find that acquiring firms using stock financing have abnormal returns of −24.2 percent over the five-year period after the merger, whereas the abnormal return is 18.5 percent for cash mergers.

Another grouping that produces a large difference in long-term abnormal returns is based on the book-to-market equity ratio. Firms classified on the basis of high book-to-market are commonly referred to as "value" firms, and tend to have higher returns on average. Firms identified as low book-to-market are referred to as "growth" or "glamour" firms, and have relatively low returns on average. Interpretations of these findings vary. For example, Fama and French (1992, 1993) argue that the relatively high returns of value firms are due to increased risk, perhaps related to distress. On the other hand, Lakonishok, Shleifer and Vishny (1994) argue that the differential returns of value and growth stocks are not related to risk, but instead arise because investors mistakenly estimate future performance by extrapolating from past performance. Using the value/growth distinction, Rau and Vermaelen (1998) calculate three-year abnormal returns of −17.3 percent for glamour acquirers and 7.6 percent for value acquirers over the period 1980-1991.

There are a number of methodological concerns with long-term event studies (Barber and Lyon, 1997; Kothari and Warner, 1997; Fama, 1998; Mitchell and Stafford, 2000; Brav, 2000). These papers question every aspect of the long-term event studies, from the calculation of the point estimates to the assumptions required to assess statistical significance. The basic concern stems from all tests of long-term abnormal performance being joint tests of stock market efficiency and a model of market equilibrium (Fama, 1970). This problem is not a major one for short-window event studies where three-day expected returns are virtually zero regardless of what model of expected returns is used. Announcement period returns of 1 to 3 percent over three days are easy to reject as normal returns when the expected return is on the order of 0.05 percent. However, the model of expected returns becomes increasingly important as the holding period is lengthened, becoming crucial for multiyear horizons. Three-year expected returns can easily range from 30 percent to 65 percent, depending on the model used, making it very difficult to determine whether an abnormal return of 15 percent is statistically significant. The bottom line is that if long-term expected returns can only be roughly estimated, then estimates of long-term abnormal returns are necessarily imprecise.

An additional statistical concern with many long-term event studies is that the test statistics assume that abnormal returns are independent across firms. However, major corporate actions like mergers are not random events, and thus event samples are unlikely to consist of independent observations. As noted earlier, mergers cluster through time by industry. This clustering leads to positive cross-correlation of abnormal returns, which in turn means that test statistics that assume independence are severely overstated.

In addition to questioning the statistical reliability of long-term event studies, Mitchell and Stafford (2000) provide estimates of long-term abnormal returns that are robust to the most common statistical problems, including cross-sectional dependence. Table 5 displays three-year post-merger abnormal returns for 2,068 acquiring firms. The abnormal returns are calculated for both equal- and value-weight portfolios of acquiring firms in the three-years following the merger completion. First, the abnormal return estimates shown in Table 5 are considerably

Table 5
Three-Year Post-Merger Abnormal Returns for Acquiring Firms, 1961 to 1993

Portfolio Composition	*Equal-Weight*	*Value-Weight*
Full Sample	−5.0%[a]	−1.4%
Financed with Stock	−9.0%[a]	−4.3%
Financed without Stock	−1.4%	3.6%
Growth Firms	−6.5%	−7.2%
Value Firms	−2.9%	1.1%

Source: Mitchell and Stafford (2000).
Note: Statistical significance at the 5 percent level is denoted by [a].

closer to zero than in most studies that use samples covering shorter time periods, and the dramatic differences in performance based on financing and the value/growth distinction are greatly reduced. Second, significant abnormal returns are only found for the equal-weight portfolios, suggesting that post-merger abnormal stock price performance is limited to the smallest acquirers. In fact, almost all reliable abnormal stock price performance comes from firms in the smallest quintile of firms. Fama and French (1993) report that the firms in the smallest quintile (based on NYSE breakpoints) account for only 2.8 percent of the value of the CRSP value-weight stock market, on average. Although this represents a large number of firms, it is not clear how economically important this portion of the market is for assessing overall stock market efficiency.

The long-run literature on abnormal stock price performance has added to the profession's knowledge of market efficiency and empirical asset pricing. This literature has not focused on long-term performance following mergers, per se, but rather has examined all types of corporate events ranging from initial public offering to stock splits. Given the serious methodological concerns with the long-run empirical literature as outlined above, we are reluctant to accept the results at face value. With respect to mergers, it is our view that the long-run abnormal performance results do not change our priors that result from the announcement-period analyses, namely, that mergers create value for the stockholders of the combined firms.

Pre- and Post-merger Profitability

Operating performance studies attempt to identify the sources of gains from mergers and to determine whether the expected gains at announcement are ever actually realized. If mergers truly create value for shareholders, the gains should eventually show up in the firms' cash flows. These studies generally focus on accounting measures of profitability, such as return on assets and operating margins. Ravenscraft and Scherer (1989) and Healy, Palepu and Ruback (1992) are two operating performance studies that have been particularly influential in reinforcing perceptions about the gains to acquiring firms. These two papers reach different conclusions about gains from mergers. However, each study has data limitations which raise concerns about the generality of the findings.

Ravenscraft and Scherer (1989) examine target firm profitability over the period 1975 to 1977 using Line of Business data collected by the Federal Trade Commission. The FTC collected data for 471 firms from 1950 to 1976 by the business segments in which the firms operated. Ravenscraft and Scherer find that the target lines of business suffer a loss in profitability following the merger. They conclude that mergers destroy value on average, which directly contradicts the conclusion drawn from the announcement-period stock market reaction.

Healy, Palepu and Ruback (1992) examine post-merger operating performance for the 50 largest mergers between 1979 and 1984. In particular, they analyze the operating performance for the combined firm relative to the industry median. They find that merged firms experience improvements in asset productivity, leading to higher operating cash flows relative to their industry peers. Interestingly, their results show that the operating cash flows of merged firms actually drop from their pre-merger level on average, but that the non-merging firms in the same industry drop considerably more. Thus, the post-merger operating performance improves *relative* to the industry benchmark.

The recent evidence on industry clustering of merger activity is important for interpreting the findings of operating performance studies. First, selecting an appropriate expected performance benchmark in the absence of a merger is crucial. Simply using the same firm's pre-merger performance will be unsatisfying if the merger transaction comes in response to an industry shock that changes the prospects for a meaningful fraction of the firms in the industry. An industry-based benchmark as employed by Healy, Palepu and Ruback (1992) will help absorb this effect. Second, the tendency for merger activity to cluster through time by industry means that a short sample period will contain observations from only a few industries, making it difficult to generalize from these samples. Finally, if there is a common shock that induces merger activity at a particular point in time, there is no reason for it to be limited to just one industry or to affect all firms in an industry. Therefore, controlling for industry may not be sufficient to account for all cross-sectional correlation. A sample spanning a longer time period allows for statistical techniques that are better able to account for cross-sectional dependence.

Table 6 reports results from a time series of annual cross-sections methodology, which is similar in spirit to one employed by Fama and MacBeth (1973). This methodology requires a longer time series, but the test statistics account for cross-sectional dependence in performance measures, and should therefore be immune to the effects of industry clustering of merger activity. The sample includes roughly 2,000 mergers from 1973 to 1998, for which accounting data are available on Compustat.

The first row of Table 6 replicates the main findings of Healy, Palepu and Ruback (1992) that post-merger operating margins (cash flow to sales) are on average improved relative to industry benchmarks. In particular, we report the

Table 6
Pre- and Post-Merger Abnormal Operating Performance (AOP)

$t-1$	$t+1$	$t+2$
2.92%[a]	3.27%[a]	3.15%[a]
[2,012]	[2,101]	[1,796]
	$AOP(t+1) = a + b\,AOP(t-1)$	
A	b	R^2
1.07%[a]	0.804[a]	0.551[a]

Note: Statistical significance at the 5 percent level is denoted by [a].

average abnormal operating performance, where we measure abnormal operating performance as the difference between the combined firm's operating margin and the corresponding industry median operating margin.[9] The results suggest that the combined target and acquirer operating performance is strong relative to their industry peers prior to the merger, and improves slightly subsequent to the merger transaction.

The second row of Table 6 reports results from a regression analysis in which we regress the post-merger abnormal operating performance measure on the pre-merger abnormal operating performance measure.[10] The intercept measures the average post-merger abnormal operating performance after controlling for the persistence of this measure through time. On average, there is an improvement in operating margins following the merger, on the order of 1 percent, which is statistically significant at the 1 percent level.[11] The improvement in post-merger cash flow performance is consistent with the positive announcement-period stock market returns to the combined target and acquirer firms.

Where We Stand

Earlier review papers of the evidence on mergers by Jensen and Ruback (1983) and in this journal by Jarrell, Brickley and Netter (1988) survey the pre-1980

[9] The pre-merger unit of observation is the sales-weighted average of the acquirer and target abnormal operating performance measures. Following the merger, the unit of observation is simply the acquirer.
[10] This analysis also uses the Fama and MacBeth (1973) time-series of cross-sections methodology.
[11] The 1 percent increase in operating performance may be a lower bound on the gains to merger. Following Mitchell and Mulherin (1996) and Andrade and Stafford (1999), we have shown that industry shocks are a primary source of takeover activity. To the extent that the benchmark firms are also undertaking value-enhancing mergers or otherwise restructuring internally in response to industry shocks, the measured change in operating performance will be biased down.

and 1980s empirical literature, respectively, and conclude that mergers create value for the stockholders of the combined firms, with the majority of the gains accruing to the stockholders of the target. Both studies base their conclusion on the announcement-period stock price reaction to mergers. Our analysis of the immediate stock market response to more than 4,000 mergers completed during the 1973-1998 concurs with these prior reviews.

At the time of the Jensen and Ruback (1983) paper, the empirical literature largely consisted of computing the average returns to merger announcements. By the mid- to late 1980s, merger research as summarized by Jarrell, Brickley and Netter (1988) also studied the redistribution aspects of mergers. Specifically, were the gains to shareholders simply reflective of wealth transfers from bondholders, employees, or communities? Jarrell, Brickley and Netter argue that there is virtually no empirical evidence that gains to shareholders are due to losses from other stakeholders. They therefore conclude that the gains to shareholders must be real economic gains via the efficient rearrangement of resources. We are inclined to defend the traditional view that mergers improve efficiency and that the gains to shareholders at merger announcement accurately reflect improved expectations of future cash flow performance. But the conclusion must be defended from several recent challenges.

A first challenge is the research findings of a negative drift in acquiring firm stock prices following merger transactions, which would imply that the gains from mergers are overstated or nonexistent. As noted in our earlier discussion, we are very skeptical of these studies, which have been shown to be fraught with methodological problems. The fundamental problem is that to measure long-term abnormal returns reliably, one must first be able to measure long-term expected returns precisely—and no one has provided a convincing way to do this. Furthermore, the evidence on long-term returns conflicts with the results, reported here, that mergers improve the long-term cash flow performance of the merging parties, relative to their industry peers.

A second challenge is that the underlying sources of the gains from mergers have not been identified. Here, the large sample nature of most studies, which tend to combine transactions with different motivations, and the inherent noisiness of the accounting data, have made it nearly impossible for traditional research methods to address the issue. The positive effect of the merger is recognized by the stock market, but it is difficult for economic researchers to identify the sources of the gains with their much coarser information sets. In an attempt to overcome these limitations and to understand better the sources of value creation and destruction arising from mergers, there have recently been several studies that try to improve on the evidence arising from accounting-based data by examining more detailed information.

One set of studies have analyzed total factor efficiency and other productivity changes following mergers, using plant-level input and output data from the Longitudinal Research Database at the Bureau of the Census. The general conclusion is that ownership changes are positively related to productivity improvements at the plant-level, but the relationship is not present in firm-level data. For example, McGuckin and Nguyen (1995) find that recently acquired plants experience productivity improvements, while the acquirer's existing plants suffer productivity losses, making the net change for the acquiring firm essentially zero. Schoar (2000) confirms this result.

Along these same lines, in 1996, the NBER commissioned a group of academic researchers headed by Steven Kaplan to conduct in-depth case studies of a small number of mergers. The studies were published in *Mergers and Productivity* (Kaplan, 2000). The purpose of the clinical research was to fill in the gaps left out by the prior large-sample stock returns and accounting performance studies. The studies revealed a richness in the economic data surrounding mergers that cannot be captured by large-sample studies. At the same time, these studies did not generate substantial insights into exactly how mergers create value, and thus do not satisfactory fill the research gap as intended. This area of investigation is wide open, spanning the fields of corporate finance, industrial organization, organizations, and strategy.

A third challenge to the claim that mergers create value stems from the finding that all of the gains from mergers seem to accrue to the target firm shareholders. We would like to believe that in an efficient economy, there would be a direct link between causes and effects, that mergers would happen for the right reasons, and that their effects would be, on average, as expected by the parties during negotiations. However, the fact that mergers do not seem to benefit acquirers provides reason to worry about this analysis.

Part of the issue here may be that an acquiring firm can seek a merger for a mix of reasons. Many firms mention mergers as their main strategic tool for growth and success, and point to possible economies of scale, synergies, and greater efficiency in managing assets. Alternatively, there is the somewhat contradictory evidence that mergers can be evidence of empire-building behavior by managers. If mergers could be sorted by true underlying motivations, it may be that those which are undertaken for good reasons do benefit acquirers, but in the average statistics, these are cancelled out by mergers undertaken for less benign reasons.[12]

Furthermore, the mere presence of competing bidders (or the potential for them to appear) could allow targets to extract full value from the eventual winner. Of course this cannot fully explain why acquirers rarely gain, since many contests, particularly in the 1990s, only feature one bidder. Also, if the term synergy is to have any meaning in a merger context, then it should imply that there is a common gain from *uniquely* joining the target and bidder, a benefit that cannot be appropriated by competing acquirers. In that case, it is still puzzling that in the data, targets appear to keep all synergistic benefits of the pairing to themselves.

The hardest task here is to make an argument for what the abnormal returns

[12] For example, Mitchell and Lehn (1990) provide empirical evidence that there are both good and bad mergers from the viewpoint of the stockholders of the acquirer, where the bad acquirers are eventually punished in the takeover market itself.

for acquiring firms should be. An abnormal return reflects the unexpected future economic rents arising from the transaction. In other words, an abnormal return of zero reflects a fair rate of return on the merger investment from the acquirer's point of view. Empirical studies of other investment decisions, such as research and development, capital expenditures, joint ventures, and product introductions, typically report very small (less than 1 percent) abnormal returns at the announcement of the investment decisions.[13] In the light of such evidence, the announcement period abnormal returns of 0.4 percent for non-stock acquirers look pretty much the same as those for other types of investments. Ultimately, what the evidence shows is that it is hard for firms to consistently make investment decisions that earn large economic rents, which perhaps should not be too surprising in a competitive economy with a fairly efficient capital market.

■ *The authors thank Timothy Taylor, Judy Chevalier, J. Bradford De Long, and Michael Waldman for helpful comments.*

References

Andrade, Gregor and Erik Stafford. 1999. "Investigating the Economic Role of Mergers," Harvard Business School working paper.

Barber, Brad M. and John D. Lyon. 1997. "Detecting Long-Run Abnormal Stock Returns: The Empirical Power and Specification of Test Statistics." *Journal of Financial Economics.* 43, pp. 341-72.

Bikchandani, Sushil, David Hirshleifer and Ivo Welch. 1992. "A Theory of Fads, Fashion, Custom, and Cultural Change in Informational Cascades." *Journal of Political Economy.* 100, pp. 992-1026.

Brav, Alon. 2000. "Inference in Long-Horizon Event Studies: A Parametric Bootstrap Approach with Application to Initial Public Offerings." *Journal of Finance.* 55, pp. 1979-2016.

Chan, Su, John Martin and John Kensiger. 1990. "Corporate Research and Development Expenditures and Share Value." *Journal of Financial Economics.* 26, pp. 255-76.

Fama, Eugene F. 1970. "Efficient Capital Markets: A Review of Theory and Empirical Work." *Journal of Finance.* 25, pp. 383-417.

Fama, Eugene F. 1998. "Market Efficiency, Long-Term Returns, and Behavioral Finance." *Journal of Financial Economics.* 49, pp. 283-306.

Fama, Eugene F. and Kenneth R. French. 1992. "The Cross-Section of Expected Stock Returns." *Journal of Finance.* 46, pp. 427-65.

Fama, Eugene F. and Kenneth R. French. 1993. "Common Risk Factors in the Returns on Stocks and Bonds." *Journal of Financial Economics.* 33, pp. 3-56.

Fama, Eugene F. and James MacBeth. 1973. "Risk, Return, and Equilibrium: Empirical Tests." *Journal of Political Economy.* 71, pp.607-36.

Gort, Michael. 1969. "An Economic Disturbance Theory of Mergers." *Quarterly Journal of Economics.* 83, pp. 624-42.

Healy, Paul M., Krishna G. Palepu and Richard S. Ruback. 1992. "Does Corporate Perfor-

[13] See McConnell and Muscarella (1985) for evidence on capital expenditure announcements and Chan, Martin and Kensinger (1990) on R&D investments.

mance Improve after Mergers?" *Journal of Financial Economics.* 31, pp. 135-75.

Jarrell, Gregg A., James A. Brickley and Jeffrey M. Netter. 1988. "The Market for Corporate Control: The Empirical Evidence Since 1980." *Journal of Economic Perspectives.* 2, pp. 49-68.

Jensen, Michael C. 1986. "Agency Costs of Free Cash Flow, Corporate Finance, and Takeovers." *American Economic Review.* 76, pp. 323-29.

Jensen, Michael C. 1993. "The Modern Industrial Revolution, Exit, and Control Systems." *Journal of Finance.* 48, pp. 831-80.

Jensen, Michael C. and Richard S. Ruback. 1983. "The Market for Corporate Control: The Scientific Evidence." *Journal of Financial Economics.* 11, pp. 5-50.

Kaplan, Steven N. 2000. "Introduction," in Steven N, Kaplan, ed. *Mergers and Productivity.* Chicago: University of Chicago Press / NBER.

Lakonishok, Josef, Andrei Shliefer and Robert Vishny. 1994. "Contrarian Investment, Extrapolation, and Risk." *Journal of Finance.* 49, pp. 1541-1578.

Loughran, Tim and Anand M. Vijh. 1997. "Do Long-Term Shareholders Benefit from Corporate Acquisitions?" *Journal of Finance.* 52, pp. 1765-1790.

McConnell, John and Chris Muscarella. 1985. "Corporate Capital Expenditure Decisions and Market Value of the Firm." *Journal of Financial Economics.* 14, pp. 399-422.

McGuckin, Robert and Sang Nguyen. 1995. "On Productivity and Plant Ownership Change: New Evidence from the Longitudinal Research Database." *Rand Journal of Economics.* 26, pp. 257-76.

Mitchell, Mark L. and Kenneth Lehn. 1990. "Do Bad Bidders Become Good Targets?" *Journal of Political Economy.* 98, pp. 372-98.

Mitchell, Mark L. and J. Harold Mulherin. 1996. "The Impact of Industry Shocks on Takeover and Restructuring Activity." *Journal of Financial Economics.* 41, pp. 193-229.

Mitchell, Mark L. and Erik Stafford. 2000. "Managerial Decisions and Long Term Stock Price Performance." *Journal of Business.* 73, pp. 287-329.

Morck, Randall, Andrei Shleifer and Robert W. Vishny. 1988. "Characteristics of Hostile and Friendly Takeovers," in Alan J. Auerbach, ed. *Corporate Takeovers: Causes and Consequences.* Chicago: University of Chicago Press / NBER.

Mulherin, J. Harold and Audra L. Boone. 2000. "Comparing Acquisitions and Divestitures." *Journal of Corporate Finance.* 6, pp. 117-39.

Nelson, R. 1959. *Merger Movements in American Industry, 1895-1956.* Princeton: Princeton University Press / NBER.

Rau, P. Raghavendra and Theo Vermaelen. 1998. "Glamour, Value, and the Post-Acquisition Performance of Acquiring Firms." *Journal of Financial Economics.* 49, pp. 223-53.

Ravenscraft, David J. and F. M. Scherer. 1989. "The Profitability of Mergers." *Journal of Industrial Economics.* 7, pp. 101-16.

Schwert, G. William. 2000. "Hostility in Takeovers: In the Eyes of the Beholder?" *Journal of Finance.* 55, pp. 2599-2640.

Schoar, Antoinette. 2000. "Effects of Corporate Diversification on Productivity." MIT Sloan School Working Paper.

ELSEVIER Journal of Corporate Finance 6 (2000) 189–214

Journal of CORPORATE FINANCE

www.elsevier.com/locate/econbase

The valuation effects of bank mergers

David A. Becher *

Department of Finance, Northern Illinois University, DeKalb, IL 60115, USA

Abstract

This paper examines the valuation effects of a sample of 558 bank mergers from 1980–1997. The overall results indicate that bank mergers create wealth. On average over a 36-day (−30, +5) event window, targets gain over 22%, bidders break even, and combined firms gain 3%. The results further indicate that mergers in the 1990s, which have not been extensively studied in prior work, have positive effects. In the 1990s over the 36-day window: target gain significantly, bidder returns are positive and statistically larger than the mid-1980s, and combined firm returns are significantly positive. These results are consistent with the notion that bank mergers occur for synergistic reasons and are not the result of empire building. However, bidder returns are sensitive to the event window implemented. Examining returns over an 11-day (−5, +5) window, target returns remain significantly positive, while bidder returns are statistically negative, and combined firm returns are statistically positive. Results over both windows indicate that overall wealth effects from bank mergers are positive over time, particularly in the 1990s. © 2000 Elsevier Science B.V. All rights reserved.

JEL classification: G34; G21; G14

Keywords: Mergers and acquisitions; Banking; Valuation effects

1. Introduction

This paper studies the valuation effects of mergers and acquisitions in the banking industry for the 1980–1997 period. The research is motivated by the significant increase in merger activity that has accompanied the widespread

* Tel.: +1-815-753-0317; fax: +1-815-753-0504.

E-mail address: becher@niu.edu (D.A. Becher).

PII: S0929-1199(00)00013-4

deregulation in the banking industry. Specifically, the number of bank mergers in the 1990s has increased 215% from the early 1980s. Moreover, bank merger activity has nearly doubled from 8% of all public mergers in the early 1980s, to over 15% in the first 8 years of the 1990s. This increase in merger activity is consistent with analysis of Jensen (1993), Mitchell and Mulherin (1996), and Weston et al. (1998) who document that industry changes induced by such factors as deregulation (among others) have led to increased merger activity.

Deregulation in the banking industry sets up a natural experiment to test two distinct merger theories: synergy vs. hubris. If mergers have enabled synergies previously prohibited by regulation, then one would expect the more recent mergers to add to target, bidder and combined firm shareholder wealth. By contrast, if the more recent mergers are an example of hubris and empire building, then one would expect that while target shareholders may gain, bidder shareholders should experience a decline in wealth and shareholders of the combined firm should not experience overall gains.

Much of the prior work on bank mergers has focused on relatively short time periods of 5-year intervals in the mid- to late 1980s with small samples (Cornett and De, 1991 — 153 acquisitions; Neely, 1987 — 26 acquisitions; Trifts and Scanlon, 1987 — 21 acquisitions; and Houston and Ryngaert, 1994, 1997 — 196 and 212 acquisitions, respectively). This paper extends the prior research by comparing mergers over an extended period of time (1980–1997) for a large data set of 558 bank mergers. This larger sample size allows for a broader test of the two competing bank merger hypotheses. Moreover, by including the 1990s, we can more completely address the question of what are the returns from bank mergers. Including the earlier years in this analysis provides a benchmark for studying these effects in the 1990s.

My results demonstrate that bank mergers create wealth over the 1980–1997 period. Moreover, returns in the early 1980s and 1990s are the most supportive of this notion of wealth creation. The magnitude of any valuation, however, is sensitive to the length of the event window employed. For targets, returns are significantly positive regardless of the methodology or time period studied over both a 36-day (−30, +5) and 11-day (−5, +5) event window around the initial merger announcement date. For bidders, returns are highly dependent on the choice of event window ranging from statistically negative to insignificantly positive. For combined firms, cumulative abnormal returns are significantly positive across time using either event window.

Finally, this paper attempts to address why we observe the type of patterns in intertemporal returns. It is possible that the positive wealth effects are merely a function of the changing aspects of the mergers. As a result, this paper provides cross-sectional sensitivity analysis to address these patterns and ensure that the results for the 1990s are robust. Patterns in intertemporal returns may be due to, among others, changes in terms of payment, competitiveness of takeover bidding, overlap in operations, or management team incentives. Results indicate that such factors as method of payment and number of bids per acquisition alone cannot account for the variation in returns over time, while the geographic location of merger participants may be related to overall returns.

The remainder of this paper proceeds as follows: Section 2 reviews the literature on bank mergers. Section 3 describes the data and descriptive statistics on the bank merger sample. Section 4 reports the event study analysis and results. Section 5 provides cross-sectional sensitivity analysis. Section 6 summarizes and provides some implications of the findings.

2. Literature review

A number of studies have analyzed the wealth effects of bank mergers. Table 1 provides a representative sample of six studies on bank merger activity. When examining these studies, three important issues concerning the prior literature are evident: the analysis is based on early time periods; the sample sizes are limited; and the measured wealth effects for merger participants are mixed.

Table 1 documents that most of the studies on bank merger activity focuses on relatively short time periods of 5-year intervals in the early to mid-1980s. Only Houston and Ryngaert (1994,1997) extend their analysis past 1986 with studies covering 1985–1991 and 1985–1992. In addition, many of these studies have relatively small sizes. Trifts and Scanlon (1987) examine 21 mergers over 4 years, while Neely (1987) studies 26 acquisitions over 7 years and James and Wier (1987) examine 60 out of 264 potential acquisitions over a 9-year period.

Finally, Table 1 shows that there is some variation in analysis across these six studies. For example, James and Wier (1987) focus only on bidder returns while the others examine returns to both targets and bidders. In addition, only Houston and Ryngaert (1994) provide results of the combined firms' returns. The other studies do not examine combined firm returns, focusing instead on bidder and target firms separately.

Taking the simple averages of each study in Table 1 indicates that target firms gain (20.48%) and bidder firms roughly break even (−0.57%). However, variation does exist among these measurements of wealth effects. While all studies find that target firms gain significantly, returns to targets range from 9.66% (Cornett and De, 1991) to 36.22% (Neely, 1987). In addition, two studies find bidder returns significantly positive, two insignificantly negative, and two others significantly negative. In all, returns to bidder firms range from significantly negative (−3.25%) to significantly positive (3.12%). Although Houston and Ryngaert (1994) measure combined firm abnormal returns, there are some questions to the overall gain from bank mergers as these returns are, on average, insignificantly positive (0.46%) over a 5-day event window.

Extending the analysis to a much larger data set (558 mergers) over a longer time period (1980–1997) will provide a better opportunity to measure the full

Table 1
Comparison of event studies on bank mergers

Number	Authors	Time period	Number of observations	Target return (%)	Bidder return (%)	Combined firm return (%)
1	James and Wier (1987)	1972–1983	60 acquisitions (264 potential)	N.D.[a]	1.77	N.D.[a]
2	Neely (1987)	1979–1985	26 acquisitions	36.22	3.12	N.D.[a]
3	Trifts and Scanlon (1987)	1982–1985	21 mergers	21.37	−3.25	N.D.[a]
4	Cornett and De (1991)	1982–1986	152 bidders, 37 targets	9.66	−0.40	N.D.[a]
5	Houston and Ryngaert (1994)	1985–1991	153 mergers (22 not completed)	14.77	−2.25	0.46
6	Houston and Ryngaert (1997)	1985–1992	184 mergers	20.40	−2.40	N.D.[a]
			Simple averages	20.48	−0.57	N.M.[b]

This table provides an overview of the results of six event studies on bank mergers. Authors, time period, number of observations, target return, bidder return, and combined firm return are all variables taken from the original studies. Simple averages are the sum of all the available returns for target or bidder firms divided by the number of papers. Since there is only one paper that calculates combined firm returns, there is no simple average for the combined firm.

[a]N.D. = not done in original study.

[b]N.M. = not meaningful.

wealth effects from bank mergers and any intertemporal variation that may occur. With extremely small data sets, results can easily be influenced by one or two unusual mergers. Moreover, much of the previous analysis does not include more recent mergers from the 1990s. Using an expanded database will allow for specific analysis of the effects in the 1990s, with the 1980s serving as a benchmark.

3. Mergers and acquisitions database and sample statistics

3.1. The bank merger sample

To create a sample of mergers[1] during the 1980–1997 period, all firms from the Center for Research in Security Prices (CRSP) tapes that had a delist code in the 200s (merger) or 300s (exchange) were selected. To focus on banks, all firms with a three-digit SIC code of 602 (banks) or 671 (holding companies) were chosen. This resulted in a preliminary sample of 771 observations.

SIC code 671X includes various types of holding companies (for example, both Transco Energy and Shawmut, the bank holding company for Shawmut National Bank, have an SIC code of 6710). As a result, each company with an SIC code of 671X was examined to determine its primary business. Primary business was determined from *Mergers and Acquisitions*, *MergerStat Review*, and the *Wall Street Journal Index*. If there was a discrepancy among these three sources as to the nature of the company, that company was cross-checked further until a consensus was reached. From the preliminary sample of 771 firms, 164 were deleted because they were not *bank* holding companies (i.e., they were instead insurance companies, thrifts, shipping conglomerates, etc.).

An additional 24 firms were removed from the sample for technical reasons: 11 were mergers in which both firms were included, thus one of the merger partners had to be reclassified as not a target firm[2]; four were duplicate listings of a firm; four were firms that repurchased all shares outstanding (and in two cases, converted into a BHC); three were government bailouts of failing institutions; one

[1] Unless noted otherwise, throughout this paper the terms merger, acquisition, and takeover are used interchangeably.

[2] These 11 firms can be considered mergers of equals (Houston and Ryngaert, 1994 detail the criteria for determining mergers of equals). In these cases, both bidders and targets are listed as the acquired firm. The firm designated as the bidder firm was the firm who retained more board seats after the merger or otherwise appeared to maintain the upper hand (i.e., with the Chase-Chemical merger, the combined entity was named Chase, but the new board was heavily influenced with Chemical executives including the CEO). Analysis was also conducted switching target and bidder designations for these 11 merger of equals and the results were qualitatively the same.

was the termination of a voting trust in exchange for capital stock; and one was the sale of several units of the firm, but the original target remained intact.

As a result, there are 583 bank mergers from 1980–1997 in my sample. By design, this sample consists only of mergers that are ultimately successful. While this exclusion of unsuccessful mergers may lead to a bias in the results, the unique nature of the banking industry most likely precludes this. Due to regulatory constraints, hostile takeovers are a rarity in the banking industry. Most mergers are friendly and are likely to be consummated. Moreover, once a takeover attempt has been made on a particular firm, it is highly probable that firm will be taken over within the next few years.[3]

For the 583 sample firms, the following variables were collected: target cusip, bidder cusip, announcement date, shareholder approval date, regulatory approval date, completion date, dollar value of merger, target share price, bidder share price, exchange ratio (target to bidder), method of payment, target state, bidder state, and event type (acquisition or merger of equals). In addition, further outside information was gathered. For example, if there was any announcement or hint of a merger prior to the actual announcement date, this was recorded as the rumor date.[4] In addition to the sources listed above, information was gathered from the following sources: *Capital Changes Reporter*, Predicasts: *F and S Index plus Text*, *Merger and Acquisition Sourcebook*, Moody's *Banking and Finance Manual*, Moody's *Industrial Manual*, the *New York Times Index*, the *American Bank*er, *Lexis-Nexis, and Dow Jones News Retrieval.*

Of the 583 sample firms, 59 are missing some data. In particular, 19 bidders are foreign; 24 bidders are private entities with no returns available; nine cases do not have the value of the acquisition; three cases have no announcement date; two cases have no completion date; and two case have no information on how the acquisition was funded. For different parts of the analyses, these missing variables reduce the overall sample size. For example, in calculating returns around announcement dates, both targets and bidders were excluded if the bidder cusip and/or the announcement dates were missing.[5] This reduced the number of mergers from 583 to 558. For consistency, this base sample of 558 mergers was used for all analyses.

[3] In a separate analysis, I study 125 banks that have at least one unsuccessful takeover attempt since 1980. In nearly all cases, the target was eventually taken over, merged with another firm, or went out of business within the next few years. Thus, excluding unsuccessful mergers is not likely an issue for this analysis.

[4] For example, the column in *The Wall Street Journal*, Heard on the Street, frequently lists rumors of pending mergers where the bidder (or occasionally the target) is not known.

[5] Abnormal returns for targets were qualitatively the same when calculated with a variety of different sample sizes. For example, if targets are excluded only when the announcement date is not available (as opposed to when both bidder cusips and announcement dates are missing) returns are the same.

Table 2
Summary statistics on bank mergers by year

Year	Number of mergers	Value of mergers (US$ millions)	CPI index (82–84 = 100)	Value of mergers (US$ millions) adjusted	Mean value of merger (US$ millions)	Mean value of merger (US$ millions) adjusted	Median value of merger (US$ millions)	Median value of merger (US$ millions) adjusted
1980	4	160.40	0.824	194.66	40.10	48.67	27.50	33.37
1981	5	312.46	0.909	343.74	62.49	68.75	47.20	51.93
1982	12	1119.05	0.965	1159.64	74.60	77.31	64.00	66.32
1983	18	2552.80	0.996	2563.05	134.36	134.90	66.00	66.27
1984	20	3512.30	1.039	3380.46	175.62	169.02	138.50	133.30
1985	20	5645.50	1.076	5246.75	245.46	228.12	202.00	187.73
1986	38	6932.56	1.096	6325.33	198.07	180.72	119.20	108.76
1987	27	10,426.33	1.136	9178.11	325.82	286.82	116.25	102.33
1988	40	10,904.80	1.183	9217.92	265.97	224.83	81.00	68.47
1989	20	2880.87	1.240	2323.28	144.04	116.16	65.00	52.42
1990	20	5623.19	1.307	4302.36	234.30	179.27	97.80	74.82
1991	21	10,079.13	1.362	7400.24	530.48	389.49	74.39	54.62
1992	32	9116.12	1.403	6497.59	284.88	203.05	122.25	87.13
1993	49	10,224.04	1.445	7075.46	213.00	147.41	95.00	65.74
1994	56	14,970.38	1.482	10,101.47	258.11	174.16	83.11	56.08
1995	51	26,151.90	1.524	17,160.04	493.43	323.77	81.70	53.61
1996	65	30,010.49	1.569	19,127.14	576.36	367.34	86.00	54.81
1997	60	37,049.50	1.605	23,083.80	617.50	384.74	91.55	57.04
All	558	187,671.82			336.33		92.38	

This table provides summary statistics for the sample of 558 bank mergers in the 1980–1997 period. Bank mergers are all completed acquisitions of any banking firm (with an SIC code = 612_, 671_) listed on the CRSP tapes denoted by a delist code in the 200s or 300s. The value of a merger is determined by multiplying the number of shares outstanding times the price of the stock at completion of a merger as defined in articles from various financial sources. The CPI Index is the consumer price index (not seasonally adjusted) for the US city average of all items with the average of 1982–1984 as the base year. Source of CPI data is the Bureau of Labor Statistic's web page, http://stats.bls.gov.

3.2. Sample statistics

Table 2 provides summary statistics for the bank merger sample by year, including number of mergers, as well as mean and median values. The number of mergers rose through the 1980s and reached a record high of 65 public mergers in 1996. The mean value of merger activity follows a similar pattern to that of the number of mergers. Table 1 shows that adjusting mean values by the CPI Index (average of 1982–1984 as base year) rescales the values, but does not change the pattern. Moreover, (adjusted) median values indicate that the pattern is similar.

This increase in the number and value of bank mergers over time is expected, in large part due to the on-going deregulation in the banking industry. In particular, in the early 1980s, merger activity was limited by strict state interstate branching laws. In the mid-1980s, various groups of states formed regional

Table 3
Comparison of all public mergers and bank mergers by year

Year	Number of all public mergers	Number of bank mergers	% Bank mergers of public	Value of all public mergers (US$ millions)	Value of bank mergers (US$ millions)	% Bank mergers of public
1980	n.a.	4	n.a.	n.a.	160.4	n.a.
1981	156	5	3.21	56,569.4	312.5	0.55
1982	176	12	6.82	31,501.8	1119.1	3.55
1983	181	18	9.94	39,471.4	2552.8	6.47
1984	204	20	9.80	82,731.0	3512.3	4.25
1985	321	20	6.23	116,675.5	5645.5	4.84
1986	352	38	10.80	89,866.2	6932.6	7.71
1987	267	27	10.11	85,924.9	10,426.3	12.13
1988	436	40	9.17	156,112.9	10,904.8	6.99
1989	320	20	6.25	121,870.6	2880.9	2.36
1990	175	20	11.43	48,214.9	5623.2	11.66
1991	144	21	14.58	31,668.0	10,079.1	31.83
1992	178	32	17.98	31,171.5	9116.1	29.25
1993	191	49	25.65	111,041.5	10,224.0	9.21
1994	291	56	19.24	109,101.3	14,970.4	13.72
1995	395	51	12.91	202,916.8	26,151.9	12.89
1996	454	65	14.32	285,185.0	30,010.5	10.52
1997	564	60	10.64	374,399.5	37,049.5	9.90
All	4805	558	11.61	1,974,422	187,671.8	9.51

This table compares bank mergers with overall public merger activity in the 1980–1997 period. The number and value of all public mergers are defined as all completed acquisitions by publicly traded companies as defined by *MergerStat Review*. Bank mergers are all completed acquisitions of any banking firm (with an SIC code = 612_, 671_) listed on the CRSP tapes with a delist code in the 200s or 300s. The value of bank mergers is determined by multiplying the number of shares outstanding times the price of the stock at completion of a merger as defined in articles from various financial sources. % Bank mergers of public is the number (or value) of bank mergers divided by the number (or value) of all public mergers.

compacts (i.e., Northeast and Southeast Compacts) that allowed banks headquartered within the region to acquire other banks headquartered within the same region (but, at the same time, prevented banks headquartered outside of the area from participating). By the beginning of the 1990s, many states had replaced these regional compacts with national interstate branching laws where banks from any other state could enter their state as long as banks within their own state were allowed to enter these other states.

Table 3 illustrates the relative importance of bank mergers over time by comparing merger activity for all public firms with that of banking firms. Public bank mergers, on average, represent nearly 12% of all public mergers and 10% of the total value. In some years, the value of bank mergers constitutes nearly a third of all dollar-value merger activity (31.8% for 1991 and 29.3% for 1992). Thus, bank mergers are not only increasing over time, but represent a larger portion of public mergers.

4. Event study analysis

4.1. Testable hypotheses

One force behind the growth in bank mergers documented above is deregulation (coupled with changes in technology and scale economies). Regulatory changes at both the state and federal level have made it easier for banking firms to merge. This deregulation enables tests of two distinct hypotheses of mergers that have been presented in the previous literature: see for example, Jensen and Ruback (1983), Malatesta (1983), Roll (1986) and Jarrell et al. (1988) the synergy hypothesis and the hubris or empire building hypothesis. Table 4 outlines the expected returns to target, bidder, and combined firms based on each of the two hypotheses.

First, mergers may allow for gains or synergies that were previously prevented because of restrictions on branching and banking activity. The *synergy* hypothesis

Table 4
Testable hypotheses and expected effects for bank mergers

Firms	Hubris or empire building hypothesis	Synergy hypothesis	Hubris and synergy hypothesis
Target	Positive	Positive	Positive
Bidder	Negative	Non-negative	Negative
Combined	Non-positive	Positive	Positive

This table details two testable hypotheses as to why bank mergers occur as well as the combination of the two: the hubris or empire building hypothesis and the synergy hypothesis. For each hypothesis, the expected effects for target, bidder, and the combined firms are indicated. The hubris and empire building hypothesis states that mergers are not wealth-creating events, but are motivated by bidder firms attempting to build empires. By contrast, the synergy hypothesis states that mergers are wealth-creating events. The combination of the two hypotheses indicates that mergers are wealth-creating events, but bidder firms may overpay to obtain these gains.

predicts that target firm returns should be positive, bidder returns should be non-negative, and the combined firm returns should be positive.

Alternatively, mergers may be a function of empire building and hubris. Analysis by Roll (1986) posits that mergers are not wealth-creating activities and are motivated by hubris. The *hubris* hypothesis would predict that, on average, target firm returns are positive, bidder firm returns are negative, and the combined firm returns are non-positive. Under this hypothesis, mergers are not wealth-creating events, but attempts by bidder firms to build dynastic empires.

A third alternative explanation may be that mergers are a function of both the synergy and hubris hypotheses. If mergers are a function of both hypotheses, then this would predict a positive revaluation for the combined firm with negative bidder firm returns. Under this *combined synergy and hubris* hypothesis, positive synergies may be associated with a merger, however, a bidder firm might overpay for the acquisition of these synergies.

4.2. Cumulative abnormal returns

A basic event study is utilized to calculate abnormal returns for target and bidder firms. I focus on two different event periods: a 36-day window $(-30, +5)$ and an 11-day window $(-5, +5)$ around each *initial* announcement date. For these periods, all missing values are removed. For target firms, the *initial* announcement date is the first date any acquisition attempt is made (within 2 years of the announcement date that was ultimately successful). For bidder firms, however, the initial announcement date is the first date *for that bidder* that an acquisition attempt is made. If there is only one bidder, the *initial* announcement dates for bidder and target firms are the same.

The base method used to calculate cumulative abnormal returns is net-of-market returns where abnormal returns are calculated by subtracting a market index from the firms' raw returns. The value-weighted index is used as the base index for market returns. Cumulative abnormal returns are determined using a geometric process. Geometric returns are found by multiplying the product of that day's return times the previous cumulative product, $((1 + r_i) * (1 + r_{i-1}))$, and then subtracting off one from the final product, where r_i is the ith day return and r_{i-1} is the cumulative product of all the days returns prior to the ith day over the event window.[6]

[6] Cumulative abnormal returns were also calculated using an arithmetic or simple process (sum of abnormal returns over the 11- and 36-day event windows). There is the potential, however, that summing the net-of-market returns will lead to positively biased returns if there is some bid-ask bounce in the stock of the banks being analyzed. In addition, cumulative abnormal returns were calculated using a market model (geometric and arithmetic returns) plus three other methods, cumulative daily returns, holding period daily returns, and abnormal holding period returns. In all cases, mean returns for both target and bidder firms were qualitatively the same. In order to conserve space, these tables are omitted.

Cumulative abnormal returns of the combined firm (target firms plus bidder firms) are calculated by following the method outlined in Houston and Ryngaert (1994):

$$\text{Combined Cumulative Abnormal Returns} = \frac{(V_{ib}\text{CAR}_{ib}) + (V_{it}\text{CAR}_{it})}{(V_{ib} + V_{it})} \tag{1}$$

where V_{ib} is the value of the ith bidder firm -30 days before the initial announcement date, V_{it} is the value of the ith target firm -30 days before the initial announcement date, CAR_{ib} is the cumulative abnormal return for the ith bidder firm over the 36-day window, and CAR_{it} is the cumulative abnormal return for the ith target firm over the 36-day window.

To gauge statistical significance, a t-test and subsequent p-value are calculated from the mean assuming a normal distribution. Although not emphasized in the text, a Wilcoxon signed rank test is also performed (with p-value) which relaxes the assumption of normality, but assumes a symmetric distribution. A sign test and p-value sign statistic are determined from the median with both assumptions of normality and symmetry being relaxed.

4.3. Results

4.3.1. Target and bidder returns

In Table 5, cumulative abnormal normal returns are provided over a 36-day $(-30, +5)$ and an 11-day $(-5, +5)$ event window. As reported in Panel A, cumulative abnormal returns for the full 1980–1997 period are 22.6% for target firms (p-value = 0.00). For bidders, cumulative abnormal returns are -0.10% (p-value = 0.80). Median returns for bidders and targets are nearly the same. These results indicate that, on average, target firms gain and bidder firms break even.

Panel B of Table 5 shows that cumulative abnormal returns over the 11-day event window for the full period are 17.1% for targets (p-value = 0.00) and -1.08% for bidder firms (p-value = 0.00). These results suggest that, on average, targets still gain while bidder firm returns are now statistically negative.

To measure the effects of bank mergers over time and to examine the 1990s in particular, cumulative abnormal returns are estimated for three time periods: 1980–1985, 1986–1990, and 1991–1997. For the three periods, there are 102, 135, and 321 firms, respectively. These three periods were chosen to approximate the changes of regulation in the banking industry. The first two periods are determined by the creation of regional compacts. By 1985, several regional compacts had formed (i.e., Northeast and Southeast Compacts) and spurred an increase in the number of mergers, as reported in the prior section. The third

Table 5
Target, bidder, and combined firm cumulative abnormal returns by time period

Time period	Mean (%)	*t*-Statistic	*p*-Value	Signed rank	*p*-Value signed rank	Median (%)	Sign statistic	*p*-Value sign statistic
Panel A: Cumulative abnormal returns − 30 days before to + 5 days after the initial announcement date								
Targets								
1980–1997	22.64	25.32	0.00	70,131.5	0.00	21.68	212.0	0.00
1980–1985	21.84	9.28	0.00	2329.5	0.00	21.15	38.0	0.00
1986–1990	20.49	10.29	0.00	3762.0	0.00	19.89	41.5	0.00
1991–1997	23.68	16.74	0.00	23,154.5	0.00	20.41	125.5	0.00
Bidders								
1980–1997	−0.10	−0.25	0.80	−4168.5	0.24	−0.41	−8.5	0.49
1980–1985	−0.08	−0.09	0.93	−56.5	0.85	−0.47	−2.0	0.77
1986–1990	−2.14	−2.49	0.01	−1757.0	0.00	−3.46	−20.5	0.00
1991–1997	0.06	0.14	0.89	−1877.5	0.26	−0.41	−10.5	0.26
Combined firms								
1980–1997	3.03	7.184	0.00	20,410.0	0.00	1.67	45.5	0.00
1980–1985	4.42	4.964	0.00	1158.0	0.00	3.68	13.0	0.01
1986–1990	0.86	0.890	0.37	−230.5	0.59	−1.35	−8.0	0.19
1991–1997	3.53	6.615	0.00	8490.5	0.00	2.39	40.5	0.00
Panel B: Cumulative abnormal returns − 5 days before to + 5 days after the initial announcement date								
Targets								
1980–1997	17.10	22.57	0.00	68,148.0	0.00	15.33	194.0	0.00
1980–1985	15.95	11.01	0.00	2337.5	0.00	16.29	37.5	0.00
1986–1990	18.33	10.60	0.00	3939.0	0.00	15.31	44.5	0.00
1991–1997	16.94	16.97	0.00	22,620.0	0.00	15.02	112.0	0.00
Bidders								
1980–1997	−1.08	−4.71	0.00	−19582.5	0.00	−0.90	−61.5	0.00
1980–1985	−0.96	−1.69	0.09	−426.5	0.13	−0.48	−5.5	0.31
1986–1990	−1.64	−3.01	0.00	−1765.5	0.00	−1.85	−24.0	0.00
1991–1997	−0.88	−3.26	0.00	−5776.0	0.00	−0.86	−32.0	0.00
Combined firms								
1980–1997	1.80	5.67	0.00	13,194.0	0.00	0.63	21.5	0.07
1980–1985	2.56	3.96	0.00	1018.0	0.00	2.48	15.0	0.00
1986–1990	1.09	1.44	0.15	−71.5	0.87	−0.26	−1.0	0.93
1991–1997	1.87	4.67	0.00	4380.5	0.00	0.42	7.5	0.42

period reflects the continued deregulation in the banking industry throughout the 1990s where more states allowed unrestricted interstate bank mergers. This change in policy led to a further increase in the number of mergers in the 1991–1997 period.

Cumulative abnormal returns for both bidders and targets across the three time periods are reported in Table 5. Panel A details that over the 36-day window, returns to targets over the three periods are all similar, ranging from 21.8% (p-value = 0.00) in the 1980–1985 period to 20.5% (p-value = 0.00) in the 1986–1990 period to 23.7% (p-value = 0.00) in the 1991–1997 period. Median values are nearly identical.

For bidder firms, returns fluctuate around zero, falling from −0.08% (p-value = 0.93) in the 1980–1985 period to −2.1% (p-value = 0.01) in the 1986–1990 period and then rising to 0.06% (p-value = 0.89) in the 1991–1997 period. Similar results are found when examining median values for the three periods as well.

In Panel B of Table 5, over the 11-day event window, returns to targets over the three time periods are all similar, ranging from 16.0% to 18.3% (with all three having p-values of 0.00). For bidder firms, returns range from −1.6% to −0.9% (all three are significantly negative). Median values for target and bidder firm returns are all nearly identical.

4.3.2. The combined firm returns

Cumulative abnormal returns are also calculated for the combined firm. As with target and bidder firm returns, results using the various estimation techniques are qualitatively the same. For simplicity, only geometric net-of-market returns (using a value-weighted index for market returns) are presented for the overall period and the three time periods in Table 5.

In Panel A, over the 36-day (−30, +5) event window cumulative abnormal returns to the combined firm are, on average, 3.0% (p-value of 0.00). The median value is slightly lower, but still highly significant. This 3.0% average increase in the combined firms' returns translates into approximately a six billion-dollar increase in total value for the entire sample.

Notes to table 5:

This table reports mean and median net-of-market cumulative abnormal returns around 558 bank merger announcements for target, bidder, and combined firms from 1980 to 1997 and for three time periods: 1980–1985, 1986–1990, and 1991–1997. For the three periods, there are 102, 135, and 321 firms, respectively. Returns are calculated over two event windows. Panel A details returns over a 36-day event window (−30, +5) around the *initial* announcement date. Panel B provides returns over an 11-day event window (−5, +5). For target firms, the initial announcement date is the first date an acquisition attempt is made. For bidder firms, the initial announcement date is the first date *for that bidder* that an acquisition attempt is made. Mean and median returns are geometric cumulative abnormal returns from a value-weighted index. Geometric cumulative abnormal returns are found by multiplying the product of that day's return times the previous cumulative product, $((1+r_i)*(1+r_{i-1}))$, and then subtracting off one from the final product, where r_i is the ith day return and r_{i-1} is the cumulative product of all the day returns prior to the ith day. The CRSP value-weighted return index (including all distributions) was used to calculate abnormal returns.

Panel A also details returns to the combined firm over the same three time periods used for target and bidder firms. Mean cumulative abnormal returns are 4.4% (p-value = 0.00) for the 1980–1985 period, 0.9% (p-value = 0.37) for the 1986–1990 period, and 3.5% (p-value = 0.00) for the 1991–1997 period. For the 1990s, this 3.5% increase translates into nearly a five billion-dollar increase in total value for 321 mergers.

Panel B indicates that over the 11-day event window, cumulative abnormal returns to the combined firm, on average, are 1.8% (p-value of 0.00). These combined firm returns are still highly significantly positive. Over the three time periods, cumulative abnormal returns for the combined firm range, on average, from 2.56% in the 1980–1985 period to 1.09% in 1986–1990 to 1.87% in the 1991–1997 period (only returns in the 1986–1990 period are not statistically significant with a p-value of 0.15).[7]

4.3.3. Comparing time periods

Table 6 formally tests for differences in wealth effects over time. A parametric t-test between two samples is used comparing cumulative abnormal returns in 1980–1985 vs. 1986–1990, 1980–1985 vs. 1991–1997, and 1986–1990 vs. 1991–1997 for bidders, targets and the combined firm. The t-test provides test statistics and p-values for variances of unequal sizes. The results are qualitatively the same when variances are assumed to be equal.

Over the 36-day event window (Panel A of Table 6), target returns trend upward in the 1990s; yet the difference among abnormal returns in the three time periods are all statistically insignificant. For bidders, returns also appear to be greater in the 1990s. Statistical tests show that while the 1980–1985 and 1986–1990 periods and 1980–1985 and 1991–1997 periods are indistinguishable, the 1991–1997 period differs from 1986–1990 (p-value = 0.03). This difference implies that bidder returns in the 1990s are statistically more positive than in the mid-1980s. For the combined firm, cumulative abnormal returns follow a similar pattern to bidder returns. In particular, the combined firm returns are more positive in the 1990s than in the mid-1980s (p-value of difference of means is 0.02).

Over the 11-day event window (Panel B of Table 6), there is still no significant difference among target firm abnormal returns in the three time periods. For

[7] Prior evidence suggests that to calculate cumulative abnormal returns around mergers, a longer event window is needed to capture the run-up in target returns prior to a merger announcement. However, there is some concern in using the longer event window in calculating bidder firm returns as there is less public ruminations about a bidder getting ready to make a bid. As a result, I also examined combined firm returns using a 36-day (−30, +5) window for target firms, but an 11-day (−5, +5) event window for bidders. The results indicate that with these event windows, combined firm returns are, on average, significantly positive across time and over the three time periods and that returns from the 1990s are significantly larger than those in the mid-1980s.

Table 6
Statistical significance among time periods for target, bidder, and combined firms

Firms	1980–1985 vs. 1986–1990	1980–1985 vs. 1991–1997	1986–1990 vs. 1991–1997
Panel A: t-Tests for cumulative abnormal returns, − 30 days before to + 5 days after announcement date			
Target	0.79	0.25	0.14
Bidder	0.20	0.51	0.03
Combined	0.02	0.66	0.02
Panel B: t-Tests for cumulative abnormal returns − 5 days before to + 5 days after announcement date			
Target	0.29	0.57	0.49
Bidder	0.40	0.89	0.16
Combined	0.14	0.36	0.32

This table provides parametric t-tests between two samples to compare returns from 558 bank mergers in the period 1980–1997. Panel A details p-values of t-tests for returns calculated over a 36-day event window $(-30, +5)$. Panel B provides p-values of t-tests for returns calculated over an 11-day event window $(-5, +5)$. p-Values for target, bidder, and the combined firms are provided. t-Tests are constructed comparing returns from 1980–1985 vs. 1986–1990, 1980–1985 vs. 1991–1997, and 1986–1990 vs. 1991–1997. The t-tests provide p-values for variances of unequal sizes. In all cases, the results are virtually the same when variances are equal. Net-of-market cumulative abnormal returns are calculated using a geometric process with a value-weighted market index. Geometric cumulative abnormal returns are found by multiplying the product of that day's return times the previous cumulative product, $((1+r_i)*(1+r_{i-1}))$, and then subtracting off one from the final product, where r_i is the ith day return and r_{i-1} is the cumulative product of all the day returns prior to the ith day. The CRSP value-weighted return index (including all distributions) was used to calculate abnormal returns.

bidders, however, the 1990s are now no longer statistically larger than the mid-1980s (p-value of difference is 0.16). For the combined firm, returns over the three time periods are all insignificantly different as well.

4.4. Summary of cumulative abnormal returns

Results from the event study analysis indicate that target returns over a 36-day event window are continually positive across time and different from zero in the magnitude of roughly 23%. Examining returns over an 11-day window demonstrates that target returns are still positive and statistically significant. These significantly positive returns are similar to prior work on mergers in general as described in Weston et al. (1998).

For bidder firms, results are sensitive to the event window selected. Over a 36-day event window, returns are insignificantly different from zero across time. Over an 11-day event window, however, returns are statistically negative. For the combined firm, returns overall are positive across time for either event window selected. Moreover, combined returns appear to be improving in the 1990s.[8]

5. Cross-sectional analysis

Analysis of bank merger activity in the 1990s, in particular, indicates that the effects from these mergers are positive to merger participants. However, it is possible that the returns in the 1990s are due to changing aspects of the mergers (for example, method of payment, multiple bids, geographic location, etc.). In particular, it is important to address why we observe specific patterns in intertemporal returns. These patterns may be a function of several key factors: (1) changes in terms of method of payment, (2) changes in the competitiveness of bidding in mergers (which may effect the division of gains more than total combined firm returns), (3) increased technological opportunities for cost savings coupled with overlap in market operations that may permit greater synergies, and (4) changes in management teams whose incentives may have become more aligned with shareholder interests due, in part, to deregulation of the banking industry. As a result, this section details cross-sectional sensitivity analysis in attempts to determine the source of patterns in returns and ensure that the results from the 1990s are robust.

5.1. Method of payment

One factor that may affect returns is the method of payment (cash, stock, or a mixture) used to finance the merger. If stock mergers are a negative signal and worse for bidders, then in those periods when more mergers are financed with stock, on average, bidder returns should be statistically lower. The prior literature

[8] These results, however, may be a function of how cumulative abnormal returns are calculated. In particular, Canina et al. (1998) document that using daily equal-weighted returns over a long event window can lead to a bias in returns. This bias is due, in part, to the illiquidity of small firms. As a result, cumulative abnormal returns for both bidders and targets are calculated over the three time periods using both an equal- and value-weighted daily market index to calculate cumulative abnormal returns over a 36-day event window. For the 1980s, returns are nearly identical using the two indices. For the 1990s, however, there is roughly a 2.6% difference between returns using an equal- and value-weighted daily market index. Examining the 1990s by year, the difference between returns using the two indices is, on average, 19% per year, 1.6% per month, and approximately 2.6% over 36 days (the length of the event window implemented in this analysis). Thus, the average difference between bidder and target cumulative abnormal returns using the value- vs. equal-weighted index of 2.6% appears to be directly the result of market index and the daily, equal-weighted index should not be used.

Table 7
Fraction of mergers by method of payment by time period

Time period	Cash + Mix (%)	Stock only (%)
Panel A: Bank mergers		
1980–1997	40.34	59.66
1980–1985	63.22	36.78
1986–1990	48.37	51.63
1991–1997	30.88	69.12
Panel B: All public mergers		
1980–1997	62.65	37.35
1980–1985	76.99	23.01
1986–1990	77.52	22.47
1991–1997	47.47	52.53

This table provides the fraction of mergers by method of payment from 1980–1997 and for three time periods: 1980–1985, 1986–1990, and 1991–1997. Panel A details the fraction of bank mergers by method of payment and Panel B details the fraction of all public mergers by method of payment. Bank mergers are all completed acquisitions of any banking firm (with an SIC code = 612_, 671_) listed on the CRSP tapes with a delist code in the 200s or 300s. All public mergers are defined as all completed acquisitions by publicly traded companies as defined by *MergerStat Review*. Method of payment is determined by examining all announcements (in the *Wall Street Journal* and other financial sources) concerning a merger, and recording how the bidder determined to finance the merger: stock, cash, or mix. The number of mergers Cash + Mix is defined as all mergers using either cash only or more than one source of payment: a combination of cash, stock, and/or debt. Stock only indicates that the merger was financed with stock only.

has found that mergers financed using stock have lower returns than those financed with cash or a mixture of cash and stock.[9]

Table 7 examines the fraction of mergers by method of payment from 1980–1997 and over the three time periods. Panel A focuses on bank mergers, while Panel B examines all public mergers. Public bank mergers are all completed acquisitions of any bank (SIC code = 612_, 671_) listed on the CRSP tapes with a delist code in the 200s or 300s. All public mergers are defined as all completed acquisitions by publicly traded companies as defined by *MergerStat Review*. The method of payment is determined by examining all announcements (in the *Wall Street Journal* and other financial sources) concerning a merger, and recording how the bidder determined to finance the merger: stock, cash or mix. The method of payment *mix* is defined as all mergers using more than one source of payment; a combination of cash, stock, and/or debt.

[9] See Houston and Ryngaert (1997), Amihud et al. (1990), Martin (1996) and Travlos (1983) for more discussion on method of payment. Houston and Ryngaert (1997) and Amihud et al. (1990) document that classifying mergers by method of payment to control for signaling or agency effects has a noise element. In particular, they find that negative bidder returns are associated with the degree to which the target's returns are sensitive to changes in the bidder's stock price while the merger is pending and the level of managerial ownership.

Panel A demonstrates that stock is the main choice of payment method for bank mergers over time. Nearly 60% of all bank mergers are financed using stock only. In addition, stock mergers have increased, rising from 36.1% in 1980–1985 to 69.1% in the 1990s. Panel B of Table 7 indicates that the fraction of *all public mergers* financed with stock only also increases; more than doubling from 23.0% in 1980–1985 to 52.5% in 1991–1997. As a result, it appears that mergers financed with stock-only are increasing in all mergers, not just bank mergers.

Cumulative abnormal returns to targets and bidders are calculated by method of payment. Returns are calculated as detailed in Section 4, segmented into a 36-day (−30, +5) and an 11-day event window (−5, +5). Table 8 documents that both

Table 8
Mean cumulative abnormal returns by method of payment

Time period	36-Day (−30, +5) event window			11-Day (−5, +5) event window		
	Cash + Mix (%)	Stock only (%)	*p*-Value of *t*-test: Cash + Mix vs. Stock	Cash + Mix (%)	Stock only (%)	*p*-Value of *t*-test: Cash + Mix vs. Stock
Target cumulative abnormal returns						
1980–1997	25.38	20.84	0.01	19.07	15.88	0.05
1980–1985	23.74	17.33	0.07	17.57	13.34	0.16
1986–1990	25.76	16.41	0.02	23.14	14.49	0.01
1991–1997	26.28	22.86	0.21	17.41	16.76	0.79
Bidder cumulative abnormal returns						
1980–1997	0.65	−1.04	0.02	−0.32	−1.55	0.01
1980–1985	−0.03	−0.86	0.61	−0.47	−1.76	0.30
1986–1990	0.65	−3.94	0.01	−0.26	−2.74	0.02
1991–1997	1.12	−0.12	0.20	−0.25	−1.12	0.15

This table provides mean net-of-market cumulative abnormal returns by method of payment around 558 bank merger announcements for targets and bidders. This table also provides parametric *t*-tests between two samples to compare returns by method of payment. *t*-Tests are constructed comparing returns from cash + mix vs. stock only. The *t*-tests provide *p*-values for variances of unequal sizes. In all cases, the results are virtually the same when variances are equal. Returns are calculated over a 36-day (−30, +5) and an 11-day (−5, +5) event window around the *initial* announcement date. For target firms, the initial announcement date is the first date an acquisition attempt is made. For bidder firms, the initial announcement date is the first date *for that bidder* that an acquisition attempt is made. Mean and median returns are geometric cumulative abnormal returns from a value-weighted index. Geometric cumulative abnormal returns are found by multiplying the product of that day's return times the previous cumulative product, $((1+r_i)*(1+r_{i-1}))$, and then subtracting off one from the final product, where r_i is the ith day return and r_{i-1} is the cumulative product of all the day returns prior to the ith day. The CRSP value-weighted return index (including all distributions) was used to calculate abnormal returns. Method of payment is determined by examining all announcements (in the *Wall Street Journal* and other financial sources) concerning a merger, and recording how the bidder determined to finance the merger. The number of mergers Cash + Mix is defined as all mergers using either cash only or more than one source of payment: a combination of cash, stock, and/or debt. Stock only indicates that the merger was financed with stock only.

target and bidder returns are higher, on average, for mergers financed by a mixture than stock-only using either event window (p-value of differences all 0.01 to 0.05). Given that stock acquisitions are more poorly received than cash offers and that there are more stock acquisitions in the 1990s, the higher returns to back acquisitions in the 1990s are not attributable to changes in financing of mergers.

5.2. Number of bids per target firm

A second factor that may affect returns is the number of bids per target firm. James and Wier (1987), Cornett and De (1991), and others posit that premiums should be different to firms with multiple bids. If a group of firms all bid on the same target, then the overpayment hypothesis would predict that the successful bidder would overpay in order to win the bidding war. If multiple bids are a signal of overpayment, then bidders, on average, should have statistically lower returns when there are multiple bidders.

Table 9 examines target and bidder firms by the number of public bids a target firm receives. All public bids are determined as follows: for every bank acquired over the 18-year time period, I search the previous 2 years prior to the announcement date for any other takeover attempt.[10] This provides the number of takeover attempts each target faces including the takeover bid that is ultimately successful. The numbers of bids is then separated into two groups for analysis: one bid and two or more bids.

Panel A of Table 9 examines the *fraction* of mergers by number of bids. This table demonstrates that the majority of target firms receive only one public bid over time (on average 85%). In addition, the number of mergers with only one bid has increased from 73.8% in 1980–1985 to nearly 93% in 1991–1997.

Panel B of Table 9 details *cumulative abnormal returns* to targets and bidders by number of bids. Returns to targets with only one bid are, on average, 23% over time vs. nearly 20% for targets with more than one bid. In the 1990s, returns to targets with only one bid are nearly 25%, while returns to targets with multiple bids are just under 16%. These results appear counter-intuitive to the overpayment hypothesis. If bidder firms are overpaying for target firms when there are multiple bidders, then target returns for mergers with two or more bids should be greater than returns for mergers with only one bid, not less.

For bidders who face no competition (one bid), cumulative abnormal returns are −0.43% over time. For mergers with two or more bids, bidder returns are approximately zero (−0.11%). In the 1990s, for mergers with only one bid, bidder

[10] In searching for all public takeover attempts, I examine the *Wall Street Journal Index*, *Lexis-Nexis*, the *New York Times Index*, *Dow Jones News Retrieval*, *Mergers and Acquisitions*, and *MergerStat Review*.

Table 9
Bank mergers by number of bids by time period

Time period	Number of bids 1 (%)	2+ (%)	p-Value of t-test: 1 vs. 2+
Panel A: Fraction of bank mergers			
1980–1997	87.93	12.07	
1980–1985	73.81	26.19	
1986–1990	84.97	15.03	
1991–1997	92.71	7.29	
Panel B: Cumulative abnormal returns			
Targets			
1980–1997	23.01	19.48	0.17
1980–1985	21.30	21.23	0.99
1986–1990	20.34	21.78	0.78
1991–1997	24.49	15.94	0.04
Bidders			
1980–1997	−0.43	−0.11	0.76
1980–1985	−0.58	0.46	0.61
1986–1990	−1.83	−2.30	0.84
1991–1997	0.14	1.21	0.50

This table details 558 bank mergers by number of bids from 1980–1997 and for three time periods: 1980–1985, 1986–1990, and 1991–1997. Panel A provides the fraction of bank mergers by number of bids. Panel B details mean net-of-market cumulative abnormal returns over a 36-day event window (−30, +5) around the *initial*announcement date. In addition, column three of Panel B provides parametric t-test between two samples to compare returns from the two groups (one bid or two or more bids). Number of bids is the number of takeover attempts each target faces including the takeover bid that is ultimately successful. The number of bids a target receives is separated into two groups: one bid and two or more bids. For target firms, the initial announcement date is the first date an acquisition attempt is made. For bidder firms, the initial announcement date is the first date *for that bidder* that an acquisition attempt is made. Mean and median returns are geometric cumulative abnormal returns from a value-weighted index. Geometric cumulative abnormal returns are found by multiplying the product of that day's return times the previous cumulative product, $((1+r_i)*(1+r_{i-1}))$, and then subtracting off one from the final product, where r_i is the ith day return and r_{i-1} is the cumulative product of all the day returns prior to the ith day. The CRSP value-weighted return index (including all distributions) was used to calculate abnormal returns.

returns are 0.14%, while bidder returns for mergers with multiple bids are 1.21%. These results suggest that returns for bidders in mergers with multiple bids are *higher* than for those with only one bid, which is contrary to the overpayment hypothesis.

Panel B of Table 9 also tests for differences in returns over time. A parametric t-test between two samples is used comparing cumulative abnormal returns from one bid vs. two or more. For targets overall, differences in returns are not statistically significant. Moreover, returns in the 1991–1997 period are statistically higher for firms with one bid vs. two or more bids (p-value = 0.04), which is

Table 10
Number of intrastate vs. interstate bank mergers by time period

Time period	Intrastate (%)	Interstate (%)
Panel A: Intra- vs. interstate mergers, banks headquartered in same state		
1980–1997	49.82	50.18
1980–1985	66.67	33.33
1986–1990	46.67	53.33
1991–1997	45.79	54.21
Panel B: Intra- vs. interstate mergers, banks with branches in same state		
1980–1997	68.46	31.54
1980–1985	71.57	28.43
1986–1990	57.78	42.22
1991–1997	71.96	28.04

This table details the fraction of mergers by geographic area for 558 bank mergers for 1980–1997 and for three time periods: 1980–1985, 1986–1990, and 1991–1997. Panel A details the fraction of mergers based on whether the bidder firm is headquartered in the target's headquarter state prior to the *initial* announcement date. Panel B provides the fraction of mergers based on whether the bidder firm has branches in the target's headquarter state prior to the *initial* announcement date. Bidder branch locations are obtained from Rand McNally Bankers Directory (1980–1990)/Thomson Bank Directory (1991–1997). Intrastate mergers are defined as those mergers that take place between firms within the same state. Interstate mergers are defined as those mergers that take place among bidder firms that are not in the same state as the target firm they are acquiring.

counter-intuitive to the overpayment hypothesis. For bidders, returns between firms with one bid vs. multiple bids are not statistically significant in all cases. Returns are not lower for firms with multiple bids in the 1990s. Hence, even though there are fewer multiple bid episodes in the 1990s, this does not appear to be the cause of higher bidder returns during this period.

5.3. Geographic location

Another factor that may explain the cross-sectional variation in bank merger returns is the geographic location of the banks involved in the mergers. The prior literature suggests that mergers that are more geographically focused have higher returns than mergers that are across large geographic borders; returns are higher in periods where more in-market mergers occurred.[11]

Table 10 tests this hypothesis, by examining the number of intrastate vs. interstate bank mergers over time as a proxy for market overlap. *Intrastate mergers* are defined as those mergers that take place between targets and bidders within the same state. *Interstate mergers* are defined as those mergers that take

[11] See for example, DeLong (1999), Houston and Ryngaert (1994), Houston et al. (1999), and Hawawani and Swary (1990).

place among bidder firms that are not in the same state as the target firm they are acquiring.

Some bidders headquartered out-of-state may still have some operations that overlap in the target's home state. To this degree, this overlap would underestimate the number of in-market mergers. As a result, intrastate and interstate mergers are defined using two methods.

Panel A details the fraction of mergers based on whether the bidder firm is headquartered in the target's headquarters state prior to the *initial* announcement date. Panel B provides the fraction of mergers based on whether the bidder firm has branches in the target's state prior to the *initial* announcement date.[12] Bidder branch locations are obtained from *Rand McNally Bankers Directory* (1980–1990)/*Thomson Bank Directory* (1991–1997).

Panel A of Table 10 indicates that, on average, 49.8% of the mergers are among bidders and targets headquartered in the same state. Examining the three time periods, the number of intrastate mergers has decreased over time, from 66.7% to 45.8%. Comparing the 1990s with the 1980s, the percentages of interstate mergers are roughly the same in the 1990s and the late 1980s, but is much higher in the 1990s as compared to the 1980–1985 period (54.2% vs. 33.3%).[13]

Panel B of Table 10 indicates that, on average, 68.5% of the mergers are among bidders and targets where the bidder has branches in the target's headquarters state. Examining the three time periods, the number of intrastate mergers fluctuate over time, from 71.7% in 1980–1985 to 57.8% in 1986–1990 to 72.0% in 1991–1997. The percentages of interstate mergers in the 1990s are nearly the same as the early 1980s and much lower than in the 1986–1990 period.

Examining returns by geographic location, if in-market mergers are more profitable than out-of-market mergers, then returns in the 1980–1985 period should be similar to returns in the 1990s, and the 1986–1990 period should be considerably different from both of these periods (see Table 5). Results from Panel A suggest that the percentage of in-market mergers cannot explain the cross-sectional variation in bank merger returns. However, focusing on Panel B which more accurately reflects intra- vs. interstate mergers, the results now indicate that returns are significantly higher in the 1990s than in the 1986–1990 period (and there is no difference between the 1990s and the 1980–1985 period). Thus, it seems likely that, as Houston et al., (1999) suggest, the percentage of in-market mergers may help to explain the cross-sectional variation in bank merger returns.

[12] This expanded definition of intrastate mergers still does not fully capture market overlap. See Houston et al. (1999) for a more detailed treatment of in-market mergers.

[13] Twenty-six acquisitions involving foreign bidders acquiring domestic targets are classified as interstate mergers (four percent of all mergers). Interstate mergers are about 48% if acquisitions by foreign bidders are excluded.

5.4. Board structure and compensation

Finally, variation in target, bidder, and/or combined firm returns may be due to firm-specific variables such as ownership structure, board composition, compensation, CEO age/tenure, among others. A wide variety of analyses have been conducted that examine the relation of these variables to returns from bank mergers.

It is possible that returns are related to a learning curve for mergers and the management teams whose incentives have become more aligned with shareholders in the 1990s. Several studies demonstrate that deregulation of the banking industry has been accompanied by improved pay-for-performance. Crawford et al. (1995) and Hubbard and Palia (1995) examine the relationship between bank CEO compensation and that bank's performance around bank deregulation. The authors test the hypothesis that the CEO's compensation becomes more sensitive to the CEO's performance as banks become less regulated (deregulation hypothesis).

Overall, the authors determine that CEO pay and firm performance have a stronger relationship after the introduction of banking deregulation. Furthermore, these studies document higher levels of pay in markets that allow for interstate banking; stronger pay-performance relationship in deregulated states; and increased CEO turnover after deregulation.

Results from these studies indicate that the deregulation of the banking industry has been accompanied by improved pay-for-performance among banking executives. These results suggest that the deregulation of the banking industry over the last two decades and subsequent merger activity has not led to negative wealth effects and *may* explain why bidder firms fare better in the 1990s.

6. Conclusion and implications

This paper studies a large sample of 558 bank mergers over the 1980–1997 period to determine the wealth effects of mergers in a particular industry. This analysis provides direct tests of the synergy vs. hubris hypotheses. I find that, on average, targets gain, bidders break even, and the combined firm gains over a 36-day event window. Over an 11-day window, targets gain, bidders lose, and the combined firm still gains.

Moreover, the analysis of mergers over an extended period of time (1980–1997) also provides a direct inquiry as to whether merger activity in the banking industry has created greater synergies and more benefits to merger participants through time. Existing theory indicates that deregulation should provide benefits to banking firms. I find that in the 1990s, when merger activity is dramatically increasing in the banking industry, the wealth effects over a 36-day event window to targets are statistically positive, bidder returns are non-negative and statistically larger than the mid-1980s, and combined firm returns are significantly positive and statistically larger than the mid-1980s as well. Over the 11-day window, target returns remain positive, bidder returns are negative and the same across time, and the combined firm returns are significantly positive but indistinguishable across time.

Prior research clearly suggests that in calculating cumulative abnormal returns for target firms, a longer event window is needed to capture run-up prior to the merger announcement. Nonetheless, there is concern about using this longer window in calculating bidder returns. Combining the 36-day window for target firms and 11-day window for bidders, combined firm returns are statistically positive and significantly greater in the 1990s than in the late 1980s.

These results suggest that bank mergers occur for synergistic reasons and not because of empire building alone. Moreover, analysis across the three time periods imply that the deregulation of the banking industry has not had a negative effect on banks and add further support to the synergy interpretation of bank mergers. However, bidder returns are sensitive to the length of the event window implemented. The use of 11-day window returns still suggests that bank mergers create positive wealth effects and occur for synergistic reasons (combined firm returns are statistically positive), but bidders may overbid in order to obtain these gains.

Finally, while results from the 1990s indicate that mergers create positive wealth effects (regardless of the event window), it is possible that these higher returns are due to changing aspects of the mergers (for example, method of payment, multiple bids, geographic location, etc.). As a result, I provide cross-sectional sensitivity analysis to examine the sources of patterns in intertemporal returns and to ensure that results from the 1990s are robust. Results demonstrate that the method of payment or number of bids per merger alone do not account for the variation in returns over time. However, examination of mergers by geographic location does suggest that returns are related to whether the merger occurs within the target's home state. Future work should also examine more closely the effects of board structure, compensation, and other variables. Nonetheless, the overall results appear consistent. The wealth effects from bank mergers are positive over time and particularly in the 1990s.

Acknowledgements

Earlier versions of this paper were presented at the 1998 meetings of the Financial Management Association and the Southern Finance Association under the title of ''Mergers in the Banking Industry: 1980–1996''. I thank the SFA for acknowledging this paper at its 1998 meetings with an Outstanding Doctoral Student Paper Award. This paper is based on a portion of my dissertation at Penn State University. I am particularly grateful to Harold Mulherin (Chair) as well as Ray Lombra, Chris Muscarella, and Dennis Sheehan for helpful suggestions. I would like to thank the editor, Mike Ryngaert and an anonymous referee for their input. I also thank Marcia Cornett, Jeffrey Mercer, Jim Miles, Steven Seelig, Henri Servaes, seminar participants at Penn State University, Babson College, Northern Illinois University, the Federal Reserve Bank of Atlanta, the Office of the Comptroller of the Currency, the University of Virginia, the 1998 FMA meetings, the 1998 SFA meetings, and participants of the 1998 FMA Doctoral Student Seminar.

References

Amihud, Y., Lev, B., Travlos, N.G., 1990. Corporate control and the choice of investment financing: the case of corporate acquisitions. Journal of Finance 45, 603–616.

Canina, L., Michaely, R., Thaler, R., Womack, K., 1998. Caveat compounder: a warning about using the daily CRSP equal-weighted index to compute long-run excess returns. Journal of Finance 53, 403–416.

Cornett, M.M., De, S., 1991. Common stock returns in corporate takeover bids: evidence from interstate bank mergers. Journal of Banking and Finance 15, 273–295.

Crawford, A.J., Ezzell, J.R., Miles, J.A., 1995. Bank CEO pay-performance relations and the effects of deregulation. Journal of Business 68, 231–256.

DeLong, G.L., 1999. Stockholder gains from focusing versus diversifying bank mergers. Journal of Financial Economics, to be published.

Hawawani, G., Swary, I., 1990. Mergers and Acquisitions in the U.S. Banking Industry: Evidence from the Capital Markets. North-Holland, Amsterdam.

Houston, J.F., Ryngaert, M.D., 1994. The overall gains from large bank mergers. Journal of Banking and Finance 18, 1155–1176.

Houston, J.F., Ryngaert, M.D., 1997. Equity issuance and adverse selection: a direct test using conditional stock offers. Journal of Finance 52, 197–219.

Houston, J.F., James, C.M., Ryngaert, M.D., 1999. Why are value enhancing mergers in banking so hard to find? Working Paper.

Hubbard, R.G., Palia, D., 1995. Executive pay and performance: evidence from the U.S. banking industry. Journal of Financial Economics 39, 105–130.

James, C., Wier, P., 1987. Returns to acquirers and competition in the acquisition market: the case of banking. Journal of Political Economy 95, 355–370.

Jarrell, G.A., Brickley, J.A., Netter, J.M., 1988. The market for corporate control: the evidence since 1980. Journal of Economic Perspectives 2, 49–68.

Jensen, M.C., 1993. Presidential address: the modern industrial revolution, exit, and the failure of internal control systems. Journal of Finance 48, 831–880.

Jensen, M.C., Ruback, R.S., 1983. The market for corporate control: the scientific evidence. Journal of Financial Economics 11, 5–50.

Malatesta, P.H., 1983. The wealth effect of merger activity and the objective functions of merging firms. Journal of Financial Economics 11, 155–181.

Martin, K.J., 1996. The method of payment in corporate acquisitions, investment opportunities, and management ownership. Journal of Finance 51, 1227–1247.

Mitchell, M.L., Mulherin, J.H., 1996. The impact of industry shocks on takeover and restructuring activity. Journal of Financial Economics 41, 193–229.

Neely, W.P., 1987. Banking acquisitions: acquirer and target shareholder returns. Financial Management, 66–74.

Roll, R., 1986. The hubris hypothesis of corporate takeovers. Journal of Business 59, 197–216.

Trifts, J.W., Scanlon, K.P., 1987. Interstate bank mergers: the early evidence. The Journal of Financial Research 10, 305–311.

Travlos, N.G., 1987. Corporate takeover bids, method of payment, and bidding firms' stock returns. Journal of Finance 42, 943–963.

Weston, J.F., Chung, K.S., Siu, J.A., 1998. Takeovers, Restructuring, and Corporate Governance. 2nd edn. Prentice-Hall, Englewood Cliffs, NJ.

Part II
Takeover Bidding

[5]

Do Bad Bidders Become Good Targets?

Mark L. Mitchell and Kenneth Lehn

Securities and Exchange Commission

This paper empirically examines one motive for takeovers: to change control of firms that make acquisitions that diminish the value of their equity. Firms that subsequently become takeover targets make acquisitions that significantly reduce their equity value, and firms that do not become takeover targets make acquisitions that raise their equity value. Within the sample of acquisitions by targets, the acquisitions that reduce equity value the most are those that are later divested either in bust-up takeovers or restructuring programs to thwart the takeover. This evidence is consistent with theories advanced by Marris, Manne, and Jensen concerning the disciplinary role played by takeovers.

I. Introduction

Since Berle and Means (1933), it has been widely recognized that a potential divergence of interest exists between managers and stockholders in corporations characterized by diffusely held equity. In recent years, economists have probed institutional arrangements that

Mitchell is on leave from Clemson University; Lehn from Washington University (St. Louis). We are grateful to Steve Belitti, Joe Burschinger, David du Mars, John Mawickee, Bill Sanders, John Tortora, and Connie Wilson for research assistance. This paper has benefited from comments by Bernie Black, Robert Comment, Larry Harris, Louis Lowenstein, Robert McCormick, Mike Maloney, Wayne Marr, Michael Ryngaert, and Rick Smith; and from seminar participants at the University of Chicago, Columbia University, University of California at Los Angeles and Davis, Ohio State University, Wichita State University, George Mason University, University of Florida, University of South Carolina, Washington University, University of Illinois, Department of Justice, and the Hayek Symposium in Freiburg, West Germany. Annette Poulsen suggested the title. The views expressed herein are those of the authors and do not necessarily reflect the views of the Securities and Exchange Commission or of the authors' colleagues on the staff of the SEC.

[*Journal of Political Economy*, 1990, vol. 98, no. 2]

mitigate this potential conflict and attempted to understand why these arrangements vary from firm to firm. Among the forces that mitigate the manager-stockholder conflict are competitive labor and product markets, managerial compensation plans, the structure of equity ownership, and the threat of corporate takeovers.[1] This paper focuses on the extent to which one of these forces, corporate takeovers, disciplines managers in firms with a specific type of manager-stockholder conflict, namely, a conflict concerning the firms' acquisition programs.

Our interest in this question emerges from general theoretical arguments by Marris (1963) and Manne (1965) and a more specific argument by Jensen (1986). Independently, Marris and Manne argue that the stock prices of firms in which managers deviate from profit maximization are less than they otherwise could be. They argue that this difference between actual and potential stock prices creates incentives for outside parties to acquire these firms and operate them in profit-maximizing ways.

More recently, Jensen argues that takeovers mitigate manager-stockholder conflicts that are especially severe in firms that generate substantial free cash flow (i.e., cash flow in excess of what is necessary to finance positive return investment projects).[2] Jensen asserts that managers in such firms often use free cash flow to finance unprofitable ventures, such as value-reducing acquisitions, rather than pay it out to stockholders in either dividends or stock buy-backs. Therefore, according to Jensen, takeovers are not only a "problem" but also a "solution." He argues that many takeovers are designed, at least in part, either to undo previous unprofitable acquisitions by target firms or to prevent these firms from making future unprofitable acquisitions.

Although numerous studies of corporate takeovers have documented that stockholders of target firms benefit from these transactions,[3] little evidence exists on the extent to which these gains reflect the reduction of agency problems of the type discussed by Marris, Manne, and Jensen. In a 1983 review article, Jensen and Ruback

[1] See, among others, Marris (1963), Manne (1965), Alchian and Demsetz (1972), Jensen and Meckling (1976), Fama (1980), Demsetz (1983), Fama and Jensen (1983*a*, 1983*b*), the June 1983 issue of the *Journal of Law and Economics,* Demsetz and Lehn (1985), Murphy (1985), and Jensen (1986).

[2] Lehn and Poulsen (1989), Mahle (1989), Maloney, McCormick, and Mitchell (1989), and Lang, Stulz, and Walkling (in press) provide empirical evidence consistent with Jensen's hypothesis.

[3] For a review of the literature on the effects of takeovers on stock prices, see Jensen and Ruback (1983) and Jarrell, Brickley, and Netter (1988). Several studies also show that legislation that restricts takeovers adversely affects stock prices (see Ryngaert and Netter 1988; Schumann 1988; Mitchell and Netter, in press).

conclude that "knowledge of the source of takeover gains still eludes us" (p. 47); a more recent survey article by Jarrell et al. (1988) concurs. To partially fill this gap of knowledge, this study addresses a testable question that emerges from Marris, Manne, and Jensen: Are takeover targets distinguished from other firms by the profitability of their prior acquisitions? Specifically, do target firms, relative to other firms, systematically make acquisitions that the stock market judges harshly?

Anecdotal evidence suggests that the *raison d'être* of some takeovers is the poor acquisition record of target firms. For example, one stated motive of Sir James Goldsmith's unsuccessful hostile takeover attempt of Goodyear Tire and Rubber Company in October 1986 was his desire to sell Goodyear's petroleum and aerospace divisions and concentrate Goodyear's attention on its tire and rubber operations. Goldsmith offered a premium of approximately $1.13 billion (roughly 30 percent of the preoffer equity value of Goodyear).

Although Goodyear, originally a tire and rubber company, had diversified into the aerospace business earlier, its 1983 purchase of Celeron Oil for approximately $800 million was its first major petroleum acquisition. On the day of the acquisition announcement, February 8, 1983, Goodyear's stock price suffered an abnormal decline of 10.04 percent, resulting in a loss of $249 million for Goodyear stockholders. Over a narrow event window surrounding the announcement (5 trading days before the announcement through 1 trading day after the announcement), Goodyear's stock price declined 14.83 percent, resulting in shareholder losses of $359 million.[4] The premium offered by Goldsmith may have recouped losses sustained by Goodyear shareholders 3 years earlier when Goodyear began its diversification into the oil industry.[5] Goodyear successfully defeated Goldsmith's takeover attempt, but its stock price did not fall to the preoffer level since it instituted a major restructuring program that was similar to the one that Goldsmith promised. Not surprisingly, the

[4] Over a longer window surrounding this announcement (5 trading days before the announcement through 40 trading days after the announcement), Goodyear's stock price declined 23.68 percent.

[5] The Standard & Poor's 500 index increased by approximately 61 percent from 5 days before the first announcement of Goodyear's acquisition of Celeron Oil in February 1983 through 20 days before the first announcement of Goldsmith's bid for Goodyear in October 1986. If the shareholder losses ($249 million [day of announcement], $359 million [−5, 1 window], and $573 million [−5, 40 window]) associated with Goodyear's energy acquisition had been invested in the S & P 500 during this period, they would have increased to $401 million, $578 million, and $923 million, respectively. Hence, the premium offered by Goldsmith would have restored much of the equity value in Goodyear that had been depreciated earlier when Goodyear's management made these acquisitions.

restructuring program included the sale of a substantial part of Celeron Oil.

To determine whether the Goodyear case generalizes to a large sample of takeovers, we examine the stock price reactions to acquisitions made by two sets of firms during 1982–86: firms that become targets of takeover attempts after their acquisitions (i.e., "targets") and a control group of firms that do not receive takeover bids during the sample period (i.e., "nontargets"). Within the sample of targets, we estimate the stock price effects associated with acquisitions of firms that later receive hostile bids (i.e., "hostile targets") and acquisitions of firms that later receive friendly bids (i.e., "friendly targets"). The following results are revealed.

1. For the entire sample, the average stock price effect associated with acquisition announcements is not significantly different from zero: 0.14 percent measured over the period of 5 trading days before the announcements through 1 trading day after the announcements ([−5, 1] window), and 0.70 percent measured over the period of 5 trading days before the announcements through 40 trading days after the announcements ([−5, 40] window).

2. Significant differences exist between the average stock price effect associated with acquisitions made by targets and the corresponding effect associated with acquisitions made by nontargets. The stock prices of targets decline significantly when they announce acquisitions (−1.27 percent over the [−5, 1] window and −3.38 percent over the [−5, 40] window), and the stock prices of nontargets increase significantly when they announce acquisitions (0.82 percent and 3.32 percent, respectively). Within the sample of targets, this stock price effect is similar in magnitude for hostile targets (−1.34 percent and −3.37 percent, respectively) and friendly targets (−1.17 percent and −3.39 percent, respectively).

3. For the entire sample of acquisitions, the average stock price effect associated with acquisitions that subsequently are divested is significantly lower (−1.53 percent and −4.01 percent, respectively) than the corresponding stock price effect associated with acquisitions that are not subsequently divested (0.56 percent and 1.89 percent, respectively). This difference is especially striking for the sample of acquisitions by target firms. The average stock price effect associated with acquisitions made by targets that subsequently are divested following the reception of their bids, either by their acquiring firms or by themselves, is −2.07 percent and −7.04 percent, respectively; the corresponding average stock price effect associated with other acquisitions made by targets is −0.72 percent and −0.87 percent, respectively.

4. Estimates from a logit equation reveal that, with equity value and

the percentage of equity held by management held constant, the probability that a firm is a target, especially a hostile target, during 1982–88 is inversely and significantly related to the stock price effects associated with announcements of the firm's acquisitions: the more negative these effects, the higher the likelihood of a subsequent takeover attempt.

These results suggest that one source of value in many corporate takeovers, especially hostile takeovers, is recoupment of target equity value that had been lost because of the targets' poor acquisition strategies prior to the reception of their bids. They also support the argument that hostile bust-up takeovers promote economic efficiency by reallocating the target's assets to higher-valued uses. Hence, these results support the theories by Marris, Manne, and Jensen concerning the disciplinary role of corporate takeovers. Additionally, the divestiture findings suggest that when companies announce acquisitions, the stock market provides an unbiased forecast of the likelihood that the assets will be ultimately divested.

II. Description of Data

The sample for this study consists of 1,158 public corporations in 51 industries covered by *Value Line* during the fourth quarter of calendar year 1981.[6] The modified sample excludes two highly regulated industries (financial services and electric utilities) covered by *Value Line* and industries that contain fewer than 10 firms. The sample includes 64.4 percent of the companies in the 1981 S & P 500 index and 75.2 percent of the companies in the 1981 *Fortune* 500.

Each of the 1,158 firms was classified into one of four groups on the basis of whether the firm was a takeover target during January 1980–July 1988: (1) nontargets, (2) hostile targets, (3) friendly targets, and (4) miscellaneous firms. Table 1 displays a frequency distribution for these four groups. The 600 nontarget firms (51.8 percent of the sample) did not receive friendly or hostile bids, pay greenmail, file for bankruptcy, significantly restructure, or become subject to large unsolicited open-market purchases. The hostile target group consists of 228 firms (19.7 percent) that were targets of successful and unsuccessful hostile tender offers, proxy contests (in which the dissenting shareholder sought control), and large unsolicited open-market purchases in which the purchaser attempted to secure control. The friendly target group contains 240 firms (20.7 percent of the sample)

[6] Every quarter, *Value Line* examines the financial prospects of approximately 1,500 firms in more than 65 industries. Each week during every quarter, it publishes a financial summary for a subset of the firms that it covers.

TABLE 1

FREQUENCY OF DIFFERENT TYPES OF CONTROL TRANSACTIONS, 1980–88

	Number	Percentage
Nontargets (N = 600):		
No control transaction	600	51.8
Hostile targets (N = 228):		
Successful hostile tender offer	58	5.0
Unsuccessful hostile tender offer	69	6.0
Unsuccessful hostile tender offer, followed by merger	51	4.4
Unsuccessful hostile tender offer, followed by leveraged buy-out	21	1.8
Unsuccessful hostile tender offer, ending in greenmail	7	.6
Proxy fight	21	1.8
Unsolicited large open-market purchase	1	.1
Friendly targets (N = 240):		
Merger or friendly tender offer	163	14.1
Leveraged buy-out	53	4.6
Unsuccessful leveraged buy-out	10	.9
Unsuccessful leveraged buy-out, followed by merger	14	1.2
Miscellaneous (N = 90):		
Greenmail, without a tender offer	11	.9
Large targeted repurchase (possible greenmail)	10	.9
Large open-market purchases	16	1.4
Bankruptcy filings or NYSE suspensions	26	2.2
Significant corporate restructuring	27	2.3
Total sample	1,158	100.0

that were targets of successful and unsuccessful friendly tender offers, mergers, and leveraged buy-outs. The miscellaneous category contains 90 firms (7.8 percent) that paid greenmail (without a tender offer), filed for bankruptcy, were subject to large open-market purchases in which the purchaser expressed no interest in securing control, made large targeted stock repurchases (without a takeover attempt), or significantly restructured (without a takeover attempt).

The Dow Jones Broadtape was then examined for announcements of acquisitions by the 1,158 firms during 1982–86, including acquisitions of other public companies, acquisitions of private companies, and purchases of assets, divisions, subsidiaries, and stock of other companies.[7] We limit the sample to acquisitions in which the disclosed

[7] Both the New York Stock Exchange (NYSE) and American Stock Exchange (AMEX) require member firms to disclose to Dow Jones any information such as an acquisition that might be expected to significantly affect their stock prices. Dow Jones transmits the disclosed information across the Broadtape to subscribers across the country. Subsequent editions of the *Wall Street Journal* include most of the Broadtape stories.

purchase price was at least 5 percent of the market value of the acquiring firm's common equity 20 trading days prior to the first announcement of the acquisition.

While we examine the stock price effects of acquisitions made during 1982–86, we record control transactions for the firms in the sample from 1980 through July 1988. Extending control transactions beyond the last year in the acquisition sample allows time for a takeover attempt to occur in response to prior value-reducing acquisitions. In addition, some firms may not have received a takeover offer during 1982–88, but received an offer during 1980–81. Acquisitions by these firms during 1982–86 will have occurred after takeover offers for themselves. Since the objective of this study is to examine the extent to which the market for corporate control disciplines firms that make value-reducing acquisitions, it seems inappropriate to include these acquisitions in the target category. It also seems inappropriate, however, to include these acquisitions in the nontarget category for obvious reasons; hence, we opt for including these acquisitions in the miscellaneous category.[8]

Although the first three groups of firms are well defined, the fourth group is a residual group lying between target firms and nontarget firms. We examine the stock price reactions to acquisition announcements by all four groups, although our principal interest lies in differences in the stock price effects of acquisitions made by the first three groups.

Table 2 lists the number of firms that made acquisitions and the number of acquisitions that they made for the four groups, the entire sample, and all target firms. The data in this table reveal that most firms in the sample did not make acquisitions of an amount that was at least 5 percent of their equity value during 1982–86. During this period, 280 firms (24 percent of the sample) made 401 acquisitions. Included in this sample of acquisitions are (1) 232 acquisitions by 166 nontargets (28 percent of all nontargets), (2) 113 acquisitions by 77 targets (16 percent of all targets), (3) 70 acquisitions by 48 hostile targets (21 percent of all hostile targets), (4) 43 acquisitions by 29 friendly targets (12 percent of all friendly targets), and (5) 56 acquisitions by 38 miscellaneous firms (42 percent of all miscellaneous firms).

Although these data might appear to indicate that nontarget firms make acquisitions more often than targets, it is inappropriate to com-

[8] For example, Houston Natural Gas made two acquisitions in November 1984, after successfully defeating a hostile tender offer by Coastal Corp. earlier in the year. In 1985, Houston Natural Gas merged with Internorth. Although the acquisitions by Houston Natural Gas could be classified as acquisitions by a friendly target, we chose to classify them as miscellaneous acquisitions since they followed an unsuccessful hostile bid. The empirical results are invariant with respect to this decision.

TABLE 2

SUMMARY STATISTICS FOR ACQUISITIONS, 1982–86

CATEGORY	NUMBER OF FIRMS*	NUMBER OF ACQUIRING FIRMS†	NUMBER OF ACQUISITIONS‡	AVERAGE AND MEDIAN RELATIVE SIZE OF ACQUISITIONS§	FORM OF FINANCING					
					All Cash‖	All Stock	Cash and Stock	Cash and Notes	Cash and Target Debt	Other
Total sample	1,158	280	401	.37	254	45	49	21	18	14
		(.24)	(.35)	(.18)	(.63)	(.11)	(.12)	(.05)	(.04)	(.03)
Nontargets	600	166	232	.36	144	27	27	12	13	9
		(.28)	(.39)	(.18)	(.62)	(.12)	(.12)	(.05)	(.06)	(.04)
All targets	467	77	113	.35	79	13	11	5	3	2
		(.17)	(.24)	(.17)	(.70)	(.12)	(.10)	(.04)	(.03)	(.02)
Hostile targets	228	48	70	.30	50	9	6	1	3	1
		(.21)	(.31)	(.18)	(.71)	(.13)	(.09)	(.01)	(.04)	(.01)
Friendly targets	240	29	43	.42	29	4	5	4	0	1
		(.12)	(.18)	(.15)	(.67)	(.09)	(.12)	(.09)	(.00)	(.02)
Miscellaneous	170	38	56	.44	31	5	11	4	2	3
		(.22)	(.33)	(.22)	(.55)	(.09)	(.20)	(.07)	(.04)	(.05)

* The number of firms in the entire sample (1,158) is less than the number of firms (1,238) obtained by adding the firms in the four categories. This discrepancy occurs because of the inclusion of some of the firms in the target categories and the miscellaneous category (see n. 8). Similarly, the number of acquiring firms in the entire sample (280) is less than the number of acquiring firms (281) obtained by adding the acquiring firms in the four categories.

† Numbers in parentheses indicate the proportion of firms in each category that made acquisitions.

‡ Numbers in parentheses indicate the number of acquisitions as a proportion of the number of firms in each category.

§ Median relative sizes of acquisitions are shown in parentheses below average relative sizes.

‖ Numbers in parentheses indicate the proportion of acquisitions that made up the various forms of financing for each category.

pare these frequencies directly since the sample period is effectively longer for nontargets than for targets. For target firms, we record only acquisitions made from January 1982 through 3 months prior to the first announcement of their suitor's interest in acquiring control. For example, if the first announcement of a bid for a target firm occurred in June 1984, we record acquisitions for only two years (1982 and 1983) and part of one year (January 1984–March 1984). One conclusion, however, does emerge directly from table 2. Since 79 percent of the hostile targets did not make a large acquisition during the period preceding the reception of their bids, at best, the bad-bidder explanation of hostile takeovers can explain only part of the reason for these transactions.

Table 2 also displays the mean and median ratio of the purchase price of the acquisitions to the equity value of the acquiring firms for the six groups of firms. For the entire sample, the mean value of this ratio is 0.37. The mean value of the acquisition relative size variable for the subgroups ranges from 0.30 for the hostile target category to 0.44 for the miscellaneous category. As with the full sample, the mean ratio exceeds the median ratio for every subgroup. Tests for differences in means indicate that the mean ratios for the various groups are not significantly different from one another and thus make comparable the empirical results reported in the next section.

Several modes of payments can be used in making acquisitions. For each acquisition, we collected the form of payment from *Mergers and Acquisitions* and the *Wall Street Journal.* The data indicate that pure cash offers are the predominant form of payment, accounting for 254 (63 percent) of the acquisitions. At least some cash is used in 354 (88 percent) of the acquisitions.[9] In contrast, pure stock transactions account for only 45 (11 percent) of the acquisitions, and at least some stock is used in 103 (26 percent) of the acquisitions.

Asquith, Bruner, and Mullins (1987) and Travlos (1987) find that form of payment is correlated with the market's reaction to an acquisition announcement. For a sample of 343 mergers and tender offers that occurred during 1973–83, Asquith et al. observe positive stock price reactions to acquiring firms for cash offers and negative reactions for stock offers. Travlos reports insignificant stock price reactions to acquiring firms for cash offers and negative reactions for stock offers for a sample of 167 mergers and tender offers during

[9] The "other" category includes 12 acquisitions partly financed by cash. This category is composed of cash, stock, and notes (8); cash notes and assumption of target debt (1); notes (1); cash and assets (1); cash and debentures (2); and stock and assumption of target debt (1).

1972–81.[10] Among nontargets, hostile targets, and friendly targets, for which comparison will be made in the following sections, the frequency distributions of form of payment do not differ significantly. The form of payment for the miscellaneous category does differ somewhat from the other categories since the miscellaneous category contains relatively fewer pure cash acquisitions. Since the primary focus of this study is to distinguish between acquisitions by target firms and acquisitions by nontarget firms, the form of payment should not bias the comparisons reported in the remainder of the paper.

III. Stock Market Analysis of Acquisitions

A. *Event-Study Methodology*

We employ event-study methodology to measure the stock price effects associated with announcements of acquisitions. Using the Center for Research in Security Prices (CRSP) daily returns tapes, we estimate the abnormal return (ar_{it}) for each acquiring firm during the period 20 days preceding the event date through 40 days following the event date. Abnormal returns are computed as

$$ar_{it} = r_{it} - \hat{\alpha}_t - \hat{\beta}_i r_{mt},$$

where r_{it} is the return to firm i at time t, r_{mt} is the return to the CRSP value-weighted index of NYSE and AMEX stocks, and $\hat{\alpha}_t$ and $\hat{\beta}_i$ are market model parameter estimates from the period 170 through 21 trading days preceding the event date.

The event date for each acquisition is the first date on which the Dow Jones Broadtape reports a story about the acquisition. These initial stories range from reports that the acquiring firm is rumored to be interested in making the acquisition, often with no price disclosed, to reports that both the bidder and the target definitively agreed to the acquisition. We then average the daily abnormal returns across firms in each group to obtain the portfolio abnormal return, $\text{AR}_t = \Sigma_{i=1}^{N} ar_{it}/N$, where N is the number of firms in each portfolio of interest, and cumulate over various windows to obtain the cumulative abnormal return, $\text{CAR} = \Sigma_{t=1}^{T} \text{AR}_t$, where T is the length of the event

[10] We find a higher proportion of cash offers in our study than Asquith et al. and Travlos do. They focus on mergers and tender offers, whereas our study examines all acquisitions, including purchases of assets and divisions, which are generally cash offers.

window. In the absence of abnormal performance, the expected value of the AR and CAR equals zero.[11]

In the tables that follow, we report the AR for the acquisition announcement date [0] and the CAR for the corresponding four windows: (1) 1 day before the event date through 1 day after the event date, [−1, 1], (2) 5 days before the event date through 1 day after the event date, [−5, 1], (3) 5 days before the event date through 40 days after the event date, [−5, 40], and (4) 20 days before the event date through 40 days after the event date, [−20, 40].

B. Stock Price Performance of Acquiring Firms

Table 3 displays the announcement day AR and corresponding CARs (*z*-statistics are in parentheses, with the percentage positive listed below *z*-statistics) associated with the announcements of acquisitions made by each of six groups of firms. In addition to examining the stock price effects of the four groups discussed earlier (hostile targets, friendly targets, nontargets, and miscellaneous), we also report the stock price effects associated with acquisitions by all targets and by the entire sample.

The announcement day AR corresponding to the acquisitions made by the entire sample of 401 acquisitions is −0.21 percent and is statistically significant at the .05 level. The CARs corresponding to the other four windows range from −0.08 percent ([−1, 1]) to 0.70 percent ([−5, 40]), and none of these is significantly different from zero. These results suggest that, on average, acquiring firms earn a normal rate of return on their investments, a finding consistent with a competitive market for corporate control.[12]

[11] We construct standardized test statistics to assess the statistical significance of stock market abnormal performance. We divide each abnormal return by the square root of its forecast variance:

$$\sigma_{ar} = \left\{\sigma^2\left[1 + \frac{1}{L} + \frac{(R_{mt} - \bar{R}_m)^2}{\text{CSSR}_m}\right]\right\}^{1/2}$$

(where σ^2 is the estimated residual variance for the estimation period, L is the number of observations in the estimation period, $\bar{R}_m$ is the estimation period mean of the market return, and CSSR_m is the corrected sum of squares of the market return during the event window), to form a standardized abnormal return, $sar_{it} = ar_{it}/\sigma_{ar}$. The test statistic for the AR is $Z_t = (\sqrt{N}/N)\,\Sigma_{i=1}^{N}\, sar_{it}$, and the test statistic for the CAR is $(1/\sqrt{T})\,\Sigma_{t=1}^{T} Z_t$, where T is the length of the event window. We also conduct nonparametric tests to test the robustness of the results reported. These tests include a test for the percentage of the abnormal returns that are positive and the Wilcoxon signed rank test. The statistical significance of the results reported throughout the text is robust with respect to these nonparametric tests. As with all other results mentioned but not reported in the text, they are available on request.

[12] See Bradley, Desai, and Kim (1988) and Jarrell and Poulsen (1989) for studies of returns to acquiring firms and target firms in tender offers.

TABLE 3

ABNORMAL STOCK MARKET PERFORMANCE ASSOCIATED WITH FIRMS ANNOUNCING ACQUISITIONS DURING 1982–86

	EVENT WINDOW				
CATEGORY	[0]	[−1, 1]	[−5, 1]	[−5, 40]	[−20, 40]
Entire sample	−.21**	−.08	.14	.70	.57
(N = 401)	(−2.18)	(−.45)	(.53)	(1.05)	(.75)
	42.39	46.63	50.37	54.11	53.12
Nontargets	.09	.49**	.82**	3.32***	3.48***
(N = 232)	(.66)	(2.19)	(2.42)	(3.80)	(3.46)
	44.83	48.71	56.03	62.93	62.07
All targets	−.78***	−.93***	−1.27***	−3.38***	−3.46***
(N = 113)	(−4.59)	(−3.16)	(−2.82)	(−2.93)	(−2.60)
	39.82	39.82	38.05	38.05	38.94
Hostile targets	−.95***	−1.50***	−1.34**	−3.37**	−3.19**
(N = 70)	(−4.64)	(−4.22)	(−2.46)	(−2.42)	(−2.00)
	38.57	37.14	35.71	38.57	40.00
Friendly targets	−.50*	−.01	−1.17	−3.39*	−3.91*
(N = 43)	(−1.68)	(−.02)	(−1.47)	(−1.67)	(−1.67)
	41.86	44.19)	41.86	37.21	37.21
Miscellaneous	−.31	−.69	.14	−1.93	−3.33
(N = 56)	(−1.01)	(−1.32)	(.17)	(−.94)	(−1.42)
	37.50	51.79	51.79	50.00	44.64

NOTE.—z-statistics are in parentheses and percentage abnormal returns that are positive are listed below z-statistics.

* Significant at the 10 percent level.

** Significant at the 5 percent level.

*** Significant at the 1 percent level.

The results listed in table 3, however, reveal that the stock price effects associated with announcements of acquisitions made by target firms differ significantly from the stock price effects associated with announcements of acquisitions made by nontarget firms. The announcement day AR associated with 113 acquisitions made by all target firms is −0.78 percent. The CAR ranges from −3.46 percent ([−20, 40]) to −0.93 percent ([−1, 1]). All these estimates are statistically significant at the .01 level. Furthermore, the CAR becomes significantly more negative when the event window extends beyond the acquisition announcements. These data indicate that the market reacted negatively to the initial announcements of these acquisitions and suggest that as the market learned more about these acquisitions during the succeeding weeks (e.g., purchase price, definitiveness of the acquisition, and resulting synergy), the market further devalued the acquiring firms.

Within the group of target firms, the results are especially significant for hostile targets. The announcement day AR associated with

70 acquisitions made by hostile targets is −0.95 percent, and the CAR ranges from −3.37 percent ([−5, 40]) to −1.34 percent ([−5, 1]). All the estimates are significant at the .05 level or higher. These results compare with the corresponding results for acquisitions by friendly targets. The AR on the announcement day for 43 acquisitions made by friendly targets is −0.50 percent and is significant at the .10 level. The CAR ranges from −3.91 percent ([−20, 40]) to −0.01 percent ([−1, 1]) and is significant at the .10 level for the two longest windows. The pattern of returns is similar for both hostile targets and friendly targets; both sets of returns become considerably more negative when the event window extends beyond day 1.

The abnormal stock price performance associated with 232 acquisitions made by nontarget firms contrasts sharply with the results for target firms. The announcement day AR for nontarget firms is 0.09 percent, and the CAR ranges from 0.49 percent ([−1, 1]) to 3.48 percent ([−20, 40]). With the exception of the announcement day AR, all these estimates are significant at the .05 level or higher. The CAR for nontargets increases and remains statistically significant when the event window extends beyond the day after the announcement of the acquisitions, a result that contrasts sharply with the corresponding result for target firms.

Finally, the results reveal that the 56 acquisitions made by the group of miscellaneous firms had no statistically significant effect on their stock prices, regardless of the window used to measure the effect. The announcement day AR for these firms is −0.31 percent, and the CAR for the four other windows ranges from −3.33 percent ([−20, 40]) to 0.14 percent ([−5, 1]).

The empirical results from table 3 indicate that the stock market negatively values acquisitions by firms that become takeover targets, especially hostile targets, whereas it positively values acquisitions by firms that never did become takeover targets during the sample period. Figure 1 graphically depicts the difference in the serial pattern of CARs for hostile targets, friendly targets, nontargets, miscellaneous firms, and the entire sample for the [−5, 40] window. Though the difference in abnormal stock price performance between nontargets and the other groups is obvious, no difference appears to exist among the hostile target, friendly target, and miscellaneous groups. Recall, however, that the estimates are statistically significant in all event windows for the hostile target category, but not significant in two of the windows for the friendly target category and any of the windows for the miscellaneous category.

The results in table 3 imply that the difference in abnormal stock returns associated with acquisitions by targets and nontargets also is significant. Table 4 lists the differences in the announcement day AR

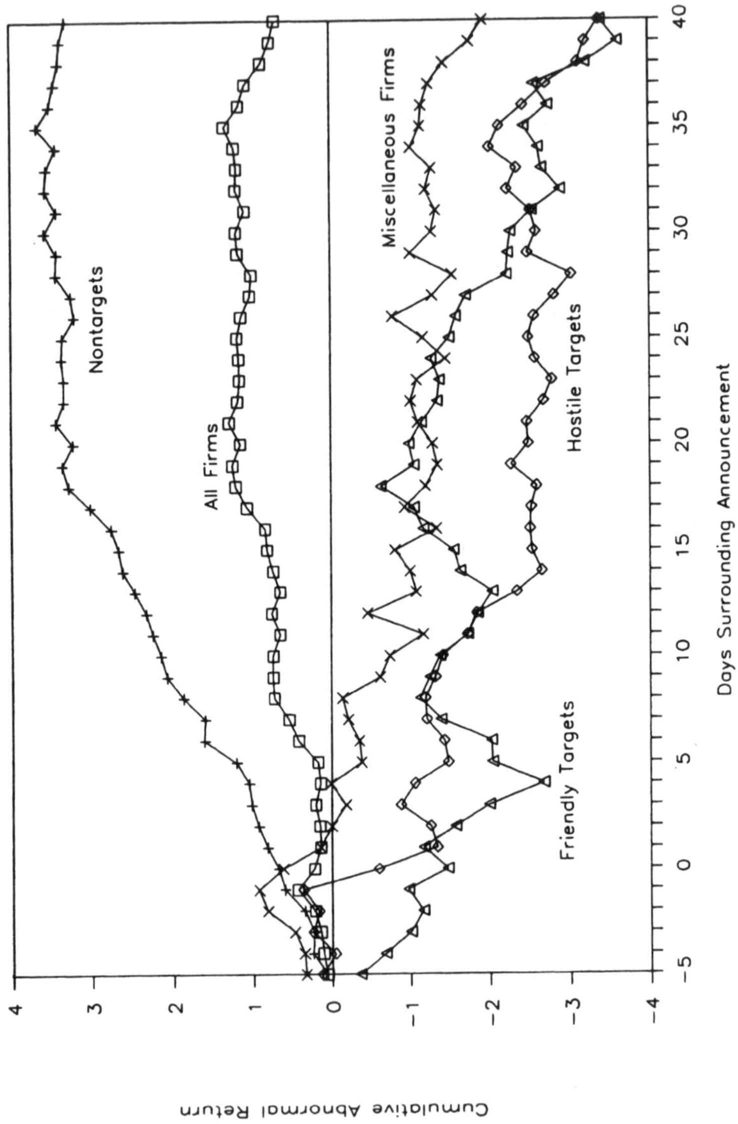

Fig. 1.—Stock price reactions to acquisition announcements, 1982–86

TABLE 4

DIFFERENCES IN ABNORMAL RETURNS ASSOCIATED WITH ANNOUNCEMENTS OF ACQUISITIONS, 1982–86

COMPARISON OF ABNORMAL RETURNS	EVENT WINDOW				
	[0]	[−1, 1]	[−5, 1]	[−5, 40]	[−20, 40]
All targets	.87***	1.42***	2.09***	6.70***	6.94***
vs. nontargets	(3.99)	(3.84)	(3.71)	(4.63)	(4.16)
Hostile targets	1.04***	1.99***	2.16***	6.69***	6.67***
vs. nontargets	(4.23)	(4.74)	(3.37)	(4.07)	(3.54)
Friendly targets	.59*	.50	1.99**	6.71***	7.39***
vs. nontargets	(1.80)	(.91)	(2.30)	(3.04)	(2.90)

NOTE.—*z*-statistics are in parentheses.
* Significant at the 10 percent level.
** Significant at the 5 percent level.
*** Significant at the 1 percent level.

and corresponding CARs associated with acquisitions made by (*a*) all targets and nontargets, (*b*) hostile targets and nontargets, and (*c*) friendly targets and nontargets.[13] The difference in stock price abnormal performance is statistically significant at the .01 level for the comparisons involving all targets and nontargets, and hostile targets and nontargets, for all five event windows. The difference is significant for friendly targets and nontargets at the .10 level or higher for all but the [−1, 1] window.

C. Stock Price Performance of Acquiring Firms for Subsequently Divested Acquisitions

The results presented so far show that, on average, targets, especially hostile targets, make acquisitions that diminish their stock prices, whereas nontarget firms make acquisitions that increase their stock prices. Two plausible explanations exist for the negative abnormal stock price performance associated with acquisitions made by targets: either targets systematically acquire assets that the market believes will reduce the combined operating profits of the acquired assets and themselves, or targets systematically overpay for acquisitions that the market believes will increase the combined operating profits of the acquired assets and themselves. Both explanations are consistent with the theory that takeovers often discipline managers who do not max-

[13] Note that we do not compare targets or nontargets with the miscellaneous category. Our aim is to compare the differences between targets and nontargets. In Sec. II, we observed that the firms in the miscellaneous category do not belong in either the target or nontarget categories. Furthermore, as shown in table 3, the stock price effects for the miscellaneous category are not statistically different from zero for any of the event windows.

imize stockholders' wealth. The former explanation suggests that the motive behind many takeovers is to undo inefficient acquisitions previously made by the targets. The latter explanation suggests that takeovers can serve to restrain managers in target firms from persistently overpaying for acquisitions in the future.[14]

Although it is difficult to measure the extent to which the latter explanation prevails, the relative importance of the former explanation can be examined by comparing the rate at which acquisitions made by targets are subsequently divested with the corresponding rate for nontargets during the sample period.[15] The target divestiture sample consists of acquisitions made by targets that are divested during a period ranging from 3 months prior to the reception of their bids through the end of the sample period. The target divestiture sample includes divestitures by targets to defend against takeovers, divestitures as part of restructuring programs after defeating takeover attempts, and divestitures by acquiring firms following successful takeovers of the targets. The nontarget divestiture sample consists of acquisitions that are divested by the end of the sample period.

If the former explanation is important, then the divestiture rate should be higher for targets than for nontargets. In addition, if the former explanation holds, then the abnormal returns associated with acquisitions that subsequently are divested should be significantly lower than the abnormal returns associated with acquisitions that are not subsequently divested. This relationship should hold not only for the group of targets but also for the entire sample and each of the subsamples.

Data on subsequent divestitures of acquisitions in the sample come from four sources: annual issues of *Mergers and Acquisitions,* the *Wall Street Journal Index,* and *Standard & Poor's Directory of Corporate Affiliations* during 1982–88 and telephone conversations with representatives of the acquiring companies themselves.[16] The data reveal that 81 of the 401 acquisitions during 1982–86, or 20.2 percent of the sample, were subsequently divested during 1982–88.

[14] According to Roll (1986), bidder overpayment results from hubris on the part of managers of acquiring firms (see also Black 1989).

[15] Porter (1987) and Ravenscraft and Scherer (1987) show that acquisitions made by firms in conglomerate mergers during the 1960s and 1970s were subsequently divested at a high rate. Neither study, however, examines divestiture rates for target and nontarget firms.

[16] Although we are confident that these four sources allow us to identify most divestitures, we are not certain that we have identified them all. Some divestitures may not have been reported in *Mergers and Acquisitions,* the *Wall Street Journal Index,* or *Standard & Poor's Directory of Corporate Affiliations,* and in some cases, we were unable to receive definitive information from the companies themselves. We have no reason to believe that the unidentified divestitures bias the results above.

A significant difference in the divestiture rate exists between nontargets and targets. Whereas only 9.1 percent (21/232) of the acquisitions made by nontargets are subsequently divested, 40.7 percent (46/113) of the acquisitions made by targets are subsequently divested, either in response to or following successful or unsuccessful takeover attempts (the *z*-statistic for the difference in divestiture rates is 6.34). No significant difference in divestiture rates exists between hostile targets and friendly targets; this rate is 41.9 percent (18/43) for acquisitions made by friendly targets and 40 percent (28/70) for acquisitions made by hostile targets (the *z*-statistic for the difference in divestiture rates is 0.20).[17]

It is noteworthy that only two of the friendly targets and none of the hostile targets divested previously acquired units prior to the threat of a takeover. Since we are interested in whether one motive for takeovers is to undo acquisitions made by target firms, these two acquisitions made by friendly targets are excluded from the friendly target divestiture sample.

Table 5 displays abnormal returns for two sets of acquisitions for each group of firms: acquisitions that subsequently were divested during the sample period and those that were not. For the entire sample, the announcement day AR associated with 81 acquisitions that subsequently were divested is −1.26 percent and is significant at the .01 level. The CAR for the corresponding four windows ranges from −5.59 percent ([−20, 40]) to −1.53 percent ([−5, 1]), and all these estimates are significant at the .01 level. The announcement day AR for the 320 acquisitions that were not subsequently divested is 0.05 percent and is not statistically significant. The corresponding CARs for announcements of acquisitions that were not divested range from 0.35 ([−1, 1]) to 2.13 ([−20, 40]), and all these estimates are significant at the .10 level or higher.

The findings of negative and significant abnormal returns associated with acquisitions that subsequently are divested during the sample period and positive and significant abnormal returns associated with acquisitions that are not subsequently divested during the sample period deliver a strong message of market efficiency. On average, the market is able to immediately provide an unbiased forecast of the likelihood that the assets will ultimately be divested, long before any cash flows from the resulting business combination are known. Table 6 displays the difference in abnormal returns for these two groups; they range from 1.31 percent for the announcement day to 7.72

[17] Both hostile and friendly targets exhibit significantly higher divestiture rates than nontargets. The *z*-statistic is 5.03 for the hostile target and nontarget comparison, and 4.23 for the friendly target and nontarget comparison.

TABLE 5

ABNORMAL STOCK MARKET PERFORMANCE ASSOCIATED WITH FIRMS ANNOUNCING ACQUISITIONS DURING 1982–86 THAT ARE SUBSEQUENTLY DIVESTED VERSUS ACQUISITIONS DURING 1982–86 THAT ARE NOT SUBSEQUENTLY DIVESTED

	EVENT WINDOW				
CATEGORY	[0]	[−1, 1]	[−5, 1]	[−5, 40]	[−20, 40]
	A. Acquisitions That Are Subsequently Divested				
Entire sample	−1.26***	−1.75***	−1.53***	−4.01***	−5.59***
(N = 81)	(−6.15)	(−4.93)	(−2.81)	(−2.88)	(−3.48)
	35.80	30.86	38.27	35.80	32.10
Nontargets	−1.16***	−1.66**	−.57	2.55	2.48
(N = 21)	(−2.86)	(−2.30)	(−.53)	(.92)	(.78)
	42.86	28.57	47.62	61.90	57.14
All targets	−1.45***	1.56***	−2.07***	−7.04***	−8.91***
(N = 46)	(−5.58)	(−3.46)	(−3.01)	(−3.99)	(−4.38)
	30.44	30.44	34.78	23.91	21.74
Hostile targets	−2.01***	−2.59***	−1.84**	−4.96***	−6.35***
(N = 28)	(−7.13)	(−5.30)	(−2.46)	(−2.59)	(−2.88)
	28.57	21.43	32.14	28.57	28.57
Friendly targets	−.58	.04	−2.44*	−10.27***	−12.90***
(N = 18)	(−1.19)	(.05)	(−1.89)	(−3.09)	(−3.37)
	33.33	44.44	38.89	16.67	11.11
Miscellaneous	−.75	−2.38**	−.45	−3.21	−5.91
(N = 12)	(−1.16)	(−2.11)	(−.26)	(−.73)	(−1.16)
	50.00	41.67	41.67	33.33	25.00
	B. Acquisitions That Are Not Subsequently Divested				
Entire sample	.05	.35*	.56**	1.89***	2.13**
(N = 320)	(.50)	(1.90)	(1.99)	(2.63)	(2.57)
	44.06	50.63	53.44	58.75	58.44
Nontargets	.21	.70***	.96***	3.40***	3.58***
(N = 211)	(1.59)	(3.07)	(2.78)	(3.80)	(3.47)
	45.02	50.71	56.87	63.03	62.56
All targets	−.32	−.50	−.72	−.87	.28
(N = 67)	(−1.47)	(−1.33)	(−1.26)	(−.59)	(.17)
	46.27	46.27	40.30	47.78	50.75
Hostile targets	−.25	−.77*	−1.00	−2.31	−1.08
(N= 42)	(−.94)	(−1.70)	(−1.45)	(−1.31)	(−.53)
	45.24	47.62	38.10	45.24	47.62
Friendly targets	−.45	−.05	−.25	1.56	2.56
(N = 25)	(−1.24)	(−.08)	(−.27)	(.64)	(.91)
	48.00	44.00	44.00	52.00	56.00
Miscellaneous	−.18	−.23	.30	−1.58	−2.63
(N = 44)	(−.56)	(−.40)	(.34)	(−.71)	(−1.02)
	34.09	54.55	54.55	54.55	50.00

NOTE.—z-statistics are in parentheses and percentage abnormal returns that are positive are listed below z-statistics.

* Significant at the 10 percent level.
** Significant at the 5 percent level.
*** Significant at the 1 percent level.

TABLE 6

DIFFERENCES IN ABNORMAL RETURNS ASSOCIATED WITH ANNOUNCEMENTS OF ACQUISITIONS, 1982–86

COMPARISON OF ABNORMAL RETURNS	EVENT WINDOW [0]	[−1, 1]	[−5, 1]	[−5, 40]	[−20, 40]
Divestitures vs. nondivestitures	1.31*** (5.75)	2.10*** (5.25)	2.09*** (3.41)	5.90*** (3.77)	7.72*** (4.27)
All target divestitures vs. nontarget nondivestitures	1.66*** (5.69)	2.26*** (4.47)	3.03*** (3.94)	10.44*** (5.28)	12.49*** (5.48)
Hostile target divestitures vs. nontarget nondivestitures	2.22*** (7.13)	3.29*** (6.10)	2.80*** (3.40)	8.36*** (3.96)	9.93*** (4.08)
Friendly target divestitures vs. nontarget nondivestitures	.79 (1.56)	.66 (.79)	3.40** (2.54)	13.67*** (3.97)	16.48*** (4.16)

NOTE.—z-statistics are in parentheses.
** Significant at the 5 percent level.
*** Significant at the 1 percent level.

percent for the [−20, 40] window, and they are all statistically significant at the .01 level.

The results from the sample of 46 target firm acquisitions that are subsequently divested support the argument that the motive behind many takeovers is to undo inefficient acquisitions previously made by targets. The announcement day AR associated with these acquisitions is −1.45 percent and is significant at the .01 level. The corresponding CARs range from −8.91 percent ([−20, 40]) to −1.56 percent ([−1, 1]), and all these estimates are significant at the .01 level. In contrast, the announcement day AR associated with 67 acquisitions made by targets that are not divested is −0.32 percent and is not statistically significant. The corresponding CARs range from −0.87 percent ([−1, 1]) to 0.28 percent ([−20, 40]), and none of these estimates is statistically significant.

Significant differences in CARs associated with acquisitions that are and are not subsequently divested exist for both friendly and hostile targets, although the relatively small size of the subsamples within each of these groups should be noted. In short, the data reveal that the average negative stock price effect associated with acquisitions made by targets is driven almost exclusively by the subset of acquisitions that subsequently are divested either in bust-up takeovers or during or following an unsuccessful takeover attempt. This evidence suggests that this stock price effect reflects more than overpayment by the target firms in their acquisitions.

The results from the nontarget and miscellaneous categories are also of interest. The announcement day AR associated with 21 acquisitions made by nontargets that subsequently are voluntarily divested is −1.16 percent and is significant at the .01 level. The corresponding CARs range from −1.66 percent ([−1, 1]) to 2.55 percent ([−5, 40]), and only the negative CAR associated with the [−1, 1] window is significant (.05 level). In contrast, the announcement day AR associated with 211 nontarget acquisitions that are not divested is 0.21 percent, though it is not significant. The corresponding CARs range from 0.70 percent ([−1, 1]) to 3.58 percent ([−20, 40]), and all these estimates are significant at the .01 level. On average, these results indicate that nontarget firms voluntarily divest relatively less profitable acquisitions. Similar results hold for the miscellaneous category: the abnormal returns associated with acquisitions subsequently divested are more negative than the acquisitions that are not divested.

We noted earlier that while the divestiture rate is significantly higher for targets (40.7 percent, 46/113) than for nontargets (9.1 percent, 21/232), there are only two divestitures by target firms prior to a takeover attempt for themselves. Thus the voluntary divestiture rate for targets (1.8 percent, 2/113) is actually considerably lower than the divestiture rate for nontargets (z-statistic = 3.23). Given the results reported in tables 3–5, this finding suggests that those nontargets that divested acquisitions may have avoided takeover attempts by divesting less profitable acquisitions, whereas had the target firms divested their bad acquisitions, a takeover attempt might not have resulted.

In conjunction with this reasoning, table 6 shows the difference in abnormal returns associated with the following paired subsamples of acquisitions: the 211 acquisitions made by nontargets that subsequently are not divested and (*a*) the 46 acquisitions made by targets that subsequently are divested, (*b*) the 28 acquisitions made by hostile targets that subsequently are divested, and (*c*) the 18 acquisitions made by friendly targets that subsequently are divested. These data reveal that, with the exception of the abnormal returns estimated over the two shortest windows for the last pairing, the differences in the abnormal returns across all paired subsamples are highly significant. These results indicate that the stock market provides a much different evaluation of acquisitions by nontargets that are retained versus acquisitions by target firms that are retained until a takeover attempt results in a divestiture either by a disciplining acquirer or through restructuring efforts to thwart off the takeover.

D. *Do Value-reducing Acquisitions Increase the Likelihood of Becoming a Takeover Target?*

To examine the effect that value-reducing acquisitions have on the probability of becoming a takeover target, we estimate three sets of logit equations, which differ by the dependent variable and the sample used for the estimate. The dependent variables and the samples corresponding to the three sets of equations are (1) the logistic transformation of the probability that a firm is a target, hostile or friendly, for the sample of targets and nontargets; (2) the logistic transformation of the probability that a firm is a hostile target, for the sample of hostile targets and nontargets; and (3) the logistic transformation of the probability that a firm is a friendly target, for the sample of friendly targets and nontargets. Within each set, five equations are estimated in which one of the independent variables is the sum of the abnormal returns associated with each firm's acquisitions. For example, 77 firms made 113 acquisitions in the target category; thus we have 77 target firm acquisition observations. These five equations differ only by the five windows over which the abnormal returns are estimated. We anticipate an inverse relationship between this independent variable and the likelihood of being a target, especially a hostile target.

Two other variables, the logarithm of the market value of the firms' equity (SIZE) and the percentage of equity held by the firms' managers (MGTHOLD),[18] both computed as of the end of 1981, are included as regressors in the logit equations.[19] Palepu (1986) finds an inverse relationship between firm size and the likelihood of becoming a target during 1971–79. Since our sample period is 1982–88, a period that witnessed the advent of hostile takeovers for large corporations, we expect a weaker and perhaps insignificant relationship between SIZE and the likelihood of becoming a target.

The expected sign of the estimated coefficient on MGTHOLD is more ambiguous. First, MGTHOLD proxies for the extent to which managers own sufficient shares to defeat takeover attempts; in this respect, we expect a negative estimated coefficient on MGTHOLD. In addition, if equity ownership by management and corporate take-

[18] The management ownership data come from proxy filings. Data were not available for Royal Dutch Petroleum, an acquiring firm in the nontarget group.

[19] Although the partial correlation coefficient between SIZE and MGTHOLD is negative (−.329) and significant (p = .0001), we are not concerned with the simultaneous inclusion of these variables in the logit equations since we are primarily interested in the estimated coefficient on the abnormal returns. Potentially more troubling is a statistically significant, partial correlation coefficient between each of the abnormal returns and MGTHOLD (.159 [p = .013], .159 [p = .013], .125 [p = .053], .130 [p = .043], and .104 [p = .108] for the abnormal returns computed over the [0], [−1, 1], [−5, 1], [−5, 20], and [−20, 40] windows, respectively). This direct correlation between the returns to acquiring firms and MGTHOLD is consistent with Lewellen, Loderer, and Rosenfeld (1985) and You et al. (1986) and suggests that managers are less likely to make value-reducing acquisitions when they bear a larger proportion of the wealth consequences of their decisions. Although this significant correlation might suggest the use of a recursive system, the magnitude of the correlation seems low enough to allow us to draw meaningful inferences from a single-equation logit model.

overs are alternative means of mitigating manager-stockholder conflicts, we expect firms with low managerial holdings to receive more takeover bids; this also leads us to expect a negative estimated coefficient on MGTHOLD. However, MGTHOLD may have a counteracting positive effect on the likelihood of being a target: where managers own a large percentage of equity and thus bear a relatively larger proportion of the wealth consequences associated with their decisions, they may have stronger incentives to seek out bids, and they may have less incentive to resist bids and their accompanying premiums.[20] Hence, the relationship between MGTHOLD and the likelihood of being a target is ambiguous a priori. The relationship between MGTHOLD and the likelihood of being a hostile target seems unambiguous since the argument in favor of a positive coefficient estimate on MGTHOLD holds only for friendly bids. Hence, we expect an inverse relationship between MGTHOLD and the likelihood of being a hostile target.[21]

The results displayed in table 7 show that the likelihood of being a takeover target, either friendly or hostile, is significantly and inversely related to the abnormal stock price performance with the firm's acquisitions. The estimated coefficient has a negative sign in all the equations, and all these coefficients are significant at the .05 level or higher. Both SIZE and MGTHOLD enter with negative estimated coefficients in all five equations, but none of these estimates is significant.

The abnormal returns associated with the firms' acquisitions also enter with negative, significant coefficients in the set of equations in which the dependent variable is the transformed probability that the firm is a hostile target. In four of the five equations, the estimated

[20] Although MGTHOLD may be a good approximation of the extent to which managers directly bear the wealth consequences of their decisions, other measures may be more appropriate. Specifically, the proportion of a manager's wealth that consists of equity in his firm might be a better proxy for the extent to which his interests are directly aligned with stockholders. However, this measure also has its drawbacks. Theoretically, if a manager's entire wealth consists of equity in his firm, he may be more risk averse than other, diversified stockholders. In order to diversify his wealth while maintaining his equity ownership in the firm, he may diversify the firm's activities in ways that do not necessarily maximize stockholder value. Hence, it is not obvious that as this proportion increases, managers' interests are more directly aligned with the interests of other stockholders. As a practical matter, this variable cannot be measured directly since the personal wealth of managers is not publicly available information. Since our principal interest in this paper lies elsewhere, we did not attempt an approximation of this variable (e.g., the ratio of the value of a manager's stockholdings to the value of his salary).

[21] Walkling and Long (1984) find that the probability that a takeover attempt is hostile, as opposed to friendly, is inversely related to the percentage of equity owned by managers. Morck, Shleifer, and Vishny (1988) find that management of hostile targets owns significantly less equity than management of friendly targets.

TABLE 7

LOGIT ESTIMATES OF PROBABILITY THAT FIRM BECAME TARGET

	Event Window				
	[0]	[−1, 1]	[−5, 1]	[−5, 40]	[−20, 40]
	A. Dependent Variable Is Transformed Probability That Firm Became Hostile or Friendly Target (vs. Nontarget) (N = 242)				
Intercept	1.059	.882	1.020	1.007	.995
	(.55)	(.39)	(.51)	(.45)	(.45)
Abnormal stock price performance around acquisition announcements	−7.886**	−5.070**	−6.016***	−3.701***	−2.776***
	(4.85)	(4.80)	(8.47)	(14.62)	(11.88)
MGTHOLD	−1.136	−1.087	−1.137	−1.029	−1.202
	(.77)	(.69)	(.73)	(.55)	(.76)
SIZE	−.139	−.124	−.134	−.133	−.131
	(1.62)	(1.30)	(1.51)	(1.37)	(1.35)
Model chi-square	6.58	6.61	10.60	18.68	15.11
	B. Dependent Variable Is Transformed Probability That Firm Became Hostile Target (vs. Nontarget) (N = 213)				
Intercept	.640	.595	.663	1.195	.931
	(.13)	(.11)	(.13)	(.39)	(.25)

continued over

Abnormal stock price performance around acquisition announcements	−7.446*	−6.500**	−5.771**	−4.478***	−3.178***
	(3.09)	(5.30)	(5.45)	(11.63)	(8.63)
MGTHOLD	−4.968**	−4.930**	−5.198**	−5.492**	−5.502**
	(4.05)	(4.10)	(4.33)	(4.71)	(4.76)
SIZE	−.124	−.121	−.123	−.163	−.141
	(.82)	(.79)	(.82)	(1.29)	(1.00)
Model chi-square	9.96	12.49	12.52	20.53	16.66
	C. Dependent Variable Is Transformed Probability That Firm Became Friendly Target (vs. Nontarget) ($N = 194$)				
Intercept	.828	.594	.872	.669	.652
	(.19)	(.10)	(.21)	(.12)	(.11)
Abnormal stock price performance around acquisition announcements	−6.953	−2.804	−6.767**	−3.714***	−2.765***
	(1.85)	(.69)	(5.16)	(8.17)	(7.02)
MGTHOLD	1.159	1.163	1.397	1.689	1.442
	(.64)	(.63)	(.88)	(1.19)	(.89)
SIZE	−.216	−.195	−.221	−.206	−.203
	(2.15)	(1.78)	(2.25)	(1.86)	(1.85)
Model chi-square	4.74	3.53	8.22	12.02	10.49

NOTE.—Chi-squared statistics are in parentheses.
* Significant at the 10 percent level.
** Significant at the 5 percent level.
*** Significant at the 1 percent level.

coefficient on the abnormal returns is negative and significant at the .05 level or higher; in the equation containing the announcement day AR, this estimate is negative and significant at the .10 level. As anticipated, MGTHOLD enters with a negative and significant (at the .05 level) estimated coefficient in all these equations. However, SIZE does not enter any of these equations with a significant estimated coefficient. Weaker results hold when the dependent variable is the transformed probability that the firm is a friendly target. The estimated coefficient on the abnormal returns is negative in all five equations, but it is not significant in the equations containing the announcement day AR and the CAR computed over the [−1, 1] window. The variable MGTHOLD enters each equation with a positive but insignificant coefficient estimate, and SIZE enters each of these equations with a negative but insignificant coefficient estimate.

In summary, the logit equations show that the results presented in tables 3 and 4 remain robust after firm size and management ownership are controlled for. Firms that make bad acquisitions are more likely to receive a takeover offer than firms that make good acquisitions.

IV. Conclusion

The evidence in this paper is consistent with the argument, developed originally by Marris (1963) and Manne (1965), that one motive for corporate takeovers is to discipline managers who operate their firms in ways that do not maximize profits. It is also consistent with a more specific argument, developed by Jensen (1986), that many takeovers discipline managers who use free cash flow to make value-reducing acquisitions.

The evidence is also relevant for arguments made by critics of hostile takeovers. First, although critics often lament the advent of hostile "bust-up" takeovers (i.e., takeovers that are followed by large divestitures of the target firms' assets), this paper supports the argument that hostile bust-up takeovers often promote economic efficiency by reallocating the targets' assets to higher-valued uses. Second, these results cast new light on evidence concerning the effect of takeovers on the equity value of acquiring firms. Critics of hostile takeovers often argue that although target shareholders fare well in takeovers, these transactions frequently diminish the equity value of acquiring firms. Our evidence suggests that takeovers can be both a "problem" and a "solution." Although, in the aggregate, we find that the returns to acquiring firms are approximately zero, the aggregate data obscure the fact that the market discriminates between "bad" bidders, which are more likely to become takeover targets, and "good" bidders, which are less likely to become targets.

References

Alchian, Armen A., and Demsetz, Harold. "Production, Information Costs, and Economic Organization." *A.E.R.* 62 (December 1972): 777–95.

Asquith, Paul; Bruner, Robert F.; and Mullins, David W., Jr. "Merger Returns and the Form of Financing." Manuscript. Cambridge, Mass.: Harvard Univ., 1987.

Berle, Adolf A., and Means, Gardiner C. *The Modern Corporation and Private Property.* New York: Macmillan, 1933.

Black, Bernard S. "Bidder Overpayment in Takeovers." *Stanford Law Rev.* 41 (February 1989): 597–660.

Bradley, Michael; Desai, Anand; and Kim, E. Han. "Synergistic Gains from Corporate Acquisitions and Their Division between the Stockholders of Target and Acquiring Firms." *J. Financial Econ.* 21 (May 1988): 3–40.

Demsetz, Harold. "The Structure of Ownership and the Theory of the Firm." *J. Law and Econ.* 26 (June 1983): 375–90.

Demsetz, Harold, and Lehn, Kenneth. "The Structure of Corporate Ownership: Causes and Consequences." *J.P.E.* 93 (December 1985): 1155–77.

Fama, Eugene F. "Agency Problems and the Theory of the Firm." *J.P.E.* 88 (April 1980): 288–307.

Fama, Eugene F., and Jensen, Michael C. "Agency Problems and Residual Claims." *J. Law and Econ.* 26 (June 1983): 327–49. (*a*)

———. "Separation of Ownership and Control." *J. Law and Econ.* 26 (June 1983): 301–25. (*b*)

Jarrell, Gregg A.; Brickley, James A.; and Netter, Jeffry M. "The Market for Corporate Control: The Empirical Evidence since 1980." *J. Econ. Perspectives* 2 (Winter 1988): 49–68.

Jarrell, Gregg A., and Poulsen, Annette. "Returns to Acquiring Firms in Tender Offers: Evidence from Three Decades." *Financial Management* 18 (Autumn 1989): 12–19.

Jensen, Michael C. "Agency Costs of Free Cash Flow, Corporate Finance, and Takeovers." *A.E.R. Papers and Proc.* 76 (May 1986): 323–29.

Jensen, Michael C., and Meckling, William H. "Theory of the Firm: Managerial Behavior, Agency Costs and Ownership Structure." *J. Financial Econ.* 3 (October 1976): 305–60.

Jensen, Michael C., and Ruback, Richard S. "The Market for Corporate Control: The Scientific Evidence." *J. Financial Econ.* 11 (April 1983): 5–50.

Lang, Larry; Stulz, Rene M.; and Walkling, Ralph A. "Tobin's *Q* and the Gains from Successful Tender Offers." *J. Financial Econ.* (in press).

Lehn, Kenneth, and Poulsen, Annette. "Free Cash Flow and Stockholder Gains in Going Private Transactions." *J. Finance* 44 (July 1989): 771–87.

Lewellen, Wilbur; Loderer, Claudio; and Rosenfeld, Ahron. "Merger Decisions and Executive Stock Ownership in Acquiring Firms." *J. Accounting and Econ.* 7 (April 1985): 209–31.

Mahle, Steven. "Agency Costs and Acquiring Firm Excess Returns: An Empirical Test of the Free Cash Flow Hypothesis." Manuscript. Iowa City: Univ. Iowa, 1989.

Maloney, Michael T.; McCormick, Robert E.; and Mitchell, Mark L. "Managerial Decision Making and Capital Structure." Manuscript. Clemson, S.C.: Clemson Univ., 1989.
Manne, Henry G. "Mergers and the Market for Corporate Control." *J.P.E.* 73 (April 1965): 110–20.
Marris, Robin. "A Model of the 'Managerial' Enterprise." *Q.J.E.* 77 (May 1963): 185–209.
Mitchell, Mark L., and Netter, Jeffry M. "Triggering the 1987 Stock Market Crash: Antitakeover Provisions in the Proposed House Ways and Means Tax Bill?" *J. Financial Econ.* (in press).
Morck, Randall; Shleifer, Andrei; and Vishny, Robert W. "Characteristics of Targets of Hostile and Friendly Takeovers." In *Corporate Takeovers: Causes and Consequences,* edited by Alan J. Auerbach. Chicago: Univ. Chicago Press (for NBER), 1988.
Murphy, Kevin J. "Corporate Performance and Managerial Remuneration: An Empirical Analysis." *J. Accounting and Econ.* 7 (April 1985): 11–42.
Palepu, Krishna G. "Predicting Takeover Targets: A Methodological and Empirical Analysis." *J. Accounting and Econ.* 8 (March 1986): 3–35.
Porter, Michael E. "From Competitive Advantage to Corporate Strategy." *Harvard Bus. Rev.* 65 (May/June 1987): 43–59.
Ravenscraft, David J., and Scherer, F. M. "Life after Takeovers." *J. Indus. Econ.* 36 (December 1987): 147–56.
Roll, Richard. "The Hubris Hypothesis of Corporate Takeovers." *J. Bus.* 59, no. 2, pt. 1 (April 1986): 197–216.
Ryngaert, Michael, and Netter, Jeffry M. "Shareholder Wealth Effects of the Ohio Antitakeover Law." *J. Law, Econ. and Organization* 4 (Fall 1988): 373–83.
Schumann, Lawrence. "State Regulation of Takeovers and Shareholder Wealth: The Case of New York's 1985 Takeover Statutes." *Rand J. Econ.* 19 (Winter 1988): 557–67.
Travlos, Nickolaos G. "Corporate Takeover Bids, Methods of Payment, and Bidding Firms' Stock Returns." *J. Finance* 42 (September 1987): 943–63.
Walkling, Ralph A., and Long, Michael S. "Agency Theory, Managerial Welfare, and Takeover Bid Resistance." *Rand J. Econ.* 15 (Spring 1984): 54–68.
You, Victor; Caves, Richard; Smith, Michael; and Henry, James. "Mergers and Bidders' Wealth: Managerial and Strategic Factors." In *The Economics of Strategic Planning: Essays in Honor of Joel Dean,* edited by Lacy Glenn Thomas III. Lexington, Mass.: Lexington Books, 1986.

[6]

Richard Roll
University of California, Los Angeles

The Hubris Hypothesis of Corporate Takeovers*

The hubris hypothesis is advanced as an explanation of corporate takeovers. Hubris on the part of individual decision makers in bidding firms can explain why bids are made even when a valuation above the current market price represents a positive valuation error. Bidding firms infected by hubris simply pay too much for their targets. The empirical evidence in mergers and tender offers is reconsidered in the hubris context. It is argued that the evidence supports the hubris hypothesis as much as it supports other explanations such as taxes, synergy, and inefficient target management.

> Finally, knowledge of the source of takeover gains still eludes us. [Jensen and Ruback 1983, p. 47]

I. Introduction

Despite many excellent research papers, we still do not fully understand the motives behind mergers and tender offers or whether they bring an increase in aggregate market value. In their comprehensive review article (from which the above quote is taken), Jensen and Ruback (1983) summarize the empirical work presented in over 40

* The earlier drafts of this paper elicited many comments. It is a pleasure to acknowledge the benefits derived from the generosity of so many colleagues. They corrected several conceptual and substantive errors in the previous draft, directed my attention to other results, and suggested other interpretations of the empirical phenomena. In general, they provided me with an invaluable tutorial on the subject of corporate takeovers. The present draft undoubtedly still contains errors and omissions, but this is due mainly to my inability to distill and convey the collective knowledge of the profession. Among those who helped were C. R. Alexander, Peter Bernstein, Thomas Copeland, Harry DeAngelo, Eugene Fama, Karen Farkas, Michael Firth, Mark Grinblatt, Gregg Jarrell, Bruce Lehmann, Paul Malatesta, Ronald Masulis, David Mayers, John McConnell, Merton Miller, Stephen Ross, Richard Ruback, Sheridan Titman, and, especially, Michael Jensen, Katherine Schipper, Walter A. Smith, Jr., and J. Fred Weston. I also benefited from the comments of the finance workshop participants at the University of Chicago, the University of Michigan, and Dartmouth College, and of the referees.

(*Journal of Business*, 1986, vol. 59, no. 2, pt. 1)

0021-9398/86/5902-0001$01.50

papers. There are many important details in these papers, but Jensen and Ruback interpret them to show overall "that corporate takeovers generate positive gains, that target firm shareholders benefit, and that bidding firm shareholders do not lose" (p. 47).

My purpose here is to suggest a different and less conclusive interpretation of the empirical results. This interpretation may not turn out to be valid, but I hope to show that it has enough plausibility to be at least considered in further investigations. It will be argued here that takeover gains may have been overestimated if they exist at all. If there really are no aggregate gains associated with takeovers, or if they are small, it is not hard to understand why their sources are "elusive."

The mechanism by which takeover attempts are initiated and consummated suggests that at least part of the large price increases observed in target firm shares might represent a simple transfer from the bidding firm, that is, that the observed takeover premium (tender offer or merger price less preannouncement market price of the target firm) overstates the increase in economic value of the corporate combination. To see why this could be the case, let us follow the steps undertaken in a takeover.

> First, the bidding firm identifies a potential target firm.
>
> Second, a "valuation" of the equity of the target is undertaken. In some cases this may include nonpublic information. The valuation definitely would include, of course, any estimated economies due to synergy and any assessments of weak management et cetera that might have caused a discount in the target's current market price.
>
> Third, the "value" is compared to the current market price. If value is below price, the bid is abandoned. If value exceeds price, a bid is made and becomes part of the public record. The bid would not generally be the previously determined "value" since it should include provision for rival bids, for future bargaining with the target, and for valuation errors inter alia.

The key element in this series of events is the valuation of an asset (the stock) that already has an observable market price. The preexistence of an active market in the identical item being valued distinguishes takeover attempts from other types of bids, such as for oil-drilling rights and paintings. These other assets trade infrequently and no two of them are identical. This means that the seller must make his own independent valuation. There is a symmetry between the bidder and the seller in the necessity for valuation.

In takeover attempts, the target firm shareholder may still conduct a valuation, but it has a lower bound, the current market price. The bidder knows for certain that the shareholder will not sell below that; thus when the valuation turns out to be below the market price, no offer is made.

Consider what might happen if there are no potential synergies or other sources of takeover gains but when, nevertheless, some bidding firms believe that such gains exist. The valuation itself can then be considered a random variable whose mean is the target firm's current market price. When the random variable exceeds its mean, an offer is made; otherwise there is no offer. Offers are observed only when the valuation is too high; outcomes in the left tail of the distribution of valuations are never observed. The takeover premium in such a case is simply a random error, a mistake made by the bidding firm. Most important, the observed error is always in the same direction. Corresponding errors in the opposite direction are made in the valuation process, but they do not enter our empirical samples because they are not made public.

If there were no value at all in takeovers, why would firms make bids in the first place? They should realize that any bid above the market price represents an error. This latter logic is alluring because market prices do seem to reflect rational behavior. But we must keep in mind that prices are averages. There is no evidence to indicate that every individual behaves as if he were the rational economic human being whose behavior seems revealed by the behavior or market prices. We may argue that markets behave as if they were populated by rational beings. But a market actually populated by rational beings is observationally equivalent to a market characterized by grossly irrational individual behavior that cancels out in the aggregate, leaving the trace of the only systematic behavioral component, the small thread of rationality that all individuals have in common. Indeed, one possible definition of irrational or aberrant behavior is independence across individuals (and thus disappearance from view under aggregation).

Psychologists are constantly bombarding economists with empirical evidence that individuals do not always make rational decisions under uncertainty. For example, see Oskamp (1965), Tversky and Kahneman (1981), and Kahneman, Slovic, and Tversky (1982). Among psychologists, economists have a reputation for arrogance mainly because this evidence is ignored; but psychologists seem not to appreciate that economists disregard the evidence on individual decision making because it usually has little predictive content for market behavior. Corporate takeovers are, I believe, one area of research in which this usually valid reaction of economists should be abandoned; takeovers reflect individual decisions.

There is little reason to expect that a particular individual bidder will refrain from bidding because he has learned from his own past errors. Although some firms engage in many acquisitions, the average individual bidder/manager has the opportunity to make only a few takeover offers during his career. He may convince himself that the valuation is right and that the market does not reflect the full economic value of the combined firm. For this reason, the hypothesis being offered in this paper to explain the takeover phenomenon can be termed the "hubris hypothesis." If there actually are no aggregate gains in takeover, the phenomenon depends on the overbearing presumption of bidders that their valuations are correct.

Even if gains do exist for some corporate combinations, at least part of the average observed takeover premium could still be caused by valuation error and hubris. The left tail of the distribution of valuations is truncated by the current market price. To the extent that there are errors in valuation, fewer negative errors will be observed other than positive errors. When gains exist, a smaller fraction of the distribution will be truncated than when there are no gains at all. Nonetheless, truncation will occur in every situation in which the gain is small enough to allow the distribution of valuations to have positive probability below the market price.

Rational bidders will realize that valuations are subject to error and that negative errors are truncated in repeated bids. They will take this into account when making a bid. Takeover attempts are thus analogous to the auctions discussed in bidding theory wherein the competing bidders make public offers. In the takeover situation, the initial bidder is the market, and the initial public offer is the current price. The second bidder is the acquiring firm who, conscious of the "winner's curse," biases his bid downward from his estimate of value. In fact, he frequently abandons the auction altogether, allowing the first bidder to win.

In a standard auction, we would observe all cases, including those in which the initial bid was victorious. Theory predicts that the winning bid is an accurate assessment of value. In takeovers, however, if the initial bid (by the market) wins the auction, we throw away the observation. If all bidders accounted properly for the "winner's curse," there would be no particular bias associated with discarding bids won by the market; but if bidders are infected by hubris, the standard bidding theory conclusion would not be valid. Empirical evidence from repeated sealed bid auctions (Capen, Clapp, and Campbell 1971; and Dougherty and Lohrenz 1976), indicates that bidders do not fully incorporate the winner's curse. Unless there is something curative about the public nature of corporate takeover auctions, we should at least consider the possibility that the same phenomenon exists in them.

The hubris hypothesis is consistent with strong-form market efficiency. Financial markets are assumed to be efficient in that asset prices reflect all information about individual firms. Product and labor markets are assumed efficient in the sense that (*a*) no industrial reorganization can bring gains in an aggregate output at the same cost or reductions in aggregate costs with the same output and (*b*) management talent is employed in its best alternative use.

Most other explanations of the takeover phenomenon rely on strong-form market inefficiency of at least a temporary duration. Either financial markets are ignorant of relevant information possessed by bidding firms, or product markets are inefficiently organized so that potential synergies, monopolies, or tax savings are being ineffectively exploited (at least temporarily), or labor markets are inefficient because gains could be obtained by replacement of inferior managers. Although perfect strong-form efficiency is unlikely, the concept should serve as a frictionless ideal, the benchmark of comparison by which other degrees of efficiency are measured. This is, I claim, the proper role for the hubris hypothesis of takeovers; it is the null against which other hypotheses of corporate takeovers should be compared.

Section II presents the principal empirical predictions of the hubris hypothesis and discusses supportive and disconfirming empirical results. Section III concludes the paper by summarizing the results and by discussing various objections to the hypothesis.

II. Evidence for and against the Hubris Hypothesis

If there are absolutely no gains available to corporate takeovers, the hubris hypothesis implies that the average increase in the target firm's market value should then be more than offset by the average decrease in the value of the bidding firm. Takeover expenses would constitute the aggregate net loss. The market price of a target firm should increase when a previously unanticipated bid is announced, and it should decline to the original level or below if the first bid is unsuccessful and if no further bids are received.

Implications for the market price reaction of a bidding firm are somewhat less clear. If we could be sure that (*a*) the bid was unanticipated and (*b*) the bid conveys no information about the bidder other than that it is seeking a combination with a particular target, then the hubris hypothesis would predict the following market price movements in bidding firms:

1. a price decline on announcement of a bid;
2. a price increase on abandoning a bid or on losing a bid; and
3. a price decline on actually winning a bid.

It has been pointed out by several authors, most forcefully by Schipper and Thompson (1983), that condition *a* above is by no means assured in all cases. Bids are not always surprises. As Jensen and Ruback (1983, pp. 18–20) observe, this alone complicates the measurement of bidder firm returns.

The possibility that a bid conveys information about the bidding firm's own operations, that is, violation of condition *b*, is an equally serious problem (cf. Jensen and Ruback 1983, p. 19 and n. 14). For example, the market might well interpret a bid as signaling that the bidding firm's immediate past or expected future cash flows are higher than previously estimated, that this has actually prompted the bid, and that, although the takeover itself has a negative value, the combination of takeover and new information is on balance positive.

Similarly, abandoning a previous bid could convey negative information about the bidding firm's ability to pay for the proposed acquisition, perhaps because of negative events in its own operations. Losing a bid to rivals could signal limited resources. These problems of contaminating information make it difficult to interpret bidding firm price movements and to interpret the combined price movements of bidder and target.

A. *The Evidence about Target Firms*

Let us first examine, therefore, the more straightforward implications of the hubris hypothesis for target firms. Bradley, Desai, and Kim (1983*b*) present results for target firms in tender offers that are consistent with the implications. Target firms display increases in value on the announcement of a tender offer, and they fall back to about the original level if no combination occurs then or later.

A similar pattern is observed in Asquith's (1983) sample of target firms in unsuccessful mergers. These firms were targets in one or more merger bids that were later abandoned and for whom no additional merger bids occurred during the year after the last original bid was withdrawn. The original merger bid announcement was accompanied by a 7.0% average increase in target firm value that appears to be almost entirely reversed within 60 days (fig. 1, p. 62). By the date when the last bid is abandoned, the target's price decline amounts to 8.1% (table 9, p. 81), slightly more than offsetting the original increase.

The result may be partially compromised by the following problem. The "outcome date" of an unsuccessful bid is the withdrawal date of the final offer following which no additional bid is received for 1 year. Thus as of the outcome date the market could not have known for certain that other bids would not arrive. However, if the market had known that no other bids would arrive, the price decline would likely have been ever larger, so perhaps this partial use of hindsight was not material. In summary, target firm share behavior, as presented in Bradley et al. (1983*b*) for tender offers and in Asquith (1983) for mergers, is consistent with the hubris hypothesis.

B. *The Evidence about Total Gains*

The central prediction of the hubris hypothesis is that the total combined takeover gain to target and bidding firm shareholders is nonpositive. None of the evidence using returns can unambiguously test this prediction for the simple reason that average returns of individual firms do not measure average dollar gains, especially in the typical takeover situation in which the bidding firm is much larger (cf. Jensen and Ruback 1983, p. 22). In some cases, the observed price increase in the target would correspond to such a trivial loss to the bidder that the loss is bound to be hidden in the bid/ask spread and in the noise of daily return volatility.

In an attempt to circumvent the problem that returns cannot measure takeover gains when bidder and target have different sizes, Asquith, Bruner, and Mullins (1983) take the unique approach of regressing the bidder announcement period return on the relative size of target to bidder. They reason that, if acquisitions benefit bidder firms, large acquisitions should show up as having larger return effects on bidder firm returns. They do find this positive relation for bidding firms. The same relation is not significant for target firms, although, as usual, target firms have much larger average returns. The positive relation for bidding firms is consistent with more than one explanation. It is consistent with the bidding firm losing on average, but losing less the larger the target. Perhaps a more accurate valuation is conducted when the stakes are large and this results in a smaller percentage loss to the bidder. Perhaps large targets are less closely held so that the takeover premium can be smaller relative to the preoffer price and still convince shareholders to deliver their shares. Perhaps bidders for larger targets have fewer rivals and can thus get away with a bidder-perceived "bargain."

The absence of any relation for target firms is puzzling under every hypothesis unless the entire gain accrues to the target firm shareholders (and Asquith et al. [1983] interpret their results to indicate that takeover gains are shared). If synergy is the source of gains, for example, target shareholder's returns would increase with the relative size of its bidder-partner.

Several studies have attempted to measure aggregate dollar gains directly. Halpern (1973) finds average market adjusted gains of $27.35 million in a sample of mergers between New York Stock Exchange–listed firms (p. 569); the gain was calculated over a period 7 months prior to the first public announcement of the merger through the merger consummation month. The standard error of this average gain, assuming cross-sectional independence, was $19.7 ($173.2/$\sqrt{77}$ [see table 3, p. 569]). In 53 cases out of 77, there was a dollar gain.

Bradley, Desai, and Kim (1982) present dollar returns for a sample of 162 successful tender offers from 20 days before the announcement until 5 days after completion. The average combined dollar increase in value of bidder plus target was $17 million, but this was not statistically significant. The $17 million gain was divided between a $34 million average gain by targets and a $17 million average loss to bidders. The authors note that the equally weighted average rate of return to bidders is positive, though the dollar change is a loss; they argue that this can be explained by skewness in the distribution of dollar changes.

In a revision of their 1982 paper, Bradley, Desai, and Kim (1983*a*) present slightly different results. The sample is expanded from 162 and 183 tender offer events, although the underlying data base appears to be the same (698 tender offers from October 1958 to December 1980). The only stated difference in the selection of samples is that the earlier paper excludes offers that are not "control oriented" (cf. Bradley et al. 1982, p. 13; and Bradley et al. 1983*a*, pp. 35–36). This sample change resulted in an average gain to targets of $28.1 million and to bidders to +$5.8 million (table 9). The authors say, however, that "the distributional properties of our dollar gain measures preclude any meaningful inferences about their significance" (p. 58).

Malatesta (1983) examines the combined change in target and bidder firms before, during, and after a merger. Jensen and Ruback summarize Malatesta's results as follows: "Malatesta examines a matched sample of targets and their bidders in 30 successful mergers and finds a significant average increase of $32.4 million ($t$ = 2.07) in their combined equity value in the month before and the month of outcome announcement. . . . This evidence indicates that changes in corporate control increase the combined market value" (1983, p. 22).

Malatesta (1983) himself does not reach so definite a conclusion. In fact, his overall interpretation of the evidence is that "the immediate impact of merger per se is positive and highly significant for acquired firms but *larger in absolute value and negative* for acquiring firms" (p. 155; emphasis added). Jensen and Ruback were referring to smaller samples of matching pairs. Even for this sample, Malatesta says, the results "provide *weak* evidence that successful resolution of these mergers had a positive impact on combined shareholder wealth" (p. 170; emphasis added). In 2 months culminating in board approval of the merger, the combined gain was positive, but "over the entire interval −60 to 0 [months], the cumulative dollar return is a trivial 0.29 million dollars" (p. 171). Of course, this could be due to selection bias; bidding or acquired firms or both may tend to be involved in mergers after a period of poor performance. According to Asquith's (1983) results, however, this is true only for targets. The opposite is true for bidders; they tend to display superior performance prior to the merger bid announcement. During the culminating merger months, the acquiring firms' gains in Malatesta's sample were not statistically significant (although the acquired firms' were).

Malatesta's month zero is when the board announced merger approval, not when the merger proposal first reached the public. Even if the merger per se has no aggregate value, the price reaction on approval could be positive because it signals that court battles, further bids to overcome rivals, and other costly events associated with hostile mergers will not take place in this case, although their possibility was signaled originally by the merger proposal. Malatesta does not present evidence about the dollar reactions of the combined firm on the first announcement of the merger proposal.

Firth (1980) presents the results of a study of takeovers in the United Kingdom. In his sample, target firms gain, and bidding firms lose, both statistically significantly. The average total change in market value of the two firms in a successful combination, from a month prior to the takeover bid through the month of acceptance of the offer, is £−36.6 million. No *t*-statistic is given for this number, but we can obtain a rough measure of significance by using the fact that 224 of 434 cases displayed aggregate losses. If these cases were independent, the *t*-statistic that the true proportion of losing takeovers is greater than 50% is about .67.

The relative division of losses was examined by Firth (1980) in an ingenious calculation that strongly suggests the presence of bidding errors. The premium paid to the target firm (in £) as a fraction of the size of the bidding firm was cross-sectionally related to the percentage loss in the bidding firm's shares around the takeover period. The regression coefficient was −.89 ($t = -5.94$). Firth concludes (p. 254), "This supports the view that the stock market expects zero benefits from a takeover, that the gains to the acquired firm represent an 'overpayment' and that the acquiring company's shareholders suffer corresponding losses."

Using dollar-based matched pairs of firms, Varaiya (1985) finds that the aggregate abnormal dollar gain of targets is $189.4 million while the average abnormal dollar loss of bidders is $128.7 million for 121 days around the takeover announcement. The aggregate gain of $60.7 ($189.4 − 128.7) is not statistically significant, on the basis of a parametric test, though a nonparametric test does indicate significance. Varaiya also reports a cross-sectional regression that indicates that, the larger the target's dollar gain, the larger the bidder's dollar loss. The regression coefficient was −.81 ($t = -2.81$).

To summarize, the evidence about total gains in takeovers must be judged inconclusive. Results based on returns are unreliable. Malatesta's dollar-based results show a small aggregate gain in the months just around merger approval in a small matched sample and an aggregate loss in a larger unmatched sample. The interpretation of Malatesta's results is rendered difficult by the possibility of losses or gains in prior months, after announcement of a merger possibility but before final approval is a certainty. Dollar-based results presented by Bradley et al. (1982, 1983*a*) show a small and insignificant aggregate gain. Firth's (1980) British results show an insignificant aggregate loss. Both Firth (1980) and Varaiya (1985) present persuasive evidence for the existence of overbidding. But, on balance, the existence of either gains or losses to the combined firms involved in corporate combinations remains in doubt.

This mixed and insignificant evidence is made even less conclusive (if that is possible) by potential measurement biases. There is a potential upward bias in the measured price reaction of bidding firms (and thus of the aggregate) caused by contaminating information. There is a potential downward bias due to prior anticipation of the takeover event, as explained by Schipper and Thompson (1983), and another potential downward bias in some studies due to an improper computation of abnormal returns (Chung and Weston 1985). These biases will be discussed in detail next, in connection with the empirical findings for bidding firms.

C. Evidence about Bidding Firms: The Announcement Effect

The hubris hypothesis predicts a decrease in the value of the bidding firm. As pointed out previously, this decrease may not be completely reflected in a market price decline because of contaminating information in a bid, because the bid has been (partly) anticipated, or simply because the economic loss is too small to be reliably reflected in prices.

The data contain several interesting patterns. Asquith (1983) finds that bidding firm shares show "no consistent pattern" around the announcement date, but, "in summary, bidding firms appear to have small but insignificant positive excess returns at the press day" (p. 66). Some of Asquith's other results are understandable under the hubris hypothesis. Before the first merger bid, for instance, firms who become successful bidders have much larger price increases than firms whose bids are unsuccessful. One would expect a higher level of hubris and thus more aggressive pursuit of a target in firms that had experienced recent good times.

Asquith's results are in conflict with those of Dodd (1980), who finds statistically significant negative returns at the bid announcement. Jensen and Ruback (1983) noted the difference in results, and they asked Dodd to check his data and computer program, which they report (Jensen and Ruback 1983, p. 17, n. 12) he did without finding an error.[1]

Negative bidder returns were also found by Eger (1983) in her study of pure exchange (noncash) mergers. Bidding firm stock prices de-

1. Recently, Chung and Weston (1985) suggested that part of the difference in results could be explained by an improper calculation of "abnormal" returns around the merger announcement. Chung and Weston point out that the premerger period generally displays statistically significant positive returns for bidding firms. If data from this period are used to estimate abnormal returns at merger announcement, the measured announcement effect will be biased downward. The reported diffrence between, say, Dodd (1980) and Asquith (1983) would be reduced by a recalculation by Dodd excluding the preannouncement period. However, it probably would not be entirely eliminated; the bias appears to be only a small fraction of Dodd's observed announcement effect.

clined, on average by about 4%, from 5 days prior to merger bid announcement to 10 days afterward (Eger 1983, table 4, p. 563). The decline was statistically significant. Eger suggests that the difference between her results and Asquith's (1983) might be attributable to a difference between mergers involving cash and pure stock exchange mergers; and she notes that tender offers, which often involve cash, seem to display more positive bidder stock price reactions (see below).

In his study of United Kingdom takeovers, Firth (1980) reports statistically significant negative bidding firm returns in the month of the takeover announcement. Eighty percent of the bidders had negative abnormal returns during that month, and the t-statistic for the average return was about -5.0 (cf. Firth 1980, table 5, p. 248).

Varaiya (1985) also finds statistically significant negative returns for bidding firms on the announcement day. He reports also that the bidder's loss is significantly larger when there are rival bidders.

A recent paper by Ruback and Mikkelson (1984) documents announcement effects of corporate purchases of another corporation's shares according to the stated purpose of the acquisition (filed on form 13-D with the Securities and Exchange Commission). The 2-day announcement effect for acquiring firms was positive and statistically significant for the 370 firms whose stated purpose was not a takeover. In contrast, for 134 acquiring firms indicating an intention to effect a takeover, the announcement effect was negative and significant (table 4, p. 17).

Studies of individual cases have been mixed. For example, Ruback (1982) argues that DuPont's large stock price decline in announcing a bid to take over Conoco could be an indication that managers (of DuPont) "had an objective function different from that of shareholder wealth maximization" (p. 24). However, he rejects this explanation because of "the magnitude of Conoco's revaluation and the lack of evidence that DuPont's management benefitted from the acquisition" (p. 24). He also rejects every other explanation except inside information possessed by DuPont and not yet appreciated by the market; but even this hypothesis "cannot be confirmed since the nature of the information is unknown" (p. 25).

One interesting aspect of the DuPont/Conoco case is that DuPont's decline was more than offset by Conoco's gain; that is, the total gain was positive (although the bidding firm lost). This suggests that nonhubris factors were indeed present, bringing a total gain to the corporate combination, but that overbidding was present too, resulting in a loss to DuPont shareholders.

The other case study by Ruback (1983) finds only a small negative effect for Occidental Petroleum in its bid for Cities Service. Cities Service's stock price increased by a relatively small amount for a target firm, and the total effect was positive. Apparently, there was little significant hubris evidenced by Occidental (who offered only a small premium). An interesting sidelight was the performance of Gulf Oil, a rival bidder who withdrew. It suffered a loss far in excess of Cities Service's gain.

Schipper and Thompson (1983) find a positive price reaction around the announcement that a firm is embarking on a program of conglomerate acquisitions. Also they observe negative price reactions of such firms to antimerger regulatory events. The two findings are interpreted as at least consistent with the proposition that acquisitions are positive net present value projects for the bidding firm. However, the authors emphasize the tentative nature of their conclusion (pp. 109–11). For example, they note that the announcement of an acquisition program is sometimes accompanied by "announcements of related policy decisions, such as de-emphasis of old lines of business, changes in management, changes in capital structure or specific merger proposals" (p. 89). Even without such explicit contaminating information, announcement of the program could be interpreted as good news about the future profitability of the bidder's current assets rather than about the prospect of an undisclosed future target firm to be obtained at a bargain price.

The possibility of contaminating information is a central problem in interpreting the price movement of a bidding firm on the announcement date of an intended acquisition. Bidders are activists in the takeover situation, and their announcements may convey as much information about their own prospects as about the takeover. To mention one example of the measurement problem, mergers are usually leverage-increasing events. It is well documented from studies of other leverage-increasing events, such as exchange offers (Masulis 1980) and share repurchases (Vermaelen 1981), that positive price movements are to be expected. Thus to measure properly that part of the gain of a bidding firm in a merger that is attributable to the merger per se and not to an increase in leverage, we ought to deduct the price increase that would have been obtained by the same firm through independently increasing its leverage by the same amount.[2]

The measurement problem induced by the disparate sizes of target and bidder is the subject of a paper by Jarrell (1983). Jarrell argues that, when a bidder is several times larger than a target, a gain to the bidder equal in size to the gain observed in the target can be hidden in the noise of the bidder's return variability; that is, the t-statistic for the bidder's effect is likely to be much smaller than for the target's effect. Jarrell suggests solving this problem by adjusting the bidder's t-statistic upward by a factor proportional to the relative sizes of bidder and target. When he makes the adjustment in his sample, bidding firms

2. I am grateful to Sheridan Titman for pointing out this possibility.

display significantly positive price movements from 30 days prior to 10 days after the takeover announcement. The mean abnormal return prior to adjustment is 2.3%; after adjustment it is 9.2%. Similarly, the combined bidder and target returns become more statistically significant.

The problem with the Jarrell adjustment is that it can be applied to any sample in order to render a sample mean of either sign statistically significant. For example, if Firth (1980) had adjusted his bidding firm returns downward according to the relative sizes of bidder and target, he could have concluded that British takeovers had significant aggregate negative effects on shareholders. This does not imply that Jarrell's conclusions are incorrect, but we are certainly entitled to remain skeptical. Several studies have reported positive bidder gains, and several others have reported losses. Applying the Jarrell technique indiscriminately to all of them could make the gains or losses more "significant," but this would simply create more confusion since the now "significant" results would disagree across studies.

D. *Evidence about Bidding Firms: Resolution of Doubtful Success*

There is some evidence available to help isolate the reevaluation of a bidding firm's own assets induced by the bid but not caused by the proposed corporate combination itself. Asquith's (1983) sample of bidding firms in mergers is separated into successful and unsuccessful bidders, and both samples are examined prior to bid announcement, between announcement and merger outcome, and after outcome. For the successful group, merger outcome is the actual date when the target firm is delisted; this is presumably the effective date of the merger. At the original bid announcement, the market cannot know for sure whether such firms actually will consummate the merger, that is, be in the "successful" group. There is only a probability of success. Between the bid announcement and the final outcome this probability goes to 1.0 for firms in the successful group. Thus if the combination itself has value for the bidder, these bidding firms should increase in value over this interim period. They do not. On average, successful bidding firms decline in value by .5% over the interim period (see Asquith 1983, fig. 4, p. 71; table 9, p. 81). The decrease in value is small and statistically insignificant, but the result has economic significance because the opposite sign must be observed if the corporate combination per se has value. If the combination has substantial value, one might have expected to observe a statistically significant upward price movement between bid announcement and outcome, provided, of course, that the upward revision in probability of success is large enough to show up.

Firms in Asquith's successful bidder group have very large prebid returns; abnormal returns average 14.3% over a 460-day period ending

20 days before the bid announcement. They have small positive returns (.2%) on the announcement date. The entire sequence of returns for successful bidding firms is consistent with the hubris hypothesis. In the prebid period, excellent performance endows management with both hubris and cash. A target is selected. The bid itself signals a small upward revision in the market's estimate of the bidding firm's current assets that is not completely offset by the prospect of paying too much for the target. Then there is a small downward revision in bidder firm value as it becomes more probable and then certain that the target will be acquired (at too high a price).

Eckbo (1983) reports a small and insignificant decline during the 3 days subsequent to the initial merger bid. But Eckbo's "successful" bidder is defined as one who is unchallenged on antitrust grounds; this may be a less relevant representation of actual success for our purposes here.

Eger (1983, p. 563) finds significant negative bidder firm returns averaging −3.1% in the 20 days after the original announcement of a merger that is ultimately successful. Most of this decline occurs in the first 10 days after the merger announcement. The bonds of these firms also decline slightly in price over the same period. This is consistent with a price decline in the total value of the bidding firm as it becomes more certain that the merger will succeed.

The most significant price decline between merger proposal and outcome is reported by Dodd (1980). Successful bidding firms decline in value by 7.22% from 10 days before the bid is announced until 10 days after the merger outcome, where outcome is defined as target stockholder approval of merger bid. The price decline is statistically significant. In the 20 days prior to the outcome date, successful bidder firms in Dodd's sample fall in price by about 2% (p. 124).

Evidence from papers using monthly data is more difficult to interpret, but the patterns do seem consistent with a negative price movement between merger announcement and successful outcome. For example, Langetieg's (1978, p. 377) bidding firms show a significant price decline continuing in the combined firm after the merger outcome. Similarly, Chung and Weston (1982, p. 334) report price declines between merger announcement month and merger completion in pure conglomerate mergers. However, the decline is not statistically significant.

Similar evidence is given in Malatesta (1983, table 4, p. 172). Acquiring firms in this sample have significant negative price performance in the period after the first announcement of a merger proposal. Since the data are monthly, the merger outcome date could be included somewhere in the sample period. This means that part of the puzzling post-outcome negative performance detected by Langetieg (1978) and Asquith (1983) might be included in Malatesta's table 4 results. In tables 5 and 6 Malatesta presents performance results for acquiring firms after the "first announcement of board/management approval of the merger" (p. 170). The returns are strongly negative in this period. This might not be such a puzzle if "board/management approval" still leaves open the possibility of withdrawal, for then the absolute certainty of merger (and the concomitant price drop expected under the hubris hypothesis) would occur sometime after this particular event date.

In summary, during the interim period between initial bid and successful outcome, the average price movement of successful merger bids is small, so it is not possible to draw strong implications. However, the pattern is generally consistent with the hubris hypothesis, which predicts the observed loss in value of bidding firm's shares. The loss is statistically insignificant in Asquith's sample but is significant in the samples of Dodd (1980) and Eger (1983) and in the monthly data samples of Langetieg (1978) and Malatesta (1983).

Evidence about the interim period from tender offer studies is mixed. One study seems to be clearly inconsistent with hubris alone; Bradley's (1980) sample of 88 successful bidding firms shows a price rise after the announcement data and before the execution date. The number is not given, but the plot of the mean abnormal price index (p. 366) indicates that the gain is approximately 2%–3%.

The interim price movement of the successful acquiring firm is reported by Ruback and Mikkelson (1984) as −1.07% with a *t*-statistic of −2.34 (table 6). Their sample is not dichotomized by merger versus tender offers, however, and it probably contains some of both types of takeovers.

The results given by Kummer and Hoffmeister (1978) for a 17-firm matched sample of tender offers are more difficult to interpret because the data are monthly and, apparently because of the small size of the cross-sectional sample, the time series of prices relative to the event data appears to be more variable. Abnormal returns are positive and largest in the announcement month but are also positive in months +1 and +2. If the tender offer is revolved sometime during these 2 months, the results are basically the same as Bradley's (1980). Months +3 to +12 witness a decline of about 4%. If the success of the tender offer is not known until sometime during this period, an interpretation could be made similar to the one discussed above concerning Asquith's and Dodd's samples of successful merger bids.

An identical set of nonconclusive inferences can be drawn from the monthly data of Dodd and Ruback (1977). There appears to be a positive price movement by successful bidders just after the announcement month followed by a price decline later. The decline over the 12 months after a bid amounts to −1.32%, but it is not statistically significant.

Bradley's daily results probably represent the best available evidence against the hubris hypothesis. The detected movement is small, but, unlike the case of merger's, the bidding firm's price does increase on average in Bradley's sample. This is consistent with the proposition that tender offers increase aggregate value and that some of the increase accrues to tender offer bidders. Whether the evidence is sufficiently compelling, particularly when balanced against evidence of an opposite character, is up to further investigation to decide definitely.

One other piece of evidence from the interim period between announcement and outcome is worthy of comtemplation. This is the price behavior of the first bidder's stock on the announcement of a rival bid. In their study of unsuccessful tender offers, Bradley et al. (1983*b*) report a significant price drop in the first bidder's stock. In contrast, Ruback and Mikkelson (1984) report a significant price increase (table 5); however, the latter sample consists not only of ultimately unsuccessful bidders in tender offers but of all corporate investors in other stock (including many who are not contemplating a takeover).

A price drop in the first takeover bidder's stock on the announcement of a rival bid is explainable by hubris. The rival bid may set off a bidding war that the market expects to result in a large loss for the winner. It would be extremely informative to observe the price reaction of the first bidder when it becomes evident that the rival bidder has won.

Finally, it should be noted that the price change after the resolution of a successful bid (either merger or tender offer) is almost uniformly negative (cf. Jensen and Ruback 1983, table 4, p. 21) and is relatively large in magnitude. This is a result that casts doubt on all estimates of bidding firm returns because it suggests the presence of substantial measurement problems.

III. Summary and Discussion

The purpose of this paper is to bring attention to a possible explanation of the takeover phenomenon of mergers and tender offers. This explanation, the hubris hypothesis, is very simple: decision makers in acquiring firms pay too much for their targets on average in the samples we observe. The samples, however, are not random. Potential bids are abandoned whenever the acquiring firm's valuation of the target turns up with a figure below the current market price. Bids are rendered when the valuation exceeds the price. If there really are no gains in takeovers, hubris is necessary to explain why managers do not abandon these bids also since reflection would suggest that such bids are likely to represent positive errors in valuation.

The hubris hypothesis can serve as the null hypothesis of corporate takeovers because it asserts that all markets are strong-form efficient.

Financial markets are aware of all information. Product markets are efficiently organized. Labor markets are characterized by managers being employed in their best operational positions.

Hubris predicts that, around a takeover, (*a*) the combined value of the target and bidder firms should fall slightly, (*b*) the value of the bidding firm should decrease, and (*c*) the value of the target should increase. The available empirical results indicate that the measured combined value has increased in some studies and decreased in others. It has been statistically significant in none. Measured changes in the prices of bidding firms have been mixed in sign across studies and mostly of a very small order of magnitude. Several studies have reported them to be significantly negative, and other studies have reported the opposite. Target firm prices consistently display large increases, but only if the initial bid or a later bid is successful. There is no permanent increase in value for target firms that do not eventually enter a corporate combination.

The interpretation of bidding firm returns is complicated by several potential measurement problems. The bid can convey contaminating information, that is, information about the bidder rather than about the takeover itself. The bid can be partially anticipated and thus result in an announcement effect smaller in absolute value than the true economic effect. Since bidders are usually much larger than targets, the effect of the bid can be buried in the noise of the bidder's return volatility. There is weak evidence from the interim period between the announcement of a merger and the merger outcome that the merger itself results in a loss to the bidding firm's shareholders; but the interim period in tender offers shows some results that favor the opposite view. Both findings have minimal statistical reliability.

The final impression one is obliged to draw from the currently available results is that they provide no really convincing evidence against even the extreme (hubris) hypothesis that all markets are operating perfectly efficiently and that individual bidders occasionally make mistakes. Bidders may indicate by their actions a belief in the existence of takeover gains, but systematic studies have provided little to show that such beliefs are well founded.

Finally, I should mention several issues that have arisen as objections by others to the hubris idea. First, the hubris hypothesis might seem to imply that managers act consciously against shareholder interests. Several recent papers that have examined nontakeover corporate control devices have concluded that the evidence is consistent with conscious management actions against the best interests of shareholders.[3] But the hubris hypothesis does not rely on this result. It is

3. See Bradley and Wakeman (1983), Dann and DeAngelo (1983), and DeAngelo and Rice (1983). Linn and McConnell (1983) disagree with the last paper. The possibility that managers do not act in the interest of stockholders has frequently been associated with the takeover phenomenon. For example, in a recent review, Lev (1983, p. 15) concludes

sufficient that managers act, de facto, against shareholder interests by issuing bids founded on mistaken estimates of target firm value. Management intentions may be fully consistent with honorable stewardship of corporate assets, but actions need not always turn out to be right.

Second, it might seem that the hubris hypothesis implies systematic biases in market prices. One correspondent argued that stock prices would be systematically too high for reasons similar to those advanced in E. M. Miller's (1977) paper. This implication is not correct, however, for the simple reason that firms can be either targets or bidders. If bidders offer too much, their stock price will fall ex post while their target's price will rise. On average over all stocks, this cancels. Unless one can predict which firms will be targets and which will be bidders, there is no bias in any individual firm, and there is certainly no bias on average over all firms.

Third, an argument can be advanced that the hubris hypothesis implies an inefficiency in the market for corporate control. If all takeovers were prompted by hubris, shareholders could stop the practice by forbidding managers ever to make any bid. Since such prohibitions are not observed, hubris alone cannot explain the takeover phenomenon.

The validity of this argument depends on the size of deadweight takeover costs. If such costs are relatively small, stockholders would be indifferent to hubris-inspired bids because target firm shareholders would gain what bidding firm shareholders lose. A well-diversified shareholder would receive the aggregate gain, which is close to zero.

Fourth, and finally, a frequent objection is that hubris itself is based on a market inefficiency defined in a particular way; in the words of one writer, "It seems to me that your hypothesis does not rest on strong form efficiency, because it presumes that one set of market bidders is systematically irrational" (private correspondence). This argument contends that a market is inefficient if some market participants make systematic mistakes. Perhaps one of the long-term benefits of studying takeovers is to clarify the notion of market efficiency. Does efficiency mean that every individual behaves like the rational, maximizing ideal? Or does it mean instead that market interactions generate prices and allocations indistinguishable from those that would have been generated by rational individuals?

References

Asquith, P. 1983. Merger bids, uncertainty, and stockholder returns. *Journal of Financial Economics* 11 (April): 51–83.

by saying, I think we are justified in doubting . . . the argument that mergers are done to maximize stockholder wealth." Foster (1983) seems to share this view or at least the view that bidders make big mistakes. Larcker (1983) presents interesting results that managers in large takeovers are more likely to have short-term, accounting-based compensation contracts. He finds that, the more accounting-based the compensation, the more negative is the market price reaction to a bid. Larcker also suggests that managers who own less stock in their own company are more likely to make bids.

Asquith, P.; Bruner, R. F.; and Mullins, D. W., Jr. 1983. The gains to bidding firms from merger. *Journal of Financial Economics* 11 (April): 121–39.

Bradley, M. 1980. Interfirm tender offers and the market for corporate control. *Journal of Business* 53 (October): 345–76.

Bradley, M.; Desai, A.; and Kim, E. H. 1982. Specialized resources and competition in the market for corporate control. Typescript. Ann Arbor: University of Michigan, Graduate School of Business.

Bradley, M.; Desai, A.; and Kim, E. H. 1983*a*. Determinants of the wealth effects of corporate acquisition via tender offers: Theory and evidence. Typescript. Ann Arbor: University of Michigan, Graduate School of Business.

Bradley, M.; Desai, A.; and Kim, E. H. 1983*b*. The rationale behind interfirm tenders offers: Information or synergy? *Journal of Financial Economics* 11 (April): 183–206.

Bradley, M., and Wakeman, L. Mac. 1983. The wealth effects of targeted share repurchases. *Journal of Financial Economics* 11 (April): 301–28.

Capan, E. C.; Clapp, R. V.; and Campbell, W. M. 1971. Competitive bidding in high risk situations. *Journal of Petroleum Technology* (June), pp. 641–53.

Chung, K. S., and Weston, J. F. 1982. Diversification and mergers in a strategic long-range planning framework. In M. Keenan and L. I. White (eds.), *Mergers and Acquisitions*. Lexington, Mass.: D. C. Heath.

Chung, K. S., and Weston, J. F. 1985. Model-created bias in residual analysis of mergers. Working paper. Los Angeles: University of California, Los Angeles, Graduate School of Management.

Dann, L. Y., and DeAngelo, H. 1983. Standstill agreements, privately negotiated stock repurchases, and the market for corporate control. *Journal of Financial Economics* 11 (April): 275–300.

DeAngelo, H., and Rice, E. M. 1983. Antitakeover charter amendments and stockholder wealth. *Journal of Financial Economics* 11 (April): 329–60.

Dodd, P. 1980. Merger proposals, managerial discretion and stockholder wealth. *Journal of Financial Economics* 8 (June): 105–38.

Dodd, P., and Ruback, R. 1977. Tender offers and stockholder returns: An empirical analysis. *Journal of Financial Economics* 5 (December): 351–74.

Dougherty, F. L., and Lohrenz, J. 1976. Statistical analysis of bids for Federal offshore leases. *Journal of Petroleum Technology* (November), pp. 1377–90.

Eckbo, B. E. 1983. Horizontal mergers, collusion and stockholder wealth. *Journal of Financial Economics* 11 (April): 241–73.

Eger, C. E. 1983. An empirical test of the redistribution effect in pure exchange mergers. *Journal of Financial and Quantitative Analysis* 18 (December): 547–72.

Firth, M. 1980. Takeovers, shareholder returns and the theory of the firm. *Quarterly Journal of Economics* (March): 235–60.

Foster, G. 1983. Comments on M & A analysis and the role of investment bankers. *Midland Corporate Finance Journal* 1 (Winter): 36–38.

Halpern, P. J. 1973. Empirical estimates of the amount and distribution of gains to companies in mergers. *Journal of Business* 46 (October): 554–75.

Jarrell, G. A. 1983. Do acquirers benefit from corporate acquisition? Typescript. Chicago: University of Chicago, Center for the Study of the Economy and the State.

Jensen, M. C., and Ruback, R. S. 1983. The market for corporate control. *Journal of Financial Economics* 11 (April): 5–50.

Kahneman, D.; Slovic, P.; and Tversky, A. 1982. *Judgment under Uncertainty: Heuristics and Biases*. New York: Cambridge University Press.

Kummer, D. R., and Hoffmeister, J. R. 1978. Valuation consequences of cash tender offers. *Journal of Finance* 33 (May): 505–16.

Langetieg, T. C. 1978. An application of a three-factor performance index to measure stockholder gains from merger. *Journal of Financial Economics* 6 (December): 365–83.

Larcker, D. 1983. Managerial incentives in mergers and their effect on shareholder wealth. *Midland Corporate Finance Journal* 1 (Winter): 29–35.

Lev, B. 1983. Observations on the merger phenomenon and review of the evidence. *Midland Corporate Finance Journal* 1 (Winter): 6–16.

Linn, S. C., and McConnell, J. J. 1983. An empirical investigation of the impact of "antitakeover" amendments on common stock prices. *Journal of Financial Economics* 11 (April): 361–99.

Malatesta, P. H. 1983. The wealth effect of merger activity and the objective functions of merging firms. *Journal of Financial Economics* 11 (April): 155–81.
Masulis, R. W. 1980. The effects of capital structure change on security prices: A study of exchange offers. *Journal of Financial Economics* 8 (June): 139–77.
Miller, E. M. 1977. Risk, uncertainty and the divergence of opinion. *Journal of Finance* 32 (September): 1151–68.
Oskamp, S. 1965. Overconfidence in case study judgments. *Journal of Consulting Psychology* 29 (June): 261–65.
Ruback, R. S. 1982. The Conoco takeover and stockholder returns. *Sloan Management Review* 14 (Winter): 13–33.
Ruback, R. S. 1983. The Cities Service takeover: A case study. *Journal of Finance* 38 (May): 319–30.
Ruback, R. S., and Mikkelson, W. H. 1984. Corporate investments in common stock. Working paper. Cambridge: Massachusetts Institute of Technology, Sloan School of Business.
Schipper, K., and Thompson, R. 1983. Evidence on the capitalized value of merger activity for acquiring firms. *Journal of Financial Economics* 11 (April): 85–119.
Tversky, A., and Kahneman, D. 1981. The framing of decisions and the psychology of choice. *Science* 211 (January 30): 453–58. Reprinted in Peter Diamond and Michael Rothschild. 1978. *Uncertainty in Economics*. New York: Academic Press.
Varaiya, N. 1985. A test of Roll's Hubris Hypothesis of corporate takeovers. Working paper. Dallas, Tex.: Southern Methodist University, School of Business.
Vermaelen, T. 1981. Common stock repurchase and marketing signalling: An empirical study. *Journal of Financial Economics* 9 (June): 139–84.

[7]

Toeholds, Bid Jumps, and Expected Payoffs in Takeovers

Sandra Betton
Concordia University

B. Espen Eckbo
Dartmouth College

We estimate sequentially outcome probabilities and expected payoffs associated with first, second, and final bids in a large sample of tender offer contests. Rival bids arrive quickly and produce large bid jumps. Greater bidder toeholds (prebid ownership of target shares) reduce the probability of competition and target resistance and are associated with both lower bid premiums and lower prebid target stock price runups. The expected payoff to target shareholders is increasing in the bid premium and in the probability of competition, but decreasing in the bidder's toehold. The initial bidder's expected payoff is significantly positive in the "rival-bidder-win" outcome, in part reflecting gains from the pending toehold sale. Despite these dramatic toehold effects, only half of the initial bidders acquire toeholds.

There is substantial theoretical support for the notion that the size of the bidder's toehold (preoffer ownership stake in the target) plays an important role in the formulation of optimal bidding strategies. In Shleifer and Vishny (1986), Hirshleifer and Titman (1990), and Chowdry and Jegadeesh (1994), a toehold helps overcome the free-rider problem among target shareholders described by Grossman and Hart (1980). Owning a toehold gives a bidder a profit from a successful takeover, even if it has to pay the expected full value

---

Earlier drafts of this article were entitled "Toeholds, Competition, and State-Contingent Payoffs in Takeovers" and "State-Contingent Payoffs in Takeovers: New Structural Estimates" [Betton and Eckbo (1997)]. We are grateful for the comments and suggestions of Jonathan Berk, Larry Dann, Wayne Ferson, Robert Hansen, Robert Harris, Cliff Holderness, Burton Hollifield, Robert Jennings, Charles Kahn, Paul Malatesta, Øyvind Norli, Enrico Perotti, Jay Ritter, David Smith, Barbara Spencer, Matthew Spiegel, Rene Stulz, Sheridan Titman (the editor), Theo Vermaelen, Joseph Williams, Robert White, an anonymous referee, and seminar participants at Boston College, Boston University, Dartmouth College, Gothenburg University, INSEAD, the Norwegian School of Economics, Norwegian School of Management, Securities and Exchange Commission, Simon Fraser University, Stockholm School of Economics, Southern Methodist University, University of Aarhus, University of Amsterdam, University of British Columbia, University of Illinois at Urbana-Champaign, University of Florida at Gainesville, University of California at Riverside, University of Southern California, University of Vienna, University of Washington, University of Toronto, and the meetings of the European Finance Association, the American Finance Association, the Nordic Symposium on Corporate and Institutional Finance (Oslo), the Utah Winter Finance Conference, and the Lisabon Conference on Corporate Finance of the Center for Economic Policy Research (CEPR, London). Address correspondance to B. Espen Eckbo, Tuck School at Dartmouth, Hanover, NH 03755. The authors' e-mail addresses are b.espen.eckbo@dartmouth.edu and betton@vax2.concordia.ca.

The Review of Financial Studies Winter 2000 Vol. 13, No. 4, pp. 841–882

for any shares bought in the tender offer.[1] In Burkart (1995), Singh (1998), and Bulow, Huang, and Klemperer (1999), the dual nature of the offer price as a bid for the remaining shares and an ask for the toehold leads to aggressive bidding behavior.[2] Intuitively the toehold reduces the number of target shares that must be purchased at a costly premium, and it provides a capital gain should a rival bidder win the contest and purchase the toehold.

Despite the substantial theoretical interest in toeholds, available empirical evidence on the impact of toeholds on takeover bids is sparse. Examining block purchases that exceed 5% and therefore trigger 13d disclosures with the Securities and Exchange Commission (SEC), the evidence in Mikkelson and Ruback (1985), Choi (1991), and Barclay and Holderness (1991) suggests that stock price runups observed prior to takeover bid announcements are in part driven by these early toehold acquisitions. Bradley, Desai, and Kim (1988) report average toeholds of 10% at the time of the takeover bid, and Jennings and Mazzeo (1993) report that toeholds decrease the probability of target management resistance. There is little evidence on the effect of toeholds on bidder returns, and the evidence on target returns is ambiguous: Target returns are found to either decrease with toeholds [Eckbo and Langohr (1989) and Jarrell and Poulsen (1989)], increase [Franks and Harris (1989)], or have no effect [Stulz, Walkling, and Song (1990)].

This article provides evidence on the size and impact of premiums and toeholds on outcome probabilities and expected payoffs using a comprehensive sample of 2,335 takeover bids taking place in 1,353 tender offer contests from 1971 to 1990. Our main contribution is threefold: First, we structure the empirical analysis around *entire tender offer contests* so that it closely replicates the actual bidding environment. Existing studies of tender offers tend to offer systematic information on final—but not on initial—bids and thus are not as well suited to examine bidding arguments.[3] We provide information on the speed of arrival of rival bids, the size of the bid jumps, and on the duration and final outcome of the entire auction. We show that rival bids arrive quickly, typically within 15 days,[4] and generate substantial bid jumps: between the first and the second bid, the premium increases on average 31%.

[1] In these models, all of a bidder's profit is accounted for by gains on its toehold. In the Shleifer–Vishny and Hirshleifer–Titman models, increasing the toehold reduces the successful bid price, while it increases the successful offer price in the Chowdry–Jegadeesh model. The empirical analysis below addresses these predictions.

[2] In the Bulow–Huang–Klemperer model with common value bidders, such aggressiveness increases the winner's curse for a nontoeholder and makes *its* bid more conservative in an ascending auction. This in turn reduces the toeholder's winner's curse and allows it to be more aggressive still, creating a potentially powerful feedback loop. "So owning a toehold can help the bidder win an auction, and win cheaply" (p. 428). These models also imply that bidders sometimes rationally "overpay" for the targets ex post, without appealing to managerial hubris or agency problems. See also Chowdry and Nanda (1993) and Eckbo and Thorburn (2000b) in the context of debt-financed bidding.

[3] For example, Bradley, Desai, and Kim (1988) sample successful (and thus *final*) bids only, thus ignoring information on earlier bids in multiple-bid contests. Similarly, although Jennings and Mazzeo (1993) and Schwert (1996) sample unsuccessful as well as successful bids, they do not identify the bid sequence in multiple-bid contests.

[4] Under the Williams Act, the initial tender offer must be outstanding at least 20 days.

Second, our empirical analysis explicitly accounts for the joint impact of four key offer characteristics: The offer premium, the toehold, target shareholder tender precommitments (which increases the bidder's *effective* toehold), as well as the payment method (cash versus stock). Several models suggest that these offer parameters are important in the takeover process. For example, in Giammarino and Heinkel (1986), Fishman (1988), and Hirshleifer and Png (1989), a high initial bid premium signals a high bidder valuation which deters competition in an environment where bidding is costly. In Fishman (1989), the choice of payment method also affects competition as the unconditional nature (with respect to the true target value) of a cash payment can be used as a signal by high-valuation bidders. Focusing on single-bidder environments, Hansen (1987), Berkovitch and Narayanan (1990), Eckbo, Giammarino, and Heinkel (1990), and Brown and Ryngaert (1992) also stress the signaling benefit of cash as a payment method. However, structural tests of the signaling argument have so far failed to provide much empirical support [Eckbo, Giammarino, and Heinkel (1990)].

We find that toeholds are largest in successful, single-bid contests (average 20%) and smallest in multiple-bid contests (average 5%). Simultaneous equation estimation indicates that toeholds and offer premiums are negatively correlated, which is consistent with the comparative statics results of Shleifer and Vishny (1986) and Hirshleifer and Titman (1990), but fails to support the signaling argument of Chowdry and Jegadeesh (1994). Moreover, we find that toeholds are smaller the greater the prebid run-up in the target's share price, which fails to support the model of Ravid and Spiegel (1999).[5] When the initial bid fails to deter competition, the first and the second bidder turn out to own similar toeholds, a possibility that is addressed by the model in Bulow, Huang, and Klemperer (1999).

The model of Bulow, Huang, and Klemperer (1999) also implies that if two or more bidders have toeholds, offer prices will be highest if all bidders have toeholds of similar size. Thus it may pay the target firm to "level the playing field" by giving a rival bidder the opportunity to buy a toehold cheaply. Our evidence shows that the target enters into a share tender agreement with the initial bidder—which is one way for the target to equalize effective toeholds in anticipation of rival bids—in 23% of the cases. However, these initial bids attract competition (or are revised) at a much lower rate than the typical initial bid. Thus we cannot conclude that these share tender agreements are designed to increase competition among rival bidders. Overall, while there appears to be significant benefits for the initial bidder to acquire a toehold,

[5] A toehold purchase that creates rumors of a pending takeover bid results in a run-up in the target share price. In Ravid and Spiegel (1999), this run-up increases the total cost (premium) of the takeover because the legally permissible amount of dilution in a minority freeze-out merger is constrained by the preoffer price.

a puzzling 47% of all initial bidders in the sample enter the contest with a zero toehold.[6]

Third, a major objective of this article is to perform a sequential, forward-looking estimation of offer outcome probabilities and expected payoffs as a function of offer characteristics. This analysis requires a structure outlining the most relevant outcomes facing *any* initial bidder and, for this purpose, we use the contest tree shown in Figure 1. The tree structure in Figure 1 exploits the large dataset as each of the 11 outcomes (nodes) in the tree contains a substantial number of sample bids (shown in parentheses). If the market uses the same tree structure to price the bid, then the stock price reaction to the bid announcement equals the product of the probabilities and payoffs summed across all the nodes in the tree. We use this assumption to estimate the payoffs at each individual node as parameters in cross-sectional regressions of announcement returns on outcome probabilities. These parameter estimates in turn allow us to compute the expected value of the offer conditional on a given offer configuration (bid premium, toehold, payment method, etc.).

We find that at the time of the initial bid, the probability of a successful single-bid contest increases with the size of the offer premium, the toehold, with the presence of a prebid tender agreement. Following the entry of a rival bidder, *none* of these offer parameters are significant predictors of which bidder (if any) will eventually win the contest. Thus it appears that the "strategic" effect of key offer characteristics such as the bid premium and toehold is limited to the initial bid. Contrary to the finding of Jennings and Mazzeo (1993) and others, the payment method is not found to be a significant determinant of the outcome probabilities anywhere in the contest tree. It appears that the marginal impact of the payment method is swamped by toehold effects.

We also find that the payoff to target shareholders increases with the probability of a successful contest, with the probability of multiple bids, and with the probability that a rival bidder eventually wins the contest. Our results generalize to an ex ante framework the well-known finding in the literature that target gains are on average greater in multiple-bid contests than in single-bid contests [e.g., Bradley, Desai, and Kim (1988)]. However, we also show that the toehold size plays a fundamental role in producing this effect. Ex ante, target gains decrease with the size of the initial bidder's toehold because the greater the toehold, the greater the probability of the relatively low target payoff in the single-bid success outcome.

As to bidder firms, there is no evidence that the expected value of the initial bid is significantly different from zero. This is consistent with the generally insignificant ex post average abnormal returns to bidders reported in

[6] In their sample of 236 successful tender offers, Bradley, Desai, and Kim (1988) also report that a substantial proportion (66%) of the bidders have zero toeholds.

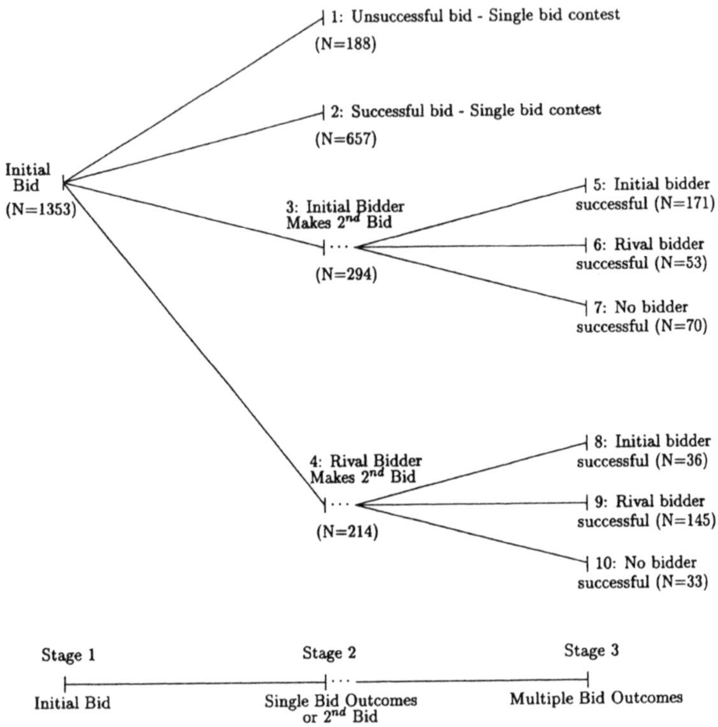

Figure 1
Sequence of outcomes and sample size (*N*) in tender offer contest tree
There are up to 10 sample bids in a single contest between stage 2 and stage 3.

the literature.[7] However, again this conclusion appears to depend on the initial toehold: The initial bidder's payoff is found to be significantly positive in the "rival bidder wins" outcome of the contest tree. Since there is no evidence of significantly negative initial bidder payoff in any of the successful outcomes, nor is there evidence of a positive bidder payoff when the target rejects *all* bids, there is no direct evidence of "overbidding." A consistent interpretation of the positive payoff associated with the "rival bidder wins" outcome is that it reflects expected gains from selling the initial toehold to the successful rival bidder.

The rest of the article is organized as follows. Section 1 details our contest event tree structure and the sample selection procedures. Section 2 describes

[7] See Eckbo and Thorburn (2000a) for a review of the literature and large-sample evidence of significantly positive average bidder gains in domestic acquisitions in Canada.

The Review of Financial Studies / v 13 n 4 2000

the basic characteristics of the tender offer contests in terms of duration, time between successive bids, average offer premiums, and toeholds. Section 3 details the structural estimation of the contest tree in Figure 1, while Section 4 concludes.

1. Sample Selection and Contest Characteristics

1.1 Sample of tender offer contests

To make a tender offer, the bidder must file a 14d statement with the SEC, which forms our initial sample source. We identified a total of 2,001 14d filings from January 1971 to December 1990, using the following three sources: (1) The *Austin* database, which includes 14d filings from January 1971 to December 1986. Filings which indicated a transaction value of less than $1 million or initial holdings of greater than 90% were excluded, resulting in 1643 filings. (2) The *Simon* database, obtained from the Dialog Electronic service (File #548, M & A Filings), which contains 14d filings for the period from January 1986 to December 1990. In order to be included, the filings had to have an indicated value of at least $1 million and be for at least 5% of the target shares, resulting in 261 filings. (3) The *Mergerstat Review*, which supplements the Simon data for 1987–1990 with an additional 97 filings.

For a given 14d filing, bids in the same *takeover contest* are identified by searching the *Wall Street Journal* index (WSJI) for bids or "continuation events" during the three calendar months before or after the tender offer announcement date. A continuation event is defined as any event that indicates that the contest is continuing, for example, due to additional bids, announcements that the target and bidder are negotiating, lawsuits are occurring, targets are searching for new bidders, etc. Announcement dates and contest beginning dates are taken from the WSJI. The WSJI information on ending dates is supplemented with information from the University of Chicago Center for Research in Security Prices (CRSP) tapes and the Commerce Clearing House (CCH) Corporate Capital Structure Changes Reporter. The 7-month search procedure is repeated for each identified bid or continuation event, and the starting and ending dates are given by the earliest and latest dates in the group of identified bids.[8] Note that this procedure identifies *all* bids for the target during the moving 7-month window, including unsuccessful initial merger bids that were followed by a 14d tender offer, tender offers that were withdrawn within 5 days and which according to SEC rules do not require a 14d filing, and any merger bid following an initial 14d tender offer.

[8] If information on the ending date is missing from the WSJI, we use the maximum of the latest announcement date and the latest identified ending date in the group of bids to define the duration of the contest. To the extent that this procedure also fails to produce an ending date, we consult the CRSP tape (for delisting dates) and the CCH Corporate Capital Structure Changes Reporter. The above procedure produces ending dates for all but 38 contests in the sample. For these 38 contests, the ending date is estimated as the median length of other contests occurring in the same year.

Of the 2,001 14d filings, 627 are excluded from the sample due to missing WSJ information on tender offer announcement dates and beginning and ending dates of the tender offer contests. Finally, another 21 contests are excluded because the initial bidder held more than 80% of the target prior to the offer. Sample firms which announced supermajority charter provisions during the sample period all required 80% shareholder support in order for a bidder to force a merger. Thus the 80% screen eliminates from the sample all minority buyouts in firms with supermajority provisions. The 80% screen also rules out tax-free stock swaps. The final sample consists of 1,353 tender offer contests over the period 1971–1990. The 1,353 contests represent 2,335 bids for 1,271 different targets. Sixty-four percent of all bids and 87% of all initial bids are represented by 14d filings.

1.2 Contest design and characteristics

Figure 1 shows the distribution of the final sample across the 10 potential outcomes in the contest tree following the initial bid. The tree includes only the most central events in a typical contest, and we focus in particular on the *initial*, *second*, and *final* bids (as it turns out, the configuration of other intermediate bids do not materially affect the final outcome probabilities). Moreover, for the purpose of the subsequent event study, we require each node in the tree to be identifiable in terms of a calendar date. As a result, there is no separate node for "target resistance," as signs of resistance typically emerge gradually between the initial and second bid. Instead, direct information on target management resistance is used as a determinant of the outcome probabilities conditional on a second bid in the contest (when the degree of resistance is typically known).

The contest tree in Figure 1 has three distinct stages. Stage 1 (node $n = 0$) reveals the vector of initial bid characteristics $\mathbf{x}$. This bid results in one of four possible events (stage 2):

- The contest ends with only one bid having been made. The initial bidder is either unsuccessful (node $n = 1$) or successful (node $n = 2$).
- A second bid is made in the contest, either by the initial bidder (node $n = 3$) or by a rival bidder (node $n = 4$).

Thus at stage 2, a decision is made whether or not to revise the initial bid, or for rival bidders to enter the contest. This decision in turn implies observed changes in the values of the initial bid vector $\mathbf{x}$. Finally, stage 3 reveals the outcome of multiple-bid contests, which may follow a number of rival bids and counterbids. The initial bidder wins (nodes $n = 5$ and $n = 8$), a rival bidder wins (nodes $n = 6$ and $n = 9$), or no bidder succeeds in acquiring the target (nodes $n = 7$ and $n = 10$).

The annual number of contests across each of the final outcome nodes ($n = 1, 2, 5, \ldots, 10$) is shown in Table 1 (for clarity, we are preserving the tree structure in terms of stages and nodes in several of our tables

The Review of Financial Studies / v 13 n 4 2000

Table 1
The number of takeover contests classified by the number of bidders and by the final outcome of the contest, 1971–1990

	Single bid contests[a]			Multiple bid contests[a]										
				2nd bid by initial bidder				2nd bid by rival bidder						
Year	S	U	All	S	SR	U	All	S	SR	U	All	Contest total	Bidder firms total	Takeover bids total
1971	10	9	19	0	0	0	0	0	0	0	0	19	18	19
1972	8	10	18	0	0	0	0	0	1	0	1	19	20	20
1973	34	17	51	2	0	0	2	1	3	0	4	57	60	67
1974	35	16	51	5	0	4	9	3	6	2	11	71	78	104
1975	15	8	23	7	1	0	8	1	1	0	2	33	32	48
1976	36	13	49	4	3	0	7	2	10	1	13	69	80	112
1977	42	26	68	11	2	9	22	2	4	4	10	100	116	157
1978	57	5	62	15	2	5	22	2	3	0	5	89	95	132
1979	54	4	58	5	5	0	10	4	9	1	14	82	101	123
1980	31	2	33	2	1	0	3	2	6	1	9	45	53	62
1981	32	8	40	6	2	3	11	3	10	1	14	65	78	118
1982	25	5	30	11	2	3	16	3	11	0	14	60	80	121
1983	14	6	20	7	3	0	10	2	7	0	9	39	56	83
1984	54	7	61	10	1	8	19	1	13	3	17	97	118	154

continued over

Table 1
(continued)

1985	39	3	42	9	3	5	17	2	14	2	18	77	104	145
1986	73	9	82	24	3	6	33	5	16	4	25	140	166	247
1987	36	12	48	20	11	6	37	0	13	7	20	105	138	222
1988	27	18	45	20	13	15	48	3	8	5	16	109	138	273
1989	23	7	30	12	1	3	16	0	9	2	11	57	78	102
1990	12	3	15	1	0	3	4	0	1	0	1	20	22	26
1971–1990	657	188	845	171	53	70	294	36	145	33	214	1353	1631	2335
Percent	48	14	62	13	4	5	22	3	11	2	16	100		
Maximum number of bids				11	12	9		6	12	8				
Maximum number of bidders				3	3	4		4	5	4				
Average number of bids				2.51	3.87	2.96		3.39	2.99	2.82				
Average number of bidders				1.08	2.09	1.36		2.11	2.29	2.24				

The sample sources are the Austin database (14d filings from 1971 to 1986) and the Simon database (14d filings from 1986 to 1990), supplemented with information from the *Mergerstat Review* and the University of Rochester MERC database. In order to be included in the sample, there must be a 14d filing for the target firm, and it must be possible to determine the starting date of the contest in the WSJI. Furthermore, offers must be for at least $1 million and minimum 5% of the target shares, and the bidder's prior toehold in the target must be less than 80%. Takeover bids are identified from 14d filings as well as from information in the WSJI. A takeover *contest* is a group of one or more bids for the same target firm. The 1,353 contests involve a total of 1,271 different target firms and 1,249 *different* bidder firms. Sixty-nine targets and 277 bidders were involved in more than one contest. Our sample contains a total of 1,457 14d filings for the 1,271 targets, that is, there are multiple filings for some targets. The duration of a contest is determined based on a search of the WSJI over 7 calendar months centered on each reported takeover bid for the target.

[a] Variable definitions: S, the first bidder wins the contest; SR, a rival bidder wins the contest; U, no bidder wins (target is not taken over). A bidder is classified as successful (wins the contest) if the bid increased the bidder's holding of target shares by at least 5%. In 6 of the 1,353 cases, this definition creates multiple winners. Fortunately, in each case one bidder later went on to acquire a controlling share, which we designate as the successful bidder. In the 774 cases with data available on the percent of the target sought by the bidder, the average percent sought is 66% and the average percent held by the successful bidder after the contest is 83%.

throughout the article). Based on the target's major four digit Standard Industrial Classification (SIC) codes for the year prior to the offer, about half of the contests are in manufacturing industries, and another 10% in the financial industry. The distribution of the number of multiple-bidder contests across industries and across time is similar to the distribution for single-bidder contests, again with the bulk of the offers occurring in manufacturing industries.

Of the 1,353 contests, 62% are single-bid. The solid line in Figure 2 shows the frequency distribution of the duration of these single-bid contests (days from initial bid to final outcome). The average duration is 40 trading days with a median of 29. The 80th percentile is 52 days and the 90th percentile is 73 days. Figure 2 also shows the frequency of the duration of multiple-bid contests from the first to the second bid, and from the initial bid to the final contest outcome. Looking first at the total contest duration, the average (median) is 70 (51) days, and 80% of the multiple-bid contests lasts less than 98 days. The 90th percentile is 142 days, and a handful of cases last more than 200 days, primarily due to court challenges and various delay tactics instituted by target management (the sample maximum is 443 days).

When a contest develops multiple bids, the second bid arrives on average after 14.5 days, with a median of 14. Moreover, in Figure 2, the 80th percentile for the time to the second bid is 40 days. In general the expected time to arrival of a second bid depends on the cost to rival bidders of becoming informed of their own valuation of the target, as well as the time it takes to file a formal offer. Unless the initial bid was largely anticipated by the rival bidders, a median of 14 days appears "short" unless the source of the target value is relatively easily established (e.g., eliminating inefficient management, free cash flow, reduced bankruptcy costs, etc.). In other words, the nature of the source of expected takeover gains is a likely determinant of the expected time to the second bid.

We classify target management reaction to bids based on information in the WSJI and the 14d filings. The target management response is categorized as supportive, neutral, or opposed, as follows: (1) Supportive: Target management states that the offer is fair, equitable, or that the bid is friendly. Alternatively, it is announced that the bidder has agreed to acquire the target, possibly following negotiations with target management. (2) Neutral: No management reaction is reported in the WSJI, or the report is neutral. (3) Opposed: Target management states that the offer is unfair, fraudulent, inadequate, unfriendly, that it is suing or otherwise intending to fight the takeover, or that it has received or been denied an injunction against the bidder. With these definitions, target management opposes the initial bid in 30% of the total sample. The proportion of bids that elicits target management opposition is significantly higher in multiple-bid than in single-bid contests: 54% versus 14%. Thus a contest develops multiple bids in part to fend off a negative target management reaction to the initial bid.

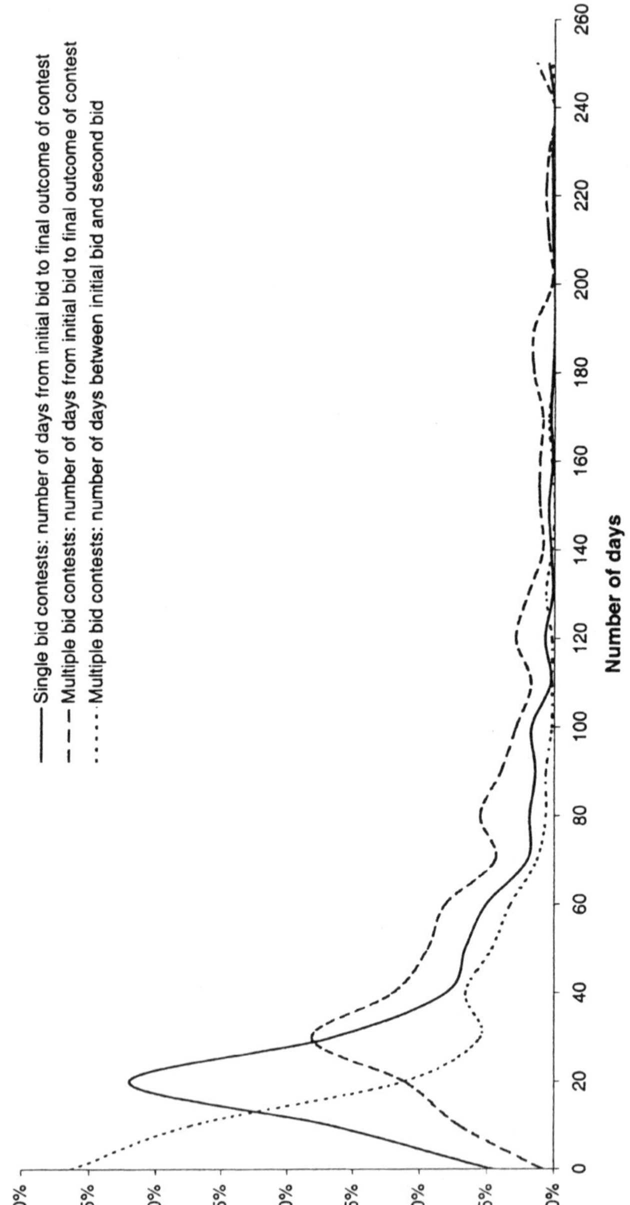

Figure 2
Frequency plots of the number of days from the initial bid to the second bid and to the final contest outcome in 1,353 U.S. tender offer contests, 1971–1990

The Review of Financial Studies / v 13 n 4 2000

Of the multiple-bid contests, 41% have only one bidder, where the initial bidder revises the initial bid. In these cases, the bidder raises the initial offer, although a rival bidder is never observed to enter the contest. Such bid revisions are first observed in the sample year 1974, and approximately 40% of the cases occur in the three-year period from 1986 through 1988. These bid revisions could be induced by *rumors* that a second bidder might launch a competing bid. However, a search of the WSJI for reports of such rumors reveals rumors in 5% of the single-bid contests and in only 6% of the multiple-bid, single-bidder contests. These two frequencies are both low and insignificantly different from each other.[9] Thus we cannot conclude that rumored competition is an important explanation for bid revisions in what turns out to be single-bidder contests. It is also possible that these bid revisions occur in response to rumors that the target board intends to decline the initial bid, or will give a hostile response. We do not, however, have any empirical evidence to support this explanation.

The overall (unconditional) success rate of the bids is 79%, with successful bidders acquiring an average of 80% of the target shares.[10] The average number of bids per contest is 2.5 when the initial bidder is successful and 3.9 when a rival bidder succeeds, and the maximum number of bids is 12. The corresponding average number of bidders is 1.1 and 2.3, with a maximum of 5.

We now turn to descriptive information on toeholds and offer premiums, and we perform regression analyses indicating the major determinants of these two offer parameters within single-bid and multiple-bid contests.

2. Toeholds, Premiums, and Bid Jumps

Table 2 lists the offer premiums of the first and final bids, classified by the type of contest and the target management response. If p_o denotes the offer price per share, the offer premium is calculated as $(p_o - p_{-60})/p_{-60}$, where p_{-60} is the target share price (corrected for dividends and stock splits) 60 days prior to the offer date. As illustrated in Figure 3 (the estimation procedure behind Figure 3 is described below), the price on day -60 shows

[9] The significance is tested using a standard Z test for comparing the proportions of two independent samples:

$$Z = \frac{\hat{p}_1 - \hat{p}_2}{\sqrt{\hat{p}(1-\hat{p})(1/N_1 + 1/N_2)}},$$

where Z is a standard normal. Sample i has N_i observations and the proportion of interest is denoted p_i. The overall proportion (in the combined sample) is denoted by $\hat{p}$.

[10] Our definition of success requires purchase of a minimum of 5% of the target shares. However, the frequency distribution of acquired shares is heavily skewed to the right, with almost every successful bidder acquiring 50% or more of the target. Moreover, for any given contest, our definition of success leads to multiple successful bidders in six cases only. Bidder share holdings following the contest are collected from the WSJI and company filings. If the acquisition is described by the WSJ as "done," "completed," or "successful," and there is no specific information available from the filing, then the bidder is assumed to have acquired the desired number of shares (typically 100% of the target).

Table 2
Percent initial and final offer premiums, classified by contest outcome and target management response to the initial bid, 1971–1990

				Multiple bid contests							
	Single bid contests			2nd bid by initial bidder				2nd bid by rival bidder			
Management reaction	S	U	All	S	SR	U	All	S	SR	U	All
I: Initial offer premium											
Target management supportive											
Average	60.02	64.26	60.39	55.69	107.20	29.94	59.98	58.67	46.65	71.67	54.52
Median	54.15	48.14	53.46	45.45	93.81	16.30	45.45	62.61	37.26	66.67	52.99
Sample	237	23	260	8	2	2	12	7	17	6	30
Target management neutral											
Average	50.06	34.84	47.96	48.79	37.30	50.85	47.81	61.022	41.00	22.54	41.22
Median	42.35	25.93	40.50	45.88	36.59	45.46	45.46	49.22	36.75	14.98	37.93
Sample	287	46	333	53	11	21	85	11	56	11	78
Target management opposed											
Average	40.27	38.43	39.21	47.01	46.16	49.45	47.39	48.69	41.93	58.10	45.29
Median	31.58	36.47	35.78	39.56	46.48	47.37	42.59	35.48	34.15	49.99	37.58
Sample	44	60	104	90	37	39	166	14	60	12	86
All contests											
Average	53.46	41.75	51.29	48.10	46.65	49.30	48.10	55.11	42.14	47.48	45.08
Median	45.05	35.78	44.00	43.09	46.19	45.46	44.68	48.15	36.75	42.83	38.29
Sample	568	129	697	151	50	62	263	32	133	29	194

Table 2
(continued)

	Single bid contests			Multiple bid contests							
				2nd bid by initial bidder				2nd bid by rival bidder			
Management reaction	S	U	All	S	SR	U	All	S	SR	U	All
II. Final offer premium											
Target management supportive											
Average				56.30	120.73	43.74	64.94	82.53	57.67	104.24	72.78
Median				59.47	70.87	28.20	59.47	70.21	54.83	111.11	66.58
Sample				8	2	2	12	7	17	6	30
Target management neutral											
Average				61.99	64.71	67.69	63.75	81.83	65.61	32.60	63.24
Median				68.07	62.16	53.99	59.46	66.99	58.89	23.61	54.9
Sample				53	11	21	85	11	56	11	78
Target management opposed											
Average				65.95	73.21	70.99	68.75	90.09	83.02	81.98	84.03
Median				60.60	86.06	72.09	63.08	80.33	72.06	69.11	79.10
Sample				90	37	39	166	14	60	12	86
All contests											
Average				64.05	73.24	68.99	66.96	85.60	72.45	67.86	73.93
Median				60.60	78.55	59.28	62.16	73.05	68.48	53.81	66.72
Sample				151	50	62	263	32	133	29	194

See Table 1 for data sources. All offer premiums are defined relative to the target share price 60 days before the start of the contest. The final offer premium uses the offer price in the final offer in the contest. The sample in this table is restricted to firms listed on the CRSP NYSE/AMEX and Nasdaq daily tapes. S indicates that the first bidder wins the contest, SR that a rival bidder wins the contest, and U that no bidder wins (target is not taken over).

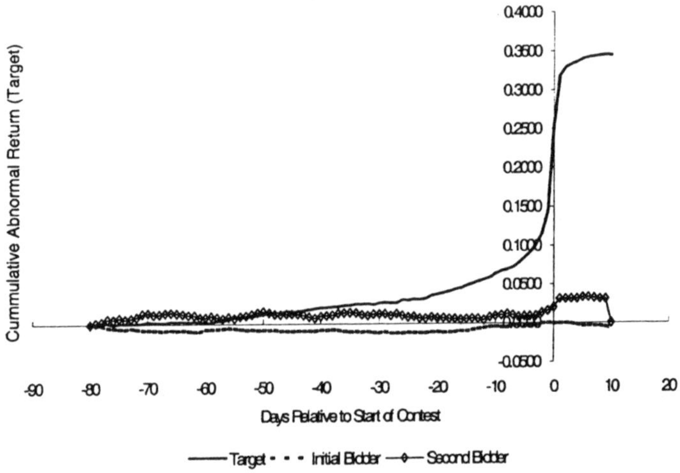

Figure 3
Average cumulative abnormal stock return to targets, initial bidders, and rival bidders in 1,353 tender offer contests, 1971–1990

little evidence of anticipating the subsequent takeover bid and is therefore a reasonable representation of a noninformative base price for offer premium calculations. In comparison, Bradley (1980) use day −40, while Schwert (1996) identifies day −42 as the preanticipation day.

In single-bid contests, the initial (and final) offer premium averages 51%. The average premium is substantially lower in single-bid contests opposed by target management than in contests not opposed by management (39% versus 60% in offers receiving target management support). This suggests that one reason for target management resistance is a low initial bid. In multiple-bid contests, the average offer premium increases from 45% in the initial bid to 74% in the final bid. Again, target management tends to oppose initial offers with a relatively low premium, on average driving the final offer premium to 84%.

If single-bid and multiple-bidder tender offer contests are drawn from the same distribution, and if single-bid contests are the result of preemptive bidding as suggested by the theory in Fishman (1988), then one would expect the offer premium in single-bid contests to exceed the *initial* offer premium in multiple-bid contests. This proposition receives some support in Table 2 since the average initial offer premium in single-bidder contests is 51%, compared to the average initial offer premium of 45% in multiple-bid contests. Looking beyond the "all contest" category, it is seen that the support for the preemptive bidding argument is limited to the sample of offers that did not generate target management opposition. Thus a relatively high initial offer premium appears to preempt target management opposition as well as rival bids.

Table 3 shows the median values of the bid jump between the first and second bids, between the second and final bids, and of the average jump per bid in the contest. The table shows bid jumps in terms of percent change in the initial bid *price* as well as the percent change in the initial bid *premium*. As shown in panel I, the median increase in the bid price from the first to the second offer is 10.0%, which corresponds to a median increase in the initial offer premium of 31%. Moreover, the median values of the average bid price and bid premium jumps across all bids in the contest equal 5.3% and 16.7%, respectively. Thus the greatest bid jumps typically occur between the first and second bids in the contest. Moreover, panels II and III show that the bid jumps are generally lower when the second bid in the contest is made by the initial bidder. The second bid in the contest typically jumps by 13.9% over the first bid (corresponding to a 45.2% premium increase) when a rival bidder enters and makes the second bid. This bid jump evidence is consistent with the presence of significant bidding costs as well as private bidder values in these auctions.

Table 4 lists average bidder toeholds classified by type of contest and the target management response. Toehold information is required in 14d filings, and we merge the 14d information with information in the WSJI, the *Mergerstat Review*, and the MERC database. The initial bidder toehold is zero in 46% of the sample, and less than 10% in 64% of the contests. Substantial toeholds are also present in the sample; in 36% of the sample, the toehold is greater than or equal to 10%, and in 11% of the cases the bidder's initial toehold exceeds 50% of the target shares.

Table 3
Median percentage bid jumps in multibid contests, 1971–1990

	Sample size	Offer price revision (%)[a] $(P_O - P_I)/P_O$	Premium revision (%)[b] $(P_O - P_I)/(P_I - P_{-60})$
I. All multibid contests			
Jump from first to second bid	454	10.00	30.77
Jump from first to final bid	457	14.29	65.08
Average bid jump througout contest	457	5.43	16.67
II. Contests where second bid is by initial bidder			
Jump from first to second bid	264	7.91	24.40
Jump from first to final bid	264	13.21	35.93
Average bid jump throughout contest	264	5.00	14.97
III. Contests where second bid is by rival bidder			
Jump from first to second bid	190	13.90	45.20
Jump from first to final bid	193	17.86	59.70
Average bid jump throughout contest	193	6.67	22.99

[a] P_I is the initial bid price price and P_O is either the second or the final bid price. Thus this column shows the percent change in the initial bid *price*.

[b] P_{-60} is the no-information target share price 60 days prior to the initial bid. Thus this column shows the percent change in the initial bid *premium*.

Table 4
The number of tender offer contests classified by the toehold of the initial bid, target management reaction, and contest outcome, 1971–1990

Reaction and toehold (%)	Single bid contests			Multiple bid contests: 2nd bid by initial bidder				Multiple bid contests: 2nd bid by rival bidder				All contests
	S	U	All	S	SR	U	All	S	SR	U	All	
I: Target management supportive												
Initial bidder toehold (%)												
$0 = x$	119	14	133	6	2	2	10	6	17	5	28	171
$0 < x < 5$	11	0	11	0	0	0	0	2	1	0	3	14
$5 \leq x < 20$	30	3	33	1	0	0	1	0	1	1	2	36
$20 \leq x < 50$	68	10	78	3	0	1	4	0	0	1	1	83
$50 \leq x$	34	5	39	0	0	0	0	0	0	0	0	39
Total	262	32	294	10	2	3	15	8	19	7	34	343
Average %	18.26	21.48	18.61	10.41	0.00	10.33	9.01	0.15	0.89	4.99	1.56	16.50
II: Target management neutral												
Initial bidder toehold (%)												
$0 = x$	138	55	193	21	7	12	40	7	45	10	62	295
$0 < x < 5$	18	3	21	4	0	4	8	1	4	2	7	36
$5 \leq x < 20$	34	6	40	14	4	5	23	2	9	0	11	74
$20 \leq x < 50$	82	8	90	13	2	2	17	2	5	0	7	114
$50 \leq x$	75	14	89	10	0	0	10	0	0	0	0	99
Total	347	86	433	62	13	23	98	12	63	12	87	618
Average %	22.51	14.31	20.88	19.27	6.21	5.68	14.35	7.65	3.92	0.47	3.96	17.47

Table 4
(continued)

Reaction and toehold (%)	Single bid contests			Multiple bid contests: 2nd bid by initial bidder				Multiple bid contests: 2nd bid by rival bidder				All contests
	S	U	All	S	SR	U	All	S	SR	U	All	
III: Target management opposed												
Initial bidder toehold (%)												
$0 = x$	18	32	50	38	15	19	72	7	27	8	42	164
$0 < x < 5$	5	10	15	22	7	7	36	3	14	0	17	68
$5 \leq x < 20$	13	20	33	30	16	14	60	4	18	4	26	119
$20 \leq x < 50$	9	7	16	7	0	3	10	2	4	2	8	34
$50 \leq x$	3	1	4	2	0	1	3	0	0	0	0	7
Total	48	70	118	99	38	44	181	16	63	14	93	392
Average %	13.64	6.85	9.61	7.10	4.20	6.91	6.44	7.46	5.32	8.41	6.15	7.33
Overall average %	20.85	13.21	19.43	11.56	4.60	6.58	9.06	5.69	4.11	5.46	4.58	14.57

See Table 1 for sample sources. S indicates that the first bidder wins the contest, SR that a rival bidder wins the contest, and U that no bidder wins (target is not taken over). Target management reaction is based primarily on information in the WSJI, supplemented by 14d filings. The classifications are illustrated as follows: *Supportive*: Target management states that the offer is fair, equitable, or that the bid is friendly. Alternatively, it is announced that the bidder has agreed to acquire the target, possibly following negotiations with target management. *Neutral*: No management reaction is reported in the WSJI, or the report is neutral. *Opposed*: Target management states that the offer is unfair; fraudulent; inadequate; unfriendly; that it is suing or otherwise intending to fight the takeover; or that it has received or been denied an injunction against the bidder.

The initial bidder's toehold is on average greater in single-bid contests (19%), and greater in multiple-bid contests with a single bidder than with multiple bidders (11% versus 5%). In multiple-bid contests, very few toeholds exceed 20%. While not shown in Table 4, there is also an association between the size of the toehold and the order of the bids in the contest. For the overall sample, the average toehold of the first bidder is 14%, which contrasts with average toeholds of subsequent rival bidders of between 5% and 8%. The initial bidder in multiple-bidder contests holds, on average, less than 5% of the target at the start of the contest. Furthermore, rival bidders enter such contests with approximately the same toehold as the initial bidder.

Prior to the initial bid, the bidder negotiated a tender-agreement with target management and/or a major target blockholder in a total of 311 cases (23% of the sample). Of these, only 47 cases (14.6%) developed into multiple-bid contests, and only one case (.40%) was opposed by target management. While we do not have data on the exact magnitude of the size of the tender precommitments specified in these agreements, the agreements effectively increase the size of the bidder's initial toehold. As shown below, there is strong evidence that the presence of a negotiated tender agreement increases the initial bidder's chance of single-bid success.

Tables 5 and 6 show the results of regressing the initial bidder's toehold on various contest characteristics. Table 5 presents a single-equation estimation, while Table 6 shows the parameters in a two-equation system where the toehold and the offer premium are determined simultaneously. The regression equation in Table 5 is as follows:

$$Toehold = \alpha_0 + \alpha_1 Runup + \alpha_2 Premium + \alpha_3 Hostile + \alpha_4 Iwin + \alpha_5 Rwin + \alpha_6 Irevise + \alpha_7 Onebid + \epsilon, \quad (1)$$

Table 5
Parameter estimates in a cross-sectional model for the initial bidder's toehold, 1971–1990

Constant	Runup	Premium	Hostile	Iwin	Rwin	Irevise	Onebid	
I. OLS estimation								
3.81	−11.16	0.01	−4.42	6.00	1.53	−6.00	8.05	R-square
(1.01)	(−2.67)	(1.07)	(−2.76)	(3.21)	(0.48)	(−3.02)	(2.88)	0.11
II. Truncated Tobit estimation								
−20.10	−15.40	0.02	−1.99	11.30	4.10	−8.43	15.30	Log-likelihood
(−2.98)	(−3.58)	(0.82)	(−0.69)	(3.83)	(0.73)	(−2.43)	(2.91)	−1992

t-Statistics in parentheses.
Variable definitions:
Toehold: Toehold of initial bidder.
Runup: Target abnormal stock return from day −60 through day −1.
Premium: Initial offer premium relative to target stock price on day −60.
Hostile: Dummy variable with value 1 if target management opposed initial bid and zero otherwise.
Iwin: Dummy variable with value 1 if initial bidder wins the contest.
Rwin: Dummy variable with value 1 if rival bidder wins the contest.
Irevise: Dummy variable with value 1 for single-bidder, multiple-bid contests.
Onebid: Dummy variable with value 1 for single-bid contests.

The Review of Financial Studies / v 13 n 4 2000

Table 6
Simultaneous equation (three-stage least squares) estimation of a cross-sectional model for the bidder's toehold and the initial offer premium

Constant	Runup	Markup	Multibid	Hostile	lnTsize	Toehold	Zero-Toe
Equation 1: Dependent variable: initial bidder's toehold							
β_0	β_1		β_3	β_4	β_5		
18.05	−4.25		−8.72	−5.34	0.08		
(5.4)	(−1.8)		(−6.0)	(−3.6)	(0.3)		
Equation 2: Dependent variable: initial offer premium							
γ_0		γ_2	γ_3	γ_4		γ_6	γ_7
4.80		0.90	−2.11	−1.33		−0.24	0.01
(1.4)		(4.3)	(−2.8)	(−1.3)		(−2.1)	(0.0)
System $R^2 = 0.58$, $\chi^2 = 667.14$ with 9 df							

Variable definitions:
Toehold: Toehold of initial bidder.
ZeroToe: Dummy variable with value of 1 if toehold equals zero and zero otherwise.
Multibid: Dummy variable with value 1 if multiple-bid contest.
Hostile: Dummy variable with value 1 if target management opposes the initial bid.
lnTsize: The log of total market value of target equity measured 60 trading days before the initial bid.
Runup: Abnormal stock return over the 60 days prior to initial bid.
Markup: Abnormal stock return over the 2 days ending with the announcement of the initial bid.

where *Runup* is the target cumulative abnormal stock return over days −60 through −1 relative to initial bid announcement, and *Premium* is the initial offer premium (relative to day −60). The remaining six regressors are zero-one binary variables: *Hostile* equals one if the target management opposes the initial bid, *Iwin* equals one if the initial bidder wins the contest, *Rwin* equals one if a rival wins the contest, *Irevise* equals one for single-bidder, multiple-bid contests, *Onebid* equals one for single-bidder contests, and ϵ is a mean zero error term.

The results in Table 5 are significant whether one uses OLS or a truncated Tobit regression.[11] Toeholds are *lower* the greater the precontest target run-up, which fails to support the model of Ravid and Spiegel (1999), where *Runup* is modeled as a result of toehold purchases.[12] The significantly positive coefficients for *Iwin* and *Onebid* strongly confirm the earlier finding in Table 4 that toeholds are higher in single-bid successful contests. Similarly the significantly negative coefficients of *Hostile* and *Irevise* confirm that toeholds are significantly lower in contests where the initial bid develops competition, either from rival bidders or (hostile) target management.

The regressions in Table 5 fail to indicate a significant relationship between the toehold and the offer premium. Given the potentially joint nature of the toehold-premium decision, Table 6 shows the results of three-stage least

[11] The truncated Tobit regression [see, e.g., Maddala (1983)] is motivated by the fact that the observed toehold may differ from the bidder's actual toehold position, in part due to a potential short position in the target and in part because of our 80% upper limit on toeholds.

[12] We also checked a two-equation setup for the simultaneous determination of the toehold and the run-up. The conclusion in the text remains unaffected.

squares estimation of two simultaneous equations for the toehold (first equation) and the initial offer premium (second equation):

$$
\begin{aligned}
Toehold &= \beta_0 + \beta_1 Runup + \beta_3 Multibid + \beta_4 Hostile + \beta_5 lnTsize \\
Premium &= \gamma_0 + \gamma_2 Markup + \gamma_3 Multibid + \gamma_4 Hostile \\
&\quad + \gamma_6 Toehold + \gamma_7 ZeroToe,
\end{aligned}
\tag{2}
$$

where *Markup* is the abnormal target stock return over the s-day period ending with the bid announcement day, *Multibid* is a binary variable for multiple bids, *lnTsize* is the logarithm of the total equity size of the target, and *ZeroToe* is a binary variable for zero toeholds. Again, the first equation confirms that toeholds are significantly lower for hostile bids and when the initial bids attract rival bidder entry. The initial offer premium (second equation) is increasing in *Markup*, decreasing in the target equity size and, as discussed earlier, is lower for resisted offers. Of interest, the premium is also significantly lower the greater the toehold. The latter result is consistent with the models of Shleifer and Vishny (1986) and Hirshleifer and Titman (1990), but fails to support the signaling argument of Chowdry and Jegadeesh (1994).

While the results in Tables 5 and 6 are interesting, they do not indicate the marginal impact of the offer characteristics on either the outcome probabilities or on the expected value of the bid. For example, while Table 6 shows that there is a negative trade-off between the toehold and the offer premium, an even more interesting question is how the offer parameters jointly determine the value and outcome of the bid. To answer this question, we now turn to a structural, forward-looking analysis that closely replicates the actual bidding environment.

3. Conditional Expected Value of the Bid: Structural Estimation

In this section we use the contest tree structure depicted in Figure 1 to estimate the impact of the vector of offer characteristics, $\mathbf{x}$, on the vector of outcome probabilities, $\mathbf{p(x)}$, and the vector of payoffs at each node of the tree, μ. As stated in the introduction, if the market prices the bid using the tree structure in Figure 1, then the bid announcement-induced abnormal stock return, Γ, equals the product of the outcome probabilities and payoffs: $\Gamma = \mu'\mathbf{p(x)}$.

Below, we first estimate $\mathbf{p(x)}$ using multinomial logit. Second, we estimate Γ for each takeover bid using the time series of bidder and target stock returns. Third, we recover the vector μ embedded in the estimate of Γ by a (normalized) cross-sectional regression of Γ on $\mathbf{p(x)}$. Finally, we use the estimates to form the predicted value of the bid, $\Gamma(\mathbf{x}) \equiv \mu'\mathbf{p(x)}$, and compute the derivative $\partial\Gamma(\mathbf{x})/\partial\mathbf{x}$, thus allowing examination of the marginal impact of the offer parameters on the expected value of the bid.

This entire analysis is performed first using the information available at the beginning of the contest only (stage 1 in the contest tree), and subsequently repeated using the (updated) information available at the arrival of the second bid (stage 2, nodes 3 or 4 of the tree).[13]

3.1 Outcome probabilities [p(x)]

3.1.1 Econometric procedure. Let $p^s_{jn} \equiv p^s_n(\mathbf{x_j})$ denote the probability that bidder j will reach node n from node s in the contest tree, conditional on the offer characteristics $\mathbf{x_j}$. We estimate p^s_{jn} using multinomial logit. With a total of $\mathcal{E}^s$ possible nodes in Figure 1 following node s, the multinomial model is given by

$$p^s_{jn} = \exp(\mathbf{x_j}'\delta^s_n) / \sum_{n \in \mathcal{E}^s} \exp(\mathbf{x_j}'\delta^s_n), \tag{3}$$

where δ^s_n is a K-vector of parameters. At stage 1 in the event tree, there are a total of $\mathcal{E}^0 = 4$ nodes (i.e., nodes 1–4). At stage 2 there are $\mathcal{E}^3 = 3$ nodes (nodes 5–7) when one arrives from node 3, and $\mathcal{E}^4 = 3$ nodes (nodes 8–10) conditional on arriving from node 4. At each stage of the contest tree, there are a total of $K\mathcal{E}^s$ different parameters to be estimated.

The multinomial model in Equation (3) differs from the binomial (two outcome) probability estimation typically reported in the literature. Several articles present binomial probability estimates for what is essentially a subset of the outcomes in Figure 1, such as the probability of success versus failure, and the probability of competition versus single-bid auction.[14] By inspection of Figure 1, the former probability estimates exclude the no bidder wins outcome, while the latter excludes bid revisions by the initial bidders as a separate outcome. Binomial estimates that omit relevant outcomes are biased [Maddala (1983)]. Our research indicates that *all* of the nodes in Figure 1 are statistically relevant and the structural analysis thus requires multinomial estimation.

Equation (3) cannot be estimated directly, as the parameters δ^s_n are determined only up to an additive constant (i.e., one can add a constant α to each δ^s_n without altering the estimated value of p^s_{jn}). The solution is to fix the set of parameters associated with one of the outcomes and rescale the remaining parameters relative to that "numeraire" outcome. For the stage 1 probability estimates, we select node 1 (unsuccessful single-bid contest) as the numeraire outcome. Similarly, the "no bidder successful" outcomes (nodes 7 and 10) are numeraire events for the probability estimates in stage 2 of the event tree. Let $\dot{\delta}^s_n$ denote the parameter value rescaled in this manner. Thus at stage 1 of

[13] One could in principle update the estimates at each of the (up to 11) new bids. However, as discussed below, we find that the offer characteristics $\mathbf{x}$ affect the outcome probabilities only at stage 1. Thus our stage 1 and 2 estimation captures the essence of the impact of $\mathbf{x}$.

[14] See, for example, Walkling and Long (1984), Walkling (1985), Jennings and Mazzeo (1993).

the tree, $\dot{\delta}_1^0 = 0$ and $\dot{\delta}_n^0 = \delta_n^0 - \delta_1^0$, for $n > 1$. The multinomial logit model used for stage 1 estimation is then

$$p_{j1}^0 = 1 \Big/ \left[1 + \sum_{n=2}^{4} \exp(\mathbf{x_j}'\dot{\delta}_n^0)\right], \tag{4}$$

$$p_{jn}^0 = \exp(\mathbf{x_j}'\dot{\delta}_n^0) \Big/ \left[1 + \sum_{n=2}^{4} \exp(\mathbf{x_j}'\dot{\delta}_n^0)\right] \text{ for } n = 2, \ldots 4. \tag{5}$$

The multinomial logit equation is similarly defined for the stage 2 estimation of the outcome probabilities.[15]

3.1.2 Parameter estimates. Table 7 reports estimates of the coefficient vector δ_n^s as well as the average probability estimates. At stage 1 ($s = 0$) the vector of offer characteristics $\mathbf{x}$ includes the initial offer premium (*Premium*), the initial toehold (*Toehold*), and three dummy variables for zero toehold (*Zero-Toe*), cash as payment method (*Payment*), and the presence of a negotiated prebid tender agreement (*Negotiated*). At stage 2 ($s = 3, 4$), $\mathbf{x}$ is augmented by the dummy variable *Hostile*, indicating observed target management opposition to the initial bid. Moreover, stage 2 regressions use as *Premium* the second offer price relative to the target share price on day −60, and *Toehold* is now the second bidder's initial toehold level.

The values of the likelihood ratio test statistics (LRT) in Table 7 indicate that the stage 1 parameter estimates are jointly highly significant (LRT = 300.55 with 15 degrees of freedom).[16] In contrast, stage 2 estimates are largely insignificant whether estimated from node $s = 3$ or node $s = 4$. In other words, the offer parameters included in $\mathbf{x}$ have a significant impact on the subsequent transition probabilities only at the first stage of the contest ($s = 0$). After the initial bidder finds it necessary to revise upwards the initial bid (node $s = 3$), or when the initial bid attracts competition (node $s = 4$), it appears that the strategic impact of the offer parameters on the subsequent outcome probabilities is limited. The only exception to this is the coefficient for *Negotiated*, which shows that a pre-initial bid tender precommitment significantly reduces the probability that a rival bidder will win the contest also after the rival bid has emerged.

[15] Generally, the likelihood function is determined by defining an index y_{jn}^s that equals 1 if bid j results in node n from node s, and zero otherwise. Then for a total of $\mathcal{E}^s$ nodes and N bids, the likelihood function is

$$L^s = \prod_{j=1}^{N} \prod_{n \in \mathcal{E}^s} p_{jn}^{y_{jn}^s},$$

which (with the logit function) has a unique maximum. Note also that a (Hausman) test fails to reject the "independence of irrelevant alternatives" assumption underlying the multinomial logit model for our contest tree. See Hausman and Wise (1977) and Maddala (1983).

[16] The likelihood ratio test (LRT) compares the performance of the model to a model with only constants. The test is distributed as χ^2 with degrees of freedom equal to the number of additional explanatory variables.

The Review of Financial Studies / v 13 n 4 2000

Table 7
Estimated parameters δ_n^s in a multinomial logit model determining tender offer outcome probabilities p_n^s from node s to node n in the tender offer contest tree, 1971–1990

Outcome probabilities		Explanatory variables in multinomial model[a]							Probability at mean x[b]
		Constant	Premium	Toehold	Zero-Toe	Payment	Negotiated	Hostile	
I: Stage 1 outcome probabilities from "initial bid" ($s = 0$)[c]									
p_2^0:	Successful initial bid	.4796 (1.13)	.7710 (2.58)	.0194 (2.95)	.1578 (.59)	−.0122 (−.03)	1.0638 (3.97)		.533
p_3^0:	Second bid by initial bidder	1.5628 (3.55)	.6352 (1.95)	−.0288 (−3.56)	−.8940 (−3.21)	−.3505 (−.89)	−1.2495 (−3.20)		.200
p_4^0:	Second bid by rival bidder	1.2070 (2.60)	.1781 (.51)	−.0490 (−4.24)	−.2903 (−.97)	−.3545 (−.88)	−.0784 (−.24)		.141
$N = 1, 154$, log likelihood $= -1270.1$, LRT $= 300.16$, $df = 15$									
II: Stage 2 outcome probabilities from "initial bidder makes second bid" ($s = 3$)[d]									
p_5^3:	Initial bidder successful	.3286 (.52)	−.0037 (−.01)	.0273 (1.75)	.0267 (.07)	.2450 (.46)	.7465 (.88)	.1002 (.30)	.593
p_6^3:	Rival bidder successful	.5108 (.68)	−.5255 (−1.10)	−.0331 (−1.11)	−.2053 (−.42)	−.5717 (−.99)	.4884 (.45)	.4816 (1.08)	.166
$N = 263$, log likelihood $= -246.01$, LRT $= 20.75$, $df = 12$									

Table 7
(continued)

III: Stage 2 outcome probabilities from "rival bidder makes second bid" ($s = 4$)[d]

p_8^4:	Initial bidder	−1.1380	.7257	−.0268	.8368	.3283	−.0863	−.2149	.140
	successful	(−.93)	(1.09)	(−.58)	(.82)	(.39)	(−.12)	(−.34)	
p_9^4:	Rival bidder	1.8806	.3526	−.0203	−.7933	.5710	−1.5587	−.3706	.715
	successful	(2.38)	(.65)	(−.85)	(−1.21)	(.87)	(−2.53)	(−.75)	

$N = 191$, log likelihood $= -148.86$, LRT $= 22.94$, $df = 12$

Asymptotic t-values in parentheses.

The multinomial logit model has the following general form:

$$p_{jn}^s = \exp(\mathbf{x}_j{}'\delta_n^s) / \sum_{n>s}^{\mathcal{E}^s} \exp(\mathbf{x}_j{}'\delta_n^s),$$

where there are $K = 7$ bid-specific characteristics in the ($K \times 1$) vector of determinants $\mathbf{x}_j$, δ_n^s is the (7×1) vector of parameters, and there are a total of $\mathcal{E}^s$ possible events (nodes) conditional on node s. At each stage of the event tree, there are a total of $7\mathcal{E}^s$ different parameters to be estimated. At stage 1 in the contest tree, there are a total of $\mathcal{E}^0 = 4$ nodes (i.e., nodes 1–4). At stage 2, there are $\mathcal{E}^3 = 3$ nodes (nodes 5–7) when one arrives from node 3, and $\mathcal{E}^4 = 3$ nodes (nodes 8–10) conditional on arriving from node 4. The sample is restricted to contests with sufficient data to estimate premiums (i.e., targets listed on both NYSE/AMEX and Nasdaq exchanges).

[a]Variable definitions:

Premium = offer price relative to the target's price 60 days before the announcement of the initial offer. In Stage 2 estimates, the premium is the second offer price relative to the target's price 60 days before the initial offer.

Tochold = initial bidder's level of ownership in the target prior to the announcement of the initial offer. In Stage 2 estimates, the toehold is the second bidder's initial level of ownership in the target.

Zero-Toe = dummy variable which equals one if the toehold is zero.

Payment = dummy variable which equals one if the payment method of the initial bid includes securities.

Negotiated = dummy variable which equals one if the initial bidder negotiated a tender precommitment with the target management or a major target shareholder prior to the bid.

Hostile = dummy variable which equals one if the target management opposes the bid.

The likelihood ratio test (LRT) compares the performance of the model to a model with only constants. The test is distributed as χ^2 with degrees of freedom equal to the number of additional explanatory variables.

[b]This is the probability computed using the mean value of the vector of characteristics $\mathbf{x}$.

[c]Stage 1 probabilities are normalized relative to p_1^0, that is, the probability of an unsuccessful single-bid contest. The average estimated probability of this node is .1118 with a standard error of .0327. Using the mean value of the vector of characteristics $\mathbf{x}$, the probability is .126.

[d]Stage 2 probabilities are normalized relative to p_7^3 (the probability of no bidder successful conditional on initial bidder making the second bid) and p_{10}^4 (the probability of no bidder successful conditional on rival bidder making the second bid), respectively. The average estimated probabilities are .2357 and .1466, with standard errors of .0481 and .0641. Using the mean value of the vector of characteristics $\mathbf{x}$, these two probabilities are .241 and .145, respectively.

The Review of Financial Studies / v 13 n 4 2000

Since the probabilities at each stage sum to one, the parameters δ_n^s reported in Table 7 do not represent partial derivatives of the probabilities with respect to each of the offer characteristics. That is, a change in the kth offer characteristic changes *all* the probabilities simultaneously, so that the partial for one probability becomes

$$\partial p_n^s / \partial x_k = p_n^s \left(\delta_{kn}^s - \sum_{e \in \mathcal{E}^s} \delta_{ek}^s p_e^s \right). \tag{6}$$

Table 8 shows the value of this partial derivative for all the probabilities and all the offer characteristics, along with the imputed t-statistics. At stage 1 (the initial bid), the probability of a successful initial bid (p_2^0) increases with *Premium, Toehold*, and *Negotiated*, while the variables *Toehold* and *Negotiated* also significantly decrease the probability of multiple bids in the contest. There is evidence of a nonlinear impact of *Toehold* on the probability of multiple bids, as *Zero-Toe* receives a significantly negative coefficient in the estimation of p_2^0 and p_3^0.

At stage 2 (the second bid), there is evidence that greater toeholds positively affect the probability that the initial bidder will be successful, conditional on making the second bid in the contest. Moreover, when the second bid in the contest is made by a rival bidder, the probability of rival bidder success is significantly lower if the rival bidder's toehold is zero. Interestingly, the value of the (revised) offer premium in the second bid has no statistically significant impact on the subsequent success probabilities. It is also interesting that target management opposition (*Hostile*), which is known at this time, also has no significant impact on any of the stage 2 probabilities.

As shown in panel III of Table 8, having obtained a tender precommitment from target management or a large shareholder prior to the initial bid is clearly of value if the contest develops rival bids. When the second bid in the contest is coming from a rival bidder, the presence of a tender precommitment tends to increase the initial bidder's chance of eventually succeeding (p_8^4) and significantly reduces the chance of the rival bidder being successful (p_{10}^4).

3.2 Offer-induced abnormal stock return (Γ)

3.2.1 Econometric procedure. The stock prices of the bidder and the target firms react to each new offer announcement in a given contest by generating an abnormal return, Γ, relative to its preoffer price. Since both the number of bids and the number of days between bids vary across contests, we use the flexible "variable window" estimation procedure in Eckbo and Langohr (1989) to estimate Γ. In Eckbo and Langohr (1989), the average

Table 8
Partial derivatives of the outcome probabilities with respect to the vector of offer characteristics x evaluated at the mean of x

Outcome probabilities		Explanatory variables in multinomial model[a]							Probability at mean x
		Constant	Premium	Toehold	Zero-Toe	Payment	Negotiated	Hostile	
I: Stage 1 outcome probabilities from "initial bid" ($s = 0$)									
p_1^0 :	Unsuccessful single bid	−.0929 (−2.00)	−.0709 (−2.11)	.0003 (.41)	.0171 (.62)	.0159 (.41)	−.0386 (−1.28)		.126
p_2^0 :	Successful single bid	−.1379 (−1.97)	.1108 (2.44)	.0116 (8.49)	.1564 (3.51)	.0610 (1.04)	.4039 (8.28)		.533
p_3^0:	Second bid by initial bidder	.1648 (3.46)	.0144 (.43)	−.0053 (−4.40)	−.1516 (−4.35)	−.0445 (−1.01)	−.3111 (−4.48)		.200
p_4^0:	Second bid by rival bidder	.0660 (1.68)	−.0543 (−1.76)	−.0066 (−3.64)	−.0218 (−.82)	−.3212 (−.99)	−.0542 (−1.81)		.141
II: Stage 2 outcome probabilities from "initial bidder makes second bid" ($s = 3$)									
p_5^3:	Initial bidder successful	.0291 (.23)	.0507 (.69)	.0098 (2.77)	.0266 (.35)	.1153 (1.08)	.1321 (.80)	−.0231 (−.33)	.593
p_6^3:	Rival bidder successful	.0383 (.44)	−.0723 (−1.19)	−.0073 (−1.55)	−.0310 (−.52)	−.1031 (−1.50)	−.0059 (−.05)	.0567 (1.02)	.166
p_7^3:	No bidder successful	−.0674 (−.60)	.0215 (.34)	−.0026 (−.87)	.0044 (.07)	−.0122 (−.13)	−.1262 (−.82)	−.0336 (−.57)	.241

Table 8
(continued)

Outcome probabilities		Explanatory variables in multinomial model[a]							Probability at mean x
		Constant	Premium	Toehold	Zero-Toe	Payment	Negotiated	Hostile	
III: Stage 2 outcome-probabilities from "rival bidder makes second bid" ($s = 4$)									
p_8^4:	Initial bidder	−.3252	.0521	−.0012	.1801	−.0176	.1456	.0112	.140
	successful	(−1.85)	(.83)	(−.24)	(1.44)	(−.21)	(1.75)	(.20)	
p_9^4:	Rival bidder	.4972	−.0008	−.0015	−.2454	.0835	−.3091	−.0540	.715
	successful	(3.55)	(−.01)	(−.29)	(−2.08)	(.76)	(−2.82)	(−.72)	
p_{10}^4:	No bidder	−.1720	−.0513	.0027	.0653	−.0659	.1635	.0428	.145
	successful	(−1.50)	(−.76)	(.85)	(.78)	(−.81)	(1.86)	(.67)	

t-values in parentheses.

The model for the outcome probabilities is $p_n^s = \exp(\mathbf{x}'\delta_n^s)/\sum_{n>s}^{\mathcal{E}^s}\exp(\mathbf{x}'\delta_n^s)$, where $\mathbf{x}$ is the K-vector of offer characteristics, δ_n^s is the corresponding K-vector of parameters (reported in Table 7), and $\mathcal{E}^s$ is the total number of possible outcomes following node s. The partial derivatives reported in the table are given by

$$\partial p_n^s/\partial x_k = p_n^s\left(\delta_{kn}^s - \sum_{e=1}^{\mathcal{E}^s}\delta_{ek}^s p_e^s\right).$$

[a]Variable definitions:

Premium = offer price relative to the target's price 60 days before the announcement of the initial offer. In stage 2 estimates, the premium is the second offer price relative to the target's price 60 days before the initial offer.

Toehold = initial bidder's level of ownership in the target prior to the announcement of the initial offer. In stage 2 estimates, the toehold is the second bidder's initial level of ownership in the target.

Zero-Toe = dummy variable which equals one if the toehold is zero.

Payment = dummy variable which equals one if the payment method of the initial bid includes securities.

Negotiated = dummy variable which equals one if the initial bidder negotiated a tender precommitment with the target management or a major target shareholder prior to the bid.

Hostile = dummy variable which equals one if the target management opposes the bid.

daily abnormal return over event window w, γ_{jw}, is estimated directly as a parameter in the following market model:

$$r_{jt} = \alpha_j + \beta_j r_{mt} + \beta'_j d_{mt} r_{mt} + \sum_{w=1}^{W_j} \gamma_{jw} d_{jwt} + \epsilon_{jt}, \tag{7}$$

where r_{jt} is the continuously compounded rate of return to firm j over day t, r_{mt} is the continuously compounded rate of return on the value weighted market index over day t, d_{mt} is a dummy variable which equals one if day t is greater than or equal to day -60 relative to the announcement of the initial bid in the contest, and zero otherwise, d_{jwt} is one of W_j dummy variables, where each dummy takes on a value of one if day t is within event window w and zero otherwise,[17] and ϵ_{jt} is a regression error term, assumed to be normally, identically, and independently distributed.[18]

Letting ω_{jw} denote the number of trading days within event window w for contest j, then the cumulative abnormal return over the wth window is given by $\omega_{jw}\gamma_{jw}$. As discussed below, there is evidence of significant average abnormal stock price behavior as early as 60 days prior to initial bids, thus we start the cumulation at day $I - 60$. The total abnormal return from event day -60 through node s in the contest tree is given by

$$\Gamma_{js}^{-60} \equiv \sum_{w=1}^{s^*} \omega_{jw}\gamma_{jw}, \tag{8}$$

where s^* is the event window in calendar time that ends with node s. For example, when we look at the initial bid ($s = 0$), $s^* = 2$ and Γ_{j0}^{-60} cumulates over event parameters γ_{j1} and γ_{j2}. The estimation uses OLS with White's heteroscedastic-consistent covariance matrix.[19] The estimation period starts

[17] The length of each event window captured by dummy variables (d_{jwt}) is as follows. For all contests, the first event window (defining d_{j1t}) is the 59-day period $[I - 60, I - 2]$ relative to the announcement of the initial bid (I = day 0), and thus reflects possible preannouncement rumors about the pending offer. The second event window (d_{j2t}) is the two-day period $[I - 1, I]$, reflecting the news of the initial bid in the *Wall Street Journal*. Each subsequent bid in multiple-bid contests adds two event windows, one covering the interim period from the day after the previous offer announcement day through day -2 relative to the new bid, and another covering the two-day window $[-1, 0]$ for the new bid. Finally, the three last event periods (for both single-bid and multiple-bid contests) cover (i) the interim period from the last bid to day $E - 2$, where E is the contest expiration date, (ii) the three-day window $[E - 1, E + 1]$ centered on the expiration day, and (iii) the postexpiration window $[E + 2, \min(T, E + 20)]$, where T is the time of target delisting after a successful takeover. In sum, there are a total of five event windows in the case of a single-bid contest. Generally, with L_j bids, the total number of event windows for contest j is $W_j = 5 + 2(L_j - 1)$. For example, with three bids, which is common in multiple-bidder contests, the total number of event windows is $W_j = 9$.

[18] Abnormal returns were also estimated assuming ϵ_{jt} follows an autoregressive conditional heteroscedasticity process of order one (ARCH(1)), that is, where $\text{var}(\epsilon_{jt}) = \alpha^0 + \alpha^1 \text{var}(\epsilon_{j,t-1})$. The results of the ARCH model are qualitatively similar to the OLS-based results and are therefore not reported.

[19] White (1980) demonstrates that the variance of the coefficient estimates b can be estimated as $\hat{\sigma}^2(b) = N(X'X)^{-1}S'(X'X)^{-1}$, where X is the matrix of independent variables and N is the number of observations in the estimation. In this case $S = \sum_i e_i^2 x_i x_i'$ where e_i is the ith least square residual. The estimated variance allows appropriate inferences without specifying the form of the heteroscedasticity.

The Review of Financial Studies / v 13 n 4 2000

191 days prior to the announcement of the initial bid and ends 191 days following the ending date of the last bid [abnormal returns were also estimated using a longer period $(-381, 381)$ without altering the conclusions].

3.2.2 Parameter estimates. Table 9 shows the average cumulative abnormal returns to targets, the initial bidder and rival bidders from day -60 relative to the announcement of the first bid in the contest through node s in the contest tree, Γ_s^{-60}, $s = 0, 1, \ldots, 10$. The total contest period extends from day -60 relative to the WSJ announcement of the initial bid through 20 days following the ending date of the contest. The time series of abnormal returns for targets, the initial bidder and the second (rival) bidder (if any) from day -80 through day 10 following the initial bid is shown in Figure 3.

Cumulative abnormal returns up through the initial bid (stage 1) average 32.48% for target firms, with a strongly significant Z-value of 33.39.[20] In single-bid contests, the average abnormal return remains at 32% if the target is successful, and it drops to 15.79% by the unsuccessful outcome date. In multiple-bid contests, by the time of the second bid (stage 2), target average abnormal returns increase to 40.69% if the second bid is made by the initial bidder, and to 42.88% if the second bid in the contest is made by a rival bidder. At stage 3, ultimately successful targets realize on average 47.78% if the initial bidder wins the contest, while the total abnormal return is 37.91% if the initial bidder eventually loses out to a rival. Finally, if no bidder wins, target average abnormal returns drop to 23.56%. In sum, successful target shareholders earn large and significant total abnormal returns which are higher in multiple-bid than in single-bid contests. In addition, target abnormal returns are on average highest when it is the initial bidder that eventually wins the auction.

In contrast, both the initial and rival bidders on average make insignificant abnormal returns, with one exception in Table 9: Rival bidders earn on average a significant 6.11% abnormal return up through the date of the second bid in the auction, provided the second bid is made by the initial bidder (node $s = 3$). This gain possibly reflects information about the target as a potential profit opportunity for rival bidders, revealed by the two first bids in the contest. This initial gain to rival bidders is reversed by the time it is clear that the initial bidder wins the contest: cumulative abnormal returns to rivals average an insignificant 3.14% at nodes $s = 5$ and $s = 8$.

The evidence in Table 9 is consistent with the proposition that competition among bidder firms grants most (if not all) of the rents from merger activity to target shareholders. However, it is also widely recognized that partial

[20] The Z-statistic is for the hypothesis that the average cumulative abnormal return equals zero, where $Z_s = (1/\sqrt{N}) \sum_{j=1}^{N} \Gamma_{js}^{-60} / \sigma_{\Gamma_{js}}$, which has a standard normal distribution for large sample size N. The variance of Γ_{js}^{-60} is $\sigma_{\Gamma_{js}}^2 = \sigma^2 R(X'X)^{-1} R'$, where σ^2 is the regression residual variance, R is a vector in which $R_t = 1$ if any $d_{jnt} = 1$, and X is the matrix of independent variables in the market model of Equation (6). The conclusions of this article also reflect the results of tests of the joint hypothesis that all the abnormal returns across firms are equal to zero using the Simes (1986) and Hochberg (1988) modified Bonferroni techniques.

Table 9
Average and median cumulative abnormal returns to NYSE/AMEX listed targets, initial bidders and rival bidders, 1971–1990

Period of cumulation (through node s)	Statistic	Average cumulative abnormal return: $\Gamma_s^{-60} = \frac{1}{N}\sum_j^N \Gamma_{js}^{-60}$ Target firms	Initial bidders	Rival bidders
Stage 1: Initial bid				
Day −60 through	Mean	.3248	.0133	.0216
day of initial bid	Median	.3013	.0068	−.0012
($s = 0$)	(N, Z_s)	(780, 33.39)	(606, 0.98)	(152, 1.35)
Stage 2: Second bid in the contest				
Day −60 through	Mean	.4069	.0120	.0611
day of second bid	Median	.3984	.0176	.0602
($s = 3$)[a]	(N, Z_s)	(209, 20.76)	(122, .80)	(42, 2.47)
Day −60 through	Mean	.4288	.0297	−.0065
day of second bid	Median	.4226	−.0028	−.0230
($s = 4$)[b]	(N, Z_s)	(142, 17.93)	(92, 1.08)	(110, −.79)
Stage 3a: Final contest outcome, single-bid contests				
Day −60 through	Mean	.3200	.0112	–
outcome day, successful	Median	.3070	.0056	–
offers ($s = 2$)	(N, Z_s)	(339, 17.29)	(313, .010)	–
Day −60 through	Mean	.1579	−.0076	–
outcome day, unsuccessful	Median	.1407	−.0203	–
offers ($s = 1$)	(N, Z_s)	(88, 4.06)	(79, −.26)	–
Stage 3b: Final contest outcome, multiple-bid contests				
Day −60 through	Mean	.4778	.0260	.0314
outcome day, initial bidder	Median	.5162	−.0154	−.0107
successful ($s = 5$ and $s = 8$)	(N, Z_s)	(139, 16.44)	(84, .58)	(22, .72)
Day −60 through	Mean	.3791	−.0008	−.0289
outcome day, rival bidder	Median	.4282	−.0064	−.0123
successful ($s = 6$ and $s = 9$)	(N, Z_s)	(151, 13.83)	(87, .28)	(109, .35)
Day −60 through	Mean	.2356	.0527	.0406
outcome day, no bidder	Median	.2600	.1083	.0181
successful ($s = 7$ and $s = 10$)	(N, Z_s)	(63, 5.31)	(43, .26)	(21, .86)

Sample size and Z-value in parentheses.

Abnormal return for firm j cumulated from day −60 through mode s in the contest tree in Figure 1 is given by $\Gamma_{js}^{-60} = \sum_{w=1}^{s^*} \omega_{jw}\gamma_{jw}$, where s^* is the event window in calendar time that ends with node s in the tree, ω_{jw} is the number of trading days within event window w, and where average daily abnormal returns over each event window w are estimated directly from the W_j event parameters γ_{jw} in the following market model:

$$r_{jt} = \alpha_j + \beta_j r_{mt} + \beta'_j d_{mt} r_{mt} + \sum_{w=1}^{W_j} \gamma_{jw} d_{jwt} + \epsilon_{jt}.$$

r_{jt} is the continuously compounded rate of return to firm j over day t, r_{mt} is the continuously compounded rate of return on the value weighted market index over day t, d_{mt} is a dummy variable which equals one if day t is greater than or equal to day −60 relative to the announcement of the initial bid in the contest, and zero otherwise, d_{jwt} is one of W_j dummy variables, where each dummy takes on a value of one if day t is within event window w, and zero otherwise, and ϵ_{jt} is an error term, assumed to be normally, identically, and independently distributed. See the text for definition of the event windows. The estimation uses ordinary least squares with White's heteroscedastic-consistent covariance matrix. The estimation period starts 191 days prior to the announcement of the initial bid and ends 191 days following the ending date of last bid. Abnormal returns were also estimated using a longer period (−381, 381) as well as assuming that the residuals follow an autoregressive conditional heteroscedasticity process of order one (ARCH(1)), with qualitatively similar results. The table reports Z-values for the hypothesis that the average cumulative abnormal return Γ from the conditional market model estimation equals zero, where $Z_s = \frac{1}{\sqrt{N}} \sum_{j=1}^{N} \Gamma_{js}^{-60}/\sigma_{\Gamma_{js}}$, which has a standard normal distribution for large sample size N. The variance of Γ_{js}^{-60} is $\sigma^2_{\Gamma_{js}} = \sigma^2 R(X'X)^{-1}R'$, where σ^2 is the regression residual variance, R is a vector in which $R_t = 1$ if any $d_{jmt} = 1$, and X is the matrix of independent variables in the market model.

[a] Second bid by initial bidder.

[b] Second bid by rival bidder.

anticipation of takeover activity and relative size of the bidder and target firms may produce attenuated estimates of total bidder gains.[21] The question remains, however, whether expected gains to bidders, conditional on the offer parameters, are positive for any of the nodes in the tender offer contest tree. The subsequent analysis sheds light on this issue as well.

3.3 Conditional expected value of bid [$\Gamma(\mathbf{x}) \equiv \boldsymbol{\mu}'\mathbf{p}(\mathbf{x})$]

3.3.1 Econometric procedure. As pointed out earlier, given the assumed contest tree structure, rational pricing implies that the market impounds the abnormal return $\boldsymbol{\Gamma} = \mu'\mathbf{p}(\mathbf{x})$ into the firm's stock price upon the bid announcement. That is, the market reaction to a bid announcement represents the sum of the products of outcome probabilities and payoffs across all subsequent nodes in the contest tree. We have so far estimated, for each bid j, the value of Γ_j and $\mathbf{p}(\mathbf{x_j})$. We now extract the vector of average payoffs μ through a cross-sectional regression of Γ_j on $\mathbf{p}(\mathbf{x_j})$. Note that since the market reaction to *every* bid contains information on the subsequent values of μ and $\mathbf{p}(\mathbf{x})$, this forward-looking regression uses all sample bids.[22] As a result, our regression estimates of μ differ from the traditional average abnormal return estimates reported in Table 9 as well as in the literature generally.[23]

In order to reduce multicollinearity and improve efficiency, we normalize the regressor $\mathbf{p}(\mathbf{x})$ by the probability of the numeraire outcome n^*. As in the probability estimation above, n^* is taken to be the unsuccessful outcome. Thus, at stage 1 of the contest tree, $n^* = 1$, and at stage 2, $n^* = 7$ when arriving from node 3, and $n^* = 10$ when arriving from node 4 in Figure 1. Dividing through $\mathbf{p}(\mathbf{x})$ by the numeraire outcome produces a vector containing a constant (for the numeraire outcome) and a set of *odds* in favor of each of the remaining outcomes: $\mathbf{p}(\mathbf{x})/p_{n^*}$. Using a logarithmic transformation for the odds and dropping the vector notation yields the following cross-sectional regression specification:

$$\Gamma_{js} = \mu_r^s + \sum_{n \in \mathcal{E}^s, n \neq n^*} \mu_n^s \ln\left(\frac{p_{jn}^s}{p_{jn^*}^s}\right) + \epsilon_j, \quad j = 1, \dots, N, \tag{9}$$

where ϵ_j is a random variable reflecting the estimation error in Γ_{js}.

[21] Eckbo and Thorburn (2000a) present large-sample evidence that the measured gains to bidders tend to increase when the total equity size of the bidder relative to the target decreases.

[22] The probability estimates reported above are generated assuming stationarity over the sample period. As shown in an earlier draft, subperiod estimations provide similar inferences.

[23] The traditional average abnormal return estimates are analogous to parameter μ obtained by regressing Γ on a vector $\mathbf{d}$ of dummy variables that takes on a value of one corresponding to the (ex post known) outcome and zero otherwise. For example, if Γ is defined as the abnormal return induced by the offer announcement, then μ is estimated with hindsight [since $\mathbf{p}(\mathbf{x}) \equiv \mathbf{1}$] and it ignores the bid information $\mathbf{x}$. Thus traditional abnormal return estimates cannot be used to compute the marginal change in the expected value of a bid from a marginal change in the bid structure. Moreover, traditional abnormal return estimates represent relatively *noisy* estimates of the various payoffs, since abnormal returns must be cumulated over the entire tender offer contest period and are thus affected by random events following the bid announcement.

Note that, in Equation (9), the slope coefficient μ_n^s represents the marginal change in the bid's expected return by changing the log-odds in favor of outcome n.[24] Moreover, the constant term μ_r^s equals the expected value of a bid for which all the log-odds are equal to zero. This is a bid that generates *equal probabilities* for all outcomes (so that the odds equal 1), which we refer to as the *reference bid.* In other words, the payoff estimate μ_n^s measures the change in payoffs resulting from altering the log-odds (through the offer configuration $\mathbf{x}$) relative to the reference bid.

We perform the above cross-sectional regression at each stage s of the contest tree:

$$\begin{aligned} s=0: \quad & \Gamma_{j0}^{-60} = \mu_r^0 + \textstyle\sum_{n=2}^{4} \mu_n^0 \ln\left(\frac{p_{jn}^0}{p_{j1}^0}\right) + \epsilon_{j0}, \\ s=3: \quad & \Gamma_{j3}^{-60} = \mu_r^3 + \textstyle\sum_{n=5}^{6} \mu_n^3 \ln\left(\frac{p_{jn}^3}{p_{j7}^3}\right) + \epsilon_{j3}, \\ s=4: \quad & \Gamma_{j4}^{-60} = \mu_r^4 + \textstyle\sum_{n=8}^{9} \mu_n^4 \ln\left(\frac{p_{jn}^4}{p_{j10}^4}\right) + \epsilon_{j4}. \end{aligned} \tag{10}$$

Each equation is estimated separately, in conjunction with the associated probability estimates. We report estimates using a two-step procedure, where Γ_{js}^{-60} and the probability p_{jn}^s is estimated in the first step and the payoff μ_n^s from the corresponding equation in the above system in the second step.[25]

Moreover, the predicted value (abnormal return) of an offer with characteristics $\mathbf{x}$, $\hat{\Gamma}_s(\mathbf{x})$ is computed as

$$\hat{\Gamma}_s(\mathbf{x}) = \hat{\mu}_r^s + \sum_{n \in \mathcal{E}^s,\, n \neq n^*} \hat{\mu}_n^s \ln\left(\frac{p_n^s(\mathbf{x})}{p_{n^*}^s(\mathbf{x})}\right), \tag{11}$$

where $\hat{\mu}_r^s$ is estimated using Equation (10). Finally, we also report the partial derivative of the predicted offer value with respect to the kth offer parameter, $\partial\hat{\Gamma}_s/\partial x_k$, which is given by

$$\partial\hat{\Gamma}_s(\mathbf{x})/\partial x_k = \sum_{n \in \mathcal{E}^s,\, n \neq n^*} \hat{\mu}_n^s \hat{\delta}_k^s, \tag{12}$$

[24] The logarithmic form of the odds regressors makes it possible to interpret the coefficients μ_n^s as partial derivatives with respect to changes in the odds, despite the fact that the probabilities themselves sum to one. For example, starting with the reference bid at stage 1, suppose we increase p_2/p_1 to 2, holding the remaining odds constant at one. The new probabilities are $p_2 = .4$ and $p_1 = p_3 = p_4 = .2$, that is, with the remaining three odds unchanged. More generally, define $r_n^s = \ln(p_n^s/p_1^s)$, $n > s$. Thus $p_n^s = p_1^s \exp(r_n^s)$ and, since the probabilities sum to one, $p_1^s = 1/\sum_{n>s,\, n\neq 1} \exp(r_n^s)$. Consequently, as one changes one of the log-odds, all the probabilities change, however, the remaining log-odds remain fixed.

[25] In an earlier draft, we also reported results of a joint estimate of the payoffs and the probability [a system of two "seemingly unrelated" (SUR) equations, the first the multinomial model and the second the appropriate equation in Equation (10)]. The joint estimation avoids the errors in variables that is present in the two-step estimation procedure. The joint estimation further restricts the sample, and we experienced some convergence problems. However, the evidence from the joint estimation appears consistent with the results reported here. We also reestimated Equation (10) with different numeraire outcomes for the definitions of the odds ratio. Altering the numeraire outcome has little impact on the payoff estimates.

where $\hat{\delta}_n^s$ is the vector of parameter estimates from the multinomial logit model. This expression for the partial derivative uses the fact that the odds $(p_n^s/p_{n^*}^s)$ equal $\exp(\mathbf{x_j}'\delta_n^s)$ and the log-odds equal $\mathbf{x_j}'\delta_n^s$.

3.3.2 Estimated values. Table 10 reports weighted least squares, two-step estimates of the payoffs μ_n^s defined in Equation (10). Note that when the true payoff is positive, the log-transformation of the odds will produce a negative coefficient μ_n^s whenever the average odds is less than one. There are three such cases in Table 10 [see $\ln(p_6^3/p_7^3)$ in panel II and $\ln(p_8^4/p_{10}^4)$ in panel III], and to clearly signal these cases the table also reproduces the value of the mean log-odds associated with each node in the regression.

The regressions in all three panels of Table 10 are highly significant for targets (adjusted regression R^2s ranging from .14 to .32), while they are generally much less significant for bidders. For the 753 targets at stage 1, payoffs are positive and significant for all three outcomes ($n = 2 - 4$). This indicates that an offer which increases (relative to the reference bid) the log-odds in favor of outcomes 2–4 significantly increases target payoffs. Outcome 2 (successful single-bid contest) has the greatest target payoff, with a highly significant $\hat{\mu}_2^0 = .29$ ($t = 17.69$). When the contest develops multiple bids, the target payoff estimates are $\hat{\mu}_3^0 = .19$ ($t = 13.74$) for the event that the second bid is made by the initial bidder, and $\hat{\mu}_4^0 = .05$ ($t = 5.39$) when the second bid in the auction is made by a rival bidder.

Target payoffs at stage 2 of the contest tree are also for the most part large and significant, as expected. For example, stage 2 estimation from "second bid by initial bidder" produces $\hat{\mu}_6^3 = -.28$ ($t = -5.83$) for "rival bidder successful" (which represents a positive average payoff since the mean log-odds is negative). Moreover, stage 2 estimation from "second bid by rival bidder" yields $\hat{\mu}_8^4 = .18$ ($t = 6.97$) for the "initial bidder successful" outcome, and $\hat{\mu}_9^4 = .09$ ($t = 3.31$) for the "rival bidder successful" outcome.

As indicated earlier, there is little evidence of significant payoffs to bidders throughout Table 10. There is one exception, however, in panel II of the table, which shows a significant bidder payoff for the outcome where a rival bidder wins the auction (node $n = 6$). As for targets, the average log-odds is negative in this regression, so that the payoff is actually positive. Positive initial bidder gains when the initial bidder loses the contest to a rival is consistent with negative initial bidder gains when the outcome is successful. However, since there is no evidence of negative bidder payoffs in the successful states, nor is there evidence of a positive bidder payoff when the target rejects *all* bids, the significantly positive value of $\hat{\mu}_6^3$ most likely reflects expected gains from selling the toehold to the successful rival bidder. As was shown in Table 2, when the initial bidder loses to a rival, the rival purchases the initial bidder's toehold (or, in a partial bid, a prorated portion of the toehold) at a premium which averages 73% over the preoffer target share price.

We now turn to the predicted offer values, conditional on the vector of offer characteristics $\mathbf{x}$, $\hat{\Gamma}(\mathbf{x})$ shown in Table 11. To reiterate, this is the offer value

Table 10
Weighted least squares estimates of payoffs (μ_n^s) associated with potential outcomes in typical tender offer contests, 1971–1990

Dependent variable	Constant[a]	Log odds regressors: Successful initial bid ($\ln(p_2^0/p_1^0)$)	Second bid by initial bidder ($\ln(p_3^0/p_1^0)$)	Second bid by rival bidder ($\ln(p_4^0/p_1^0)$)
I. Stage 1 estimation from "initial bid" ($s = 0$)				
Targets ($N = 753$, adjusted $R^2 = .32$)				
Γ_0^{-60}	−.2371	.2877	.1859	.0522
	(−8.85)	(17.69)	(13.74)	(5.39)
Mean log-odds		1.29	.51	.20
Initial bidders ($N = 516$, adjusted $R^2 = -.002$)				
Γ_0^{-60}	−.0194	.0107	.0098	−.0060
	(−.95)	(.98)	(.99)	(−.87)
Mean log-odds		1.60	.32	.05

Dependent variable	Constant[b]	Log odds regressors: Initial bidder successful ($\ln(p_5^3/p_7^3)$)	Rival bidder successful ($\ln(p_6^3/p_7^3)$)
II. Stage 2 estimation from "second bid by initial bidder" ($s = 3$)			
Targets ($N = 203$, adjusted $R^2 = .14$)			
Γ_3^{-60}	.5133	−.2845	−.2827
	(8.80)	(−3.78)	(−5.83)
Mean log-odds		.86	−.27
Initial bidders ($N = 108$, adjusted $R^2 = .03$)			
Γ_3^{-60}	.0047	−.0307	−.0796
	(.11)	(−.55)	(−2.12)
Mean log-odds		.82	−.27

Dependent variable	Constant[c]	Log odds regressors: Initial bidder successful ($\ln(p_8^4/p_{10}^4)$)	Rival bidder successful ($\ln(p_9^4/p_{10}^4)$)
III. Stage 2 estimation from "second bid by rival bidder" ($s = 4$)			
Targets ($N = 137$, adjusted $R^2 = .29$)			
Γ_4^{-60}	.2398	.1832	.0932
	(4.97)	(6.97)	(3.31)
Mean log-odds		−.17	1.58
Initial bidders ($N = 77$, adjusted $R^2 = .01$)			
Γ_4^{-60}	.0747	−.0184	−.0448
	(1.65)	(−.68)	(−1.61)
Mean log-odds		.04	1.50

The payoffs μ_n^s are estimated using the following cross-sectional regression equation with log-odds as regressors:

$$\Gamma_{js}^{-60} = \mu_r^s + \sum_{n>s, n \neq n^*}^{\mathcal{E}^s} \mu_n^s \ln\left(\frac{p_{jn}^s}{p_{jn^*}^s}\right) + \epsilon_{js} \quad j =, 1, \ldots, N.$$

where Γ_{js}^{-60} is the abnormal return to firm j cumulated from day −60 relative to the initial offer date and through node s in the contest tree, $\mathcal{E}^s$ is the number of nodes in the tree following node s, p_{jn}^s is the outcome probability of node n conditional on node s, n^* is the numeraire (unsuccessful contest) outcome, and ϵ_{js} is an error term. The constant term μ_r^s is the expected payoff to a bid which generates equal outcome probabilities (and therefore zero log-odds ratios). The dependent variable and the probabilities used to form the log-odds ratios are estimated as in Tables 7 and 9, and the WLS weights are the standard errors of the estimates of Γ_{js}.

[a]This constant term is the expected payoff to a bid generating $p_1^0 = p_2^0 = p_3^0 = p_4^0 = 1/4$ (and thus zero log-odds).

[b]This constant term is the expected payoff to a bid generating $p_5^3 = p_6^3 = p_7^3 = 1/3$ (and thus zero log-odds).

[c]This constant term is the expected payoff to a bid generating $p_8^4 = p_9^4 = p_{10}^4 = 1/3$ (and thus zero log-odds).

The Review of Financial Studies / v 13 n 4 2000

computed using the estimated parameters in Table 10 and a given offer configuration **x**. The first three columns of Table 11 shows predicted offer values for three alternative bid structures, while the last six columns lists the partial derivatives $\partial\hat{\Gamma}_s(\mathbf{x})/\partial x_k$, $s = 0, 3, 4$, $k = 1, \ldots, 6$. Thus this table addresses questions concerning the impact on the expected value of a bid from, for example, increasing the toehold, fully accounting for the payoffs as well as the marginal impact of the toehold increase on the relevant outcome probabilities. Note that because the payoffs for bidder firms in Table 10 are statistically insignificant (with the one exception noted above), Table 11 shows results for target firms only.

The first column of Table 11 shows the expected value of the reference bid by repeating the constant term μ_r^0 from the regressions in Table 10. Notice first the significantly negative value of the reference bid for targets in panel I

Table 11
Predicted offer value ($\hat{\Gamma}$(x)) and its partial derivative ($\partial\hat{\Gamma}$(x)/∂x_k) for target firms in tender offer contests, 1971–1990

Predicted offer value ($\hat{\Gamma}(\mathbf{x})$)			Partial derivatives:[a] $\partial\hat{\Gamma}(\mathbf{x})/\partial x_k$					
At reference bid[b]	At mean log-odds[c]	At mean probabilities[d]	Premium	Toehold	Zero-Toe	Payment	Negotiated	Hostile
I: First bid in contest ($s = 0$)								
−.2371	.2406	.3430	.3492	−.0023	−.1360	−.0872	.0697	
II: Second bid in contest, bid made by initial bidder ($s = 3$)								
.5133	.3434	.3209	.1496	.0016	.0504	.0919	−.3505	−.1647
III: Second bid in contest, bid made by rival bidder ($s = 4$)								
.2398	.3558	.4080	.1658	−.0068	.0794	.1134	−.1611	−.0739

The predicted value (abnormal return) of an offer with characteristics **x**, $\hat{\Gamma}_s(\mathbf{x})$, is computed as

$$\hat{\Gamma}_s(\mathbf{x}) = \hat{\mu}_r^s + \sum_{n \in \mathcal{E}^s, n \neq n^*} \hat{\mu}_n^s \ln\left(\frac{p_n^s(\mathbf{x})}{p_{n^*}^s(\mathbf{x})}\right),$$

where $\hat{\mu}_n^s$ are the payoff estimates from Table 10. There are $K = 7$ bid-specific characteristics in the $(K \times 1)$ vector of determinants **x**, and there are a total of $\mathcal{E}^s$ possible events (nodes) conditional on node s. The partial derivative of the predicted offer value with respect to the kth offer parameter, $\partial\hat{\Gamma}_s(\mathbf{x})/\partial x_k$, is given by

$$\partial\hat{\Gamma}_s(\mathbf{x})/\partial x_k = \sum_{n \in \mathcal{E}^s, n \neq n^*} \hat{\mu}_n^s \hat{\delta}_k^s.$$

where $\hat{\delta}_n^s$ is the (7×1) vector of parameter estimates from the multinomial logit model reported in Table 7. This derivative follows since $(p_n^s/p_{n^*}^s) = \exp(\mathbf{x}_j{}'\delta_n^s)$ and thus the log-odds equal $\mathbf{x}_j{}'\delta_n^s$.

[a]Variable definitions:

Premium = offer price relative to the target's price 60 days before the announcement of the initial offer. In stage 2 estimates, the premium is the second offer price relative to the target's price 60 days before the initial offer.

Toehold = initial bidder's level of ownership in the target prior to the announcement of the initial offer. In stage 2 estimates, the toehold is the second bidder's initial level of ownership in the target.

Zero-Toe = dummy variable which equals one if the toehold is zero.

Payment = dummy variable which equals one if the payment method of the initial bid includes securities.

Negotiated = dummy variable which equals one if the initial bidder negotiated a tender precommitment with the target management or a major target shareholder prior to the bid.

Hostile = dummy variable which equals one if the target management opposes the bid.

[b]The value of the reference bid equals the constant term $\hat{\mu}_r^s$ and is reproduced here from Table 10. The reference bid represents an offer which produces equal outcome probabilities across all outcomes in the contest tree and thus zero log-odds.

[c]The estimated value of $\Gamma(\mathbf{x})$ is computed using the mean of log odds observed for that sample (i.e., the log odds used to estimate the μs.

[d]The estimated value of $\Gamma(\mathbf{x})$ is computed using the mean of the probabilities estimated using the full sample of bids.

($\mu_r^0 = -.24$, with a t value of -8.85 as shown in Table 10). In other words, the expected value to target shareholders of the reference bid is lower than the expected value of the average bid in the sample. The explanation for this is that the reference bid places a higher probability (equal to .25) on the "target unsuccessful" outcome at stage I of the contest tree (node 1 in Figure 1): Recall from Table 7 that the average sample probability of this outcome is only .11. Moreover, we reported earlier that the average abnormal return to targets from day −60 through the unsuccessful outcome at node 1 is only .16 (Table 9), which is substantially lower than the average abnormal return to the various successful outcome nodes in the contest tree. In sum, by placing too much weight on the relatively low-payoff, unsuccessful outcome, the expected value of the reference bid, relative to the average bid in the sample, is negative.

Our finding of a negative target expected payoff from the reference bid is interesting in light of the evidence in Bradley, Desai, and Kim (1983) of a reversal of initial gains to ultimately unsuccessful targets. Target losses in the unsuccessful outcome nodes of the contest tree are consistent with the hypothesis that takeover gains anticipated prior to the offer date (over the period from day −60 through day 0) are conditioned on a control change in the target firm. Note, however, the methodological difference: While Bradley–Desai–Kim arrive at their conclusion based on average abnormal returns in a subsample of ex post unsuccessful targets (much as in our Table 9), our inferences are based on the estimated *expected* payoff to the reference bid. In our analysis, this expectation is a product of the estimated outcome probabilities and the cumulative abnormal returns from day −60 through day 0 across *all* bids in the sample.

The second and third columns in Table 11 show the expected payoffs to target shareholders of (1) the bid which produces the average estimated log-odds, $\overline{\ln}(p_n^s/p_{n^*}^s)$, and (2) the bid which generates the average estimated probabilities $\bar{p}_n^s(\mathbf{x})$. For target firms at stage I (the initial bid), the value of $\hat{\Gamma}_s^{-60}(\mathbf{x})$ is .24 for the former offer and .34 for the latter offer type. Recall also from Table 9 that the average target abnormal return from day −60 through the offer announcement day (Γ_0^{-60}) is .33. Thus when we combine the payoff estimates from Table 10 with the average estimated outcome probabilities, we generate an expected offer value that is very close to the unconditional sample average abnormal return for target firms at the initial stage of the contest.

The partial derivatives $\partial\hat{\Gamma}_s(\mathbf{x})/\partial x_k$ shown in Table 11 are also interesting. As expected, raising the offer price increases the expected return to targets whether it is at the first or at the second bid in the contest. However, if the initial bidder increases the toehold, the expected value of the offer to target shareholders is generally reduced at the time of the first bid, and increased at the time of the second bid. The reduced target value from an increase in the toehold at the time of the initial bid reflects the significantly positive

The Review of Financial Studies / v 13 n 4 2000

impact of the toehold on the probability of single-bid success (which generates lower target gains) shown earlier in Table 8. The increased target value of a larger bidder toehold at the time of the second bid most likely reflects the finding (Table 8) that greater toeholds at this stage reduces the probability of an altogether unsuccessful target (nodes 7 and 10 in the contest tree). It is also interesting to note that the presence of a negotiated tender agreement increases the expected value of the offer to target shareholders at the initial offer but not at the second bid.

Finally, the results indicate that target management resistance *reduces* the expected value of the second bid in the tender offer contest, whether the second bid is made by the initial or by the rival bidder. In other words, target shareholders are better off (in terms of the expected value of the bid) if the initial bid attracts competing offers without target management signaling a hostile reaction to the initial bid.

4. Conclusions

Corporate takeover bids occur in sequential auctions that have a variety of potential outcomes. This article designs an empirically tractable contest tree structure capturing much of the complexity of such auctions. With a sample of 2,335 bids in 1,353 tender offer contests over the post-Williams Act period of 1971–1990, we estimate outcome probabilities throughout the contest tree as a function of key decision variables under the bidder's control. These include the offer premium, the toehold, the payment method, and whether or not the bidder negotiates a partial tender agreement with a major target shareholder. We then use the estimated outcome probabilities to generate payoff estimates embedded in the market reaction to the initial and second bid announcements. The latter estimation exploits the notion that the market reaction to a bid announcement represents the sum of the product of outcome probabilities and payoffs across every node in the contest tree. The estimation permits a systematic examination of the marginal impact of various offer parameters on expected payoffs to bidder and target firms, using only information available at the time of the bid.

Our information on the duration, bid jumps, and success rates in tender offer contests can be summarized as follows:

Contest duration and bid jumps. *(C1) The average single-bid contest lasts 40 days, while the average duration for multiple-bid contests is 70 days. (C2) In multiple-bid contests, the number of bids ranges from 2 to 12, with an average of 3. (C3) The average number of days between the first and second bid is 15, and the typical bid jump from initial to second bid is 10%, representing a premium increase of 31%. (C4) Offer premiums in successful single-bid contests are on average higher than the average initial offer premium in multiple-bid contests. (C5) The initial bidder's rate of success is*

78% in single-bid contests, but only 41% when the first bid attracts competition.

The relatively rapid entry of a competing bid, combined with the large bid jump (C3), suggests that tender offer contests have common value elements (rival bidders quickly determine their own valuation of the target) and that bidding is costly (making large bid jumps optimal). We also find that the initial bidder frequently revises the initial bid before the entry of a rival bidder, possibly to avoid a negative reaction to the bid by the target board. Result (C4) is consistent with the model of Fishman (1988) in which the relatively high-value initial bidders in private value auctions with costly bidding raises the bid to deter competition.

We also show that toehold effects are significant:

Bidder toeholds. *(T1) Of the 1,353 initial bidders, only 53% have toeholds. Initial bidder toeholds are largest in single-bid contests (average 20%) and lowest in multiple-bid contests (average 5%). (T2) In multiple-bidder contests, the initial and rival bidders on average enter with similar toehold levels. (T3) Toeholds and offer premiums are negatively correlated, and toeholds are smaller the greater the prebid run-up in the target share price. (T4) Greater toeholds increase the probability of single-bid success, and lowers both the probability of rival bidder entry and target management resistance.*

These results have implications for bidding models focusing on the toehold decision. For example, (T1) and (T4) are consistent with multiple-bidder models in which acquiring a toehold provides a competitive advantage [e.g., Burkart (1995), Singh (1998), and Bulow, Huang, and Klemperer (1999)]. As argued by Bulow, Huang, and Klemperer (1999), in common-value auctions, (T2) implies the greatest level of competition among rival bidders and may therefore be the result of a deliberate target "level the playing field" strategy. However, our evidence on prebid target tendering agreements does not support this conjecture. The first part of (T3) is consistent with Shleifer and Vishny (1986) and Hirshleifer and Titman (1990), but inconsistent with Chowdry and Jegadeesh (1994). The second part of (T3) is inconsistent with the model of Ravid and Spiegel (1999).

Multinomial logit estimation of the probabilities for each of the nodes in the contest tree in Figure 1 reveals the following:

Contest tree outcome probabilities. *(P1) The offer premium, toehold, and the prebid tender agreement all significantly affect the outcome probabilities, while the payment method is insignificant. (P2) The impact of the offer parameters on the outcome probabilities is almost exclusively restricted to the initial bid in the contest. (P3) At the initial bid, the derivative of the probability of single-bid success is positive with respect to the offer premium, the toehold, and the prebid tender agreement.*

The insignificance of the payment method (P1) differs from previous studies such as by Walkling (1985), Asquith (1992), and Jennings and Mazzeo (1993), who find some evidence that use of cash increases the probability of a succsessful bid. Also, Jennings and Mazzeo (1993) report that the probability of a competing bid increases with the proportion of cash used in the initial bid. However, Jennings–Mazzeo and others present binomial probability estimates that omit relevant branches of Figure 1 and which therefore are biased. Moreover, since they do not include the remaining four offer parameters, our finding may simply indicate that the effect of the payment method is small when considered jointly with the remaining offer parameters. Results (P2) and (P3) are also new, produced by the sequential nature of our probability estimation.

Finally, our ex ante payoff estimates at each node across the contest tree can be summarized as follows:

Contest tree payoffs and expected value of bid. *(S1) Target payoffs are positive and large in all successful nodes in the contest tree, and greater when the initial bid attracts competition. (S2) An offer that generates a higher than average probability of an unsuccessful single-bid contest has a much lower expected value to target shareholders than an offer generating average outcome probabilities. (S3) Increasing the offer premium increases the expected value of the offer to target shareholders, while increasing the initial bidder's toehold reduces target payoffs. (S4) Target management resistance reduces the expected value of the second bid to target shareholders. (S5) The expected payoff to initial bidders is insignificantly different from zero, as are bidder payoffs for all the successful states. (S6) Expected payoff to initial bidders is significantly positive when a rival bidder wins the auction, most likely reflecting the expected gain from the ensuing toehold-sale to the successful rival.*

Result (S1) is consistent with results reported by Bradley, Desai, and Kim (1988) for their sample of 236 successful tender offers. (S2) is consistent with a target management entrenchment hypothesis under which takeover gains require a transfer of control to new management. This inference is qualitatively similar to that of Bradley, Desai, and Kim (1983), who find that share prices of ex post unsuccessful targets tend to fall back to their preoffer levels. However, (S2) provides new information because it is founded on the market reaction to the *initial* offer announcement and does not use hindsight. Result (S3) is explained by the finding that an increased toehold at the initial stage of the contest increases the probability of single-bid success, which in turn is associated with lower target payoffs. The negative effect of toeholds on target payoff is consistent with Jarrell and Poulsen (1989) and Eckbo and Langohr (1989), but contradicts Franks and Harris (1989) and Stulz, Walkling, and Song (1990). Result (S4) indicates that target shareholders are better off with a second bid that materializes without target management having resorted to hostilities vis-á-vis the takeover attempt. Finally, our structural estimation also sheds new light on the controversial issue of gains to bidder firms. Abnormal returns to bidder firms are typically found to be insignificantly different from zero in the literature. Result (S5) is consistent with results reported elsewhere. However, (S6) possibly reflects gains from selling the target toehold at a premium to the winning rival bidder, which in turn reinforces the value to bidders of acquiring toeholds.

References

Asquith, D., 1992, "Essays on Tender Offers," Ph.D. dissertation, University of California at Los Angeles.

Barclay, M. J., and C. G. Holderness, 1991, "Negotiated Block Trades and Corporate Control," *Journal of Finance*, 46, 861–878.

Berkovitch, E., and M. P. Narayanan, 1990, "Competition and the Medium of Exchange in Takeovers," *Review of Financial Studies*, 3, 153–174.

Betton, S., and B. E. Eckbo, 1997, "State-Contingent Payoffs in Takeovers: New Structural Estimates," working paper, Tuck School at Dartmouth.

Bradley, M., 1980, "Interfirm Tender Offers and the Market for Corporate Control," *Journal of Business*, 53, 345–376.

Bradley, M., A. Desai, and E. Han Kim, 1983, "The Rationale behind Inter-firm Tender Offers: Information or Synergy?," *Journal of Financial Economics*, 11, 141–153.

Bradley, M., A. Desai, and E. Han Kim, 1988, "Synergistic Gains from Corporate Acquisitions and their Division between the Stockholders of Target and Acquiring Firms," *Journal of Financial Economics*, 21, 3–40.

Brown, D. T., and M. D. Ryngaert, 1992, "The Mode of Acquisition in Takeovers: Taxes and Asymmetric Information," *Journal of Finance*, 46, 653–670.

Bulow, J., M. Huang, and P. Klemperer, 1999, "Toeholds and Takeovers," *Journal of Political Economy*, 107, 427–454.

Burkart, M., 1995, "Overbidding in Takeover Contests," *Journal of Finance*, 50, 1491–1515.

Choi, D., 1991, "Toehold Acquisitions, Shareholder Wealth, and the Market for Corporate Control," *Journal of Financial and Quantitative Analysis*, 26, 391–408.

Chowdry, B., and N. Jegadeesh, 1994, "Pre-Tender Offer Share Acquisition Strategy in Takeovers," *Journal of Financial and Quantitative Analysis*, 29, 117–129.

Chowdry, B., and V. Nanda, 1993, "The Strategic Role of Debt in Takeover Contests," *Journal of Finance*, 48, 731–745.

Eckbo, B. E., R. M. Giammarino, and R. L. Heinkel, 1990, "Asymmetric Information and the Medium of Exchange in Takeovers," *Review of Financial Studies*, 3, 651–676.

Eckbo, B. E., and H. Langohr, 1989, "Information Disclosure, Method of Payment, and Takeover Premiums: Public and Private Tender Offers in France," *Journal of Financial Economics*, 24, 363–403.

Eckbo, B. E., and K. S. Thorburn, 2000a, "Gains to Bidder Firms Revisited: Domestic and Foreign Acquisitions in Canada," *Journal of Financial and Quantitative Analysis*, 35, 1–25.

Eckbo, B. E., and K. S. Thorburn, 2000b, "Toeholds and Fire-Sales in Bankruptcy Auctions," working paper, Tuck School at Dartmouth.

Fishman, M. J., 1988, "A Theory of Preemptive Takeover Bidding," *Rand Journal of Economics*, 19, 88–101.

Fishman, M. J., 1989, "Preemptive Bidding and the Role of the Medium of Exchange," *Journal of Finance*, 44, 41–57.

Franks, J., and R. Harris, 1989, "Shareholder Wealth Effects of Corporate Takeovers: The U.K. Experience," *Journal of Financial Economics*, 24, 225–250.

Giammarino, R. M., and R. L. Heinkel, 1986, "A Model of Dynamic Takeover Behavior," *Journal of Finance*, 41, 465–480.

Grossman, S. J., and O. D. Hart, 1980, "Takeover Bids, the Free Rider Problem and the Theory of the Corporation," *Bell Journal of Economics*, 11, 42–64.

Hansen, R., 1987, "A Theory for the Choice of Exchange Medium in Mergers and Acquisitions," *Journal of Business*, 60, 75–95.

Hausman, J. A., and D. A. Wise, 1977, "Social Experimentation, Truncated Distributions and Efficient Estimation," *Econometrica*, 45, 919–939.

Hirshleifer, D., and I. P. L. Png, 1989, "Facilitation of Competing Bids and the Price of a Takeover Target," *Review of Financial Studies*, 2, 587–606.

Hirshleifer, D., and S. Titman, 1990, "Share Tendering Strategies and the Success of Hostile Takeover Bids," *Journal of Political Economy*, 98, 295–324.

Hochberg, Y., 1988, "A Sharper Bonferroni Procedure for Multiple Tests of Significance," *Biometrika*, 75, 800–802.

Jarrell, G. A., and Annette B. Poulsen, 1989, "Stock Trading Before the Announcement of Tender Offers: Insider Trading or Market Anticipation?," *Journal of Law, Economics, & Organization*, 5, 225–228.

Jennings, R. H., and M. A. Mazzeo, 1993, "Competing Bids, Target Management Resistance, and the Structure of Takeover Bids," *Review of Financial Studies*, 6, 883–910.

Maddala, G. S., 1983, *Limited-Dependent and Qualitative Variables in Econometrics*, Econometric Society Monographs 3, Cambridge University Press, Cambridge, UK.

Mikkelson, W. H., and R. S. Ruback, 1985, "An Empirical Analysis of the Interfirm Investment Process," *Journal of Financial Economics*, 14, 523–553.

Ravid, S. A., and M. Spiegel, 1999, "Toehold Strategies, Takeover Laws and Rival Bidders," *Journal of Banking and Finance*, 23, 1219–1242.

Schwert, G. W., 1996, "Markup Pricing in Mergers and Acquisitions," *Journal of Financial Economics*, 41, 153–192.

Shleifer, A., and R. W. Vishny, 1986, "Large Shareholders and Corporate Control," *Journal of Political Economy*, 94, 461–488.

Simes, R. J., 1986, "An Improved Bonferroni Procedure for Multiple Tests of Significance," *Biometrika*, 73, 751–754.

Singh, R., 1998, "Takeover Bidding with Toeholds: The Case of the Owner's Curse," *Review of Financial Studies*, 11, 679–704.

Stulz, R. M., R. A. Walkling, and M. H. Song, 1990, "The Distribution of Target Ownership and the Division of Gains in Successful Takeovers," *Journal of Finance*, 45, 817–833.

Walkling, R. A., 1985, "Predicting Tender Offer Success: A Logistic Analysis," *Journal of Financial and Quantitative Analysis*, 20, 461–478.

Walkling, R. A., and M. Long, 1984, "Agency Theory, Managerial Welfare, and Takeover Bid Resistance," *Rand Journal of Economics*, 15, 54–68.

White, H., 1980, "A Heteroscedasticity Consistent Matrix Estimator and a Direct Test for Heteroscedasticity," *Econometrica*, 48, 817–838.

[8]

AUCTIONS OF COMPANIES

ROBERT G. HANSEN*

Auctions of companies are conducted in ways that contradict received auction theory. The major puzzles are: (1) sellers restrict the number of bidders; (2) sellers restrict the number of bidders; (3) bidders are screened by an initial round of nonbinding bids; and (4) bidders offer—and sellers sometimes accept—preemptive bids. Puzzles (1), (2), and (4) are explained by assuming that some information concerning the company can, if released, reduce the value of the company. Puzzle (3) is explained as a way for sellers to select the highest-valued bidders; equilibrium is maintained by using the initial bids to set a reserve price for the final bidding round. (*JEL* D44, D82, G34)

I. INTRODUCTION

From 1989 to 1998, 19,593 private companies were reported to be bought and sold in the United States, many through an auction process. The total value of these transactions was in excess of $315 billion.[1] In addition, from 1989 to 1998, there were 13,134 reported divestitures of divisions, subsidiaries, or product lines; the value of these transactions was in excess of $900 billion. Perhaps not surprisingly, an industry of advisors/auctioneers exists to facilitate these transactions, and the institutional framework by which auctions of companies are conducted has become somewhat standardized. The purpose of this article is to apply auction theory to explain this standardized institutional framework. The article proceeds as follows: section II describes the standardized process used for selling private companies or divisions of public companies; points out how these practices conflict with certain aspects of received auction theory; and presents initial arguments that explain the rationality of the practices. In section III, a more formal model is developed to show how some of the standard corporate auction practices can be explained. Section IV deals with what may be the most intriguing institutional practice—the use of preliminary, nonbinding indications of interest. Section V concludes the article with a preliminary discussion of entry fees and preemptive bidding.

*Many of the ideas in this paper were generated when the author worked as a consultant with LEK Consulting. The research was given financial support by the Tuck Associates. I would like to thank the editor, an anonymous reviewer, Rajesh Aggarwal, and participants at the Tuck School Finance/Economics workshop for useful comments.

Hansen: Norman W. Martin 1925 Professor of Business Administration and Senior Associate Dean, Tuck School, Dartmouth College, Hanover, NH 03755. Phone 1-603-646-2079, E-mail Robert.hansen@dartmouth.edu

1. *Mergerstat Review*, 1999. I purposely exclude tender offers for entire publicly traded companies as the auction process for such transactions is not as structured as for private transactions.

II. THE "TYPICAL" AUCTION PROCESS AND CONSISTENCY WITH AUCTION THEORY

The typical process for selling a private company or division of a public company runs as follows.[2] Upon making the decision to sell, the selling company will retain (or will already have retained) an advisor who will serve as de facto auctioneer. The auctioneer, drawing on knowledge of the selling company, will draw up a preliminary list of potential bidders; this list will probably include competitors, suppliers, customers, and acquisition-oriented conglomerates or leveraged buyout houses. The advisor will also exercise his judgment at this time as to whether or not a prospective bidder will be willing and able to complete a transaction at a "satisfactory" price. If a negative judgment is made, that potential bidder

2. Much of my information on this process derives from my experience as a management consultant. Macy (1990) contains a description of some aspects of the process. I also have on file two documents produced by investment banks that describe the divestiture process.

Economic Inquiry
(ISSN 0095-2583)
Vol. 39, No. 1, January 2001, 30–43

will likely be excluded from further participation. The remaining prospective bidders will receive a very cursory description of the selling company and will be offered a more in-depth offering memorandum if they sign a confidentiality agreement. Although the first cursory description may not even include the selling company's name, the offering memorandum will be quite detailed, including the sort of information that would typically be in a public corporation's Securities and Exchange Commission 10K filing as well as traditionally confidential information on current issues at the selling company, overview of costs, plans for market and product developments, and so on. The next step is for the prospective bidders to submit preliminary, nonbinding "indications of interest" for the selling company. These indications will be either a number or a range of numbers that are supposed to represent "bidders' first approximations of their estimates of the value of the target."[3] The preliminary indications are then used by the auctioneer to further reduce the number of bidders who will proceed further: "Only the top bidders on their list are permitted to go forward"[4] Although the screening is clearly not as straightforward as the preceding passage presumes, there is no doubt that the likelihood of admittance to the next round increases with the preliminary bid—even though that bid is nonbinding.[5]

Since explaining this institutional practice of requiring submission of preliminary, nonbinding indications of interest is a primary purpose of this paper, it is important to establish that the practice is indeed common. Besides the references to Macy (1990), I have spoken with numerous investment bankers who confirm that a round of preliminary indications of interest is standard practice. A representative quote is as follows: "When our firm is engaged by a selling company to conduct an auction, we always ask potential buyers to submit preliminary, nonbinding indications of interest. These indications are typically ranges of values, and those potential buyers with low ranges are more likely to be excluded from the ensuing auction than buyers with higher ranges, *ceteris paribus*. This is standard practice at all investment banks with which I am familiar."[6] I have also reviewed two documents from major New York City investment banks that spell out a typical auction process. The process as described in these documents is entirely consistent with the description given here.

For those potential buyers who sign confidentiality agreements and are qualified by their preliminary indications, the next round of the selling process ensues with more extensive dissemination of information. This process includes visits with and presentations by senior management of the selling company; plant and site visits; and review of financial, legal, and other documents that are assembled by the selling company and its advisor in a "data room." Information released in this phase of the selling process is quite detailed and definitely of use to potential buyers in their valuation of the selling company. Some of the headings in one investment bank's "Information Request" (given to the selling company to prepare for visits with potential buyers) are as follows:

- Other market trends, including changes in unit pricing
- Historical and projected volume of units sold for each major product and/or product line
- A descriptive list of the company's key customers, which includes dollar amount and percentage of sales attributable to each, and special concessions given
- Description of any products and/or product lines presently in development stage, including expected dates of introduction, results of any testing, and expected financial results
- Description of each major component of cost-of-sales and a detailed list of direct general, selling, and administrative expenses attributable to each major product

3. Macy (1990), 95.
4. Macy (1990), 95.
5. Bidders themselves will also choose to not participate in the auction; such self-selection can occur at any stage of the process. Presumably bidders will opt out when they perceive the costs of participating as being greater than the expected benefits. Thus, there is an implicit *a priori* equilibrium along the lines of French and McCormick (1984), wherein the number of potential bidders who participate in each step of the auction process is endogenously determined. Although this aspect of the process is not modeled here, the idea is important, for it implies that there is not an unlimited number of willing bidders and that bidders who enter the process have positive expected profit.

6. Quote by Alex Fuchs of Morgan Stanley & Co., Inc.

• Description of the terms of any long-term supply contract or any other major commitment regarding the purchase of raw materials

• Major items of equipment and facilities used in the production process, including age and condition, total available production capacity, and amount of capacity used

• Specialized projected income statements for the next five years by product and/or product line and by geographic region

Although much of this information will be presented in the offering memorandum in a way designed by the selling company's advisor, original documents (for example, internal accounting data and actual supply contracts) will be available in the data room for review by potential buyers.

It is important to note that although the information given to potential buyers is extensive, it is not complete. Throughout the auction process, potential buyers may ask for information that the selling company will view as too confidential to reveal. The divestiture manual I reviewed notes this and adds that such information will generally be "that which is believed to be advantageous to competitors, or cost information believed to threaten relations with suppliers or employees."

The final step in the auction is for bidders to submit sealed bids for the purchase of the company. Because these bids may not be purely cash bids, choosing the best bid might represent a valuation problem for the selling company. Also, it is important to note that any time during this process a bidder might make a preemptive bid to short-circuit the sale. The most likely time for a preemptive bid, however, is before the last round of intensive information gathering.

There are aspects of this auction process that are interesting as they stand, but the process calls more strongly for explanation because it conflicts with standard results in auction theory and/or with what would appear to be rational behavior on the part of bidders. More explicitly, let me arrange the stylized facts of the auction process in this manner:

Stylized Fact #1: Sellers restrict the number of bidders.

Stylized Fact #2: Sellers restrict the flow of information to bidders.

Stylized Fact #3: Sellers choose the set of final-round bidders by staging an initial round of nonbinding bidding; the probability of getting into the final round increases with the initial round bid.

Stylized Fact #4: Bidders sometimes offer preemptive bids that sellers sometimes accept.

Stylized Fact #1 contradicts a basic tenet of auction theory: having more bidders increases the expected selling price. Although there are auction models where it pays the seller to restrict bidders by charging entry fees, these do not explain the practice observed in corporate auctions because no entry fees are charged in these auctions.[7] Also, standard auction models imply an optimal reserve price for the seller that implicitly limits the number of bidders (those with value less than the reserve price will not bid) but the limitation in these models is passive: bidders elect to participate or not; they are not told by the seller that they cannot participate. In the absence of entry fees, existing auction models give no rationale for excluding bidders.

Stylized Fact #2 contradicts a result by Milgrom and Weber (1982) on prices and information that has been conveniently restated by McAfee and McMillan (1987): "The seller can increase his expected revenue by having a policy of publicizing any information he has about the item's true value."[8] The intuition for this price-increasing effect is that divulging information tends to reduce the variance of bidders' value estimates, and this variance gives bidders the incentive to strategically reduce their bids. Yet in corporate auctions we see sellers purposely withholding relevant information.

Stylized Fact #3 is difficult to understand in the face of bidder rationality. If getting into the final round has any value at all (and it cannot be negative, for the bidder could always elect to drop out), then why not bid

7. In the model of French and McCormick (1984), for instance, a seller could increase revenues by charging an entry fee and thereby restricting the number of bidders, but it would never pay the seller to restrict bidders without an entry fee. See also the discussion in Macy (1990).

8. McAfee and McMillan (1987), 722.

high enough in the first round to ensure participation in the final round? But if everyone does this, the initial round bidding must escalate indefinitely, and the seller would not be able to use the initial-round bids to select bidders any more efficiently than random selection. Perhaps the most commonly heard rationale for existence of equilibrium is that "reputation effects" keep bidders from bidding "too high." But for many bidders an auction of this sort is likely to be a one-shot affair, so concern over reputation should be minimal. Also, determining when "cheating" has occurred—when a bidder opportunistically bids high just to get in the final round—must be extremely difficult; after all, the initial round bids must be nonbinding to allow for the possibility that, after seeing more information, a bidder decides the company is worth less than he or she originally thought. Yet bids in these initial rounds do appear to represent some measure of a bidder's valuation, and sellers do select bidders on the basis of their initial-round bids.

Stylized Fact #4—preemptive bidding—contradicts a finding by Riley and Samuelson (1981) that the seller cannot improve expected revenue by employing multiple rounds of bidding.[9] Preemptive bidding, after all, can be thought of as another initial round of bids; the seller stands ready to accept a bid in this initial preemptive round if it is high enough. Although it may seem profitable for a seller to use multiple rounds, with declining reservation prices, it turns out that after accounting for how bidders will behave in the initial round (i.e., they will bid low because they anticipate a next round), the seller's expected revenue will actually decline with such a scheme. Yet we see preemptive bids made and accepted.

In this article, I argue that the overall process by which companies are sold represents a balance between the benefits of getting more bidders and of releasing more information against what I term the *competitive information cost*. The idea is very simple: to accurately value a selling company, a potential buyer needs more than just projections or summary statistics, such as aggregate sales, profits, or valuations done by third parties. Because many potential buyers will be involved in the same industry as the selling company (as a competitor, supplier, or customer) the question will often be how the selling company will fit in with the buyer's existing operations. Thus, financial details on products and product lines, geographic distribution of sales, research and development plans, state of production facilities, and contracts with suppliers, customers, and employees, will be critical—just the sort of information noted above as being in a typical information request. Information such as the "recipe" for a product would probably not be critical to a buyer's valuation, for the effect of the recipe can be seen in summary statistics, such as sales data, and the recipe itself would be available on conclusion of the purchase. Where the product is sold, to whom, and for how much will be much more important, for a buyer may want to get, for example, a marketing/distribution network that is complementary to its own network.

The problem, however, is that the information relevant to an accurate valuation may also be valuable to potential buyers in their role as competitors, suppliers, or customers of the selling company. Releasing information to a set of potential buyers that includes competitors, suppliers, and customers may in fact reduce the value of the selling company. This is what I refer to as the competitive information effect: a negative relationship between the amount of information given out, the number of bidders that information is given out to, and the selling company's value to any one of the bidders.[10]

9. Bulow and Klemperer (1996) show that an auction of a company is always preferable to a negotiation so long as the auction attracts at least one additional bidder. They do not, however, consider the potential cost of releasing proprietary information, which is the crucial assumption of this article. From discussions with investment bankers, the decision to negotiate rather then auction does seem to hinge on the existence of proprietary information that, if released, could damage value.

10. For a competitive information effect to exist, the selling company and the bidders must be competing on some front, and that competition must be imperfect due to uncertainty. Disclosure of information in the auction process can then affect that competition, benefiting the bidders and destroying value of the selling company. Many game-theoretic models of competition involving the selling company and bidders would yield a competitive information effect. One possibility would be the following: Envision the selling company as procuring inputs via a sealed bid process. If one of the input suppliers finds out another supplier's current bid (through the selling company's disclosure), it could use that information to its advantage and the selling company's disadvantage. Entry models could also yield

Given this, the selling company will find it optimal to limit both the number of bidders and the amount of information it divulges; this explains Stylized Facts #1 and #2. Furthermore, the seller will increase profits if he can limit the number of bidders in a way that screens out low-valued bidders and admits high-valued bidders. I find that an initial round of nonbinding bids can serve this purpose *if the seller also uses the initial-round bids to set a reserve price for the final-round auction*. In this way, bidders are discouraged from bidding too high in the first round: the higher the bid in the first round (for any bidder) the higher the reserve price in the final round, and hence the lower the expected profits for the bidder.[11] Indeed, it turns out that the seller can elicit honest revelation of bidders' initial value estimates by a suitable choice of functional relationship between initial round bids and the final round reserve price.

This idea is just a formalization of a basic business tenet that I believe most people would subscribe to: "When buying something, do nothing to make the seller think that the item is worth a lot to you." In either a negotiated or auction context, if the seller believes that the item is worth a lot to a buyer, then the seller will generally find it optimal to raise the reservation price or to bargain harder. Thus, bidders in the initial round of a corporate auction must balance the benefits of a higher bid (increased probability of entry in the final round) against the costs (increased reserve price in the final round). Of course, there are certain conditions that must hold for an equilibrium to obtain; these are detailed below.

The final issue is that of preemptive bidding. Preemptive bidding can also represent rational equilibrium behavior for bidders and the seller in the presence of a competitive information cost. If the cost of releasing information in the final round is large, then the seller may find it better to accept any preemptive bid exceeding a critical level. In doing this, the seller forgoes the benefit of price determination via auction but also forgoes the value reduction due to information disclosure.[12]

I turn to a more formal model for explaining the restrictions placed on number of bidders and disclosure of information (Stylized Facts #1 and #2). The following section will deal with preliminary indications of interest—Stylized Fact #3.

III. A FORMAL MODEL FOR MANAGEMENT OF BIDDERS AND INFORMATION DISCLOSURE

A. Assumptions on Bidders, Valuations, and Information

There will be N potential bidders for the company being sold. A bidder's value for the company being sold will depend on both a bidder-specific variable (the bidder's *type*) and on a common state-variable that defines the condition of the selling company's assets.

More formally, I make the following assumptions.

Assumption 1. Bidder's value for the selling company is given as

$$\text{(1)} \qquad \text{Value to bidder } i = V(x_i; z)$$

where $V(\bullet)$ is a common valuation function; $x_i \in [\underline{x}, \bar{x}]$ is a variable denoting the bidder's type known only by bidder i, and $z \in [\underline{z}, \bar{z}]$ is a random state variable, with probability distribution $G(z)$, known by bidder i only after

a competitive information effect. One of the bidders could be considering entry into one of the selling company's product markets. In many entry models, the profitability of entry depends on the incumbent's cost. If disclosure during the auction reveals the selling company's costs, that information could be profitably used by a competitor. Other scenarios are readily envisioned: disclosure of expansion/capital expenditure plans of the selling company could lead a competitor to alter its own plans accordingly; disclosure of new marketing programs or product developments could let a competitor prepare competitive responses; and disclosure of profitability by geographic region could help a new competitor free-ride on the selling company's marketing efforts (by focusing its own efforts in those areas revealed to be most profitable and avoiding the unprofitable markets).

11. This mechanism works only if all bidders, even those with the lowest *ex ante* valuation, have positive expected profits in the final round auction. This is not the case in the standard auction model. The assumptions laid out below do allow all bidders to have positive expected profits; besides permitting equilibrium to hold in the model here, the assumptions that lead to positive expected profits for all bidders are of interest on their own.

12. Fishman (1988, 1989) also addresses the issue of preemptive bidding, but his analysis differs from mine. In Fishman's models, preemptive bidding arises out of a desire by one bidder to deter other bidders from investing in information concerning the target. Fishman's analysis and mine share the prediction that it will be high-valued bidders who make successful preemptive bids.

purchase of the company. Bidder i therefore has an *ex ante* expected value for the selling company given as

(2) Bidder i's Prior Expected Value $\equiv EV_i(x_i)$

$$= \int V(x_i; z)dG(z).$$

Each bidder views his competitors' types as independent draws from a probability distribution $F(x)$.[13]

Assumption 2. The seller has observations $y = (y_1, \ldots, y_N)$ on N random variables $(y_1, \ldots, y_N)$ that are also correlated with z. If the seller discloses m of these observations to the bidders, the bidder would update his beliefs on z using the conditional probability distribution $G(z|y_1, \ldots, y_m)$.

In words, then, a bidder's valuation depends on a component x_i that is independent and specific to himself and on a component z that is common to everyone but unknown. Bidders begin with no information on z, but the seller has potential to give them considerably more by disclosing all or part of his information $(y_1, \ldots, y_N)$. The seller's information can be thought of as that which he puts into the data room and which he provides through plant visits and management meetings.

There are two other characteristics to this seller's information set that are crucial, however. First, I assume that disclosure of the seller's information to more than just the winning bidder has the effect of reducing the value of the selling company to all of the bidders. As discussed above, the rationale for this is that much of the seller's information is of a competitive nature so that its disclosure to nonowners would lessen the economic viability of the company. The second characteristic is a logical corollary to the first: that the seller's information is itself of value to the bidders. That is, if the seller's information is competitive in nature, then the bidders would be willing to pay to get it.

In more formal terms:

Assumption 3. If $(y_1, \ldots, y_m)$ is observed by n bidders, then the net value of the selling company to bidder i becomes

(3) Net value to bidder i

$$= V(x_i, z) - f(n, m)$$

where $\partial f/\partial n > 0$ and $\partial f/\partial m > 0$.

Assumption 4. The competitive value to bidder i of observing $(y_1, \ldots, y_m)$ is d. Thus, all bidders place the same value on the information.[14]

B. Expected Sales Prices and the Optimal Number of Bidders and Information Disclosure

The expected price that the seller receives if it auctions the company will depend on m, its information disclosure; n, the actual number of bidders; and the auction rule (open, sealed bid, etc.) used. In the example that follows shortly, I will assume an open auction, but the results of the article are not at all dependent on the specific auction form used.

Because of the way information is assumed to affect valuations—it simply reduces every bidder's value by the fixed amount $f(n, m)$—it is straightforward to show that for any auction rule used, the competitive information cost reduces the seller's proceeds by exactly $f(n, m)$. It will therefore be convenient to talk about the gross sales price as the price before considering the competitive information effect and the net sales price as being the gross price less $f(n, m)$. The gross expected price will be denoted as $E_A(p|n, m)$, where the subscript A is simply a reminder that the expected price will depend on the auction rules used.

13. Though this set-up is similar to that of Milgrom and Weber (1982), it differs in that no restrictive assumptions are placed on the $V(x_i; z)$ function. In particular, Milgrom and Weber assume that the $V(\bullet)$ function is nondecreasing in all its variables. This precludes reversals in the ranking of bidders' valuations: if $x_i > x_j$, then $V(x_i; z) > V(x_j; z)$ for all z. As will be seen below, it is critical in the model here that the ranking of bidders' valuations depend on the state. The model as set up bears some resemblance to "almost common-values" assumptions—see, for instance, Klemperer (1998). In "almost common-values" auctions one bidder is given a slight valuation advantage. In the model here, one bidder will be given a slight advantage; the additional twist is that which bidder has the advantage depends on the state.

14. It would be more realistic to have d as an increasing function of m and, possibly, a declining function of n. These changes would complicate the model but would not alter the essential conclusions.

Following well-known results in auction theory, we know that having more bidders raises the gross expected price, so if $n_1 > n_2$, then

$$(4) \qquad E_A(p|n_1, m) \geq E_A(p|n_2, m).$$

Another well-known result in auction theory is that disclosure of information also raises the expected price. Some benefit to the seller of information disclosure is critical to the analysis here in order to create a tension between disclosure versus withholding of information by the seller. (If there is no benefit to the seller of disclosing information, and if there is any cost at all to disclosure, then no disclosure would be the best policy. This certainly conflicts most strongly with observed practice.) Although the intuitive reasons for the price-enhancing effects of disclosure are clear, the effect is assured only with certain valuation and informational assumptions—if the x_i variables and z were affiliated, and if $V(x_i; z)$ had certain features, as in Milgrom and Weber (1982). As will be made clear below, we do not wish to constrain the $V(x_i; z)$ function in the way that would ensure the price-enhancing effect of disclosure. This said, the assumptions we make do not preclude a price-enhancing effect of information and in the numerical example provided a price-enhancing effect does exist. Also in this regard, there is another very important legal benefit to sellers from disclosing information: withholding relevant information could be grounds for a claim of fraud. This legal aspect by itself would create the tension between the benefits and costs of disclosure at the heart of this article.

We will then assume that disclosure of information has a (gross) benefit to the seller: if $m_1 > m_2$, then

$$(5) \qquad E_A(p|n, m_1) \geq E_A(p|n, m_2).$$

With this groundwork established, the institutional facts of how companies are sold are easy to justify. Although adding more bidders does increase the "gross" expected selling price, the net price—after subtracting the information cost—may actually decline. Indeed, because it is likely that the gross selling price increases at a decreasing rate in the number of bidders, there is likely to be an interior optimum with the actual number of bidders less than the total available. Similarly, as the seller reveals more information, the marginal benefit of disclosure is likely to fall, so that there will be an optimum level of disclosure that is less than complete.

Two extreme cases are worth mentioning at this point, for they emphasize that the explanation given here for the "typical" auction process assumes a significant but not overwhelming importance of the competitive information cost. At one extreme, there would be little or no competitive information cost, so the optimal policy for the seller would be to have as many bidders as possible and to disclose fully. At the opposite extreme, the competitive information cost would be so high that the most attractive option for the seller would be to negotiate solely with one bidder but to give complete information. Because only the sole bidder receives the information, there is no cost to giving him everything, and this is likely to increase the price that can be negotiated. Thus, with companies where disclosure of even little information could reduce the value of the company significantly, we should not be surprised to see negotiated one-on-one sales. Section V discusses this idea further along with the related one of preemptive bidding.

IV. SCREENING BIDDERS VIA AN INITIAL ROUND OF BIDDING

A. Introduction

In the previous section it was suggested that an interior optimum exists for the number of bidders, but no mechanism was given for how the actual bidders would be selected. We now inquire as to whether the seller can somehow select final bidders in an efficient fashion, selecting the ones of better type (higher prior expected value, EV_i). One approach would be to qualitatively evaluate the potential bidders, focusing on how they might evaluate the selling company. The goal here would be to try to choose those bidders that have the most "synergy" with the selling company, that is, are most likely to place a higher value on it.

Although this kind of screening undoubtedly does occur, my focus here is on another process that could be complementary to the qualitative screening: screening bidders through the use of an initial round of nonbinding bids. My argument is that the selling company commits itself to set a *reserve price* in the final round of bidding that depends (positively) on the bids received in the initial round. Because bidders' expected profits are *decreasing* in the reserve price, this imposes a cost of bidding high in the first round.[15]

Furthermore, the cost imposed by a higher reserve price falls most heavily on bidders with lower *ex ante* expected values, for they are more likely to have a value that is less than the reserve price. This induces low-valued bidders to put in lower first-round bids than bidders with higher *ex ante* expected values, thereby creating a positive relation between initial-round bids and *ex ante* expected values. Choosing the highest initial-round bids then will ensure the seller of having a set of final-round bidders with the highest *ex ante* expected values—and to the extent that higher *ex ante* values lead to higher *ex post* values, this will maximize the final selling price.

15. A higher reserve price with unchanged bidding strategies lowers expected profits by reducing each bidder's probability of winning. A higher reserve price will, at least with sealed bids, also lead all bidders to increase their bids (conditional on expected valuations). Thus, the new equilibrium bid strategy also implies lower expected profits for bidders. The chance that the item remains unsold, of course, means that the seller's expected revenue does not increase monotonically with the reserve price. See Riley and Samuelson (1981).

The issue of commitment by an auctioneer is important—see, for example, the extensive discussion by McAfee and McMillan (1987, 703–04). In a first-price sealed-bid auction, a seller has incentive to renege on the stated policy of selling to the highest bidder at his bid, for upon seeing the highest bid the seller could (theoretically) infer the bidder's true value and demand a price equal to that value. (More practically, the seller would at least know that the winner would be willing to pay something more than the received bid.) All auction theory assumes that auctioneers can commit to a set of auction rules. I follow in this tradition by assuming that the auctioneer commits to a reserve price policy that is based on information revealed by the bidders in the first round. Although it might be true that the auctioneer could profit from reneging on his commitment and using the information revealed in a more opportunistic fashion, I assume that long-term considerations by the auctioneer (in my case, investment banks) prevent this. It should also be noted that the reserve price policy I propose is rational for the seller, if the seller is presumed to not know the distribution function of bidders' values: an *ex post* optimal reserve price will be higher, the higher are bidders' values. See Riley and Samuelson (1981).

TABLE 1
Type, States, and Valuations

	State	
Bidder Type	**1**	**2**
HI	80	140
LO	90	120

B. An Illustrative Example

Before proceeding to a general model showing the equilibrium of the first-round auction, it will be useful to develop a very simple example of a two-stage auction that clearly shows the principles at work. The example will also highlight the importance of one assumption concerning the interaction between information and bidder's valuations.

This example will have five potential bidders, with each bidder being characterized by their type. Type will take on one of two values, call them HI and LO. There will also be a state variable, which will also take on one of two values. Table 1 shows how type and state together determine a bidder's valuation (their value for the company being sold).

We assume that bidders' types are privately known and that the probability of any bidder being HI or LO is 1/2. The state variable is meant to cover the economic conditions of the company being sold; state will be unknown to the bidders *ex ante* but will be revealed by the seller in the second round of the auction through disclosure of proprietary information. *Ex ante*, bidders believe each state to be equally likely. Thus, HI bidders have an expected value of the company of 110, whereas expected value for LO type bidders is 105.

Note that this set-up fits the general assumptions described above. Value to a bidder is $V(x_i; z)$ where x_i is type and z is the state variable.

A very important aspect of these assumptions is that the *ranking of bidder's valuations depends upon the state*. As already noted (see note 13), this is unusual in auction theory. It is also critical for equilibrium in the model. For both of these reasons, the rationale for the underlying assumptions deserves discussion.

Let me turn first to why the assumption is critical for the model's equilibrium. This article argues that preliminary, nonbinding bids can reveal useful information to the seller (the bidder's types—HI or LO) if there is a cost to the bidders of dishonest reporting. The cost being considered works through the setting of the reserve price in the final round: High initial bids lead to higher reserve prices. For this mechanism to work, all bidders must see the possibility of positive expected profits in the final round; otherwise an increase in the reserve price could have no impact. Yet in received auction theory, the bidder of lowest type *ex ante* knows they will always be the lowest-valued bidder and must therefore have zero expected profit.[16]

With the assumptions here, neither a HI or LO bidder knows *ex ante* that they will be the low-valued bidder on disclosure of the state variable—ranking of the bidders' valuations is state-dependent. Both types of bidders therefore have the potential for positive expected profit in the final-round auctions, and there is therefore the ability of a reserve price mechanism to reduce that expected profit and induce honest revelation through initial bids.

More important than just the preservation of an equilibrium, the assumption on state/valuation interaction is economically reasonable, and it has implications for efficiency in auctions.

On the assumption's reasonableness, note that all that is being assumed is that the state variable affects bidders differentially. Both types view state-2 as being better than state-l, but HI-type bidders view state-l more unfavorably and state-2 more favorably than LO-type bidders. Put differently, HI-types are more sensitive to the state variable. From a general point of view, different utility functions could give rise to these valuation differences. In the context of corporate auctions, the different types of bidders could reasonably lead to valuations that exhibit such differences. Suppose the state-variable corresponds to the fundamental financial viability of the selling company, and suppose a HI-type bidder is another industrial firm while a LO-type bidder is a leveraged buyout house specializing in corporate restructuring. An industrial buyer might well be more sensitive to underlying financial viability, having a very high valuation if the company is solid and a very low valuation if the company is not viable. Or, to take another example, suppose the state variable corresponds to an underlying resource or marketing capability of the selling company. State-1, for example, could be a poor state of new product development, while state-2 could be new products almost ready for market. If new products are very important for a HI-type bidder, they would naturally have a valuation that was more sensitive to that state variable.

Numerous other situations could be envisioned: the state-variable could correspond to the state of management talent, geographic distribution of marketing and distribution resources, capacity utilization of plants, etc. For all of these variables, it would seem reasonable, if not likely, for bidder's valuations to respond differently.

Another view on the assumption being made further supports its economic rationale and its importance to economic efficiency. As pointed out, an implication of the interaction between state and value interaction is that the identity of the highest-valued bidder depends upon the state. Again, from a general utility/preference point of view this would not seem surprising: who is the highest-valued user of a resource cannot be ascertained without knowing the state (characteristics) of the resource itself. But in regard to economic efficiency, there is now a social value to information disclosure that is absent in received auction models (for an extreme example, consider the common-value model, where information has no allocative role to play since all bidders have the same valuation no matter the state). That information in auctions can be important to allocative efficiency seems intuitively appealing, but it cannot be unless the identity of the high-valued bidder depends upon the state.[17]

Proceeding then with analysis of a two-stage auction under those assumptions, we assume that in the initial round each bidder

16. See, for example, Milgrom and Weber (1982) and the discussion of that model in note 13.

17. As a further twist on this, it is easy to see that with assumptions that permit ranking of valuations to depend on the state, disclosure of information may reduce the seller's expected price. In the example, and with just two bidders, one HI and one LO, expected price in a second-price auction is 105 without disclosure of state and is 100 with disclosure. Thus, a tension exists between a seller's revenue and economic efficiency in relation to disclosure of information.

puts in a nonbinding bid of either 105 or 110.[18] The actual value of the bids is immaterial, but we choose them to equal the two bidders' *ex ante* expected values. Five initial bids will be received, and the seller will select the four highest to proceed into the second and final round. Ties will be broken randomly. Before the final round, the seller discloses proprietary information that reveals the state variable; in the final round bidders therefore know their valuation (still privately). The final-round auction will be an open auction (for ease of computing prices and profits). Most important, there will be a reserve price in the final round that depends on the initial bids: The reserve price will equal 80 if three or fewer initial bids come in at 110, but the reserve price will jump to 90 if four or more initial bids come in at 110.

With these auction rules, LO-type bidders will elect to put in a bid of 105 in the initial round and HI-type bidders will put in an initial bid of 110. Thus, the auction elicits honest revelation of bidders' *ex ante* expected values. LO-types do not mimic HI-types because the expected increase in the reserve price from a high initial bid affects the LO-types too much. To confirm this equilibrium, we must check that honest revelation is optimal for both types. This verification entails assuming that all other bidders are following the proposed equilibrium strategy and seeing if unilateral defection pays for one bidder.

First consider a HI-type. A HI-type can earn profit in the final round only if he or she is the only HI-type. Assuming equilibrium behavior by the other bidders, this implies that the other four bidders must all be LO-types, and it also implies that the reserve price will be 80 in the final auction. By not honestly revealing in the initial round, this HI-type would only forfeit a certainty of entry into the final round in the one instance where he could make a profit, for if he dishonestly reported 105 in the initial round, he would be indistinguishable from the other four LO-types. And there is absolutely no benefit in other situations for an initial bid of 105: Although this would reduce the reserve price in some cases, there were already zero expected profits in those cases because of the presence of other HI-types. A HI-type is therefore strictly better off with an initial bid of 110.

Next consider a LO-type bidder. A LO-type, by bidding 110 instead of 105 in the initial round, may increase the likelihood that they get into the final-round auction. The only case, however, where a LO-type can make a profit is when they are the only LO-type in the final round. By bidding 110 in the initial round rather than 105, a LO-type can increase the likelihood that he or she gets into those final-round auctions with three HI-types (with two LO-types and three HI-types, a defecting LO-type assures entry in the final round.) The problem is that with four initial bids of 110 in these cases, the reserve price becomes 90, eliminating the possibility of a LO-type making a profit. Thus, there is only a net cost to bidding 110 instead of 105, and a LO-type will honestly report his *ex ante* valuation in the initial round. (There are other cases where defection by a LO-type increases their likelihood of entry into the final round, but with other LO-types present in the final round, there is no profit in these cases.)[19]

In this example, then, the seller can select four out of five bidders to receive additional proprietary information and participate in a final round auction. The two-stage process limits the number of bidders in the final round so as to reduce potential for value destruction through disclosure of competitive information, and it ensures that the higher-valued bidders are selected—a HI type is always selected over a LO type.[20]

18. For clarity of presentation, we ignore in the example both the strategic information cost and the competitive value of information to bidders. The strategic information cost is implicit for that is why the seller wants to restrict bidders. The competitive value of information could exist, so long as it was not too great, and the equilibrium would still hold.

19. An important characteristic of the example is that LO-types win against HI-types in State 1, which is the low-value state for both types of bidders. Because the reserve price is binding only in the low-value state, this causes the LO-types to put in the lower initial-round bids.

20. The last question would be whether, in this example, the seller is indeed better off with the two-stage procedure than with just selling without disclosure but with all five bidders. The first thing to note here is if there is a legal cost to nondisclosure, then the two-stage procedure could definitely be better. Without a legal cost to nondisclosure, the question comes down to any price-enhancing effect of disclosure and any benefit to selection based on initial bids. In this example, there is a price-enhancing effect of disclosure; in the absence of a reserve price, the sellers expected revenue is higher with four bidders and disclosure than with five bidders and no disclosure. However, the reserve price affects this, for

C. A More General Formulation

Let me turn then to a more general characterization of this process of screening bidders via an initial round of nonbinding initial bids. The model will be set up as an honest revelation game; we will determine the actions that the seller must take to elicit as initial bids the true initial expected values from the bidders. There will be N potential bidders, each of whom has a valuation function as described earlier. The seller asks for initial bids b_i from each bidder. The seller is committed to a reserve price policy according to

$$r = h(b_1) + \cdots + h(b_N) \tag{6}$$

where b_i is the i-th bidder's initial bid. The seller also commits to an entry policy that specifies a relationship between a bidder's initial bid and the likelihood of that bidder being admitted to the final round. This relationship will be described by the function $p(b)$, where $p(b)$ is the probability of final-round entry given an initial bid of b. It is assumed that $p(b)$ is increasing in b.

Initial round bids will be chosen by bidders to maximize

$$\text{Bidder } i\text{'s expected profit} = p(b_i)(E(\pi_i|EV_i, b_i) + d) \tag{7}$$

where EV_i is bidder i's *ex ante* expected value, itself a function of the bidder's type x_i; $E(\pi_i|EV_i, b_i)$ is bidder i's expected profit in the final round conditional on his type and initial bid; and d is expected value of information to bidder released in final round.

Equation (7) is a compressed version of the typical bidder's overall expected profit. It is important to note that $E(\pi_i)$ is itself a function of b_i, for b_i affects the expected reserve price in the final round and the reserve price affects expected profit. Taking the first derivative of equation (7) with respect to b_i and setting to zero, we have

$$(dp(b_i))/(db_i)(E(\pi_i|EV_i, b_i) + d) + p(b_i)(dE(\pi_i|EV_i, b_i))/(db_i) = 0 \tag{8}$$

or

$$(dE(\pi_i|EV_i, b_i))/(db_i) = (-dp(b_i)/db_i(E(\pi_i|EV_i, b_i) + d)) / (p(b_i)) \tag{9}$$

Equation (8) has a simple interpretation. The first term represents the marginal benefit of raising the initial bid: A higher bid increases the probability of receiving $(E(\pi_i|EV_i, b_i) + d)$. The second term of (8) depicts the marginal cost of raising the initial bid: $p(b_i)$ multiplied by the reduction in final-round expected profit due to the expected higher reserve price. Note that the marginal cost of bidding higher will be decreasing in EV_i: For higher-value bidders, the impact of a higher reserve price is lower. Thus, bidders with higher EV_i will choose to put in higher initial bids because the marginal cost of higher bids is lower.[21]

To elicit honest revelation, that is, $b_i = EV_i$, the seller must set $p(b)$ and $r = h(b_1) + \cdots h(b_N)$ such that equation (9) holds for all values of EV_i when bidders set $b_i = EV_i$. If we make the substitution $b_i = EV_i$ in (9), and assume for now an arbitrary $p(b)$ function, then equation (9) becomes a first-order differential equation that, when solved, yields the $h(b)$ function that elicits honest revelation. This can be seen by noting that Leibniz's Rule allows us to write

$$\begin{aligned}(dE(\pi_i|EV_i, b_i))/(db_i) &= E[(d\pi_i(EV_i, b_i))/(db_i)] \\ &= E[((d\pi_i(EV_i, b_i))/(dr))((dr)/(db_i))] \\ &= (dh)/(db_i)E[(d\pi_i(EV_i, b_i))/(dr)]\end{aligned} \tag{10}$$

where the last step is made possible from the definition $r = h(b_1) + \cdots + h(b_N)$, so that

in some instances the seller does not sell the item (this occurs in state 1 with at least four HI bidders, so the reserve price is 90.) The seller is better off with the two-stage procedure (versus nondisclosure but five bidders) so long as the value of the selling company to the seller is at least 63.33 in state 1. It is also of interest to note that because of the expected-value differences between the bidder types, random selection of four bidders is worse than selection based on initial bids.

21. Note that with the model as formulated, there is no possibility of a bidder having a high EV_i simply because he got a high signal for the unknown state variable z. That is, in the model, all bidders start with common information on z. In a more general formulation, bidders could start with private information on z; this would allow for the interesting possibility of selecting bidders through initial bids who are just overestimating value—the classic winner's curse.

$dr/db_i = dh/db_i$, and this is independent of other bids.

Thus, we can rewrite equation (9) (with the honest revelation condition $b_i = EV_i$) as

$$(11)\ (dh(b_i = EV_i))/(db_i) = [(-dp(b_i = EV_i))/(db_i) \times [E(\pi_i | EV_i, b_i = EV_i) + d]] / [p(b_i = EV_i) E[(d\pi_i(EV_i, b_i = EV_i))/(dr)]]$$

Equation (11), a first-order differential equation, is the main incentive-compatibility constraint for the direct revelation game for the first-round auction. For a given $p(b)$, equation (11) can be solved to yield the $h(b)$ function, which will induce each bidder to report his true prior expected-value, EV_i, as his first-round bid. Note that dp/db is assumed to be positive and $d\pi_i/dr$ must be negative, hence dh/db must be positive: The reserve price increases with the initial bids. As is often true in auction theory, it is not possible to analytically solve (11) for the general form of the $h(b)$ function.[22] However, as the example illustrates, reserve price functions consistent with incentive compatibility can be found for specific cases.

One important caveat remains to be explored, however, that will further develop the incentive-compatibility constraints for this model. I have implicitly assumed that all bidders find an interior optimum according to equation (11). This may not always be the case. Suppose a bidder considered raising his initial bid beyond $b_i = EV_i$. Doing so increases the expected reserve price and reduces expected final-round profits, $E(\pi_i | EV_i, b_i)$. There may come a point where a bidder's expected final-round profit goes to zero as higher initial bids are contemplated. If this occurs, then higher initial bids serve to *increase* overall expected profit, for they simply increase the chance of getting the competitive information value, d. In such a case, the bidder would have to compare overall expected profit with initial bid $b_i = EV_i$ (a local maximum) to overall expected profit with initial bid $b_i = \bar{b}$, where $\bar{b}$ is the highest possible initial bid, in order to determine the overall best bid. (Overall expected profit in the latter case will be just $p(\bar{b})d$.)

Figure 1 can be used to develop the condition that ensures that the corner solution $b_i = \bar{b}$ does not yield greater overall profit to any bidder than $b_i = EV_i$. This analysis also tells us something about how much the seller can differentiate between bidders in regard to their entry into the final round.

When bidding $b_i = EV_i$, an arbitrary bidder has overall expected profit $p(b_i = EV_i)(E(\pi_i | EV_i, b_i = EV_i) + d)$, denoted as point B in Figure 1. Let us suppose for ease of exposition that $p(b)$ is linear. Then in considering higher initial bids, this bidder finds that at some bid b^*, his *final round* expected profit, $E(\pi_i | \bullet)$ becomes zero (because of the implied increase in reserve price); after this point, his overall expected profit increases linearly with b_i. At the highest feasible initial bid, his overall expected profit would be $p(\bar{b})(d)$, indicated by point C in the diagram. For the seller to elicit honest revelation, we must have the following inequality hold for all possible EV_i in addition to the main incentive-compatibility constraint (equation 11):

$$(12)\quad p(b_i = EV_i)(E(\pi_i | EV_i, b_i = EV_i) + d) \geq p(\bar{b})d$$

Equation (12) illustrates once again the importance of all bidders having positive expected profits in the final-round auction, when they honestly bid their initial expected value. If some bidders did not have positive

FIGURE 1

Interior Optimum Initial Bid

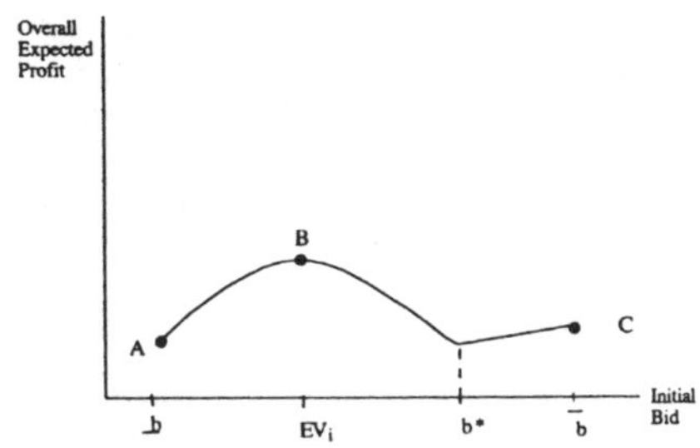

22. In Hansen (1988) for example, comparison of different auction rules is accomplished entirely through comparison of the differential equations that define equilibrium bidding strategies. No general solution of the differential equations is required and, indeed, would add little to the understanding of the model.

expected profits, then (12) could not hold and this bidder would find it most profitable to put in an initial bid equal to $\bar{b}$ just to ensure getting into the final round to capture the value of the information to be released in that round.

Equation (12) can also be viewed as a restriction on the $p(b)$ function, or more intuitively, on how discriminating the seller can be with his screening policy. Consider a bidder with the lowest possible EV_i, who in equilibrium must submit an initial bid equal to this minimum expected value and therefore have the lowest probability of entry into the final round. For this initial bid to indeed be the global optimum for the bidder, equation (12) must hold. To make (12) hold, the seller may have to flatten the $p(b)$ function, that is, make the difference between $p(b)$ and $p(\bar{b})$ smaller. Such a flattening will eliminate the incentive for this bidder to deviate from honest revelation. However, doing so also reduces the discrimination inherent in the initial round of bids, for a low-valued bidder becomes relatively more likely to gain admittance to the final round.

V. DISCUSSION

This article does not claim that the observed set of auction practices is the single best mechanism for selling a company, only that the set of practices yield a net selling price in excess of what an unrestricted auction (in terms of bidder participation) would yield if the competitive information cost is sufficiently high. Although the practices seem to be reasonable in these terms, they should be compared to at least one other set of practices that might yield similar if not improved results: Instead of screening bidders via initial round bidding that produces no revenue by itself, why should the seller not ask bidders to submit cash bids for the right to see the second round of information and get into the final bidding round? The seller could then select only those bidders who bid above a certain amount, thereby accomplishing a reduction in the set of bidders; the seller would also receive revenues directly from this initial round auction.

There are several possible explanations for why entry into the final round is determined via a preliminary round of bidding rather than via entry fees. One likely explanation has to do with incentive-compatibility on the part of the selling company. With screening accomplished via initial bids, the seller gets no revenue unless he carries through with the final auction. If screening is accomplished via entry fees, the selling company would receive significant revenues even before selling the company. There is certainly the possibility that some companies would entertain the option of beginning an auction process only to collect entry fees.[23] Another problem with entry fees relates to the optimal number of bidders in the final round. If entry fees are used to get the same number of final bidders as nonbinding bids, then there will necessarily be less overall expected profit for the bidders—with the same number of bidders in the final round, profits in that stage must be the same, but entry fees have already been paid. This decrease in expected profits for bidders will have to impact some decisions made by bidders on an *ex ante* basis. A likely area of impact is how much effort will be put into evaluation of the company in the initial round. If bidders put less resources into initial evaluations, then screening via entry fees will be less efficient at selecting final-round bidders and the selling company may be worse off overall.

Returning to another issue mentioned previously, corporate auctions are sometimes short-circuited by one bidder offering a preemptive bid. Generally, these bids will take this form: A bidder will indicate a range of prices that they are willing to pay for the selling company, subject only to review of certain information. As quid pro quo, the selling company must then negotiate exclusively with the preempting bidder; in particular, the selling company must not disclose any more information to other bidders.

This last point is what makes dealing with only one bidder potentially mutually beneficial: the competitive information effect can be avoided by disclosing the information to only one bidder. If the cost of disclosure is high, the seller should weigh the price-enhancing effects of an auction against the value destruction due to disclosure. Having

23. One must note that problems in commitment plague almost any auction rule. The point here is just that entry fees would create one more level to the selling company's commitment.

only one bidder may well be optimal,[24] and it could be that it is one of the bidders, through a preemptive bid, who forces the seller to consider the trade-off.

Several outstanding questions concerning preemptive bids remain, however. If the seller agrees to disclose to only one bidder and negotiate exclusively with that bidder, what keeps that bidder from behaving opportunistically *ex post* (offering a final price outside the lower range of the preemptive bid); how should the seller choose which bidder if any to negotiate with exclusively; and should the selling company move to a more formal "preemptive" auction, asking bidders to submit nonbinding bids for the right to negotiate exclusively? As preemptive bids certainly do occur, the general topic would be a rich one for further research.

REFERENCES

Bulow, J., and P. Klemperer. "Auctions vs. Negotiations." *American Economic Review*, 86(1), 1996, 180–94.

Cramton, P., and A. Schwartz. "Using Auction Theory to Inform Takeover Regulation." *Journal of Law, Economics and Organization*, 7, 1991, 27–53.

Fishman, M. J. "A Theory of Preemptive Takeover Bidding." *Rand Journal of Economics*, 19(1), 1988, 88–101.

———. "Preemptive Bidding and the Role of the Medium of Exchange in Acquisitions." *Journal of Finance* 44(1), 1989, 41–57.

French, K. R., and R. E. McCormick. "Sealed Bids, Sunk Costs, and the Process of Competition." *Journal of Business* 57(4), October 1984, 417–41.

Hansen, R. G. "Auctions with Endogenous Quantity." *Rand Journal of Economics*, 19(1), 1988, 44–58.

———. "Socially Productive Information and Expected Prices in Auctions." Tuck School mimeo, 1991.

Hirschleifer, J., and J. G. Riley. *The Analytics of Uncertainty and Information*. Cambridge: Cambridge University Press, 1992.

Klemperer, P. D. "Auction Theory: A Guide to the Literature." *Journal of Economic Surveys*, 13(3), 1999, 227–60.

Klemperer, P. D. "Auctions with Almost Common Values." *European Economic Review*, 42, 1988, 757–69.

Macy, J. R. "Auction Theory, MBOs and Property Rights in Corporate Assets." *Wake Forest Law Review*, 25, 1990, 85–119.

McAfee, P. R., and J. McMillan. "Auctions and Bidding." *Journal of Economic Literature*, 25(2), 1987, 699–738.

Milgrom, P., and R. J. Weber. "A Theory of Auctions and Competitive Bidding." *Econometrica*, 50(5), 1982, 1089–1122.

Reece, D. K. "Competitive Bidding for Offshore Petroleum Leases." *Bell Journal of Economics* 9(2), 1978, 369–84.

Riley, J. G., and W. F. Samuelson. "Optimal Auctions." *American Economic Review*, 71(3), 1981, 381–92.

24. As a simple example, suppose with two bidders in the final auction the net price would be \$0.70 (think of this as a gross expected price of \$1 reduced by a competitive information effect of \$0.30). If by negotiating with only one bidder the seller could avoid the competitive information effect and receive (net) anything greater than \$0.70, then negotiating with one bidder would be optimal.

Part III
Corporate Restructuring

[9]

ELSEVIER

Journal of Corporate Finance 6 (2000) 117–139

Journal of CORPORATE FINANCE

www.elsevier.com/locate/econbase

Comparing acquisitions and divestitures

J. Harold Mulherin *, Audra L. Boone

Department of Finance, Smeal College of Business, Penn State University, University Park, PA 16802, USA

Abstract

We study the acquisition and divestiture activity of a sample of 1305 firms from 59 industries during the 1990–1999 period. Consistent with the importance of restructuring activity during the 1990s, we find that half of the sample firms are acquired or engage in a major divestiture. Consistent with the notion that economic change is a source of the observed restructuring activity, we find significant industry clustering in both acquisitions and divestitures. We also study the announcement effects of the two forms of restructuring and find that both acquisitions and divestitures in the 1990s increase shareholder wealth. Moreover, the wealth effects for both acquisitions and divestitures are directly related to the relative size of the event. The symmetric, positive wealth effects for acquisitions and divestitures are consistent with a synergistic explanation for both forms of restructuring and are inconsistent with nonsynergistic models based on entrenchment, empire building and hubris. © 2000 Elsevier Science B.V. All rights reserved.

JEL classification: G14; G34
Keywords: Acquisitions; Equity carve-outs; Spinoffs; Asset sales; Synergy

1. Introduction

In this paper, we study the causes and effects of acquisitions and divestitures during the 1990s. The general purpose of our analysis is to bring new evidence to bear on the contrasting views of corporate restructuring that have been presented

* Corresponding author. Tel.: +1-814-865-9201; fax: +1-814-865-3362.
E-mail address: jhml4@psu.edu (J.H. Mulherin).

0929-1199/00/$ - see front matter
PII: S0929-1199(00)00010-9

in research on earlier time periods.[1] We study whether corporate restructuring can best be typified as an efficient response to economic shocks or instead is better described as an imperfect reaction to management entrenchment and hubris.

Our initial analysis gauges the impact of economic shocks on corporate restructuring activity by studying whether there are industry patterns in acquisitions and divestitures. We follow the premise of recent studies of merger patterns by Mitchell and Mulherin (1996) and Andrade and Stafford (1999) that the clustering of restructuring activity in particular industries emanates from fundamental economic shocks. Our work can be distinguished from the other research by our emphasis on the 1990s and by our consideration of both acquisitions and divestitures. Consistent with the importance of economic shocks for restructuring activity, we find that both acquisitions and divestitures exhibit significant industry clustering.

To more directly determine the importance of economic shocks for acquisitions and divestitures, the main body of the paper uses event study analysis to empirically distinguish between two broad sets of theories of corporate restructuring: the nonsynergistic theory and the synergistic theory. The joint consideration of acquisitions and divestitures facilitates more refined tests of the two theories than can be attained by studying either acquisitions or divestitures in isolation. In particular, we study whether acquisitions and divestitures have an asymmetric or symmetric effect on shareholder wealth.

The first set of models that we test can collectively be labeled the nonsynergistic theory. These include models based on management entrenchment, empire building, and managerial hubris (see, e.g., Jensen, 1986; Roll, 1986; Shleifer and Vishny, 1989). Although differing in assumptions and emphasis, these theories generally predict an asymmetric relation between the wealth effects of acquisitions and divestitures. In the models, divestitures create wealth by increasing specialization and reducing agency costs, while acquisitions lower wealth by protecting management from market forces and by lessening corporate focus.

A second set of theories poses synergistic reasons for both acquisitions and divestitures. The origin of this line of thought is usually traced to Coase (1937) who theorizes that the size of the firm responds over time to factors that affect the relative costs of market pricing and internal management decisions. As an example, Coase (1937, Footnotes 31 and 32) argues that technological change will alter the efficient size of the firm and, by implication, affect the decision to engage in acquisitions or divestitures. Subsequent analysis has extended these insights. Klein et al. (1978) argue that acquisitions and divestitures represent reactions to changes in the transaction costs created by specialized assets. Bradley et al. (1988,

[1] Jensen and Ruback (1983) and Jarrell et al. (1988) provide the seminal surveys of acquisitions research. The Appendix to this paper highlights some of the more recent research on acquisitions as well as selected research on divestitures.

p. 4) posit that mergers occur when bidding firms attempt "to exploit a profit opportunity created by a change in economic conditions." Jensen (1993) more specifically relates the restructuring activity of the 1980s to changes in technology, input prices, and regulation. In contrast to the nonsynergistic theory, the synergistic models predict that both acquisitions and divestitures create wealth.

We test the predictions of the nonsynergistic and synergistic theories by studying the announcement effects of acquisitions and divestitures during the 1990s. We find that both acquisitions and divestitures create wealth. Moreover, the wealth effects for acquisitions and divestitures are directly related to the size of the restructuring event. The symmetric, positive wealth effects for both acquisitions and divestitures are consistent with a synergistic explanation for the two restructuring events and are inconsistent with nonsynergistic models based on management entrenchment, empire building, and hubris.

The sample used in our analysis is described in the following section. Section 3 characterizes the overall restructuring activity for the sample firms during the 1990s and Section 4 reports the industry patterns in acquisitions and divestitures. The fifth section presents the evidence on wealth effects. The final section summarizes the results and offers concluding comments.

2. The sample

The intent of our analysis is to study the causes and effects of acquisitions and divestitures during the 1990s. To implement our research design, we begin with a sample of firms covered by the Value Line Investment Survey and track their restructuring activity between 1990 and 1999. Our general procedure bears resemblance to recent research, such as Mitchell and Mulherin (1996) and Andrade and Stafford (1999), and allows us to estimate the rate of acquisitions and divestitures both in aggregate and at the industry level. The firms listed on Value Line are heavily followed in the media, allowing us to precisely pinpoint the incidence and nature of particular restructuring events. The use of Value Line also enables accurate assignment of firms to industries and avoids the ambiguity created from the reliance on SIC codes reported in CRSP and Compustat (see Kahle and Walkling, 1996).

The use of Value Line as the basis for our sample also facilitates comparisons of the wealth effects of acquisitions and divestitures. Rather than draw the two forms of restructuring from heterogeneous sets of firms, the acquisitions and divestitures are taken from a common universe. As reported below, this ensures that the relative size of the sample acquisitions and divestitures are of a comparable order of magnitude.

To form our sample, we begin with 1681 firms listed in the Value Line Investment Survey in the 1st quarter of 1990. We delete 376 firms for the following reasons: Value Line industries with fewer than nine US firms (110 deletions), particular Value Line categories, such as Diversified Company, Investment Company, REIT, and Unassigned (159 deletions), and non-US firms tracked by Value Line (107 deletions).

The resulting sample of 1305 firms is characterized in Table 1. The firms come from 59 industries spanning Aerospace/Defense to Trucking. By number of firms, the Electric Utility industry has the greatest representation with 102 firms. In terms

Table 1
The sample

Industry	Firms		Industry	Firms	
	Number	Value (US$ billions)		Number	Value (US$ billions)
Aerospace/defense	32	47	Medical services	9	10
Air transport	12	17	Medical supplies	37	58
Apparel	17	8	Metal fabricating	16	8
Auto parts	20	11	Metals and mining	12	21
Bank	50	97	Natural gas (dist)	28	14
Bank (Midwest)	23	28	Natural Gas (div)	22	45
Broadcasting/cable	10	28	Newspaper	13	30
Building materials	26	17	Office equipment	20	15
Chemical (basic)	10	68	Oilfield services	19	28
Chemical (diversified)	12	36	Packaging and contain	15	8
Chemical (specialty)	35	31	Paper	27	51
Computer and peripherals	37	105	Petroleum (integrate)	23	216
Computer software	17	21	Petroleum (produce)	18	22
Drug	19	153	Precision instrument	25	21
Electric utility	102	199	Publishing	17	30
Electrical equipment	20	98	Railroad	9	28
Electronics	38	15	Recreation	18	35
Environmental	11	32	Restaurant	17	18
Financial services	22	43	Retail store	27	85
Food processing	45	95	Retail (special lines)	49	34
Furniture	12	5	Securities brokerage	13	12
Grocery Store	19	20	Semiconductor	15	21
Homebuilding	11	2	Shoe	12	7
Hotel/gaming	14	13	Steel	25	19
Household products	10	42	Telecommunications	23	259
Industrial services	26	11	Textile	9	2
Insurance	47	105	Thrift	16	16
Machine tool	10	5	Toiletries/cosmetics	9	11
Machinery	32	16	Trucking	12	6
Machinery (constr.)	11	16	Full sample	1305	2514

This table reports the number and value of the sample firms by industry. The sample is formed from the firms covered by the Value Line Investment Survey in the 1st quarter of 1990. Industries with at least nine US firms are included in the analysis. The industries are reported in alphabetical order. Value (in US$ billions) is the sum of the equity value of the firms in an industry at year-end 1989 and is taken from the Daily Stock Price Record.

of equity value at year-end 1989, the Telecommunications industry is the largest at US$259 billion. The total value of the 1305 sample firms at year-end 1989 is US$2.5 trillion, which is 71% of the combined equity value of the listings on the NYSE, AMEX, and NASDAQ in 1989. The average firm in the sample has a value of US$1.9 billion at year-end 1989.

3. Overall acquisition and divestiture activity in the 1990s

For each of the sample firms, we track acquisition and divestiture activity during the 1990s. Relying on the Wall Street Journal Index, Lexis/Nexis, Mergers and Acquisitions, and other financial and news media, we determine whether and when a sample firm is acquired. Using the same sources, we also determine whether a sample firm engaged in any major divestitures, including corporate spinoffs, equity carve-outs and asset sales. The spinoffs and carve-outs in the sample are readily classifiable. By contrast, the choice of asset sales to include in the sample is somewhat more problematic, due to the substantial variation in the size of both the sample firms and their assets divested via direct sale. Our criterion in classifying an asset sale as ''major'' is that the sold assets were either worth at least US$100 million in absolute terms or represented at least 5% of the equity value of the divesting parent.

The results on overall acquisition and divestiture activity during the 1990s are reported in Table 2. A total of 335 firms (25.7% of the sample) are acquired but do not engage in a divestiture. In addition, 222 firms (17%) undertake a major

Table 2
Overall acquisition and divestiture activity

	# of Firms	Fraction of sample (%)	Average firm value (US$ billions)
Acquired	335	25.7	1.1
Divest	222	17.0	4.7
Both	46	3.5	2.9
Neither	702	53.8	1.4
Full sample	1305	100	1.9

This table reports the overall acquisition and divestiture activity for the sample firms in the 1990–1999 period. Acquisition and divestiture activity is determined by consulting the Wall Street Journal Index, Lexis/Nexis, Mergers and Acquisitions, and other financial and news media. Acquired reports — the firms that were acquired and did not engage in a major divestiture during the 1990–1999 period. Divest reports — the firms that engaged in at least one major divestiture (including spinoffs, equity carve-outs, and asset sales) but were not acquired. Both reports the firms that had at least one divestiture and were also acquired. Neither reports the firms that were not acquired and did not have a major divestiture. Average Firm Value reports the average equity value of the firms in a particular category as of year-end 1989.

divestiture but are not acquired. Finally, 46 firms (3.5%) engage in a divestiture and are later acquired.

As a whole, roughly half (46%) of the sample firms are acquired and/or engage in a major divestiture during the 1990s. These results indicate that the restructuring in the most recent decade has some comparability to the significant wave that occurred in the 1980s. As a comparison, Mitchell and Mulherin (1996) estimate that 48% of their sample firms were acquired or engaged in a defensive asset restructuring during the 1982–1989 period.

Table 2 also reports some characteristics of firms that turn out to be acquisition or divestiture candidates. Based on equity values at the time of the formation of the sample, firms that are acquired are smaller than average; the average value of the acquired firms as of year-end 1989 is US$1.1 billion. By contrast, the firms engaging in divestitures are much larger; the average value of a firm undertaking a major divestiture is US$4.7 billion. In results not reported in the table but available upon request, these relations hold at the industry level; acquired firms are generally smaller than their industry peers while divesting firms are larger than their industry counterparts. We report further data on the relative value of targets to bidders and divested subsidiaries to parents later in the text.

4. Acquisition and divestiture activity by industry

We next estimate whether there are industry patterns in the rate of acquisition and divestiture activity during the 1990s. Our analysis is motivated by the theory of the firm (e.g., Coase, 1937), which argues that firm size responds to changing economic conditions. Subsequent theory by Jensen (1993) more specifically relates corporate restructuring to changes in technology, input prices and regulation. Mitchell and Mulherin (1996) support the theory of the firm by finding significant patterns in acquisitions across industries in the 1980s. We provide further evidence by studying acquisitions in the 1990s and by extending the analysis to industry patterns in divestiture activity.

4.1. Industry patterns in acquisition activity

Table 3 reports the fraction of firms acquired for each of the 59 Value Line industries in the sample. In the median industry, 29% of the firms are acquired during the 1990s. But there is a notable variation in the rate of acquisitions across industries. Virtually every firm, 10 out of 11 or 91%, in the Environmental industry is acquired. By contrast, no firms in Homebuilding are acquired.

The variation in the rate of acquisitions is statistically significant. We compute the Pearson χ^2 that tests the null of no variation in the frequency of acquisition

Table 3
Acquisition activity by industry

Industry	% Acquired	Industry	% Acquired
Environmental	91	Recreation	28
Bank (Midwest)	57	Natural gas (div)	27
Bank	54	Industrial services	27
Broadcasting/cable	50	Paper	26
Petroleum (produce)	50	Auto Parts	25
Medical services	44	Machinery	25
Toiletries/cosmetics	44	Office equipment	25
Thrift	44	Financial services	23
Telecommunications	43	Food processing	22
Grocery store	42	Retail store	22
Electrical equipment	40	Textile	22
Electronics	39	Natural gas (dist)	21
Aerospace/defense	38	Oilfield services	21
Steel	36	Electric utility	20
Hotel/gaming	36	Metal fabricating	19
Publishing	35	Apparel	18
Computer and peripherals	35	Restaurant	18
Building materials	35	Petroleum (integrated)	17
Packaging and contain	33	Air Transport	17
Railroad	33	Chemical (diversified)	17
Trucking	33	Furniture	17
Precision instrument	32	Metals and mining	17
Insurance	32	Retail (special lines)	16
Drug	32	Household products	10
Securities brokerage	31	Machinery (constr.)	9
Chemical (basic)	30	Shoe	8
Machine tool	30	Newspaper	8
Medical supplies	30	Semiconductor	7
Computer software	29	Homebuilding	0
Chemical (specialty)	29	Full sample	29

This table reports the fraction of sample firms acquired in each industry in the 1990–1999 period. The data are sorted by the percent of industry members acquired. Acquisition activity is determined by consulting the Wall Street Journal Index, Lexis/Nexis, Mergers and Acquisitions, and other financial and news media.

activity across industries. The statistic is defined as Σ_i $(\text{Actual}_i - \text{Expected}_i)^2/\text{Expected}_i$, where i represents the 59 industries in the sample and expected$_i$ equals the product of the average acquisition activity for the full sample, 29.2%, times the number of firms in the ith industry. The value of the statistic is 103 ($df = 58$, p-level = 0.001), indicating a rejection of the null.

A natural query is whether any of the sources of the inter-industry variation in acquisition activity can be identified. Jensen (1993) argues that the restructuring in the 1980s was induced by changes in regulation as well as a desire to eliminate industry overcapacity. In support of these conjectures, Mitchell and Mulherin (1996) find that the rate of takeover activity by industry is higher in deregulated industries and in low-tech industries with little or no research and development or other growth options.

We consider whether acquisition activity in the 1990s is driven by similar factors as the 1980s. We regress the rate of acquisition activity by industry on two variables. The first is a dummy variable equal to one for seven industries that underwent federal deregulation in the 1990s. The federal deregulation and the affected industries are: Riegle-Neal Act of 1994: Bank, Bank (Midwest) and Thrift, Telecommunications Act of 1996: Broadcasting/Cable TV and Telecommunications, Energy Policy Act of 1992: Electric Utility, and termination of the Interstate Commerce Commission: Railroad.

The second explanatory variable is the average R&D/Sales in a given industry in 1989 (obtained from Compustat). This variable tests whether the clustering of acquisitions in the 1990s is driven, in part, by the variation in underlying technology and growth options across industries.

The results of this regression are (t-statistic in parentheses):

$$\text{Acquisition activity} = 0.27(12.3) + 0.16\,(2.75)\,\text{Dereg Dummy} + 0.015(0.03)\,\text{R\&D/sales},$$

$N = 59$; F-value $= 3.89$ ($p = 0.03$); Adjusted $R^2 = 0.09$.

The positive and significant coefficient for the Deregulation Dummy indicates that, consistent with the 1980s, deregulation has a significant, positive effect on the acquisition activity in the 1990s. Of course, the affected industries differ over time. In the 1980s, deregulation induced significant merger activity in industries, such as air transport, natural gas and trucking. In the 1990s, deregulation was directed toward sectors including banking, electric utilities, and telecommunications. Indeed, past research has often excluded industries, such as banking, telecommunications and electric utilities due to heavy regulation. The removal of the regulatory burdens in these industries allows them to become part of mainstream merger analysis.

The coefficient for R&D/Sales is not significantly different from zero. In contrast to the 1980s, merger activity in the 1990s is not restricted to industries with low growth options. Indeed, some of the industries shown in Table 3 to have the highest rate of acquisition activity during the 1990s include Telecommunications, Electrical Equipment, and Electronics that are in high-tech, growing sectors. These results are consistent with related findings in Andrade and Stafford (1999) and indicate that mergers can facilitate both industry consolidation and industry expansion.

As a more direct analysis of acquisition activity in the 1980s and 1990s, we compare the rate of activity across industries in the two decades. Our sample has 42 industries that overlap those studied by Mitchell and Mulherin (1996, Table 3) for the 1980s. The simple correlation coefficient of the rate of acquisition activity between the two samples from the two decades is 0.25 ($p = 0.11$). This confirms that while there was significant restructuring activity in both the 1980s and 1990s, there was not a one-to-one relation in the affected industries.

4.2. Industry patterns in divestiture activity

We next analyze whether there are industry patterns in divestiture activity. Table 4 reports the results. For the median industry, 18% of the firms engaged in at least one major divestiture in the 1990–1999 period. Like acquisitions, however, there is a wide variation in divestiture activity across industries. In the Chemical (Diversified) industry, 67% of the firms undertook a major divestiture. By contrast, several industries, including Toiletries/Cosmetics, refrained from any measurable divestiture activity.

To determine whether the frequency of divestiture activity significantly differs across industries, we compute the Pearson χ^2 statistic. The value of the statistic is 110 ($df = 58$, p-level = 0.001), indicating a rejection of the null of no difference in divestiture activity across industries.

The estimates of acquisition and divestiture activity by industry in Table 3 and Table 4 allow us to do some analysis as to the nature of the shocks that induce the two forms of restructuring. If the underlying shocks are identical, then there will be a high, positive correlation between the rate of acquisitions and divestitures. Alternatively, if the underlying shocks are dissimilar, then there will be a strong, negative correlation between the relative occurrence of the two forms of restructuring at the industry level. The estimated correlation coefficient of the rate of acquisitions and divestitures is -0.08 (p-level = 0.53). Hence, acquisitions and divestitures are neither direct substitutes nor direct complements at the industry level. The estimate indicates, instead, that acquisitions and divestitures are induced by both common and dissimilar industry shocks. For example, exactly half of the 30 firms at the median or above in the ranking of acquisition activity in Table 3 are also at the median or above in the ranking of divestiture activity in Table 4. Dasgupta et al. (1999) report similar findings for a sample of mergers and divestitures in the 1986–1994 period.

The comparison of industry patterns in acquisitions and divestitures is somewhat crude as acquired firms, by the nature of our research design, cannot subsequently engage in a divestiture. To account for sample attrition due to acquisitions, we reestimated the rates of divestiture activity based on the available firm years for each industry. For example, in our sample, the Shoe industry has 12 firms, or a total of 120 firm years in the 1990–1999 period. But one firm in the industry was acquired in 1995, reducing the available firm years to 116. After accounting for sample attrition due to acquisitions, our estimates for the adjusted rate of divestiture by industry are also insignificantly related to the industry rate of acquisitions; the correlation coefficient is -0.03 (p-level = 0.84).

Table 4
Divestiture activity by industry

Industry	% Divesting	Industry	% Divesting
Chemical (diversified)	67	Restaurant	18
Chemical (basic)	50	Chemical (specialty)	17
Petroleum (integrate)	48	Air transport	17
Telecommunications	48	Petroleum (produce)	17
Medical services	44	Shoe	17
Natural gas (div)	41	Bank	16
Drug	37	Building materials	15
Electrical equipment	35	Office equipment	15
Paper	33	Retail store	15
Railroad	33	Natural gas (dist)	14
Trucking	33	Computer and peripherals	14
Financial services	32	Packaging and contain	13
Newspaper	31	Machinery	13
Insurance	30	Metal fabricating	13
Medical supplies	30	Computer software	12
Publishing	29	Electric utility	12
Electronics	26	Textile	11
Metals and mining	25	Machine tool	10
Food processing	24	Environmental	9
Retail (special lines)	22	Machinery (constr.)	9
Recreation	22	Furniture	8
Hotel/gaming	21	Semiconductor	7
Oilfield services	21	Thrift	6
Broadcasting/cable	20	Apparel	6
Household products	20	Auto parts	5
Precision instrument	20	Bank (Midwest)	0
Steel	20	Grocery store	0
Industrial services	19	Securities brokerage	0
Aerospace/defense	19	Toiletries/cosmetics	0
Homebuilding	18	Full sample	21

This table reports the fraction of the sample firms in each industry that engaged in at least one major divestiture (spinoff, equity carve-out, or asset sale) in the 1990–1999 period. The data are sorted by the percent of industry members performing at least one divestiture. Divestiture activity is determined by consulting the Wall Street Journal Index, Lexis/Nexis, Mergers and Acquisitions, and other financial and news media.

The similarity in results for both the unadjusted and adjusted rates of divestitures is due, in part, to the fact that a majority of the acquisitions in the sample occur in the second half of the 1990s. Table 5 reports that 33% of the acquisitions were completed in the 1990–1994 period, compared with 67% in the 1995–1999 period.

Overall, the analysis in this section finds significant industry clustering in both acquisitions and divestitures. These results are consistent with the theory of the firm, which predicts that corporate restructuring is a function of industry shocks

Table 5
Acquisition and divestiture activity by year

Year	Acquisitions		Divestitures	
	Number	Percentage (%)	Number	Percentage (%)
1990	38	10	22	6
1991	23	6	33	9
1992	21	6	36	10
1993	26	7	40	11
1994	19	5	47	13
1995	49	13	37	10
1996	41	11	53	14
1997	61	16	39	11
1998	61	16	36	10
1999	42	11	27	7
Total	381	100	370	100

This table reports the number and fraction of acquisitions and divestitures by year during the 1990–1999 period. Acquisitions and divestitures are assigned to the year of completion. Activity is determined by consulting the Wall Street Journal Index, Lexis/Nexis, Mergers and Acquisitions, and other financial media.

and changing economic conditions. In the next section, we estimate whether the reaction to changing economic conditions is wealth enhancing.

5. Wealth effects of acquisitions and divestitures

A large body of research has studied the wealth effects of acquisitions and divestitures. Much of the research on acquisitions is reviewed by Jensen and Ruback (1983) and Jarrell et al. (1988). The Appendix A to this paper notes some of the more recent research on acquisitions as well as selected research on divestitures.

In this section, we expand on the prior work by estimating the wealth effects of acquisitions and divestitures in the 1990s. Our joint consideration of acquisitions and divestitures allows us to distinguish between nonsynergistic and synergistic theories of corporate restructuring. In particular, we study whether acquisitions and divestitures have an asymmetric or symmetric effect on shareholder wealth.

5.1. Data used to estimate the wealth effects of acquisitions and divestitures

Our analysis of the wealth effects of acquisitions and divestitures employs standard event study techniques. As such, our only data requirement is stock price information around the announcement of the restructuring events. For acquisitions

Table 6
Data used to estimate wealth effects of acquisitions and divestitures

	No. of observations
Panel A. Data availability for acquisitions	
Total number of targets	381
Targets with stock price data	376
Acquisitions with available bidder data	281
Panel B. Data availability for divestitures	
Total Number of Divestitures	370
Spinoffs	106
Equity carve-outs	125
Asset sales	139

This table reports the data available for the estimation of the wealth effects of acquisitions and divestitures. Panel A reports data availability for acquisitions. Of the 381 target firms in the sample, 5 are delisted prior to being acquired, leaving 376 targets with available stock price data. Of these 376 targets, 63 are acquired by foreign bidders and 32 are acquired by private bidders, leaving 281 that are acquired by US publicly traded bidders, which have available stock price data. Panel B reports the number of observations in the full sample of divestitures as well as the subsamples for spinoffs, equity carve-outs and asset sales. For both acquisitions and divestitures, data from 1990–1998 are obtained from CRSP. Data from 1999 are obtained from the Daily Stock Price Record.

and divestitures in the 1990–1998 period, we obtain the data from CRSP. For events in 1999, we obtain the data from the Daily Stock Price Record.

Table 6 sketches the data available for the estimation of wealth effects. Panel A reports data availability for acquisitions. As reported previously in Table 2, a total of 381 sample firms are acquired in the 1990–1999 period. Five of these firms, however, are delisted prior to the announcement of their acquisition, leaving 376 target firms available for the analysis of wealth effects. Within this sample, 281 of the targets are acquired by US publicly traded firms having available stock price data to be used to estimate the wealth effects for the bidders as well as the combined target and bidder return.

Panel B of Table 6 reports the data availability for divestitures. As reported previously in Table 2, a total of 268 sample firms engaged in at least one major divestiture in the 1990–1999 period. Because some firms undertook more than one divestiture over the sample period, there are a total of 370 divestitures that can be used in the analysis of wealth effects. As noted in Table 6, within this divestiture sample, there are 106 corporate spinoffs, 125 equity carve-outs, and 139 asset sales.

5.2. The relative value of acquisitions and divestitures

Table 7 provides information on the relative size of the acquisitions and divestitures in the sample. Panel A reports the relative value of the acquisitions,

Table 7
Relative value of acquisitions and divestitures

Panel A. Relative value of acquisitions

Target value/bidder value	
Mean	42%
Median	27%
N	281

Panel B. Relative value of divestitures (subsidiary/parent)

	All	Spinoffs	Carve-outs	Asset sales
Mean	26%	22%	37%	18%
Median	13%	14%	17%	11%
N	370	106	125	139

This table reports information on the relative value of the sample acquisitions and divestitures. Panel A reports the relative value of the sample acquisitions, defined as the ratio of the equity value of the target divided by the equity value of the bidder, both measured 2 days prior to the initial announcement of the acquisition bid. Data are available for the 281 acquisitions where the bidding firm is a US publicly traded firm with available stock price data. Panel B reports the relative value of the sample divestitures. For spinoffs, the relative value is the equity value of the spinoff on the first day of trading divided by the equity value of the parent on the day before the spinoff. For equity carve-outs, the relative value is the equity value of the carve-out (offer price times total shares outstanding) divided by the equity value of the parent on the offer date. For asset sales, the relative value is the reported price of the asset sale divided by the asset value of the parent at the year-end prior to the announcement of the asset sale. For both acquisitions and divestitures, data from 1990–1998 are obtained from CRSP and Compustat. Data from 1999 are obtained from the Daily Stock Price Record and SEC filings.

defined as the equity value of the target divided by the equity value of the bidder, both measured two days prior to the initial announcement of the acquisition bid. Data are available for the 281 acquisitions with both target and bidder equity value. The average target firm is 42% as large as the average bidder. The median relative value is 27%. The median size of the target to the bidder is somewhat larger than that reported by Jarrell and Poulsen (1989, Exhibit 1) for acquisitions in the 1970s and 1980s (though not the 1960s), which is expected since we sampled the acquisition targets from firms covered by Value Line.

Panel B of Table 7 reports the relative value of the 370 sample divestitures. For spinoffs, the relative value is defined as the equity value of the spinoff on the first day of trading divided by the equity value of the parent on the day before the spinoff. The mean estimate for the relative value of spinoffs is 22% and the median is 14%.

To provide a comparable measure for equity carve-outs, the relative value is defined as the equity value of the carve-out (offer price times total shares outstanding) divided by the equity value of the parent on the offer date. The mean estimate for the relative value of carve-outs is 37% and the median is 17%. An alternative measure for the relative value of the sample carve-outs based on offer proceeds rather than total equity value of the subsidiary, not reported in the table, generates a mean of 16% and a median of 7%.

For asset sales, the relative value is defined as the reported price of the asset sale divided by the asset value of the parent at the year-end prior to the announcement of the asset sale. We choose to weight asset sales by parent asset value because using parent equity value can lead to relative values larger than 100%, especially for parents experiencing financial difficulty (see Brown et al., 1994). The mean estimate for the relative value of asset sales is 18% and the median is 11%.

Across all 370 observations, the average divestiture comprises 26% of the parent firm. The median relative value of the sample divestitures is 13%. Although there is some variation in the mean relative size across the three types of divestitures, the median relative values are comparable across divestiture types.

Overall, the data in Table 7 indicate that both the acquisition and divestiture samples entail important events. The relative value of target firms and divested firms are both more than 25% of the value of the bidding firm and the divesting parent, respectively. This facilitates a direct comparison of the wealth effects of the two forms of restructuring.

5.3. Wealth effects for the sample acquisitions and divestitures

In this section, we estimate the wealth effects of acquisitions and divestitures. Our primary objective is to test two contrasting theories of corporate restructuring: the nonsynergistic theory and the synergistic theory. Within the nonsynergistic theory, we group models based on management entrenchment, empire building, and managerial hubris. Within the synergistic theory, we include models such as Coase (1937), Klein et al. (1978), and Bradley et al. (1988). Our joint analysis of acquisitions and divestitures enables tests that directly distinguish between the two theories. In particular, the nonsynergistic theory predicts asymmetric wealth effects of acquisitions and divestitures (see, e.g., Shleifer and Vishny, 1989), while the synergistic theory predicts that both acquisitions and divestitures create wealth.

Table 8 sketches the specific analysis used to test the two competing theories. As noted in Panel A, both theories predict that the announcement effect of corporate divestitures will be positive. By contrast, the nonsynergistic theory predicts that the combined bidder–target return in acquisitions will be negative, while the synergistic theory predicts that the combined wealth effect in acquisitions will be positive.

As outlined in Panel B of Table 8, the two theories also make contrasting predictions regarding the relation between wealth effects and the relative size of the event. The nonsynergistic theory predicts that larger divestitures will have a more positive effect on shareholder wealth while larger acquisitions will be

Table 8
Predictions from models of corporate restructuring

	Nonsynergistic	Synergistic
A. Announcement effects		
Divestitures	positive	positive
Acquisitions (combined)	negative	positive
B. Relation between announcement effect and relative size of the event		
Divestitures	positive	positive
Acquisitions (combined)	negative	positive

This table compares and contrasts the predictions from two sets of theories offering nonsynergistic and synergistic models of corporate acquisitions and divestitures. Panel A reports the predictions of the two theories for the wealth effects at the announcement of acquisitions and divestitures. Panel B reports the predicted relation in regressions of announcement effects on the relative size of the corporate events.

relatively more detrimental to shareholders, as the acquisition of a larger target will induce greater management entrenchment. The synergistic theory predicts that larger acquisitions and divestitures will both have relatively more positive effects on shareholder wealth.

In our analysis of the wealth effects of acquisitions and divestitures, we estimate changes in equity value at the time of the announcement of the two restructuring events. Because we want to isolate on the specific market reaction to the two events, we focus on a narrow window of the (−1, +1) period around the events, where day 0 is the initial announcement as determined from Lexis/Nexis, the Wall Street Journal Index, and other financial and news media. Because of the employment of this narrow window, we simply rely on net-of-market estimates of the abnormal returns. In results available upon request, we also employ other estimation techniques, such as the market model and obtain findings comparable to those reported in the text. Similarly, the use of longer event windows does not alter the inferences drawn in the text. For events from the 1990–1998 period, the market index is the CRSP value-weighted index. For events in 1999, the market index is the S&P 500.

Table 9 reports the wealth effects for the sample acquisitions. Panel A reports the wealth effects for the entire sample of 376 targets with available stock price data. On average, the equity value of a target firm appreciates 21.2%, net-of-market, in the three days around the initial announcement of the acquisition. The median abnormal return in the (−1, +1) period is 18.4%. The significant, positive return for the sample targets is consistent with research from earlier time periods.

Panel B of Table 9 reports the wealth effects for the 281 acquisitions with available data for both targets and bidders. The results for the targets resemble the full sample of all acquisitions. On average, targets gain more than 20% at the announcement of an acquisition.

Table 9
Wealth effects for the sample acquisitions

Panel A. Wealth effects for the full sample of acquisitions

	Target
Mean	21.20%
(t-Stat.)	(16.8)
Median	18.40%
(p-Level)	(0.0001)
N	376

Panel B. Wealth effects for the acquisitions with available bidder data

	Target	Bidder	Combined
Mean	20.2%	−0.37%	3.56%
(t-Stat.)	(14.0)	(−0.69)	(6.23)
Median	17.4%	−0.87%	1.99%
(p-Level)	(0.0001)	(0.004)	(0.0001)
N	281	281	281

This table reports the wealth effects for the sample acquisitions. All estimates are net-of-market, cumulative abnormal returns for the (−1, +1) period, where day 0 is the date of the initial announcement of the acquisition bid, as determined from Lexis/Nexis, the Wall Street Journal Index, and other financial and news media. Panel A reports the wealth effects for the 376 targets with available stock price data. Panel B reports the wealth effects for the 281 acquisitions where the bidder is a US publicly traded firm with available stock price data. Note that bidder returns are based on the date of the first mention of the bidder in the financial press, which may be later than the initial announcement date for the target. The Combined Return is the value-weighted CAR, defined as: (target value × target CAR + bidder value × bidder CAR)/(target value + bidder value), where bidder and target values are the equity value 2 days prior to the initial acquisition announcement. Data from 1990–1998 are obtained from CRSP and the market index is the CRSP value-weighted index. Data from 1999 are obtained from the Daily Stock Price Record and the market index is the S&P 500. The t-statistic tests the null hypothesis that the mean CAR equals zero. The p-level is for the Wilcoxon sign rank test that the median differs from zero.

Bidders, on average, experience an insignificant mean change in wealth at the announcement of the acquisition. The median is also small in absolute terms, although the estimate is significantly negative. As in the prior research reviewed in the Appendix A, the bidder returns are somewhat sensitive to the event window. For example, in results not reported in the table, the net-of-market bidder return for the (−42, +1) period is positive but insignificant: 0.65% ($t = 0.91$). The small magnitude of the bidder returns is consistent with prior research and is generally interpreted as reflecting a competitive market for corporate control (see, e.g., Mitchell and Lehn, 1990).

To measure the total wealth effect of the acquisitions, we estimate the combined return, defined as the value-weighted CAR:

$$(\mathrm{TV}_i \times \mathrm{TCAR}_i + \mathrm{BV}_i \times \mathrm{BCAR}_i)/(\mathrm{TV}_i + \mathrm{BV}_i),$$

where $TCAR_i$ is the cumulative abnormal return for the ith target over the (−1, +1) period, $BCAR_i$ is the cumulative abnormal return for the ith bidder over the (−1, +1) period, and TV_i and BV_i are equity values for the ith target and bidder, respectively, 2 days prior to the initial acquisition announcement. The results indicate that the acquisitions in the sample create wealth. The combined return to targets and bidders averages 3.56%. This positive combined wealth effect for acquisitions is consistent with the synergistic theory.

Table 10 reports the wealth effects for the sample divestitures. On average, the divestitures create wealth. For the full sample of 370 divestitures, the average net-of-market return for the (−1, +1) period is 3.04%. The median abnormal return is 1.75%. The positive wealth effects hold for all three types of divestitures. The mean abnormal return is 4.51% for corporate spinoffs, is 2.27% for equity carve-outs, and is 2.60% for asset sales. These results are comparable in magnitude to research on divestitures from earlier time periods.

In results not reported in the table, we further study the subset of asset sales with data available for the buyers of the assets. Of the 139 asset sales in the sample, there are 56 cases where the buyer is either a foreign firm or a private US firm, leaving 83 cases where the buyer is a publicly traded US firm. In this subsample, the asset sales also create wealth. The mean CAR for the seller is 1.75% ($t = 2.57$) and for the buyer is 1.34%. The mean, value-weighted CAR for the buyer and the seller is 1.18% ($t = 2.88$).

Overall, the results on wealth effects indicate that both acquisitions and divestitures create wealth. These findings are consistent with the synergistic theory of corporate restructuring. The results indicate that corporate decisions to expand and to contract both benefit shareholders, on average, in the 1990s. These findings on wealth effects are consistent with the results in Maksimovic and Phillips (1999) that both mergers and asset sales improve total factor productivity.

Table 10
Wealth effects for the sample divestitures

	All	Spinoffs	Carve-outs	Asset sales
Mean	3.04%	4.51%	2.27%	2.60%
(t-Stat.)	(7.96)	(7.55)	(3.54)	(3.75)
Median	1.75%	3.64%	0.84%	1.58%
(p-Level)	(0.0001)	(0.0001)	(0.0002)	(0.0001)
N	370	106	125	139

This table reports the wealth effects for the sample divestitures. All estimates are net-of-market, cumulative abnormal returns for the (−1, +1) period, where day 0 is the date of the initial announcement of the divestiture, as determined from Lexis/Nexis, the Wall Street Journal Index, and other financial and news media. Data from 1990–1998 are obtained from CRSP and the market index is the CRSP value-weighted index. Data from 1999 are obtained from the Daily Stock Price Record and the market index is the S&P 500. The t-statistic tests the null hypothesis that the mean CAR equals zero. The p-level is for the Wilcoxon sign rank test that the median differs from zero.

5.4. Wealth effects and the relative value of acquisitions and divestitures

The basic results on wealth effects indicate that the average acquisition and the average divestiture in the 1990s create wealth. While consistent with the synergistic theory, the results do not indicate the sources of wealth gains from corporate restructuring. Moreover, the results do not conclusively reject the nonsynergistic theory, as the average returns do not account for the size of the particular restructuring events (see, e.g., Roll, 1986). To provide cross-sectional tests that distinguish between the synergistic and nonsynergistic theories, we estimate whether the wealth gains in the sample acquisitions and divestitures are related to the relative size of the restructuring events.

There is some prior analysis of this relation between wealth effects and the relative size of acquisitions and divestitures. Servaes (1991) finds that the combined return to targets and bidders is positively related to the relative size of the target. The papers on divestitures listed in the Appendix A generally report that the abnormal returns in corporate divestitures are directly related to the relative size of the divested entity. We extend this analysis by jointly studying acquisitions and divestitures in the 1990s.

Column (1) of Table 11 reports the results for the 281 acquisitions with available target and bidder data. The analysis entails an OLS regression that estimates the relation between the combined target and bidder return at acquisition

Table 11
Wealth effects and the relative value of acquisitions and divestitures

	(1)	(2)
	Acquisitions	Divestitures
Constant	0.022	0.022
(t-Stat.)	(3.11)	(4.79)
Relative value	0.033	0.031
(t-Stat.)	(3.45)	(3.01)
N	281	370
F-value	11.9	16.7
(p-Level)	(0.0007)	(0.0001)
Adjusted R^2	0.04	0.04

This table reports OLS regressions that estimate the relation between the relative value of acquisitions and divestitures and the wealth effects from the two events. Column (1) reports the results for acquisitions, where the dependent variable is the combined bidder and target net-of-market return at the announcement (days −1, +1) of the acquisition and the independent variable is the relative value of the acquisition (target value/bidder value), as defined in Panel A of Table 7. Column (2) reports the results for divestitures, where the dependent variable is the net-of-market return for the parent at the announcement (days −1, +1) of the divestiture and the independent variable is the relative value of the divestiture (divested entity/parent value), as defined in Panel B of Table 7. Data from 1990–1998 are obtained from CRSP and the market index is the CRSP value-weighted index. Data from 1999 are obtained from the Daily Stock Price Record and the market index is the S&P 500.

announcement and the relative value of the acquisition. The coefficient for Relative Value is positive and more than three standard errors different from zero. Hence, the combined target and bidder returns in the sample are directly related to the relative value of the acquisition.

Column (2) of Table 11 reports comparable analysis for the sample of 370 divestitures. Similar to the acquisition sample, the coefficient of Relative Value is positive and significant in the divestiture regression. Consistent with prior research, the wealth creation at the announcement of corporate divestitures is directly related to the relative size of the divestiture.

Interestingly, the estimated parameters in columns (1) and (2) of Table 11 are virtually identical. Hence, whether expanding or downsizing, the impact on shareholder wealth is comparably related to the relative size of the restructuring event. The results provide further support for the synergistic theory of acquisitions and divestitures and are not consistent with the nonsynergistic models.

6. Summary and concluding comments

In this paper, we compare the acquisition and divestiture activity of a sample of 1305 firms from 59 industries in the 1990–1999 period. We find a significant occurrence of these two forms of restructuring during the 1990s. Roughly half of the sample firms are acquired or engage in a major divestiture in the sample period.

We also find significant industry clustering in acquisition and divestiture activity during the 1990s. Consistent with results for the 1980s, we find that acquisition activity is greater in industries undergoing deregulation, although the specific industries affected by deregulation differ between the 1980s and 1990s. In contrast to the evidence for the 1980s, we find that acquisitions in the 1990s are not restricted to industries with low growth options.

We find that the acquisitions and divestitures in the 1990s create wealth. Indeed, the wealth creation from the two restructuring events is comparable in magnitude. The combined target and bidder return at the announcement of an acquisition averages 3.5%, while the announcement return for corporate divestitures averages 3.0%. Moreover, the wealth creation for both acquisitions and divestitures is directly related to the relative size of the restructuring event.

As a whole, these results are consistent with the predictions of the synergistic theory of the firm that changing economic conditions and industry shocks are at play in restructuring activity. Indeed, the results indicate that firms efficiently respond to economic change, whether such changes induce an expansion (via merger) or a reduction (via divestiture) in firm size. The symmetric relation for both acquisitions and divestitures is inconsistent with nonsynergistic models based on management entrenchment, empire building and managerial hubris, which argue that firms expand for reasons other than wealth creation. In the 1990s, the

Appendix A

A. Selected event studies of acquisitions that report target and bidder returns

Study	Time period	# Targets	# Bidders	Window	Target (%)	Bidder (%)	Combined
Bradley et al. (1988)	1963–1984	236	236	(−5, +5 last bid)	31.77	0.97	7.43%
Kaplan and Weisbach (1992)	1971–1982	209	271	(−5, +5 last bid)	26.90	−1.49	3.74%
Asquith et al. (1990)	1973–1983	157	343	(−1, 0)	18.04	−0.85	not reported
Jarrell and Poulsen (1989)	1963–1986	526	462	(−20, +10)	28.99	1.29	not reported
Servaes (1991)	1972–1987	704	384	(−1, resolve)	23.64	−1.07	3.66%
Schwert (2000)	1975–1996	2,296	1,286	(−63, 126)	22.00	−1.00	not reported

B.1. Selected event studies of spinoffs that include analysis of CARs and relative size of the spinoff

Study	Source	Time period	# Obs	Window	CAR (%)	Relative size	Effect of relative size on CAR
Miles and Rosenfeld (1983)	Moody's Div Record	1963–1980	55	(0, +1)	3.34	median = 10%	larger spinoffs have greater CAR
Hite and Owers (1983)	S&P Div Record	1963–1981	123	(−1, 0)	3.30	median = 6.7%	positive regression coefficient
Schipper and Smith (1983)	CRSP Dist Codes	1963–1981	93	(−1, 0)	2.84	mean = 19.7%	positive correlation
Krishnaswami and Subramaniam (1999)	CRSP Dist Codes	1979–1993	118	(−1, +1)	3.28	median = 13.8%	positive regression coefficient

B.2. Selected event studies of carve-outs that include analysis of CARs and relative size of the carve-out

Study	Source	Time Period	# Obs	Window	CAR (%)	Relative size	Effect of relative size on CAR
Schipper and Smith (1986)	SEC ROS tape	1965–1983	76	(−4, 0)	1.83	median = 8%	positive correlation
Allen and McConnell (1998)	SEC, IDD, SDC	1978–1993	188	(−1, +1)	1.90	median = 14%	positive regression coefficient
Vijh (1999)	SDC, M and A	1980–1997	336	(−3, +1)	2.29	median = 7.9%	positive regression coefficient

B.3. Selected event studies of asset sales that include analysis of CARs and relative size of the asset sale

Study	Source	Time period	# Obs	Window	CAR (%)	Relative size	Effect of relative size on CAR
Klein (1986)	Mergers and Acquisitions	1970–1979	202	(−2, 0)	1.12		positive regression coefficient
Lang et al. (1995)	SEC Form 8K	1984–1989	93	(−1, 0)	1.41	median = 23%	positive regression coefficient

This appendix summarizes selected prior research on acquisitions and divestitures. Panel A reviews selected papers that study the announcement returns for targets and bidders in acquisitions. Panels B.1 to B.3 review selected papers on corporate spinoffs, equity carve-outs, and asset sales that include analysis of the effect of the relative size of the divestiture and wealth effects.

corporate restructuring decisions made by management, whether downsizing or expansion, on average benefit shareholders.

Our results on the incidence and wealth effects of corporate restructuring in the 1990s have important policy implications. Many have interpreted the abrupt reversal of corporate takeovers at the end of the 1980s as evidence that entrenched managers could rely on antitakeover provisions and state laws to inhibit the market for corporate control. Our results of an active corporate control market in the 1990s, however, support Comment and Schwert's (1995) forecast that the decline in takeovers in the late 1980s and early 1990s would prove to be driven by economic conditions rather than legal burdens.

Our results also have implications for corporate finance, which extend beyond the basic wealth effects emphasized in the paper. A growing body of research has presented evidence of systematic mispricing in long windows following corporate events, such as those studied in this paper (see Mitchell and Stafford, 1999 for a recent survey). Our evidence that both acquisitions and divestitures cluster in particular industries adds to the growing cautions being applied to the long-run performance studies. Such clustering indicates that the assumptions of independence that frame much of the statistical tests of long-run studies are misapplied.

Finally, there is clearly much to be gained from more detailed study of acquisitions and divestitures in the 1990s. One query raised by Klein and Murphy (1997) is the nature of gains from large vertical mergers, such as Merck's acquisition of Medco and Disney's acquisition of Capital Cities/ABC. A further line of study raised by our own findings of the industry clustering of acquisitions and divestitures is a comparison of the sources of gains from restructuring in industries with high growth options vis-à-vis low growth industries. More broadly, are the sources of gains from restructuring in the 1990s the same as in prior decades? Along these lines, Boone (1999) reports that the source of gains from corporate divestitures is sensitive to time period. Clearly, an ongoing comparison of acquisitions and divestitures will continue to enlighten us on the causes and effects of corporate restructuring.

Acknowledgements

We thank Ted Boone, Laura Field, Gordon Hanka, Kathy Kahle, Bill Kracaw, Jeff Netter, Kim Rodgers, Dennis Sheehan, and seminar participants at the University of South Florida for comments on prior drafts. We especially acknowledge the detailed comments and suggestions provided by Mike Ryngaert.

References

Allen, J.W., McConnell, J.J., 1998. Equity carve-outs and managerial discretion. Journal of Finance 53, 163–186.

Andrade, G., Stafford, E., 1999. Investigating the Economic Role of Mergers. Unpublished manuscript, Harvard Business School.

Asquith, P., Bruner, R.F., Mullins Jr., D.W., 1990. Merger Returns and the Form of Financing. Unpublished manuscript, Massachusetts Institute of Technology.

Boone, A.L., 1999. Can Focus Explain Carve-Out Gains? Unpublished manuscript, Penn State University.

Bradley, M., Desai, A., Kim, E.H., 1988. Synergistic gains from corporate acquisitions and their division between the stockholders of target and acquiring firms. Journal of Financial Economics 21, 3–40.

Brown, D.T., James, C.M., Mooradian, R.M., 1994. Asset sales by financially distressed firms. Journal of Corporate Finance 1, 233–257.

Coase, R.H., 1937. The nature of the firm. Economica 4, 386–405.

Comment, R., Schwert, G.W., 1995. Poison or placebo? Evidence on the deterrence and wealth effects of modern antitakeover measures. Journal of Financial Economics 39, 3–43.

Dasgupta, S., Goyal, V., Tan, G., 1999. Active Asset Markets, Divestitures and Divisional Cross-Subsidization. Unpublished manuscript, Hong Kong University of Science and Technology.

Hite, G.L., Owers, J.E., 1983. Security price reactions around corporate spin-off announcements. Journal of Financial Economics 12, 409–436.

Jarrell, G.A., Poulsen, A.B., 1989. The returns to acquiring firms in tender offers: evidence from three decades. Financial Management 18, 12–19.

Jarrell, G.A., Brickley, J.A., Netter, J.M., 1988. The market for corporate control: the empirical evidence since 1980. Journal of Economic Perspectives 2, 49–68.

Jensen, M.C., 1986. Agency costs of free cash flow, corporate finance, and takeovers. American Economic Review 76, 323–329.

Jensen, M.C., 1993. The modern industrial revolution: exit, and the failure of internal control systems. Journal of Finance 48, 831–880.

Jensen, M.C., Ruback, R.S., 1983. The market for corporate control: the scientific evidence. Journal of Financial Economics 11, 5–50.

Kahle, K.M., Walkling, R.A., 1996. The impact of industry classifications on financial research. Journal of Financial and Quantitative Analysis 31, 309–335.

Kaplan, S.N., Weisbach, M.S., 1992. The success of acquisitions: evidence from divestitures. Journal of Finance 47, 107–138.

Klein, A., 1986. The timing and substance of divestiture announcements: individual, simultaneous and cumulative effects. Journal of Finance 41, 685–696.

Klein, B., Murphy, K.M., 1997. Vertical integration as a self-enforcing contractual arrangement. American Economic Review 87, 415–420.

Klein, B., Crawford, R.G., Alchian, A.A., 1978. Vertical integration, appropriable rents, and the competitive contracting process. Journal of Law and Economics 21, 297–326.

Krishnaswami, S., Subramaniam, V., 1999. Information asymmetry, valuation, and the corporate spin-off decision. Journal of Financial Economics 53, 73–112.

Lang, L., Poulsen, A., Stulz, R., 1995. Asset sales, firm performance, and the agency costs of managerial discretion. Journal of Financial Economics 37, 3–37.

Maksimovic, V., Phillips, G., 1999. The Market for Corporate Assets: Who Engages in Mergers and Asset Sales and are there Efficiency Gains. Unpublished manuscript, University of Maryland.

Miles, J.A., Rosenfeld, J.D., 1983. The effect of voluntary spin-off announcements on shareholder wealth. Journal of Finance 38, 1597–1606.

Mitchell, M.L., Lehn, K., 1990. Do bad bidders become good targets? Journal of Political Economy 98, 372–398.

Mitchell, M.L., Mulherin, J.H., 1996. The impact of industry shocks on takeover and restructuring activity. Journal of Financial Economics 41, 193–229.

Mitchell, M.L., Stafford, E., 1999. Managerial decisions and long run stock price performance. Journal of Business, (forthcoming).

Roll, R., 1986. The Hubris theory of corporate takeovers. Journal of Business 59, 197–216.
Schipper, K., Smith, A., 1983. Effects of recontracting on shareholder wealth: the case of voluntary spin-offs. Journal of Financial Economics 12, 437–467.
Schipper, K., Smith, A., 1986. A comparison of equity carve-outs and seasoned equity offerings: share price effects and corporate restructuring. Journal of Financial Economics 15, 153–186.
Schwert, G.W., 2000. Hostility in takeovers: in the eyes of the beholder? Journal of Finance, (forthcoming).
Servaes, H., 1991. Tobin's Q and the gains from takeovers. Journal of Finance 46, 409–419.
Shleifer, A., Vishny, R.W., 1989. Managerial entrenchment: the case of manager-specific investments. Journal of Financial Economics 25, 123–139.
Vijh, A.M., 1999. The Positive Announcement-Period Returns of Equity Carveouts: Asymmetric Information or Divestiture Gains? Unpublished manuscript, University of Iowa.

[10]

THE JOURNAL OF FINANCE • VOL. LVI, NO. 6 • DEC. 2001

The Market for Corporate Assets: Who Engages in Mergers and Asset Sales and Are There Efficiency Gains?

VOJISLAV MAKSIMOVIC and GORDON PHILLIPS*

ABSTRACT

We analyze the market for corporate assets. There is an active market for corporate assets, with close to seven percent of plants changing ownership annually through mergers, acquisitions, and asset sales in peak expansion years. The probability of asset sales and whole-firm transactions is related to firm organization and ex ante efficiency of buyers and sellers. The timing of sales and the pattern of efficiency gains suggests that the transactions that occur, especially through asset sales of plants and divisions, tend to improve the allocation of resources and are consistent with a simple neoclassical model of profit maximizing by firms.

In the United States there is a large and active market for corporate assets, from individual plants and divisions up to sales of entire corporations. Each year over the period 1974 to 1992, an average 3.89 percent of the large manufacturing plants in the country changed ownership.[1] This average masks substantial procyclical time variation, so that in expansion years, an average of 6.19 percent of manufacturing plants are involved in mergers and acquisitions and asset sales in each year. While the literature has succeeded in providing many insights about the gains and losses in mergers, mergers comprise only about one half of the total number of assets traded.[2] Much less is known about partial-firm asset sales.[3]

* Robert H. Smith School of Business, The University of Maryland. This research was supported by NSF Grant #SBR-9709427. We thank Judy Chevalier, John Graham, Peter MacKay, Steven Michael, Harold Mulherin, René Stulz, Michael Vetsuypens, an anonymous referee, and seminar participants at Duke, Illinois, NYU, The National Bureau of Economic Research, Stanford, University of Texas at Austin, University of Texas at Dallas, Virginia Tech, and the Western Finance Association meetings for helpful comments. We also thank Sang Nguyen and researchers at the Center for Economic Studies for their comments and help with the data used in this study. The research was conducted at the Center for Economic Studies, U.S. Bureau of the Census, Department of Commerce. The authors alone are responsible for the work and any errors or omissions.

[1] These statistics are described in detail below.

[2] For a comprehensive survey see Jensen and Ruback (1983) and also Ravenscraft and Scherer (1987).

[3] Early studies are Alexander, Benson, and Kampmeyer (1984), and Hite, Owers, and Rogers (1987). The number of transactions in these studies has been fairly small because the data is difficult to obtain. Schlingemann, Stulz, and Walkling (2002) also analyze segment sales.

In this study, we treat mergers, acquisitions, and asset sales as components of the overall market for firm assets in manufacturing industries. Using detailed plant-level data from the Longitudinal Research Database (LRD) compiled at the Census Bureau, we track sales of individual plants and benchmark their efficiency against that of other plants in the industry. We ask several questions: Does the market facilitate the reallocation of assets to more efficient uses? How big is the market for plants, and each of the segments (individual plants, divisions, and entire firms)? What are the factors that drive mergers and asset sales? We also ask whether firm organization affects how firms participate in the market for assets. Does the subsequent productivity of the transacted plants vary by the buying and selling firms' organizational characteristics?

An influential view in the literature is that major investment and takeover decisions of firms are influenced by conflicts of interest between managers and the owners of the firm.[4] This view suggests that many acquisitions are undertaken for empire building and managerial entrenchment by managers, and that they serve little economic purpose. Morck, Shleifer, and Vishny (1990) provide evidence that the stock market reacts negatively to diversifying acquisitions and to acquisitions where the bidder's managers perform poorly prior to the acquisitions. For asset sales, Jain (1985) finds that sell-off announcements are greeted positively by the market and that they proceed a period of negative returns for the sellers. Lang, Poulsen, and Stulz (1995) find asset sales follow poor firm-level performance. John and Ofek (1995) find that the remaining assets of the firm improve in performance after asset sales that subsequently leave the firm more focused. These studies suggest that transactions either follow inefficient investments by firms or act to unwind such investments.

An alternative view, modeled in Maksimovic and Phillips (2002), posits that firms grow and purchase assets efficiently across the industries in which they operate.[5] This model is also consistent with existing evidence.[6] The model makes specific testable predictions about the timing and the direction of sales. In our model, firms become focused when their prospects in their main industry significantly improve. They may optimally choose to remain unfocused if their prospects in their main industry are not as good as other firms that choose to become focused. Firms sell assets in their less productive divisions following positive demand shocks for these divisions.

[4] See Jensen (1986) and Hart and Moore (1995).

[5] The model is based on Lucas (1978). Lucas (1978) and Williamson (1985) stress the costs of managing a larger organization.

[6] We do not have transaction prices or stock price data. Thus, we cannot test whether one party gains or loses in the stock market as a result of the transaction. The advantage of our study is that we look at actual productivity changes while stock market data includes a response to the price paid and prior expectations, in addition to the value of any productivity changes.

The intuition for the Maksimovic and Phillips (2002) model is simple. Some firms are more productive and can produce more than other firms from a given number of plants. Firms adjust in size until the marginal benefit is equal to the marginal cost of production. As output prices increase, the more productive firms have a larger gain in value from the assets they control. As a result, they find it optimal to acquire plants from less productive firms in the industry, even when that entails some increase in the costs of management. By the same token, a positive shock in an industry increases the opportunity cost of operating as an inefficient producer in that industry. Thus, industry shocks alter the value of the assets and create incentives for transfers to more productive uses. Given the generally positive upward trend in GDP in the U.S. economy during the mid- and late 1980s, the model can explain the trend towards increased focus over this period.

Empirically we find that the pattern of transactions (procyclical sales and subsequent increases in productivity) is consistent with this model. Our empirical results show that assets are more likely to be sold (1) when the economy is undergoing positive demand shocks, (2) when the assets are less productive than their industry benchmarks, (3) when the selling division is less productive, and (4) when the selling firm has more productive divisions in other industries. For mergers and acquisitions, we find evidence that the less productive firms tend to sell at times of industry expansion. Firms are more likely to be buyers when they are efficient and are more likely to purchase additional assets in industries that experience an increase in demand.

Sellers *and* buyers of individual plants and divisions tend to be large conglomerates. A firm's internal organization has a significant effect on the probability that an asset is sold. Assets are significantly more likely to be sold by peripheral divisions than by main divisions of conglomerates. The sales of main divisions are much rarer events, perhaps because only divisions in which the firm has a core competency become main divisions. For conglomerates, we find that the probability of the whole firm being sold off is negatively correlated with firm size and with firm focus.

Our results show that most transactions in the market for assets result in productivity gains. The average productivity of the buyer's and seller's existing assets is an important determinant of the gain to trade, suggesting that firms have differing levels of ability to exploit assets, and that their comparative advantage is in their main industries. The subsequent observed increase in productivity of the transferred assets is consistent with these gains offsetting the increased costs to the purchasing firm of managing a larger organization.[7] Thus, the market for corporate assets facilitates the redeployment of assets from firms with a lower ability to exploit them to firms with a higher ability. There is less support for the hypothesis that

[7] Thus, the existence of measurable productivity gains following a transfer does not imply that the transfer's timing is not optimal. A full dynamic model would be necessary to address the question of the optimal timing of transfers.

empire building predominantly drives asset purchases. However, because measured gains are negative for a minority of transactions, we cannot reject the possibility that some transactions may be motivated by agency considerations.

Our evidence primarily relates to two literatures: the literature on asset sales and the literature on mergers. Our paper views and considers these two types of transactions as part of a larger market for assets. The literature on sales of plants and divisions is relatively small. Alexander et al. (1984), Jain (1985), and Hite et al. (1987) have found a positive stock market response to asset sales. Lang et al. (1995) have shown these asset sales follow poor firm-level performance and that the stock-market gains are positive for firms that pay out the proceeds instead of reinvesting within the firm.[8] John and Ofek (1995) show that the remaining assets of the firm improve in performance after asset sales that subsequently leave the firm more focused. Maksimovic and Phillips (1998) show that firms in Chapter 11 tend to sell their most efficient plants, whereas firms in a control sample tend to sell their least efficient plants.

Schlingemann, Stulz, and Walkling (2002) (SSW) examine sales of divisions. They compare firms that report the sale of one or more whole segments with a control sample of firms which do not divest. Working with accounting data, they predict how firms choose which segments to divest. SSW's principal finding is that the liquidity of the market for assets plays an important role in determining which asset is divested. The probability that a segment is divested is higher if the asset is in an industry with a liquid market for assets and if it performs poorly. The divested segments are on average smaller than segments that are retained.

There is a large literature on the gains from mergers that has examined the gains to the bidders and targets in the stock market. Lang, Stulz, and Walkling (1991) show that the total stock market gains in tender offers are highest when the bidder has a high Tobin's q and the target has a low q. This is consistent with the notion that gains are highest when well-managed firms take over badly managed firms. Less is known about the gains in partial firm sales. Several studies have examined the cash flow performance of firms before and after mergers. Matsusaka (1993) examines the ex ante financial performance of firms before they merge and Ravenscraft and Scherer (1987) examine the ex post financial performance of mergers using FTC line-of-business data. Other studies that have documented performance changes following mergers using the LRD include Lichtenberg and Siegel (1992) and McGuckin and Nguyen (1995, 1999). McGuckin and Nguyen (1999) show

[8] The advantage over using stock market data and event studies is that a stock market response reflects the price paid relative to anticipated gains. Gains in productivity can still occur if the excess stock market return equals zero if the seller captures the gains. Similarly a combined positive stock market response (for buyers and sellers) may reflect information being revealed about the assets' value in the future and may not represent any real productivity gains.

that whether a firm is multiplant or single plant affects observed productivity gains. Kaplan and Weisbach (1992) track firms after they merge and find that divestiture rates by purchasers of unrelated firms are higher than purchasers of related firms. Even the firms that were broken up, however, show positive combined stock market responses (buyer and seller) at the time of the acquisition and do not show declines in operating performance before they are broken up. Our theory predicts that firms will buy assets outside of their main areas of expertise during recessions and sell unrelated assets to firms expanding their core business units during booms. Fluck and Lynch (1999) also predict that conglomerate firms maximizing shareholder value will buy firms outside of their primary area of expertise during recessions.

Following Jensen (1986), several authors argue that firm investment and growth can be explained by managers' tendency to overinvest in projects that yield private gains. Using data on bidding firms, Lang et al. (1991) show that the shareholders do not benefit if acquisitions are made using free cash flows. Scharfstein (1997) and Rajan, Servaes, and Zingales (2000) argue that investment distortions are endemic within conglomerates. A similar logic might suggest that firms acquire plants and divisions that they cannot run efficiently. By contrast, our view of acquisitions is based on Maksimovic and Phillips (2002), who show that the growth by conglomerates' divisions is consistent with a simple profit-maximizing model with scarce managerial or organizational ability. Graham, Lemmon, and Wolf (2002) show that conglomerate firms purchase firms that have lower Tobin's q than the firms that remain single-segment firms. Chevalier (1999) also shows that conglomerate firms purchase firms that have a different sensitivity of cash flow to investment than firms that conglomerates choose not to purchase. These results are consistent with our model and evidence that conglomerate firms, given productivity differences, make selective acquisitions of certain types of firms.[9]

Two recent studies by Mitchell and Mulherin (1996) and Andrade and Stafford (1999) show that industry characteristics such as technological changes and capacity utilization are strongly associated with the incidence of mergers, takeovers, and investment. We are able to exploit plant-level data to obtain a more detailed picture of intraindustry firm-level determinants of asset transactions. Our evidence suggests that firm organization and efficiency drives most of the intraindustry trades.

The remainder of this paper is organized as follows. We discuss our analytical framework of analysis in Section I. The data is discussed in Section II. Section III presents the descriptive statistics of the market for assets. The firm's decisions to buy and sell and the gains from the transaction are analyzed in Sections IV and V, respectively. Section VI concludes.

[9] The evidence in Maksimovic and Phillips (2002) shows that conglomerates grow their more productive segments faster.

I. Framework for Analyzing Trades in Assets

The hypotheses that we examine are motivated by a neo-classical model of firm organization across multiple markets, advanced by Maksimovic and Phillips (2002). Firms sell some or all their assets when there is an expected gain in productivity if the assets are operated by another firm. These trades occur because firms differ in organizational ability and these differences determine their productivity in different industries. The model shows how a profit-maximizing firm chooses the quantity of capacity to employ in each industry and how demand shocks in one industry affect capacity decisions in other industries. It provides predictions on how firm organization affects who trades assets, and the magnitude of the gains from such activity. These predictions differ from the predictions of models that assume that firms acquire assets outside their main industry because managers engage in empire building behavior. Thus, the predictions of the model can be used to test the hypothesis that the trade in assets by multiindustry firms allocates assets to more productive uses. This section describes the model and sets out the hypotheses motivated by the model.

Consider first the market for assets when firms maximize profits and financial market imperfections are not material. Following Lucas (1978), Maksimovic and Phillips (2002) argue that management teams of firms or firm organizations differ in their ability to operate plants efficiently.[10] Management teams of all abilities find it more difficult to manage a large firm than a small firm. Thus, a high quality management team may operate a marginal plant in a large firm only as efficiently as a low quality management team operates a marginal plant in a small firm. Firm size and the scope of a firm's operations adjust until the profit from operating the marginal plant is equalized across all firms in the industry. As industry conditions change, a firm's comparative advantage in operating plants also changes. As a result, there are gains to trading assets, and trade occurs until the profit from operating the marginal plant is again equalized. In the equilibrium, firms with more skilled managers or organizations still have a higher average productivity than firms managed by less skilled managers.

The model focuses on how changes in industry demand affect the marginal value of plant production in single-segment and in multisegment firms, and thus the direction and the gains to trade in plants. As demand increases, output prices also increase, and the ability to produce more output per unit input becomes relatively more valuable. The increased value of output is now greater than the increased cost of operating the firm at a larger size. More productive firms can sell the output at a price that is high enough to compensate for the diseconomies of operating at a larger size. This raises the

[10] More generally, their model can be reinterpreted as positing the existence of a fixed firm-specific factor of production that induces diminishing returns to scale. Following Lucas (1978), they identify this factor with managerial, or more generally, organizational ability.

price of capacity in the market for physical assets and less productive managers will find it more advantageous to sell their plants to more productive managers instead of producing output themselves.

Thus the model predicts that assets flow from more productive to less productive firms when demand increases.[11] The divisions with more skilled management teams thus gain in size relative to divisions managed by less skilled managers in the same industry. The volume of sales is higher when the technology in the industry is such that productivity does not decrease steeply as a firm acquires more capacity in the industry. The magnitude of transactions in response to such demand shocks depends, in part, on whether or not there are significant diseconomies of scale.

When demand falls, the costs of managing a large firm outweigh the benefits of high productivity and at the margin firms may shed assets. However, if the overall trend in the economy exhibits positive growth, we would expect the magnitude of this flow to be lower empirically. Firms would expect such transactions to be reversed subsequently when economic growth resumes. In addition, the existence of transaction costs would reduce the incentive to engage in such transactions, as the opportunity cost of an asset being operated outside its best use is lower in a recession. Under these conditions, the incentives to engage in transactions will be larger after positive industry shocks, giving rise to more transactions when demand increases.

To summarize, the profit-maximizing model suggests tests of the following predictions.

HYPOTHESIS 1: *Sales of assets are more likely to occur when the industry receives a positive demand shock. The higher (lower) the productivity of a division (or a single-segment firm) the higher the probability that it buys (sells).*

Trade-offs between managerial ability and size also hold within multisegment firms. A firm grows its segments until the value of a marginal investment is equalized across industries in which it operates. Thus, the growth and efficiency of a segment may affect a firm's decision to buy or sell plants in another segment. The model predicts that a firm reduces its capacity in an industry by selling assets when the value of these assets to another firm is higher. The opportunity cost may be high either because other firms in the industry can better use the assets, or because the selling firm has better prospects in other industries. Thus, a multisegment firm sells plants in a segment when its other segments are growing fast and it is an efficient producer in these other segments. It may also sell a segment when the segment is not an efficient producer, but the industry is doing well and the plant is relatively more valuable to other, more efficient, producers. These predictions are summarized in the following hypothesis.

[11] The model allows buying of new capacity from an external market with an upward sloping supply curve. An upward sloping supply curve can be justified given adjustment costs for new capacity, or through time-to-build, or given increasing costs of needed inputs to build new capacity. Firms may also scrap assets if the demand in the industry is sufficiently low.

HYPOTHESIS 2: *Asset trades in multisegment firms follow a specific pattern: There is an increased probability that a segment is sold (purchased), when (1) the firm has lower (higher) productivity in an industry and this industry receives a positive demand shock, and (2) the firm's other segments have higher (lower) relative productivity and these other industries receive positive demand shocks.*

The asset purchase decision works similarly to the sale decision. Multisegment firms may purchase plants in an industry if their other segments are less productive producers in industries that receive a positive demand shock. In that case, these less productive segments optimally sell out to more productive producers in their respective industries, and the firm expands faster in its remaining segments. Firms may also purchase plants in an industry when their prospects elsewhere diminish. This occurs if they are more productive producers in other industries and these industries suffer negative demand shocks.

This prediction may also be used to distinguish the neoclassical model from several hypotheses about the acquisition decisions of multisegment firms when managers act opportunistically or when there are material financial market imperfections. Lamont (1997), for example, suggests that firms would be more likely to invest outside their main divisions when their main division receives a positive demand shock. Thus, if the main division of firms is more efficient than peripherals, this prediction on the effect of demand shocks on the purchase and sale decisions in other industries is opposite to that of our model.

Jensen's (1986) free cash flow theory suggests that when firms have excess cash flow, they tend to use it to acquire additional assets that they cannot operate efficiently. More recently Rajan et al. (2000) and Scharfstein and Stein (2000) have also argued that the organizational structure of conglomerates makes them likely to waste assets. Although we cannot identify the dissipation of shareholder wealth from managers overpaying for acquisitions or the appropriation of cash flows from assets, our empirical tests will detect the extent to which the dissipation of free cash flows in multisegment firms leads to acquisition patterns that differ from those predicted by efficient allocation across industries.

These predictions regarding the flow of assets between firms have implications for the analysis of firm organization and restructuring. Profit-maximizing firms grow more in industries in which they have a comparative advantage. Thus, on average, the larger divisions of multisegment firms are predicted to have a higher mean productivity than smaller, peripheral divisions.[12] As a result, in the long run, main divisions are more likely to be buyers and peripheral divisions are more likely to be sellers. For the same

[12] Maksimovic and Phillips (2002) examine this prediction and show it to be consistent with segment-level data constructed from underlying plant-level census data.

reason the expected gain in productivity is higher when the plant is sold by a peripheral division and purchased by a buyer's main division than if the purchase is of a plant in a buyer's peripheral division.

The differences in productivity between main and peripheral units of the same firm are also likely to create an association between organizational structure and trades following a demand shock. When the main division of a multisegment firm receives a positive demand shock, the firm will sell capacity in the peripheral divisions. When the main unit receives a negative demand shock, the firm will acquire assets in peripheral units.[13] We summarize these predictions in the following hypothesis.

HYPOTHESIS 3: *Multisegment firms increase their focus through acquisitions when demand is high in their main industries, and decrease their focus when demand is low. The probability that an asset is sold and the expected gain from the sale are higher for assets operated by peripheral divisions of firms.*

Our model does not make a distinct prediction for transactions involving the whole firm—such as mergers—and transactions involving only some plants or divisions. In fact, we expect the model to predict mergers less well than partial firm transactions: Mergers or acquisitions of multidivisional firms may involve the transfer of some divisions that do not fit under new ownership and that would not have occurred in isolation.[14]

II. Data

We use data from the Longitudinal Research Database (LRD), maintained by the Center for Economic Studies at the Bureau of the Census.[15] The LRD database contains detailed plant-level data for manufacturing plants (SIC codes 2000–3999) on the value of shipments produced by each plant, investments broken down by equipment and buildings, and the number of employees. The LRD tracks approximately 50,000 manufacturing plants every year in the Annual Survey of Manufactures (ASM). This database is only a survey for smaller plants. The ASM covers all plants with more than 250 employees. In addition, it also includes smaller plants that are randomly selected every fifth year to complete a rotating five-year panel. Once selected, plants

[13] We would also expect to see similar effects on other divisions when peripheral units receive demand shocks. However, because peripheral units are smaller than main units, these effects are less likely to be detectable.

[14] Another model that has implications for the timing of asset sales is Shleifer and Vishny (1992). Shleifer and Vishny stress the importance of asset sales that occur by firms with high debt when industries become temporarily distressed. We do not examine the predictions of this model in this paper given that this database does not have financial structure variables.

[15] For a more detailed description of the Longitudinal Research Database (LRD) see McGuckin and Pascoe (1988).

are required by U.S. law to answer the questions. Many data items used (e.g., the number of employees, employee compensation, total value of shipments) also represent items that are also reported to the IRS, increasing the accuracy of the data.

There are several advantages to this database. First, it covers both public and private firms in manufacturing industries. Second, coverage is at the plant level, and output is assigned by plants at the four-digit SIC code level. Thus, firms that produce under multiple SIC codes are not assigned to just one industry. Third, plant-level coverage means that we can track plants even as they change owners. In addition to a plant-level identifier, the database contains a code that identifies which assets change ownership. These two features are key to our study, as they allow us to identify assets that have changed hands from year to year. Thus, plants have to be part of an ASM panel for the plants to remain in our study.

We confine our analysis to the period 1974 through 1992. We use 1974 as the starting year of our analysis because it is the first year of a five-year panel; 1992 is the last year of data available to us. We aggregate plants into firm-level business segments at the three-digit SIC code level and exclude segments that are less than $1 million in real value of shipments in 1982 dollars. Our regressions contain observations beginning in 1979 given we use five years of lagged data in order to calculate productivity for each plant in each year.

III. The Basic Facts

Before preceding to test the hypotheses from the prior section, we first describe the data and present some basic facts about the market for assets.

A. The Number and Types of Transactions

We classify firms as single segment or multiple segment based on three-digit SIC codes. If a firm produces 97.5 percent of its sales or higher in one three-digit SIC code, we classify that firm as a single-segment firm and exclude the small peripheral segment. We classify all other firms as multiple-segment firms. For these firms, we also classify each segment as either a main segment or a peripheral segment. Main segments are segments whose real value of shipments (in 1982 dollars) is at least 25 percent of the firm's total shipments.

We classify transactions into three types: single-plant transactions by single-plant firms, multiplant transactions broken into full divisions and partial divisions (at the three-digit SIC code level), and full-firm transactions. We break transactions into these three categories as it seems plausible that transactions in which a single plant changes hands between multiplant firms in the same industry are marginal investment transactions that have the least implications for both future investment policy and corporate control.

Transactions in which a division is sold have greater implications for managerial control. Finally whole-firm transactions (mergers and acquisitions) include the purchase of a whole multisegment firm, and thus buyers may obtain extra assets outside of their area of expertise that they would not otherwise acquire. Gains may thus differ across transaction types.

Table I presents summary statistics for asset reallocations in our data set between 1974 and 1992. We break out the transactions into whole-firm dispositions (mergers and takeovers) and sales of assets by firms that remain in existence.[16]

Table I shows that from 1974 to 1992, the total number of plants reallocated in mergers and takeovers was approximately equal to the total number of plants reallocated in sales by ongoing firms. On average, 1.95 percent of plants are reallocated annually through takeovers and mergers, whereas 0.95 percent and 0.99 percent are reallocated through sales of entire and partial divisions, respectively. In each case, the plants reallocated tend to be below average in size (real value of shipments) for their industry. More plants than not are sold to buyers whose major focus is producing in the same industry, defined at the three-digit SIC code level.[17] The proportion of same industry buyers is lowest for whole-firm dispositions, and highest for partial-division sales. Table I also shows that more transactions occur in industries that are in expansion than in recession.

Table I also shows the two-digit SIC code industries with the highest and lowest rates of reallocations in our sample. The highest annual rate is 4.72 percent, for Rubber and Plastics, followed by Electronics, Primary Metal products, Optical Equipment, and Processed Food Products. The lowest annual reallocation rate is 2.77 percent, for Leather and Leather Products, followed by Clothes and Apparel, Printing and Publishing, Lumber and Wood products, and Oil Refining. Comparing the types of transactions across industries, it is evident that the rates of partial- and full-division sales in particular differ considerably within these industries. Thus, for example, the full-division sales rates for Rubber and Plastics and Leather and Leather Products are 1.33 percent and 0.68 percent, respectively. The corresponding rates for partial-division sales are 1.36 percent and 0.46 percent, respectively.

B. Who Are the Buyers and Sellers?

Table II shows the characteristics of the firms that sell and acquire assets, by transaction category. In the table, we also break out mergers and acquisitions into those that involve sellers with just one plant, sellers in just one industry, and sellers who operate in more than one industry. In all cases, the characteristics are measured in the year prior to the transaction. The acquiring firm in the case of partial and full divisional sales is the buying

[16] Thus, a firm that sells its only division is classified as a merger.

[17] More precisely, buyers for whom that industry is one of the top two industries in which they operate, and who produce at least 25 percent of their output in that industry.

Table I

Asset Reallocations: Summary Statistics

Sample characteristics for asset reallocations for the years 1974 to 1992. Reallocations include partial firm asset sales and sales through mergers and acquisitions in which the selling firm disposes of all its assets. Plant-level data is obtained from the Annual Survey of Manufactures from the Bureau of the Census, U.S. Department of Commerce. The average annual percentage of plants reallocated is the number of plants reallocated in a given year divided by the total plants, averaged over all years. The percentage sold to buyer inside industry excludes plant sales to buyers with no existing plants in manufacturing prior to the purchase. Average plant sizes are the total value of shipments in thousands of dollars for each plant deflated by three-digit SIC code deflators from the Bureau of Economic Analysis.

	Sample of Firms			
			Asset Sales	
	Total	Mergers and Acquisitions	Full Segment	Partial Segment
Panel A: Reallocation rates across and within industries				
Full period: 1974 to 1992				
Number of plants reallocated	35,291	17,720	8,556	9,015
Average annual % of plants reallocated	3.89%	1.95%[a,c]	0.95%	0.99%
% Plants sold to buyer inside industry				
Same three-digit SIC code	56.8%	54.1%[b,c]	55.5%	63.1%
Same four-digit SIC code	47.7%	44.9%[a,c]	47.9%	53.0%
Average plant size (Real $ in thousands, value of shipments)	$30,332	$28,435	$30,916	$33,506
Average industry plant size (Real $ in thousands, value of shipments)	$35,790	$34,569	$36,440	$37,574

continued over

	Sample of Firms			
			Asset Sales	
	Total	Mergers and Acquisitions	Full Segment	Partial Segment
Panel B: Reallocation rates by 2-digit SIC code				
Industry reallocations: Highest quartile				
SIC Code: 30, Rubber and plastic products	4.72% (2167)	2.03% (974)	1.33% (577)	1.36% (616)
Yearly percentage plant sales (number of sales)				
SIC Code: 36, Electronics/communications	4.61% (3037)	2.12% (1397)	1.28% (840)	1.21% (800)
Yearly percentage plant sales (number of sales)				
SIC Code: 33, Primary metal products	4.49% (1663)	1.95% (732)	1.33% (487)	1.20% (444)
Yearly percentage plant sales (number of sales)				
SIC Code: 38, Scientific/optical equipment	4.38% (1113)	2.22% (570)	1.32% (332)	0.83% (211)
Yearly percentage plant sales (number of sales)				
SIC Code: 20, Processed food products	4.24% (2358)	2.23% (2358)	0.58% (603)	1.40% (1491)
Yearly percentage plant sales (number of sales)				
Industry reallocations: Lowest quartile				
SIC Code: 29, Oil refining	3.21% (307)	2.13% (307)	0.51% (71)	0.58% (82)
Yearly percentage plant sales (number of sales)				
SIC Code: 24, Lumber and wood products	3.04% (1436)	1.54% (743)	0.59% (273)	0.90% (420)
Yearly percentage plant sales (number of sales)				
SIC Code: 27, Printing and publishing	2.99% (1104)	1.84% (1104)	0.57% (331)	0.57% (344)
Yearly percentage plant sales (number of sales)				
SIC Code: 23, Clothes and apparel	2.95% (1495)	1.78% (893)	0.55% (275)	0.62% (327)
Yearly percentage plant sales (number of sales)				
SIC Code: 31, Leather and leather products	2.77% (253)	1.63% (143)	0.68% (63)	0.46% (47)
Yearly percentage plant sales (number of sales)				

[a], [b] Test of whether the proportion of mergers is significantly different from the proportion of full-segment sales at the 1 percent and 5 percent levels, respectively, using a two-tailed test.

[c] Test of whether the proportion of mergers is significantly different from the proportion of combined full- and partial-segment sales at the 1 percent level using a two-tailed test.

Table II

Asset reallocations: Summary Statistics

Sample characteristics for asset reallocations for the years 1974 to 1992. Reallocations include partial firm asset sales and sales through takeovers and mergers in which the selling firm disposes of all its assets. Plant-level data is obtained from the Annual Survey of Manufactures from the Bureau of the Census, U.S. Department of Commerce. Recession (expansion) years are the three years classified as having the largest decline (expansion) in the aggregate real value of industrial production. Industry capacity utilization quartiles are yearly quartiles based on the rates reported by the Department of the Census. Long-run industry growth/decline quartiles are calculated using growth rates for aggregate industry shipments over a 15-year period, with beginning and ending periods representing three-year averages for 1974 to 1976 and 1990 to 1992.

	Sample of Firms			
			Asset Sales	
	Total	Mergers and Takeovers	Full Division	Partial Division
Transactions by aggregate economy conditions				
Recession years (1981, 1982, 1991)				
Average % reallocated (total number)	3.57% (5,148)	2.16% (3,112)	0.70% (1,003)	0.72% (1,033)
Expansion years (1986, 1987, 1988)				
Average % reallocated (total number)	6.19% (8,989)	2.69% (3,904)	1.73% (2,509)	1.77% (2,576)
Indeterminate Years	3.21%	1.73%	0.70%	0.78%
Transactions by industry capacity utilization				
Low industry capacity utilization (bottom quartile)				
Average % reallocated (total number)	3.86% (8,618)	1.90% (4,244)	0.99% (2,210)	0.97% (2,164)
High industry capacity utilization (top quartile)				
Average % reallocated (total number)	3.69% (8,413)	1.92% (4,375)	0.87% (1,977)	0.90% (2,061)
Transactions by long-run industry growth/decline				
Quartile 1: Declining industry growth				
Average % reallocated (total number)	4.01% (6,290)	1.95% (3,058)	1.09% (1,707)	0.97% (1,525)
Quartile 2				
Average % reallocated (total number)	3.86% (5,250)	1.96% (2,666)	1.05% (1,425)	0.85% (1,160)
Quartile 3				
Average % reallocated (total number)	3.52% (10,008)	1.80% (5,131)	0.88% (2,505)	0.83% (2,372)
Quartile 4: High industry growth				
Average % reallocated (total number)	4.03% (15,746)	2.01% (7,870)	0.87% (3,405)	1.14% (4,471)

firm. In the case of mergers and acquisitions, these are the surviving firms. For mergers we also report the characteristics of buyers who operate in multiple three-digit SIC code industries.

Firms that sell full and partial divisions tend to be quite large (average revenues of $1.328 and $1.849 billion) and operate in an average of approximately eight three-digit industries. Sellers of partial divisions tend to operate a greater number of plants (an average of 31.48 in contrast to an average of 23.72 plants operated by sellers of entire divisions). Only approximately a quarter of the plants sold in the sales of entire divisions belong to one of the seller's main divisions, whereas approximately half of plants sold in partial division sales belong to one of the seller's main divisions.

Buyers of entire divisions are of similar size and operate a similar number of plants as the sellers, whereas the buyers of partial divisions are on average about two thirds as large as the sellers. Buyers in both categories tend to be slightly more focused than the sellers, operating in an average of approximately six three-digit SIC code industries. The buyers' main divisions acquired 53.8 percent and 63.1 percent of the plants purchased in entire and partial-division transactions, respectively. Thus, the market for asset sales is one in which both the buyers and sellers are conglomerate firms. The sellers sell peripheral divisions and marginal plants to the main divisions of the buyers. Although the buyers are somewhat smaller and more focused than the sellers, the differences between them are not large.

In contrast, the average seller in a merger operates 1.78 plants and has sales of $51 million. Approximately 80 percent of all full-firm sales (mergers and purchases) involve the sale of small, one-plant firms. About 10 percent of all mergers involve multiplant single-industry firms (average number of plants, 5.15) and approximately 10 percent involve multiple-industry firms. Even in this last category, the sellers have an average of only 7 plants, have sales of $239 million, and operate in an average of approximately three three-digit SIC code industries. Buyers of whole firms are larger than the sellers. On average, they operate 16.64 plants, produce in 4.66 three-digit SIC code industries, and have annual sales of $856 million. About a half of the acquired plants are operated by the buying firms' main divisions.

To summarize, we find several differences between the buyers in partial firm dispositions and mergers. On average, buyers of full or partial divisions tend to be larger than buyers in mergers, they operate more plants, and tend to operate in a larger number of industries. These differences arise because a larger proportion of buyers in mergers are single-industry firms. The subset of buyers in mergers who operate in multiple industries are slightly bigger in size and in the number of industries in which they operate.

C. *Aggregate and Industry Demand and Asset Reallocations*

We compare asset reallocations during economic expansions and recessions. We classify years as recession or expansion years by using aggregate and aggregate-detrended industrial production. Detrended industrial production is defined as the actual less predicted industrial production, where we calculate predicted industrial production from a regression of industrial production on a yearly time trend. Recession years are years in which both real and detrended industrial production decline relative to the previous year. We classify years as expansion years when both real and detrended industrial production increase relative to the previous year.

This procedure gives us results similar to the NBER recession dating procedure, which the NBER does quarterly. This procedure also allows us to classify a year such as 1980, which, according to the NBER, had a recession of less than six months. Using this procedure, we classify 1981, 1982, and 1991 as recession years. For comparability, we also take the top three expansion years—1986 through 1988. (Other expansion years were 1976 through 1978 and 1984 through 1985.) Given that actual and detrended industrial production did not move in the same direction, 1979, 1980, 1983, 1989, and 1992 are indeterminate years.

Table III shows that more assets are reallocated in expansions. The rates of reallocations during expansion years (the three years with the highest increases in the aggregate real value of industries production) and recession years (the three years with the largest decline in the aggregate real value of industries production) are 6.20 percent and 3.57 percent, respectively. The rates of full- and partial-division sales, in particular, are much higher in expansions (1.73 percent and 1.78 percent, respectively), than in recession years (0.70 percent and 0.72 percent, respectively). The reallocations rate due to mergers is somewhat higher in expansions than in recessions (2.69 percent compared to 2.16 percent). By contrast, the total reallocation rate in the remaining indeterminate years is 3.21 percent, the reallocation rate due to mergers is a low 1.73 percent, whereas the partial- and full-division sales rates are 0.78 percent and 0.70 percent, respectively. Thus, the partial- and full-division sales are sharply higher in expansion years.

We find that the number of transactions is sharply higher in expansions. The fact that transactions are lower in recessions is consistent with the overall positive growth trend in the economy causing firms to expect to need more capacity in the future, when growth resumes. In addition, transactions in recessions may result in gains that are less likely to offset transactions costs because the opportunity cost of an asset being operated outside its best use is lower in a recession.

We next explore differences in capacity utilization on the rate of transactions. We use industry-level capacity utilization data from the Bureau of the Census. For each year we use capacity utilization to classify into quartiles all the three-digit SIC industries. We report the average rate of transactions over the sample period for the top and bottom quartile. As Table II shows, the rates of reallocation do not differ materially across capacity utilization quartiles.

We also report the rates of reallocations by long-run industry growth. As Table III shows, more reallocations take place in the fastest growing industries—15,746 in the fastest growing quartile compared to 6,290 in the

Table III

Buyer and Seller Characteristics

Sample characteristics of purchasing firms prior to asset purchases for the years 1974 to 1992. Data is aggregated to firm-level from individual manufacturing plants. Plant-level data is from the Annual Survey of Manufactures from the Bureau of the Census, U.S. Department of Commerce. Buyers without any prior manufacturing plants (foreign buyers, outside manufacturing buyers) are excluded as prepurchase characteristics can not be calculated. Average buyer and seller size is the average value of total shipments deflated by industry price deflators from the Bureau of Economic Analysis. 1992 was the last year available at the time the study was conducted.

	Sample of Firms				
	Asset Sales		Mergers and Takovers		
	Full Division	Partial Division	Firms with Plants = 1	Firms with Plants > 1	Multiple Industry Firms (Three-digit SIC Code)
Seller characteristics prior to sale					
Full period: 1974 to 1992					
Number of selling firms	3,774	4,205	9,480	2,204	1,224
Average number of plants	23.72	31.48	1.00	5.15	7.0
Average seller size (millions $)	1,328	1,849	22	176	239
Average number of three-digit industries	7.56	7.77	1.00	2.21	3.17
Average number of four-digit industries	9.58	10.56	1.00	2.53	3.61
% of plants sold by seller in its primary line of business					
Seller's primary three-digit line(s)*	28.2%	50.8%	100.0%	70.6%	62.2%
Seller's primary four-digit line(s)*	25.6%	36.3%	100.0%	61.6%	54.9%
Buyer characteristics prior to purchase					
Full period: 1974 to 1992					
Number of buyers	2,267	2,755	1,648	4,530	3,627
Average number of plants	23.50	23.38	1.00	22.33	26.80
Average buyer size (millions $)	1,307	1,357	27.9	1,157	1,410
Average number of three-digit industries	6.24	5.75	1.00	6.00	7.24
Average number of four-digit industries	8.21	7.58	1.00	7.87	9.51
% of plants bought that are in buyer's home industry					
At the three-digit SIC code	53.8%	63.1%	59.1%	30.8%	26.3%
At the four-digit SIC code	47.9%	55.2%	49.9%	21.0%	17.4%

* If the seller (buyer) produces in multiple industries, the seller's (buyer's) home industries are those industries that have at least 20 percent of the firm's sales.

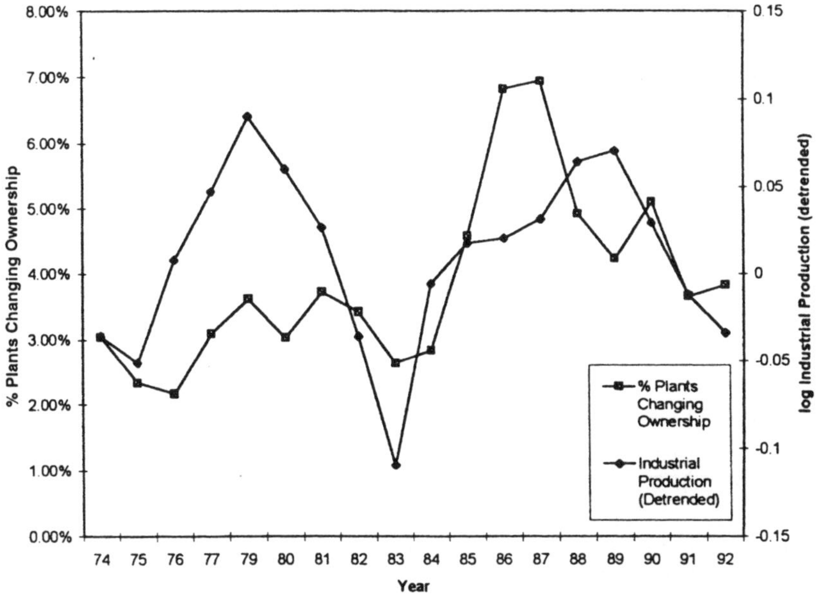

Figure 1. Left-hand scale is the total percentage of plants changing ownership by year. Right-hand scale is aggregate real industrial production detrended.

slowest growing quartile of industries. However, the overall rate of transactions is similar at approximately four percent. There is some limited evidence that industries which have more moderate growth rates have a somewhat lower rate of transactions, but the effect, if it exists, is relatively small.

We also subclassify the reallocations into those that occurred in years in which the industry (at the three-digit SIC level) was in expansion, and those that occurred in years in which the industry was in recession. For an industry to be classified as being in expansion, its real production in that year has to increase and its real level of output has to exceed its long-term trend level. For an industry to be classified as being in recession, the industry's real output has to decline in that year and the real level of output has to be below the long-term trend level.

Table III suggests that the average rate of reallocations, and in particular the rate of partial firm sales, is higher in periods of macroeconomic expansion. There is less evidence that differences in industry conditions have a material effect.

A similar pattern emerges when the time series of sales is plotted. Figure 1 shows both the annual rate of reallocations and detrended aggregate industrial production. Detrended industrial production is calculated as described earlier.

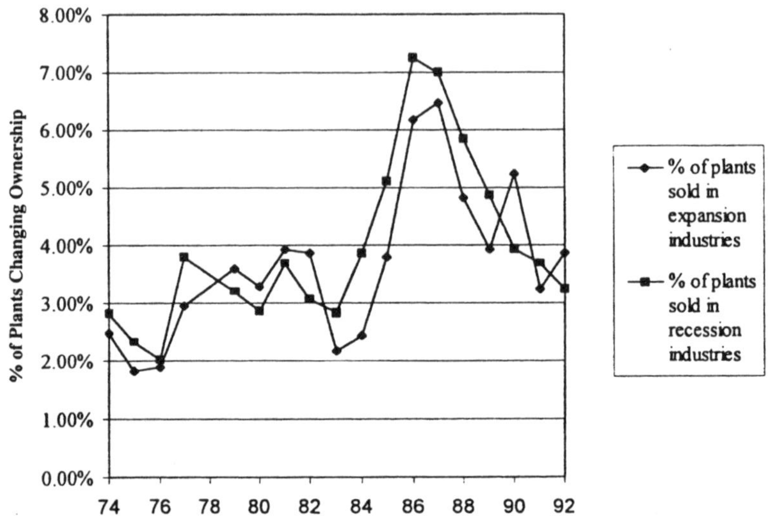

Figure 2. Change of ownership by type of industry. Expansion (recession) industries are the industries in which real and detrended value of shipments at the industry level increase (decline).

Figure 1 shows that, consistent with Table II, the annual percentage of plants that transferred ownership is high in expansions. It is highest in 1986 and in 1987, when nearly seven percent of the plants change ownership (adding up mergers and full- and partial-firm asset sales). The proportion of transactions that occur in industries that are in expansion also varies considerably, and is procyclical. In 1987 and 1988, when few industries are in recession, the number of plants transacted in these industries clearly declines.

However, when we plot the time series of the proportion of plants transacted in industries that were in recession and expansion in Figure 2, we find that the proportions are very similar. The reason for this result is that few industries are in recession when the overall economy is in expansion. Those that are in recession have a similar proportion of plants transacted. Thus, time series variation in the overall rate of asset reallocations is driven by economy-wide factors.

We next examine the time series variation in the percentage of plants broken down by mergers and acquisitions, division sales and partial-division sales. Figure 3 breaks the transactions into these categories. In particular, mergers are strongly procyclical, rising in the years before the 1982 recession to over three percent of plants, before falling to one percent of plants in 1984. The rate of mergers and acquisitions increased again to almost four percent of plants by 1987. Partial-firm asset sales vary less year by year; however they still hit a peak of over four percent (combining full and partial segment sales) in 1987.

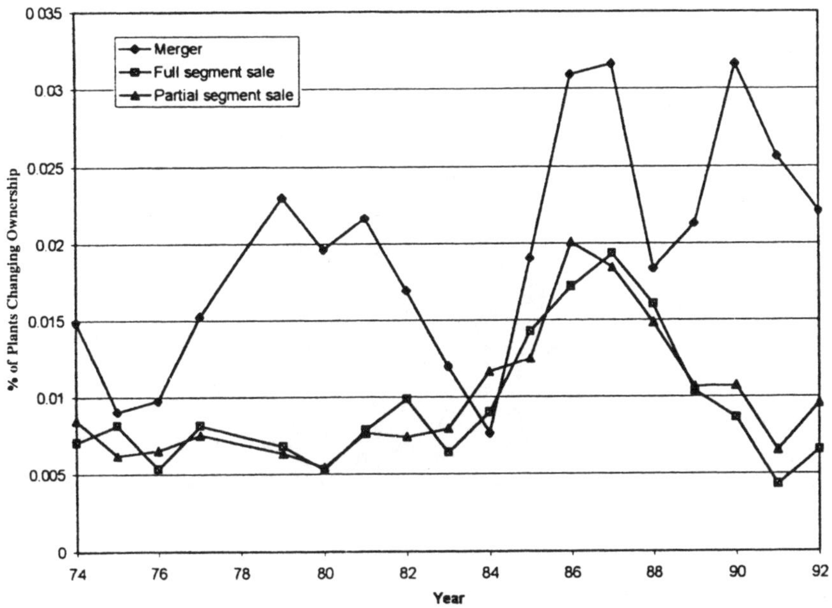

Figure 3. Percentage of plants reallocated through mergers, full-segment sales, and partial-segment sales by year.

The summary statistics suggest that the rate of asset sales, and in particular of full- and partial-divisions sales, is affected by economy-wide factors. There is less evidence that the average rate of transactions is affected by industry factors, such as capacity utilization and long-term growth. We next explore how within-industry and within-firm characteristics affect which firms sell plants and what plants firms choose to sell.

IV. The Probability of an Asset Sale

A. *How Sales Vary with Firm Organization*

In Figure 4, we show how the proportion of assets sold by division rank, where rank equals one for the largest segment by real value of shipments.

For firms with a given number of segments, as the segment rank of a particular segment increases, the proportion of its assets sold also increases sharply. The plants in the largest segment of a firm are the least likely to be sold. For example, the proportion of largest segment plants sold is less than one percent for firms with seven or more segments, whereas the proportion of plants that these firms sell in their smallest segments rises to three and four percent. Schlingemann et al. (2002) find using accounting data on whole

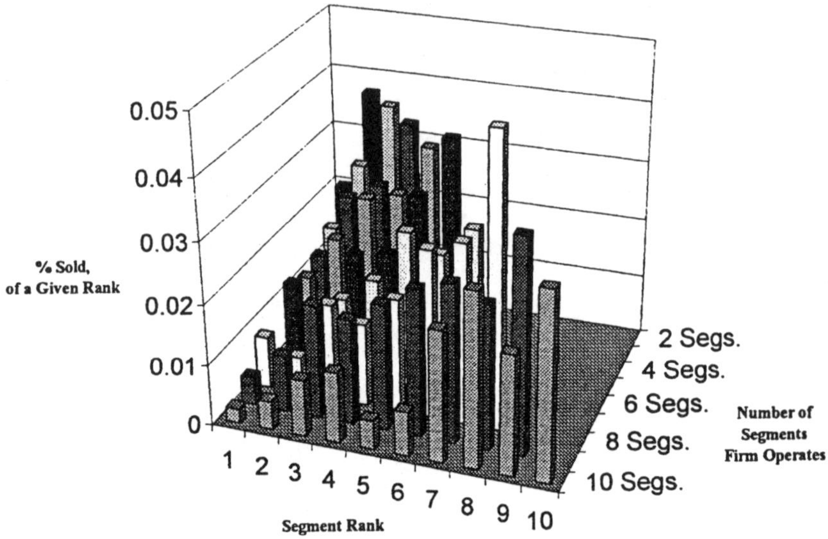

Figure 4. Percentage of plants sold via asset sale by segment rank as the number of segments the firm operates increases. Segment rank equals one for the largest segment a firm operates.

segments that a firm is more likely to sell small rather than large segments. Maksimovic and Phillips (2002) find that there is an inverse relation between the rank of a segment and its efficiency, and that the equally ranked segments of larger firms tend to be more efficient than those of smaller firms. Thus, Figure 4 accords well with the hypothesis that firms are more likely to sell their least efficient plants and also that, holding segment ranks constant across firms, the rate of plant sales is lower for more efficient segments.

There also exists an inverse relation between the number of segments a firm possesses and the probability that it will be acquired. Three percent of single-segment firms are bought out or merged, whereas only 1.5 percent of firms with six and seven segments are merged.

B. Measurement of Productivity and Demand in Business Segments

To analyze the relation between demand and firms' productivity on asset sales, we need measures of both these variables. We discuss our measures next.

B.1. Productivity of Business Segments

We calculate productivity for all firm segments at the plant level. Our primary measure of performance is total factor productivity (TFP). TFP takes the actual amount of output produced for a given amount of inputs and compares it to a predicted amount of output. "Predicted output" is what the plant should have produced, given the amount of inputs it used and the mean industry production technology in place. A plant that produces more than the predicted amount of output has a greater-than-average productivity. This measure is more flexible than a cash-flow measure of performance, and does not impose the restrictions of constant returns to scale and constant elasticity of scale that a "dollar in, dollar out" cash-flow measure requires.

In calculating the predicted output of each plant, we assume that for each industry there exists a production function that defines the relation between a plant's inputs and outputs. Then, for each industry, we estimate this production function using an unbalanced panel with plant-level fixed effects, using all plants in the industry within our 1974 to 1992 time frame. If a plant changes owners, we effectively treat the years under each owner as separate plants, allowing plant-level fixed effects to differ by each owner. For each industry, we calculate productivity using up to five years of lagged data. Thus we can calculate productivity for the 1979 to 1992 period. In addition, each plant has to have at least two years of productivity to be included. Finally, each input has to have a nonzero reported value.

In calculating productivity, we assume that the plants in each industry have a translog production function.[18] This functional form is a second-degree approximation to any arbitrary production function, and therefore takes into account interactions between inputs. To estimate predicted outputs, we take the translog production function and run a regression of log of the total value of shipments on the log of inputs, including cross-product and squared terms:

$$\ln Q_{it} = a_i + A + \sum_{j=1}^{N} a_j \ln L_{jit} + \sum_{j=1}^{N} \sum_{k=j}^{N} a_{jk} \ln L_{jit} \ln L_{kit}, \qquad (1)$$

where Q_{it} represents output of plant i in year t, a_i is a plant-level fixed effect, and L_{jit} is the quantity of input j used in production for plant i for time period t. The parameter A is a technology shift parameter, assumed to be constant by industry, and $a_j = \sum_{i=1}^{N} a_{ji}$ indexes returns to scale. Plants that change ownership have a different fixed effect for each owner, allowing the plant-level fixed effect to differ by owner.

Our measure of TFP is the residual from equation (1) plus the plant-level fixed effect. We standardize plant-level TFP by dividing by the standard deviation of TFP for each industry. Thus, our comparisons of plants' TFP are not driven by differences in the dispersion of productivity within each industry. We discuss the details of the variables used and present some summary statistics from our estimation of TFP in the Appendix.

To check robustness of our regression results, we also use two alternative measures of productivity. First we use value added per worker. Value added per worker is defined as total sales less materials cost of goods sold, divided

[18] See Caves and Barton (1990) and especially Jorgenson (1986) for more details and extensive references on estimating firm production functions.

by the number of workers. This measure has been used in McGuckin and Nguyen (1995). Second, we use cash flow per dollar of sales. Cash flow is defined as sales less the sum of the materials cost of goods sold and the capital expenditures, all divided by the value of sales. Neither of these measures has the desirable theoretical properties of TFP. However, they have the advantage of being familiar, and since they are not computed from a regression, may have desirable statistical properties.

B.2. Demand in Business Segments

To examine the effect of demand on asset sales, we include measures of both aggregate and industry demand. For aggregate demand we use detrended aggregate industrial production, as described earlier.[19] We capture changes in demand for an industry's output using an indicator of economic activity in downstream industries. By using a downstream demand indicator we avoid potential endogeneity problems that may arise if we were to use changes in the value of an industry's own shipments to proxy for demand shocks. Our measure of downstream industry demand is based on a four-digit industry measure of downstream economic activity from Baily, Bartelsman, and Haltiwanger (1998). This measure is constructed by using the 1977 input–output matrix to construct a weighted average index of downstream economic activity, with weights equal to the share of total shipments from the industry in question.[20]

C. Probability of Asset Sales

We next analyze how seller characteristics and firm organization influence partial firm sales. We separately examine sellers who are single-segment firms, and those that are multiple-segment firms. To be included in the subsample of firms that might have a partial-firm sale, the single-segment firms must have at least two plants. The regressions in this table (and all subsequent tables) cover the years from 1978 to 1992.[21]

Hypothesis 2 above suggests that a multiple-segment firm's decision to sell plants or an entire segment is influenced by its performance in other segments. We test for this effect, and for the effect of industry- and economy-

[19] Results are similar using actual industrial production. We use detrended industrial production to capture the idea that reallocations take place in response to a shock to the marginal value of production.

[20] The measure was first used in Bartelsman, Caballero, and Lyons (1994) (BCL). The BCL measure is still subject to simultaneity bias if a demand shock to the upstream industry affects activity in the downstream industry. To avoid this problem, in constructing each upstream industry's index of downstream demand, we exclude all downstream industries from the index if they purchase a large share of their inputs from that upstream industry (see Shea (1993)). Our results are similar using either this series or the original one constructed by BCL. We would like to thank John Haltiwanger for kindly providing both of these data series to us.

[21] The beginning year for these regressions is 1978 as that is the first year the change in downstream industry demand is available. A previous version of the paper used the change in own industry shipments (beginning in 1975) and found similar results. We also included industry profitability in the regressions. This variable is insignificant when added to the existing variables.

wide conditions.[22] In each case, we run an unbalanced panel probit regression allowing for correlated residuals within panel units, and we report heteroskedasticity-consistent standard errors. We control for firm size, number of plants, and relative segment rank. Relative segment rank is defined as the segment rank, with the largest segment having rank equal to one, divided by the total number of segments.

The results in Table IV show that demand at the aggregate level affects the probability of a partial sale of plants. Plants and segments are more likely to be sold when aggregate industrial production is high. This effect is stronger for multiple-segment firms.

Productivity strongly affects the probability a plant is sold for multisegment firms. The probability of a sale declines as the plant productivity increases and as the plant's segment productivity increases. This is consistent with the firm selling its worst plants in its worst divisions.[23] Thus, the behavior of sellers is consistent with the hypothesis that they are selling plants for which they do not have superior expertise.

For multisegment firms, a firm's other segments' productivity affects the probability of a plant sale. The probability of sale is positively and significantly related to the segment's rank within the firm: The probability that a plant in a smaller segment is sold is higher, holding industry shocks and productivity constant. The probability of a plant sale is also higher if the firm's other segments are more productive. This effect is strongly significant. In addition, the probability that a plant is sold is higher when the firm's other segments are productive *and* the firm's other industries have a positive increase to demand. The estimated magnitude of this effect can be shown by varying the magnitude of the other segments' weighted TFP while holding all the remaining variables at their median values. The predicted probability that the segment is sold is 3.35 percent when the other segments' weighted TFP is relatively low (at the 10th percentile) and the other segment's relative demand is high. This probability increases to 4.16 percent when the other segments' weighted TFP is relatively high (at the 90th percentile), and relative demand is also high.

In Table V, we present robustness tests of our results using two alternative measures of efficiency: value added per worker and plant cash flow. The alternative measures of productivity yield similar results as those in Table IV.

In sum, the results in Tables IV and V confirm the importance of aggregate demand on the rate of transactions. They are also consistent with profit maximizing behavior by sellers. Plants are more likely to be sold when they

[22] In unreported regressions, we also analyze partial-segment and full-segment sales separately. We have also estimated the equation for main and peripheral divisions of multiple-segment firms separately. In all material respects, the results are qualitatively similar. In addition we analyzed alternative specifications in which the firm multiple segment variables were weighed by the size of each segment. The results do not differ in any material respect.

[23] In unreported regressions, we also examine the choice of which plant to sell within a segment. The probability that a plant is sold is negatively related to the difference between its productivity and that of the other plants in the segment.

Table IV

Partial Firm Sales

Regressions test the effects of plant-level productivity and industry-level demand on the decision to sell plants for single-segment and multiple-segment firms. The dependent variable is a binary variable that indicates that the firm sells a plant, while still remaining in operation the next year. Observations are at the plant level for all firms. Detrended aggregate industrial production is actual minus predicted U.S. aggregate industrial production where predicted industrial prediction is obtained by regressing industrial production on a yearly time trend. Productivity variables are industry and year adjusted. Segment variables are aggregated into three-digit SIC codes for industry segments from underlying plant-level data. We estimate the regressions using unbalanced panel probit regressions allowing for correlated residuals within panel units. Significance tests are conducted using heteroskedasticity consistent standard errors. Data are yearly from 1979 to 1992. (p-values are in parentheses.)

	Dependent Variable: Plant Sale		Test for Significant Diff.:
Variable	Single segment firms (with >1 Plant)	Multiple segment firms	Single vs. Conglomerate Firms (p-Value)[a]
Constant	−6.162	−1.774	
	(0.000)*	(0.000)*	(0.000)*
Aggregate industrial production	0.831	1.104	
(detrended)	(0.000)*	(0.000)*	(0.000)*
Industry sensitivity to aggregate	0.009	−0.006	
industrial production	(0.277)	(0.003)*	(0.056)***
Lagged productivity (TFP) of plant[b]	−0.021	−0.075	
	(0.797)	(0.001)*	(0.042)**
Lagged segment TFP	0.026	−0.338	
	(0.705)	(0.000)*	(0.000)*
Segment TFP * change in	−0.055	0.000	
downstream industry demand	(0.317)	(0.987)	(0.812)
Lagged firm size (coefficient * 10,000,000)	0.642	−0.038	
	(0.000)*	(0.000)*	(0.000)*
Average number of plants per	−0.002	−0.022	
industry segment	(0.378)	(0.000)*	(0.000)*
Firm multiple segment variables			
Segment rank/number of segments		0.080	
		(0.000)*	
Other segment's weighted TFP[c]		0.240	
		(0.000)*	
Relative demand * other segments		0.073	
weighted TFP[d]		(0.003)*	
Total plant years	45,959	259,065	
Chi-squared statistic	108.44	1940.91	
Significance level (p-value)	<1%	<1%	

*, **, *** Significantly different from zero at the 1 percent, 5 percent, and 10 percent levels, respectively, using a two-tailed test.

[a] Significance test for a multiple-segment dummy variable interacted with each independent variable in a regression with all firms with greater than one plant.

[b] Total Factor Productivity (TFP) is calculated using a translog production function.

[c] Other segments' productivity is weighted average of the firm's other segment(s) weighted by the segment(s) sales.

[d] Relative industry demand equals one (zero, minus one) when the segment's change in downstream industry demand is greater (equal, less) than the change in downstream demand of the firm's median segment. Relative industry demand is interacted with the firm's other segments' weighted TFP.

Table V

Robustness Tests: Alternative Measures of Efficiency

Regressions test the effects of plant-level efficiency measures and industry-level demand on the decision to buy out another firm for single-segment and multiple-segment firms. The dependent variable is a binary variable which indicates that the firm sells a plant, while still remaining in operation the next year. Observations are at the plant level for all firms. Efficiency variables are industry and year adjusted. Segment variables are aggregated into three-digit SIC codes. Detrended aggregate industrial production is actual minus predicted U.S. aggregate industrial production where predicted industrial prediction is obtained by regressing industrial production on a yearly time trend. Columns one and two use value added per worker as the measure of efficiency. Value added is sales less materials divided by the number of workers. Columns three and four use plant cash flow as the measure of efficiency. Cash flow is sales less materials cost of goods sold less capital expenditures divided by sales. We estimate the regressions using unbalanced panel probit regressions allowing for correlated residuals within panel units. Significance tests are conducted using heteroskedasticity consistent standard errors. Coefficients for the value added measure of efficiency are multiplied by one hundred. (*p*-values are in parentheses.)

	Dependent Variable: Plant Sale			
	Efficiency measure: Value added per worker		Efficiency measure: Plant cash flow	
Variable	Single-segment Firms (with >1 Plant)	Multiple-segment Firms	Single-segment Firms (with >1 Plant)	Multiple-segment Firms
Constant	−6.364	−6.236	−6.004	−1.799
	(0.000)*	(0.000)*	(0.000)*	(0.000)*
Aggregate industrial production	0.880	0.980	0.802	1.100
(detrended)	(0.000)*	(0.000)*	(0.000)*	(0.000)*
Lagged plant efficiency measure	−0.166	−0.184	−0.404	−0.363
	(0.000)*	(0.000)*	(0.003)*	(0.000)*
Lagged segment efficiency measure	−0.004	−0.001	0.345	−0.162
	(0.597)	(0.670)*	(0.040)**	(0.015)**
Lagged segment efficiency * change in	0.061	0.046	−0.449	0.325
downstream industry demand	(0.661)	(0.633)	(0.147)	(0.748)
Lagged firm size (coefficient * 10,000,000)	0.710	0.066	0.671	−0.037
	(0.000)*	(0.000)*	(0.000)*	(0.000)*
Average number of plants per	−0.003	−0.024	−0.003	−0.022
industry segment	(0.184)	(0.000)*	(0.224)	(0.000)*
Firm multiple segment variables				
Segment rank/number of segments		0.489		0.124
		(0.000)*		(0.000)*
Other segment's weighted efficiency[a]		0.006		0.109
		(0.792)		(0.097)***
Relative demand * other segments		0.129		−0.040
weighted efficiency[b]		(0.005)*		(0.450)
Total plant years	45,959	259,065	45,959	259,065
Chi-squared statistic	115.66	1561.24	95.39	623.74
Significance level (*p*-value)	<1%	<1%	<1%	<1%

*, **, *** Significantly different from zero at the 1 percent, 5 percent, and 10 percent levels, respectively, using a two-tailed test.

[a] Other segments' efficiency is weighted average of the firm's other segment(s) weighted by the segment(s) sales.

[b] Relative industry demand equals one (zero, minus one) when the segment's change in downstream industry demand is greater (equal, less) than the change in downstream demand of the firm's median segment. Relative industry demand is interacted with the firm's other segments' weighted TFP.

are not productive, when their segment is less productive, and when the firm has better performing assets elsewhere. This finding supports our Hypotheses 2 and 3.

In Table VI we analyze the economic significance of our regression results. Specifically, we analyze how the probability of a sale by a single-segment firm or a division of a conglomerate varies as the level of industrial production and the productivity of the asset vary, holding all other variables at their sample medians. The probability of a sale is derived using regression coefficients computed in Tables IV and V.

Panel A of Table VI shows how the probability that an asset is sold depends on the initial owner's corporate structure and the asset's productivity. In general, the probability that an asset is sold by a conglomerate firm rather than by a single-segment firm is higher by a factor of approximately four. Using our standard productivity measure, TFP, the probability that a median level asset is sold by a conglomerate firm in any year is 3.71 percent, whereas the corresponding probability for a single-segment firm is 0.85 percent. Assets operated by peripheral divisions of conglomerates are sold at a somewhat higher rate.[24] We also find that more efficient assets at the 90th percentile have a lower probability of being sold than less efficient assets (10th percentile). The results are not sensitive to the choice of productivity measure used. The table also shows that smaller peripheral divisions are more likely to be sold. The probability a division with segment rank equal to the 90th percentile is sold is 4.13 percent at the median productivity.

Panel B shows how variation in the real level of aggregate industrial production affects the probability of sale. We present results for the median level of detrended industrial production and for levels that correspond to the 90th and 10th percentiles, respectively. The rate of asset sales is very responsive to the variation in aggregate industrial production. Thus, for example, when the aggregate production is at the 90th percentile (the second highest year), the probability that an asset of a conglomerate firm is sold is 4.03 percent, whereas it is only 3.20 percent when the level of industrial production is at the 10th percentile (the second lowest year). The corresponding statistics for single-segment firms are 1.26 percent and 0.57 percent, again illustrating their lower participation in the market for partial-firm asset sales.

Panel C shows the combined effect of the variation in productivity and aggregate industrial production. A low productivity plant owned by a peripheral division of a conglomerate has a 4.82 percent probability of being sold when industrial production is high, whereas a high productivity plant at a time of low aggregate production has a probability of being sold of only 2.50 percent. The corresponding probabilities for single-segment firms are 1.46 percent and 0.48 percent, respectively.

[24] The difference between single-segment and conglomerate rates may arise in part because the exit from an industry is classified as a partial-firm sale for a multisegment firm, but a whole-firm sale in the case of a single-segment firm. We return to this point in our discussion of Table IX.

Table VI

Probability of an Asset Sale

Predicted probability of an asset sale varying performance measures and industrial production using the regression coefficients from Tables IV and V. Panel A presents results varying performance measures from the 10th to 90th percentiles. Panel B presents results varying detrended industrial production from its median value using yearly data from 1979 to 1992. Panel C varies both productivity and aggregate industrial production at their median values. We hold all other variables at their sample medians.

Panel A: Varying Initial Productivity/Performance

	10th Percentile	Median Level	90th Percentile
Single-segment firms			
Varying productivity (Table IV, column 1)	1.08%	0.85%	0.66%
Varying value added per worker (Table V, column 1)	1.02%	0.88%	0.72%
Varying cash flow (Table V, column 3)	0.99%	0.87%	0.77%
Conglomerate firms			
Varying productivity (Table IV, column 2)	4.32%	3.71%	2.86%
Also decreasing segment rank to 10% (main divisions)	4.11%	3.52%	2.71%
Also increasing segment rank to 90% (peripheral divisions)	4.80%	4.13%	3.20%
Varying value added per worker (Table V, column 2)	4.06%	3.66%	3.08%
Varying cash flow (Table V, column 4)	4.19%	3.59%	3.04%

Panel B: Varying Industrial Production

	10th Percentile	Median Level	90th Percentile
Single-segment firms (Table IV, column 1)	0.57%	0.85%	1.26%
Conglomerate firms			
All divisions (Table IV, column 2)	3.20%	3.71%	4.03%
Also decreasing segment rank to 10% (main divisions)	3.02%	3.52%	3.81%
Also increasing segment rank to 90% (peripheral divisions)	3.64%	4.13%	4.56%
All divisions (Table V, column 2)	3.21%	3.66%	4.09%
All divisions (Table V, column 4)	3.15%	3.59%	4.02%

Panel C: Varying Industrial Production and Productivity

	Productivity 10th and Industrial Production 90th percentile	Mean Level	Productivity 90th and Industrial Production 10th percentile
Single-segment firms			
Varying productivity (Table IV, column 1)	1.46%	0.85%	0.48%
Varying value added per worker (Table V, column 1)	1.39%	0.88%	0.51%
Varying cash flow (Table V, column 3)	1.32%	0.87%	0.56%
Conglomerate firms			
All divisions (Table IV, column 2)	4.82%	3.71%	2.50%
Also decreasing segment rank to 10% (main divisions)	4.59%	3.52%	2.36%
Also increasing segment rank to 90% (peripheral divisions)	5.34%	4.13%	2.80%
All divisions (Table V, column 2)	5.53%	3.66%	2.70%
All divisions (Table V, column 4)	4.67%	3.59%	2.66%

Taken together, the estimates in Table VI suggest that the probability that a plant is transferred is considerably higher if the plant belongs to a multisegment firm, particularly a small division of a multisegment firm. Inefficient plants are more likely to be sold than efficient plants, and there are considerably more sales in times of high production. These observations are consistent with the view that the market for plants facilitates the transfer of assets to productive uses, and that transfers occur at times when the marginal value of capital is high. There is no evidence that managers of conglomerate firms are less willing to sell assets than managers of single-segment firms.

D. Probability of Mergers and Acquisitions

In Table VII we analyze mergers and whole firm sell-offs. As before, we split the sample of selling firms into single-segment and multiple-segment firms. Because the majority of selling firms are small single-plant firms, we also analyze these separately.

The results in Table VII show that industry demand strongly influences mergers and acquisitions. The rate of mergers and firm sell-offs is higher when aggregate demand is high and in industries whose demand is sensitive to aggregate output shocks. In contrast to the case of partial firm sales, the role of productivity in predicting mergers is less clear-cut. The probability that a single-plant firm is sold decreases with its productivity. We find do not find similar significant effects with the sales of other firms. However, we do find that the probability that a multiple-segment firm is sold falls if the firm's productivity is high and when the industries in which it operates experience higher demand. This finding is consistent with the first hypothesis in this paper, that firms are more likely to sell in good times when they are less productive.

The significance of the relation between firm size and the probability of sale also differs across the categories in Table VII. There is a significant positive relation between firm size and the probability of sale for single-plant firms, no relation for multiple-plant single-segment firms, and a significant negative relation for multiple-segment firms. Controlling for size, focused firms are less likely to be sold then diversified firms.

E. Buyer Characteristics and the Probability of a Purchase

In Table VIII we examine the buyers of whole firms. We consider single-segment and multisegment firms separately. To investigate whether the motives for focus-increasing and diversifying purchases are the same, we classify multisegment buyers into those for whom the purchase increases firm focus and those for whom it decreases focus, as measured by the firm's herfindahl index across the segments it operates.

With only the exception of single-plant firms, we find that the probability that a firm is a buyer in a particular industry increases with the buying

Table VII

Mergers and Firm Selloffs: Selling Firm Characteristics

Regressions test the effects of plant-level productivity and industry-level demand on the decision to sell out or merge with another firm for single-segment and multiple-segment firms. The dependent variable is a binary variable that indicates that the firm sells to another firm. Productivity variables are industry and year adjusted. Firm-level variables are aggregated from plant-level data by weighting each plant by its real value of plant shipments. Industry-level variables are constructed for each firm using as weights the real value of that firm's industry production. We estimate the regressions using unbalanced panel probit regressions allowing for correlated residuals within panel units. Significance tests are conducted using heteroskedasticity-consistent standard errors following Huber–White. (p-values are in parentheses.)

	Dependent Variable: Firm Selloff			
Variable	Single-segment Firms with 1 Plant	Single-segment Firms with >1 Plant	Multiple-segment Firms	Test for Significant Diff.: Multiple-segment Interaction Variable (p-value)[a]
Constant	−1.833	−1.987	−1.808	
	(0.000)	(0.000)*	(0.000)*	(0.644)
Aggregate industrial production (detrended)	0.723	0.716	0.743	
	(0.000)*	(0.035)**	(0.006)*	(0.952)
Industry sensitivity to aggregate industrial production	0.012	0.013	0.018	
	(0.000)*	(0.054)***	(0.002)*	(0.519)
Lagged productivity of firm (TFP)[b]	−0.023	−0.018	−0.014	
	(0.041)**	(0.526)	(0.549)	(0.600)
Firm TFP * downstream industry shipments	0.181	0.070	−0.568	
	(0.191)	(0.864)	(0.028)**	(0.615)
Lagged firm size (coefficient * 10,000,000)	2.500	0.299	−0.145	
	(0.000)*	(0.186)	(0.042)**	(0.166)
Dispersion (herfandahl) across industries			−0.223	
			(0.000)*	
Total firm years	96,961	24,772	42,524	
Chi-squared statistic	56.12	11.62	39.36	
Significance level (p-value)	<1%	0.040	<1%	

*, **, *** Significantly different from zero at the 1 percent, 5 percent, and 10 percent levels, respectively, using a two-tailed test.

[a] Significance test for a multiple-segment dummy variable interacted with each independent variable in a regression with all firms with >1 plant.

[b] Total Factor Productivity (TFP) is calculated using a translog production function.

Table VIII

Mergers and Firm Selloffs: Buying Firm Characteristics

Regressions test the effects of plant-level productivity and industry-level demand on the decision to buy out another firm for single-segment and multiple-segment firms. The dependent variable is a binary variable that indicates that the firm buys another firm. Observations are at the firm level for all firms. Productivity variables are industry and year adjusted. Segment-level variables are aggregated from plant-level data by weighting each plant by its real value of plant shipments. Industry-level variables are constructed for each firm using as weights the real value of a firm's industry production. We estimate the regressions using unbalanced panel probit regressions allowing for correlated residuals within panel units. Focus-increasing (decreasing) purchases are transactions that result in the buying firm's sum of squared industry market shares (herfandahl) increasing (decreasing). Significance tests are conducted using heteroskedasticity-consistent standard errors following Huber–White. (p-values are in parentheses.)

	Dependent Variable: Firm Purchase			
	Single-segment Firms		Multiple-segment Firms	
Variable	With 1 Plant	With >1 Plant	Focus-increasing Purchase	Focus-decreasing Purchase
Constant	−2.381	−2.094	−2.122	−1.987
	(0.000)*	(0.000)*	(0.000)*	(0.000)*
Aggregate industrial production	0.551	0.450	0.914	0.817
(detrended)	(0.044)**	(0.206)	(0.001)*	(0.001)*
Industry sensitivity to aggregate	0.007	−0.008	−0.006	−0.004
industrial production	(0.216)	(0.318)	(0.371)	(0.512)
Lagged productivity of industry	−0.048	0.271	0.249	0.290
segment (TFP)[a]	(0.413)	(0.004)*	(0.100)***	(0.000)*
Firm TFP * downstream	0.618	0.884	0.062	−0.047
industry shipments	(0.580)	(0.643)	(0.549)	(0.412)
Lagged firm size	4.330	0.650	0.196	0.166
(coefficient * 10,000,000)	(0.000)*	(0.105)	(0.091)***	(0.051)**
Average number of plants per		0.027	0.090	0.075
industry segment		(0.000)*	(0.000)*	(0.000)*
Total plant years	77,713	24,774	40,152	40,498
Chi-squared statistic	21.33	99.85	141.37	144.31
Significance level (p-value)	<1%	<1%	<1%	<1%

*, **, *** Significantly different from zero at the 1 percent, 5 percent, and 10 percent levels, respectively, using a two-tailed test.

[a] Total Factor Productivity (TFP) is calculated using a translog production function.

firm's segment TFP, size, and with the number of plants the firm already owns. Acquisitions are more likely when aggregate industrial production is high. These results indicate that buying firms are growing in industries in which they are productive when demand is high.

Table IX calculates economic significance of the previous regressions in Tables VII and VIII. The table shows how the predicted probabilities of mergers or full firm purchases are affected by variation in firm productivity and

Table IX

Probability of Mergers

Predicted probability of a merger or full-firm purchase varying performance measures and industrial production using the regression coefficients from Tables VII and VIII. Panel A presents results varying performance measures from the 10th to 90th percentiles. Panel B presents results varying detrended industrial production from its median value over 1979 to 1992. Panel C varies both productivity and aggregate industrial production at their median values. We hold all other variables at their sample medians.

Panel A: Selling Firms

Varying productivity	10th Percentile	Median	90th Percentile
Single-segment selling firms	2.63%	2.55%	2.45%
Conglomerate selling firms	3.21%	3.01%	2.77%
Varying industrial production	**10th Percentile**	**Median**	**90th Percentile**
Single-segment selling firms	2.33%	2.55%	2.75%
Conglomerate selling firms	2.74%	3.01%	3.25%
Varying productivity & industrial production	**Productivity 10th, Industrial Production 90th Percentile**	**Median Level**	**Productivity 90th, Industrial Production 10th Percentile**
Single-segment selling firms	2.83%	2.55%	2.26%
Conglomerate selling firms	3.46%	3.01%	2.53%

Panel B: Buying Firms

Varying productivity	10th Percentile	Median	90th Percentile
Single-segment buying firms	1.85%	2.13%	2.56%
Conglomerate buying firms: Focus increasing	2.30%	2.47%	2.94%
Conglomerate buying firms: Focus decreasing	2.92%	3.27%	3.95%
Varying industrial production	**10th Percentile**	**Median**	**90th Percentile**
Single-segment buying firms	1.93%	2.13%	2.17%
Conglomerate buying firms: Focus increasing	2.03%	2.47%	2.56%
Conglomerate buying firms: Focus decreasing	2.76%	3.27%	3.37%
Varying productivity & industrial production	**Productivity 10th, Industrial Production 90th Percentile**	**Median Level**	**Productivity 90th, Industrial Production 10th Percentile**
Single-segment buying firms	1.78%	2.13%	2.60%
Conglomerate buying firms: Focus increasing	2.22%	2.47%	3.04%
Conglomerate buying firms: Focus decreasing	2.87%	3.27%	4.01%

demand conditions. For the case of buying firms, the explanatory variables and their variation parallel those discussed in the case of partial firm sales in Table VI.

Panel A shows the predicted probabilities of whole firms sales. As in the case of partial firm sales, whole single-segment firms are less likely to be sold than multisegment firms, at 2.55 percent and 3.01 percent, respectively. The difference between the two types of firms is less than the difference for asset sales. Taken together with the results on partial-firm sales in Table VII, our estimates predict that assets owned by conglomerate firms appear to be "in play" to a greater extent than assets owned by single-segment firms. Overall, predicted sales of multisegment firms are very sensitive to variations in both productivity and aggregate industrial demand.

Panel B shows predicted variation in the probability of purchase. Again, the predicted purchases by multisegment firms are higher than by single-segment firms. The predicted probability that a firm is a buyer varies with the firm's productivity. However, the predicted probability that a multisegment firm engages in a focus-decreasing purchase depends somewhat more on the buying firm's productivity. Both the probability of a purchase by a single-segment firm and of a focus-decreasing purchase by a multisegment firm are also higher when aggregate industrial output is high. Focus-increasing mergers by multisegment firms are not as sensitive to changes in aggregate industrial production.

V. Are There Productivity Gains and What Determines the Gains?

In this section, we examine the productivity change (industry adjusted in each year) surrounding the asset sales—both for full-firm mergers and sales and for partial-firm sales. To begin the analysis, we first present simple summary statistics on the change in productivity for the manufacturing plants involved in purchases subsequent to the transactions.

In Table X, we analyze the changes in productivity using a three-by-three matrix to capture the internal organization characteristics of the buyer and the seller. We classify both the buyer and the seller as a single-segment firm, or as a main or peripheral division of a multisegment firm. Because the results in Table VII suggest that single-plant firms may behave differently than the rest of the firm population, in the case of mergers we further subclassify single-segment sellers into firms with one plant and firms with more than one plant.

In this table, and in our subsequent tables analyzing productivity changes, we require that both buyer and seller ex ante data exist for each transaction. Transactions for which we have no ex ante data for buying firms include foreign firms purchasing assets for the first time in the United States, non-manufacturing firms purchasing manufacturing assets, new firms formed to purchase existing assets, assets spun off or carved out from existing firms,

Table X

Summary Statistics for Change in Productivity for Assets Sold or Merged

The change in productivity, industry and year adjusted, for three years surrounding asset sales, mergers, or full-firm sales (year −1 to year +2). Values represent sample means for transactions between buyers and sellers. (Standard error of the mean in parentheses.) Third row is the number of plants transacted.

Panel A: Partial-Firm Sales

	Selling Firm Characteristics		
	Multidivision Firm		
	Main Division	Peripheral Division	Single-segment Firm
Buying firm characteristics			
Multidivision buyer adds to			
Main division	0.062	0.103*	0.127
	(0.039)	(0.036)	(0.092)
	444	580	87
Peripheral division	−0.008	0.047**	0.033
	(0.027)	(0.021)	(0.076)
	857	1,544	122
Single-segment buyer	0.019	0.107**	−0.038
	(0.052)	(0.042)	(0.069)
	275	382	126

Panel B: Full-Firm Mergers and Acquisitions

	Selling Firm Characteristics			
	Multidivision Firm		Single-segment Firm	
	Main Division	Peripheral Division	with 1 Plant	with >1 Plant
Buying firm characteristics				
Multidivision buyer adds to				
Main division	0.087**	0.143***	−0.020	−0.039
	(0.041)	(0.083)	(0.039)	(0.043)
	396	89	420	234
Peripheral division	−0.017	−0.020	−0.051***	0.058
	(0.020)	(0.025)	(0.028)	(0.039)
	1,278	914	723	401
Single-segment buyer	−0.044	0.037	0.053	−0.011
	(0.049)	(0.067)	(0.029)	(0.050)
	237	108	677	219

*, **, *** Significantly different from zero at the 1 percent, 5 percent, and 10 percent levels, respectively, using a two-tailed test.

and small firms outside of the ASM sample that purchase larger plants. Given that our subsequent regressions analyze the effect of differences between ex ante buyer and seller productivity, we also only analyze transactions for which we have ex ante productivity data for both buying and selling firms.[25] After these requirements are taken into account, we are able to analyze productivity changes for 10,109 transactions.

We calculate the industry adjusted change in productivity from the year before the transaction to two years after the transaction, year −1 to year +2, where year 0 is the year of the transaction. For our sample, the mean industry adjusted change in productivity is 0.02, and is significantly different from zero at the one percent significance level. The median change in productivity is also positive. Thus, the majority of the transactions in our sample have led to increases in productivity. Productivity changes for the transaction types are given in Table X.

Panel A of Table X presents the change in productivity for partial-firm asset sales. We find that all sales from peripheral divisions have significant positive ex post changes in productivity, regardless of the buyer's organizational characteristics. For single-segment sellers, no transactions resulted in a significant increase in productivity. There is no evidence that any category of transactions leads to significant declines in productivity of the assets sold.

Panel B presents the change in productivity for full-firm sales and mergers. Several facts emerge: We find significant productivity gains only when buyers add capacity to their main divisions—increasing the focus of their firm. Purchases by single-segment firms, although very frequent, do not result in increased productivity of the purchased assets. Thus, there is evidence that restructuring that involves sales from multisegment firms to single-segment firms does not result in gains. Productivity significantly decreases in only one class of transactions: purchases of single-plant firms by the peripheral divisions of multisegment firms.

The differences in the observed gains in Table X may exist because some types of buyers are more efficient in improving assets. The differences may also occur if, in some types of transactions, there is a higher incidence of inefficient sellers and efficient buyers, who have the expertise or resources to improve the assets. To examine the latter possibility, we classify transactions into those where the productivity of the buyer's assets in the industry exceeds that of the acquired plants, and into those where it does not.

For partial-firm asset sales, the buyer's existing plants are more productive than the acquired plants in 59.6 percent of the transactions. For mergers and acquisitions, 57.2 percent of the total transactions have buyers that are more productive than the plants they purchase. These proportions are significantly different from each other at the 1.5 percent level. Looking at differences based on firm organization, we also find significant differences. For example, for asset sales, we find that when firms add assets to their main divisions, their existing plants are more productive in 62.9 percent of the transactions. By contrast, for peripheral divisions 59.6 percent of buyers are more productive than purchased plants and for single segment firms

[25] This also eliminates transactions occurring prior to 1979, given that we calculate productivity in each industry using five years of lagged data.

54.9 percent are more productive than the purchased plants. In all cases the proportion of transactions is significantly greater than 50 percent at the 1 percent level.

We next examine if these differences between the buyer's and seller's productivity significantly affect productivity gains of the purchased plants in a multivariate regression. To test whether the transaction type affects productivity gains after controlling for productivity differences, we also allow for a differential effect for the difference in seller and buyer productivity based on the type of transaction. We regress the change in productivity of the purchased plants on the difference between the initial productivity of the buyer and the productivity of the plants purchased, buyer's and the seller's respective firm sizes, and the selling firm's initial productivity.

We expect the productivity of acquired plants to increase when they are acquired by a buyer who has higher productivity. However, the productivity of acquired plants may not increase when the buyer's productivity is lower. To examine whether this occurs, we interact the difference between buyer and seller productivity with an indicator variable that equals one when the purchased plant is more productive than the buyer. This variable allows the slope coefficient on the difference in buyer and seller productivity to change when buyers are less productive than the plants they purchase.

Lastly, to test whether there is a differential affect by type of transaction, we interact the difference in productivity between the buyer and seller with indicator variables identifying the different transaction categories from Table X. The interaction variables measure how the effect of the difference between the buyer's and seller's initial productivity on the asset's change in productivity depends on whether the transaction is a partial sale or a merger, and on the organizational structure of the buyer and the seller. The interaction variables thus allow different types of transactions to have larger or smaller sensitivities to the difference between initial buyer and seller productivity.

Table XI shows that the productivity gain following a transaction depends on the productivities of the selling and buying firms. Assets increase in productivity when the productivity of the buying firm is higher than the productivity of the assets purchased. This finding suggests that the earlier stock market evidence of Lang, Stulz, and Walkling (1989), which shows total stock market gains of tender offers when high q firms acquire low q targets, is not caused just by tax differences or by purely financial gains. However, when assets are purchased by a buyer with a lower productivity, the purchased assets' productivity falls. Gains in productivity are positively related to the seller's size and inversely related to the initial seller productivity.

None of the 17 estimated transaction interaction variables is statistically significant. Thus, there is little evidence that the type of transaction affects productivity gains, after controlling for the initial buyer's and seller's productivity.

The fact that some buyers acquire assets that are more productive than their existing assets, and that the acquired assets' productivity declines subsequently, may initially appear puzzling. One possible explanation is that

Table XI

Change in Productivity Based on Buying & Selling Firm Characteristics

This table presents a single regression that tests the joint effects of buyer and selling firm organization characteristics on the change in plant productivity over a three-year horizon from the year prior to the asset sale or merger (year −1) to the end of the second year (year +2) after the transaction. Total Factor Productivity (TFP) variables are calculated using a translog production function. Lagged firm productivity variables are aggregated up from individual plants. All productivity variables are industry and year adjusted. Transaction type variables are indicator variables that show whether the transaction was from a seller's main or peripheral division or from a single-segment firm to a buyer's main, peripheral, or to a single-segment buyer. Transaction type dummy variables are then interacted with the difference in productivity between the buying firm and the assets purchased. We estimate the regressions using ordinary least squares. Significance tests are conducted using heteroskedasticity-consistent standard errors. (p-values in parentheses.)

	Dependent Variable: Change in Productivity Year −1 to +2	
	Transaction Type	
Variable	Partial Firm Sale	Merger/Acquisition
Productivity and transaction size		
Lagged productivity (year −1)	−0.453	
of selling firm's plants	(0.000)*	
Difference in productivity (year −1)	0.399	
buying firm—productivity of plants purchased	(0.000)*	
Difference in productivity (year −1) * Indicator	−0.084	
variable for negative difference in productivity	(0.004)*	
Buyer size (coefficient * 10,000,000)	−0.003	
	(0.834)	
Seller size (coefficient * 10,000,000)	0.123	
	(0.000)*	
Difference in productivity interacted with transaction characteristics		
Sale from seller's main division	−0.009	0.000
to buyer's main division	(0.931)	(0.907)
Sale from seller's main division	−0.014	−0.043
to buyer's peripheral division	(0.894)	(0.676)
Sale from seller's main division	−0.032	−0.119
to a single segment buyer	(0.776)	(0.282)
Sale from seller's peripheral division	0.119	omitted
to buyer's main division	(0.268)	
Sale from seller's peripheral division	−0.002	−0.058
to buyer's peripheral division	(0.987)	(0.572)
Sale from seller's peripheral division	−0.090	−0.165
to a single segment buyer	(0.400)	(0.179)
Sale from single segment firm	0.021	−0.034
to buyer's main division	(0.883)	(0.750)
Sale from single segment firm	0.065	−0.045
to buyer's peripheral division	(0.620)	(0.662)
Sale from single segment firm	−0.034	−0.155
to a single segment buyer	(0.786)	(0.131)
Constant		−0.066
		(0.000)*
Total transactions:		
Partial firm sales and merger and acquisitions	10,109	
R^2	0.21	
F-test all coefficients = 0 (p-value)	<1%	

* Significantly different from zero at the 1 percent levels using a two-tailed test.

Table XII

Change in Buyer Productivity

Buyer's change in productivity, industry and year adjusted, for three years surrounding asset purchases, mergers, or acquisitions (year −1 to year +2). Values represent sample means for transactions. We construct a firm-level weighted average of buyer's plants, with weights equal to an individual plant's value of shipments. For the existing assets' change in productivity, we present the weighted average change in productivity for plants in the same industry as the purchased assets. (Standard error of the mean is in parentheses.)

		Cases where	
	Overall Change in Productivity	Initial Buyer Productivity > Productivity of Assets Purchased	Initial Buyer Productivity < Productivity of Assets Purchased
Panel A: Change in Productivity of Buyer's Existing Assets (Excluding Purchased Assets)			
All transactions	0.004	−0.027**	0.053*
	(0.009)	(0.011)	(0.015)
Asset purchases	0.008	−0.028***	0.065*
	(0.014)	(0.016)	(0.023)
Mergers & acquisitions	0.000	−0.027***	0.044**
	(0.012)	(0.016)	(0.019)
Panel B: Change in Productivity of All Assets of Buyer (Including Purchased Assets)			
All transactions	0.020*	0.028*	−0.010
	(0.006)	(0.008)	(0.011)
Asset purchases	0.048*	0.056*	0.002
	(0.009)	(0.010)	(0.014)
Mergers & acquisitions	−0.003	0.004	−0.028**
	(0.007)	(0.009)	(0.013)
Number of buying firms	6905	5366	1539

*, **, *** Significantly different from zero at the 1 percent, 5 percent, and 10 percent levels, respectively, using a two-tailed test.

managers of these buying firms are destroying value by making inefficient acquisitions. However, such a conclusion would be unwarranted if the acquired assets provide synergies that increase the value of the buyers' existing assets.

To check whether this is the case, we calculate the industry- and year-adjusted changes in productivity of the buyer's assets for three years surrounding asset purchases (year −1 to year + 2). In Panel A of Table XII we present the changes in the productivity of buyers' existing plants in the same industry in which plants are acquired. The data is broken down into three categories: all transactions, partial-firm purchases, and whole-firm purchases. We further present productivity changes for transactions for the case in which the buyer's initial productivity exceeds that of the assets purchased, and for the case in which it does not.

Panel A shows that for all transactions, and for partial- and whole-firm transactions taken separately, there is no overall change in the productivity of the buyers' existing assets in the same industry. However, the buyers' assets exhibit a significant decline in productivity in those cases where the initial buyers' productivity exceeds that of the purchased assets. By contrast, buyers' existing assets in a segment show a significant increase in productivity when more productive plants are acquired in that segment.

The pattern of gains is consistent with the notion that the addition of a less productive plant to a segment increases control costs and lowers the productivity of existing assets. A majority of transactions are of this type. The fact that the acquisition of a more productive plant results in gains to the existing assets and a decline in productivity of the acquired plants is consistent with buyer purchasing expertise or productive ability that can be transferred to existing assets.

To determine whether the total gains in productivity outweigh the losses, we compute the total changes in the productivity of the buying firm around the period of the transaction. This calculation, which includes the purchased assets, shows the full effect of the purchase on all of the buyer's manufacturing operations. To get a firm-level measure of the productivity gain, we construct a weighted average of all plants of the buyer. We weight each plant's productivity by its initial value of shipments.

Panel B shows the buyers' total productivity gains at the firm level. The results show that there is a significant firm-level productivity gain in partial-firm sales when the buyer's productivity exceeds the productivity of the acquired plants. Thus, the productivity gain of the acquired plant(s) outweighs the productivity loss on the firm's existing assets. Panel B also shows that a significant firm-level productivity loss only occurs in the case when less productive firms acquire more productive firms. In this case, the productivity gain that the buying firm experiences is outweighed by the loss in productivity of the assets purchased. There are no significant firm-level productivity effects in whole-firm sales when the buyer is more efficient than the seller, or in partial-firm sales when the buyer acquires more efficient plants.

These results, combined with the summary statistics that show significant increases in productivity, are consistent with the hypothesis that the market for assets works well for asset sales and for the majority of mergers. Assets that are transacted result in significant gains, consistent with Hypothesis 1 presented earlier. Contrary to the hypothesis that these divisions get subsidized by their parent firms, multidivisional firms are more likely to sell less productive divisions and these sales to other firms result in subsequent productivity increases. Our results support the conclusion that assets change hands as the prospects in the overall economy and in their other industries improve and their owners discover that they do not have a comparative advantage in running these assets. There is significant firm-level fall in productivity surrounding a transaction in cases where more efficient firms are acquired by less efficient firms—a minority of transactions.[26]

Overall these results show that, as suggested by our first hypothesis, there are significant gains for assets being redeployed from less productive sellers to productive buyers. The results on the timing of transactions are consistent with our second hypothesis, which predicts that more productive firms will expand their operations in good times and when their prospects in a given industry look better than the other industries in which they operate.

VI. Conclusions

In this paper, we analyze the market for corporate assets (plants, divisions, and whole firms) in manufacturing industries. We analyze both the buyers and sellers. We show that the market for both full and partial firms is extensive. On average, 3.89 percent of plants change ownership in each year in our study. The total number of transactions varies with the economy and is strongly procyclical. In expansion years, close to 7 percent of plants annually change ownership. Approximately the same number of plants are sold through partial-firm asset sales as in mergers and acquisitions. The buyers and sellers in the partial-firm asset sale market are typically large multisegment firms, in contrast to the merger and acquisition market where the buyers are much bigger than the sellers.

We analyze the factors that are associated with the probability that assets transfer ownership. We have three main results on the probability assets are sold:

1. For multiple-division firms, the probability of a firm selling assets decreases with both the asset's and the segment's productivity. The probability that assets are sold is higher for peripheral divisions. The probability of mergers and firm sell-offs is higher when the selling firm is less productive and the industry experiences a positive demand shock.
2. The selling firm's productivity in other divisions impacts the probability of a sale. A division is more likely to be sold the better the prospects of the other divisions.
3. We find that the probability that a firm is a buyer of additional assets increases with its efficiency and size.

[26] In unreported results, we have also calculated the total effect of acquisitions at the segment level. These calculations measure the changes of productivity of the new and existing assets of the segment that acquires the new assets. The qualitative results at the segment level are the same as the results at the firm level.

In addition, we show that ex post productivity changes occur for assets transacted and these productivity changes are associated with buyer and seller initial productivity and firm organization. We also examine the overall changes in buyer productivity for purchasing firms. Our primary findings for changes in productivity for assets transacted are:

1. The gain in productivity of assets under new ownership is higher when the selling firm's productivity is low and is higher the more productive the buyer.
2. A firm's internal organization is also associated with observed changes in productivity of the asset sold. Asset sales from peripheral divisions of sellers to both main and peripheral divisions of buyers show significant productivity gains. For mergers and acquisitions, assets that are acquired by the buyer's main divisions from other multiple-segment firms show significant gains. These gains are primarily explained by the differences in the initial productivity of buying and selling divisions.
3. When we take into account both the purchased and existing assets, the change in productivity is positive for partial-firm asset purchases and is insignificantly different from zero for mergers and acquisitions.
4. When firms purchase assets of lower productivity, existing assets increase in productivity but the acquired assets decline in productivity. At the firm level, these losses on the acquired assets are offset by the productivity increases of the purchased assets. Overall firm productivity increases for partial-firm purchases and is insignificant for mergers and acquisitions.
5. When firms purchase assets of higher productivity, the acquired assets decline and the existing assets increase in productivity. At the firm level, the change in productivity is not significantly different from zero for partial-firm purchases by less efficient producers. Firm-level productivity declines for one category of transactions: mergers and acquisitions by less efficient firms.

These findings suggest that firms have differing levels of ability to exploit assets, and that their comparative advantage is in their main industries. The low productivity of firms' peripheral divisions prior to the sale, however, does not necessarily imply inefficient ownership. They may optimally operate these divisions until demand is high, at which point more efficient buyers acquire these assets.

The productivity gains we document are consistent with buying firms being able to offer a premium in part because of the gains in real productivity that occur. The results are also consistent with more skilled buying firms being able to transfer skill and improve the assets they purchase. There is no evidence that managers of conglomerate firms are less willing to sell assets than managers of single-segment firms.

The timing of sales and the pattern of productivity gains suggests that most transactions that occur in the market for plants and divisions tend to improve the allocation of resources and are consistent with profit maximizing by firms across the divisions they operate. Thus, the pattern is consistent with profit-maximizing behavior. However, our results do not disprove the existence of agency conflicts within firms. We identify one category of transactions, full-firm acquisitions by buyers with lower productivity than that of the assets they purchase, for which overall firm productivity declines. Moreover, if managers are able to appropriate the gains of productivity from any acquisitions, there might not be a gain to shareholders.

Our results would indicate that efficient firms refocusing in booms may produce the highest gains to transactions. Boards of directors should be more willing to accept productivity explanations for these types of transactions, particularly for partial firm acquisitions.

Despite our finding that most transactions result in gains in productivity, this does not refute the proposition that sometimes managers undertake transactions that, even given rational expectations, reduce value at the time the transaction is undertaken. For example, our research would also suggest that mergers and acquisitions by inefficient firms, presumably with lower stock market valuations relative to industry peers, should receive closer scrutiny by boards of directors. Further research should examine the link between acquirer and seller stock market valuations and subsequent productivity gains.

Overall, our results suggest that most transactions in the market for assets result in an increase in productive efficiency. We conclude that the market for corporate assets facilitates the redeployment of assets from firms with a lower ability to exploit them to firms with higher ability.

Appendix

In estimating the TFPs in our sample, we use data for approximately 50,000 plants each year. We are able to calculate lagged productivity for plants from 1979 to 1992 as we use five years of lagged data to calculate productivity. In the productivity regression for each industry, we include three different types of inputs: capital, labor, and materials, as explanatory variables for each plant. All these data exist at the plant level. We include plants if plants have at least two years of data. In addition, all observations must have nonzero values for all inputs and outputs. After productivity is calculated, we report and use these numbers in regressions after excluding the top and bottom one percent of the calculated productivities. We also only include plants if the total value of firm shipments is at least 10 million real 1982 dollars.[27] After imposing these restrictions, we end up with over 400,000 plant-level productivity measures.[28] In calculating productivity, the capital variable used

[27] We also find similar results changing this requirement to one million real 1982 dollars.

[28] The regressions in Table IV use 305,024 observations. Single-plant firms, representing 95,916 observations, are not included in Table IV. In addition, 15,874 observations are excluded as we also exclude outliers based on alternative measures of efficiency presented in Table V. The tables for mergers use firm-level observations obtained by aggregating these plant-level observations up to the firm level.

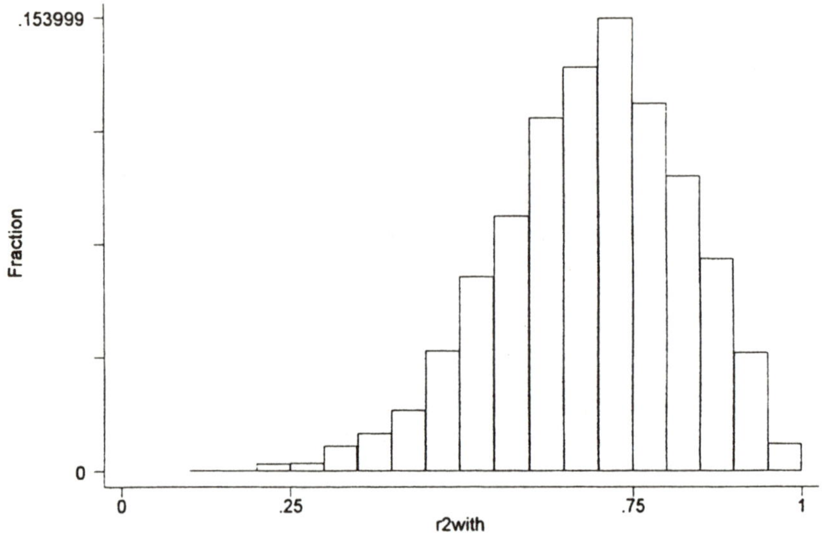

Figure A1. Histogram of R-squares from TFP within regressions run each year using five years of lagged data.

is plant's capital stock that is available to be used in production. To account for depreciation of beginning of period capital stock, we use data from the Bureau of Economic Analysis to make depreciation adjustments for beginning period capital stock at the two-digit level. To the beginning of period capital stock, we add the real dollars (in real 1982 dollars) spent on capital expenditures for additions to the capital stock. In addition, to capture vintage effects of capital, we include plant age in our productivity calculations. Plant age is either the first year in which the plant appeared in the database, or 1972 (the first year of the database), if the plant existed in 1972. For the dependent variable, output, the ASM does not state the actual quantity shipped by each plant, but shows only the value (in current period dollars) of shipments. We adjust all nominal dollar variables for inflation by using four-digit SIC code price deflators for output, materials, and capital from the Bartelsman and Gray (1994) database. Kovenock and Phillips (1997) describe these inputs and the method for accounting for inflation and depreciation of capital stock in more detail.

To measure the productivity for a firm's entire business segment, we construct a weighted average of individual plant productivity, in which the weights are the predicted plant-level real value of shipments. The variable for the productivity of the firm's other segments is the weighted average of all of the firm's other plants outside of the segment in question. Again, the weights are the predicted plant-level real value of shipments.

Table AI

Total Factor Productivity

Table reports mean coefficients from yearly regressions by industry. Each regression is repeated in each year for each industry using the last five years of data. Coefficients in column one represent the average coefficients from regressions estimated in each year for each industry (1,726 total regressions). Columns two and three represent illustrative industries for 1978. In each year, productivity is the residual plus the firm-specific fixed effect obtained from regressing the real value (deflated) of output on a plant's age, the value of materials and inputs, the real value of a plant's capital stock and the hours of labor utilized. Adjustments for depreciation for capital stock are made each year using depreciation deflators from the Bureau of Economic Analysis. All dollar amounts are deflated to 1982 dollars using deflators for the National Bureau of Economic Research. (p-values in parentheses).

Independent Variable: Real Value of Output			
Variable	Mean Coefficient	Meat Packing SIC 2011	Oil Refining SIC 2911
Age	0.013	0.019	0.169
	(0.061)***	(0.587)	(0.009)*
Inputs	0.108	0.003	1.661
	(0.000)*	(0.972)	(0.000)*
Capital stock	0.044	0.084	0.306
	(0.000)*	(0.124)	(0.001)*
Labor	0.674	0.773	−0.072
	(0.000)*	(0.000)*	(0.600)
$(\text{Inputs})^2$	0.074	−0.001	0.009
	(0.000)*	(0.825)	(0.043)**
$(\text{Capital stock})^2$	0.000	0.075	0.007
	(0.631)	(0.000)*	(0.411)
$(\text{Labor})^2$	0.020	0.085	−0.024
	(0.000)*	(0.000)*	(0.039)**
Inputs * capital stock	−0.029	−0.005	0.003
	(0.000)*	(0.640)	(0.856)
Inputs * labor	−0.110	−0.005	−0.040
	(0.000)*	(0.503)	(0.003)*
Capital stock * labor	0.044	−0.144	−0.000
	(0.000)*	(0.000)*	(0.999)
Constant	3.352	2.819	−3.765
	(0.000)*	(0.000)*	(0.000)*
R^2		0.92	0.74

*, **, *** For column one mean value of the coefficient is significantly different from zero at the 1, 5, 10 percent levels, respectively, using a two-tailed t-test. For columns two and three, significance test is whether coefficient is significantly different from zero using a two tailed t-test.

We also include other firm and segment-level variables in our regressions to provide additional controls for unmeasured productivity differences and other factors, such as size, that can influence firm growth. We include the lagged firm size and the number of plants operated by a firm at the beginning of the year. We define firm size as the total value of shipments in real 1982 dollars. We exclude all industry segments with real value of shipments smaller than one million dollars from our regressions.

To allow for technical change, each regression is repeated for each industry for each year using data for the current year and the preceding four years, giving us a rolling panel of data for each year. Thus we can calculate productivity for the 1978 to 1992 period. We use the earlier years of data, 1974 to 1977, only for calculating the first year of productivity.[29] Thus, there are 1,726 separate regressions. Figure A1 shows the distribution of adjusted R^2 for the regressions.

In Table AI we present the means of the coefficients for the 1,726 separate regressions covering the whole sample and also the coefficients for two sample industries.

The coefficients for the sample industries are for 1979, the first year for which a five-year panel is available. The first industry, SIC 2011 Meat Packing, was selected because it is the first industry in our sample when industries are ranked by SIC codes. Because meat packing is labor intensive, the second industry, SIC 2911 Oil Refining was selected to illustrate a capital intensive industry. The means of the coefficients in the whole sample are significantly different from zero. The coefficients of the two sample industries reflect their technologies. As expected, labor inputs have a more significant role in the meat packing equation and capital stock inputs are more important in oil refining.

REFERENCES

Alexander, Gordon J., George P. Benson, and Joan M. Kampmeyer, 1984, Investigating the valuation effects of announcements of voluntary corporate selloffs, *Journal of Finance* 39, 503–517.

Andrade, Gregor, and Erik Stafford, 1999, Investigating the economic role of mergers, Working paper, Harvard Business School.

Baily, Martin Neil, Eric J. Bartelsman, and John Haltiwanger, 1998, Labor productivity: Structural change and cyclical dynamics, Working paper 98-7, Center for Economic Studies.

Bartelsman, Eric J., Ricardo J. Caballero, and Richard K. Lyons, 1994, Customer and supplier-driven externalities, *American Economic Review* 84, 1075–1084.

Bartelsman, Eric J., and Wayne Gray, 1994, The NBER Manufacturing Productivity Database, Working paper, The Center for Economic Studies.

Caves, Richard E., and David R. Barton, 1990, Efficiency in U.S. manufacturing. (MIT Press, Cambridge, MA)

Chevalier, Judith, 1999, Why do firms undertake diversifying mergers? An examination of the investment policies of merging firms, Mimeo, University of Chicago.

Fluck, Zsuzsanna, and Anthony W. Lynch, 1999, Why do firms merge and then divest: A theory of financial synergy, *Journal of Business* 72, 319–346.

Graham, John, Michael Lemmon, and Jack Wolf, 2002, Does corporate diversification destroy value? forthcoming, *Journal of Finance* 57.

Hart, Oliver, and John Moore, 1995, Debt and seniority: An analysis of the role of hard claims in constraining management, *American Economic Review* 85, 567–585.

[29] In an earlier version of this paper, we calculated TFPs using the entire sample period for each industry. The two methodologies yielded very similar qualitative results.

Hite, Gailen, James E. Owers, and Ronald C. Rogers, 1987, The market for interfirm asset sales: Partial sell-offs and total liquidations, *Journal of Financial Economics* 18, 229–252.

Jain, Prem C., 1985, The effect of voluntary sell-offs announcements on shareholder wealth, *The Journal of Finance* 40, 209–224.

Jensen, Michael C., 1986, The agency costs of free cash flow: Corporate finance and takeovers, *American Economic Review* 76, 323–329.

Jensen, Michael C., and Richard S. Ruback, 1983, The market for corporate control: The scientific evidence, *Journal of Financial Economics* 11, 5–50.

John, Kose, and Eli Ofek, 1995, Asset sales and the increase in focus, *Journal of Financial Economics* 37, 105–126.

Jorgenson, Dale W., 1986, Econometric methods for modeling producer behavior; in Zvi Griliches and Michael D. Intriligator, eds.: *Handbook of Econometrics*, vol. 3. (North Holland, Amsterdam).

Kaplan, Steven N., and Michael Weisbach, 1992, The success of acquisitions: Evidence from divestitures, *The Journal of Finance* 47, 107–138

Kovenock, Daniel, and Gordon Phillips, 1997, Capital structure and product market behavior: An examination of plant exit and investment behavior, *Review of Financial Studies* 10, 767–804.

Lamont, Owen, 1997, Cash flow and investment: Evidence from internal capital markets, *Journal of Finance* 52, 83–109.

Lang, Larry H. P., Annette Poulsen, and René Stulz, 1995, Asset sales, firm performance, and the agency costs of managerial discretion, *Journal of Financial Economics* 37, 3–38.

Lang, Larry H. P., René Stulz, and Ralph A. Walkling, 1989, Managerial performance, Tobin's *q*, and the gains from successful tender offers, *Journal of Financial Economics* 24, 137–155.

Lang, Larry H. P., René Stulz, and Ralph A. Walking, 1991, A test of the free cash flow hypothesis: The case of bidder returns, *Journal of Financial Economics* 29, 315–335.

Lichtenberg, Frank R., and Donald Siegel, 1992, Takeovers and corporate overhead; in Frank R. Lichtenberg, ed.: *Corporate Takeovers and Productivity* (MIT Press, Cambridge, MA).

Lucas, Robert, 1978, On the size distribution of business firms, *Bell Journal of Economics* 9, 508–523.

Maksimovic, Vojislav, and Gordon M. Phillips, 1998, Asset efficiency and reallocation decisions of bankrupt firms, *Journal of Finance* 53, 1619–1643.

Maksimovic, Vojislav, and Gordon M. Phillips, 2002, Do conglomerate firms allocate resources efficiently across industries: Theory and evidence, forthcoming, *Journal of Finance* 57.

Matsusaka, John G., 1993, Takeover motives during the conglomerate merger wave, *RAND Journal of Economics* 24, 357–379.

McGuckin, Robert H., and Sang V. Nguyen, 1995, On productivity and plant ownership change: New evidence from the LRD, *RAND Journal of Economics* 26, 257–276.

McGuckin, Robert H., and Sang V. Nguyen, 1999, Exploring the role of acquisition in the performance of firms: Is the "firm" the right unit of analysis; in Silvia Biffignandi, ed.: *Micro- and Macrodata of Firms* (Physica-Verlag, New York).

McGuckin, Robert H., and George Pascoe, 1988, The longitudinal research database: Status and research possibilities, *Survey of Current Business* 68, 30–37.

Mitchell, Mark L., and Harold J. Mulherin, 1996, The impact of industry shocks on takeover and restructuring activity, *Journal of Financial Economics* 41, 193–229.

Morck, Randall, Andrei Shleifer, and Robert W. Vishny, 1990, Do managerial objectives drive bad acquisitions? *Journal of Finance* 45, 31–48.

Rajan, Raghuram G., Henri Servaes, and Luigi Zingales, 2000, The cost of diversity: The diversification discount and inefficient investment, *Journal of Finance* 55, 35–80.

Ravenscraft, David, and F. M. Scherer, 1987, *Mergers, Sell-offs, and Economic Efficiency* (Brookings Institution, Washington, DC).

Scharfstein, David S., 1997, The dark side of internal capital markets II, Mimeo, MIT.

Scharfstein, David S., and Jeremy C. Stein, 2000, The dark side of internal capital markets: Divisional rent-seeking and inefficient investment, *Journal of Finance* 55, 2537–2564.

Schlingemann, Frederik, P., René M. Stulz, and Ralph A. Walkling, 2002, Asset liquidity and segment divestitures, forthcoming , *Journal of Financial Economics*.

Shea, John, 1993, Do supply curves slope up? *Quarterly Journal of Economics* 108, 1–32.

Shleifer, Andrei, and Robert W. Vishny, 1992, Liquidation values and debt capacity: A market equilibrium approach, *Journal of Finance* 47, 1343–1365.

Williamson, Oliver, 1985, *The Economic Institutions of Capitalism: Firms, Markets, Relational Contracting*, The Free Press, New York.

[11]

THE JOURNAL OF FINANCE • VOL. LVII, NO. 2 • APRIL 2002

Does Corporate Diversification Destroy Value?

JOHN R. GRAHAM, MICHAEL L. LEMMON, and JACK G. WOLF*

ABSTRACT

We analyze several hundred firms that expand via acquisition and/or increase their number of business segments. The combined market reaction to acquisition announcements is positive but acquiring firm excess values decline after the diversifying event. Much of the excess value reduction occurs because our sample firms acquire already discounted business units, and not because diversifying destroys value. This implies that the standard assumption that conglomerate divisions can be benchmarked to typical stand-alone firms should be carefully reconsidered. We also show that excess value does not decline when firms increase their number of business segments because of pure reporting changes.

DOES CORPORATE DIVERSIFICATION destroy value? Several recent papers attempt to answer this question by comparing the market value of firms that operate multiple lines of business to the value of a portfolio of stand-alone firms operating in the same industries as the conglomerate's divisions. Lang and Stulz (1994) use this approach and find that multisegment firms have low values of Tobin's q compared to stand-alone firms. Similarly, Berger and Ofek (1995) find that U.S. conglomerates are priced at a mean discount of about 15 percent. Lins and Servaes (1999) find similar discounts in Japan and the United Kingdom. Indeed, based on the Berger and Ofek methodology, diversified firms with valuation discounts had aggregate value losses of $800 billion in 1995. The magnitude of the value loss suggests that operating the divisions of conglomerates as stand-alone firms would create significant value. In this paper, we provide new evidence on whether the act of corporate diversification destroys value, or whether the divisions that make up conglomerates would trade at a discount, even if they operated as stand-alone firms.

* Graham is from Duke University, Lemmon is from the University of Utah, and Wolf is from Clemson University. We thank three anonymous referees, George Benston, Hank Bessembinder, Judy Chevalier, Rick Green, Owen Lamont, Gordon Phillips, Marlene Plumlee, Henri Servaes, René Stulz, and seminar participants at the 2000 NBER Corporate Finance Summer Workshop, and at Carnegie Mellon, Clemson, Emory, the University of Kentucky, the University of Texas–Austin, the University of Utah, William and Mary, the 2000 meetings of the Western Finance Association and the Southern Finance Association, and the 2001 meeting of the American Economics Association for helpful comments. Graham gratefully acknowledges financial support from the Alfred P. Sloan Research Foundation.

In concluding that diversification destroys value, the prior literature implicitly assumes that stand-alone firms are a valid benchmark for valuing the divisions of conglomerates. The main point of our paper is that the diversification discount calculation can be misleading if there are systematic differences between the divisions of conglomerates and the stand-alone firms to which they are benchmarked. Failure to account for these differences can lead to incorrect inferences regarding the effect of corporate diversification on firm value. To assess the extent to which these selection bias issues are important, we examine two samples of firms that expand via acquisition and/or increase their reported number of business segments.

The first sample consists of firms involved in mergers and acquisitions (M&A) for which we can identify the market value of the acquirer and target prior to the acquisition. We find that the mean combined announcement return for the acquirer and target is three percent, indicating that overall the market views these mergers positively. Using the methodology of Berger and Ofek (1995), however, the mean excess value of the acquiring firms declines by approximately seven percent over the two-year period surrounding the acquisition. To investigate the source of the decline in excess value, we examine the targets prior to acquisition and find that they have excess values of approximately −10 percent on average in their last year of operation as stand-alone firms. The addition of an already discounted unit reduces the excess value of the acquiring firm as measured by the excess value methodology, even if combining the firms does not destroy any value.

For the M&A sample, we find that almost all of the seven percent reduction in excess value for the acquirers can be traced directly to the addition of already "discounted" targets. Moreover, the reduction in excess value from the acquisition of a discounted target appears for many different types of firms: (a) those involved in both related and unrelated acquisitions, (b) those that increase their number of segments and those that do not, and (c) those that end up single segment or multisegment after the M&A event. These findings indicate that in our sample, the units that are combined into other firms are systematically different than stand-alone firms, and suggest that methodologies that benchmark divisions of conglomerates to stand-alone firms might overstate the magnitude of the diversification discount.

Much of the prior literature on the diversification discount (e.g., Lang and Stulz (1994), Berger and Ofek (1995), and Servaes (1996)) defines conglomerates as firms that report operations in multiple business segments. Somewhat surprisingly, only 16 percent of the firms in our M&A sample increase their number of reported business segments following the merger, even though most of the merger events are large enough to qualify for segment reporting. Chevalier (2000) also finds relatively few segment increases in her M&A sample. To better understand how our findings for the M&A sample are related to the multisegment discount, we gather data for a second sample: firms that begin as single-segment and then increase their number of business segments. Nearly two-thirds of these firms increase their number of segments via acquisitions, while the remaining one-third increase their number of business segments because of internal expansion or reporting changes. We obtain many more segment increases in this sample, because unlike in the M&A sample, we include some firms for which we cannot exactly identify the acquired unit prior to acquisition.

For the segment-increasing firms that expand via acquisition, the mean excess value changes from about 0 to −14 percent over the two-year period surrounding the segment increase. Because we cannot directly identify the acquired units in this sample, we assign excess values using a method similar in spirit to the standard benchmarking assumption of the segment-based literature: To proxy for the excess values of the new segments, we use a multiple of the median value among all same-industry stand-alone COMPUSTAT firms that were targets of completed acquisitions. Our results suggest that about half of the 14 percent "value loss" in these diversifying firms is explained by the parent adding an already discounted unit. We also examine the one-third of firms that increase their reported number of segments because of internal growth or due to pure reporting changes.[1] These firms do not experience a decline in excess value at the time of the segment increase, which provides additional support for the view that the diversification discount is linked to the characteristics of acquired firms.

Overall, our findings suggest that the benchmarks for valuing conglomerate firms should be carefully chosen, and that one should interpret cautiously conglomerate valuations that rely on comparisons to stand-alone firms. In the conclusion, we discuss strengths and weaknesses related to interpreting our results in the context of the multisegment discount literature.

Several other papers investigate issues related to interpreting the diversification discount. Lang and Stulz (1994), Campa and Kedia (1999), and Hyland (2001) provide evidence that diversifying firms are poor performers prior to conglomeration, indicating that the act of diversifying does not necessarily cause the entire discount observed in conglomerates. Schoar (2000) finds that the industry-q of new units is lower than the average industry-q of a firm's initial segments. Lamont and Polk (2001) show that conglomerate firms have higher required rates of return and that this can account for approximately one-third of the diversification discount. Using plant level data, Maksimovic and Phillips (2002) find that the growth of most conglomerates is consistent with optimal behavior; they do not find evidence that headquarters protects peripheral divisions inefficiently. Whited (2001) argues that much of the evidence that links the diversification discount to inefficient cross-subsidization suffers from problems related to measurement error.

Our paper is also related to other research that examines the endogeneity of the diversification decision. Villalonga (2000) compares conglomerates to

[1] Piotroski (1999) finds that firms that increase their number of segments as a pure reporting change (with no real alteration of company structure) exhibit significant positive stock price performance in the periods following the segment increase. Hyland (2001) also distinguishes between reporting changes and other segment-increasing events.

portfolios of single-segment firms with a high "propensity to diversify" (rather than matching to the actual business units that become part of the larger firm like we do in our M&A analysis). In results similar to ours, she finds that the diversification discount is reduced when conglomerates are compared to stand-alone firms with similar propensities to diversify. In contrast to our paper, however, her focus is on the valuations of diversifying firms and not on the divisions that they add. Our paper also complements the analysis in Chevalier (2000). In a sample similar to our subset of unrelated M&A firms, she finds that investment patterns commonly attributed to cross-subsidization between divisions are apparent in pairs of merging firms prior to their mergers.

The remainder of the paper is organized as follows. Section I presents a numerical example that summarizes our main point. Section II describes the data. Section III reports ex ante excess values for acquiring and acquired firms, and Section IV shows the extent to which the preacquisition discounts of acquired units explain the change in excess values of the acquiring firms. Section V reports ex ante excess values for segment-increasing firms and those removed from COMPUSTAT because they are acquired, and Section VI relates these figures to the reductions in excess values of the segment-increasing firms. Section VII summarizes and discusses implications for other corporate diversification studies.

I. Measuring the Effect of Diversification on Firm Value

To value multisegment firms, Berger and Ofek (1995) impute values for each segment of a diversified company using valuation multiples from the median stand-alone firm in the same industry as the segment being valued. On average, they find that the actual market value of conglomerates is less than the weighted sum of the imputed divisional values, a negative "excess value." The key assumption in this valuation approach is that "typical" single-segment firms are a valid benchmark against which to compare the divisions of conglomerates.

The main point of our paper is that a firm's excess value can decline if it acquires an already discounted unit, even if the actual act of combining the units destroys no value. Therefore, conglomeration might not be as bad as is commonly thought. We use a numerical example to illustrate this intuition. Assume that an acquiring firm A with sales of 100 acquires a new unit T with sales of 65. The market values of the acquiring and target firms are 115 and 70, respectively, as shown in Table I. To determine the excess value of these firms, we compare each unit's market-to-sales ratio to the benchmark ratio for the median firm in its own industry. The market-to-sales ratio for firm T is 1.08 in comparison to 1.25 for the median firm in its industry, implying an excess value of -15 percent ($= \ln(1.08/1.25)$). In contrast, the excess value of firm A is 0 percent. The rightmost column in Table I shows that the mathematical combination of the two businesses results in an excess value of -6 percent for the conglomerate.

Table I

Example of Negative Excess Value with No Value Destruction

This table shows how acquiring target Firm T could affect Firm A's excess value. By construction, total market value is conserved so no market value is destroyed. The benchmark represents the median market-to-sales ratio of single-segment same-industry firms.

	Firm A	Firm T	Combination
Sales[a]	100.00	65.00	165.00
Market value	115.00	70.00	185.00
Benchmark market-to-sales ratio	1.15	1.25	
Imputed value	115.00	81.25	196.25
Excess value	0.000	−0.15[b]	−0.06[c]

[a] This could be book value of assets if an asset multiplier is used.
[b] Excess value is calculated as $\ln[70/(65*1.25)] = \ln[70/81.25] = -0.15$.
[c] Excess value is calculated as $\ln[(115 + 70)/(100*1.15 + 65*1.25)] = -0.06$.

In this example, the acquisition does not destroy value, and the acquiring firm does not make an inefficient decision when it purchases firm T at market value. And yet, the excess value calculation makes it appear that the acquirer's value has been reduced by six percent. If, on average, firms that choose to diversify or the divisions that they add are discounted prior to acquisition, then this valuation methodology may erroneously attribute (too much) value loss to the act of combining the two firms. This example highlights that it is important to consider the characteristics of individual divisions of conglomerate firms before concluding (a) that the population of undiversified firms is an appropriate benchmark against which to value conglomerate divisions, and (b) that corporate diversification destroys value.

II. Sample Selection and Description

To investigate the potential selection bias issue described above, we examine a sample of firms making acquisitions. We use the Securities Data Corporation (SDC) Mergers and Acquisitions database to identify an initial sample of 2,457 publicly traded acquirers that completed an acquisition of 100 percent of the shares of a publicly traded target firm over the period 1980 to 1995. We require that both the acquirer and the target are listed in the 1996 active, research, or historical COMPUSTAT Industry Segment files. These files contain segment-level data from 1978 through 1995 and include companies reclassified or removed from the annual industrial files. A total of 755 acquisitions meet these criteria. We refine this sample by applying the same criteria used by Berger and Ofek (1995). We eliminate firm-years with any segment in a financial services industry (SIC code between 6000 and 6999), with total sales less than $20 million, or if the sum of segment sales is not within one percent of the firm's total sales. This leaves a sample of 356 acquisitions. When assets are not completely allocated across business segments, we prorate the unallocated assets to divisions based on the division's relative asset size.

A. Excess Value Measures

We define excess value using the two-step methodology in Berger and Ofek (1995). In the first step, an imputed value is calculated for each division by multiplying each segment's sales (assets) by the median market-to-sales (market-to-assets) ratio of single-segment firms in the same industry for the same year. These benchmark multipliers are based on all single-segment firms, including those that are removed from COMPUSTAT due to merger, acquisition, bankruptcy, or other reasons. To ensure that the multipliers are representative, at least five companies in the industry must have data for that year. If less than five firms match at the four-digit SIC level, the three-digit SIC level is examined and so on until the median of the tightest SIC level with at least five observations is found. In the second step, the excess value is calculated as the log of the ratio of the firm's actual market value to the sum of its divisions' imputed values. There are potential valuation problems related to purchase versus pooling accounting when using asset multipliers.[2] Therefore, in describing our results we focus on sales-based calculations, though we show asset results in the tables.

B. Diversification Measures

We group firms based on two different measures of the type of diversification. First, if the acquirer and the target share any four-digit SIC codes, according to the COMPUSTAT segment information, we classify the acquisition as related. If the acquirer and target have no common four-digit SIC codes, the acquisition is classified as unrelated. Similar classification schemes are used by Morck, Shleifer, and Vishny (1990) and Chevalier (2000). For our sample, 226 of the acquisitions are unrelated and 130 are related.

Second, we classify the firms according to whether or not the acquisition corresponds to an increase in the number of reported business segments. Fifty-seven of our acquisitions correspond to segment increases as of the year following the acquisition ($t = +1$).[3] Chevalier (2000) also reports few segment

[2] With purchase accounting, book asset values are marked-to-market, effectively resulting in a market-to-book asset value of 1.0. This accounting change induces a negative bias into excess value calculations when these altered market-to-book asset ratios for conglomerates are benchmarked to unaltered ratios for stand-alone firms (see Plumlee and Wolf (2000)). The effect of accounting methodology is important in our analysis because half of our sample firms use purchase accounting and we study diversification at the time of acquisition. The issue would exist but be less important if the acquisition had occurred in the more distant past. Importantly, sales are not marked-to-market, so the market-to-sales ratio does not suffer from this same problem.

[3] Another 12 firms record segment increases in year $t = +2$. Using this broader definition of segment increases does not qualitatively alter the reported results.

increases for a similar sample of mergers. The fact that so few acquisitions correspond to segment increases is somewhat surprising, given that more than half of the acquisitions appear to be large enough to warrant reporting as a separate segment (according to the accounting rules described in Section V.A).

Although there are relatively few segment increases directly associated with acquisitions in our sample, 186 of our acquiring firms report operations in multiple business segments in year $t = +1$. Even without segment increases, the fact that over half of the acquirers in our sample are multisegment firms links our results to studies of the conglomerate discount. (Another link, that we discuss in Section V, is that nearly two-thirds of firms that increase from one segment to more than one do so via acquisition.) Finally, because our sample contains a number of firms that remain single-segment following the acquisition, the M&A sample also allows us to investigate whether the valuation issues we identify apply more generally.

C. *Event Study Returns*

To provide preliminary evidence on the expected valuation effects of the acquisitions in our sample, we compute event study returns over the three-day $\{-1, +1\}$ period surrounding the announcement date of the acquisitions as reported in SDC. The abnormal returns are computed using the residuals from a market model estimated over the period beginning 200 days and ending 51 days prior to the announcement. The mean three-day announcement period cumulative abnormal return of the targets in our sample is 22.51 percent, while for the bidders it is −0.78 percent. The mean combined abnormal returns of the acquirer and target (weighted according to the pre-announcement market values of equity) is 3.4 percent. All of these returns are statistically significant at the 0.01 level. We also find positive combined returns in both related and unrelated acquisitions, as well as those that result in single- or multisegment firms ex post.[4]

These abnormal returns are similar to those reported elsewhere. Andrade, Mitchell, and Stafford (2001), Chevalier (2000) and Kaplan and Weisbach (1992) find small negative acquirer returns, large positive target returns, and moderate positive combined returns. Based on the combined returns, these studies and our results indicate that, at the time of the announcement, the market does not view acquisitions as destroying value.

III. Excess Values of Acquiring and Acquired Firms in the Merger and Acquisition Sample

In this section we examine the excess values of our merging firms. Because the thrust of our paper is to examine the valuation effects of diversification, we focus on the change in the excess value of the acquirer over the period

[4] Like in Morck et al. (1990), the acquiring firms in our M&A sample experience negative announcement returns in unrelated deals in the 1980s; however, combined returns are positive even for this subset.

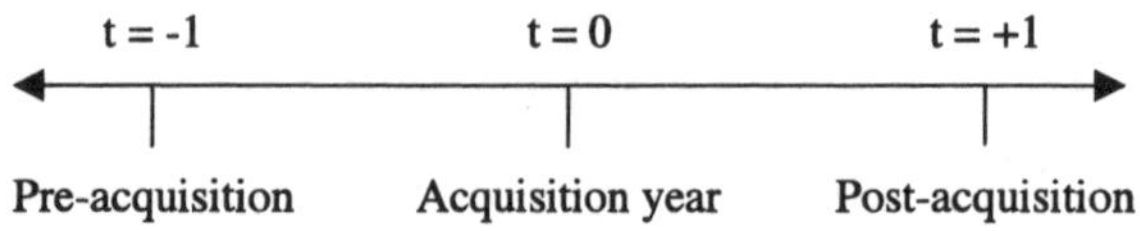

Figure 1. Timing conventions for measuring the change in excess values. We examine the preacquisition ($t = -1$) to postacquisition ($t = +1$) change in excess value.

surrounding the acquisition. We require that our sample firms have three years of data available, centered on the year in which the acquisition is completed. The timing conventions are illustrated in Figure 1.

We focus on the first full year after the acquisition ($t = +1$). We exclude year zero because the excess value measures rely on accounting data, and the effective year of the acquisition ($t = 0$) does not represent a full year of sales revenue for the combined company for the majority of our sample firms.

A. Excess Values of Acquiring Firms

Table II presents excess values for the acquiring firms in the M&A sample. For the full sample of 356 firms (Panel A) in the last year in operation as a stand-alone company ($t = -1$), the mean (median) excess value based on sales multipliers is 14.02 percent (11.03 percent). These excess values are significantly different from zero, indicating that, in the year prior to the acquisition, the acquiring firms are valued at a premium relative to the median single-segment firms in their industries. Chevalier (2000) also finds that acquirers trade at a premium.

By $t = +1$, the first full year after the acquisition, the excess values of the acquiring firms have dropped substantially. The sales multiplier mean (median) excess value is 7.09 percent (6.14 percent). We emphasize that the acquisitions are associated with large declines in excess values. Examining firm-by-firm the change in excess value from $t = -1$ to $t = +1$, the mean (median) change is -6.93 percent (-4.35 percent). These changes are statistically significant at the 0.01 level. In unreported analysis, we find that the changes in excess value are uncorrelated with the event study returns documented in Section II.C.

Panels B through E of Table II explore whether the reductions in excess value are related to the type of diversification strategy. Among firms making related acquisitions (Panel B), the mean (median) sales multiplier change in excess value from $t = -1$ to $t = +1$ is -10.44 percent (-7.75 percent), significantly different from zero at the 0.01 level. In contrast, firms that make unrelated acquisitions (Panel C) exhibit much smaller changes in excess value. For the unrelated acquisition group, the mean (median) change in excess value is -4.92 percent (-1.62 percent), and only the mean is reliably different from zero at the 0.10 level. Comparing the changes in excess value across the related and unrelated acquisition groups, only the median change based on asset multipliers is statistically different across the two groups at the 0.10 level.

Table II

Excess Values for Acquirers

This table reports excess values for the year prior to and the year following the acquisition. The sample consists of 356 firms that completed acquisitions between 1980 and 1995 with sufficient data to calculate excess values as defined in Berger and Ofek (1995). Acquisitions are classified as related when the acquirer and target firms share a four-digit SIC code prior to the acquisition. Acquisitions are classified as segment increasing if the number of reported segments is greater at $t = +1$ than at $t = -1$. Differences ($EV_{+1} - EV_{-1}$) are the firm-specific differences from period $t = -1$ to period $t = +1$. Panel A reports results for the full sample. Panels B through E examine subsamples. Statistical significance for means is based on Robust-Cluster standard errors and statistical significance for medians is based on the Wilcoxon sign-rank test.

	Sales Multiplier		Asset Multiplier	
	Mean	Median	Mean	Median
Panel A: Full Sample (356 firms)				
EV_{-1}	0.1402***	0.1103***	0.0753**	0.0214***
EV_{+1}	0.0709**	0.0614***	0.0183	−0.0334
$EV_{+1} - EV_{-1}$	−0.0693***	−0.0435***	−0.0570***	−0.0379***
Panel B: Related Acquisition (130 firms)				
EV_{-1}	0.1749***	0.1026***	0.0712**	0.0255**
EV_{+1}	0.0705	0.0000***	−0.0198	−0.0378
$EV_{+1} - EV_{-1}$	−0.1044***	−0.0775***	−0.0909***	−0.0847***
Panel C: Unrelated Acquisition (226 firms)				
EV_{-1}	0.1203**	0.1185***	0.0776**	0.0173**
EV_{+1}	0.0711	0.0730**	0.0402	−0.0327
$EV_{+1} - EV_{-1}$	−0.0492*	−0.0162	−0.0374*	−0.0169
Panel D: No Segment Increase (299 firms)				
EV_{-1}	0.1525***	0.1230***	0.0920***	0.0410***
EV_{+1}	0.0971***	0.0833***	0.0345	−0.0207
$EV_{+1} - EV_{-1}$	−0.0554**	−0.0313**	−0.0576***	−0.0378***
Panel E: Segment Increase (57 firms)				
EV_{-1}	0.0974	0.0912	−0.0126	−0.0193
EV_{+1}	−0.0554	−0.0855*	−0.0665***	−0.0918***
$EV_{+1} - EV_{-1}$	−0.1528**	−0.1210***	−0.0539	−0.0381

*, **, and *** indicate significantly different from zero at the 10, 5 and 1 percent levels, respectively.

For acquisitions in which the number of reported business segments remains unchanged (Panel D), the mean (median) change in excess value from $t = -1$ to $t = +1$ is −5.54 percent (−3.13 percent), both of which are significantly different from zero at the 0.05 level. When the acquisition is accompanied by an increase in the number of reported business segments (Panel E), the decline in excess value is considerably larger. For the segment-increasing group, the mean (median) change in excess value is −15.28 percent (−12.10 percent), both significantly different from zero. We cannot, however, reject the hypothesis that the changes in excess value are equal at the 0.10 level for the segment-increasing and no-segment-increase groups.

In summary, the acquiring firms in our sample experience a reduction in excess value following the acquisition. One possible interpretation is that acquisitions destroy value. An alternative explanation is that the addition of an already discounted unit causes a decline in the excess value measure, even if no value is destroyed in the acquisition. To investigate this possibility, we study the characteristics of the acquired firms to see what role they play in explaining the decline in excess value.

B. Excess Values of Target Firms

Table III presents summary statistics of the excess values of the target firms in the M&A sample prior to acquisition. We compute the excess values using the market value of equity based on the last stock price available prior to delisting. This measure includes the valuation effects of the acquisition announcement.

For the full sample, based on sales multipliers, the mean (median) excess value of the targets is −10.16 percent (−7.68 percent), and both are significantly less than zero at the 0.01 level.[5] These findings indicate that target firms in acquisitions are poor performers (in terms of excess value) relative to "typical" stand-alone firms. The table also reports the relative size of the acquisition, calculated as the ratio of target sales to the combined sales of the acquirer and target at $t = -1$. The acquisitions are fairly large. The mean (median) ratio of target to combined sales is 24.87 percent (21.21 percent). Given the negative excess values of the targets, it is natural to expect that the excess value of the acquiring firms will decline as these fairly large, poorly performing companies are merged into existing operations, even if the acquisitions do not destroy value.

Panels B through E report excess values and relative acquisition sizes for the various subgroups. The most striking result is that the patterns in target firm excess value and relative size in Table III closely parallel the declines in acquiring firm excess value documented in Table II. Namely, target firms in related acquisitions are larger and more deeply discounted relative to targets in unrelated acquisitions. In the related acquisition group (Panel B), the mean sales multiplier excess value of the target firms is −20.58 percent. In comparison, the corresponding mean excess value in the unrelated acqui-

[5] We also compute excess values using the market value of equity one month prior to the acquisition announcement. The mean (median) preannouncement excess value of the targets is −35.89 percent (−35.11 percent). The difference in the preannouncement and the postannouncement excess values shown in the tables reflects the large wealth gains of target shareholders in acquisitions.

Table III

Excess Values for Targets and Relative Sizes of Acquisitions

This table reports excess values of target firms in the year prior to being acquired. The sample consists of 356 firms that were acquired between 1980 and 1995 with sufficient data to calculate excess values as defined in Berger and Ofek (1995). The excess value is based on the last stock price available prior to the date the target is delisted. The relative size of the acquisition is the ratio of the target's sales (assets) to the combined sales (assets) of the target and acquirer at the end of the year preceding the acquisition. Acquisitions are classified as related when the acquirer and target firms share a four-digit SIC code prior to the acquisition. Acquisitions are classified as segment increasing if the number of reported segments is greater at $t = +1$ than at $t = -1$. Panel A reports results for the full sample while Panels B through E examine subsamples. Statistical significance for means is based on Robust-Cluster standard errors and statistical significance for medians is based on the Wilcoxon sign-rank test.

	Sales Multiplier		Asset Multiplier	
	Mean	Median	Mean	Median
Panel A: Full Sample (356 firms)				
EV_{-1}	−0.1016***	−0.0768***	−0.0120	−0.0268
Relative size	0.2487	0.2121	0.2273	0.1774
Panel B: Related Acquisition (130 firms)				
EV_{-1}	−0.2058***	−0.1489***	−0.0765**	−0.0681***
Relative size	0.2941	0.2697	0.2654	0.2362
Panel C: Unrelated Acquisition (226 firms)				
EV_{-1}	−0.0417	−0.0325	0.0251	0.0000
Relative size	0.2226	0.1577	0.2053	0.1446
Panel D: No Segment Increase (299 firms)				
EV_{-1}	−0.1055***	−0.0840***	−0.0138	−0.0260
Relative size	0.2308	0.1902	0.2125	0.1578
Panel E: Segment Increase (57 firms)				
EV_{-1}	−0.0812	−0.0768	−0.0024	−0.0401
Relative size	0.3425	0.2966	0.3048	0.2654

** and *** indicate significantly different from zero at the five and one percent levels, respectively.

sition group is −4.17 percent (Panel C). Additionally, the ratio of target to combined sales of the mean related acquisition (29.41 percent) is larger than that for the mean unrelated acquisition (22.26 percent). Panels D and E report the results for the subsamples based on whether the acquisition leads to a segment increase. The mean excess value of target firms in the group with no segment increases is −10.55 percent, compared to a mean excess value of −8.12 percent for targets in acquisitions associated with segment increases. The ratio of target to combined sales of the mean acquisition in the no segment increase group is 23.08 percent, compared to a mean of 34.25 percent for the group with segment increases.[6]

The finding that the targets have low excess values is consistent with other research. For example, Hasbrouck (1985) finds that the average q-ratio of acquired firms is lower than that of a control group. Lang, Stulz, and Walkling (1989) find that the q ratios of target firms in tender offers decline significantly over the five years preceding the offer. Hubbard and Palia (1999) note that acquired units are often financially constrained. Maksimovic and Phillips (2001) show that acquired plants have lower productivity than the productivity of the selling firm's other plants, and that acquired plants experience subsequent gains in productivity. Schoar (2000) finds that acquired plants have lower productivity than the median plant in their same industry, and that productivity and excess value are positively correlated.

IV. Explaining the Apparent Value Loss in Acquisitions

In this section, we determine the portion of the reduction in acquiring firm excess value that is attributable to acquiring a unit with low excess value. Our strategy is straightforward. We compute the excess value the combined firm would have if its parts were merged instantaneously at $t = -1$, prior to the actual acquisition. This calculation estimates the excess value of the sum of the combined firm's parts, before the acquisition could have possibly destroyed any value.

More specifically, we define P_{+1}, the projected excess value at $t = +1$, as

$$P_{+1} = \ln\left(\frac{MVA_{-1} + MVT_{-1}}{IVA_{-1} + IVT_{-1}}\right), \tag{1}$$

where MVA_{-1} and IVA_{-1} are the market value and imputed value of the acquirer at $t = -1$, and MVT_{-1} and IVT_{-1} are the corresponding quantities for the target. The imputed values are calculated using the methodology of Berger and Ofek (1995). We compare the change in the projected excess value to the actual change in excess value of the combined firm to determine whether the acquisition has an effect on the value of the firm, beyond what can be accounted for by the ex ante excess values of the acquirer and the target.[7]

[6] Though not reported in the tables, we also examine firms that end up as single- or multisegment ex post. In each case, these firms experience decreases in excess value following the acquisition, and the decreases are tied to the size and discount of the acquired unit. The same patterns hold in firms that end up with positive excess value ex post, negative excess value ex post, multisegment and negative excess value ex post, and so forth.

[7] One data issue occurs in some unrelated acquisitions. When an unrelated acquisition does not result in the reporting of a new business segment, the ex post excess value of the combined firm is benchmarked to the industries of the original business segments of the acquirer. The projected excess value, however, is benchmarked in part to the industries of the target's business segments, via IVT_{-1} in equation (1). For these observations, this issue might introduce some noise into the ability of the projected excess value to predict ex post excess values.

Table IV

Actual and Projected Changes in Excess Values for Acquirers

This table reports changes in excess values from the year prior to the acquisition to the year following the acquisition. The sample consists of 356 firms that completed acquisitions between 1980 and 1995 with sufficient data to calculate excess values as defined in Berger and Ofek (1995). Statistical significance for means is based on Robust-Cluster standard errors and statistical significance for medians is based on the Wilcoxon sign-rank test.

	Sales Multiplier		Asset Multiplier	
	Mean	Median	Mean	Median
	Full Sample (356 firms)			
Actual change ($EV_{+1} - EV_{-1}$)	−0.0693***	−0.0435***	−0.0570***	−0.0380***
Projected change ($P_{+1} - EV_{-1}$)	−0.0738***	−0.0176***	−0.0326***	−0.0087***
Difference ($EV_{+1} - P_{+1}$)	0.0045	−0.0133	−0.0244	−0.0168

*** indicates significantly different from zero at the one percent level.

Table IV reports the actual and projected changes in the excess values of the acquiring firms from $t = -1$ to $t = +1$. For the full sample, the mean (median) actual change in excess value based on sales multipliers is −6.93 percent (−4.35 percent). The mean (median) projected change is −7.38 percent (−1.76 percent). The difference between the actual and projected excess values can be interpreted as the value created or destroyed by acquisition that is not accounted for by the mechanical effect of adding a low valued target. The differences are very close to zero, indicating that the addition of a discounted target explains most of the decline in excess value for the acquirer.[8]

Though not reported in tables, we also analyze various subsamples. For the related acquisition group, the mean (median) differences between the actual and projected changes in excess value are −0.84 percent (−4.01 percent). The negative differences suggest that some additional value loss occurs beyond simply adding a low-valued unit; however, neither difference is statistically different from zero. Comparing the unexplained change in excess value to the actual change indicates that the mechanical valuation effect explains approximately 92 percent (1 − [−0.0084/−0.1044]) of the mean change in excess value of the acquirers. In the unrelated acquisition group, the mean (median) differences between the actual and projected excess values are 1.19 percent (0.71 percent), but neither is significantly different from zero.

For acquisitions with no segment increase, the results are similar to those in the full sample: The mechanical effect of adding a discounted target explains nearly all of the actual change in excess value following the acquisi-

[8] The finding that there is no significant difference between the value of the pieces and the value of the conglomerate is consistent with a result in Burch and Nanda (2001). In a study of spin-offs, they find that the combined excess value of the parent and spun-off unit is statistically indistinguishable from the excess value of the firm prior to spin-off.

Table V

Relation Between Projected and Actual Excess Values

This table reports regression results examining how well the projected excess values actually predict the ex post excess value. The sample consists of 356 firms that completed acquisitions between 1980 and 1995 with sufficient data to calculate excess values as defined in Berger and Ofek (1995). The regression model is:

$$(EV_{+1} - EV_{-1}) = \alpha + \beta(P_{+1} - EV_{-1})$$

where EV_{+1} is the actual ex post excess value, P_{+1} is the projected ex post excess value, and EV_{-1} is the ex ante excess value. Robust-Cluster standard errors are presented in parentheses. P-values for the null hypotheses that $\alpha = 0$ and $\beta = 1$ are reported in brackets.

	Adj. R^2	Intercept	Coefficient on Projected Change $(P_{+1} - EV_{-1})$
Actual change in sales multiplier $(EV_{+1} - EV_{-1})$	0.2636	0.0039	0.9968
		(0.0190)	(0.1192)
		[0.839]	[0.979]
Actual change in asset multiplier $(EV_{+1} - EV_{-1})$	0.1516	−0.0238	1.0231
		(0.0165)	(0.1044)
		[0.170]	[0.827]

tion. For the segment-increasing subsample, the results are somewhat different. The mean (median) difference in the actual and projected change in excess value is −4.15 percent (−2.79 percent). Although these differences are not statistically different from zero, they provide weak evidence that segment-increasing acquisitions exhibit additional value loss beyond that which can be explained by the characteristics of the target. In the case of segment-increasing acquisitions, the mechanical valuation effect explains about 71 percent (1 − [−0.0415/−0.1428]) of the average decline in the excess value of the acquirers.

To further explore how much decline in the excess value of acquiring firms is attributable to a purely mechanical effect of adding low valued targets, Table V presents results from regressing the actual change in excess value on the projected change in excess value. Statistical significance is based on Robust-Cluster standard errors. Using sales multipliers, the R^2 indicates that the projected change in the value loss explains 26.36 percent of the variation in the actual change. Moreover, the estimated regression coefficient on the projected value loss term is not statistically different from one (p-value = 0.979), indicating that the projected change in excess value is an unbiased predictor of the actual change. The intercept in the regression is 0.0039, which is not statistically different from zero (p-value = 0.839). The intercept measures the unexplained portion of the change in excess value and indicates that, on average, essentially no additional value loss remains after accounting for the characteristics of the acquired firm.

Table VI

Relation Between Projected and Actual Excess Values

This table reports regression results examining how well the projected excess values predict actual ex post excess value. The sample consists of 356 firms that completed acquisitions between 1980 and 1995 with sufficient data to calculate excess values as defined in Berger and Ofek (1995). The regression models are:

$$(EV_{+1} - EV_{-1}) = \alpha + \beta(P_{+1} - EV_{-1}) + \lambda I(\cdot)$$

where EV_{+1} is the actual ex post excess value, P_{+1} is the projected ex post excess value, EV_{-1} is the ex ante excess value, and $I(\cdot)$ is an indicator variable for relatedness or segment increase. The relatedness indicator equals one if the acquisition is classified as related. The segment increase indicator equals one when the acquisition results in an increase in the number of reported business segments. Robust-Cluster standard errors are presented in parentheses. *P*-values for the null hypotheses that $\alpha = 0$ and $\beta = 1$ and $\lambda = 0$ are reported in brackets.

	Adj. R^2	Intercept	Coefficient on Projected Change $(P_{+1} - EV_{-1})$	Coefficient on Indicator Variable $I(\cdot)$
Panel A: Relatedness Indicator				
Actual change in sales multiplier	0.2620	0.0110	0.9937	−0.0200
$(EV_{+1} - EV_{-1})$		(0.0261)	(0.1173)	(0.0353)
		[0.678]	[0.958]	[0.579]
Actual change in asset multiplier	0.1517	−0.0127	1.0118	−0.0313
$(EV_{+1} - EV_{-1})$		(0.0206)	(0.1039)	(0.0267)
		[0.545]	[0.911]	[0.260]
Panel B: Segment Increase Indicator				
Actual change in sales multiplier	0.2637	0.0126	0.9907	−0.0579
$(EV_{+1} - EV_{-1})$		(0.0237)	(0.1237)	(0.0541)
		[0.603]	[0.941]	[0.302]
Actual change in asset multiplier	0.1500	−0.0196	1.0296	−0.0254
$(EV_{+1} - EV_{-1})$		(0.0179)	(0.1040)	(0.0303)
		[0.290]	[0.780]	[0.415]

Table VI presents analysis regressing the actual change in excess value on the projected change and two indicator variables. In Panel A, the indicator is set equal to one if the acquisition is related. We include the relatedness indicator because other research has found that unrelated diversification is worse than related diversification (e.g., Berger and Ofek (1995)). Based on sales multipliers, the estimated coefficient on the projected value loss is not significantly different from one (p-value = 0.958). The estimated intercept is 0.0110 (p-value = 0.678), indicating that for unrelated acquisitions the characteristics of the acquired unit account for almost all of the observed change in excess values. For related acquisitions, the coefficient estimate on the indicator variable is −0.0200, which is insignificant.

In Panel B, the indicator variable is set equal to one if the acquisition leads to a segment increase. The coefficient on the segment-increase indicator is −0.0579, but is not significantly different from zero (p-value = 0.302). The negative coefficient on the indicator variable provides weak evidence that segment-increasing acquisitions result in value loss beyond that explained by the characteristics of the target.

Our M&A evidence shows that the excess values of acquiring firms decline following acquisition, which we attribute to acquired units having significantly negative excess values. This result suggests that the types of firms that are absorbed into other firms differ systematically from the stand-alone firms to which conglomerates are typically benchmarked. By accounting for the preacquisition value of the target firms, we explain most of the negative valuation effects associated with mergers.

On the surface, our not leaving any unexplained reduction in excess value might seem at odds with the evidence of long-term negative drift in acquiring firm stock prices following mergers (e.g., Loughran and Vijh (1997) and Rau and Vermaelen (1998)). Note, however, that there is not necessarily a relation between stock returns and excess value measures. The latter are industry-adjusted ratios of market value to an accounting item. Even if the firm's stock returns decline following the merger, the excess value measure need not decline because the firm's sales or assets (or stock returns of the industry benchmark) may also decline. Moreover, our analysis focuses on the first year following the merger, while the typical long-run returns paper examines between three and five years ex post.

V. Segment-increasing Firms

Much of the diversification discount literature defines conglomeration as operation in multiple business segments, and there are relatively few segment increases in the M&A sample. To comment more directly on the valuation effects associated with operating in multiple business segments, and also to assess the robustness of the M&A results, we examine a sample of firms that increase their number of business segments from one to more than one. Relative to the M&A sample, the criteria to be included in the segment-increasing sample are not as restrictive in that we do not require being able to exactly identify the acquired unit(s).

A. Segment-increasing Sample

From the set of firms listed in the 1996 COMPUSTAT Industry Segment file, including the research and historical files, we identify those that change from reporting one segment (in $t = -1$) to reporting multiple segments. We require that these firms have three years of data and that they report more than one segment in periods $t = 0$ and $t = +1$. We concentrate on these firms, in part, because Lang and Stulz (1994) and Servaes (1996) show that the largest drop-off in q occurs between single-segment and two-segment firms. We also require that the firms meet all of the Berger and Ofek (1995) requirements (as described in Section I). We begin the sample period in 1984 because Lexis/Nexis does not have annual reports for periods earlier than 1984.

Firms increase their number of reported segments for a variety of reasons. Financial Accounting and Standards Board (FASB) Statement 14 requires firms to report data for individual lines of business that represent more than 10 percent of the firm's total revenues, assets, or profits. New segments may result from the acquisition of a new line of business, the internal growth of an operation that passes one of these thresholds, or simple restructuring of existing operations. Based on annual reports, 10-Ks, and Investor Dealers' Digest Merger & Acquisition reports from Lexis/Nexis, we group our sample firms into three categories related to the reason for the increase in the number of reported business segments.

Under Generally Accepted Accounting Principles (APB 16, August 1970), firms are required to discuss acquisitions in the footnotes of their filings. When the footnotes mention an acquisition, we place a firm into one of two categories. If the acquired unit operates in an industry related to the existing operations of the diversifying firm based on the four-digit SIC code listed in COMPUSTAT, we categorize the segment increase as a related acquisition. Otherwise, the acquisition is classified as unrelated. We delete 32 observations because either the size or industry of the new business segment does not match the description of the acquired firm(s). If we find no evidence of an acquisition, we include the segment increase in the "no acquisition" group. Firms in this group may have added segments due to internal growth, a decision to begin reporting a previously existing division, and so forth.

The majority of segment increases in our sample result from acquisitions. Of the final sample of 225 segment increases, 124 result from unrelated acquisitions, 17 result from related acquisitions, and the remaining 84 segment increases are the result of internal growth and reporting changes. These proportions are similar to those in Hyland (2001), who reports that 150 out of 227 firms in his sample of firms that increase from one segment to more than one segment do so via acquisition.

The primary difference between the M&A and segment-increasing samples is that in the former we only keep firms for which we can identify the acquired unit.[9] In contrast, in the segment-increasing sample, we do not require exact identification of the acquired unit that leads to the segment increase. In many cases, the segment increases result from partial acquisitions, acquisitions of private firms, or multiple acquisitions that occur over several years.

[9] Two other differences are that the segment-increasing sample only includes firms that start with a single unit, and the segment-increasing sample contains some firms that increase their number of reported segments, even though they did not make an acquisition (the "no acquisition" group).

Table VII

Excess Values for Firms That Increase the Number of Reported Segments

This table reports excess values for the year prior to and the year following the first year in which more than one segment is reported. The sample consists of 225 firms that changed from reporting one segment in year $t = -1$ to reporting more than one segment in years $t = 0$ and $t = +1$. Excess values are calculated as defined in Berger and Ofek (1995). Differences ($EV_{+1} - EV_{-1}$) are the firm-specific differences from period $t = -1$ to period $t = +1$. Panel A reports results for the full sample while Panels B through D examine subsamples. Statistical significance for means is based on Robust-Cluster standard errors and statistical significance for medians is based on the Wilcoxon sign-rank test.

	Sales Multiplier		Asset Multiplier	
	Mean	Median	Mean	Median
Panel A: Full Sample (225 firms)				
EV_{-1}	0.0472	0.0000	0.0323	0.0000
EV_{+1}	−0.0899**	−0.0708***	−0.0481*	−0.0811***
$EV_{+1} - EV_{-1}$	−0.1371***	−0.0707***	−0.0870***	−0.0397***
Panel B: No Acquisition (84 firms)				
EV_{-1}	0.0418	0.0000	−0.0022	0.0029
EV_{+1}	−0.0230	−0.0093	−0.0389	−0.0688
$EV_{+1} - EV_{-1}$	−0.0648	−0.0158	−0.0387	−0.0195
Panel C: Unrelated Acquisitions (124 firms)				
EV_{-1}	0.0330	0.0000	0.0464	−0.0080
EV_{+1}	−0.1326**	−0.1075***	−0.0598*	−0.0874**
$EV_{+1} - EV_{-1}$	−0.1656***	−0.0852***	−0.1063***	−0.0416**
Panel D: Related Acquisitions (17 firms)				
EV_{-1}	0.1778	0.0860	0.1781*	0.0080
EV_{+1}	−0.1085	−0.0324	−0.0074	−0.0511
$EV_{+1} - EV_{-1}$	−0.2863**	−0.2216***	−0.1855**	−0.1793***

*, **, and *** indicate significantly different from zero at the 10, 5, and 1 percent levels, respectively.

B. Excess Values of Segment-increasing Firms

Table VII presents excess values centered on the year of the segment increase. For the full sample of 225 firms (Panel A) in the last year in operation as a focused company ($t = -1$), the mean (median) excess value based on sales multipliers is 4.72 percent (0.00 percent). These excess values are not significantly different from zero, indicating that, in the year prior to diversifying, the sample firms are not valued at a discount relative to the median single-segment firms in their industries. These results are similar to those reported in Lang and Stulz (1994), who find that diversifying firms have industry-adjusted Tobin's q values that are not significantly different from zero. Our results differ from those reported in Campa and Kedia (1999), who find that diversifying firms have negative excess values prior to diversification.[10]

By $t = +1$, the first full year after conglomeration, the diversifying firms exhibit a statistically and economically significant diversification discount. The sales multiplier mean (median) excess value is −8.99 percent (−7.08 percent), which are reliably negative at the 0.10 level or better. More importantly, diversification is associated with large declines in excess value. Firm by firm, the mean (median) change in excess value from $t = -1$ to $t = +1$ is −13.71 percent (−7.07 percent), which are significant at the 0.01 level.

In Panels B through D of Table VII, we examine whether the change in excess value varies by the type of segment increase. Note that much of the existing literature defines diversification based on the number of reported segments. One therefore might expect to observe a decline in excess value whenever a firm begins to report additional segments. In some instances, however, firms begin to report new business segments because of internal growth or a change in filing practice. (For example, Cybex International reports a single segment, "medical and fitness eq." in 1992. In 1993, Cybex operates two segments, "exercise equipment" and "medical equipment." Total assets of the company increased only $5 million, from $104 million in 1992 to $109 million in 1993.) In these "no acquisition" cases, the firm has not changed substantially, even though the number of segments has increased, so we do not expect to find a significant decrease in excess value.

Firms that add segments because of internal growth or reporting changes start with excess values that are indistinguishable from zero and, consistent with our expectation, do not exhibit a significant reduction in excess value (Panel B). The mean (median) sales multiplier change in excess value for the no acquisition group is −6.48 percent (−1.58 percent), and neither is reliably different from zero. Therefore, there does not appear to be loss in value when the increase in the number of business segments is attributable to internal growth or reporting changes.

Firms that increase their number of business segments through unrelated acquisitions also have excess values that are indistinguishable from zero prior to diversification, but exhibit large changes in excess value after increasing their number of segments. For the unrelated acquisition group, the mean (median) change in excess value from $t = -1$ to $t = +1$ is −16.56 per-

[10] Campa and Kedia (1999) find that firms that diversify once from one to more than one segment trade at a discount of seven percent (two percent) using sales (asset) multipliers in the year prior to the segment increase. One difference between their approach and ours is the choice of benchmark to calculate excess values. Campa and Kedia restrict the benchmark group to firms that always operate as a single segment. In contrast, we assume no foreknowledge of the firms' future choices about whether to operate as a focused or diversified firm and thus avoid any potential look-ahead bias.

Table VIII

Excess Values for Single-segment Firms That Are Removed from COMPUSTAT Because of Merger or Acquisition

This table reports excess values for the three years before the firm was removed from COMPUSTAT due to merger or acquisition. The sample consists of 653 firms that are removed from the COMPUSTAT active tapes because of merger or acquisition over the period 1984 to 1995. Excess values are calculated as defined in Berger and Ofek (1995). Statistical significance for means is based on Robust-Cluster standard errors and statistical significance for medians is based on the Wilcoxon sign-rank test.

	Sales Multiplier		Asset Multiplier	
	Mean	Median	Mean	Median
EV_{-3}	−0.0574***	−0.0511***	−0.0020	−0.0056
EV_{-2}	−0.1251***	−0.1131***	−0.0408***	−0.0386***
EV_{-1}	−0.1596***	−0.1601***	−0.0593***	−0.0526***

*** indicates significantly different from zero at the one percent level.

cent (−8.52 percent), both significantly less than zero at the 0.01 level. Companies making related acquisitions have the largest decline in excess value. The related acquisition group has positive excess values in year $t = -1$, and large negative excess values in year $t = +1$. The mean (median) change in sales-based excess value is −28.63 percent (−22.16 percent), and both are significantly less than zero at the 0.01 level. This finding is consistent with our results for the M&A sample, where related acquisitions are associated with large declines in excess values. However, the related acquisition group has only 17 observations, so these numbers should be treated cautiously.[11]

C. Excess Values of Acquired Firms

The acquired units in the M&A sample are valued at a significant discount relative to same-industry stand-alone firms. To examine whether this finding can be generalized, Table VIII presents excess values for the population of firms that are removed from COMPUSTAT because they are acquired. COMPUSTAT footnote number 35 indicates whether firms on the annual industrial files are removed due to acquisition or merger (codes 01 or 04).

[11] We statistically reject the hypothesis that the mean and median changes in excess value in Panels B through D are equal across the three groups at the 0.05 level. In pairwise comparisons based on sales multipliers, the mean changes in excess value are not equal for the no acquisition and unrelated acquisition groups at the 0.10 level. The differences in the medians are not significant. The differences in the mean (median) changes in excess values across the no acquisition and related acquisition subsamples are significant at the 0.05 (0.01) level. The differences in the mean changes in excess values across the related and unrelated groups are not significant, but the differences in the medians are significant at the 0.05 level.

Two key points stand out. First, the excess values are significantly below zero in year $t = -1$, just prior to when the firm is acquired. Second, there is a notable downward trend in the years leading up to the firm's acquisition.[12] The mean excess values based on sales multipliers are -5.74 percent in year $t = -3$, -12.51 percent in year $t = -2$, and -15.96 percent in year $t = -1$.[13] These excess values are all significantly different from zero at the 0.01 level. With discounts of this magnitude, it is natural to expect that the excess value of segment-increasing firms will decline as poorly performing companies are merged into existing operations, even if diversification itself does not destroy value.

VI. Explaining (Part of) the Apparent Value Loss in Segment-increasing Firms

To determine the portion of the ex post discount for segment-increasing firms that is attributable to the acquisition of a unit with negative excess value, we follow the strategy that we used on the M&A sample. We project the excess value that the conglomerate would have if its parts were merged instantaneously at $t = -1$, prior to the actual segment increase. The only difference is that, for the sample of segment-increasing firms, we calculate the imputed value of the new segment(s) using the median excess value at $t = -1$ from the population of acquired firms in the same industry.[14] In other words, we assume that the excess values of the new segments are similar to those of other acquired firms in the same industry, which is similar in spirit to the benchmarking assumption made in other conglomeration analyses. We use the respective actual sizes of the conglomerate segments as of $t = +1$ to weight the $t = -1$ excess values of the initial segment and proxied new segment(s). This calculation determines the projected excess value of the conglomerate after the segment increase, under the null hypothesis that the act of diversification itself does not affect value.

We only perform this calculation for the unrelated acquisition group. The comparison is not feasible for the firms making related acquisitions because the original parent division of these firms is often dissolved in conjunction

[12] As noted earlier, Lang et al. (1989) find that the q ratios of target firms in tender offers decline significantly over the five years preceding the offer.

[13] In spite of the decline in the excess values of acquired firms, there is only limited evidence that target firms have low stock returns in the period preceding the acquisition. For example, Agrawal and Jaffe (2001) only find evidence of underperformance in subsamples of target firms involved in acquisitions where disciplining of management is likely. However, as noted previously, there need be no relation between stock returns and excess value measures, because the latter are industry-adjusted ratios of market value to an accounting item.

[14] There are only 653 single-segment firms with sufficient data to calculate excess value that are removed from the COMPUSTAT active file because of merger or acquisition during 1984 to 1995, and in many industries, only a few firms are removed. Therefore, for this part of the paper only, we define industry based on one-digit SIC code, to ensure that we have enough acquired firms in any given industry.

Table IX

Regressions of Actual Changes in Excess Value on Projected Changes in Excess Value for Segment-increasing Firms

This table reports regression results examining how well the projected excess values predict the ex post excess value. The sample consists of 124 firms that changed from reporting one segment at year $t = -1$ to reporting more than one segment during years $t = 0$ and $t = +1$ as the result of an unrelated acquisition. Excess values are calculated as defined in Berger and Ofek (1995). The regression model is

$$(EV_{+1} - EV_{-1}) = \alpha + \beta(P_{+1} - EV_{-1})$$

where EV_{+1} is the actual ex post excess value, P_{+1} is the projected ex post excess value, and EV_{-1} is the ex ante excess value. Robust-Cluster standard errors are presented in parentheses. P-values for the null hypotheses that $\alpha = 0$ and $\beta = 1$ are reported in brackets.

	Adj. R^2	Intercept	Coefficient on Projected Change $(P_{+1} - EV_{-1})$
Actual change in sales multiplier $(EV_{+1} - EV_{-1})$	0.3304	−0.0926	0.8192
		(0.0363)	(0.0647)
		[0.029]	[0.0191]
Actual change in asset multiplier $(EV_{+1} - EV_{-1})$	0.3265	−0.0783	0.6797
		(0.0257)	(0.2179)
		[0.012]	[0.172]

with the increase in the number of reported business segments. Specifically, of the 17 firms making related acquisitions, the segment ID at $t = -1$ of the original parent continues to exist at $t = +1$ for only 6 firms.

To examine how much of the actual value loss is mechanically attributable to the acquisition of a discounted unit, we calculate the actual and projected changes in excess value for the segment-increasing firms (not tabulated). Based on sales multipliers, the mean actual change in excess value from $t = -1$ to $t = +1$ is −16.56 percent, while the mean projected change is −8.91 percent, implying that approximately 50 percent of the observed value loss can be accounted for by the addition of an already discounted unit. Based on asset multipliers, we explain approximately 40 percent of the mean decline in excess value.

Table IX presents results from regressing the actual change in excess value on the projected change. Based on R^2, the projected change explains 33 percent of the variation in the actual value loss. Moreover, the estimated regression coefficient on the projected value loss term is close to (though statistically different from) 1.0, indicating that the projected value loss estimates do a reasonable job capturing the cross-sectional variation in the actual changes in excess values. The intercept in the regression is −0.0926, which is significantly different from zero (p-value = 0.029). The intercept indicates that the unexplained portion of the 16.56 percent change in excess value is approximately 9.26 percent. Our results indicate that only about one-half of the discount in our sample of segment-increasing firms can be attributed to negative valuation consequences associated with diversification. This result is generally consistent with our findings from the subsample of M&A firms with segment increases.

Finally, we perform an unreported robustness check to investigate the effect of our proxying for the excess value of the acquired units in the segment-increasing sample. We repeat the analysis on the M&A sample pretending that we do not know the identity of the actual acquired unit but instead proxying with the median same-industry single-segment firm among acquired units.[15] That is, we repeat on the M&A sample the experiment that we use on the segment-increasing sample (except that we use $t + 1$ weights in this robustness check). As in Table V, the adjusted R^2 for the regression of the actual change in excess value on the projected change is around 20 percent and the beta coefficient is indistinguishable from 1.0; however, the intercept equals -0.049. Interestingly, when we proxy for the acquired units in the M&A sample, we do not explain the entire value loss, which corresponds to the pattern we observe when we use the same methodology on the segment-increasing sample. Overall, this suggests that proxying for the acquired unit (as in the segment-increasing analysis) does not induce substantial bias into projecting the change in excess value, although it does reduce the portion of the value loss that we can explain.

VII. Conclusions

During the 1990s, academic research and popular press reports generally argued that corporate diversification destroys value. Based on methodologies that compare the values of conglomerates to proxies for the valuations of their individual divisions, the literature indicates that conglomerate firms are discounted by as much as 15 percent from the value that could be attained by breaking them up and operating the divisions as stand-alone companies.

An implicit assumption in the common valuation methodologies is that divisions of conglomerate firms are similar to "typical" stand-alone firms. We contend that if the divisions of conglomerates systematically differ from the stand-alone firms to which they are benchmarked, failure to account for these differences can lead to incorrect inferences regarding the valuation effects of corporate diversification. Our evidence suggests that these selection biases are important.

We show that units that are combined into firms through merger or acquisition are priced at significant discounts (relative to the median stand-alone firm in the same industry) prior to becoming part of the larger firm. When this discounted unit is added to an existing firm, not surprisingly, it has a negative effect on the excess value of the combined business as measured using the standard methodology. In a sample of acquisitions, we dem-

[15] We thank Owen Lamont for suggesting this experiment.

onstrate that accounting for the characteristics of the acquired units explains nearly all of the reduction in the acquirer's excess values for all types of acquisitions (related or unrelated and segment-increasing or not) and firms (whether they are single- or multisegment ex post). In a sample of segment-increasing firms, we proxy for the preacquisition discount of acquired units and account for about half of the reduction in excess value following the segment increase. Consistent with the view that the characteristics of acquired units are an important factor in determining the valuation discount, we find that excess value is not reduced when a firm increases its number of business segments without making an acquisition.

A strength of our M&A analysis is that we are able to directly value the acquired business units. However, our M&A firms are priced at a premium prior to the acquisition and relatively few acquisitions directly result in segment increases. These facts imply that our results cannot be applied one-for-one to the overall corporate diversification literature; however, we feel that our analysis has important implications for that literature. First, half of our M&A firms are multisegment ex post, and the valuation of these firms (which are included in typical diversification discount studies) is artificially low according to the standard methodologies because they contain a unit that would be valued at a discount even if it stood alone. Second, nearly two-thirds of the firms that increase their number of segments do so via acquisition in our sample, and only firms that become multisegment via acquisition experience a reduction in excess value. In her broad sample of firms, Schoar (2000) finds that already diversified firms are relatively likely to continue making acquisitions and that they expand more frequently via acquisition than they do via internal growth. These points indicate that corporate diversification is closely tied to the acquisition process and link our M&A findings to the corporate diversification literature.

A weakness of our segment-increasing analysis is that we cannot explicitly value the acquired units because many segment increases result from partial acquisitions, acquisitions of private firms, or multiple acquisitions. We proxy for the value of the acquired units using information about public firms that become inactive due to merger or acquisition. Our approach is therefore similar to that used in most diversification studies, which use information on publicly traded stand-alone firms to value the divisions of conglomerates. Moreover, Schoar's (2000) analysis implies that, were it available, using valuations of private and partial acquisitions might produce results similar to what we report. Schoar finds that acquired plants (many of which are privately held) have lower productivity than the median plant in their industry and that plant-level productivity is positively related to excess value.

To the extent that our results carry over to the broader sample of conglomerate firms, they have important implications about whether conglomeration destroys value in the typical multisegment firm. At a minimum, our results suggest that the standard assumption that conglomerate divisions can be benchmarked to firms that remain as stand-alone needs to be carefully reconsidered. Moreover, they also suggest that the distribution of excess values for multisegment firms should be centered closer to 0, instead of near −15 percent as implied by some previous research. Even if the distribution is centered at 0, however, much research remains to be done explaining the cross-sectional distribution of excess values.

In terms of measuring the diversification discount, we offer a new approach to benchmarking the divisions of conglomerate firms: Compare conglomerate divisions that arise via acquisition to stand-alone firms that disappear from the public record because they are merged or acquired. Other researchers can potentially use this same methodology, especially if they are able to identify the conglomerate divisions that are created via acquisition.

Another issue that we believe deserves attention in future research involves better understanding the relation between the economic event of diversifying through adding a business unit in a new industry and the accounting event of reporting a new business segment. Hayes and Lundholm (1996) suggest that segment reporting is often subject to strategic managerial motives, which calls into question the approach of defining corporate diversification strictly on the basis of the number of business segments. We have attempted to cover all the bases in our paper by examining firms that experience the accounting event of increasing the number of reported business segments, while also examining firms that experience the economic event of making a diversifying acquisition.

REFERENCES

Agrawal, Anup, and Jeffrey Jaffe, 2001, Do takeover targets underperform, Working paper, University of Alabama.

Andrade, Gregor, Mark Mitchell, and Erik Stafford, 2001, New evidence and perspectives on mergers, *Journal of Economic Perspectives* 15, 103–120.

Berger, Philip, and Eli Ofek, 1995, Diversification's effect on firm value, *Journal of Financial Economics*, 37, 39–65.

Burch, Timothy, and Vikram Nanda, 2001, Divisional diversity and the conglomerate discount: The evidence from spin-offs, Working paper, University of Miami.

Campa, Jose, and Simi Kedia, 1999, Explaining the diversification discount, Working paper, Harvard Business School.

Chevalier, Judith, 2000, What do we know about cross-subsidization? Evidence from the investment policies of merging firms, Working paper, University of Chicago.

Hasbrouck, Joel, 1985, The characteristics of takeover targets: *q* and other measures, *Journal of Banking and Finance* 9, 351–362.

Hayes, Rachel, and Russell Lundholm, 1996, Segment reporting to the capital market in the presence of a competitor, *Journal of Accounting Research* 34, 261–279.

Hubbard, R. Glenn, and Darius Palia, 1999, A reexamination of the conglomerate merger wave in the 1960s: An internal capital markets view, *Journal of Finance* 54, 1131–1152.

Hyland, David, 2001, Why firms diversify: An empirical examination, Working paper, University of Texas, Arlington.

Kaplan, Steven, and Michael Weisbach, 1992, The success of acquisitions: Evidence from divestitures, *Journal of Finance* 47, 107–138.

Lamont, Owen, and Christopher Polk, 2001, The diversification discount: Cash flows versus returns, *Journal of Finance* 56, 1693–1721.

Lang, Larry, and René Stulz, 1994, Tobin's *q*, corporate diversification and firm performance, *Journal of Political Economy* 102, 1248–1280.

Lang, Larry, René Stulz, and Ralph Walkling, 1989, Managerial performance, Tobin's q, and the gains from successful tender offers, *Journal of Financial Economics* 24, 137–154.

Lins, Karl, and Henri Servaes, 1999, International evidence on the value of corporate diversification, *Journal of Finance* 54, 2215–2239.

Loughran, Tim, and Anand Vijh, 1997, Do long-term shareholders benefit from corporate acquisitions? *Journal of Finance* 52, 1765–1790.

Maksimovic, Vojislav, and Gordon Phillips, 2001, The market for corporate assets: Who engages in mergers and asset sales and are there efficiency gains? *Journal of Finance* 56, 2019–2065.

Maksimovic, Vojislav, and Gordon Phillips, 2002, Do conglomerate firms allocate resources inefficiently across industries? Theory and evidence, *Journal of Finance* 57, 721–767.

Morck, Randall, Adrei Shleifer, and Robert Vishny, 1990, Do managerial objectives drive bad acquisitions? *Journal of Finance* 45, 31–48.

Piotroski, Joseph, 1999, The impact of newly reported segment information on market expectations and stock prices, Working paper, University of Michigan.

Plumlee, Marlene, and Jack Wolf, 2000, Purchase or pooling? The impact of accounting choice on the calculation of excess value, Working paper, University of Utah.

Rau, P. Raghavendra, and Theo Vermaelen, 1998, Glamour, value, and the post-acquisition performance of acquiring firms, *Journal of Financial Economics* 49, 223–253.

Schoar, Antoinette, 2000, Effects of corporate diversification on productivity, Working paper, Massachusetts Institute of Technology.

Servaes, Henri, 1996, The value of diversification during the conglomerate merger wave, *Journal of Finance* 51, 1201–1225.

Villalonga, Belén, 2000, Does diversification cause the diversification discount? Working paper, UCLA.

Whited, Toni, 2001, Is it inefficient investment that causes the diversification discount? *Journal of Finance* 56, 1667–1691.

Journal of Financial Economics 27 (1990) 557–580. North-Holland

Consolidating corporate control

Dual-class recapitalizations versus leveraged buyouts*

Kenneth Lehn

U.S. Securities and Exchange Commission, Washington, DC 20549, USA

Jeffry Netter and Annette Poulsen

University of Georgia, Athens, GA 30602, USA

Received December 1989, final version received May 1990

Dual-class recapitalizations and leveraged buyouts have similar effects on ownership of corporate voting rights but very different effects on ownership of residual claims. We predict that firms with greater growth opportunities, lower agency costs, and lower tax liability are more likely to consolidate control through dual-class recapitalizations. We find strong support for the growth hypothesis and weaker support for the other hypotheses. These results increase our understanding of the causes of change in organizational form by illustrating that the method and effects of consolidating corporate control are systematically related to firm attributes.

1. Introduction

We compare two types of transactions that consolidate corporate control: dual-class recapitalizations and going-private transactions. In dual-class recapitalizations (hereafter, dual-class recaps), insiders acquire or solidify con-

*We thank Daniel Asquith, David Blackwell, David Brown, Mary Dehner, Leo Herzel, Robert Kieschnick, Wayne Marr, J. Harold Mulherin, James Musumeci, Greg Niehaus, Roberta Romano, Michael Ryngaert, Richard Ruback (the editor), Kathleen Weiss, the referee, and participants in seminars at UCLA, the University of Florida, Georgetown University, and the Western Finance Association meetings for helpful comments. In addition, the paper benefited from discussions at the Harvard Conference on the Structure and Governance of Enterprise. Ekkehart Boehmer provided excellent research assistance. The Securities and Exchange Commission as a matter of policy disclaims responsibility for any private publication or statement by any of its employees. The views expressed here are those of the authors and do not necessarily reflect the views of the Commission or Lehn's colleagues on the staff of the Commission.

trol by increasing their ownership of voting rights without simultaneously increasing their ownership of a firm's residual claims. In going-private transactions [hereafter, leveraged buyouts (LBOs)], insiders or third parties consolidate control by proportionately increasing their ownership of both voting rights and residual claims. Comparison of the two transactions increases our understanding of what motivates changes in corporate control and how the changes affect firm performance.[1]

Dual-class recaps and LBOs grew in popularity during the 1980s, a trend presumably related to the increase in takeover activity. Although dual-class recaps are often thought of as antitakeover devices and LBOs as a form of takeover, this characterization masks some important similarities between the two. Both are antitakeover devices in that they can be motivated by the threat of a takeover by outsiders. Similarly, both are a form of takeover, since both involve a 'takeover' of voting control. For our purposes, the salient distinction between the two transactions is their different effect on the relationship between ownership of voting rights and ownership of residual claims.

Gilson (1987) focuses on why some firms choose a dual-class recap to consolidate control while others choose an LBO. Recognizing that both transactions can either promote efficiency or exploit shareholders, Gilson emphasizes their different effects on stock prices – shareholders typically receive hefty premiums in LBOs but not in dual-class recaps. Although Gilson states that the data cannot distinguish between the efficiency and exploitation explanations, he argues that they suggest exploitation in dual-class recaps and calls for a regulatory response that eliminates the possibility of such exploitation.

Gilson's argument raises the question of why insiders of some firms pay a premium for control (as they do in LBOs) while insiders in other firms (those adopting dual-class recaps) do not. One explanation is that the choice between the two methods of consolidating control is governed by firm attributes that make dual-class recaps efficient for some firms and LBOs efficient for others. A second explanation is that the cost of coordination among outside shareholders is higher in firms adopting dual-class recaps (thereby allowing coercion) than among firms going private through LBOs. We examine these alternative, but not necessarily competing, explanations.

Since the costs and benefits associated with consolidating control via the two means presumably vary from firm to firm, we discuss salient differences between dual-class recaps and LBOs that may govern the choice. These differences lead to several predictions about firm attributes that would make one choice more desirable than the other. Among these attributes are the

[1]See Jensen and Ruback (1983) and Jarrell, Brickley, and Netter (1988) for reviews of the empirical evidence on corporate control.

firms' growth opportunities, agency costs, and tax liabilities, and insiders' information about stock prices.

We test our predictions on a sample of 380 firms that either adopted a dual-class recap or went private through an LBO from 1977 through 1987. In short, we find:

- Firms that adopt dual-class recaps have significantly higher growth in sales and number of employees than LBO firms. These results are consistent with the argument that fast-growing firms are more likely to have a continuing demand for external financing and hence find it unattractive to consolidate control by going private.

- The ratios of research and development (R&D) expenditures to sales and advertising expenditures to sales are significantly higher for firms adopting dual-class recaps than for firms going private through LBOs. If R&D and advertising expenditures are valid proxies for growth prospects, this result is consistent with the growth hypothesis.

- Firms that adopt dual-class recaps have lower ratios of undistributed cash flow (i.e., cash flow not distributed to bondholders and stockholders through interest and dividend payments) to equity value than LBO firms, although the difference is not statistically significant. Market-to-book ratios, however, are significantly higher in dual-class firms. Some researchers have used these measures as proxies for free cash flow and possible agency costs. The lower market-to-book ratios in LBO firms suggest that agency costs may be higher for those companies.

- Firms that adopt dual-class recaps have significantly lower pretransaction tax liability than LBO firms. This result is consistent with the argument that the value of tax savings associated with debt is less for firms recapitalizing with dual classes of stock than for LBO firms.

In addition to examining what determines the choice between dual-class recaps and LBOs, we examine the posttransaction performance for the two sets of firms, with the following results:

- Dual-class firms devote a higher percentage of their subsequent cash flow to capital expenditures than a sample of management buyouts. In addition, a large proportion of dual-class firms issues equity following the recapitalization. This suggests that the dual-class firms have more promising investment opportunities than their LBO counterparts, either because of higher payoffs associated with their projects or because of a lower effective cost of capital.

- There are significant increases in industry-adjusted operating income (divided by sales) for dual-class firms, although these are less than for a sample of management buyouts. Though LBO firms outperform dual-class firms, these results do not support the argument that dual-class recaps retard efficiency.

In the following section, we discuss further the similarities and differences between dual-class recaps and LBOs and the choice between these two transactions. In sections 3 and 4, we develop testable hypotheses and report our empirical evidence. Section 5 offers concluding remarks.

2. Comparison of dual-class recapitalizations and LBOs

2.1. Similarities and differences

Both dual-class recaps and LBOs are mechanisms for consolidating voting control of a firm in a small group, usually consisting of management. In a dual-class recap, insiders create dual classes of common stock with disparate voting rights that concentrate the high-vote stock among themselves. The recapitalization often is accomplished with an exchange offer, in which existing stockholders are offered the new class of low-vote stock and a higher dividend in exchange for their high-vote stock.[2] Insiders retain their high-vote stock and increase their voting control without proportionately increasing their ownership of residual claims.

In an LBO, shareholders of a public firm are bought out by a bidder who takes a concentrated ownership position in the new privately-held firm. The transactions are usually financed heavily with debt. LBOs are also known as going-private transactions, since the firm often loses its public status, or as management buyouts, since insiders frequently are part of the acquiring group.

Following Gilson (1987), we suggest that LBOs and dual-class recaps are alternative ways of achieving a similar goal – the consolidation of corporate control. These transactions are rarely thought of as substitutes, however, The change in distribution of voting control after a dual-class recap leads Ruback (1988, p. 153) to argue that 'dual-class plans may be the most effective universal antitakeover device ever invented'. An LBO, in contrast, is generally considered a type of takeover.

LBOs and dual-class recaps are similar, however, in that both typically insulate insiders from outside shareholders and the market for corporate control. Shleifer and Vishny (1988) suggest that management buyouts are

[2]See Partch (1987) and Jarrell and Poulsen (1988) for additional description of recapitalization methods.

often used to perpetuate control when managers are threatened by hostile takeover. Consistent with this view, Lehn and Poulsen (1989) find that 40% of 283 LBOs from 1981 through 1987 were preceded by either takeover rumors or actual bids for the firms. Hence, although LBOs are a form of takeover, they also can be viewed as antitakeover devices, much like dual-class recaps.

There are important differences between dual-class recaps and LBOs. First, in dual-class recaps, insiders increase their ownership of voting rights while usually maintaining or reducing their ownership of residual claims. In LBOs, insiders increase their ownership of both voting rights and residual claims. DeAngelo and DeAngelo (1985), Partch (1987), and Ang and Megginson (1989) find that after a dual-class recap insiders control a much smaller share of the inferior voting stock than of the superior voting stock and a greater share of voting power relative to claims on residual cash flows.

This difference could result in different managerial incentives following dual-class recaps and LBOs. Economists have argued that the stockholder gains associated with LBOs stem at least partly from the lessening of manager–stockholder conflicts that accompanies the consolidation of residual claims among insiders. In contrast, the reduced correspondence between voting control and rights to residual cash flows following dual-class recaps may attenuate managerial incentives to maximize profits, since these transactions diminish the extent to which insiders bear the wealth consequences of their decisions. As a result, critics of dual-class recaps argue that they entrench insiders and retard efficiency.

Dual-class recaps and LBOs also have very different stock-price effects. Numerous studies document that, on average, shareholders receive premiums of 35% to 50% in LBOs [see, for example, DeAngelo, DeAngelo, and Rice (1984), Lehn and Poulsen (1989), Kaplan (1989a), and Marais, Schipper, and Smith (1989)]. In dual-class recaps, insiders are able to acquire or maintain control without paying similar premiums. Partch (1987) and Jarrell and Poulsen (1988) find that shareholders do not benefit from dual-class recaps; in fact, Jarrell and Poulsen find small negative average stock-price effects associated with recaps after 1985.

Pretransaction insider holdings also differ significantly for dual-class recap and LBO firms. Insiders in firms choosing dual-class recaps control a large percentage of the shares before the transaction – in our sample, on average, insiders hold 43.1% of the common equity before dual-class recaps, compared with 23.4% in LBOs. The high insider holdings may assure passage of dual-class recap plans. These holdings also may preclude the possibility of a hostile takeover; we find that takeover rumors or bids preceded dual-class recaps in only 3 of the 97 firms.

Finally, dual-class recaps and LBOs have very different effects on capital structure. Whereas dual-class recaps have no direct effects on leverage, LBOs result in dramatic leverage increases. Marais, Schipper, and Smith (1989) find that median leverage (long-term debt/long-term debt plus shareholders' equity) increases from 26% to 85% following LBOs; Lehn and Poulsen (1988) find a corresponding increase in average debt/equity ratios from 0.457 to 5.524.

In short, dual-class recaps and LBOs share two similarities: both consolidate voting control and both have been used in response to takeover threats. The two transactions differ, however, in several respects, including a) the extent to which insiders increase their ownership of residual claims, b) their stock-price effects, c) the level of insider holdings before the transactions, and d) their capital-structure effects. We examine these and other similarities and differences to determine why some firms choose to consolidate control through a dual-class recap and others choose to do so through an LBO.

2.2. *Shareholder exploitation or promotion of efficiency?*

2.2.1. *Exploitation*

Gilson's exploitation argument views dual-class recaps as antitakeover devices through which insiders protect themselves from takeovers, thereby removing the possibility that shareholders will receive a takeover premium. Ruback (1988) argues that collective action problems can result in exploitation of shareholders.[3] His model is based on a 'prisoner's dilemma' confronting outside shareholders who exchange their high-vote stock for low-vote stock with other benefits. Each outside shareholder faces a worst-case scenario of rejecting the exchange offer while other shareholders accept. The nonexchanging shareholder retains high-vote stock with irrelevant voting power since the insiders control the high-vote stock. To avert this scenario, outside shareholders exchange their high-vote stock even though the concentration of this stock with insiders is detrimental to shareholders' collective interest.

Insiders can exploit shareholders in LBOs as well. Since insiders are both the bidders and the decisionmakers for the target firm, they have an inherent conflict of interest. As bidders, they presumably try to obtain the target at the lowest possible price. Simultaneously, they have a fiduciary duty to obtain the highest price for their shareholders. A competitive takeover market lessens the conflict, but if insiders have informational advantages or large holdings, the threat of competing bids may be small. For example, outside bidders are disadvantaged if insiders have private information about the firm's prospects. Since premiums paid in LBOs are comparable to those observed in other

[3] Gordon (1988) discusses dual-class recapitalizations within a similar framework.

takeovers, however, it does not appear that shareholders generally are exploited in LBOs.

Gilson suggests why insiders in some firms are able to consolidate control through a dual-case recap without paying a premium while insiders in the LBO firms pay a premium for control. He notes that firms that choose dual-class recaps have high pretransaction insider ownership. Thus, the insiders have effective control before the transaction and are able to impose the dual-class structure on the outside shareholders. The LBO firms, in contrast, have lower pretransaction insider ownership, limiting insiders' ability to exploit outside shareholders.

Gilson argues that the difference in stock-price effects associated with the two transactions is consistent with the exploitation hypothesis. If the primary reason for both transactions is increased efficiency associated with consolidation of control, then both should benefit outside stockholders. With low transaction costs and perfect capital markets, Gilson argues, shareholders would be equally well off in either transaction. Since shareholders receive substantial wealth gains only in LBOs, managerial exploitation deprives shareholders of the benefits associated with consolidation of control in dual-class recaps.

2.2.2. *Efficient self-selection*

In addition to the shareholder exploitation argument, Gilson offers another explanation for why some firms choose LBOs and others choose dual-class recaps, which he refers to as the efficient self-selection explanation. This argument begins with the premise that consolidation of voting control promotes efficiency, even if there is no consolidation in the ownership of residual claims. Two potential efficiency gains are suggested by DeAngelo and DeAngelo (1985).

First, consolidation of voting control may encourage managers to invest in firm-specific human capital. If threatened by a takeover that could lead to their replacement, managers may be reluctant to invest in such capital, since the returns to the investment can be appropriated outside bidders. Shareholders want managers to invest in firm-specific human capital that increases firm value.[4] Thus, to create stronger *ex ante* incentives for managers to make these investments, shareholders may wish to insulate managers from the threat of takeovers by consolidating voting control among the managers.

[4]Shleifer and Vishny (1989) argue that shareholder wealth declines after manager-specific investments designed to make it costly to remove managers. Consolidation of control in managers makes it more likely, however, that they choose positive NPV investments by reducing the benefits of investments that only serve to increase the cost of removing managers.

According to the argument, the shareholders may not require the insiders to increase their ownership of residual claims commensurately, since the costs of foregone diversification may be large. Hence, shareholders may find it optimal to raise one type of agency cost (that associated with a weaker link between ownership of voting rights and rights to residual claims) to lower another type (subpar investment in firm-specific human capital).

Consolidation of voting control also can be valuable in firms where it is difficult for insiders to communicate information about performance or investment opportunities. In these firms, managers, to avoid being replaced in a takeover, may undertake costly methods of signaling, including investing in projects that have observable payoffs even though these projects may have lower expected returns than others with less observable payoffs. Stein (1988) formally models this possibility. To avert this dissipation of value, shareholders may wish to provide management with protection in the form of voting control. Meulbroek, Mitchell, Mulherin, Netter, and Poulsen (1990) provide evidence that firms decrease R&D intensity after the introduction of shark repellents, failing to support Stein's prediction.

In sum, consolidation of voting control can promote efficiency by giving managers strong *ex ante* incentives to invest in firm-specific human capital and investment projects that are costly to monitor. Dual-class recaps and LBOs may be efficient ways of reorganizing some business firms. In the next section, we discuss several firm attributes that we expect to influence the choice between dual-class recaps and LBOs if that choice reflects efficient self-selection.

3. The choice between dual-class recaps and LBOs

We hypothesize that the choice of organizational structure is determined by firm attributes that make one form more desirable than the other. In this section, we suggest that fundamental differences in firm growth opportunities, agency costs, tax liabilities, and information asymmetries can explain why different firms choose different methods to consolidate control. We also examine the posttransaction performance of the two sets of firms to compare the effects of different organizational forms on firm performance.

3.1. Growth rates

The common equity of firms that adopt dual-class recaps continues to trade publicly. Unlike firms that go private through leveraged buyouts, these firms do not realize cost savings associated with fewer SEC filings and lower costs of servicing shareholders. Private firms, however, may face a higher cost of capital, since they have less access to public capital markets. DeAngelo and DeAngelo (1987, p. 45) discuss how the cost of capital differs for private and public companies. They note that private-firm investment is limited by:

(1) the availability of senior claim financing at acceptable terms,
(2) the amount of funds generated by company operations, and
(3) the ability and willingness of current stockholders to contribute equity capital.

In addition, they argue that managers must be compensated for holding poorly-diversified portfolios in private firms.

Since dual-class firms remain public, they can raise capital at a lower cost than their private counterparts. Firms with higher growth prospects and a desire for continued access to public capital markets are more likely to consolidate control through dual-class recaps than through LBOs. This hypothesis is consistent with the observation that many firms indicate in their proxy voting material that the purpose of their dual-class recap is to allow them to issue equity subsequently without diminishing managerial control. In fact, we find a high frequency of subsequent equity issues by firms adopting dual-class recaps, consistent with the growth hypothesis.

There is another reason that we expect dual-class firms to have greater growth prospects than LBO firms. Debt financing may be especially costly for firms with growth opportunities, since stockholders may find it easier to redistribute wealth away from creditors in these firms. Myers (1984) argues that firms with valuable growth opportunities (intangible assets) tend to borrow less than firms with mostly tangible assets.[5] Firms that adopt dual-class recaps could issue debt to raise capital without diluting control. That dual-class firms forego this alternative suggests that debt financing is more costly for these firms than for firms that consolidate control through LBOs. The difference in the relative costs of debt financing could be due to a difference in growth prospects.

The growth hypothesis has implications for interpreting the different stock-price effects associated with dual-class recaps and LBOs. In general, dual-class firms are already controlled by insiders who wish to issue equity without relinquishing control. Thus, the announcement of a dual-class recap contains two pieces of information: the firm has growth prospects that it may finance with an equity issue, and the insiders will continue to control the firm.

These two pieces of information may combine to yield small, possibly negative, stock returns at the announcement of the recap. First, since insiders

[5]Bradley, Jarrell, and Kim (1985) find evidence of a significant negative relationship between rates of investment in advertising and R&D (proxies for noncollateralizable assets) and leverage. Long and Malitz (1985) and Alchian and Woodward (1988) provide similar analysis. Titman and Wessels (1988) outline and empirically test various capital-structure theories and our findings are broadly consistent with their results.

often retain control in a dual-class recap, the announcement of these transactions contains little news about a change in control that would affect stock prices. Second, the market presumably infers from recap announcements that a subsequent equity issue is likely. Since equity issues are usually accompanied by negative stock returns, part of the stock-price reaction to announcements of dual-class recaps may reflect the market's reaction not to recapitalization per se, but to the greater probability of an equity issue. If so, the stock-price reaction to the subsequent equity issues should be less negative than the stock-price reaction to other equity issues. Hence, for reasons unrelated to the control consequences of dual-class recaps, one might expect a negative stock-price reaction to announcements of these transactions.

3.2. Agency costs

Dual-class firms and LBO firms may be distinguished by the severity of their manager–stockholder conflicts before the transactions. If part of the stockholder gain in LBOs stems from lessening of these conflicts, the absence of stockholder gains in dual-class recaps may reflect the absence of high agency costs in firms adopting this organizational form. One indication that the pretransaction agency costs are higher in LBO firms is that the percentage of equity owned by insiders is approximately twice as large in dual-class firms as in LBO firms (with a mean of 43.1% versus 24.3% and a median of 46.2% versus 17.7%). Thus, the pretransaction incentives of insiders are more closely aligned with those of outside shareholders in dual-class than in LBO firms. The different stock-price effects associated with the two types of transactions may reflect a greater reduction in agency costs in LBO firms.

Using insider ownership as a proxy for agency costs is consistent with the argument that ownership structures are endogenously determined and guided by value maximization [Demsetz and Lehn (1985)]. Firms choose ownership structures that maximize the discounted stream of the difference between revenues and costs. Since agency costs are only one component of costs, different firms can survive with different levels of agency costs. For example, small firms (in which insiders typically own a large percentage of equity) incur relatively low agency costs but forego cost savings associated with a larger scale of operations; large firms (in which insiders typically own a much smaller percentage of equity) incur higher agency costs but realize cost savings associated with larger scale. If the takeover and restructuring phenomenon of the 1980s is viewed as a technological innovation that significantly lowered the cost of resolving agency problems in firms [Jensen (1989)], we expect the benefits of the innovation to fall disproportionately upon firms with higher agency costs (i.e., firms with lower insider holdings).

A special type of agency problem, suggested by Jensen (1986), may distinguish dual-class from LBO firms. According to Jensen, targets of hostile takeovers often suffer from high agency costs associated with the use of free cash flow (i.e., cash flow beyond what is required to finance positive-return investment projects). This agency problem arises because insiders and stockholders are likely to differ over the use of free cash flow. Insiders will often prefer to retain the cash to finance investment projects that expand firm size but simultaneously reduce firm value (by definition, since all positive-return projects have been exhausted). Shareholders prefer to receive excess cash in the form of either higher dividends or stock buybacks. Jensen argues that hostile takeovers, LBOs, and leveraged recapitalizations all serve, at least in part, to discipline insiders who use free cash flow in ways that diminish the equity value of their firms.[6]

The free cash flow theory suggests another influence on the choice of a means for consolidating control. If some of the shareholder gains in LBOs stem from a lessening of manage–shareholder conflicts over the use of free cash flow, LBO firms should have more free cash than dual-class firms. This prediction builds on the previous prediction about comparative growth rates for the two samples of firms. Since dual-class firms arguably have growth opportunities that require continued access to external capital, these firms, by definition, have less excess cash to finance their investment projects.

The agency cost hypothesis has implications for posttransaction performance. If LBOs lower agency costs, we would expect the performance of LBO firms, but not that of dual-class firms, to improve following the transaction. The reduced correspondence between insider voting power and residual cash flows in dual-class firms could, in fact, suggest a decline in performance. We test these predictions by examining posttransaction performance of both sets of firms. In addition, we contrast our measures of performance with the findings of other researchers.

3.3. *Tax considerations*

The tax advantages associated with debt financing also lead to predictions about the choice between dual-class recaps and LBOs. Several studies have shown that tax savings associated with highly leveraged transactions account for a significant part of the premiums paid to stockholders in these transactions.[7] The main source of tax savings in LBOs, the tax deductibility of interest expense, is irrelevant in dual-class recaps, because these transactions do not involve issuance of debt.

[6]Several recent papers find evidence supporting the free cash flow hypothesis. See, for example, Lang, Stulz, and Walkling (1989a), Lehn and Poulsen (1989), and Mitchell and Lehn (1990). Gilson (1987, p. 831) provides an alternative to the free cash flow explanation of LBOs, suggesting that they occur in industries where management is not disciplined by product market competition.

[7]See Hayn (1989), Kaplan (1989a), Lehn and Poulsen (1988), Lowenstein (1985), Macris (1989), and Schipper and Smith (1988).

This observation suggests two testable predictions. First, firms with lower effective tax liability are likely to value the tax advantages of debt less than firms with higher liability, and are thus more likely to choose dual-class recaps than LBOs. In addition, firms with more nondebt tax shields should value the tax advantages of debt less than firms with fewer shields. Thus, the greater the nondebt tax shields, the more likely the firm is to choose a dual-class recap.

3.4. Information asymmetries

Management's possession of private information is often suggested as a major reason for corporate stock repurchases and equity issues.[8] Since management-led LBOs are extreme forms of stock repurchases, it is reasonable also to posit this information asymmetry as an explanation for many LBOs. According to this argument, insiders who know the 'true' value of corporate assets have financial incentives to propose buyouts when they believe their companies' equity is undervalued. If they have favorable information about their companies' prospects, they want to own the rights to residual cash flows, whose value will increase.

In dual-class recaps, insiders presumably do not have favorable private information about their firms' prospects, since they are not attempting to increase their ownership of residual claims. If insiders choose a dual-class recap over an LBO, it is more likely that their company's stock is overvalued. This is consistent with the observations that dual-class recaps often precede new equity issues and that these issues are often thought to signal that insiders believe their stock is overvalued.

We conjecture that insiders in firms that go private through leveraged buyouts are more likely to have private information that their firms' stock price is undervalued, whereas their counterparts in dual-class firms are more likely to have private information that their companies' stock prices are overvalued. At this time, we do not test for the presence of these information asymmetries.

In sum, several predictions about pre- and posttransaction characteristics of firms that undergo dual-class recaps and LBOs emerge:

- Dual-class firms have higher growth rates than LBO firms both before and after the transaction.
- Dual-class firms use the public capital markets after the transaction to fund investments.
- Pretransaction agency costs are lower in dual-class firms than in LBO firms. Similarly, free cash flow is lower in dual-class than in LBO firms. Thus,

[8]See, for example, Dann (1981), Vermaelen (1981), and Netter and Mitchell (1989).

LBO firms should perform better after the transaction. Performance in dual-class firms should change little.

- Dual-class firms have lower effective tax liability and more nondebt tax shields than LBO firms before the transaction.
- Insiders in dual-class firms have less positive private information about their firms' prospects than their counterparts in LBO firms.

In the next section, we present the results from our empirical analysis of all of these predictions except the last.

4. Empirical analysis

Our sample combines those used in the Jarrell and Poulsen (1988) study of dual-class recaps and the Lehn and Poulsen (1989) study of going-private transactions. Jarrell and Poulsen identify 97 firms that adopted dual-class common stock or other disparate voting provisions from 1976 through May 1987. Lehn and Poulsen collect a sample of 283 successful going-private transactions from 1980 through 1987. In addition, we compare the posttransaction performance of the dual-class firms with corresponding results obtained by Kaplan (1989b), Muscarella and Vetsuypens (1989), and Smith (1990). All financial variables are constructed from COMPUSTAT data.

The choice between dual-class recaps and LBOs is also a function of regulation. Before 1988, firms traded on the American Stock Exchange (AMEX) and NASDAQ were not restricted in their ability to recapitalize with multiple classes of common stock with disparate voting rights. New York Stock Exchange (NYSE) listed firms, however, could not do so without being delisted. This one-share one-vote requirement for listing on the NYSE dates to the 1920s [see Seligman (1988)]. The NYSE imposed a moratorium on its rule in 1984 in response to competitive pressure from the AMEX and NASDAQ. In September 1986, the NYSE proposed a modification of its listing standards to allow listed companies to have multiple classes of common stock with disparate voting rights. In response to the proposal, the Securities and Exchange Commission in July 1988 adopted Rule 19c-4, to protect existing shareholders from disenfranchisement in a dual-class recap. This rule effectively prohibited recaps with multiple classes of common stock listed on any national exchange or NASDAQ. However, in 1990 the D.C. Circuit Court decided that the SEC lacked the authority for the adoption of Rule 19c-4.

Since regulations may influence the choice between dual-class recaps and leveraged buyouts, we analyze several subsamples to reflect these considerations. We contrast firms in the pre- and postmoratorium period and also

Table 1

Number, mean equity value, median equity value, and total equity value of firms that recapitalize with dual classes of equity and LBO firms, 1976–1987.[a]

	Number				Mean equity value		Median equity value		Total equity value	
	Dual-class firms		LBO firms		Dual-class firms	LBO firms	Dual-class firms	LBO firms	Dual-class firms	LBO firms
1976	1	(1)	—		39.7	—	39.7	—	39.7	—
1977	—		—		—	—	—	—	—	—
1978	—		—		—	—	—	—	—	—
1979	2	(2)	—		64.5	—	64.5	—	129.0	—
1980	4	(3)	18	(15)	23.0	33.4	24.5	11.4	69.2	501.3
1981	3	(3)	23	(21)	50.0	103.6	28.6	22.4	149.9	2175.5
1982	4	(4)	29	(26)	22.5	75.2	8.6	49.3	90.0	1955.5
1983	14	(14)	37	(34)	123.0	111.1	65.4	56.7	1721.5	3777.7
1984	10	(9)	50	(46)	641.7	199.0	287.9	65.1	5775.2	9153.5
1985	16	(16)	42	(36)	180.4	347.2	120.2	70.2	2886.6	12500.5
1986	29	(29)	40	(34)	201.1	306.4	142.8	79.1	5832.4	10419.1
1987	14	(14)	44	(38)	610.5	218.4	170.3	59.6	8547.2	8298.4
1976–1987	97	(95)	283	(250)	265.7	195.1	101.5	52.1	25240.8	48781.5

[a]Equity values are computed as the product of common shares outstanding and closing price of common stock at end of fiscal year immediately preceding the calendar year of the transactions, as reported by COMPUSTAT. Numbers in parentheses indicate number of firms with necessary COMPUSTAT data available.

firms listed on the NYSE versus those traded on the AMEX or NASDAQ. Overall, our results are consistent across the several subsamples.

Summary statistics for number and equity value for the samples of dual-class recaps and LBO transactions are reported in table 1. The selection criteria for the respective samples represent an attempt to identify all dual-class recap and LBO firms over the period considered. The data indicate that the number and value of both dual-class recaps and LBOs increased dramatically during the 1980s. For example, in 1980 there were four dual-class recaps, involving firms with mean and total equity values of $23 million and $69.2 million. By 1987, there were 14 dual-class recaps, involving firms with mean and total equity values of 610.5 million and $8,547.2 million. Similarly, the number of LBO firms increased from 18 in 1980 to 44 in 1987. The mean equity value of these firms increased from $33.4 million to $218.4 million, and the total equity value, from $501.3 million to $8,298.4 million. Since these increases are coterminous with a dramatic increase in hostile takeover activity, these data are consistent with the argument that the increased threat of hostile takeovers induced many of the dual-class recaps and LBOs.

In the remaining tables, we report the results of our analysis of the hypothesized differences between the characteristics of firms that choose dual-class recapitalizations and those that choose LBOs. In the following subsections, we discuss the results of our empirical tests of each hypothesis.

4.1. Growth rates

We predict that firms with higher growth rates are more likely to choose dual-class recaps than LBOs. We measure growth in several ways – average annual increase in sales, in employees, and in capital expenditures, and research and development (R&D) and advertising expenditures as a percentage of sales, which are usually higher in faster growing firms. We also report average cumulative abnormal returns earned by the firms in the two samples over the year preceding and the two years preceding the control transaction.

In panel A of table 2, we report the median values for the sales, employees, and capital-expenditure growth variables, measured as the average growth rate over the five years and the year preceding the transaction. We also report the R&D and advertising intensity comparisons. Sales growth is significantly higher (using the Wilcoxon test statistic) in the dual-class sample than the LBO sample, with a median value of 14.4% in the dual-class sample, compared with 6.3% in the LBO sample. Similarly, growth in employees is significantly higher for dual-class firms (4.5%) than for LBO firms (0.0%). For the median five-year averages, we find similar results. In addition, dual-class firms spend significantly more on advertising and R&D than LBO firms.[9] In contrast, growth rates for capital expenditures are not different in the two samples in either the year preceding or the five years preceding the transaction.

Dual-class firms outperform LBOs in the stock market in the year and two years before the transaction, as also reported in panel A of table 2. The dual-class firms experience average cumulative abnormal returns of 15.0% over one year and 19.4% over two years preceding the transaction, compared with 3.6% and 0.3% for the LBO firms. The two-year cumulative abnormal returns are significantly different across the two samples, using a t-test. Since equity issues often follow dual-class recaps, the large average cumulative abnormal returns for the dual-class sample are consistent with other studies that find a significant stock-price runup before the announcement of equity issues.

The results are consistent with the hypothesis that growing firms, because of a continuing future demand for external financing, are more likely to consolidate control through a dual-class recap than through an LBO.

[9]Our findings on R&D and advertising expenditures are consistent with the results of Titman (1984) and Titman and Wessels (1988). They suggest that there are high costs when firms with unique products (indicated by R&D and advertising) liquidate, and thus uniqueness is negatively related to debt ratios.

Table 2

Median values of variables describing LBO firms and firms that recapitalize with dual classes of stock between 1976 and 1987 and corresponding Wilcoxon test statistics for differences in distribution. Number of firms for which data are available in parentheses.[a]

Variable	LBO firm	Dual-class recap	Wilcoxon test statistic
Panel A: Growth variables			
Average annual increase in sales prior to transaction			
Preceding year	0.063 (248)	0.144 (94)	4.26***
Preceding 5 years	0.083 (232)	0.121 (85)	3.37***
Average annual increase in employees prior to transaction			
Preceding year	0.000 (234)	0.045 (88)	3.74***
Preceding 5 years	0.002 (215)	0.046 (79)	3.34***
Average increase in capital expenditures prior to transaction			
Preceding year	−0.022 (236)	−0.023 (90)	−0.02
Preceding 5 years	0.257 (220)	0.300 (80)	0.70
Advertising expenditures/sales			
Preceding year	0.008 (209)	0.013 (77)	2.05**
Preceding 5 years	0.009 (171)	0.014 (62)	1.80*
R&D expenditures/sales			
Preceding year	0.000 (129)	0.009 (51)	3.14***
Preceding 5 years	0.000 (118)	0.010 (46)	2.80***
Average cumulative abnormal return in percent (test statistic = t-test)			
Preceding year	3.65 (241)	15.0 (80)	1.53
Preceding 2 years	0.35 (241)	19.4 (80)	1.97**
Panel B: Agency-cost variables			
Cash flow/equity			
Preceding year	0.112 (247)	0.093 (93)	−0.98
Preceding 5 years	0.144 (220)	0.124 (78)	−1.19
Market value of public securities/book value of assets			
Preceding year	0.748 (249)	0.931 (95)	4.45***
Preceding 5 years	0.597 (223)	0.713 (79)	2.92***
Panel C: Income-tax variables			
Income tax/equity			
Preceding year	0.064 (250)	0.044 (94)	−2.39**
Preceding 5 years	0.074 (223)	0.053 (79)	−3.07***
Nondebt tax shields (depreciation + investment tax credits)/sales			
Preceding year	0.023 (203)	0.026 (79)	0.34
Preceding 5 years	0.024 (164)	0.026 (59)	0.89

[a]The asterisks indicate:
* significantly different distribution at the 10% confidence level,
** significantly different distribution at the 5% confidence level,
*** significantly different distribution at the 1% confidence level.

4.2. Agency costs

To measure potential agency problems, whose severity may influence the means chosen to consolidate control, we use two measures. First, to approximate cash flow undistributed to securityholders, we calculate posttax cash flow minus interest expense and dividend payments, expressed as a fraction of the market value of common equity for each firm. This variable does not perfectly measure unrestricted cash flow, since it is not adjusted for the lack of positive-return investment projects. Other researchers, however, have used it as a proxy for free cash flow. Lehn and Poulsen (1989) find that cash flow is significantly higher for firms that go private than for a control sample. They also find that this cash flow can explain part of the premiums paid in LBOs. Lang, Stulz, and Walkling (1989b) use a similar measure to explain returns to acquiring firms in successful tender offers and find that acquiring-firm stock returns are negatively related to the firms' cash flow.

We also measure agency costs with the ratio of a firm's market value to the book value of its assets. On average, the higher the quality of management, the higher this ratio should be. Admittedly, this measure may be a proxy for other differences between firms, including the degree to which assets are properly valued by accounting convention and the importance of intangible assets. Our use of the market-to-book ratio parallels the use of Tobin's q by Lang, Stulz, and Walkling (1989a, b), Morck, Shleifer and Vishny (1988), McConnell and Servaes (1990), and Kole (1990) as a measure of managerial performance. Although market valuation is measured more precisely with Tobin's q since it adjusts total assets for their replacement costs, other research shows the market-to-book ratio provides a reasonable proxy for q. For example, Amit, Livnat, and Zarowin (1989) report that the market-to-book ratio and Tobin's q are highly correlated and that in their empirical tests the market-to-book ratio is a good proxy for q. We measure the market-to-book ratio as the ratio of the market value of equity plus the book value of long-term debt and preferred stock divided by the book value of assets.

The agency cost results are reported in panel B of table 2. Contrary to our hypothesis that free cash flow should be higher in LBO firms, we find no significant difference in cash flow between LBO and dual-class firms. This result may be explained by agency costs not being higher in LBO firms. Alternatively, our measure of cash flow may not measure free cash flow in fast-growing firms completely. This is a plausible interpretation when we consider the cash flow results along with the evidence that dual-class firms outgrow LBOs. If the faster growth of dual-class firms indicates that they have larger positive-return investment opportunities for the same level of cash flow, then free cash flow will be higher in LBO firms.

Market-to-book ratios are significantly higher for dual-class firms than for LBO firms, suggesting that dual-class firms have better managerial performance and lower agency costs. This result is consistent with the findings of Lang, Stulz, and Walkling (1989a) that target firms in successful tender offers have relatively low values of Tobin's q and that the gains in takeovers are negatively related to target-firm q ratios.

4.3. Tax considerations

The tax implications of LBOs and dual-class recapitalizations differ. LBO firms benefit from the tax deductibility of interest payments on their usually large debt, whereas the new equity issues that follow dual-class recapitalizations have few tax ramifications. Earlier research has indicated the importance of tax considerations in motivating LBOs. An LBO is more attractive than a dual-class recap for firms with greater returns from lowering taxes. We use effective tax liability and nondebt tax shields to measure the extent to which firms can benefit from leverage. We expect LBO firms to have higher effective tax liability and lower nondebt tax shields than the dual-class firms.

We find some support for the tax hypothesis. As reported in panel C of table 2, dual-class firms have significantly lower tax-to-equity ratios than LBO firms, with a median of 0.044, compared with 0.064, in the year preceding the transaction. We find similar results for the five years preceding the transaction (0.053 versus 0.074). We find no difference, however, in the value of nondebt tax shields for the two sets of firms.

4.4. Posttransaction performance

Posttransaction performance, measured in this section, provides insights into how consolidation of voting control (and protection from hostile takeovers) affects firms' performance and whether the effects of dual-class recaps and LBOs differ. This approach parallels the studies of management buyouts by Kaplan (1989b), Muscarella and Vetsuypens (1989), and Smith (1990). They generally find evidence that management buyouts or LBOs improve firm performance.[10]

We hypothesize that dual-class firms have more growth opportunities and hence desire greater access to public capital markets than LBO firms. We measure these growth opportunities by the growth in capital expenditures following the control transactions. In addition, we expect operating performance to improve more in LBO firms, since they potentially have greater pretransaction agency costs.

[10] Healy, Palepu, and Ruback (1989) analyze posttransaction performance for firms that merge and also find evidence of significant improvements in asset productivity. Lichtenberg and Siegel (1990) find that relative productivity of plants involved in LBOs improves significantly after the transaction.

Table 3

Posttransaction performance measured by percentage change in operating income and capital expenditures: median values for LBO firms and firms that recapitalize with dual class of stock between 1978 and 1987 (significance measured with Wilcoxon statistics). Number of firms for which data are available in parentheses.[a]

	Percent change from indicated year before transaction to after transaction		
	−1 to +1	−1 to +2	−1 to +3
Panel A: Dual-class firms			
Capital expenditures/sales			
Percentage change	12.05*** (86)	−0.94* (75)	14.81** (43)
Industry-adjusted percentage change	19.5*** (86)	3.50** (72)	12.61** (42)
Operating income/sales			
Percentage change	−0.65 (90)	−5.25 (78)	−0.97 (44)
Industry-adjusted percentage change	4.90** (89)	4.56* (72)	3.25** (43)
Panel B: LBO firms			
Capital expenditures/sales			
Percentage change	−17.5 (16)	−16.5 (11)	2.57 (4)
Industry-adjusted percentage change	10.8 (14)	7.98 (11)	196.9 (4)
Operating income/sales			
Percentage change	0.32 (16)	−6.09 (11)	33.67 (4)
Industry-adjusted percentage change	7.14 (13)	−5.87 (10)	41.59 (3)

[a]The asterisks indicate:
* significantly different from zero at the 10% confidence level,
** significantly different from zero at the 5% confidence level,
*** significantly different from zero at the 1% confidence level.

In table 3, we report several measures of posttransaction performance of dual-class firms (panel A) and LBO firms (panel B). Performance changes are reported from one year before to one year after, two years after, and three years after the transaction. We report percentage changes and industry-adjusted percentage changes in capital expenditures and operating income, standardized by sales. These variables are taken from Kaplan (1989b) and are similar to those used by other researchers. We obtain essentially the same results when we standardize by assets rather than sales. These data are obtained from COMPUSTAT, so our posttransaction LBO sample is limited by the lack of public reporting in these now-private firms.

We find significant industry-adjusted growth in capital expenditures/sales for the dual-class firms in all three measurement periods. The median value of this variable is 19.5% from year −1 to year +1, 3.50% from year −1 to +2, and 12.61% from year −1 to +3. (The unadjusted results are similar.) The change in capital expenditures/sales for LBOs, in contrast, is insignificantly different from zero according to the Wilcoxon sign test (and insignificantly different from that of the dual-class sample). The interpretation of the LBO results, however, is limited by the small sample size. The findings of Kaplan, Muscarella and Vetsuypens, and Smith suggest a difference between dual-class firms and LBOs. These authors report that management-buyout firms significantly reduce capital expenditures in the years following the transaction. Although we cannot measure the significance of the differences between our sample of dual-class firms and the other researchers' samples of management buyouts, the comparison indicates that dual-class firms increase capital expenditures substantially more than LBO firms.

Increased capital expenditures represent a demand for equity capital, however, only if operating cash flows are inadequate to fund expenditures. To test whether the dual-class firms continue to access public capital markets to fund investments, we examine the incidence of equity issuances (including common stock, convertible debt, and convertible preferred stock) following the recap. An unusually high number of the dual-class firms issue equity securities, 46 out of 97 (47%), from the time of the recapitalization through 1989. Forty of these issues occur within three years of the recap announcement. Partch (1987) also reports a high frequency of equity issuances after a dual-class recap. In contrast, Mikkelson and Partch (1986) find that between one-third to one-quarter of a random sample of firms issued equity securities from 1972 through 1982.

We test whether the negative stock-price reaction at the announcement of dual-class recaps reflects, at least in part, anticipation of subsequent equity issues. Mikkelson and Partch (1986), Asquith and Mullins (1986), and Masulis and Korwar (1986) find statistically significant two-day abnormal returns around announcements of common stock offerings ranging from −3.56% in the Mikkelson and Partch study, to −3.31 in the Masulis and Korwar study, to −3.0 in the Asquith and Mullins study. For the 34 common stock offerings subsequent to the recap for which stock return data from the Center for Research in Security Prices (CRSP) are available, the average two-day abnormal return around the announcement of these offerings is −1.97%, or about 60% of the average two-day abnormal returns found in the other three studies. The smaller abnormal returns are consistent with the argument that part of the stock reaction to these offerings occurred at the time of the recap.

In table 4, we contrast the postperformance results for dual-class firms that do and do not issue equity. We find that the firms issuing equity increase their industry-adjusted capital expenditures significantly in all three reported periods, with median values of 23.1%, 35.0%, and 46.9%, respectively. In contrast, the nonissuing firms experience a significant increase in capital expenditures in the +1 period only. The differences between the issuing and nonissuing firms are significant in the +2 and +3 periods. We also find that nonissuing firms experience negative net-of-market returns (averaging

Table 4

Posttransaction performance measured by percentage change in operating income and capital expenditures: median values for firms that recapitalize with dual classes of stock between 1976 and 1987, by later issuance of equity securities (significance measured with Wilcoxon statistics). Number of firms for which data are available in parentheses.[a]

	Percent change from indicated years before transaction to after transaction		
	−1 to +1	−1 to +2	−1 to +3
Panel A: Dual-class firms that later issue equity securities			
Capital expenditures/sales			
Percentage change	20.4** (38)	46.3*** (35)	44.2*** (25)
Industry-adjusted percentage change	23.1*** (37)	35.0*** (34)	46.9*** (24)
Operating income/sales			
Percentage change	0.66 (41)	−5.61 (37)	−0.97 (26)
Industry-adjusted percentage change	5.57** (40)	13.1** (35)	16.7** (25)
Panel B: Dual-class firms that do not later issue equity securities			
Capital expenditures/sales			
Percentage change	4.41 (48)	−16.6 (40)	−11.7 (18)
Industry-adjusted percentage change	9.41* (49)	−4.27 (38)	0.00 (18)
Operating income/sales			
Percentage change	−1.46 (49)	−3.33 (41)	−1.84 (18)
Industry-adjusted percentage change	3.82 (49)	−0.45 (37)	−2.00 (18)

[a]The asterisks indicate:
* significantly different from zero at the 10% confidence level,
** significantly different from zero at the 5% confidence level,
*** significantly different from zero at the 1% confidence level.

−12.5%) in the year following the recap announcement, in contrast to the approximately zero net-of-market returns of issuing firms. To supplement this information, we test for significant differences in the variables reported in table 2 from the pretransaction period for the issuing and nonissuing firms and find none.

Dual-class firms experience significant increases in industry-adjusted operating income/sales for each of the three periods reported in table 3, with a median value of 4.90%, 4.56%, and 3.25%. Thus, there is no evidence that dual-class recaps retard efficiency. We find insignificant changes in operating income/sales for our LBO sample. For a larger sample of MBOs, however, Kaplan finds large increases in this ratio, with median values of 12.4%, 23.3%, and 34.8% for year +1, +2, and +3.[11] The larger increases in

[11]Muscarella and Vetsuypens (1989) report a median increase of 26.2% in this ratio for a sample of 28 LBOs that later went public in a secondary initial public offering. Smith (1989) reports significant increases in similar profitability measures.

operating income for the MBOs than to dual-class firms suggest that MBOs experience greater efficiency improvements.

The significant increases in industry-adjusted operating income/sales for dual-class firms are concentrated in the firms that later issue equity securities. As reported in table 4, issuing firms experience significant median income growth of 5.57%, 13.1%, and 16.7% for year +1, +2, and +3, while the growth figures for nonissuing firms are insignificantly different from zero. Thus, while we find no significant differences between these firms in the pretransaction period, issuing firms are characterized by faster growth in both capital expenditures and income than nonissuing firms.

5. Conclusions

The proliferation of corporate takeovers and restructurings in the 1980s has provided researchers with a rich opportunity to study the causes and consequences of different forms of business organization. We examine two especially popular types of corporate reorganization: dual-class recapitalizations and LBOs. These two transactions have similar effects on ownership of voting rights but very different effects on ownership of residual claims.

We argue that the choice between dual-class recaps and LBOs is governed, at least partly, by firm attributes that make one organizational form more desirable than another. Firms with greater growth opportunities, lower agency costs, and lower tax liability are expected to be more likely to consolidate control through dual-class recaps than through LBOs. We find strong support for the growth hypothesis, and weaker support for the agency-cost and tax hypotheses.

Dual-class firms devote a higher percentage of their subsequent cash flow to capital expenditures than a sample of management buyouts. In addition, a large proportion of dual-class firms follow the recap with the issuance of equity securities. This suggests that the dual-class firms have more promising investment opportunities than their LBO counterparts, as predicted by the growth hypothesis. We also find significant increases in industry-adjusted operating income for dual-class firms, although less than for a sample of management buyouts.

References

Alchian, Armen and Susan Woodward, 1988, Review of Williamson's 'The economic institutions of capitalism', Journal of Economic Literature 26, 65–79.

Amit, Raphael, Joshua Livnat, and Paul Zarowin, 1989, A classification of mergers and acquisitions by motives: Analysis of market responses, Contemporary Accounting Research 6, 143–158.

Ang, James and William Megginson, 1989, Restricted voting shares, ownership structure, and market value of dual-class firms, Journal of Financial Research 12, 301–318.

Asquith, Paul and David Mullins, 1986, Equity issues and offering dilution, Journal of Financial Economics 15, 61–89.

Bradley, Michael, Gregg A. Jarrell, and E. Han Kim, 1984, On the existence of an optimal capital structure: Theory and evidence, Journal of Finance 39, 857–878.

DeAngelo, Harry and Linda DeAngelo, 1985, Managerial ownership of voting rights: A study of public corporations with dual classes of common stock, Journal of Financial Economics 14, 33–69.

DeAngelo, Harry and Linda DeAngelo, 1987, Management buyouts of publicly traded corporations, Financial Analysts Journal 43, 38–49.

DeAngelo, Harry, Linda DeAngelo, and Edward Rice, 1984, Going private: Minority freezeouts and stockholder wealth, Journal of Law and Economics 28, 367–401.

Dann, Larry, 1981, Common stock repurchases: An analysis of returns to bondholders and stockholders, Journal of Financial Economics 9, 113–138.

Demsetz, Harold and Kenneth Lehn, 1985, The structure of corporate ownership: Causes and consequences, Journal of Political Economy 93, 1155–1177.

Gilson, Ronald J., 1987, Evaluating dual class common stock: The relevance of substitutes, Virginia Law Review 73, 807–844.

Gordon, Jeffrey, 1988, Ties that bond: Dual class common stock and the problem of shareholder choice, California Law Review 76, 3–85.

Hayn, Carla, 1989, Tax attributes as determinants of shareholder gains in corporate acquisitions, Journal of Financial Economics 23, 121–154.

Healy, Paul M., Krishna G. Palepu, and Richard Ruback, 1989, Do mergers improve corporate performance?, Working paper (MIT, Cambridge, MA).

Herzel, Leo and Richard Shepro, 1989, Recapitalization instead of leveraged buyout, Manuscript (Mayer, Brown & Platt, Chicago, IL).

Jarrell, Gregg and Annette Poulsen, 1988, Dual-class recapitalizations as antitakeover mechanisms: The recent evidence, Journal of Financial Economics 20, 129–152.

Jarrell, Gregg A., James A. Brickley, and Jeffry M. Netter, 1988, The market for corporate control: The empirical evidence since 1980, Journal of Economic Perspectives 2, 49–68.

Jensen, Michael C., 1986, Agency costs of free cash flow, corporate finance and takeovers, American Economic Review 76, 323–329.

Jensen, Michael C., 1989, Eclipse of the public corporation, Harvard Business Review, Sept.-Oct., 61–74.

Jensen, Michael and Richard S. Ruback, 1983, The market for corporate control: The scientific evidence, Journal of Financial Economics 11, 5–50.

Kaplan, Steven, 1989a, Management buyouts: Evidence on taxes as a source of value, Journal of Finance 94, 611–632.

Kaplan, Steven, 1989b, The effects of management buyouts on operating performance and value, Journal of Financial Economics 24, 217–254.

Kieschnick, Robert, 1989, Management buyouts of public corporations: An analysis of prior characteristics, in: Y. Amihud, ed., Leveraged management buyouts: Causes and consequences (Dow Jones-Irwin, Homewood, IL).

Kole, Stacey, 1990, A reexamination of the interaction between board ownership of equity and firm performance, Working paper (Securities and Exchange Commission, Washington, DC).

Lang, Larry, Rene Stulz, and Ralph Walkling, 1989a, Managerial performance, Tobin's q, and the gains from successful tender offers, Journal of Financial Economics 24, 137–154.

Lang, Larry, Rene Stulz, and Ralph Walkling, 1989b, Free cash flows, Tobin's q, and bidder gains in successful tender offers, Working paper (New York University, New York, NY).

Lehn, Kenneth and Annette Poulsen, 1988, Leveraged buyouts: Wealth created or wealth redistributed, in: Murray Weidenbaum and Kenneth Chilton, eds., Public policy toward corporate takeovers (Transaction Books, New Brunswick, NJ).

Lehn, Kenneth and Annette Poulsen, 1989, Free cash flow and stockholder gains in going private transactions, Journal of Finance 64, 771–781.

Lichtenberg, Frank and Donald Siegel, 1990, The effects of leveraged buyouts on productivity and related aspects of firm behavior, Journal of Financial Economics, this volume.

Long, Michael and Ileen Malitz, 1985, Investment patterns and financial leverage, in: Friedman, ed., Corporate capital structure in the United States (University of Chicago Press, Chicago, IL).

Lowenstein, Louis, 1985, Management buyouts, Columbia Law Review 85, 730–784.

Macris, Robert, 1989, Leveraged buyouts and federal income tax considerations, in: Y. Amihud, ed., Leveraged management buyouts: Causes and consequences (Dow Jones-Irwin, Homewood, IL).
Marais, Laurantius, Katherine Schipper, and Abbie Smith, 1989, Wealth effects of going private for senior securities, Journal of Financial Economics 23, 155–191.
Masulis, Ronald and Ashok Korwar, 1986, Seasoned equity offerings: An empirical investigation, Journal of Financial Economics 15, 91–118.
McConnell, John and Henri Servaes, 1990, Additional evidence on equity ownership and corporate value, Journal of Financial Economics, this volume.
Meulbroek, Lisa, Mark Mitchell, J. Harold Mulherin, Jeffry Netter, and Annette Poulsen, 1990, Shark repellents and managerial myopia: An empirical test, Journal of Political Economy 98, 1108–1117.
Mikkelson, Wayne and Megan Partch, 1986, Valuation effects of security offerings and the issuance process, Journal of Financial Economics 15, 31–60.
Mitchell, Mark and Kenneth Lehn, Do bad bidders become good targets?, Journal of Political Economy 98, 372–398.
Morck, Randall, Andrei Shleifer, and Robert Vishny, 1988, Management ownership and market valuation: An empirical analysis, Journal of Financial Economics 20, 293–316.
Muscarella, Chris and Michael Vetsuypens, 1989, Efficiency and organizational structure: A study of reverse lbos, Journal of Finance, forthcoming.
Myers, Stewart, 1984, The capital structure puzzle, Journal of Finance 39, 575–592.
Netter, Jeffry and Mark Mitchell, 1989, Stock-repurchase announcements and insider transactions after the October 1987 stock market crash, Financial Management 18, 84–96.
Partch, Megan, 1987, The creation of a class of limited voting common stock and shareholders' wealth, Journal of Financial Economics 18, 313–339.
Ruback, Richard S., 1988, Coercive dual-class exchange offers, Journal of Financial Economics 20, 153–173.
Schipper, Katherine and Abbie Smith, 1988, Corporate income tax effects of management buyouts, Working paper (University of Chicago, Chicago, IL).
Securities and Exchange Commission, Office of the Chief Economist, 1987a, The effects of dual-class recapitalizations on the wealth of shareholders, June 1, 1987.
Securities and Exchange Commission, Office of the Chief Economist, 1987b, Update – The effects of dual-class recapitalizations on shareholders wealth: Including evidence from 1986 and 1987, July 16, 1987.
Seligman, Joel, 1988, Stock exchange rules affecting takeovers and control transactions, in: J. Coffee, L. Lowenstein, and S. Rose-Ackerman, eds., Knights, raiders, & targets (Oxford University Press, New York, NY).
Shleifer, Andrei and Robert W. Vishny, 1988, Management buyouts as a response to market pressure, in: Alan Auerbach, ed., Mergers and acquisitions (University of Chicago Press, Chicago, IL).
Shleifer, Andrei and Robert W. Vishny, 1989, Management entrenchment: The case of manager-specific investments, Journal of Financial Economics 25, 123–139.
Smith, Abbie, 1990, Corporate ownership structure and performance: The case of management buyouts, Journal of Financial Economics, this volume.
Stein, Jeremy, 1988, Takeover threats and managerial myopia, Journal of Political Economy 96, 61–80.
Titman, Sheridan, 1984, The effect of capital structure on a firm's liquidation decision, Journal of Financial Economics 13, 137–151.
Titman, Sheridan and Roberto Wessels, 1988, The determinants of capital structure choice, Journal of Finance 43, 1–19.
Vermaelen, T., 1981, Common stock repurchases and market signalling: An empirical study, Journal of Financial Economics 9, 139–183.

Part IV
Corporate Governance

[13]

ELSEVIER

Journal of Corporate Finance 1 (1994) 139–174

Journal of
CORPORATE
FINANCE

The economics of corporate governance: Beyond the Marshallian firm ☆

Gerald T. Garvey [a,*], Peter L. Swan [b]

[a] *Department of Economics, The Faculties, Australian National University, Canberra, ACT 0200, Australia*

[b] *Department of Finance, Faculty of Economics, University of Sydney, NSW 2006, Australia*

Abstract

It is now customary to view the corporation as a nexus of explicit and implicit contracts. Governance determines *how* the firm's top decision makers (executives) actually administer such contracts. We survey recent theory and evidence on executive behaviour and incentives and reject the standard assumption of shareholder-wealth-maximisation, either in its strict sense or in the sense implied by standard principal–agent models. Explanations for this state of affairs as an inefficient, rent-seeking outcome are contrasted with efficiency explanations, particularly those that explicitly consider the diverse claims of employees, customers, and suppliers as well as those of investors.

Key words: Corporate governance; Incomplete contracts

JEL Classification: G30

1. Introduction

Corporate governance is an issue of immense importance both to policy-makers and to individual firms. The past few years has seen a flood of articles in the business and popular press wrestling with the question of what 'good'

☆ Thanks to Jeff Borland, Ken Lehn, Oliver Hart, Bengt Holmstrom and participants at the University of Melbourne's 1993 Conference on Recent Developments in the Theory of the Firm for helpful comments.

* Corresponding author.

SSDI 0929-1199(94)00002-C

governance is and how to achieve it (e.g., *Advice and Dissent*, 1991; Dobrynski, 1993). A recent survey in *The Economist* (1994) summarizes the popular and political debate in the US, Japan, and Europe. Some commentators have even attributed the successes of the Japanese and German economies to their unique systems of corporate governance, and urge their transmission to Anglo-Saxon corporations (see, e.g., Roe, 1993, and the associated comments). This paper summarizes past achievements and future research opportunities in the corporate governance area.

Webster's International Dictionary (1971) defines the term 'governance' as follows:

(i) "to exercise arbitrarily or by established rules continuous sovereign authority over"; and

(ii) "to rule without sovereign power; to implement and carry into effect policy decisions over without having the power to determine basic policy".

In the corporate context, governance issues are thrown into stark relief by events such as takeovers, shareholder meetings and proxy contests, and controversies surrounding board composition and executive compensation. More mundane decisions involving the reallocation of physical, human, and financial resources, capital budgeting, expansion or contraction of the firm's boundaries, and labor negotiations are also strongly affected by governance.

Despite the importance of these issues, governance has not occupied a central place in economic theory. This reflects a more general tendency of economics to neglect the theory of the firm. As Demsetz (1982) points out, the perfect competition model of microeconomics is actually a model of perfect decentralization, in which no one exercises any authority or powers over anyone else. Governance has no content in such a world. Hart (1988) sharpens this argument by stressing that both the general equilibrium model of Arrow and Debreu (1954) and more recent models of incentive problems under asymmetric information assume complete contracts. In such a world there is no role for governance as all corporate decisions are effectively pre-programmed. Governance is irrelevant because a comprehensive set of 'rules and policies' are negotiated in the markets where the firm secures its inputs and sells its outputs.

Governance only matters when contracts are incomplete. A key implication, which has not been widely recognized in the literature, is that the parties who make the 'filling-in decisions' ('executives') no longer resemble the Marshallian entrepreneur. Even if an executive held 100 per cent of the firm's equity shares, she would not be a true residual claimant because her decisions affect the welfare of *other* members of the firm (investors, workers, managers and/or customers) at least in an ex post sense. [2] The case of bond

[2] The existence of competition generally ensures that these parties expect to receive at least their next-best alternative ex ante, that is, before joining the firm.

covenants provides a convenient illustration. At the time bonds are sold, the firm will often promise, not only to make fixed payments, but also to restrict its dividends, to maintain liquidity, and sometimes even to refrain from investing in certain areas (see Smith and Warner, 1979). But so long as such explicit promises are fulfilled, the bondholders bear any losses and enjoy any gains that may flow from changes in corporate policy. This simply says that bond prices will move for reasons other than exogenous realisations of 'states of nature'. The firm's actions are not perfectly controlled but only loosely guided by rules negotiated in arms-length markets, and the costs and benefits of such actions are *not* borne entirely by shareholders. To understand how such firms will operate, we must understand more than the markets in which they operate. We must understand the incentives and objectives of the 'executives' who make the 'filling-in' decisions. This paper surveys attempts to *endogenize* these objectives. Two different approaches are contrasted: 'rent-seeking' theories which explicitly or implicitly focus on ways in which executives extract wealth from other agents in the economy, and 'efficiency' theories which stress that executives help internalize the externalities which are inherent in a world of incomplete contracts.

Section 2 presents the basic theoretical framework that underpins most economic analysis of governance issues. Section 3 summarizes the relevant empirical evidence on governance structures and management objectives in order to flesh out the framework. Section 4 summarizes more detailed and specific theories which incorporate some of the newer and more troublesome evidence. Section 5 focuses on currently topical issues in governance, and Section 6 highlights some specific areas for future research.

2. An informal model

The basic structure of the model was outlined as early as Jensen and Meckling (1976). The firm begins with a single founder or entrepreneur who wishes to secure additional resources, including capital, labor and perhaps managerial talent. The founder is assumed unable to write contracts that fully map out the firm's state-contingent future. The contract will be completed by discretionary actions of other parties, including but not restricted to 'nature' (who mechanically resolves uncertainty). Actions are discretionary since there will be decisions on which the contract is silent. Essentially, the founder chooses the firm's charter provisions, its top executives, contractual terms with suppliers of capital and labor, and in a federal system such as the US, may also select the set of corporate laws by choosing the state of incorporation. Clearly, such choices do not fully determine the firm's response to a hostile takeover bid, the pay and promotion of future workers and managers, the resolution of financial distress and raising of new capital, or future joint ventures and acquisitions.

While the charter and other ex ante contractual features do not detail specific actions to be taken, the founder can exercise an indirect influence over the identity and incentives of the parties who will take various decisions. Some decisions are subject to a vote of shareholders, others are chosen by the board, and others are essentially left to managerial discretion; see Clark (1985) for a description of the standard assignment of corporate decision rights. Except where otherwise indicated, we will refer to the board and top management interchangeably as 'executives'.

While many decisions are subject to the discretion of shareholders and/or managers, we assume that *expectations* of all such actions are priced-in ex ante. That is, all affected parties form rational expectations about the actions the relevant decision-makers will take, and insist on receiving at least their expected utility levels ex ante. With the exception of the 'public choice' approach summarized in Section 4, the founder (the vestige of the Marshallian entrepreneur) will choose to set up efficient structures in order to pre-commit herself and her delegates to use decision-making authority in ways that take account of the costs and benefits the decisions will confer.

This model of governance involves an 'ex ante' stage where market prices and contracts are formed, and an 'ex post' stage where actual decisions are made; see Williamson (1988) for more on this distinction. In technical terms, we focus on the subgame perfect equilibria of 'contracting' games, all of which share the following basic structure: First, the founder chooses the legal jurisdiction plus key elements of the firm's charter; then investors, workers, and all other relevant parties decide whether or not to participate; then workers and others may choose actions; then 'executives' (the founder's delegate) take some other action (e.g., decisions on investment and/or promotions); then nature resolves uncertainty and legally binding elements of any agreement are executed. With few exceptions, this model incorporates all the theories summarized in this paper (the exceptions are those in which nature reveals information to some parties earlier than to others, i.e., signalling models). No methodological advances beyond those surveyed in Hart and Holmstrom (1987) are involved. Indeed, a central message of this paper is that governance is an area where we can fruitfully apply techniques that have been well-known since the early 1980s. Governance is essentially a contracting problem with ex ante equilibration in expected utilities. Models of this type are far easier to solve than those often encountered in the new Industrial Organization (see, e.g., Tirole, 1988).

The specific form of the appropriate model is dictated by the particular problem at hand and by existing evidence. There is in fact a great deal of evidence available to guide theoretical models, even though many studies are themselves only loosely guided by modern theory (for example, Scharfstein, 1988, represents the sole published analytical model of the notion that takeovers serve to reduce agency problems between managers and shareholders!). The next section presents a picture of the causes and consequences of existing corporate governance structures from existing studies. It is necessarily interpretative and is meant to stimulate further research. The rather bald assertions we will make about the world are deliberately intended to suggest the type of theoretical and empirical work we think would be most valuable.

Our basic empirical contention is that most large firms are importantly 'managerial', in the sense that decisions are often *not* made in the interests of shareholders (who are at least legally the equivalent of Marshall's residual claimant entrepreneur). The separation of share ownership and firm control highlighted by Berle and Means in the early 1930s is real. Moreover, we believe that there are substantially greater departures from shareholder wealth-maximisation than is suggested by the costs of risk-aversion and monitoring stressed in the traditional principal–agent models. To use the jargon, the direct costs of reducing the degree to which many managers are 'entrenched' and 'insulated' from pressures to maximize shareholder wealth are not prohibitive. Many decisions heavily weight the interests of parties other than shareholders even though it would be relatively cheap to ensure a greater role for shareholders.

This assertion is quite controversial, particularly among Chicago-style economists, because its seems to imply that governance is inefficient and would be improved by government intervention (recall that Berle and Means, 1932, argued for a wide-spread socialisation of corporate assets). Our contention is that in a world of incomplete contracts there is no reason why management 'entrenchment' should be construed as inefficient. There is a useful analogy with what Williamson (1985) termed the "inhospitality tradition" in antitrust whereby business practices that did not confirm with textbook theory were immediately interpreted as monopolistic and counter to the public interest. The point, as the courts have come increasingly to recognize, is that businesses operating under conditions that differ from those in the textbooks must adopt practices that similarly differ from those in the textbooks, *in order to be efficient* (Coase, 1972). In a world of positive transaction costs, it is efficient for many firms to adopt practices that do not resemble textbook, arms-length transactions. By the same token, if the world of corporate governance were accurately depicted as a standard principal–agent problem involving only shareholders and a top manager, *then* the observed decoupling of managers' and shareholders' wealth would be inefficient. But if the principal–agent model is not an accurate depiction of a corporation, then the conclusion that current practice is inefficient is unwarranted.

Section 4 pursues this theme further. It summarizes theories that suggest that management entrenchment is efficient, and presents the alternative notion that governance is somehow sub-optimal by reference to recent 'public choice' accounts of corporate governance. The argument is that governance isn't efficient because the initial wishes of the founder have been superseded by managers who use the political process to effectively rewrite the rules in their favour. We conclude that both the efficiency and the public choice theories need further development before any empirical test can reliably distinguish between them. Both are provocative and indeed plausible, which argues all the more for further theoretical development and empirical tests.

As should be clear by now, governance is a complex and multi-faceted phenomenon. To assess the efficiency of alternative governance mechanisms and features one must focus on individual elements and limited comparisons. Some of the key issues that have been the subject of analysis and discussion are summarized in Section 5. The focus is on recent developments in the U.S. and on comparisons between governance systems in the U.S. and other 'Anglo-Saxon' countries as opposed to those in the successful post-war economies of Germany and Japan. Section 6 concludes by indicating specific areas for future research.

3. A picture of the typical corporation from existing research

This section summarizes recent empirical studies that shed light on the question of whether the typical large corporation is run mainly in shareholders' interests and, if not, in whose interests it is in fact run.

3.1. The facts, part one: How important are shareholders?

3.1.1. Top management compensation

A wealth of studies examine the correlation between top managers' wealth and various measures of financial performance. The best-known of the recent studies is Jensen and Murphy (1990), who conclude that the average US CEO receives less than five cents for every thousand dollar increase in shareholder wealth, even taking into account managerial stock holdings, options, and the linkage between the likelihood of dismissal and share price (see also Warner, Watts and Wruck, 1988).

Compounding the relatively weak linkage between managerial and shareholder wealth is the common finding that top executives' pay is approximately three times more sensitive to firm *size* (measured as total assets or sales) than to shareholder wealth. Murphy (1985) finds this correlation holds over time as well as cross-sectionally. This implies that the size-pay relationship is not simply due to large firms hiring more able executives, as suggested by Rosen (1982). Crystal (1991) provides an illuminating account of the tactics some compensation consultants adopt to justify raises for top management even in the face of weak and declining profit performance (see Byrne,

1992, for a summary of executives' counter-arguments). These sources provide a wealth of raw material for more systematic theoretical and empirical studies.

3.1.2. Reputation effects

The assumption that managers act in shareholder interests is not always justified by reference to their explicit financial incentives. Fama (1980) takes the extreme view that even if management compensation were formally unrelated to share price, top managers would still seek to maximize shareholder wealth in order to protect or enhance their reputations in the managerial labor market. Holmstrom (1982) shows that this conclusion is quite optimistic and that reputations will rarely reduce agency costs to zero. Gibbons and Murphy (1992) find evidence consistent with the conclusion that while reputations may go some way to aligning the interests of managers and shareholders, the effects are not overwhelmingly strong, particularly for managers near the end of their careers.

More recent theoretical research casts further doubt on the notion that reputational concerns drive managers to act in shareholder interests. Holmstrom and i Costa (1986) and others show how reputation can take the form of 'career concerns' that actually *encourage* managers to act counter to the interests of their shareholders; see Borland (1992) for a survey. A related weakness with the reputational story is that it must assume that *hiring* decisions are always made in the interests of shareholders. Reputation-induced distortions are far greater if an executive believes her future employers will be Berle-Means firms that are more interested in how much her talents will contribute to the utility of incumbent managers rather than their shareholders; see Hart (1983) for one model of the interaction between 'managerial' and profit-maximising firms.

3.1.3. The threat of takeover

One of the earliest commentators on the question of whether or not corporations were run in shareholder interests made no reference to managerial reputation and only passing reference to compensation. Manne (1965) argued that competition for the *votes* that are generally attached to equity shares, or the 'market for corporate control', was the most important force driving managers to maximize shareholder wealth. Certainly many takeovers in the 1980s bear out his view that gross managerial slack can be pruned by hostile takeovers or the threat thereof (see Agrawal and Walkling, 1991; Jensen, 1988; Martin and McConnell, 1991).

While the takeover threat is clearly a force that motivates managers to look after their shareholders, it has distinct limitations. First of all, hostile takeovers are rare in Germany and Japan (eg., Kester, 1991a,c). Even in the

US, regulatory developments and the chilling of the 'junk bond' market have substantially dampened the takeover market (see, e.g., Jensen, 1991). But even before these developments there were sizeable cost barriers to hostile takeovers that served to 'insulate' or even 'entrench' incumbent managers. Bradley, Desai and Kim (1988) report that successful buyers paid an average premium of 20–30 per cent over the pre-existing price and that some 'successful' bidders actually lost share value. While it would be an overstatement to claim that the market for corporate control actually exacerbates 'managerialism' on the part of acquirers (see Mitchell and Lehn, 1990), it is clear that the threat of hostile takeover places only broad limits on the degree to which managers can run the firm in the interests of parties other than shareholders.

3.1.4. Proxy fights and shareholder 'voice'

Shareholders do not, in principle, need to sell to hostile bidders in order to influence management policy. They can exercise their voting rights to elect a new slate of directors, or even in some cases to recommend explicit actions be taken by managers (see DeAngelo and DeAngelo, 1989, for some instances).

With the chilling of the corporate control market in the 1990s, many sizeable institutional shareholders such as CalPERS have attempted, sometimes successfully, to affect corporate decisions (e.g., Pound, 1992a). But those who would mount a challenge are at a severe disadvantage relative to management, not only in terms of their own knowledge of the corporation's real situation but also in terms of their ability to communicate with their fellow shareholders and to finance a campaign (Pound, 1991; Roe, 1990). Class action suits brought by shareholders are even less rewarding for the participants (Romano, 1991).

At present, large shareholders face enormous costs in influencing the behaviour of executives. While some commentators claim that this will change with the appearance of large pension funds and other potential 'relationship investors' able to exert a major influence over corporate policies (e.g., Taylor, 1990; Drucker, 1991), to date there is little systematic evidence of such a trend. While institutional investors have come to hold a substantial fraction of many firms' shares, the institutions are themselves large organizations and it is not at all clear that the managers of institutional funds will push corporate managers to maximize the wealth of the fund's beneficiaries. Lakonishok, Shleifer and Vishny (1992) argue that large pension funds tend to underperform the market, and Murphy and Van Nuys (1993) provide evidence that pension fund managers have little incentive to actively monitor the firms in which they invest. This suggests that the highly publicized incidents of institutional activism by shareholders such as CalPERS may be the exception rather than the rule.

3.1.5. Anecdotal evidence

The preceding sketch of available evidence has, of necessity, featured a great deal of interpretation. The importance of reputation and the threat of takeover are particularly difficult to identify in statistical studies. Given these ambiguities, softer evidence such as the views of those who advise top executives can make at least some contribution. While many statements that are flagrantly inconsistent with maximising shareholder wealth can be found in the popular press, we will focus on two that have appeared in mainstream finance journals.

The first observation is made by a practising corporate lawyer who was invited to comment on studies in a recent conference volume of the Journal of Financial Economics (Herzel, 1990). His comments focused on statistical studies aimed at discovering whether employee share ownership plans (ESOPs) and related devices are intended to increase shareholder wealth or protect management from takeover. Herzel (1990, p. 582) argues

.... that leveraged ESOPs are being used as an anti-takeover device should surprise no one. In fact, that is how investment bankers sell leveraged ESOPs to prospective clients.

Courts and everyone else involved understand that leveraged ESOPs are being used as an antitakeover device.

Herzel (1990) thus argues that courts uphold management actions that are explicitly recognized as aimed at defeating and deferring takeover bids, *not* at extracting a higher price for shareholders. Such explicit recognition of acts against shareholder interests became unfashionable in the 1980s, with most managers at least avowing that, despite appearances their actions were aimed at maximising shareholder wealth (see, e.g., the panel discussions in the *Continental Bank Journal of Applied Corporate Finance* (1991; 1992)). A refreshingly candid exception is provided by Prahalad (1993), whose work on management strategy is widely acknowledged as highly influential: [3]

... in the future, the scarce resource is not going to be capital but human talent. Shouldn't we now be using talent accumulation as one of our major criteria for judging corporate success....as we enter this new world of global competition, I think we will be forced to re-examine our theory of wealth creation and its assumption of the primacy of shareholder value.

---

[3] For example, Prahalad and Hamel (1990) was voted the most important article in the Harvard Business Review that year.

3.2. *The facts, part two: Do other constituencies matter?*

The idea that corporate managers do not always act in shareholder interests is not new. The obvious problem that confronts any 'managerial' model of corporate behaviour is to specify the alternative objective function that executives actually maximize. Alchian (1965) summarizes an earlier literature that posits alternative objectives for managers, including sales maximisation and consumption of 'perquisites'. The incomplete contracts approach suggests that a more explicitly 'political' view of corporate objectives is appropriate, since members of the firm besides shareholders are affected by executive decisions (see Meyer, Milgrom, and Roberts, 1992, for one theoretical treatment in this vein). We still have little theory or direct evidence that suggests how *effective* various 'stakeholders' are in influencing managerial decisions. This section summarizes recent evidence that sheds light on the relative influence of non-shareholder constituencies.

3.2.1. *The influence of senior claimants*

Early agency models focus either on the relationship between managers and shareholders, or assume that managers act in the interests of shareholders at the expense of bondholders (Jensen and Meckling, 1976; Myers, 1977). The key idea behind the latter class of models is that shareholders with limited liability receive 'up-side' gains to firm decisions while bondholders bear some of the 'down-side' losses. The attendant problems, known as 'asset substitution' and 'underinvestment', certainly do exist in cases such as the U.S. savings and loans associations that were protected by deposit insurance (Kane, 1989). But in most corporations, the key assumption that executives treat bankruptcy or financial distress lightly is both implausible and inconsistent with some new evidence. Gilson (1989) studies a large random sample of under-performing firms, of which only a fraction had sufficient debt in their capital structures to go into default. He finds that management turnover in the 'distressed' subsample is over 3 times as great as that in the 'solvent' subsample, even though losses borne by investors *as a whole* are similar in both subsamples. He also finds that neither top managers nor outside board members displaced by insolvency, subsequently found similar positions in listed firms. Lo Pucki and Whitford (1990) find that of the 43 large firms that entered bankruptcy proceedings during the period 1979–1988, 40 top managers lost their jobs by the time negotiations were completed. Gilson and Vetsuypens (1993) find that for 77 firms that suffered financial distress almost one-third of all CEOs are replaced and that those who keep their jobs usually experience large salary and bonus reductions. Newly appointed CEOs associated with previous management are generally paid 35 per cent less than the CEOs they replace while outside replacement CEOs are paid 36 per cent more.

While there are many important research issues raised by the problem of resolving financial distress (see Aghion, Hart and Moore, 1992, for a recent contribution and summary), we wish to stress the obvious implication for solvent firms. A key objective of the management of such firms must be to *avoid* financial distress and to ensure that creditors will in fact be paid. De Fusco, Johnson and Zorn (1990) find that the introduction of managerial *stock* option plans, which increase their share of up-side gains to asset substitution and underinvestment, increase equity prices but significantly *reduce* the wealth of bondholders. The obvious implication is that managerial incentives are 'naturally' aligned with those of *bondholders* in the absence of explicit incentive schemes to the contrary; see Coffee (1986) for more implications of this view.

3.2.2. *The influence of labor*

Statements to the effect that the interests of workers, or some subset thereof, are important to top managers are easy to find; the quote from Prahalad (1993) is only one example. The notion that greater pay for workers is somehow a 'good' to managers also appears in the early managerial theories surveyed in Alchian (1965). Jensen's (1986) idea that managers tend to overinvest is also partially justified on grounds that expanding the firm provides more top management positions into which favoured subordinates can be promoted. Brumagin (1991) reports intriguing evidence that is consistent with the general argument. He shows that large conglomerates that appear to operate in unrelated businesses according to traditional measures of *output* are in fact closely related if we focus on the use of similar labor skills (measured in terms of occupational categories). [4] Aoki (1988) argues that the tendency to invest "with labor in mind" is even more pronounced in large Japanese firms.

The presence of an 'inter-industry wage structure' in which workers at large firms and firms in concentrated industries receive higher pay (e.g. Krueger and Summers, 1988) is certainly consistent with the idea that workers exert a sizeable influence over management decisions. As Krueger and Summers (1988) stress, it is very difficult to construct 'efficiency-wage' stories that reconcile their findings with shareholder wealth maximisation.

Further evidence on the relative influence of workers and investors on management decisions is provided by DeAngelo and DeAngelo (1991) who document the effect of collective bargaining on dividend and investment policy, and by Bronars and Deere (1991) who find that unionized firms tend

[4] To be sure, this finding could also suggest that conglomerate mergers are sensible from an efficiency perspective; but see Bhagat, Shleifer, and Vishny (1990) on the dismantling of conglomerates.

to have more debt in their capital structures, arguably to pre-empt excessive union wage concessions by management.

3.3. Conclusion

The picture that emerges from this section is clearly one where top managers' decisions will not entirely neglect shareholder wealth. Compensation, dismissal through takeover or board action, and reputations are to some degree linked to share price. But the evidence also suggests that creditors (through the threat of distress) and some subset of workers also strongly affect management decisions.

The implicit theoretical lens used in most studies is the legal and economic model that assumes efficiency is monotonically increasing in the degree to which actions are made in shareholder interests. That is, shareholders are the only constituency that *should* matter. This view reflects the assumption that all other corporate constituencies receive fully specified contractual claims, or at least that shareholders are a decent approximation to the Marshallian residual claimant. We return to this assumption in the next section. The main argument here is that it is far easier to interpret the evidence as reflecting a world where managers have substantial leeway, at least ex post, to depart from maximising shareholder wealth. Moreover, *other* claimants appear to exert substantial influence over corporate policy choices. The next section is devoted to assessing the efficiency of this situation. If current arrangements are in fact efficient, then they serve to maximize the ex ante wealth of shareholders as well as society. If inefficient, then wealth is transferred from shareholders both ex ante and ex post and some reform of governance is warranted.

4. Theoretical models that are consistent with the facts

4.1. Wealth redistribution theories

4.1.1. Extracting rents from bidders

The potential conflict between managers' and shareholders' interests are thrown into stark relief when the firm receives an unsolicited tender offer. Managers often vigorously resist such transactions even through shareholder wealth is almost invariably increased by a successful takeover. It has been pointed out, however, that while resistance to takeovers certainly serves target managers' interests, it can also serve the interest of shareholders by inducing bidders to pay a higher premium. The most prominent versions of this argument are Stulz (1988), Gilson (1986), Shleifer and Vishny (1986), and Berkovitch and Khanna (1990).

While it is certainly true that refusing to accept a 'first' bid could, and sometimes does, cause the bidder to pay more or encourage other bidders to enter, it is difficult to accept the theory as a general explanation for the amount of resistance we observe. While early studies of takeover defenses found little effect on target shareholder wealth (eg., Bradley and Wakeman, 1983), more recent defenses, particularly those such as poison pills that do not require shareholder approval, have clearly harmed shareholders in many cases. Also, as Herzel (1990) points out, poison pills and ESOPs are often *explicitly* intended to reduce the probability of a successful bid, not to increase the product of the probability of a bid times the premium paid in successful bids. Much of the new 'activism' evidenced by shareholders such as CalPERS has been directed towards *revoking* 'poison pills', which, broadly speaking, refer to charter amendments that increase the cost of takeover and do not require a shareholder vote (Dobrynski, 1993). More systematically, Dann and De Angelo (1988) and Ryngaert (1988) both find that most poison pill and related defences reduce shareholder wealth.

There are also two theoretical problems with the 'extracting a high price from bidders' argument. First, the earlier models of takeover bids (Grossman and Hart, 1980), argued that, if left to their own devices, shareholders would be too *loath* to tender, rather than too anxious to tender as is assumed in the models summarized so far. Their model suggests that 'dilution' measures aimed at *reducing* the premium that target shareholders demand, would be wealth-increasing. While this conclusion is still not settled theoretically (see, e.g., Holmstrom and Nalebuff, 1992), Easterbrook and Fischel (1981) raise another objection that has particular relevance for a world of diversified shareholders. They point out that if a given investor holds shares of *both* the bidder and the target, she need not gain from defensive actions that extract a higher price from the bidder. This last problem is consistent with the fact that shareholders such as CalPERS who have sizeable stakes in *many* firms are the most active opponents of takeover defences.

4.1.2. Extracting rents from product market rivals

Another rationale for management entrenchment focuses on competition in product markets. The argument is that by pre-committing to a strategy that is more 'aggressive' than the one implied by profit-maximisation, a firm can pre-empt rivals and increase its profits (Sklivas, 1987; Fershtman and Judd, 1987). While the published studies have the appealing feature that managers' pay increases in firm size (as it appears to be in the real world), the result only holds if competition is in quantities. If competition is in prices, there is the counterfactual implication that managers' pay should *decrease* in firm size. Moreover, as Katz (1991) stresses, the models all rely on the assumption that the key parameters of management compensation are common knowledge among rivals. In addition, Fumas (1992) shows how paying managers according to their performance *relative* to rival firms provides effort incentives, insurance, and a *more* aggressive output market strategy than can be achieved by size-based pay. [5] More generally, the product-market explanations for managerial slack are subject to much the same problems encountered by strategic trade theory.

4.1.3. Public choice theories: Corporate managers as a powerful interest group

The last set of wealth redistribution theories drops the idea that managers extract rents from others on behalf of their shareholders. Rather, the argument is that top managers use the political and regulatory process to tip the scales in *their* favour, *against* the interests of their shareholders. The broad contours of the theory, outlined in Grundfest (1990), and Roe (1990), follow a straightforward public choice approach. Corporate managers are argued to represent a concentrated and organized interest group, that took advantage of an existing populist suspicion of 'bankers and financiers' in the 1930s to the 1970s, to effectively free themselves from control by their investors. Roe (1993a, p. 1234) asserts:

> ...one must look beyond economics to explain the American results: America's politics of financial fragmentation, rooted in federalism, populism, and interest group pressures, pulverised American financial institutions, contributing heavily to the rise of the Berle-Means corporation.

As is the case with many public choice accounts of regulation, the story is relatively plausible overall and provides a compelling explanation of certain regulations (such as some of the state-based legislation featured in the 'second wave' of antitakeover legislation in the late 1980's; see Karpoff and Malatesta, 1991, but also Jahera and Pugh, 1991).

At its current state of development, however, the argument also exhibits the characteristic weaknesses of public choice theories of regulation. First of all, the underlying determinants of 'political power' (e.g., ability to overcome free-rider problems) are often casually spelled out, leaving open the question of why 'managers' and other parties who might be harmed by takeovers should be a more coherent political group than large institutional shareholders (see Roe, 1993b, and the ensuing discussion). The theory also relies to some extent on a pre-existing 'public' animosity toward 'Wall Street' that is not obviously grounded in sound principles. Finally, the theory makes little headway in predicting the actual forms that 'pro-management' regulation will

[5] Indeed, if one firm is believed to pay its managers solely according to relative performance, its rivals' best response is to simply profit-maximise. This leaves the relative performance firm with Stackelberg leader profits!

take. To take a particularly anomalous example, Jensen and Murphy (1990) argue that the political process places inefficiently *tight* constraints on top management compensation. It is argued that politics and 'the media' make it impossible for corporations to pay large sums of money to managers who perform superlatively well. No straightforward model of maximising behaviour would suggest that managers prefer insulation from takeovers to receiving immense personal wealth, and of course if managers are truly powerful they need not even strike a trade-off. Despite these lacunae, there is little doubt that the public choice approach to finance has much to contribute to our understanding of real-world corporate governance, and represents a fertile field for more careful and focused theoretical and empirical work.

4.2. Efficiency theories

The explanations sketched in section 4.2.1 all explained existing corporate governance and management objectives in terms of wealth-redistribution. We now turn to theories which suggest that the existing suppression of shareholder interests is efficient.

4.2.1. Direct monitoring cost explanation

The first explanation is essentially tautological: it *must* be too costly to align the interests of managers and shareholders more closely. Principal–agent theory directs our attention to the costs of having managers rather than diversified shareholders bear risk. As Baker, Jensen, and Murphy (1988) stress, the standard principal–agent model of, e.g., Holmstrom (1979) is unfortunately imprecise in its prediction about the *degree* to which managers' pay should be linked to shareholder wealth. The predictions of the model depend on the precise nature of managerial risk-preferences as well as the statistical association between profits and executive 'effort'. We now turn to theories that explicitly incorporate distinctive features of the corporate environment for more precise guidance.

4.2.2. Measurement problems

One explanation for why managers' objectives are not more closely aligned with those of shareholders refines the popular notion that stock prices reflect "short-term" interests and represent a misleading guide to managerial behaviour. The general contention is that managers who are solely concerned with their firm's stock price would take inefficient actions aimed at increasing this price. While this argument is often based on the dubious notion that equities are systematically mis-priced, it need not be. The basic insight is that investors are interested in predicting the future dividends the company will pay, and *not* with providing the most accurate possible signal of managerial effort or efficiency. Paul (1992) provides a host of examples (and references) in which managers who are paid solely according to share price will inefficiently allocate their effort and time, both between different projects and between effort and leisure. These models help rationalize the weak observed linkage between share price and managerial wealth, and also the use of accounting numbers as performance indicators even when the stock market efficiently prices corporate assets.

These studies have provided important insights and indeed may have gone nearly as far as is possible within the basic principal–agent framework. We now turn to theories that explicitly recognize that the corporation's productive actions are not taken by a single top manager, but rather by a hierarchy of employees and suppliers.

4.2.3. Models of the large corporation

To the lay person, the notion that corporations should be run in the interests of shareholders seems odd: don't other investors, workers, suppliers, and local communities have a legitimate 'voice'? Fama (1990) points out that 90% of the cashflows of the average U.S. corporation go to parties other than shareholders. The argument from traditional corporate finance, of course, is that this confuses totals and margins; the remaining 10% of cash-flows are the risky ones and those that are affected by effort choices. But as mentioned before, this effectively assumes a world of complete contracts: when contracts are incomplete residual claimant status is a matter of degree and is not restricted to shareholders. In such a world it pays to pre-commit to take account of such interests ex ante. Brander and Poitevin (1992) and John and John (1992) focus on debtholders and show how the 'low-powered' incentive schemes documented by Jensen and Murphy (1990) can be optimal.

Shleifer and Summers (1988) focus on long-term employees and suppliers in the context of hostile takeovers, which they portray as an event that reasserts the interests of shareholders to a degree *not* contemplated in the original contract. There is some evidence in favour of the Shleifer–Summers view of takeovers; see particularly Ippolito and James' (1992) and Petersen's (1992) studies of the effect of hostile takeovers and management buyouts on non-vested employee pensions. But it is also clear that wealth transfers from employees do not explain the premium paid in most hostile takeovers (see, e.g., Palepu, 1990).

The Shleifer–Summers (1988) argument is also questionable on a priori grounds. Holmstrom (1988) points out that the argument *assumes* that entrenched managers will strike efficient trade-offs in updating incomplete contracts, simply because they are insulated from shareholder demands. Garvey and Gaston (1991) present some evidence that Shleifer and Summers' (1988) leap of faith may in fact be justified, at least for employees. They find that earnings growth and non-vested pensions are significantly negatively related to the concentration of institutional shareholdings in a small sample of Australian firms. Lazear (1979) shows how growth in earnings as well as non-vested pensions constitute an incentive scheme for employees that requires them to 'trust' the firm to dismiss them only if they do not perform. Garvey and Gaston (1991) find that such schemes are more prevalent in diffusely held, 'managerial' firms. [6] In addition to the problems of small sample size and highly imperfect proxies for ownership, however, Garvey and Gaston's (1991) study also fails to identify *why* managerial firms appear to behave in a more 'trustworthy' fashion towards their labor force.

One key issue that is raised by the Shleifer–Summers argument is that the incentives and decisions of top managers are important to employees as well as shareholders. The idea that "management" may involve more than simply exerting "effort" or choosing investment projects was confronted in early attempts to apply the principal–agent model to the manager–shareholder relationship. Diamond and Verrecchia (1982) recognized:

It is probably inaccurate to model all of a firm's employees as agents directly for the stockholders. This is because information on which most employees' compensation is based is not observed by stockholders but rather by their direct supervisors. That is, most firms have a hierarchical structure. Much of the information relevant for supervised employees is observed only within the firm. Incentive schemes for supervised employees should be designed using information produced internally by the firm. This however merely shifts the problem back one level, as someone within the firm must construct the incentives for its employees. How this someone makes these decisions depends on his incentives.

Despite this recognition, Diamond and Verrecchia (1982), and other papers that followed, effectively assumed that designing and implementing an incentive scheme for subordinates was formally identical to that of exerting costly effort. Demski and Sappington (1992) show that this presumption is generally incorrect. They focus on the key problem of inducing a manager to truthfully announce his private information about a subordinate's action. Assuming that the manager is a risk-neutral, 100% residual claimant (and, therefore, a perfect agent of stockholders!), they show that it is generally impossible to design an incentive-compatible contract. The reason is that by announcing high effort on the part of subordinates the manager reduces his wealth. Hence the manager always has an incentive to under-report effort.

Prendergast and Topel (1993) stress the related but more general problem of biased supervision ratings, and point out that it might be valuable for the

[6] Management shareholdings are essentially zero in their sample.

manager *not* to be a residual claimant. [7] Garvey and Swan (1992a) show that, in fact, it is optimal for the 'manager of a subordinate' to be completely unconcerned with shareholder wealth, to have some propensity to transfer wealth to the subordinate, and to face a large penalty in the event of default on a moderate fixed financial claim. The intuition is that by performing well, the subordinate gives his superior some 'slack' which can be used for higher compensation, whereas by performing badly he backs his superior 'against a wall' and forces her to be stingy. This mechanism requires default to be costly for the top manager and also for her to use her 'breathing space' to reward her employees more generously. The model is consistent with the evidence documented in Section 3, and is extended to a multi-layered hierarchy in Garvey and Swan (1992b). It also endogenizes the view of managerial incentives featured in important work on capital structure by Grossman and Hart (1982) and Hart (1993).

A weakness of the theory is that it proves too much; it is optimal for shareholders to be completely passive and for managers to be fully entrenched. Garvey and Swan (1993) show how shareholders are 're-admitted' to an active role by making the model more 'dynamic' in the sense that the firm's performance can be affected by random shocks that, from the top manager's point of view, mimic good subordinate performance. Hence, for example, if an investment turns out well then subordinates know that the CEO 'already has' breathing space and they need not work as hard to secure their rewards. This leads to a situation analogous to Jensen's (1986) notion of free cash flow, without having to rely on exogenously imposed inefficiencies in management compensation. Rather, inefficient executive behaviour can naturally develop in an ex ante optimal world, and is redressed by the threat of takeover or shareholder activism. The intuition from the static model remains, however, and implies that there should be substantial, but not prohibitive, cost barriers to hostile takeover.

4.3. Assessment of the various theories

The common theme in all the models of this section is the recognition that shareholders are not identical to the Marshallian entrepreneur, a 100 per cent residual claimant surrounded by competitive input and output markets and completely specified contracts. Theories that stress extraction of rents from bidders or product market rivals rely on specific departures from

[7] They also summarise ways in which the internal labour market can be designed to reduce the problem of morally hazardous evaluations; see Malcolmson (1984) and Prendergast (1993) on this issue. We focus on the role of governance and endogenous management objectives.

perfect competition. These stories have received the bulk of attention in recent years, but we suspect that this will not be the case in the future. The public choice approach is, to us, the most promising of the wealth-redistribution approaches. This state of affairs is surely due, in part, to the novelty and undeveloped nature of the theory. We also suspect it has a substantial empirical relevance, a suspicion that could be tested with more careful identification of the precise conditions under which managers will be a powerful interest group.

The efficiency theories, we suspect, have at least as great empirical relevance. This view reflects, in part, a faith in the power of competition between institutional forms which tends to select out those that are mainly associated with rent-seeking. We have argued that a great deal of evidence that apparently suggests inefficiency in governance is in fact perfectly consistent with a world where the major task of managers is to administer labor contracts (to 'manage human resources'). A more convincing case would involve drawing out the empirical implications of the efficiency versus the rent-seeking approaches in the context of a particular institutional feature (such as board composition, state of incorporation, voting status of equity shares, or structure of internal labor and capital markets) or key corporate decision (such as adoption of antitakeover measures, setting of compensation policy, etc.).

The remaining two sections address these issues through differences in governance between countries and over time, and then by identifying specific areas most promising for future research.

5. Selected topics

5.1. International differences: The Japanese / German model

It is now common to distinguish between two distinct governance systems for large corporations in developed economies: the Anglo-American type and the Japanese-German type (Aoki, 1992, p. 44; The Economist, 1994, pp. S5–S11). Some argue that the Anglo-American form is dominated by shareholder interests through the market for corporate control (takeovers), boards of directors and direct intervention by large stockholders. This view has recently been questioned by Roe (1993a) who believes that managers control the reins of power because stock is diffusely held by individuals and institutions. By contrast, in the Japanese-German form the large block of stable shareholding by financial institutions (the main bank system, Sheard, 1989) and interlocking shareholding (Sheard, 1991) effectively prevent hostile takeovers and hence appears to give very little weight to the average shareholder. Nonetheless, as Roe (1993a) points out, senior managers in Japan and Germany are not all-powerful. Power is shared between managers and active financial intermediaries. Ownership of corporations does not appear to be more concentrated in Japan than in the United States but the composition of ownership is different with much greater ownership by banks in Japan (Kester, 1986).

German corporations also have a large proportion of their shares held by large banks and other stable shareholders. While the individual shareholder may be effectively locked out in Japan and Germany, both the worker (Aoki, 1992) and debtholder combined with the institutional shareholder (main bank) exercise considerable voice. Suppression of individual shareholder voice is associated with main bank control within a Keiretsu-grouping of Japanese firms (Kester, 1991b) and similarly in Germany for firms with strong relational banking links (Kester, 1992). In Germany, there is also evidence to suggest that bank involvement adds significantly to firm financial performance (Cable, 1985).

Traditional explanations for the success of the Japanese main bank system stress that financial intermediaries such as banks can serve a monitoring role and provide a substitute for the external capital market and the market for corporate control (Stiglitz, 1985; Sheard, 1989). The main bank controls both equity and debt and its influence helps to overcome the free-riding problem that confronts small shareholders and creditors. The bank not only has an incentive to monitor but can obtain access to the firm's information and internal decision making which is more difficult for participants in the external capital market (Sheard, 1989, p. 403).

While this informational-based argument sounds plausible, it is not obvious why this role should be played by banks rather than by large investors who hold only equity. For example, why could not conglomerates provide an internal capital market just as efficiently? Moreover, if conglomerates can fulfil this role efficiently why were so many conglomerates broken up during the wave of management buyouts in the 1980's in the United States?

The monitoring argument presents an additional puzzle. A large financial intermediary such as a main bank is hardly an individual person for whom, by assumption, there are no 'agency costs' of making decisions. A bank is subject to all the same internal monitoring, informational and control problems as the corporations it is supposed to be monitoring. Who effectively monitors the main banks? Hence the problem is simply pushed back one level. This suggests there may be some more fundamental explanation for the success of main banks, related more to their particular rights they exercise than to any explanation based on the assumption that they are more effective monitors in an absolute sense.

Another more cogent explanation links investor monitoring to the operation of internal labor markets in Japan and Germany. There is evidence from Japan that workers can expect to be employed with one firm for a much longer period than is the case in the United States (Hashimoto, 1989, p. 249). The employment relationship is a long-term implicit contract to an even greater degree than in the Anglo-American model. While lifetime employment with a single firm in Japan may be restricted to large, highly successful firms and a myth for the average worker, it is much closer to the truth than in the United States.

Important differences in the internal labor market are also reflected in the age-earnings profile. Over his career with the firm, a typical Japanese worker will experience a much greater rise in earnings than will the United States worker (Hashimoto, 1989, pp. 255–256). This rising age-earnings profile in Japan is more closely associated with firm-specific experience than overall experience, whereas the reverse is the case in the United States.

A rising age-earnings profile may be associated with underpayment of workers when they are young, relative to marginal product and overpayment in later years, given that productivity will not always continue to rise with age. Compensation which is deferred in this way means that employees are rewarded *after* their efforts have been made, but there is no contractual obligation on the part of the firm to identify and subsequently reward superior performance and hence the 'contract' is implicit rather than explicit (Becker and Stigler, 1974; Lazear, 1979).

Alternatively, a rising age-earnings profile may reflect rising productivity levels as workers within the firm invest in firm-specific skills. Since these skills are firm-specific, workers can not expect to get higher wages outside. Yet workers will not invest themselves in firm-specific training unless they are rewarded by higher wages. Hence the firm-specific capital and effort stories are almost identical (Kanemoto and MacLeod, 1991).

It is generally impossible for courts other outsiders to observe either the degree of past contributions by workers, or enhanced current contributions due to costs the worker has incurred in undertaking firm-specific investments. In the Marshallian firm in which the employer or 'boss' is the residual claimant, there is a strong incentive to understate the worker's past or present performance to reduce the wage or 'bonus' bill and increase profitability. The employer may refuse to pay the promised 'deferred compensation', the employee who has incurred firm-specific training costs may receive only the lower wage that other firms may offer. Unless outsiders know exactly what transpired, the employer's reputation will not be much tarnished by such behaviour. This makes reputational explanations somewhat doubtful.

One way in which the Marshallian firm could commit not to cheat performing workers who have sunk their effort or incurred firm-specific training costs is to commit to a fixed total wage bill to be allocated according to relative performance (Malcolmson, 1984). Since it is generally difficult, if not impossible, for a manager to observe helping assistance that one worker provides to another, relative performance evaluation based on a rank-order tournament between workers will have the severe drawback that cooperative helping behaviour will be discouraged and active sabotage of co-workers even encouraged. A partial solution to this problem is a narrowing of the difference between the winner's prize and loser's prize (Lazear, 1989). Such wage compression will clearly reduce individual effort incentives since in the limit a flat wage is paid irrespective of relative or absolute performance.

Relative performance evaluation is therefore most appropriate when agents are separate so that there is little opportunity for harmful interaction such as sabotage or for mutual helping. Thus unless interactions between firms are important as with attempts to maintain a cartel, it would seem likely that relative performance evaluation would be used in chief executive officer (CEO) compensation and this tends to be borne out in empirical work (Antle and Smith, 1986; Gibbons and Murphy, 1990).

However, Japanese firms employ a tournament system which extends throughout the hierarchy, with each worker assigned a well-defined grade and rank (Aoki, 1988; Kanemoto and MacLeod, 1991, p. 165). By contrast to the Anglo-American model in which workers are assigned to jobs, in Japan both rank and pay are independent of the current job. Depending on both seniority and performance, the Japanese worker's income increases as he moves up the promotional ladder. The coexistence of lifetime internal promotional tournaments in Japan with and extensive cooperation, teamwork and helping (Kanemoto and Macleod, 1991, p. 166) certainly presents a puzzle given Lazear's (1989) demonstration that relative performance evaluation encourages outright sabotage.

An important clue to the reconciliation of extensive helping behaviour with promotional tournaments is provided in a field study by Kester (1991a, p. 92) who finds evidence of a link between the financial and employment policies of large Japanese firms:

> Maintaining substantial cash balances may have been a means of making credible a company's commitment to implicit contracts with some of its major stakeholders. The promises of lifetime employment and future retirement benefits are good examples. When queried about why so much cash and marketable securities were being held, managers in the field sample most frequently cited labor considerations. As one manager put it, 'If we began paying out the cash as dividends, the employees would probably become angry and frightened. 'You are spending our future,' they would say. 'Why are you draining the company of funds rather than keeping it inside and securing our welfare?' I am sure their concerns would ultimately prevent us from giving the cash to shareholders.

Garvey and Swan (1992c) draw on this link between retained cash and corporate governance more generally on one hand, and internal labor markets on the other, to propose a hybrid system made up of a labor market tournament and a group performance bonus implemented by a manager who has no concern for share price. The manager is, however, concerned with avoiding both pay inequality and financial distress. Concern with the former leads to pay compression and hence greater efficiency when helping is important. The concern for debtholders due to costs the manager bears in bankruptcy encourages a group bonus which increases when the worker-team performs better and hence the threat of bankruptcy has been reduced. This hybrid scheme dominates the pure tournament when helping is important. The model is thus consistent with those set out in Section 4.2.3 above in which there is an efficiency explanation for manager concerns with constituencies other than shareholders.

The Japanese corporate governance system seems to be extreme in terms of suppressing the linkage between shareholder rewards and bonuses to managers. While some senior managers in Japanese firms hold equity in their employer, officers are prohibited from owning stock options. Furthermore, while managers' bonuses are often withheld if dividends are not maintained, bonuses are not increased when dividends are raised (Kester, 1986, p. 15).

Garvey and Swan (1992d) build an explicit model of the Japanese corporation which rationalizes these features of Japanese firms. A hybrid incentive scheme with both tournament-based worker compensation and a group piece-rate can only be implemented by having managers give weight to employee and debtholder interests. Any weight to shareholder interests must be outweighed by that given to debtholder interests. The model also implies that shareholdings should be relatively diffuse and takeovers quite difficult so that shareholders cannot intervene to extract cash which is retained to reward performing subordinates.

The predictions of this model are borne out by the Japanese main bank interventions documented in Sheard (1989) which occur only in the event of financial distress and by Aoki (1990) who observes that the power of Japanese banks only becomes visible in bad states.

The model also predicts that the hybrid scheme is most beneficial when helping is important and where workers are organized into relatively small teams. The free-riding problem becomes more severe for larger teams. Once again, such small teams of between three and ten workers with relatively homogenous membership (Hashimoto, 1989, p. 276) are prevalent within the Japanese corporation.

In the incentive design literature alternatives to rank-order tournaments have been considered when cooperation is required. One response is to make agents jointly responsible for output so that a group piece rate is used to encourage cooperation. [8] This approach is similar to Garvey and Swan (1992b) but without the labor tournament and debt mechanism.

5.2. Developments in the United States

Some commentators infer that the separation of ownership and control documented in Section 3 is so inefficient that the corporation will sharply decline in importance. Jensen (1989) asserts that the massive changes observed in the United States economy in the 1980's with takeovers, corporate breakups, divisional spinoffs, leveraged buyouts, and going private transactions, spell the eclipse of the public corporation. The basic cause, he asserts, is conflict between shareholders and managers over the control and use of resources.

In Jensen's (1986) framework the manager makes investment decisions on behalf of shareholders. Where internally generated cash flows are excessive and external investment prospects poor, managers interested in self-aggrandizement will invest nonetheless. The classic case of these problems was the United States oil industry which benefited from a tenfold increase in oil prices from 1973 to 1981 but had very little prospect of major new oil discoveries. The solution, according to Jensen (1986) is increased leverage to force managers to pay out excessive cash flows as interest payments rather than reinvest cash in value-destroying projects.

The problem with tying the hands of the manager by denying her cash is that ex ante it is not always obvious that investment prospects are so poor. Excessive debt will kill good prospects as well as poor prospects (Stultz, 1990; Hart and Moore, 1990). In fact, if the problem of corporate governance were simply to encourage managers to make good investment decisions, the solution would be relatively simple: either 'sell' the corporation to management so that at the margin the manager suffers the same loss of wealth as the shareholder should the manager invest where prospects are poor, or at least ensure maximal exposure to the takeover market. The Marshallian firm, rather than the highly leveraged "junk-bond" financed firm, reasserts itself as the solution to Jensen's free-cash-flow problem. Of course there are limits to such links between manager and shareholder wealth, depending on the manager's wealth, degree of risk aversion, etc. As was noted in Section 3.1.1

[8] In the principal–agent model of Holmstrom and Milgrom (1991), free-riding behaviour does not make it optimal to use joint responsibility or 'induced cooperation'. As in Garvey and Swan (1992a), the benefits of a group piece-rate diminish in large teams. Itoh (1992) assumes that a little bit of helping is relatively costless at the margin, and shows that joint responsibility is more likely to be optimal when agents must interact with each other, as they are less risk averse, and as there is less correlation between performance measurement errors. See Aoki (1992) for a more extensive survey of these and related features of the internal structure of the enterprise.

above, the observed linkage of managerial rewards to that of the shareholder is too weak to overcome Jensen's 'free-cash-flow' problem.

There is an alternative explanation for what Jensen (1989) calls the conventional model of corporate governance with a moderate debt level and without manager income being tied to shareholder income. The role of the CEO is not exclusively to make investment decisions, but rather to manage an internal labor market (Garvey and Swan, 1992a, 1992b). The capital and governance structure of the organisation is just as much about managing the human capital in the hierarchy as it is about making investment decisions and hence managing physical capital. The more important is activity lower down in the hierarchy relative to the entrepreneurial efforts of the CEO, the less onerous should be the debt level (Garvey and Swan, 1992a). That is, large hierarchical organisations should be 'blue chip'. This is because a high risk of default in such an organisation places an excessive 'bonus squeeze' on subordinates lower down in the organisation.

Despite these criticisms, Jensen (1986, 1989) seems to have accurately described the behaviour of 'cashed up' oil companies in the post 1973 period. While some degree of management entrenchment may be optimal, takeover barriers should not be prohibitive (Garvey and Swan, 1993). To stave off takeover oil companies would have had to disgorge cash to shareholders in the form of dividends or share repurchase and this would have tended to restore debt-equity ratios prior to what they were before the oil price increases. This ultimately happened but with a considerable lag. The implicit contracts story in Garvey and Swan (1993) provides one rationalisation of Jensen's free-cash-flow mechanism.

Additional support for the role of creditors as a means of disciplining management is provided by Maloney, McCormick and Mitchell (1993) who find that a favorable share price reaction to acquirers at merger announcement is positively associated with the leverage of the acquiring firm. Firms which restructure by increasing leverage also improve their acquisition performance.

Rappaport (1990) believes that the corporation will survive but the ultimate salvation is management compensation linked to shareholder value. Once again, such links restore the Marshallian firm but at the expense of sunk efforts by labor within the hierarchy who will rightly fear that their future rewards are threatened.

Perhaps more damaging to Jensen's belief that the public corporation will be eclipsed is the finding that the percentage of leveraged buyouts returning to public ownership increases over time, with LBOs remaining private for a medium time of 6.82 years (Kaplan, 1991). Hence LBOs may simply be a transitional phenomenon (see also Bhagat, Shleifer and Vishny, 1990). An interesting empirical question for future research is whether these recorporatised LBOs correspond more to Rappaport's (1990) model with management compensation tied to shareholder value or whether management interests are linked instead to labor and debtholders as in the Japanese model.

5.3. Composition and effectiveness of boards of directors

The basic findings about board composition are not at all surprising: poor stock returns lead to the departure of insiders on the board and as the CEO nears retirement insiders also leave the board. Presumably as the winning candidate is announced, the losing candidates depart. Moreover, insiders are added shortly before the CEO retires, presumably as part of a grooming period. Outsiders are more likely to be added when the CEO is newly appointed and after poor performance (Hermalin and Weisbach, 1988).

What is more controversial are the possible reasons for the departure of insiders and adding of outsiders following poor performance. Is there a monitoring explanation with outsiders disciplining poor performance, or is the advice and council of outsiders more valuable when the insiders, who are presumably more influential in decision making, are not getting it right?

The most visible monitoring role of the board is the removal of an under-performing CEO. The probability of a US CEO's departure is in fact positively influenced by poor stock performance. Moreover, board type appears to have some influence on the board's response to poor stock price performance. The responsiveness of the removal decision to poor stock performance is three times as large for outside boards, that is, for boards with more than 60 per cent outsiders (Weisbach, 1988, p. 441). However, the statistical significance of the difference is relatively small, as is the absolute relation (Warner, Smith and Wruck, 1988). When accounting earnings are used as the measure of performance, there is a statistically significant effect for outside boards but not for inside boards. This evidence is consistent with outside directors undertaking more monitoring of the CEOs performance than inside directors. An alternative explanation is that powerful CEOs appoint internal boards while weaker CEOs must appoint mainly outside boards. Nonetheless, the favourable share price reaction to replacement of the CEO following poor performance is significant only for outside boards. Thus outside boards appear to displace the CEO more effectively than inside or mixed boards (Weisbach, 1988, pp. 458–9).

More recent studies have made a distinction between 'independent' outside directors and 'affiliated' outside directors (Byrd and Hickman, 1992). Affiliated outsiders have links with insiders, including legal, banking and consulting relationships. For example, one study of the independence of audit committees found that over 25 per cent of firms sampled had committees dominated by affiliated outsiders rather than by independent outsiders. A study by Byrd and Hickman (1993) found that the share market response to bidding companies announcing tender offers was slightly more favourable for boards with independent directors compared with other boards. Independent boards also tend to pursue proportionately smaller firms and offer lower premiums.

Recent surveys of the academic literature on the impact of executive compensation on investment decisions by boards and executives (see Jarrell, 1993; Gibbons and Murphy, 1992) tend to be more optimistic that these schemes are structured sensibly to achieve efficient outcomes than is suggested by the popular critique (for example, Crystal, 1991). But as Jensen and Murphy (1990) stress, the effect is small.

5.4. Managers, institutional investors and employees as owners

Jensen and Meckling (1976) posit the shareholder as principal and manager as agent. So long as property rights to wealth creation within the internal labor market are perfectly defined, maximising the wealth of the residual claimant, the shareholder, will optimize the total wealth generated by the corporation. Since costs of self-aggrandizement and other forms of 'shirking' by managers will be borne by shareholders, the more closely are the interests of managers and shareholders aligned, the greater should be the value of the corporation. Hence the greater the share of the corporation owned by insiders such as board members, the higher should be its value.

While this alignment-of-interests hypothesis predicts an increasing relationship between management shareholdings and value, an alternative approach, the 'entrenchment' hypothesis, posits that managers may be able to control a company and hence prevent hostile takeovers without necessarily having a sizeable equity stake. For example, Malatesta and Walkling (1988) find in their sample of poison-pill introductions which decreased share value that shareholdings by insiders was below the industry average in 83 per cent of cases. Stultz (1988) and others have attempted to rationalize some of the conflicting evidence around the entrenchment hypothesis by utilising a rent-extraction-from-bidders explanation for entrenchment (see Section 4.1.1 above).

Virtually all the studies which attempt to examine the effect of ownership structure measure performance as Tobin's Q, the ratio of the market value of assets to replacement cost. Morck et al. (1988b) estimate a piecewise-linear regression between board ownership and Tobin's Q for a sample of 371 Fortune 500 firms. Performance increases sharply initially until ownership reaches 5 per cent. Performance then declines until ownership reaches 25 per cent and then increases to in excess of 80 per cent holdings. The initial sharp rise in Tobin's Q may simply reflect shares allocated to the management of highly performing companies. While Morck et al. (1988b) rationalize the range of declining performance as being due to management entrenchment, this explanation has the odd implication that firm performance can be reliably improved simply by reducing board ownership. Moreover, the Japanese-German model of corporate governance gives rise to management entrenchment but this is usually associated with above average firm performance. McConnell and Servaes (1990) include the impact of institutional and blockholder investors on Tobin's Q and this tends to push up the maximum point that inside ownership contributes to value. Craswell, Saywell and Taylor (1993), using a sample of Australian firms, test the kind of relationships found by Morck et al. (1988b) and predicted by Stultz (1988). No unambiguous support is found for insider ownership or institutional ownership as determinants of firm value.

Smith and Watts (1992) find a relationship between the opportunities that a firm has and its governance structure and policies. In particular, firms with more growth options (essentially higher Tobin Qs) have lower debt to equity ratios, lower dividend yields, higher executive compensation, and make greater use of stock option plans. These findings are consistent with Jensen (1986) in that it would appear that firms with better investment prospects rely more on internal equity funding. One of the problems here is that such firms are likely to have had greater past success and, given the reluctance of managers to bear the risk of financial distress due to debt, lower debt levels are not surprising. Moreover, larger firms have both higher dividend yields and executive compensation. Results of this sort suggest that a 'horses for courses' approach may be beneficial in which the circumstances of each firm affect its governance structure and board structure, etc.

The introduction of employee stock ownership plans (ESOPs) appears to give rise to adverse share price movements when used as a device to stave off hostile takeover threats (Gordon and Pound, 1990; Chang and Mayers, 1992). Its effects are similar to the issuance of dual-class shares in that management is able to increase voting rights while not increasing its cash-flow claims. Chang and Mayers (1992) find that ESOPs are most likely to increase shareholder wealth when managers initially control between 10 and 20 per cent of the firm's shares. While the authors interpret this finding as evidence in support of Stultz's (1988) rent-extraction hypothesis, it is also consistent with the better operation of the internal labor market. The adverse share price reaction for firms subject to the immediate threat of hostile takeover may reflect the short-term interest that shareholders have in extracting quasi-rents from the internal labor market. Cash retained to reward performing managers and workers can no longer be extracted by the raider. While there would appear to be scope here for more empirical work to sort out these effects, it would probably be of still greater value to carefully isolate the testable implications of the various theories.

6. Directions for future research

The central contention of this survey is that corporate governance cannot be understood in a world where property rights are perfectly defined, so that shareholders, as the residual claimants, represent the only group worthy of consideration. Only when contracts are incomplete do the problems of management and governance become interesting, but as a consequence shareholders are no longer true residual claimants.

Recent developments in our understanding of corporate governance pose a familiar puzzle from the economics of regulation: do unexpected features of observed corporate governance arrangements reflect rent-seeking behaviour or is there an efficiency rationale? The relatively extensive empirical work in this area to date has only loosely, if at all, been driven by theory. Partly this is the fault of the theory in that very few propositions have been developed to a testable stage. What we can normally observe presumably represents an equilibrium in which each organisation has adjusted to its circumstances. The challenge is to pinpoint the key features of a firm's environment and the specific effect that the environment is expected to have on governance structures.

In a free-market firms may have adjusted such that their corporate governance structure is ideal given their individual circumstances. Thus, for example, if each firm is optimising and Tobin's Q is a performance measure, every firm should have the same Tobin's Q. Perhaps the reason that they differ so much is because Tobin's Q is measuring something else, for example, the ratio of intangible to tangible assets. Hence to use Tobin's Q in studies of optimum ownership must imply a disequilibrium theory in which ownership structure is far from being optimal.

If the methods at our disposal are inadequate to deal with an equilibrium theory, then we may be forced to rely more on 'events' and natural experiments such as in Pound (1992b). In this instance the event consisted of a new law that imposed severe new requirements on hostile bidders but at the same time enabled potential targets to opt out of protection from hostile raiders. In the process information was revealed about the characteristics of firms choosing to opt out relative to those that prefer the new status quo.

Clearly, however, such natural experiments are scarce. Some of the new and exciting areas opened up for empirical research by recent developments include the relationship between the capital structure of firms and implicit contracts which may link their governance structure with their internal labor market. Some fascinating recent empirical research (Lazear, 1992; Baker, Gibbs and Holmstrom, 1993) makes use of individual company records providing details of their internal labor markets. Future work should focus on characterizing the internal labor markets of multiple companies with varying circumstances, and presumably appropriate governance features.

References

Advice and Dissent, 1991, Rating the corporate governance compact, Harvard Business Review, Nov.–Dec., 136–43.

Aghion, P., O. Hart and J. Moore, 1992, The Economics of Bankruptcy Reform, Journal of Law, Economics, and Organization, 8, 523–46.

Agrawal, A. and R. Walkling, 1991, Ex post settling up: The effect of acquisition bids on executive turnover and compensation, Working Paper, Ohio State University Graduate School of Business.

Alchian, A., 1965, The basis of some recent advances in the theory of management of the firm, Journal of Industrial Economics, 7, 30–41.

Alchian, A. and H. Demsetz, 1972, Production, information costs, and economic organization, American Economic Review, 62, 777–95.

Antle, R., and A. Smith 1986, An empirical investigation of the relative performance evaluation of corporate executives, Journal of Accounting Research, 24, 1–39.

Aoki, M., 1988, Information, Incentives, and Bargaining in the Japanese Economy, Cambridge University Press, Cambridge, U.K.

Aoki, M., 1992, The internal structure of the enterprise: A partial survey from comparative perspective, invited paper, session on the Internal Structure of the Enterprise, IEA Tenth World Congress, Moscow.

Arrow, K. and G. Debreu, 1954, Existence of an equilibrium for a competitive economy, Econometrica, 22, 265–90.

Baker, G., M. Gibbs and B. Holmstrom 1993, Hierarchies and compensation: A case study, European Economic Review, 37, 366–78.

Baker, G., M.C. Jensen and K.J. Murphy, 1988, Compensation and incentives: practice vs. theory, Journal of Finance, 43, 593–616.

Berkovitch, E. and N. Khanna, 1990, How target shareholders benefit from value-reducing defensive strategies in takeovers, Journal of Finance, 45, 673–91.

Berle, A. and G.C. Means, 1932, The Modern Corporation and Private Property, Macmillan, New York.

Bhagat, S., A. Shleifer and R. Vishny 1990, Hostile takeovers in the 1980's: the return to corporate specialization, Brookings Papers on Economic Activity, Microeconomics, 1–84.

Borland, J., 1992, Career concerns: incentives and endogenous learning in labor markets, Journal of Economic Surveys, 6, 251–70.

Brander, J. and M. Poitevin, 1992, Managerial compensation and the agency cost of debt, Managerial and Decision Economics, 13, 55–64.

Bradley, M. and L.M. Wakeman, 1983, The wealth effects of targeted share repurchases, Journal of Financial Economics, 11, 275–300.

Bronars, S. and D. Deere, 1991, The threat of unionization, the use of debt, and the preservation of shareholder wealth, Quarterly Journal of Economics, 106, 231–54.

Brumigan, A., 1991, Occupational skills linkages: A resource-based investigation of conglomerates, Academy of Management Proceedings: Best Papers, 7–11.

Byrd, J. and K. Hickman, 1992, The case for independent outside directors, Continental Bank Journal of Applied Corporate Finance, 5 (3), (Fall), 78–82.

Byrd, J. and K. Hickman, 1993, Do outside directors monitor managers?: evidence from tender offer bids, Journal of Financial Economics, forthcoming.

Byrne, J., 1992, What, me over-paid? CEO's fight back, Business Week, May 4, 60–66.

Cable, J., 1985, Capital market information and industrial performance: The role of west german banks, The Economic Journal, 95, 118–132.

Chang, S. and D. Mayers, 1992, Managerial vote ownership and shareholder wealth: Evidence from employee stock ownership plans, Journal of Financial Economics, 32, 103–131.

Clark, R., 1985, Agency costs and fiduciary duties, in: Pratt, J. and R. Zeckhauser (eds.), Principals and Agents: The Structure of Business, (Harvard Business School Press, Cambridge MA) 123–45.

Coase, R. 1972, Industrial organization: A proposal for research, in: V. Fuchs (ed.), Policy Issues and Research Opportunities in Industrial Organization, (NBER, New York.), 87–103.

Coffee, J.C., 1986, Shareholders versus managers: The strain in the corporate web, Michigan Law Review, 85, 1–109.

Continental Bank Roundtable, 1991, Corporate performance and management incentives, Continental Bank Journal of Applied Corporate Finance, 4, 24–48.

Craswell, A., R.A. Saywell, and S.L. Taylor, 1993, Insider ownership and corporate value: Australian evidence, working paper, Department of Accounting, University of Sydney.

Crystal, G., 1991, In Search of Excess, W.W. Norton, New York.

Dann, L. and H. DeAngelo, 1988, Corporate financial policy and corporate control: A study of defensive adjustments in asset and ownership structure, Journal of Financial Economics, 20, 87–128.

Davis, G.F. and S.K. Stout, 1992, Organisational theory and the market for corporate control: A dynamic analysis of the characteristics of large takeover targets, 1980–1990, Administrative Science Quarterly, 37, 605–633.

De Fusco, R., R. Johnson, and T. Zorn, 1990, The effect of executive stock option plans on stockholders and bondholders, Journal of Finance, 45, 617–27.

DeAngelo, H. and L. DeAngelo, 1989, Proxy contests and the governance of publicly held corporations, Journal of Financial Economics, 23, 29–59.

DeAngelo, H. and L. DeAngelo, 1991, Union negotiations and corporate policy, Journal of Financial Economics, 30, 3–43.

Demsetz, H., 1982, Economic, Legal, and Political Dimensions of Competition, North-Holland, Amsterdam.

Demski, J. and D.E.M. Sappington (1992), The make-or-buy decision with unverifiable public information, Working Paper, University of Florida, Gainesville.

Diamond, D. and R. Verrecchia, 1982, Optimal managerial contracts and equilibrium security prices, Journal of Finance, 37, 275–88.

Dobrynski, J., 1993, Relationship investing, Business Week, March 15, 38–45.

Drucker, P.F., 1991, Reckoning with the pension fund revolution, Harvard Business Review, March-April, 106–14.

Easterbrook, F. and D. Fischel, 1981, The proper role of a target's management in responding to a tender offer, Harvard Law Review, 94, 1161–1195.

Fama, E.F., 1980, Agency problems and the theory of the firm, Journal of Political Economy, 88, 288–307.

Fama, E.F., 1990, Contract costs and financing decisions, Journal of Business, 63, 571–91.

Fershtman, C. and K. Judd, 1987, Equilibrium incentives in oligopoly, American Economic Review, 77, 927–40.

Fumas, X., 1992, Relative performance evaluation of management, International Journal of Industrial Organization, 10, 473–89.

Garvey, G.T. and N.G. Gaston, 1991, Delegation, the role of managerial discretion as a bonding device, and the enforcement of implicit contracts, Advances in Econometrics, 9, 87–119.

Garvey, G.T. and P.L. Swan, 1992a, Optimal capital structure for a hierarchical firm, Journal of Financial Intermediation, 2, 376–400.

Garvey, G.T. and P.L. Swan, 1992b, The disciplinary role of debt in a hierarchical organization, Research in Finance, 10, 1–40.

Garvey, G.T. and P.L. Swan, 1992c, Managerial objectives, capital structure, and the provision of worker incentives, Journal of Labor Economics, 10, 357–79.

Garvey, G.T. and P.L. Swan 1992d, The interaction between financial and employment contracts: A formal model of japanese corporate governance, Journal of the Japanese and International Economies, 6, 247–274.

Garvey, G.T. and P.L. Swan, 1993, Shareholder activism, 'voluntary' restructuring, and the management of labor, Working Paper, A.G.S.M., University of New South Wales.

Gibbons, R. and K.J. Murphy, 1990, Relative performance evaluation for chief executive officers, Industrial and Labor Relations Review, 43, 30S–51S.

Gibbons, R. and K.J. Murphy, 1992a, Optimal incentive contracts in the presence of career concerns: theory and evidence, Journal of Political Economy, 100, 468–505.

Gibbons, R. and K.J. Murphy, 1992b, Does executive compensation affect investment?, Continental Bank Journal of Applied Corporate Finance, 5, 99–109.

Gilson, R., 1986, The Law and Finance of Corporate Acquisitions, Foundation Press, Mineola, N.Y.

Gilson, S.C., 1989, Management turnover and financial distress, Journal of Financial Economics, 25, 241–62.

Gilson, S.C. and M.R. Vetsuypens, 1993, CEO compensation in financially distressed firms: An empirical analysis, Journal of Finance, 48, 425–458.

Gordon, L. and J. Pound, 1990, ESOPs and corporate control, Journal of Financial Economics, 27, 525–555.

Grossman, S. and O.D. Hart, 1980, Takeover bids, the free-rider problem, and the theory of the corporation, Bell Journal of Economics, 11, 42–64.

Grossman, S. and O.D. Hart, 1982, Corporate financial structure and managerial incentives: in J.J. McCall (ed.), The Economics of Information and Uncertainty, (NBER, University of Chicago Press, Chicago.), 123–55.

Grundfest, J., 1990, Subordination of american capital, Journal of Financial Economics, 27, 89–114.

Hart, O.D, 1983, The market mechanism as an incentive scheme, Bell Journal of Economics, 14, 366–82.

Hart, O.D., 1988, Incomplete contracts and the theory of the firm, Journal of Law, Economics, and Organization, 4, 119–40.

Hart, O.D., 1993, Theories of optimal capital structure: A managerial discretion perspective, in: M. Blair (ed.), The Deal Decade, (The Brookings Institution, Washington, D.C.), 203–33.

Hart, O.D. and B. Holmstrom, 1987, The theory of contracts in: T. Bewley (ed.), Advances in Economic Theory, (Cambridge University Press, Cambridge, U.K.), 294–351.

Hart, O.D. and J. Moore, 1990, A theory of corporate financial structure based on the seniority of claims, NBER Working Paper No. 3431.

Hermalin, B. and M.S. Weisbach, 1988, The determinants of board composition, Rand Journal of Economics, 19, 589–597.

Herzel, L., 1990, Corporate governance through statistical eyes, Journal of Financial Economics, 27, 581–94.

Holmstrom, B., 1979, Moral hazard and observability, Bell Journal of Economics, 10, 4–29.

Holmstrom, B., 1982, Managerial incentive problems: A dynamic perspective, in: Essays in Economics and Management in Honor of Lars Wahlbeck, (Swedish School of Economics, Helsinki) 210–35.

Holmstrom, B., 1988, Comment on Shleifer and Summers in: A.J. Auerbach (ed), Corporate Takeovers: Causes and Consequences, (NBER, University of Chicago Press), 211–3.

Holmstrom, B. and P. Milgrom, 1991, Multitask principal–agent analyses: Incentive contracts, asset ownership, and job design, Journal of Law, Economics, and Organization, 7, 524–552.

Holmstrom, B. and B. Nalebuff, 1992, To the raider goes the surplus? A reexamination of the free-rider problem, Journal of Economics and Management Strategy, 1, 37–62.

Holmstrom, B. and J. Ricart i Costa, 1986, Managerial incentives and capital management, Quarterly Journal of Economics, 101, 835–60.

Ippolito, R. nd W. James, 1992, LBO's, reversions and implicit contracts, Journal of Finance, 47, 139–67.
Itoh, H., 1992, Cooperation in hierarchical organizations: An incentive perspective, Journal of Law, Economics, and Organization, 8, 321–345.
Jahera, J.S. and W. Pugh, 1991, State takeover legislation: The case of delaware, Journal of Law, Economics, and Organization, 7, 410–28.
Jarrell, G.A., 1993, An overview of the executive compensation debate, Continental Bank Journal of Applied Corporate Finance, 5, 35–43.
Jensen, M.C., 1986, Agency costs of free cash flow, corporate finance and takeovers, American Economic Review, 76, 323–29.
Jensen, M.C., 1988, Takeovers: Their causes and consequences, Journal of Economic Perspectives, 2, 21–48.
Jensen, M.C., 1989, Eclipse of the public corporation, Harvard Business Review, Sept–Oct, 60–70.
Jensen, M.C., 1991, Corporate control and the politics of finance, Continental Bank Journal of Applied Corporate Finance, 4, 13–33.
Jensen, M.C. and W.R. Meckling, 1976, Theory of the firm: managerial behaviour, agency costs and financial structure, Journal of Financial Economics, 3, 35–60.
Jensen, M.C. and K.J. Murphy, 1990, Performance pay and top management incentives, Journal of Political Economy, 98, 225–63.
John, K. and T. John, 1992, Top-management compensation and capital structure, Working Paper, Stern School of Business, New York University.
Kane, E.J., 1989, The S and L Insurance Mess: How Did it Happen?, The Urban Institute Press, Washington, D.C.
Kanemoto, Y. and W.B. MacLeod, 1991, The theory of contracts and labor practices in Japan and the United States, Managerial and Decision Economics, 12, 159–170.
Kaplan, S., 1991, The staying power of leveraged buyouts, Journal of Financial Economics, 29, 287–313.
Karpoff, J. and P. Malatesta, 1989, The wealth effects of second-generation state takeover legislation, Journal of Financial Economics, 25, 291–323.
Katz, M., 1991, Game playing agents: Unobservable contracts as precommitments, Rand Journal of Economics, 22, 307–28.
Kester, W.C., 1986, Capital and ownership Structure: A comparison of United States and Japanese manufacturing corporations, Financial Management (Spring), 5–16.
Kester, W.C. 1991a, The hidden costs of Japanese success, Continental Bank Journal of Applied Corporate Finance, 3, 90–97.
Kester, W.C., 1991b, Japanese corporate governance and the conservation of value in financial distress, Continental Bank Journal of Applied Corporate Finance, 4, 98–104.
Kester, W.C., 1991c, Japanese Takeovers: The Global Contest for Corporate Control, Cambridge, MA: Harvard Business School Press.
Kester, W.C., 1992, Governance, contracting, and investment horizons: A look at Japan and Germany, Continental Bank Journal of Applied Corporate Finance, 5, 83–98.
Lakonishok, J., A. Shleifer and R Vishny, 1992, The structure and performance of the money management industry, Brookings Papers in Economic Activity: Microeconomics, 339–92.
Lazear, E.P., 1979, Why is there mandatory retirement?, Journal of Political Economy 87, 36–54.
Lazear, E.P., 1989, Pay equality and industrial politics, Journal of Political Economy, 97, 561–80.
Lazear, E.P., 1992, The job as a concept, in: W. Bruns (ed.), Performance Measurement, Evaluation, and Incentives, (Harvard Business School Press, Boston, MA.), 9–42.
Lo Pucki, L. and W. Whitford, 1990, Bargaining over equity's share in the bankruptcy reorganization of large, publicly held companies, Pennsylvania Law Review, 134, 125–73.

Malatesta, P.H. and R.A. Walkling (1988), Poison Pill Securities: Stockholder Wealth, Profitability, and Ownership Structure, Journal of Financial Economics, 20, 347–376.
Malcolmson, J.M., 1984, Work incentives, hierarchy, and internal labor markets, Journal of Political Economy, 92, 486–507.
Maloney, M.T., R.E. McCormick and M.L. Mitchell, 1993, Managerial decision making and capital structure, Journal of Business, 66, 189–217.
Manne, H.G., 1965, Mergers and the market for corporate control, Journal of Political Economy, 75, 110–26.
Martin, K. and J. McConnell, 1991, Corporate performance, corporate takeovers and management turnover, Journal of Finance, 46, 671–87.
McConnell, J.J. and H. Servaes, 1990, Additional evidence on equity ownership and corporate value, Journal of Financial Economics, 27, 595–612.
Meyer, M., P. Milgrom, and J. Roberts, 1992, Organizational prospects, influence costs, and ownership changes, Journal of Economics and Management Strategy, 1, 9–36.
Middlestaedt, H.F., 1989, An empirical analysis of the factors underlying the decision to remove excess assets from overfunded pension plans, Journal of Accounting and Economics, 11, 394–418.
Mirrlees, J., 1976, The optimal structure of incentives and authority within an organization, Bell Journal of Economics, 7, 105–31.
Mitchell, M. and K. Lehn, 1991, Do Bad Bidders Become Good Targets?, Journal of Political Economy, 99, 237–61.
Morck, R., A. Shleifer and R. Vishny, 1988a, Characteristics of hostile and friendly takeovers, in: A.J. Auerbach (ed): Corporate Takeovers: Causes and Consequences, (NBER, University of Chicago Press), 301–27.
Morck, R., A. Shleifer and R.W. Vishny, 1988b, Management ownership and market valuation: An empirical analysis, Journal of Financial Economics, 20, 293–315.
Murphy, K.J., 1985, Corporate performance and managerial remuneration: An empirical analysis, Journal of Accounting and Economics, 7, 11–42.
Murphy, K.J. and K. Van Nuys, 1993, Public Pension Funds: Ark of the Lost Raiders?, Working paper, Harvard Business School, Cambridge, MA.
Myers, S., 1977, Determinants of corporate borrowing, Journal of Financial Economics, 9, 147–75.
Palepu, K., 1990, Consequences of leveraged buyouts, Journal of Financial Economics, 27, 247–61.
Paul, J., 1992, On the efficiency of stock-based compensation, Review of Financial Studies, 5, 471–502.
Peterson, M., 1992, Pension Reversions and Worker-Stockholder Wealth Transfers, Quarterly Journal of Economics, 108, 1032–55.
Pontiff, J., A. Shleifer and M. Weisbach, 1990, Reversions of excess pension assets after takeovers, Rand Journal of Economics, 8, 600–613.
Pound, J., 1991, Proxy voting and the SEC, Journal of Financial Economics, 29, 241–85.
Pound, J. 1992a, Raiders, targets and politics, Continental Bank Journal of Applied Corporate Finance, 5, 6–18.
Pound, J., 1992b, On the motives for choosing a corporate governance structure: A study of corporate reaction to the Pennsylvania takeover law, The Journal of Law, Economics, and Organisation, 8, 656–672.
Prahalad, C.K., 1993, Comments, Continental Bank Journal of Applied Corporate Finance, 6, 38–54.
Prahalad, C.K. and G. Hamel, 1990, The core competence of the corporation, Harvard Business Review, May–June, 74–92.

Prendergast, C., 1993, The role of promotion in inducing specific human capital acquisition, Quarterly Journal of Economics, 108, 523–34.

Prendergast, C. and R. Topel, 1993, Discretion and bias in performance evaluation, European Economic Review, 37, 355–65.

Rappaport, A., 1990, The staying power of the public corporation, Harvard Business Review, January–February, 96–104.

Roe, M., 1990, Political and legal restraints on ownership and control of public companies, Journal of Financial Economics, 27, 7–41.

Roe, M., 1993a, Some differences in corporate structure in Germany, Japan, and the U.S., Yale Law Journal, 102, 19282037.

Roe, M., 1993b, Takeover politics, in: M. Blair (ed.), The Deal Decade, (Brookings Institute, Washington, D.C.), 321–47.

Romano, R., 1991, The shareholder suit: Litigation without foundation?, Journal of Law, Economics, and Organization, 7, 55–88.

Rosen, S., 1982, Hierarchy, control, and the distribution of earnings, Bell Journal of Economics, 13, 77–98.

Ryngaert, M., 1988, The effect of poison pill securities on shareholder wealth, Journal of Financial Economics, 20, 377–418.

Scharfstein, D.S., 1988, The disciplinary role of takeovers, Review of Economic Studies, 45, 185–99.

Sheard, P., 1989, The main bank system and corporate monitoring and control in Japan, Journal of Economic Behavior and Organisation, 11, 399–422.

Sheard, P., 1991, The economics of interlocking shareholding in Japan, Ricerche Economiche, 45, 2–3, 421–448.

Shleifer, A. and L. Summers, 1988, Hostile takeovers as breaches of trust, in A.J. Auerbach (ed), Corporate Takeovers: Causes and Consequences, (NBER, University of Chicago Press.), 65–88.

Shleifer, A. and R. Vishny, 1986, Greenmail, white knights, and shareholder's interest, Rand Journal of Economics, 17, 293–309.

Sklivas, S., 1987, The strategic choice of managerial incentives, Rand Journal of Economics, 18, 452–58.

Smith, C. and J. Warner, 1979, On financial contracting: An analysis of bond covenants, Journal of Financial Economics, 7, 117–61.

Smith, C.W. and R.L. Watts, 1992, The investment opportunity set and corporate financing, dividend, and compensation policies, Journal of Financial Economics, 32, 263–292.

Stern Stewart Roundtable (1992), Management incentive compensation and shareholder value, Continental Bank Journal of Applied Corporate Finance, 110–30.

Stiglitz, J.E., 1985, Credit markets and the control of capital, Journal of Money, Credit, and Banking, 17, 133–152.

Stulz, R., 1988, Managerial control of voting rights, Journal of Financial Economics, 20, 25–59.

Stulz, R., 1990, Managerial discretion and optimal financing policies, Journal of Financial Economics, 26, 3–27.

Taylor, W., 1990, Can big owners make a big difference?, Harvard Business Review, September–October, 70–82.

Thomas, J.K., 1989, Why do firms terminate their overfunded pension plans?, Journal of Accounting and Economics, 11, 418–37.

Tirole, J., 1988, The Theory of Industrial Organization, MIT Press, Cambridge, MA.

Warner, J., R. Watts and K. Wruck, 1988, Stock prices and top management changes, Journal of Financial Economics, 20, 461–92.

Watching the Boss: A Survey of Corporate Governance, 1994, The Economist, Jan. 29, S1–S18.

Webster's Third New International Dictionary (1971), G. and L. Merriam, Springfield, MA.
Weisbach, M.S., 1988, Outside directors and CEO turnover, Journal of Financial Economics, 20, 431–460.
Williamson, O., 1985, The Economic Institutions of Capitalism, New York: The Free Press.
Williamson, O., 1988, Corporate finance and corporate governance, Journal of Finance, 43, 567–92.

[14]

ELSEVIER Journal of Financial Economics 39 (1995) 3–43

JOURNAL OF Financial ECONOMICS

Poison or placebo? Evidence on the deterrence and wealth effects of modern antitakeover measures

Robert Comment[a,b], G. William Schwert*[,a,c]

[a]*William E. Simon Graduate School of Business, University of Rochester, Rochester, NY 14627, USA*
[b]*U.S. Securities and Exchange Commission, Washington, DC 20549, USA*
[c]*National Bureau of Economic Research, Cambridge, MA 02831, USA*

(Received March 1993; final version received July 1994)

Abstract

This paper provides large-sample evidence that poison pill rights issues, control share laws, and business combination laws have not systematically deterred takeovers and are unlikely to have caused the demise of the 1980s market for corporate control, even though 87% of all exchange-listed firms are now covered by one of these antitakeover measures. We show that poison pills and control share laws are reliably associated with higher takeover premiums for selling shareholders, both unconditionally and conditional on a successful takeover, and we provide updated event study evidence for the three-quarters of all poison pills not yet analyzed. Antitakeover measures increase the bargaining position of target firms, but they do not prevent many transactions.

Key words: Poison pill; Antitakeover law; Merger; Tender offer; Takeover premium
JEL Classifications: G34; G38

*Corresponding author.

The Bradley Policy Research Center, William E. Simon Graduate School of Business Administration, University of Rochester, provided support for this research. We are grateful for suggestions from Michael Bradley, Jim Brickley, Harry DeAngelo, Craig Dunbar, Ken French, Stuart Gilson, Paul Gompers, Gregg Jarrell, Michael Jensen (the editor), Steve Kaplan (the referee), E. Han Kim, Glenn MacDonald, Wayne Mikkelson, Mitchell Peterson, Roberta Romano, Robert Vishny, Marc Zenner, Jerold Zimmerman, and participants in seminars at the American Finance Association, the NBER Summer Institute, and the Universities of Chicago, Michigan, Rochester, and Southern California. This paper is part of NBER's research program in Asset Pricing. The Securities and Exchange Commission, as a matter of policy, disclaims any responsibility for any private publication or statements by any of its employees. The views expressed herein are those of the authors and do not necessarily reflect the views of the Commission, or of the authors' colleagues on the staff of the Commission, or of the National Bureau of Economic Research.

SSDI 0304405X9400823 J

1. Introduction

At the end of the 1980s, the level of takeover activity fell dramatically. Many commentators have speculated that the demise of the market for corporate control was caused by the evolution of sophisticated antitakeover measures. This paper analyzes data on all exchange-listed firms from 1975–91 and casts doubt on the hypothesis that antitakeover measures shut down the market for corporate control.

The 1980s saw many improvements in corporate antitakeover methods. More than 1,500 firms adopted shareholder rights plans (poison pills) during the second half of the decade. These securities, issued as dividends, serve to create impossibly burdensome obligations for anyone who buys a controlling block of shares without management approval. (Bruner, 1991, provides a detailed review of the mechanics of poison pills.) Separately, states developed several forms of antitakeover statute able to pass constitutional muster: *control share laws* that restrict the voting rights of a controlling shareholder and *business combination* (merger-moratorium or freeze-out) *laws* that delay any business combination. In either variant, the prohibitions last for three to five years and, like poison pills, apply to the buyer of a controlling block of shares who buys without management approval. Ohio adopted the first business combination law in 1982 and New York adopted the first control share law in 1985. Many states have both types of law. The U.S. Supreme Court upheld Indiana's control share law in April 1987, and an appellate court upheld Wisconsin's business combination law in June 1989.[1] The appellate court ruled that investors have no constitutional right to receive tender offers and that state law need not leave bidders a meaningful opportunity for success.

The demise of the 1980s market for corporate control is closely associated with the spread of these new antitakeover methods. Fig. 1 plots the percentage of all firms listed on the New York (NYSE) or American Stock Exchange (Amex) that received initial takeover offers in each month from January 1975 to December 1991, along with the proportion covered by the three kinds of modern antitakeover measures. Coverage by business combination statutes jumped from 15% to 63% when Delaware adopted its law in January 1988 (half the exchange-listed firms are incorporated in Delaware) and reached 80% by 1991. Coverage by control share laws increased gradually to reach 24% by 1991. Coverage by poison pills, trivial before 1986, increased gradually to reach 35%. By 1991, 87% exchange-listed firms were covered by a poison pill, a business combination law, or a control share law. In comparison, takeover rates started at levels below 0.5% per month in 1975 and increased to a peak of about 1.5%

[1] See CTS Corp. v. Dynamics Corp. of Am., 481 U.S. 69, 86–87 (1987); Amanda Acquisition Corp. v. Universal Foods Corp., 877 F. 2d 496, 504–05 (7th Cir.), cert. denied, 110 S. Ct.367 (1989).

per month during 1987 and 1988. A long, gradual rise in merger and acquisition activity culminated in a sharp reversal during 1989. Takeover rates were again below 0.5% per month in 1990 and 1991.

The association seen in Fig. 1 suggests that incumbent managers used their enhanced decision rights to deter takeovers systematically. This interpretation is consistent with (1) a substantial literature that portrays managers as more interested in entrenchment than in maximizing shareholder wealth, (2) anecdotal evidence from well-publicized cases of managers relying on antitakeover measures to defeat premium-priced takeover offers, and (3) indirect evidence from many event studies that find average reductions in shareholder wealth from adoption of antitakeover measures. The aim of this study is to use large-sample evidence to test whether modern takeover defenses have been used systematically to deter takeovers.

The evidence from our direct test of deterrence provides little support for the proposition that modern antitakeover measures have been used to deter takeovers systematically. We infer from this evidence that firm-specific antitakeover

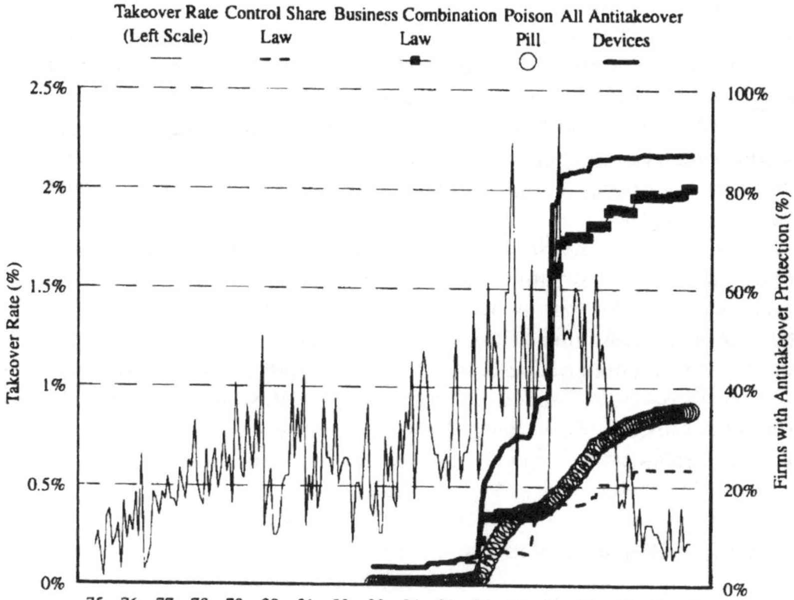

Fig. 1. Monthly time series plot of proportion of all exchange-listed firms that are covered by (1) control share laws, (2) business combination laws, (3) poison pill rights issues, (4) any of the above, and (5) the proportion of all exchange-listed firms that received initial merger proposals, merger agreements, or inter-firm tender offers each month during 1975–91 (left-hand scale).

measures played a minor role in ending the 1980s merger wave. Our evidence points instead to broad-scale political or economic forces that manifest themselves as secular variation. In addition, our review of the major takeover-related court decisions suggests that this secular variation is not due to an evolution in takeover jurisprudence.

While systematic evidence is scarce, practitioners and researchers have long acknowledged that antitakeover measures could enhance the bargaining power of incumbent management versus bidders, thereby yielding higher takeover premiums for selling shareholders. We find that selling shareholders do receive premium prices for their shares when antitakeover measures are in place. Since higher prices surely deter buyers, this result is consistent with deterrence, and yet we fail to detect such deterrence. Moreover, we find that expected premiums are higher with an antitakeover measure in place even with expected premiums calculated to account for the possibility of added deterrence. Finally, we update previous studies of the stock price effects of announcements of adoptions of poison pills and closely replicate their results. Overall, our evidence casts doubt on the view that antitakeover measures are used primarily to entrench incumbent management.

Section 2 discusses some *a priori* grounds for skepticism regarding the deterrent effect of antitakeover measures, and offers several alternate explanations, notably the credit crunch that began with the dismantling of Drexel Burnham Lambert, for the sharp reduction in takeover activity that occurred in the late 1980s. We describe our data sources in Section 3. Section 4 updates the existing evidence on the wealth effect of poison pills. In Section 5 we exploit the firm- and time-specific nature of coverage by poison pills and state antitakeover laws to decide if deterrence is observable in the takeover experience of individual firms. In Section 6 we estimate the relation between antitakeover measures and conditional and unconditional takeover premiums. Section 7 discusses various specification checks that assure the insensitivity of our results to reasonable changes in the definition of the variables or tests. In particular, evidence for deterrence is not materially enhanced when we analyze hostile takeovers rather than all transactions. Section 8 presents our conclusions. The Appendix contains a brief history of case law in Delaware and Federal courts as it pertains to takeover defenses.

2. Takeover defenses as placebos

There is much a priori ground for skepticism about the deterrent effect of modern antitakeover measures. To begin with, incumbent managers wielded considerable influence over takeover outcomes even before modern antitakeover measures, as shown by the predominance of negotiated transactions during the first half of the 1980s. Considering all takeover attempts involving tender offers for exchange-listed firms between 1981 and 84, Comment and Jarrell (1987) report that half of all bidders obtained a merger agreement before starting an offer, 22% of all transactions started as hostile but were superseded by negotiated bids, while another 12% started as hostile but ended with no shares purchased by any bidder. Few bids (the remaining 16%) were executed without management's approval. This evidence shows that deterrence is not management's main interest (eventually two-thirds of all offers were approved), and that management wielded considerable bargaining power versus bidders throughout the 1980's and not just after the spread of modern antitakeover measures.

Moreover, the burden imposed on buyers by a control share law (i.e., restricted voting rights) may be avoidable at low cost. As noted by Gilson and Black (1992), this type of law provides for a shareholder vote to decide if the law's restrictions on voting rights are to apply in a given instance. These elections are paid for by the buyer, triggered by a disclosure of intent to seek control, held within 55 days, and require a simple majority to grant the buyer full voting rights. Thus, the minimal burden imposed by a control share law is the cost of a special election and a 55-day delay (where the minimum tender-offer period is 20 days in any event). As a practical matter, bidders can make their offers conditional on the outcome of this vote, just as they might on the outcome of an antitrust review. Bidders might prefer such a vote since it would be viewed as an expression of shareholder preference that would undermine any claim of coercion as a legal rationale for antitakeover measures. For example, as an adjunct to its unnegotiated tender offer for Kansas Gas & Electric in 1990, Kansas City Power & Light sought a court order to force the target firm to comply with the Kansas Control Share Acquisitions Act by calling a special election to approve voting rights for any shares it might buy in its offer.

A corresponding provision for a shareholder vote occurs in business combination laws, but with the crucial difference that the vote is triggered by an actual purchase of shares, rather than by a stated intent to purchase. Thus, a buyer must win a vote among nontendering shareholders, rather than among all holders, to avoid the burden imposed by a business combination law (a five-year delay before cleanup mergers).

Event studies of the stock price effects of adoptions of antitakeover measures provide considerable indirect evidence regarding deterrence, and although stock prices fall, implying deterrence, the size of the decline is inconsistent with strong deterrence. The typical decline is less than 1% for most types of antitakeover measures.[2] Ryngaert (1988) examines 283 poison pills adopted through 1986

[2]Exceptional results are reported by Szewczyk and Tsetsekos (1992). They find an average return of −9.09% for 56 Pennsylvania firms during the legislative process (from October 10, 1989 through April 27, 1990) for the adoption of that state's cashout law. When cumulated over key dates, a methodology comparable to that used by Karpoff and Malatesta, the average return is −3.33%.

and finds an average two-day announcement return of − 0.34%. Malatesta and Walkling (1988) examine 132 poison pills adopted through March 1986 and find an average two-day return of − 0.92%. Romano (1993) reviews 13 studies of the wealth effects of adoptions of antitakeover laws by individual states. Pooling these events, Karpoff and Malatesta (1989) examine the average stock price effect for a sample of 1,505 firms affected by 40 different instances of an introduction of a law to a state legislature in 26 different states, and find a two-day announcement return of − 0.29%. In addition, Jarrell and Poulsen (1987) report an average announcement return of − 1.25% for 649 fair-price, classified-board, and supermajority-voting charter amendments from 1980–85, although other studies find little evidence of an adverse reaction to antitakeover charter amendments (for example, DeAngelo and Rice, 1983; Linn and McConnell, 1983).

In juxtaposition to these studies, Nathan and O'Keefe (1989) show that shareholder gains of 50% are typical in takeovers and thus typical of what is forgone with deterrence. For instance, if the probability of a takeover decreases by 10% with the adoption of an antitakeover measure, and if a 50% gain is lost, then the wealth decline on adoption should be about 5%. The empirical estimates of wealth loss generally do not approach this level. Thus, the size of the average wealth decline on the adoption of an antitakeover measure is consistent with only a modest change in takeover probability.

A substantial literature relating merger waves and business cycles provides further grounds for skepticism (see Weston, Chung, and Hoag, 1990, Ch. 11, for a review of this evidence). It is possible that the 1980s restructuring boom, like earlier booms, simply succumbed to market forces. The National Bureau of Economic Research marks the start of a recession in July 1990, which lags the decline in takeover activity in Fig. 3, but there is evidence of an earlier credit crunch. As reported by Putnam (1991), U.S. flow of funds data show a collapse in net new lending to the nonfinancial business sector by commercial banks from $33 billion in 1989 to $2 billion in 1990. Commercial banks were the dominant providers of bridge or transaction financing for large, cash acquisitions. The Securities and Exchange Commission (1986) shows that commercial banks provided over three-quarters of the immediate financing for 272 successful tender offers from 1981–85.

The availability of long-term and subordinated financing had shriveled before 1990 due to declining prices, illiquidity, and government intervention in the market for junk bonds in 1989 (see Yago, 1991, for a detailed discussion). In

This law requires a buyer of more than 20% of the shares to purchase at fair value any remaining shares that holders wish to put to them. This type of antitakeover law appears late in our sample period and only Maine and South Dakota have followed Pennsylvania in adopting a cashout law, so we lack sufficient experience with this type of law to estimate its deterrence effects.

September 1988, the S.E.C. sued Drexel Burnham Lambert, the investment bank most active in financing takeovers, alleging a secret alliance with Ivan Boesky. The impact on Drexel's ability to serve as a financial intermediary was immediate. By October, the $570 million, Drexel-financed leveraged buyout of Wickes was canceled and Drexel had to cover out of its own capital almost half its 'highly confident' commitment to raise $1.4 billion for an offer for Interco. In a December 1988 attempt at damage control, Drexel dismissed Michael Milken, pleaded guilty to six felony counts, and paid a $650 million fine. In August 1989, Congress passed the Financial Institutions Reform, Recovery and Enforcement Act (FIRREA), which penalized savings and loans for holding junk bonds and mandated their sale, while regulators issued guidelines barring commercial bank participation in highly leveraged transactions (including all acquisition loans that raised liabilities to 75% of assets, or doubled the debt ratio while raising it to 50% of assets). The junk bond market crashed in September 1989 when Campeau, which had become a major issuer of (non-Drexel) junk bonds, revealed the extent of its liquidity crisis and when UAL failed to secure buyout financing. The decline in the value of Drexel's portfolio of junk bonds triggered its declaration of bankruptcy and dissolution in February 1990. Finally, the National Association of Insurance Commissioners adopted guidelines in June 1990 requiring insurance companies to increase reserves against junk bonds not in default.

Although a formal test of a credit crunch model is beyond the scope of this paper, we do provide two illustrative charts. Fig. 2 plots the number of cash-only transactions and the number of securities-only transactions (common and preferred stock, debt, and combinations), year-by-year, from 1975 to 1991. The number of securities-only transactions remains steady at 15–25 transactions per year, so both boom and bust are attributable to cash transactions. Fig. 3 plots monthly the yield spread between long-term low-quality corporate bonds (rated below Baa) and high-quality bonds (rated Aaa), along with the takeover rates from Fig. 1.[3] The most noticeable change in the yield spread is a jump after 1988. Combined, this evidence suggests that the demise of the takeover market coincided with tighter credit.[4] In the formal tests below, we represent changing economic conditions (from 1986 on) with yearly dummy variables.

[3]Long-term monthly bond yields are from Salomon Brothers and Ibbotson Associates. The gradual increase in the junk bond yield spread from 1975–88 probably reflects a shift in the composition of the below-Baa group of bonds due to the gradual addition of a large number of original issue bonds issued in the early and mid-1980s to fund takeovers and restructurings.

[4]Tight credit conditions for takeovers could outlast any economy-wide problem. Neither Viacom nor QVC were able to borrow enough to make an all-cash offer for Paramount Communications in 1994.

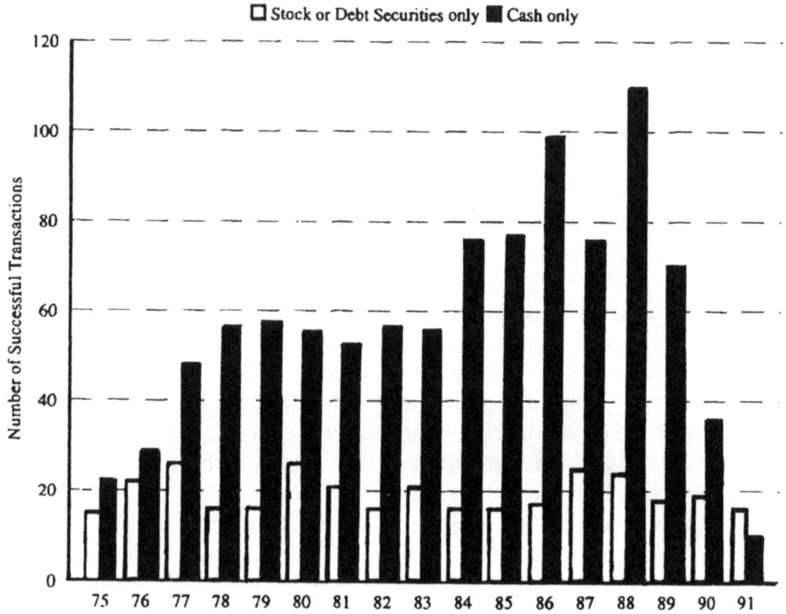

Fig. 2. Number of cash-only and securities-only successful takeovers of exchange-listed firms in the period 1975–91, by year of announcement.

3. Data sources and descriptive statistics

The information on merger and acquisition announcements comes from our proprietary mergers & acquisitions (M&A) database, which covers all exchange-listed target firms in the period 1975–91. These announcements were obtained through various keyword searches of the *Dow Jones News Retrieval* (*DJNR*) database, inspection of the *Wall Street Journal Index*, and from Commerce Clearing House's *Capital Changes Reporter* [the original source for Center for Research in Security Prices (CRSP) delisting codes]. In this study, we use the subset of records covering merger proposals, merger agreements, and interfirm tender offers. Merger proposals are distinguished from merger talks by a public disclosure of terms of purchase. We use these data to identify (1) successful takeovers, (2) announcement dates, (3) method of payment (cash versus stock), and (4) whether a target is bought in an auction (multiple, publicly revealed bidders). An announcement qualifies as the initial one (that puts the firm in play) if there has been no other qualifying announcement in the prior year.

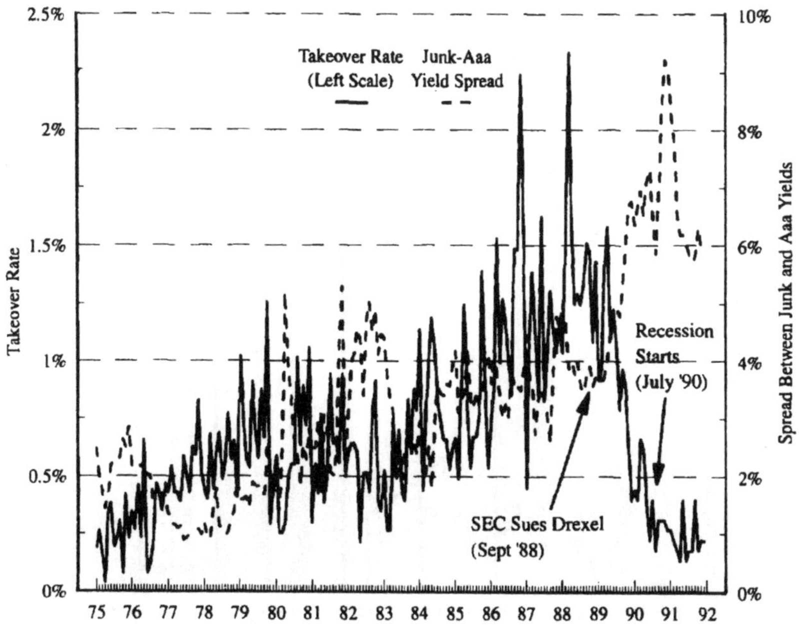

Fig. 3. Monthly time series plot of the spread between the junk (< Baa) and Aaa corporate bond yields and the proportion of all exchange-listed firms that received initial merger proposals, merger agreements, or inter-firm tender offers each month, 1975–91 (left-hand scale).

We use data from CRSP to calculate takeover premiums as the compound difference between the returns to target firms' stock and the value-weighted NYSE and Amex market portfolio during announcement periods that vary in length from target to target. We know from event-study evidence that on average the wealth effect of takeovers occurs in a period from about 10 trading days before to 10 trading days after the initial announcement of a takeover. To ensure that we capture any runup, we begin our periods 20 trading days before the initial takeover announcements. To ensure that we capture the wealth effects of multiple bids or auctions, we end our periods five days after the announcement of the successful offer.

Our information on adoptions of state antitakeover laws comes from the Investor Responsibility Research Center, and our information on states of incorporation (and reincorporations) comes from various issues of *Moody's Manuals*. Our information on adoptions of poison pills is from annual compilations contained in *Corporate Control Alert*, from various *DJNR* keyword searches, from *Capital Changes Reporter*, and from *Moody's Manuals*. We identify a total of 1,584 original poison pill rights issues made through December 1991. Of these, 60% were issued by firms listed on the NYSE or Amex at the

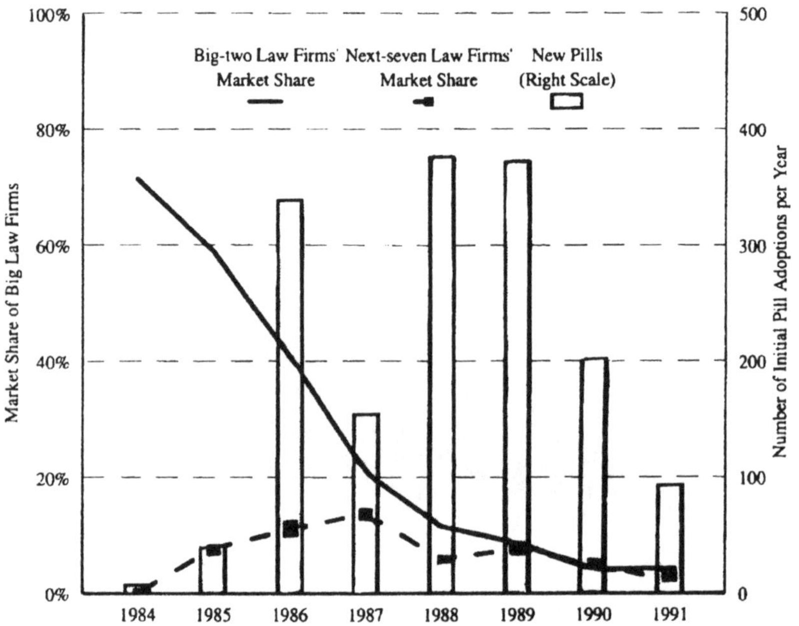

Fig. 4. Number of initial poison pill adoptions by year for all exchange-listed firms in the period 1984–91. Also, market share of large law firms used in pill adoptions. The 'big-two' law firms are Wachtell Lipton and Skadden Arps. The 'next-seven' law firms are Fried Frank Harris, Sullivan Cromwell, Cravath Swaine, Paul Weiss, Wilkie Farr, Shearman Sterling, and Jones Day.

time of issue. For purposes of determining antitakeover coverage when predicting takeovers, we account for pills adopted before exchange listing and for the handful of pills redeemed without being replaced. It is likely that we fail to account for most opt outs from state laws due to the difficulty of identifying these events. Because they have not been enforced by federal courts, we ignore provisions in some state laws that attempt to extend coverage to firms incorporated in other states.[5]

3.1. Evolution of the legal market for poison pill securities

Fig. 4 shows the number of new pills adopted each year from 1984 to 1991. Pill adoptions became common after 1985, with 1988 and 1989 being the peak years. The number of adoptions declines after this, and 1991 had the fewest

[5]The U.S. Supreme Court found such extraterritorial effects unconstitutional in Edgar v. Mite Corp., 457 U.S. 624 (1982).

adoptions since 1985. It is unlikely that the falloff in pill adoptions is due to saturation, as two-thirds of all exchange-listed firms remain without pills, consistent with our analysis of the legal treatment of antitakeover devices (in the Appendix). Because the legality of antitakeover devices depends only on the carefulness of the deliberations of the board of directors at the time that a pill is used, pills are no less valid when adopted on short notice, and the adoption itself is not a complex legal matter.

We can get a sense of the extent of specialization in the legal market for poison pills from information in *Corporate Control Alert* on the identity of the law firm that advised on the adoption. Fig. 4 shows the market shares of several large law firms that frequently advise on pill adoptions. The 'big-two' law firms are Wachtell Lipton and Skadden Arps, the market leaders. Wachtell Lipton invented the poison pill and Skadden Arps developed a popular variation. The 'next-seven' group includes the next seven firms most commonly retained to advise on pill adoptions: Fried Frank, Sullivan Cromwell, Cravath Swaine, Paul Weiss, Wilkie Farr, Shearman Sterling, and Jones Day. The big-two firms advised on about two-thirds of the pills adopted in 1984 and 1985, when pills were rare and experimental. The market shares of the two leaders fell continuously as pills became common place, ending at 7% in 1991. The market share of the next-seven law firms fell from 10% through 1986 to 7% afterwards, so that the shift over time was toward the use of in-house counsel and local law firms, suggesting that poison pills did not present complex legal issues for long.

3.2. Accounting and stock market predictors of takeover activity

Palepu (1986) uses several accounting and stock market performance measures to predict takeovers. Following his approach, we create a sample of all firm-years with data available on Compustat for exchange-listed firms with fiscal years that end December 1976 through December 1990, yielding 21,887 fiscal-year forecast periods that begin between January 1977 and January 1991. This sample approximates the population. We exclude firm-years without four years' worth of previous accounting data on Compustat, and we exclude a handful of firm-years that begin after the year of an initial takeover announcement. We use accounting and stock return variables in our prediction models to account for variation, across time and firms, in business conditions that affect the likelihood of takeovers. The variables are all calculated over the four years before each fiscal-year forecast period, and include:

abnormal stock return for firm i and day t, $u_{it} = R_{it} - \alpha_i - \beta_i R_{mt}$, averaged over four years before the forecast period (where the market model parameters α_i and β_i for the CRSP value-weighted portfolio are estimated in the fifth year before the forecast period), *sales growth* measured as the proportional change in sales over four years [Compustat item 12],

liquidity measured as a four-year average of the ratio of net liquid assets to total assets [Compustat items (4 − 5)/6],

debt/equity measured as a four-year average of the ratio of debt to equity [Compustat items 9/60],

market/book (sometimes called the 'q-ratio') measured as a four-year average of the ratio of the year-end market value of common stock to the book value of equity [Compustat items $24 \cdot 25/60$],

price/earnings measured as a four-year average of the ratio of the year-end stock price to earnings per share [Compustat items 24/58], and

size measured as the log of total assets at the start of the forecast period in millions of dollars [Compustat item 6].

Extreme outliers, such as market/book, price/earnings, or debt/equity ratios greater than 100, were omitted from the sample.

Table 1 shows means and standard deviations for these variables, along with t-tests for whether mean values differ for the 669 takeover firm-years compared with the full sample of 21,887 firm-years. Consistent with Palepu (1986), there are some modest differences. The average abnormal stock return is slightly higher for takeover targets. This could be due to anticipatory, pre-bid runups in the target's stock price, although by construction this prior return excludes any runup within the fiscal year of the announcement. In addition, target firms have below-average sales growth, higher cash positions, and lower debt/equity ratios. These results imply that target firms are poor performers that make inefficient use of their financial capital, consistent with Jensen's (1986) discussion of free cash flow. While their price/earnings ratios are not unusual, targets do have lower-than-average market/book ratios, consistent with several interpretations. One interpretation is that targets have more assets in place and fewer growth options (Myers, 1977). Another is that firms become targets because they are undervalued in the stock market, and market/book measures this undervaluation. Third, takeover targets could be run less efficiently (Lang, Stulz, and Walkling, 1989). In any event, the largest t-statistic by far is for (the log of) size, confirming the well-known fact that small firms are more likely to be acquired. Overall, these comparisons provide some reason to think that these accounting and stock market measures of performance can help predict takeover activity.

3.3. Coverage by antitakeover laws and poison pills

Since state antitakeover laws represent a legal innovation, there is ambiguity about when coverage took effect. It can be argued that control share laws took effect only after the U.S. Supreme Court ruled on the Indiana law in April 1987, and that business combination laws took effect only after the appellate court ruled on the Wisconsin law in June 1989. The fact that the S.E.C. filed a friend-of-the-court brief challenging the Wisconsin law as unconstitutional implies that some uncertainty remained even after the Supreme Court ruling. We report descriptive statistics for alternate specifications of a pill coverage dummy variable in Table 1. In our subsequent analysis we define the effective dates of these laws using the dates of these two important judicial decisions, although this choice does not much affect the results. We ignore the issue of important court decisions for pills since the relevant decision, *Moran*, occurred in 1985 before all but a handful of pills were adopted.

Table 1 reports means and standard deviations for dummy variables that equal one when a firm is covered by a law or a poison pill at the beginning of the forecast fiscal year, so that mean values represent proportions of the sample covered (i.e., exchange-listed firms). Using adoption dates yields a total of 1,263 firm-years of experience with control share laws (5.8% of the sample) and 3,417 firm-years of experience with business combination laws (15.6%). When coverage is defined to begin after the judicial decisions, for laws adopted before these decisions, coverage drops to 884 firm-years for control share laws (4.0%) and to 1,625 firm-years for business combination laws (7.4%). There are 1,779 firm-years of experience with poison pills in the sample (8.1%). We treat firm-years as covered only when an antitakeover measure is in place at the start of the year, ignoring part-year coverage from midyear adoptions.

Foreshadowing the estimates from our prediction model reported in Table 3, which show almost no deterrence, the univariate results in Table 1 show that coverage by control share laws is as frequent in the takeover sample as in the full sample (5.5% versus 5.8%, t-statistic of -0.28), while coverage by business combination laws is slightly lower in the takeover sample than in the full sample (13.5% versus 15.6%, t-statistic of -1.66). Coverage by poison pills is more frequent in the takeover sample than in the full sample (9.6% versus 8.1%, t-statistic of 1.30). The only possible evidence of deterrence in Table 1 is in business combination laws for which coverage is assumed to begin only after the June 1989 appeals court decision that validated these laws. Here, coverage is less frequent in the takeover sample than in the full sample (3.1% versus 7.4%, t-statistic of -6.33). However, this difference could also reflect a seculiar decline in the takeover market, rather than deterrence. Takeovers were unusually infrequent for fiscal years beginning in 1990 (t-statistic of -2.43) and 1991 (t-statistic of -11.00), confirming the evidence in Fig. 1.

3.4. Characteristics of successful takeovers

Table 1 describes some variables that are only defined for takeovers. Exchange-listed firms were acquired at a rate of 3.1% per year. Auctions account

Table 1

Means and standard deviations of accounting and stock market performance variables, antitakeover protection, and takeover characteristics for 21,887 firm-years beginning January 1977 through January 1991 for NYSE- and Amex-listed stocks with necessary data available in Compustat

	Full sample, 21,887 firm-years		Takeover sample, 669 firm-years		
Variable	Mean	Std. dev.	Mean	Std. dev.	T-test for equal means
Abnormal return (in % over 4 years)	0.0117	0.1777	0.0256	0.1776	2.06
Sales growth (4-year average)	0.0867	0.1272	0.0768	0.1127	– 2.30
Liquidity (4-year average)	0.2470	0.2061	0.2767	0.2190	3.57
Debt/equity (4-year average)	0.7410	1.8455	0.6063	0.9939	– 3.43
Market/book (4-year average)	1.4814	1.7316	1.3718	1.0951	– 2.57
Price/earnings (4-year average)	11.1357	11.0488	10.6688	10.4521	– 1.17
Size	5.6291	1.8596	5.1638	1.4927	– 8.12
Proportion of firm-years covered by:					
Control share law:					
Date law became effective	0.0577	0.2332	0.0553	0.2287	– 0.28
Supreme Court upheld IN law (April 1987)	0.0404	0.1969	0.0389	0.1934	– 0.21
Business combination law:					
Date law became effective	0.1561	0.3629	0.1345	0.3415	– 1.66
Circuit Court upheld WI law (June 1989)	0.0742	0.2622	0.0314	0.1745	– 6.33

Poison pill	0.0811	0.2731	0.0957	0.2944	1.30
1986	0.0632	0.2433	0.0912	0.2881	2.57
1987	0.0611	0.2396	0.0658	0.2481	0.49
1988	0.0589	0.2354	0.0822	0.2749	2.24
1989	0.0562	0.2304	0.0628	0.2427	0.71
1990	0.0495	0.2169	0.0329	0.1785	−2.43
1991	0.0462	0.2100	0.0075	0.0862	−11.00
Successful takeover (= 1)	0.0306	0.1721			
Auction (= 1 if multiple bidders)			0.2407	0.4278	
Cash (= 1)			0.6741	0.4690	
Tender offer (= 1)			0.4499	0.4979	
Market-adjusted premiums in successful takeovers	0.0107	0.0828	0.3489	0.3263	

Abnormal return is the average daily prediction error in percent from a market model regression using the CRSP value-weighted portfolio, where the parameters are estimated in the year before the measurement period (year − 5 relative to the forecast fiscal year). Sales growth is the average growth rate in sales over the four years before the fiscal year. Liquidity is the four-year average of net working capital divided by total assets. Debt/equity is the four-year average ratio of debt to equity. Market/book is the four-year average ratio of the year-end market value of stock to the book value of equity. Price/earnings is the four-year average ratio of the year-end stock price to earnings per share. Size is the log of total assets at the start of the forecast period. The control share law and business combination law dummy variables are both defined in two ways: (a) they equal one if the forecst fiscal year occurs after the effective date of the law for the state in which the company is incorporated, or (b) they equal one if that company's state has a law which is effective for the forecst period and there has already been a major judicial precedent indicating that such a law is likely to be upheld if challenged. Poison pill equals one if the firm has a shareholder rights plan in effect before the forecast period. The dummy variables 1986 through 1991 equal one in these years to show variation in the last part of the sample period. Successful takeover equals one when an initial tender offer or merger proposal that leads to a successful takeover occurs during the forecast firm-year. Auction equals one when more than one bidder tries to takeover the target firm. Cash equals one when the payment to target shareholders is in the form of cash. Tender offer equals one when the winning bid occurs in the form of a tender offer. The market-adjusted premium in successful takeovers is the compounded difference in the returns to target firm's stock and the CRSP value-weighted NYSE/Amex market portfolio during the period from 20 trading days before the first merger proposal or tender offer through five trading days after the successful offer; it equals zero for firm-years in which no takeover occurs.

for 24.1% of the 669 takeovers, cash is the only consideration paid in 67.4%, and tender offers are used 45.0% of the time. Net-of-market premiums received by target shareholders average 34.9%. We refer to this below as the conditional mean premium, conditioning on the occurrence of a successful takeover. We also calculate an unconditional mean premium using all 21,887 firm-years, assigning a takeover premium of zero to all of the firm-years with no initial announcement leading to a successful takeover. There are 669 firm-years with a mean premium of 34.5%, and 21,218 firm-years with a mean premium of zero, aggregating to a population or unconditional mean premium of 1.1% per firm-year.

The unconditional mean premium suggests the economic gain that could be forgone if the takeover market remains dormant, although future losses would be mitigated through alternate ways of regulating managerial slack, such as proxy fights or incentive pay schemes. The demise of the takeover market is often cited as a justification for greater involvement by institutional investors in corporate decisions and governance. Partly in response to the demands of institutional investors, the S.E.C. revised its proxy statement rules in October 1992 to expand disclosure of management compensation, to ease disclosure rules for communications among investors, and to facilitate partial slates of nominees to corporate boards.

4. New evidence on the wealth effect of poison pills

4.1. Poison pill announcement effects, 1983–91

In contrast to event studies of the wealth effects of adoptions of state antitakeover laws, which have been conducted for most of the firms covered by such laws, existing event studies of pill adoptions have been done for only the earliest one-quarter of all the pills adopted to date. We update the event studies of Ryngaert (1988) and Malatesta and Walkling (1988), drawing on the entire population of 1,577 original poison pills adopted through December 1991. Of these, we exclude 118 with inadequate stock return data available from CRSP.

The wealth effect of a pill adoption is a combination of a stock price decline amounting to the expected present value of future takeover premiums forgone due to deterrence, offset by the expected present value of any increase in premiums due to a gain in bargaining power versus bidders. In addition, prices can change due to a revelation of management's private information. Some managers probably wait to adopt pills until they know that an offer is imminent. They could be engaged in merger talks, for which public disclosure is not usually required, they could be aware that an investment bank is shopping the company, or they could anticipate a takeover based on undisclosed corporate performance. A good indication that investors suspect managers of basing their decisions to adopt pills on private information is that 56% of our *Dow Jones News Retrieval* stories on pill adoptions include a denial by management of knowledge of any pending takeover.

Information effects make it difficult to measure deterrence using stock prices. To address this problem, previous researchers have analyzed the subset of pill adoptions made after the market is already aware of a merger interest. Presumably, management's informational advantage regarding any outstanding merger interest is diminished when a merger interest has already been revealed. We refer to these cases below as the 'control premium' subset of pill adoptions. Even in this subset, however, it can be difficult to separate deterrence and information effects. During merger negotiations, the announcement of a pill is tantamount to a disclosure of the bad news that a deal has yet to be struck, so a decline in stock price does not necessarily imply deterrence. Subject to this caveat, our evidence on the wealth effects of pill adoptions confirms earlier studies (i.e., it is consistent with deterrence, but not strong deterrence).

Table 2 shows estimates of the effect of poison pill adoptions on shareholder wealth, measured by the three-day return on the common stock of the issuing firm, centered on the day of the announcement. To adjust for market movements, we subtract the prediction from a market model regression using the CRSP value-weighted portfolio, as estimated over the previous 253 trading days. If the *DJNR* time-stamp for a story is later than 4:00 p.m., we treat the following day as the announcement date. When we cannot find a *DJNR* mention, which happens in 8.5% of the cases, the announcement date is from the *Wall Street Journal Index* or from *Corporate Control Alert*. The *DJNR* text often provides information about coincident confounding news, pending takeover proposals, and rumors. We also check the *Wall Street Journal Index* for such items. Our sample includes 242 control premium cases (16.6% of the sample) in which the adoption was preceded within 12 months by a 13D filing, a published story about merger rumors, or an explicit takeover bid, and where no M&A event was announced simultaneously with the pill. There are 100 cases (6.9% of the sample) with a simultaneous M&A announcement.

Table 2 contains two estimates of average abnormal returns associated with announcements of poison pill adoptions. The fourth column shows the average abnormal return for each subset of the sample, and the second column shows the coefficients from a multiple regression that accounts for interaction effects among the variables. Most of the results are similar, but we focus on the multiple-regression estimates because they account for interactions among the subsamples.

The regression in Table 2 includes dummy variables for control premium cases, for simultaneous M&A news, for NASDAQ listing, and for the year of adoption. We include adoption-year dummy variables in case there is a different market reaction to more recent pills. Principally, we find that a prior control premium decreases the pill announcement effect by -2.09% (t-statistic of

Table 2

Least-squares regression showing the average wealth effect of initial poison-pill rights issues announced in the period 1983–91 for NYSE, Amex, and NASDAQ-listed stocks, by whether a 13D filing, rumors of a bid, or an explicit takeover bid make it likely that a control premium is built into the issuer's stock price at the time of announcement. Another variable measures whether merger and acquisition (M&A) news is announced at the same time as the pill. A different dummy variable indicates NASDAQ-listed firms. Dummy variables for the year of adoption represent the intercepts for each year (to distinguish the early pills from the later ones). The dependent variable is measured as the cumulative abnormal return over days − 1 to + 1 using a market model estimated with the CRSP value-weighted market portfolio during the year (trading days − 255 to − 2) prior to the pill announcement. The third column shows the proportion of the sample for which the respective dummy variables are nonzero. The right column shows the average abnormal return for each subset of the sample. White's (1980) heteroskedasticity-consistent t-statistics are in parentheses.

Variable	Regression coefficients (t-statistic)	Proportion of sample	Average return (t-statistic)
Prior control premium (= 1)	− 0.0209	0.1659	− 0.0155
	(− 6.60)		(− 5.20)
Contemporaneous M&A news (= 1)	0.0326	0.0685	0.0404
	(3.16)		(4.81)
NASDAQ-listed firm (= 1)	− 0.0076	0.3633	− 0.0022
	(− 2.40)		(− 0.92)
Year-by-year intercepts			
1984	− 0.0232	0.0062	− 0.0285
	(− 1.71)		(− 1.56)
1985	0.0068	0.0254	0.0017
	(0.81)		(0.23)
1986	0.0032	0.2255	0.0005
	(1.31)		(0.20)
1987	0.0038	0.0987	0.0022
	(0.81)		(0.45)
1988	0.0098	0.2358	0.0072
	(3.29)		(2.98)
1989	0.0023	0.2282	− 0.0014
	(0.66)		(− 0.50)
1990	0.0036	0.1206	0.0032
	(0.74)		(0.71)
1991	0.0087	0.0596	0.0060
	(1.18)		(1.09)
$\bar{R}^2$	0.048		
Standard error of regression	0.0537		
Degrees of freedom	1,448		

− 6.60). This finding confirms Ryngaert (1988), who reports an average return of − 1.51% (t-statistic of − 2.77) for his control premium group, implying either deterrence or bad news about the progress of takeover negotiations.

NASDAQ companies have lower announcement effects, all else equal, by − 0.8%. with a t-statistic of − 2.40. This result could reflect larger fractional inside ownership. McWilliams (1990) shows that the stock market reaction to adoptions of antitakeover charter amendments is negatively related to the fraction of insider ownership, based on 763 announcements by exchange-listed firms in the period 1980–84. Brickley, Coles, and Terry (1994) show that the stock market reaction to 247 pill adoptions depends on the composition of the board of directors: firms with insider-dominated boards had more negative announcement effects. They find no evidence that the takeover rate is lower for firms with insider-dominated boards. We include only NYSE- and Amex-listed companies in our analyses of deterrence and premiums (Tables 3 and 4), and this differential announcement effect for NASDAQ companies implies that our conclusions may not apply to smaller companies.

Among the yearly dummy variables, the only negative intercept estimate (− 2.3% t-statistic of − 1.71) is for 1984, which covers the first nine pills (including two from 1983). The earliest adopters may have been more likely to use poison pills to the detriment of target stockholders, or the market may have initially overestimated the deterrence effect of pills. Finally, average abnormal returns are higher by 3.3% (t-statistic of 3.16) when pills are announced jointly with M&A news. This effect is small compared to initial takeover announcements because these are usually cases in which a pill is announced after an initial takeover announcement, often as part of an announcement of management's response to a takeover attempt.

4.2. Can deterrence be measured for poison pills?

Fig. 5 shows the endogenous nature of decisions to adopt poison pills (i.e., managers often adopt pills when a takeover attempt is unusually likely). It plots (in daily event time) the cumulative proportion of pill adopters that received an initial takeover attempt within one year on either side of the adoption date. The sample consists of all 960 adoptions of original poison pills by exchange-listed firms in the period 1983–90. We exclude pills adopted after 1990 to ensure a year's worth of M&A data after every adoption. Takeover attempts include the first occurrence of a merger proposal, merger agreement, or interfirm tender offer. The plotted value for the nth event day is a count of the total number of takeover announcements in a period starting 250 trading days before an adoption and ending with the nth day relative to the adoption. This count is divided by the sample size, so the plotted values represent the cumulative proportion of pill adopters put into play within one year of adoption.

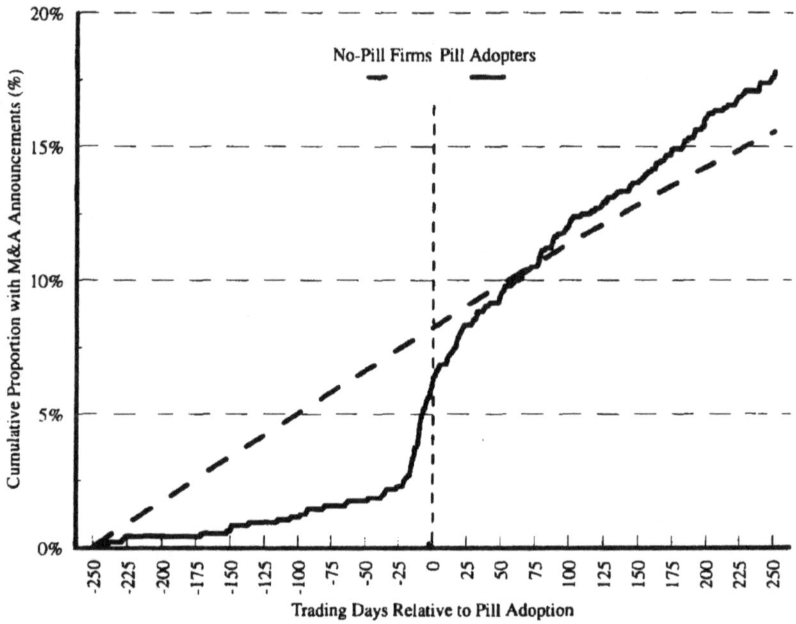

Fig. 5. Event study showing the cumulative proportion of firms receiving merger and acquisition (M&A) announcements within a year of the date of adoption of a initial poison pill, for 960 exchange-listed firms that adopted pills in the period 1983–90. The dotted line shows the cumulative fraction, over corresponding two-year periods, for exchange-listed firms that never adopted a poison pill. M&A announcements include merger proposals, merger agreements, and inter-firm tender offers, regardless of success.

For comparison, we also plot the average proportion of no-pill firms that are put into play over coincident intervals. No-pill firms are all those exchange-listed firms that did not adopt a pill. For each of the 960 adoptions, we calculate the cumulative proportion of no-pill firms in play as of the *n*th day relative to that adoption. We average these values across events to produce a series of *n* (plotted) values that can be interpreted as the proportion of firms expected to be in play as of each event day, allowing for secular variation in takeover frequency and an uneven distribution of pill adoptions over time. Since two-thirds of the exchange-listed firms are in the no-pill group, the cumulative proportion of no-pill firms that are put into play should be a smooth and continuous curve over any given two-year period. Because we average these over 960 pill-adoption periods to get the cumulative proportion of no-pill firms that are put into play in the typical period, our expected values plot as a straight line.

The tendency for managers to adopt pills when the likelihood of a takeover is unusually high shows up in Fig. 5 as a steeper slope for pill firms (solid line) than for no-pill firms (dashed line) near pill adoptions. The proportion of pill adopters that are in play increases from 2.4% one month before (day −25) to 19.4% one year after (day 250). Since the corresponding proportions for no-pill firms are 7.8% and 16.2%, the change among pill firms is about double that no-pill firms. Most of the difference arises near the pill adoption, with 6.4% of pill adopters put in play between days −25 and 25 compared with 1.7% of no-pill firms. Fig. 5 also shows a curious deficit in merger and acquisition activity before poison pills are adopted, compared with the coincident experience among no-pill firms (2.7% versus 7.8% as of day −25). This deficit is largely eliminated during the month before adoption and eliminated about three months after adoption. The proximity of the endpoints of the two curves (at the far right of Fig. 5) is consistent with a long-run rate of receiving takeover bids that is largely independent of pill adoption, and consistent with the results of our prediction analysis in Section 5. Ken French has pointed out that the low level of M&A activity before pill adoptions may be an artifact of the decision to adopt pills when management perceives that M&A activity is likely, given that the long-run rate of receiving takeover bids is not strongly related to pill adoption.

This tendency for managers to adopt poison pills when takeovers are unusually likely is less of an issue with adoptions of state antitakeover laws because these laws are less under the control of a target firm's management, although they can switch their state of incorporation, lobby for new legislation, or opt out of existing legislation. Romano (1987) notes that antitakeover laws are sometimes adopted to protect a particular firm that is already in play. Since all of the firms domiciled in that state become covered, though few are in play at the time, law adoptions are endogenous for a small fraction of firms. Thus, in Section 5, we implement a two-stage statistical procedure to address endogeneity in pill coverage, but use a standard procedure for law coverage.

5. Direct evidence of deterrence

5.1. Previous studies

Pound (1987) provides direct evidence that takeover frequency is lower for firms with antitakeover charter provisions. He compares the post-adoption takeover experience of a sample of 100 NYSE firms that adopted supermajority and classified board charter amendments (as a package) in the period 1973–79 and the takeover experience of a time-matched sample of 100 NYSE firms that did not adopt either type of amendment. Over periods that run from adoption through 1984 (averaging eight years in length), the takeover frequency is 28% for adopters and 38% for nonadopters. Ambrose and Megginson (1992) estimate a logit model using cross-sectional data on a sample of 117 exchange-listed target firms in the period 1981–86 and a time-matched sample of 214 exchange-listed firms. Their model includes (among other things) dummy variables for whether each firm has a classified board, fair price charter provision, dual class capitalization, blank check preferred stock authorization, or poison pill. Preferred stock authorizations provide the only evidence of deterrence. Bhagat and Jefferis (1993) study classified board charter provisions, poison pills, and fair price amendments adopted in 1984–85 and test whether they deterred takeovers over the following two years for 344 firms, and find little evidence that takeover defenses reduce takeover activity.

Other prediction studies do not include antitakeover measures as predictors. Hasbrouck (1985) uses a logit model to predict takeovers for a sample of 86 targets and a sample of 344 time-, size-, and industry-matched nontargets, and finds that larger market/book ratios and larger size reduce the likelihood of a takeover, but that liquidity and leverage are unimportant. Palepu (1986) provides logit estimates based on a sample of 163 target and 256 nontarget firms in the period 1971–79 using the accounting and stock-based predictors described in Section 3. He obtains negative coefficient estimates for abnormal return, sales growth, leverage, and size, so these reduce the likelihood of a takeover. He obtains a positive coefficient estimate for a growth-resource mismatch dummy variable, so mismatched firms face a higher likelihood of a takeover. Market/book, price/earnings, and liquidity do not affect the likelihood of a takeover. Mørck, Shleifer, and Vishny (1988) estimate a probit model using 1980 data for 454 Fortune-500 firms, of which 82 were takeover targets between 1981 and 1985, and find that larger size and q-ratio deter hostile takeovers, but not friendly ones. Mikkelson and Partch (1989) use a logit model and pool data as of 1973, 1978, and 1983 for 240 exchange-listed firms. They find that larger size and affiliate-firm cross-holdings deter acquisitions, but that leverage and managerial stockholdings do not affect the likelihood of a successful takeover. Shivdasani (1993) estimates a logit model using data on 193 hostile targets and 194 nontarget firms from 1980–88 and finds that size, managerial stockholdings, and affiliate-firm cross-holdings deter hostile takeovers, but that earnings growth and board composition do not matter. Size is the only predictor that is consistently successful in these studies, while mixed success has been achieved with abnormal return, sales growth, leverage, q-ratio, or market/book, and certain ownership variables.

5.2. Predicting poison pills

If managers adopt poison pills when takeovers are unusually likely, as suggested by the evidence in Fig. 5 and Table 2, then this tendency will mask the estimated deterrence effect of pills. If the tendency is severe, pills could appear to cause takeovers. Using a medical analogy, the consumption of aspirin might be a good predictor of the visible symptoms of the common cold, not because aspirin causes colds, but because people often take aspirin when they feel a cold coming on. Similarly, managers may adopt pills when they feel that a takeover is unusually likely. We mitigate this possibility by following a suggestion of Maddala (1983, p. 246). We first estimate a model to predict pill coverage, using variables that are likely to predict management's choice of whether and when to adopt a pill. This yields 'predictable' and 'surprise' components of pill coverage. The logic is that pills that are a surprise (to researchers) are the ones most likely to have been adopted when management has information about a pending takeover attempt. We hope to isolate the deterrence effect of pill coverage, in a second-stage analysis discussed below, after stripping away the surprise component.

Candidates for inclusion in the first-stage (pill) prediction model are the accounting and stock return variables listed in Table 1, along with law coverage. Since poison pills represent an innovation, we include yearly dummy variables (for 1986–91) to reflect the spread of pill coverage over time. The right panel of Table 3 shows estimates of a probit model that predicts pill coverage for all 21,887 firm-years. Since probit coefficients are difficult to interpret, Table 3 reports the marginal effect of a change in each predictor variable calculated at its sample mean (i.e., similar to the least-squares coefficient in a linear probability model).[6]

Being incorporated in a state with an antitakeover law is a good predictor of whether a firm has a poison pill. A control share law increases the likelihood of having a pill by 2.33% (t-statistic of 5.49) and a business combination law increases it by 4.81% (t-statistic of 7.88). These variables will be negatively related if one form of protection substitutes for another, and positively related if managers who prefer protection choose to both incorporate in a state with an antitakeover law and also to adopt a pill. The positive sign on these estimates implies that state laws and poison pills are more complements than substitutes.

Among the accounting and stock market predictors, only firm size is both statistically and economically significant. Larger firms are less likely to be acquired, as detailed in the next section, and more likely to have pills. An increase of just \$1.7 million (t-statistic of 20.79) in total assets, which average \$280 million, increases the probability of having a pill by 1%. For the average firm-year in our sample, this means an increase from 8.1% to 9.1% in the probability of having a pill. This positive relation between size and the probability of pill adoption is understandable if there are economies of scale in buying pill protection due to fixed costs in adopting pills, but the rapid trend toward

[6]See, for example, Greene (1993, p. 639) for a description of this calculation. The predictions from a probit model estimated using data after 1983 (when poison pills were invented) are virtually identical to those from the full sample of firm-years.

Table 3

Probit estimates of the dependence of takeover probability on accounting and stock price data, state antitakeover laws, and poison pills (left panel), and the dependence of poison pill adoptions on accounting and stock price data and state antitakeover laws (right panel), using pooled time-series cross-sectional data for exchange-listed firms and for fiscal-year forecast periods beginning January 1977 through January 1991 (21,887 firm-years). The dependent variable is either a dummy that equals one if a successful tender offer, merger proposal, or merger agreement is announced during the forecast period, or a dummy that equals one if a firm adopts an original poison pill during the forecast period. The predictor variables are all defined as of the start of the forecast period.

	Takeover dummy			Pill adoption dummy		
	Probit coefficient	Adjusted t-statistic	Marginal effect	Probit coefficient	t-statistic	Marginal effect
Poison pill	0.345	4.60	0.0234			
Predicted pills (from probit)	– 0.735	– 2.01	– 0.0498			
Surprise pills (error from probit)	0.418	5.23	0.0283			
Control share law	0.184	1.55	0.0124	0.277	5.49	0.0233
Business combination law	0.267	1.74	0.0181	0.573	7.88	0.0481
Abnormal return (in % over 4 years)	0.177	1.42	0.0120	– 0.054	– 0.46	– 0.0045
Sales growth (4-year average)	– 0.086	– 0.51	– 0.0059	– 0.450	– 3.28	– 0.0378
Liquidity (4-year average)	0.073	0.64	0.0048	0.453	4.59	0.0380

Debt/equity (4-year average)	– 0.024	– 1.30	– 0.0017	– 0.011	– 0.99	– 0.0009
Market/book (4-year average)	– 0.012	– 0.70	– 0.0008	0.011	0.96	0.0009
Price/earnings (4-year average)	– 0.001	– 0.62	– 0.0001	0.003	2.33	0.0003
Size	– 0.048	– 3.24	– 0.0032	0.231	20.79	0.0194
Constant	– 1.602	11.81	– 0.1086	– 4.997	– 31.39	– 0.4199
1986	0.216	1.61	0.0147	1.188	7.52	0.0998
1987	0.155	1.17	0.0105	2.374	17.29	0.1995
1988	0.300	2.20	0.0204	2.577	18.85	0.2165
1989	0.234	1.41	0.0159	2.866	21.04	0.2408
1990	– 0.114	– 0.58	– 0.0077	2.689	18.22	0.2260
1991	– 0.681	2.58	– 0.0462	2.746	18.19	0.2307
Log-likelihood		– 2922.89			– 3291.12	
Degrees of freedom		21,869			21,871	

Coefficient and t-statistic for the *poison pill* dummy variable are from a regression including all the other explanatory variables, except predicted pills and surprise pills. By definition, the sum of the predicted and surprise components of pills equals '*poison pill*'. For other variable definitions, see the note to Table 1. The marginal effect column transforms the probit coefficient into the marginal effect of the variable on the estimated probability, evaluated at the sample means of the explanatory variables. T-statistics in the takeover prediction model have been adjusted to account for the fact that explanatory variables are estimates from another statistical model (i.e., the pill prediction model in the right panel); see Maddala (1983, p. 247).

in-house and local counsel to advise on pill adoptions (seen in Fig. 4) suggests that the costs of adopting a pill, fixed or otherwise, are small. A positive relation could also occur if small firms have a natural or incidental immunity, perhaps due to ownership structures that are more concentrated, so that their demand for pill protection is low. By this reasoning, however, the demand for pill protection would be lower for larger firms because (as detailed below) size itself seems to be a natural or incidental deterrent.

The next-best predictors after size are sales growth and liquidity. A 1% increase in the probability of having a pill requires a decease in sales growth of 26% per year (t-statistic of -3.28), where typical sales growth is 8.7% per year. The same effect requires an increase of 27% (t-statistic of 4.59) in the ratio of net liquid assets to total assets, which would involve doubling the typical ratio of 24.7%. We do not judge either of these effects to be economically important.

5.3. Predicting takeovers

We test for the deterrence effect of antitakeover measures by including dummy variables defined on antitakeover coverage in a takeover prediction model. The power of this research design depends on dispersion in antitakeover coverage. At each time, we want some firms to be covered, while others are not. Because half of all exchange-listed firms became covered *en masse* when Delaware adopted its business combination law in January 1988, the deterrence effect of business combination laws could show up as a post-1987 drop in takeover frequency, rather than as a firm-specific phenomenon. Conversely, a late-1980s shift in takeover frequency, perhaps due to recession or regulatory intervention in credit markets, could show up as deterrence due to business combination laws. Our review of the events of the late 1980s in Section 2 favors the latter interpretation and persuades us to control for year-by-year variation in takeover frequency. Thus, our dummy variables for pills and laws tell us whether antitakeover measures had an effect *beyond* a probable secular decline in takeover activity. With one exception noted below and discussed in Section 7.2, our conclusions do not depend on the inclusion of yearly dummy variables.

The left-hand panel of Table 3 shows estimates of a model that predicts takeovers among exchange-listed firms with fiscal years beginning 1977–91 (the sample described in Section 3). We predict a dummy variable equaling one if a successful merger proposal, merger agreement, or interfirm tender offer is announced during a fiscal year. The predictors include dummy variables for coverage by antitakeover measures, seven accounting and stock market predictors, and six yearly dummy variables (1986 through 1991).

The first row of Table 3 shows that the marginal deterrence effect of a pill is 2.34% (t-statistic of 4.60). A literal interpretation of the positive sign on this estimate is that a pill increases the likelihood of a takeover, but a more plausible interpretation is that pills tend to be adopted in anticipation of a takeover attempt, and that this (private) information is not captured by the (public) accounting and stock market factors that we include. To deal with any tendency for managers to adopt pills when a takeover is unusually likely, we break the dummy variable for pills into surprise and predictable components, based on estimates of the first-stage pill prediction model reported in the right panel of Table 3. We use these components as predictors in a second-stage takeover prediction model, reported in the left panel of Table 3. Thus, the predictable component of pill coverage is an estimate of the probability of pill coverage, and the surprise component is the difference between the pill dummy variable and this prediction.

The coefficient estimate for the surprise component of pills is positive, as expected, and implies that the annual probability of takeover is higher by 2.83% (t-statistic of 5.23) when a pill is a total surprise (i.e., the predicted probability of having a pill is zero, based on publicly available accounting and stock price data). The corresponding estimate for the predictable component of pill coverage is negative and implies that the annual probability of takeover is lower by 4.98% (t-statistic of -2.01) when a pill is completely predictable (i.e., the prediction of pill coverage = 1.0). None of the pills in our sample are completely predictable, however. Even in 1991, the year with the highest average predicted pill coverage (44.2%), the pill-induced decrease in annual takeover probability is only 2.15% per year (4.87% times 44.2%) for the typical firm.[7] Moreover, when we omit the yearly dummy variables that control for secular variation, the t-statistic for the predictable component of pill coverage falls to -0.84 (see Section 7.2).

The estimated coefficients for control share laws and business combination laws are positive (t-statistics of 1.55 and 1.74), so antitakeover laws appear to increase takeover probabilities slightly, holding other factors constant (including secular variation). Since the law adoptions are motivated by takeover expectations for only a few firms, we conclude from these estimates that managers have not used these laws to deter takeovers systematically, and infer that antitakeover laws played a minor role in depressing the 1980s market for corporate control.

Few of the accounting and stock market performance variables are reliable predictors of takeovers. Size is the one exception. Larger firms are less likely to be acquired (t-statistic of -3.24) and the economic significance of the estimated

[7]The standard errors have been corrected to account for the fact that this explanatory variable is an estimate from another statistical model. See Maddala (1983, p. 247). In earlier drafts of our paper we reported uncorrected logit estimates that differed little from the corrected probit estimates reported here. Since the same variables are used to predict pills and then takeovers, there is substantial collinearity between the pill predictions and the other variables in the takeover prediction model (except for surprise pills). In fact, identification is achieved in these models only because of the nonlinearity of the prediction models.

coefficient is not trivial. A decrease of $23 million from the average level of total assets (of $280 million) increases the annual likelihood of takeover by 1%. The probability of takeover falls reliably below the sample period norm only for fiscal years that start in 1991 (t-statistic of -2.58). As discussed in Section 2, these forecast periods follow the bankruptcy of Drexel Burnham Lambert and coincide roughly with the onset of recession and the credit crunch.

6. Predicting takeover premiums

Table 4 shows estimates of the dependence of takeover premiums on antitakeover measures, the accounting and stock market performance variables (described in Section 3), and certain takeover characteristics. Huang and Walkling (1987) estimate a regression model in a sample of 204 exchange-listed target firms acquired by merger or tender offer in the period 1977–82, and find that premiums are reliably higher in all-cash transactions, but not in tender offers. Bradley, Desai, and Kim (1988) estimate a similar model for 236 tender offers for exchange-listed firms in the period 1963–84, and find that premiums are higher in auctions. Thus, we include dummy variables defined by whether the transaction is (1) an auction with multiple, publicly revealed bidders, (2) an all-cash transaction, and (3) a tender offer.

The right panel of Table 4 reports estimates based on the sample of 669 successful takeover targets (conditional premiums) and the left panel of Table 4 reports estimates of the same model using all 21,887 firm-years with the takeover premium set to zero in nontakeover firm-years (unconditional premiums). The estimated effect of antitakeover measures on the unconditional premium (left column) is of interest because it is a net effect of a decrease in the premium if antitakeover devices deter offers and an increase if they increase premiums in successful offers. The first line of Table 4 shows (*in italics*) estimates for the coefficient on a dummy variable that combines the predictable and surprise components of pill coverage (described in the previous section). These estimates imply that both conditional and unconditional premiums are higher with a pill in place. Since we control for the (positive) effect of auctions on premiums, these estimates understate the effect of pills on premiums to the extent that pills cause auctions, as their proponents claim.[8]

[8]Using probit models, similar to Table 3, to predict which successful takeovers involve auctions shows an insignificant effect on the predictable component of pills (t-statistic of -1.77) and the surprise component (t-statistic of 0.14), but reliable positive effects of control share laws (t-statistic of 3.50) and business combination laws (t-statistic of 2.10).

Table 4
Least-squares estimates of the relation of takeover premiums with state antitakeover laws, poison pills, accounting and stock price data, and characteristics of the takeover. Takeover premiums are measured as the compounded difference in the returns to target firm's stock and the CRSP value-weighted NYSE/Amex market portfolio during the period from 20 trading days before the first merger proposal or tender offer through five trading days after the successful offer. In the left panel, the sample consists of pooled time-series cross-sectional data for exchange-listed firms with fiscal-year forecast periods beginning January 1977 through January 1991 (21,887 firm-years). The right panel uses the 669 firm-years when a subsequently successful takeover begins. The predictor variables are all defined as of the start of the forecast period. The dates when important legal precedents established the effectiveness of control share laws (April 1987) and of business combination laws (June 1989) are used to define coverage by these laws (i.e., the dummy variable equals one for firm-years in which the firm was covered by a law that had already been certified by a major judicial decision). The t-statistics use White's (1980) heteroskedasticity-consistent standard errors.

	Full sample		Successful takeover sample	
Predictors	Coefficient	t-statistic	Coefficient	t-statistic
Poison pill	0.0144	4.38	0.1627	2.95
Predicted pills (from probit)	0.0024	0.30	0.4588	1.60
Surprise pills (error from probit)	0.0151	4.33	0.1453	2.31
Control share law	0.0080	1.96	0.1094	1.61
Business combination law	0.0054	2.22	0.0269	0.29
Abnormal return (in % over 4 years)	0.0059	1.71	0.0439	0.61
Sales growth (4-year average)	0.0048	1.27	0.3964	3.48
Liquidity (4-year average)	0.0096	3.18	0.0813	1.33
Debt/equity (4-year average)	− 0.0003	− 1.77	− 0.0167	− 1.37
Market/book (4-year average)	− 0.0005	− 2.52	− 0.0212	− 2.00
Price/earnings (4-year average)	− 0.0001	− 1.46	− 0.0012	− 0.97
Size	− 0.0008	− 2.38	0.0020	0.20
Constant	0.0137	5.31	0.2048	3.02
1986	0.0020	0.92	− 0.1214	− 3.74
1987	− 0.0012	− 0.48	− 0.1665	− 2.78
1988	0.0119	2.66	0.0198	0.29
1989	− 0.0007	− 0.18	− 0.2400	− 2.30
1990	− 0.0103	− 3.97	− 0.3008	− 4.42
1991	− 0.0144	− 4.21	− 0.3300	− 2.08
Auction (= 1 if multiple bidders)			0.1137	3.61
Cash (= 1)			0.0857	3.53
Tender offer (= 1)			0.1296	5.27
$\bar{R}^2$	0.005		0.192	
Standard error of regression	0.0826		0.2933	
Degrees of freedom	21,869		648	

Coefficient and t-statistic for the *poison pill* dummy variable are from a regression including all the other explanatory vaiables, except predicted pills and surprise pills. The other coefficients from that regression are not shown. The pill predictions come from the model shown in Table 3. By definition, the sum of predicted and surprise pills equals 'poison pill'. For other variable definitions, see the note to Table 1.

The surprise component of pill coverage is reliably related to higher premiums. For pills that are a total surprise (i.e., the predicted probability of pill coverage = 0.0), conditional premiums are higher by 14.5% (t-statistic of 2.31) and unconditional premiums by 1.5% (t-statistic of 4.33). Not only are takeovers more frequent the more surprising is pill coverage (from Table 3), average premiums are higher as well. With the predictable component of pills, the most we can conclude is that shareholders are not harmed, but this conclusion is important in view of the weak evidence in Table 3 that predictable pills deter takeovers. Specifically, the positive effect on conditional premiums is large, at 45.9%, but quite imprecise (t-statistic of 1.60). The effect on unconditional premiums is small but positive, 0.24% (t-statistic of 0.30), reflecting a large increase in conditional premiums and a smaller decrease in the probability of a takeover.

A control share law raises conditional premiums by 10.9% (t-statistic of 16.1) and a business combination law has almost no effect (t-statistic of 0.29). Control share and business combination laws have small positive effects on unconditional premiums, 0.8% and 0.5% respectively (t-statistic of 1.96 and 2.22). In tests that are not reported here, we find that neither law has an effect on premiums reliably different from zero when coverage is defined using the dates these laws took effect instead of judicial decision dates.

The accounting and stock market performance variables predict premiums better than they do takeovers. Recent sales growth has a modest positive effect on conditional premiums. A deviation in sales growth of 2.5% per year (from a sample mean of 7.7%) increases conditional premiums by 1% (t-statistic of 3.48), but unconditional premiums are not reliably related to sales growth (t-statistic of 1.27). Although liquidity has no reliable effect on conditional premiums, it is associated with larger unconditional premiums (t-statistic of 3.18). A higher market/book ratio reduces conditional premiums (t-statistic of − 2.00) and unconditional premiums (t-statistic of − 2.52). Although size has only a small positive effect on conditional premiums, size does predict lower unconditional premiums (t-statistic of − 2.38). This finding is no surprise since size is the one variable with reliable predictive power for takeovers. The fact that the estimates for yearly dummy variables are generally reliably negative for the years 1989–91 means that takeover premiums became much lower for unprotected targets after antitakeover protection became the norm, suggesting either a shift in the composition of the group of unprotected firms or a growing association between antitakeover measures and management bargaining power versus bidders.

We confirm a result reported by Bradley, Desai, and Kim (1988) with our finding that an auction is associated with an added takeover premium of 11.4% (t-statistic of 3.61), compared with their estimate of 13% (t-statistic of 4.23). We also confirm a result reported by Huang and Walkling (1987) with our finding that all-cash transactions are associated with an added premium of 8.6%

(t-statistic of 3.53), compared with their estimate of 12.9% (t-statistic of 3.68). Our evidence contradicts another of their results, however, since we find that tender offers are associated with an added takeover premium of 13.0% of (t-statistic of 5.27), after controlling for method of payment, compared with their estimate of -0.2%.

7. Sensitivity analysis

As a check, we estimate alternate specifications for the tests in Tables 2, 3, and 4. In the interests of parsimony, we summarize these tests below but do not report detailed results.

7.1. Hostile takeovers

There are arguments in the literature that hostile takeovers are different from friendly takeovers in the sense that the sources of gain from the two kinds of transactions are likely to be different (for example, Mørck, Shleifer, and Vishny, 1988, 1989). The takeover prediction estimates in Table 3 do not distinguish, however, between hostile and friendly transactions. By definition, antitakeover measures add nothing to management's ability to reject friendly transactions, i.e., those conditioned implicitly on management approval, so including such transactions cannot help us measure the deterrence effect of antitakeover measures. Depending on how well we can measure friendliness, filtering out friendly transactions could reduce noise. Considering how large our sample is, however, our concern over bias outweighs our concern over efficiency. Filtering would introduce a bias if stronger takeover defenses cause a substitution of negotiated for unnegotiated transactions, rather than a reduction in the frequency of transactions. Since some substitution is likely, a test of whether takeover defenses deter hostile transactions alone overstates the costs of antitakeover measures.

Despite these reservations, we estimate the effect of antitakeover measures on hostile takeovers alone using specifications of hostility that are, at least, replicable. Hostility is hard to measure in a replicable way because most initially hostile takeovers end as friendly (negotiated) transactions through a process of negotiation and competition. Thus, the stage at which hostility is measured, within this process, determines whether transactions are classified as hostile. Moreover, these negotiations typically are confidential. When they are revealed before settlement, it is often because one of the negotiating parties sees its bargaining position enhanced by presettlement publicity, and this presettlement publicity is the raw material for any measurement of hostility. We know of no way to define hostility that does not suffer from these practical difficulties.

Nonetheless, we treat takeovers as hostile if:

(1) during the 12 months before an initial merger or tender offer bid, a 13D statement is filed in which the buyer discloses an intent to seek control, or there are significant merger rumors about the target firm (suggesting an effort to put the firm in play), or there is a targeted share repurchase for more than 5% of the target company's stock;

(2) the initial bid is either an unnegotiated tender offer for control of the target firm, or a merger proposal specifying a price (a 'bear hug').

Our full sample includes 438 takeovers that fit the first description, with hostility based on pre-bid events, and 172 that fit the second description, with hostility based on the character of the opening bid.

When we replicate our takeover prediction analysis for hostile takeovers, neither of these definitions yields results (not shown here) that differ substantively from those in Table 3, although the smaller number of successful takeovers resulting from these two definitions of hostility results in less precise estimates of all of the coefficients in the model.

7.2. *Controlling for a secular trend*

Our takeover prediction model in Table 3 includes yearly dummy variables for 1986–91 because there is reason to expect a decline due to general business conditions, particularly a cash crunch, in the last few years of our sample period. When we replicate this analysis without yearly dummy variables, the estimated effects of the state antitakeover law variables are stronger. T-statistics for the control share and business combination law variables in the pill prediction equation are 19.16 and 37.78 (compared with 5.49 and 7.88 in Table 3). The marginal effect of coverage by control share and business combination laws increases the probability of pill coverage by 10.14% and 15.14%, respectively (compared with 2.33% and 4.81% in Table 3). The t-statistic for the predictable component of pill coverage in the takeover prediction model is smaller ($-$ 1.17 compared with $-$ 2.01 without the yearly dummy variables). Thus, there is no reason to believe that the yearly dummy variables substitute for the effects of the antitakeover laws or for pills to reduce the evidence for deterrence in the takeover prediction models.

Since poison pills were not introduced until 1983, and the significant legal precedents supporting state antitakeover laws also occurred after 1983, we also estimate our tests using only firm-years after 1983. The negative coefficient of the predicted component of pills and the positive coefficients for the surprise components of pills and for coverage by control share or business combination laws in the takeover prediction models are all larger and the t-statistics are larger, but the general conclusions described in Sections 5 and 6 are unchanged.

Also, Table 3 reports yearly dummy variables for only the last six years in the sample period in Table 3 to economize on the results we report. When we estimate a version of the takeover prediction model that includes dummy variables for all years (and no constant), the estimates of the yearly intercepts from 1977–85 are between − 1.379 and − 1.628 with no discernible pattern. Constraining these coefficients to be equal in Table 3 does not affect the estimates of the other coefficients in the model.

Finally, the failure of the accounting and stock market performance measures, other than size, to help explain takeovers is due neither to the inclusion of the poison pill nor state law variables nor to the inclusion of the yearly dummy variables. We estimate models using only the accounting and stock market variables separately for each year from 1977–91, and find only size helps predict takeovers in most years.

7.3. Wealth effect of pills

Szewczyk and Tsetsekos (1992, Table 4) provide evidence that the wealth effect of the adoption of the Pennsylvania antitakeover law was less negative for firms that already had a poison pill, the presumption being that the added deterrence from a state antitakeover law is lower in these cases. Reversing this, we test whether the wealth effect of the adoption of a pill is less negative for firms that are already covered by a law. Adding a dummy variable to the regression in Table 2, we find that the stock price reaction to pill announcements does not depend on whether a firm is already covered by a law (coefficients of 0.00003 and − 0.0009, with t-statistics of 0.01 and − 0.19, for business combination and control share laws, respectively). Also, since hiring expensive outside counsel to implement a pill could signal litigiousness, we included dummy variables equaling one if the adopting company retained a big-two or next-seven law firm, but these coefficients are not different from zero (coefficients of − 0.0020 and 0.0026, with t-statistics of − 0.57 and 0.41, respectively).

7.4. Effective dates for state antitakeover laws

We estimate versions of the models in Table 3 using the dates that the individual state antitakeover laws took effect (when these precede the relevant judicial decision dates). These results show even less evidence of deterrence for state laws, probably because they include more firm-years in the mid-1980s when takeover activity is high. Using the judicial decision dates, which are closer to the beginning of the crash in the market for corporate control, as we have done in Tables 3 and 4, gives the state laws a better chance to explain the time series and cross-sectional behavior of takeover rates, but that advantage still yields no reliable evidence of deterrence.

7.5. *Morning-after pills and success rates*

The endogeneity problem, or the tendency for managers to adopt poison pills shortly before impending takeover attempts (seen in Fig. 5 and discussed in Sections 4 and 5), would be worse if our measurement interval were narrower than one year. Fig. 5 shows that many poison pills are adopted close to the time of tender offers or merger bids. We call these 'morning-after pills'. When we include these pills in our takeover prediction model, after subtracting the predictable component of these pills, they have positive effects similar to those of the surprise component of pill coverage, but about half as large. As for takeover premiums, in a regression similar to Table 4 the coefficient for the surprise component of morning-after pills is 0.0366 (t-statistic of 0.61) for conditional premiums and 0.0277 (t-statistic of 4.01) for unconditional premiums. Thus, morning-after pills affect premiums much as does the surprise component of pill coverage.

We do not report on takeover success rates elsewhere in this study, but we find that takeover success rates are lower for morning-after pills than for the predictable and surprise components of pill coverage, which are in place at the start of forecast fiscal years. In Table 3 we predict successful bids within the whole sample. We can predict takeover success rates by replicating our analysis on the subset of firm-years containing initial bids, regardless of success. Doing so, the marginal effect of the surprise component of pills is 4.8% (t-statistic of 0.80) and − 17.0% (t-statistic of − 2.95) for the surprise component morning-after pills. Of the 50 firms with morning-after pills, half are acquired in the following 12 months. This compares with a 76% success rate for the 875 firm-years in which a target firm receives a tender offer or merger proposal (resulting in the 669 firm-years with successful takeovers). In summary, although takeover bids are less likely to succeed when target firm management adopts a pill after the initial bid, expected takeover premiums remain positive even for these pills, so that from the selling shareholders' point of view, it is never too late to adopt a poison pill, nor is there a clear gain from preemptive adoption.

7.6. *Clinical experience*

Clinical experience leaves little doubt that some takeovers were deterred by antitakeover measures. For example, there were 27 instances from 1985 through 1990 in which a court upheld a poison pill challenged by a bidder. Since this sample excludes negotiations that settle quickly (before lawsuits are filed or before courts rule), these tend to be deals with difficult negotiations, where pills matter. Of these target firms, 11 remained independent one year after the decision and 16 were acquired by the plaintiff or some third party.[9] Clearly, total deterrence is the less common outcome even among these obviously hostile takeovers.

8. Conclusions

If the 1980s merger wave was ended by modern antitakeover measures, evidence of deterrence should be seen in the experience of individual firms following adoption of these measures, and this evidence should survive attempts to control for secular trends in takeover activity. Otherwise, it is more likely that broad-scale political or economic forces are responsible for the demise of the market for corporate control. We find no evidence of deterrence from control share or business combination laws. There is weak evidence of deterrence from poison pills that are predictable based on publicly available information about the firm's performance. Poison pills adopted by firms that do not fit the pattern in the market (which we call surprise pills) are associated with reliably higher takeover rates. This finding probably reflects the choice by management to adopt a poison pill when it has private information that a bid is imminent. The net effect of these two motivations for adopting poison pills is a positive association with takeover rates.

Anecdotal evidence and clinical experience strongly suggest that some potential takeovers were deterred by modern antitakeover measures, but this conclusion is not supported by our systematic evidence. In its decision upholding the Indiana control share law, the U.S. Supreme Court noted that the case against the law ultimately rested on an unsubstantiated empirical claim of deterrence, and our results validate the Court's skepticism.

Our new evidence on how stock prices change with poison pill adoptions does not suggest an economically meaningful degree of deterrence. Controlling for other measures of information that reflect the likelihood of a subsequent takeover bid, only the earliest pills (before 1985) are associated with large declines in shareholder wealth on the adoption of these measures. There is

[9]Firms whose pills were upheld in court, and who stayed independent for a year following the decision (date), include CTS (4/23/86), DeSoto (2/5/90), Household International (1/19/85), Johnson Controls (3/25/85), Phillips Petroleum (6/3/86), Property Trust of America (10/2/89), Revlon (10/9/85), Sea Containers Ltd (11/27/89), Universal Foods (3/18/89), Santa Fe-Southern Pacific (3/11/88), and USG (4/28/88). Firms that were acquired within a year include Allied Stores (10/24/86), Damon (9/16/88), Facet Enterprises (4/15/88), Federated Department Stores (3/18/88), Gelco (11/10/86), Great Northern Nekoosa (12/12/89), Hayes Albion (11/25/86), Holly Farms (12/30/88), Koppers (4/1/88), Milton Roy (11/9/89), Prime Computer (12/20/88), Ryan Homes (10/24/86), Southwest Forest (3/20/85), Staley Continental (5/9/88.), T W Services (3/2/89), and Vermont American (10/13/89).

a negative reaction to pill announcements when the firm is already in play through some prior public announcement that is likely to foreshadow M&A activity. This effect could represent either deterrence or negative information about the process of ongoing negotiations.

Our new evidence that takeover premiums are higher when target firms are protected by state laws or by pills suggests that the relative bargaining positions of bidders and targets are altered by these antitakeover devices, raising the costs to the bidder and the gains to the target. This implies deterrence, but we find that target shareholders gain even after accounting for deals that are never completed.

The combination of the event study evidence in Table 2, the previous event studies on antitakeover devices in the literature, and the takeover premium evidence in Table 4 raises an interesting puzzle. Why is there ever a negative reaction to poison pills or to antitakeover laws when, based on the evidence through 1991, the net effect of takeover protection from laws and pills is positive? One possible answer is that the market misestimated the eventual effect of pills and laws, overestimating the costs of deterrence and underestimating the benefits of added bargaining power. Even in an efficient market, after all, we do not presume that investors have perfect foresight about the future evolution of takeover strategies. From this perspective, the evidence we provide about the actual takeover rate and premiums paid as a function of antitakeover devices outweighs the event study evidence in judging deterrence.

The most plausible explanations for the collapse of the market for corporate control at the end of the 1980s are that (1) the spread of modern antitakeover measures made absolute deterrence feasible and that (2) the 1990 recession and credit crunch greatly affected this market. The first explanation is buttressed by our evidence that 87% of exchange-listed firms are now covered by one or another form of modern antitakeover measure (35% by poison pills, 80% by business combination laws, and 24% by control share laws), but refuted by our failure to find direct evidence of deterrence using all available data through 1991. We therefore conclude that the demise of the market for corporate control was caused by secular trends and not the introduction, spread, and legal acceptance of poison pill rights plans, control share laws, or business combination laws. An interesting test to discriminate between these alternate hypotheses will be to see whether the market for corporate control comes back from its recent doldrums. If state laws and pills are effective deterrents, the market will not recover unless firms rescind poison pills and opt out of state law protection (or switch to states like Texas and California that do not have antitakeover laws).[10]

[10]Since the first version of this paper in January 1993, the mergers and acquisitions market has become much more active. A front page story in the October 14, 1993 *Wall Street Journal* discussed the recent merger boom, and led to a brief summary of this paper on the front page of the October 21, 1993 *Wall Sreet Journal*.

Appendix: Case law about takeover defenses

The Delaware Supreme Court established the legality of defensive measures in May 1985 when it decided that Unocal's board of directors could exclude Mesa Petroleum from a defensive self-tender offer. This decision set a standard by which courts should focus solely on the nature of the deliberative process followed by the board of directors and ignore the optimality or 'fairness' of the antitakeover measure that they happen to use. According to this (Unocal) standard, there are no legally defective antitakeover devices, only defective deliberations. This ruling explains why the takeover litigation of the 1980s never yielded a list of proscribed defensive measures, and why adjudications of takeover defenses have been commonplace and seemingly repetitive.

Specifically, the Unocal standard took the business judgement rule, the well-established principle that ordinary business decisions ought not be subject to judicial review, and extended it to court decisions regarding antitakeover measures. In takeover situations, however, the standard would allow for 'special scrutiny', where boards of directors would need to show (1) reasonable grounds for believing that a 'danger to corporate policy and effectiveness' existed and (2) that their actions are based on 'good faith and reasonable investigation'. The active involvement of independent, outside directors would show such a good faith deliberation.

The Delaware Supreme Court found an immediate application for the Unocal standard in its 1985 Moran decision, in which it upheld the adoption of a poison pill but noted that '[t]he ultimate response to an actual takeover bid must be judged by the Directors' actions at that time, and nothing we say here relieves them of their basic fundamental duties to the corporation and its stockholders'.[11] The Unocal standard was subsequently adopted by most other courts. For example, in 1986, a U.S. District Court blocked a pill adopted by CTS because the board did not adequately consider the bidder's offer and acted without sufficient independent investigation. CTS cured its defect by forming a special committee of outside directors and by obtaining advice from outside counsel and investment bankers, and then adopted another pill, which the Court upheld. In the Buckhorn case in 1987, a U.S. District Court blocked a poison pill and an ESOP-based defense because had the board made reasonable inquiries, it would have discovered that the investment bankers 'relied too much' on management's assumptions and optimistic profit projections in computing fair value.[12]

[11] Unocal Corp.v. Mesa Petroleum Co., DelSupCt 5/17/85; Moran v Household International Inc., DelSupCt 11/19/85.

[12] Dynamics Corp. v. CTS Corp., DC NIll 6/20/86; Buckhorn, Inc. v. Ropak Corp., DC SOhio, 2/11/87.

The Delaware Supreme Court added a nuance to the Unocal standard in 1986 to address the proper conduct of an auction. In its Revlon decision, the Court overturned Revlon's lockup agreement with an LBO group led by Forstmann Little. In exchange for the lockup, Forstmann agreed in part to assume certain notes that Revlon had issued in a defensive exchange offer several months earlier, and that had fallen in value. 'In reality', the Court said, 'the Revlon board ended the auction in return for very little actual improvement in the final bid. The principal benefit went to the directors, who avoided personal liability to a class of creditors [note holders] to whom the board owed no further duty under the circumstances'. The added nuance was that, once the board decided that the firm would not survive in its current form, '[t]he directors' role changed from defenders of the corporate bastion to auctioneers charged with getting the best price for the stockholders at a sale of the company'. The Delaware Supreme Court applied similar reasoning in its MacMillan decision in 1989, in which it denounced the 'illicit manipulation of a board's deliberative processes' and overturned a lockup agreement granted to a management buyout group, adding that the board's hostility toward the competing bidder was unjustified once it decided to abandon its restructuring attempts and sell the entire company.[13]

Takeovers were completed so quickly in the 1980s that most court cases were either settled or rendered moot before they were appealed. This left the Delaware Supreme Court with only a few opportunities to reinforce the notion of a corporate bastion. In its Newmont decision, in 1987, it allowed a special dividend and rapid open-market purchases (a street sweep) to block a takeover bid. The Court found it significant that these actions did not constitute an abandonment of the corporation's continued existence, that most of the directors were outsiders, and that their investment banker estimated the foreclosed bid to be 8.7% below 'fair' value.[14] This seemed to leave premium-priced offers open to question, but in the Time–Warner decision in 1990, the Delaware Supreme Court ruled that Time's board of directors could reject a premium offer, saying that 'directors are not obliged to abandon a deliberately conceived corporate plan for a short-term shareholder profit unless there is clearly no basis to sustain the corporate strategy'.[15] The Court also identified several previous lower court decisions that it thought were in error, but which had passed without review, saying that 'the Court of Chancery has suggested that an all-cash, all-shares offer, falling within a range of values that a shareholder might reasonably prefer, cannot constitute a legally recognized 'threat' to shareholder

[13]Revlon Inc. v. MacAndrews & Forbes Holdings Inc., DelSupCt, 3/13/86; MacMillan, DelSupCt, 5/3/89.

[14]Ivanhoe Partners v. Newmont Mining Corp., DelSupCt, 11/18/87.

[15]Paramount Communications Inc. v. Time Inc., DelSupCt, 2/26/90 (oral ruling 7/24/89).

interests sufficient to withstand a Unocal analysis'. This view 'represents a fundamental misconception of our standard of review under Unocal principally because it would involve the court in substituting its judgment for what is a 'better' deal for that of a corporation's board of directors'. Again, the Court was impressed by the deliberative approach taken by Time's directors to a decision 'made only after what could be fairly characterized as an exhaustive appraisal of Time's future as a corporation'.[16]

In another noteworthy case, the Delaware Supreme Court acquiesced when the Chancery Court allowed Polaroid to deter an unnegotiated tender offer by Shamrock in 1989. The main issue was Polaroid's creation of an ESOP to hold 14% of its stock, which the lower court did not see as 'unfair'. Rather, it found that Polaroid's directors acted in good faith after a reasonable investigation, noting that all but two of Polaroid's 13 board members were independent outsiders, and that the board met at least six times in a four-month period to review Shamrock's various offers and to discuss appropriate actions with financial and legal advisers.[17] Finally, the Unocal standard applies in the latest decisions. In 1993, the Delaware Chancery Court blocked a lockup provision of the merger agreement between Paramount Communications and Viacom, saying: 'In connection with [Paramount CEO] Davis's efforts to entrench himself through the Viacom merger, Paramount's directors failed adequately to inform themselves of the relevant facts and circumstances. As a result, Davis was able to secure the approval of Paramount's directors for the Lockup Agreements in breach of the directors' fiduciary duties . . . [T]he question finally becomes whether the directors have demonstrated that they were sufficiently informed to have a reasoned basis for favoring Viacom's offer. (Interestingly, regarding the lockup agreement, the Court asked: 'Why such redundancy? They already had pill protection'. The implication is that the Court believed the pill was sufficient to defeat the offer.)[18]

As an aside, we should note that courts overturned some pills because their 'flip-in' features were found to conflict with general provisions in state corporation laws that require equal treatment of shareholders.[19] The affected states subsequently modified these provisions to exclude the discriminatory effect of pills, and we ignore these 'pro-pill' antitakeover laws in our analysis.

This review of the important legal decisions regulating the use of defensive measures shows that directors have not been significantly constrained in their

[16]The lower court decisions that the Delaware Supreme Court identified as erroneous were Grand Metropolitan, PLC. v. Pillsbury Co., Del. Ch., 12/16/88, and City Capital Associates v. Interco, Inc., Del. Ch., 1988.

[17]See Shamrock Holdings, Inc. v. Polaroid Corp., Del. Ch., 1/6/89, and Del SupCt, 3/23/89.

[18]QVC Network v. Paramount Communications, Del. Ch., 10/21/93.

[19]See, for example, Amalgamated Sugar Co. v. NL Industries, Inc., DC SNY, 8/5/86.

use of poison pills (or other measures) to deter takeovers; it also shows that the treatment of antitakeover measures was stable after 1985 (see also Greene, 1991). Consequently, we take the dates that poison pills were adopted to be the dates that they became effective, and estimate the deterrence effect of poison pills as a constant over the sample period. Overall, it leaves us disinclined to attribute the secular variation that we observe in takeover rates to any discontinuity in the legal environment.

References

Ambrose, Brent W. and William L. Megginson, 1992, The role of asset structure, ownership structure, and takeover defenses in determining acquisition likelihood, Journal of Financial and Quantitative Analysis 27, 575–589.

Bhagat, Sanjai and Richard H. Jefferis, 1993, Is defensive activity effective?, Working paper (University of Colorado, Boulder, CO).

Bradley, Michael, Anand Desai, and E. Han Kim, 1988, Synergistic gains from corporate acquisitions and their division between the stockholders of target and acquiring firms, Journal of Financial Economics 21, 3–40.

Brickley, James A., Jeffrey L. Coles, and Rory L. Terry, 1994, The board of directors and the adoption of poison pills, Journal of Financial Economics 35, 371–390.

Bruner, Robert F., 1991, The poison pill anti-takeover defense: The price of strategic deterrence (Institute of Chartered Financial Analysts, Charlottesville, VA).

Comment, Robert and Gregg A. Jarrell, 1987, Two-tier and negotiated tender offers: The imprisonment of the free-riding shareholder, Journal of Financial Economics 19, 283–310.

DeAngelo, Harry and Edward M. Rice, 1983, Antitakeover charter amendments and stockholder wealth, Journal of Financial Economics 11, 329–359.

Gilson, Ronald J. and Bernard S. Black, 1992, The law and finance of corporate acquisitions: 1992 supplement (Foundation Press, Westbury, NY).

Greene, Edward F, 1991, Regulatory and legislative responses to takeover activity in the 1980s: The United States and Europe, Texas Law Review 69, 1539–1593.

Greene, William H., 1993, Econometric analysis, 2nd ed. (Macmillan, New York, NY).

Hasbrouck, Joel, 1985, The characteristics of takeover targets, Journal of Banking and Finance 9, 351–362.

Huang, Yen-Sheng and Ralph A. Walkling, 1987, Target abnormal returns associated with acquisition announcements: Payment, acquisition form, and managerial resistance, Journal of Financial Economics 19, 329–349.

Jarrell, Gregg A. and Annette B. Poulsen, 1987, Shark repellents and stock prices: The effects of antitakeover amendments since 1980, Journal of Financial Economics 19, 127–168.

Jensen, Michael C., 1986, Agency costs of free cash flow, corporate finance, and takeovers, American Economic Review 76, 323–329.

Karpoff, Jonathan M. and Paul H. Malatesta, 1989, The wealth effects of second generation state takeover legislation, Journal of Financial Economics 25, 291–322.

Lang, Larry H.P., René M. Stulz, and Ralph A. Walkling, 1989, Managerial performance, Tobin's Q, and the gains from successful tender offers, Journal of Financial Economics 24, 137–154.

Linn, Scott C. and John J. McConnell, 1983, An empirical investigation of the impact of 'antitakeover' amendments on common stock prices, Journal of Financial Economics 11, 361–399.

Maddala, G.S., 1983, Limited-dependent and qualitative variables in econometrics (Cambridge University Press, Cambridge).

Malatesta, Paul H. and Ralph A. Walkling, 1988, Poison pill securities: Stockholder wealth, profitability, and ownership structure, Journal of Financial Economics 20, 347–376.

McWilliams, Victoria B., 1990, Managerial share ownership and the stock price effects of antitakeover amendment proposals, Journal of Finance 45, 1627–1640.

Mikkelson, Wayne H. and M. Megan Partch, 1989, Managers' voting rights and corporate control, Journal of Financial Economics 25, 263–290.

Mørck, Randall, Andrei Shleifer, and Robert W. Vishny, 1988, Characteristics of targets of hostile and friendly takeovers, in: Alan J. Auerbach, ed., Corporate takeovers: Causes and consequences (National Bureau of Economic Research, Chicago, IL) 101–129.

Mørck, Randall, Andrei Shleifer, and Robert W. Vishny, 1989, Alternative mechanisms for corporate control, American Economic Review 89, 842–852.

Myers, Stewart C., 1977, Determinants of corporate borrowing, Journal of Financial Economics 5, 147–176.

Nathan, Kevin S. and Terrence B. O'Keefe, 1989, The rise in takeover premiums: An exploratory study, Journal of Financial Economics 23, 101–119.

Palepu, Krishna G., 1986, Predicting takeover targets: A methodological and empirical analysis, Journal of Accounting and Economics 8, 3–35.

Pound, John, 1987, The effects of antitakeover amendments on takeover activity: Some direct evidence, Journal of Law and Economics 30, 353–367.

Putnam, Bluford H., 1991, Regulation and capital market efficiency: Some evidence from the U.S. credit crunch of 1990, Journal of Applied Corporate Finance 4, 92–95.

Ryngaert, Michael, 1988, The effect of poison pill securities on shareholder wealth, Journal of Financial Economics 20, 377–417.

Romano, Roberta, 1987, The political economy of takeover statutes, Virginia Law Review 73, 111–199.

Romano, Roberta, 1993, Competition for corporate charters and the lesson of takeover statutes, Fordham Law Review 61, 843–864.

Securities and Exchange Commission, 1986, Noninvestment grade debt as a source of tender offer financing (Office of the Chief Economist, U.S. Securities and Exchange Commission, Washington, DC).

Shivdasani, Anil, 1993, Board composition, ownership structure, and hostile takeovers, Journal of Accounting and Economics 16, 167–198.

Szewczyk, Samuel H. and George T. Tsetsekos, 1992, State intervention in the market for corporate control: The case of Pennsylvania Senate Bill 1310, Journal of Financial Economics 31, 3–24.

Weston, J. Fred, Kwang S. Chung, and Susan E. Hoag, 1990, Mergers, restructuring, and corporate control (Prentice-Hall, New York, NY).

White, Halbert, 1980, A heteroskedasticity-consistent covariance matrix estimator and a direct test for heteroskedasticity, Econometrica 48, 817–838.

Yago, Glenn, 1991, The credit crunch: A regulatory squeeze on growth capital, Journal of Applied Corporate Finance 4, 96–100.

[15]

ELSEVIER Journal of Financial Economics 47 (1998) 279–313

JOURNAL OF Financial ECONOMICS

Proxy contests and corporate change: implications for shareholder wealth[1]

J. Harold Mulherin[a,*], Annette B. Poulsen[b]

[a] *The Mary Jean and Frank P. Smeal College of Business Administration, The Pennsylvania State University, University Park, PA 16802, USA*

[b] *Terry College of Business, University of Georgia, Athens, GA 30602, USA*

Received 5 October 1992; received in revised form 27 September 1997

Abstract

We study the shareholder wealth effects of 270 proxy contests for board seats in the 1979–1994 period. We find that proxy contests create value, with the bulk of the wealth gains stemming from firms that are acquired. Restricting analysis to firms listed on Compustat imparts a downward bias on estimated wealth effects because such a restriction excludes a sizable fraction of the firms acquired during the proxy contest. For firms that are not acquired, the occurrence of management turnover has a significant, positive effect on shareholder wealth because firms replacing management are more likely to restructure following the contest. © 1998 Elsevier Science S.A. All rights reserved.

JEL classification: G34

Keywords: Proxy contests; Market for corporate control; Management Turnover; Corporate restructuring

1. Introduction

The theory of the firm attributes the survival of the corporate form to devices such as proxy contests that constrain the potential incentive problems created

* Corresponding author. Tel.: 814/865-9201; fax: 814/865-3362; e-mail: jhm14@psu.edu.

[1] This paper has circulated under several titles and has been presented in many settings. We thank the many people who provided comments on prior drafts. We especially acknowledge our editors, Michael Jensen and William Schwert, and an anonymous referee.

PII S0304-405X(97)00046-9

by the separation of ownership and control. Alchian and Demsetz (1972, p. 97) state that '... the transfer of proxies enhances the probability of decisive action in the event current stockholders or any outsider believes that management is not doing a good job with the corporation'. In this paper, we examine whether proxy contests do indeed facilitate change at target corporations and whether any such changes benefit shareholders.

Extant empirical research indicates that shareholder wealth increases at the announcement of proxy contests (see, e.g., Dodd and Warner, 1983), with one plausible source of the positive announcement effect being that proxy contests sometimes lead to liquidation or sale of the target firm (DeAngelo and DeAngelo, 1989). But there is evidence of a negative change in shareholder wealth between contest announcement and resolution (Dodd and Warner, 1983). Moreover, the decline in shareholder wealth appears to persist following the contest, with the worst equity performance occurring when dissidents win control of the board (Ikenberry and Lakonishok, 1993). These latter results are puzzling and suggest that proxy contests do not perform the function proposed in the theory of the firm. The initial appreciation and subsequent reversal in stock returns also raise disconcerting questions of market inefficiency and investor overreaction surrounding proxy contests.

The central goal of our paper is to clarify and extend the somewhat diametric findings regarding the shareholder wealth gains associated with proxy contests. We employ a comprehensive sample of 270 proxy contests from the 1979–1994 time period. The questions we address include whether proxy contests benefit shareholders, how shareholder wealth gains are tied to outright takeovers, and whether the impact of proxy contests has changed over time.

In addition to resolving ambiguities in prior research, answers to these questions have significant policy implications. Many observers (e.g., Jarrell, 1987; Pound, 1992; Roe, 1993) predict that proxy contests will become an increasingly important means of monitoring corporate management due to the growing hurdles to tender offers raised by shark repellents, poison pills, state antitakeover laws, and the judicial deference to incumbent management. This anticipation of a heightened role for the proxy mechanism has led the U.S. Securities and Exchange Commission to promulgate the first major changes in the federal proxy rules in 40 years (Sharara and Hoke-Witherspoon, 1993).

Our data do reveal a changing role for proxy contests. Indeed, proxy contests are playing an increasingly complementary role in outright takeover bids by removing incumbent management who might otherwise use the terms of poison pills or the provisions in state laws to block an acquisition. Moreover, we find that the shareholder wealth gains associated with proxy contests are driven primarily by firms that are acquired in the period proximate to the contests.

In documenting the important interaction of proxy contests and outright acquisitions, we also address methodological issues related to sampling techniques and the estimation of shareholder wealth effects. Consistent with recent analysis by Barber and Lyon (1997) and Kothari and Warner (1997), we find that minimum data requirements can affect the inferences taken from the measurement of equity performance. In particular, our sensitivity analysis indicates that the requirement that a firm be listed on Compustat in the period proximate to the proxy contest excludes a large fraction of the firms acquired during proxy contests and thereby imparts a downward bias in the estimated effect of proxy contests on shareholder wealth.

The following section provides a more detailed review of the results from prior research and outlines our analysis. Section 3 describes our sample. Section 4 reports the overall shareholder wealth effects of proxy contests and Section 5 performs cross-sectional analysis of the sources of wealth creation in proxy contests. Section 6 analyzes the relation between management turnover and the corporate restructuring associated with proxy contests. The final section summarizes the results, relates our findings to ongoing issues in corporate governance, and notes some implications of our specific research for the general empirical analysis of corporate events.

2. Prior research and proposed analysis

A number of papers analyze the performance of target firms in the period preceding proxy contests. Most of these papers focus on accounting performance and, as a rule, find that target firms perform poorly prior to board contests. For example, in a study of 64 contests from the 1956–1960 time period, Duvall and Austin (1965) find that firms experiencing proxy contests have profit margins and a return on equity that are low relative to industry peers. Similar evidence of subpar pre-contest performance is provided in DeAngelo's (1988) analysis of 86 contests from the 1970–1983 time period, Mukherjee and Varela's (1993) analysis of 37 contests from the 1968–1983 time period, Ikenberry and Lakonishok's (1993) analysis of 97 contests from the 1968–1987 time period, and Sridharan and Reinganum's (1995) analysis of 38 contests from the 1978–1985 period. This poor performance prior to proxy contests fits the depiction of target firms in the theory of the firm.

Prior research has also estimated the effect of proxy contests on shareholder wealth. Table 1 summarizes the findings of several key studies. The table reports the time period covered by each study, the sample size, and the cumulative abnormal returns found for several event windows: (i) the period around contest announcement, (ii) the period between contest announcement and contest resolution, (iii) the full-contest period from announcement to resolution, and (iv) the period following the contest. As noted in the table, the studies differ in the definition of event windows, although these differences do not affect qualitative comparisons.

Table 1
Prior research on the shareholder wealth effects of proxy contests.

Study [source]	Sample	Sample size	Cumulative abnormal returns			
			Initiation or announcement	Post-announcement	Full contest	Post-contest
Panel A. Full sample results						
Dodd and Warner (1983) [Table 3]	1962–1978	96	11.9% (5.09) [– 60,0]	– 4.3% (– 2.63) [+ 1,resolution]	8.2% (2.78) [– 60,resolution]	n.a.
DeAngelo and DeAngelo (1989) [Table 6 and text]	1978–1985	60	18.76% (9.44) [– 40,0]	– 12.47% (– 0.77) [+ 1,resolution]	6.02% (4.32) [– 40,resolution]	n.a.
Borstadt and Zwirlein (1992) [Exhibit 4]	1962–1986	142	n.a.	n.a.	11.4% (5.83) [– 60,resolution]	– 4.5% (– 1.02) [+ 12 months]
Ikenberry and Lakonishok (1993) [Table 5]	1968–1987	95	4.27% ($p = 0.05$) [month 0]	n.a.	n.a.	– 17.24% ($p = 0.05$) [months 5 to 24]
Panel B. Results partitioned by whether dissidents win seats						
Dodd and Warner (1983) [Table 3]	Win seats	56	14.1% (4.76) [– 60,0]	– 5.9% (– 2.36) [+ 1,resolution]	8.1% (2.05) [– 60,resolution]	n.a.

continued over

	Do not win seats	40	8.6% (2.23) [– 60,0]	– 1.8% (– 1.26) [+ 1,resolution]	8.2% (1.89) [– 60,resolution]	n.a.
Ikenberry and Lakonishok (1993) [Table 5]	Win seats	50	3.43% ($p > 0.10$) [month 0]	n.a.	n.a.	– 28.57% (– 2.92) [months 5 to 24]
	Do not win seats	45	5.21% ($p = 0.05$) [month 0]	n.a.	n.a.	– 3.90% ($p > 0.10$) [months 5 to 24]
Panel C. Results partitioned by whether sale of firm is linked to dissident activity						
DeAngelo and DeAngelo (1989) [Table 6]	Sale of target linked to dissidents	15	22.36% (5.90) [– 40,0]	n.a.	15.16% (4.21) [– 40,resolution]	n.a.
	No evidence of dissident-linked sale of target	45	17.56% (7.49) [– 40,0]	n.a.	2.90% (2.54) [– 40,resolution]	n.a.

Note: t-Statistic or p-value in parentheses; [event interval in brackets].

As reported in Panel A of Table 1, the prior research consistently finds a positive appreciation in shareholder wealth at contest announcement. For example, in their study of 96 contests from the 1962–1978 period, Dodd and Warner (1983) find that in the period from 60 days prior to announcement through the day of announcement, the cumulative abnormal return for the sample firms is 11.9%. Dodd and Warner (1983, pp. 422 and 423) note that the formal date of contest announcement is often preceded by substantial dissident activity, suggesting that the appropriate event date is actually earlier than the formal announcement date. DeAngelo and DeAngelo (1989, p. 40) confirm this point by finding a cumulative abnormal return of 18.76% in the period from 40 days prior to through the date of *initial dissident activity* and smaller abnormal returns around the date of the actual contest announcement.

For the full-contest period, prior research has also found a positive and significant appreciation in shareholder wealth. For example, Dodd and Warner report a cumulative abnormal return of 8.2% in the period from 60 days prior to contest announcement to the resolution of the contest. Research by DeAngelo and DeAngelo (1989) as well as Borstadt and Zwirlein (1992) report similar findings for samples with data extending into the 1980s.

Although the results for contest announcement and the full-contest period suggest that proxy contests benefit shareholders, the reported behavior of stock returns following contest announcement tempers such conclusions. Dodd and Warner report a significantly negative cumulative abnormal return of − 4.3% ($t = -2.63$) in the period between contest announcement and contest resolution. Ikenberry and Lakonishok (1993) report an even larger decline in shareholder wealth of − 17.24% in the period from five months to 24 months following contest announcement. Borstadt and Zwirlein also report a negative drift in abnormal returns following proxy contests.

One plausible source of the post-announcement reversal in stock returns is the subset of contests in which dissidents do not attain seats. However, as reported in Panel B of Table 1, Dodd and Warner find (1983) that the post-announcement decline in shareholder wealth is more severe for contests in which dissidents gain seats. Moreover, Ikenberry and Lakonishok (1993) report a post-contest cumulative abnormal return of − 28.57% for the 50 firms in their sample in which dissidents attain seats, as compared to an insignificant change in shareholder wealth following contests in which incumbents retain all seats. The significantly negative change in shareholder wealth for the subsamples in which dissidents gain seats questions the depiction of proxy contests presented by the theory of the firm.

Dividing the data according to whether dissidents attain seats does not directly address whether proxy contests ferret out poorly performing managers. As posed by Alchian and Demsetz (1972, p. 96, emphasis added), 'The question is the probability of the *replacement of management* if it behaves in ways not acceptable to the majority of shareholders'. Hence, an alternative gauge of success is whether senior management is replaced following a proxy contest. Consistent with the importance of management turnover, Ikenberry and Lakonishok (1993) report that their confounding finding of negative post-contest abnormal returns for the subsample of contests where dissidents attain seats is driven by the cases in which incumbent management remains in place following the contest. However, Ikenberry and Lakonishok (1993) report no effect of management turnover on post-contest abnormal returns for the subsample where dissidents fail to win seats. This latter result is surprising, as DeAngelo and DeAngelo (1989) note that senior management is often replaced even when incumbent directors retain all seats in a proxy contest.

Duvall and Austin (1965), (fn. 5) elaborate on the point that attaining seats is an arbitrary measure of contest success and note that the central issue is whether the contest spurs major changes at the target firm. They relate the case of a 1957 contest involving General Realty and Utilities Corporation in which the dissidents argued that the firm should be liquidated. Although the dissidents were unsuccessful in gaining control of the board, the incumbent management itself liquidated the firm a year later.

DeAngelo and DeAngelo (1989) more systematically investigate the liquidation and sale of firms experiencing proxy contests. As reported in Panel C of Table 1, they find that the 15 firms for which subsequent sale of the firm could be linked to dissident activity had a cumulative abnormal return of 15.16% for the full-contest period, compared to a cumulative abnormal return of only 2.90% for the 45 firms with no record of a dissident-linked sale of the firm. Borstadt and Zwirlein (1992) show that the post-contest equity performance of their sample firms is also affected by whether the firms are subsequently acquired, although they differ from DeAngelo and DeAngelo (1989) by arguing that the shareholder wealth appreciation that is associated with proxy contests is not solely driven by the contests in which the target firms are acquired.

2.1. Proposed analysis

Taken as a whole, the prior empirical research on proxy contests has produced ambiguous results. As predicted by the theory of the firm, proxy contests occur at poorly performing firms and the announcement of contests is associated with shareholder wealth appreciation. However, in results that contradict theory, past research finds that shareholder wealth declines following contest announcement, with the largest declines occurring when dissidents gain seats. Some evidence suggests that contest success should be gauged not by whether dissidents attain seats but by specific corporate changes such as management turnover or sale of the target firm, but the past research is inconclusive as to whether shareholders benefit in proxy contests that are not accompanied by outright takeovers or when dissidents do not attain seats but senior management is replaced. Finally, the results of past research may be moot and not applicable to current policy issues, given the changes in the corporate governance environment in recent years (Pound, 1992; Sharara and Hoke-Witherspoon, 1993).

We clarify and extend the prior empirical research with a sample of 270 contests for board seats from the 1979–1994 period. The bulk of our analysis revisits the shareholder wealth effects of proxy contests. Our sample is twice as large as any prior study, an aspect that is important for statistical tests, especially because we wish to examine differences between sub-samples based on factors such as whether dissidents attain seats and whether senior management is replaced. Moreover, a majority of the contests in our sample comes from a period not previously studied in past research, thus mitigating concerns about data snooping. The lengthy time period of our sample also allows us to address whether the impact of proxy contests has changed over time in response to the changing corporate governance environment.

One specific focus of our analysis is the interaction between proxy contests and outright takeover bids. We document a growing complementarity of proxy contests and takeover bids in the latter half of the 1980s and find that the greatest appreciation in shareholder wealth occurs at target firms that are acquired in the period proximate to the proxy contest. We further show that this interaction between proxy contests and takeover bids raises issues of selection bias for studies that fail to account for takeover attrition.

Our analysis also extends the prior research on the link between management turnover and shareholder wealth gains in proxy contests by delving into reasons why management turnover is a beneficial outcome of proxy contests. In particular, we examine the degree to which management turnover is associated with corporate change such as asset sales, restructuring, and downsizing.

3. The proxy contest sample

Our sample comprises 270 proxy contests for board seats in the 1979–1994 period. We use two data sources to create the sample: contests in the 1979–1989 period are derived from the list of proxy solicitations (Schedule 14b) filed with the Securities and Exchange Commission (SEC) while contests in the 1990–1994 period are taken from the Proxy Fight Database of the Securities Data Company (SDC). For each of these data sources, we exclude firms not having stock returns on the Center for Research in Security Prices (CRSP) files on NYSE/Amex or Nasdaq firms. We also drop proxy solicitations that are not for board seats and firms with no mention of the occurrence of a contest in the *Wall Street Journal* or on the *Dow Jones News Retrieval Service*. The Appendix provides more detail on our sample formation procedure.

Table 2
Annual occurrence of sample contests

This table reports the annual incidence of the sample contests. The year for each contest is based on the initiation date of the contest. Equity Value is the mean value per year in millions of 1983 dollars and is computed from closing prices and the number of shares outstanding reported on CRSP 40 days prior to the initiation of the contest. Contests are classified as being accompanied by a takeover bid if the target firm was the object of an ongoing tender offer, merger, or leveraged buyout by the dissident or a third party in the period from 20 days prior to the initiation of the contest through one year following the resolution of the contest.

Year	Full sample		No takeover bid		Accompanying takeover bid	
	# Contests	Equity Value	# Contests	Equity Value	# Contests	Equity Value
1979	10	72.8	8	83.4	2	30.3
1980	12	86.0	9	72.7	3	125.8
1981	11	58.0	7	56.8	4	60.1
1982	13	74.9	11	84.6	2	22.0
1983	13	144.4	7	198.5	6	81.3
1984	13	359.6	6	487.5	7	249.9
1985	19	199.2	10	123.2	9	283.5
1986	16	155.9	6	126.9	10	173.3
1987	20	598.4	9	323.4	11	823.4
1988	28	676.6	14	804.1	14	549.2
1989	37	492.0	19	288.2	18	707.1
1990	25	465.4	13	177.3	12	777.5
1991	12	669.2	9	789.1	3	309.5
1992	17	282.9	13	353.3	4	54.3
1993	10	131.4	7	54.2	3	311.5
1994	14	326.2	6	58.5	8	526.9
All	270	354.3	154	281.3	116	451.2

Table 2 reports the annual occurrence of the sample contests. The 270 contests in the 16-year sample period imply an average of 17 contests per year. For the first five years of the sample, 1979 to 1983, the annual number of contests is below this average, ranging from ten to 13. The annual number of contests increases in the second half of the 1980s and peaks at 37 contests in 1989. From this level, the rate of contests declines in the 1990s, averaging 16 contests per year in the 1990–1994 period.

Our sample size of 270 contests for board seats is larger than that in prior studies. This stems in part from the inclusion of more recent years in our analysis. The most recent year covered in past analysis is 1987 by the Ikenberry and Lakonishok (1993) study. For the years 1988–1994, we have a total of 143 contests. Hence, a majority (53%) of our sample comes from years not previously analyzed.

Moreover, even in years that overlap with prior research, our sampling procedure derives a larger number of contests. Consider the data below:

Prior study	Period of overlap	# Contests in prior study	# Contests in current study
DeAngelo and DeAngelo (1989)	1979–1985	55	91
Borstadt and Zwirlein (1992)	1979–1986	63	107
Ikenberry and Lakonishok (1993)	1980–1987	54	117

One reason for the greater number of contests in our sample is that we employ the complete Schedule 14b list from the SEC. Another reason is that we supplement the NYSE/Amex listings used by DeAngelo and DeAngelo (1989) and Borstadt and Zwirlein (1992) with Nasdaq listings that are now more readily available on CRSP. A further reason that we have more contests than Ikenberry and Lakonishok (1993) is that our sampling procedure only requires that the firm be listed on CRSP while Ikenberry and Lakonishok (1993) impose the additional requirement that the firm be listed on Compustat.

3.1. Attributes of the sample contests

Table 3 reports descriptive statistics of the proxy contest sample. This information allows us to benchmark the characteristics of the contests in our sample relative to prior research and to determine the extent to which the underlying attributes of the sample firms change over time. Details regarding the material used to determine the attributes of the sample contests are reported in the Appendix.

To study proxy contests over time, Table 3 also reports data for three subperiods: 1979–1983, 1984–1989, and 1990–1994. The analysis of separate time periods addresses whether the nature of proxy contests has changed in response to alterations in the underlying corporate governance environment as evidenced by judicial decisions such as the validation of poison pills [*Moran v. Household International, Inc.*, 500 A.2d 1346 (Del. 1985)] and second-generation control share statutes [*CTS Corporation v. Dynamics Corporation of America*, 481 U.S. 69 (1987)]. The specific years for the subperiod analysis are motivated by the fact that 1984 marks the first occurrence of a poison pill at a sample firm and 1989 spells the decline of an active market for corporate control documented by Comment and Schwert (1995). The separate analysis of the

Table 3
Summary statistics for the proxy contest sample

This table reports descriptive statistics for the 270 contests for board seats comprising our sample and for three sub-samples partitioned by time period. Section 2 of the Appendix provides definitions of the variables reported in Panels B and C.

	Full sample	Subsamples by time period		
		1979–1983	1984–1989	1990–1994
Panel A. The sample				
# of Contests	270	59	133	78
Mean equity value ($1983)	$354 mil	$89 mil	$452 mil	$389 mil
Panel B. Attributes of the sample contests				
Steady dividend	35%	36%	35%	33%
Median dissident stake	9.1%	9.8%	9.6%	7.6%
Contest type:				
Full control	68%	64%	70%	67%
Partial control	32%	36%	30%	33%
Accompanying takeover Bid				
Yes	43%	29%	52%	38%
No	57%	71%	48%	62%
Poison pill	39%	0%	42%	62%
Panel C. Governance results of the contests				
Dissidents attain seats				
Yes	52%	56%	50%	51%
No	48%	44%	50%	49%
Management turnover				
Yes	61%	61%	62%	58%
No	39%	39%	38%	42%
Acquired				
Yes	23%	19%	27%	21%
No	77%	81%	73%	79%

1990–1994 period also controls for the use of two different source materials, the SEC and SDC.

Prior research finds that firms experiencing proxy contests exhibit poor performance. Consistent with these findings, the firms in our sample have a poor record of paying dividends. As reported in Panel B of Table 3, only 35% of the sample firms pay a steady dividend in the period from three years prior to two years following the contest. Thirty-nine percent of the sample firms pay no dividend at all during the period surrounding the contest, 20% omit a dividend in the three years prior to the contest, and 6% omit a dividend within the two years following the contest. The dividend record of the sample firms is similar across the three subperiods reported in Table 3. DeAngelo and DeAngelo (1990, pp. 1417 and 1418) cite evidence that 'annual dividend decreases are uncommon, with increases surpassing decreases by a factor of 15 or 20 to one'. The fact that only one-third of our sample firms pay a steady dividend indicates substandard performance.

In our sample, dissidents accumulate a sizable fraction of the common stock of the target firms, with a median dissident stake (reported in Table 3) of 9.1%. This stake ranges between 7.6% and 9.8% across time periods. The dissident stake is comparable to the 10% figure reported in prior studies such as Borstadt and Zwirlein (1992) and Ikenberry and Lakonishok (1993).

Proxy contests are routinely classified according to the fraction of seats sought by the dissidents. As reported for our sample in Table 3, dissidents seek to attain a majority or more of the total board seats of the target firm roughly two-thirds of the time. The fraction of contests for full control is similar across time periods and resembles the rate reported in prior research.

Table 3 also indicates that 43% of the sample contests are accompanied by an outright takeover bid. This fraction varies across time periods, ranging from 29% in the 1979–1983 period to 52% in the 1984–1989 period. This variation is consistent with the view that the changing corporate governance environment has induced a growing complementarity between proxy contests and outright takeover bids. As further evidence of an alteration in the underlying governance environment, Table 3 reports an increase over time in the fraction of firms having a poison pill from zero in the 1979–1983 period to 42% in the 1984–1989 period. By the 1990s, 62% of the firms in the sample employ a poison pill at the time of the contest.

3.2. Governance results of the contests

Panel C of Table 3 reports information on the governance results of the sample contests. A commonly reported statistic is the fraction of cases in which dissidents attain seats. In our sample, dissidents gain seats roughly half of the time. This rate is similar across time periods and resembles that reported in prior research.

We also examine actual changes at target firms by measuring the rate at which the most senior officer, normally the CEO, is replaced and the fraction of cases in which the target firm is acquired proximate to the proxy contest. We find that the senior officer is replaced 61% of the time, with similar rates of management turnover in the three subperiods. For the full sample, 23% of the firms are acquired, with the greatest rate of acquisition, 27%, occurring in the 1984–1989 period.

4. Shareholder wealth effects of proxy contests

In this section, we address the question of whether proxy contests create value. We employ event-study analysis to measure the effect of the proxy contests in our sample on shareholder wealth. In the event analysis, Day 0 is the date of contest initiation as determined by the earlier of (i) the date of the report of initial dissident activity in the *Wall Street Journal* or on the *Dow Jones News Retrieval Service* or (ii) the filing date of a Schedule 14b proxy solicitation at the SEC (or the filing date reported by SDC for the 1990–1994 contests).

Following conventional procedures, our basic empirical analysis estimates the market model over the period from 170 to 21 days prior to contest initiation and then uses the parameters from the estimated model to calculate cumulative abnormal returns (CARs) for several periods surrounding the proxy contest. The event windows include the *initiation period* from 20 days prior through five days following the initiation of dissident activity, the *post-initiation period* of six days following initiation through contest resolution, the *full-contest period* encompassing 20 days prior to initiation through contest resolution, and the *post-contest period* of one year following the contest. To measure statistical significance, z-statistics are computed from standardized prediction errors. We also report the percentage of negative CARs and the average number of days in each event window.

Recent research by Barber and Lyon (1997) and Kothari and Warner (1997) poses concerns regarding the application of conventional event-study procedures to the analysis of lengthy event windows. Since our analysis includes the estimation of shareholder wealth effects in the one year following proxy contests, we examine the sensitivity of our results to different estimation procedures. For example, we compare results employing continuous compounding with simple compounding. We also compare the use of a market index with a size-based index. Finally, we follow Barber and Lyon (1997) by also measuring post-contest abnormal performance using a matched-firm, buy-and-hold analysis.

Barber and Lyon (1997, pp. 356 and 357) and Kothari and Warner (1997, pp. 304 and 305) also caution that performance measurement can be sensitive to the survivorship bias that arises from minimum data requirements such as the imposition that the sample firms be listed on Compustat. The extent of the problem and the direction of the bias are functions of the distribution of the firms in the database used to generate the sample (e.g., Compustat data availability) and the distribution of the firms in the comparison index (e.g., a CRSP-based index). To examine the sensitivity of our results to minimum data requirements, we also estimate shareholder wealth effects for subsamples of firms listed on Compustat in various years proximate to the proxy contest.

4.1. *Wealth effects for the full sample*

Panel A of Table 4 reports the shareholder wealth effects for the full sample of 270 proxy contests when stock returns are computed from continuous compounding and the market index is the CRSP equally weighted index. On

Table 4
Shareholder wealth effects around proxy contests: full sample analysis

This table reports cumulative abnormal returns (CARs) for the full sample of 270 proxy contests. Day 0 is the date of contest initiation as determined by the earlier of (i) the date of the report of initial dissident activity in the *Wall Street Journal* or on the *Dow Jones News Retrieval Service* or (ii) the filing date of a Schedule 14b proxy solicitation at the Securities and Exchange Commission (or the filing date reported by the Securities Data Company for the 1990–1994 contests). The resolution date is the conclusion of the contest as determined from media sources. Because four firms do not trade following contest resolution, the number of observations in the post-contest period is 266. Panel A reports CARs determined from continuous compounding using the CRSP equally weighted index as the market index. Panel B reports CARs determined from simple compounding rather than continuous compounding. Panel C reports CARs with the index based on similar-sized firms rather than the CRSP equally weighted index. z-Statistics are computed from standardized prediction errors. Each cell also reports the fraction of negative CARs and the average number of days in the event window.

Sample [# contests]	Mean CAR (%), z-statistic, % negative, average days in window			
	Initiation (− 20, + 5)	Post-initiation (+ 6,resolution)	Full contest (− 20,resolution)	Post-contest (1 y post resolution)
A. Continuous compounding	8.04	− 2.82	5.35	− 3.43
	10.7	− 0.87	5.80	− 1.93
	34.4	50.7	40.7	52.2
	26	66	91	225
B. Simple compounding	8.42	− 2.94	5.60	− 1.65
	11.6	− 0.08	7.04	− 0.82
	35.5	50.7	40.0	54.1
	26	66	91	225
C. Size index	8.55	− 2.56	6.11	− 0.71
	11.6	− 0.21	6.94	− 0.25
	31.8	50.0	38.9	50.3
	26	66	91	221

average, the market responds favorably to the initiation of the contests in our sample – the average abnormal return in the initiation period is 8.04% ($z = 10.7$). Between initiation and resolution of the contest, there is a negative, but insignificant, abnormal return of − 2.82% ($z = -0.87$), reducing the average abnormal return to 5.35% ($z = 5.80$) for the full-contest period. In the year following the contest, the abnormal return is − 3.43% but is less than two standard deviations from zero.

To examine the sensitivity of the results to the estimation model, Panel B of Table 4 reports the results employing simple compounding rather than continuous compounding. For the initiation period and the full-contest period, the CARs are slightly greater under simple compounding than under continuous compounding, which is consistent with analysis of event-study methodology by Seyhun (1993) showing cases in which continuous compounding generates less positive CARs relative to those estimated using simple compounding. The post-contest CAR estimated under simple compounding is half the magnitude of the post-contest CAR estimated employing continuous compounding, which is consistent with comparisons made by Barber and Lyon (1997), (p. 350). But while the differences between simple and continuous compounding are qualitatively consistent with recent methodological research, the statistical significance of the estimates and the inferences to be garnered from the two estimation procedures are not appreciably different for our sample of proxy contests.

As a further sensitivity check, we follow Dimson and Marsh (1986) and estimate CARs with a model using a size-based index from CRSP rather than the CRSP equally weighted index. The results are reported in Panel C of Table 4. As with the prior two estimation methods, the CARs at contest initiation and for the full-contest period are positive and significant while the CARs between contest initiation and resolution and in the one year following the contest are negative but less than two standard deviations from zero. In Section 4.4, we perform additional sensitivity analysis by using a matched-firm, buy-and-hold analysis.

In summary, regardless of estimation method, the initiation of proxy contests is accompanied by a positive and significant increase in shareholder wealth that remains positive for the full-contest period. Moreover, we find no evidence of any significant decline in shareholder wealth in the one year following the contest. From the evidence reported in Table 4, we conclude that, on average, proxy contests create value.

4.2. Subsamples based on Compustat

As a further sensitivity check of the robustness of the results, we study the shareholder wealth effects of subsamples of firms listed on Compustat in the period proximate to the proxy contest. This analysis is motivated by the recent work of Barber and Lyon (1997) and Kothari and Warner (1997) which raises concerns that minimum data requirements can significantly affect performance measurement. One standard concern is that the requirement that a sample firm be listed on Compustat over a particular time period imparts a positive survivorship bias on performance measurement. In our analysis of proxy contests, however, there is reason to believe that the requirement that a firm be listed on Compustat leads to a *downward* bias in estimated wealth changes. This downward bias occurs because the Compustat requirement excludes many firms that are acquired in the period surrounding the proxy contest and thereby do not 'survive' to report accounting data for the year of or the year following the contest.

To illustrate the potential bias, we first compare the size of our full sample with subsamples based on Compustat data availability, with data availability determined by a nonzero value for assets. Our full sample has 270 contests. Imposing the restriction that the firm have data available on Compustat in the year prior to and the year of contest initiation reduces the sample size to 208 contests. The additional restriction that the firm have data available on Compustat in the year following contest initiation further reduces the sample size to 186 contests, a loss of nearly one-third of the original size.

While the loss of observations is not necessarily a source of bias, in our sample the reduction in sample size is nonrandom, being weighted toward acquired firms. For the full sample and the two subsamples based on Compustat restrictions, we compare the fraction of firms that were the object of a takeover bid and further partition the takeover-bid subsample according to whether the firm was acquired:

	Full sample	Compustat [− 1,0]	Compustat [− 1,0, + 1]
% With no takeover bid	57	63	69
% With takeover bid	43	37	31
% Acquired	23	15	6
% Not acquired	20	22	25

These data confirm that the restriction that a firm be listed on Compustat in the period proximate to the proxy contest has a nonrandom effect on the makeup of sample contests. In particular, the Compustat restriction reduces the fraction of sample firms that are acquired in the period surrounding the proxy contest. For example, while 23% of the firms in the full sample are acquired in the period surrounding the proxy contest, only 6% of the firms are acquired in the subsample restricted to firms listed on Compustat in the year prior to, the year of, and the year following contest initiation.

To examine the effects that the Compustat minimum data requirements actually have on performance measurement, Table 5 reports the shareholder

Table 5
Shareholder wealth effects around proxy contests: samples based on Compustat

This table reports cumulative abnormal returns (CARs) for samples of proxy contests taken from firms with data available on Compustat, with data availability determined by a nonzero value for assets in particular years surrounding the proxy contest. Event windows are defined in Table 4. Panel A reports CARs determined from continuous compounding and simple compounding for the 208 sample firms with Compustat data available in the year before and the year of contest initiation. Panel B reports CARs determined from continuous compounding and simple compounding for the 186 sample firms with Compustat data available in the year before, the year of, and the year following contest initiation. z-Statistics are computed from standardized prediction errors. Each cell also reports the fraction of negative CARs and the average number of days in the event window.

Sample [# contests]	Mean CAR (%), z-statistic, % negative, average days in window			
	Initiation (– 20, + 5)	Post-initiation (+ 6,resolution)	Full contest (– 20,resolution)	Post-contest (1 y post resolution)
Panel A. Firms on Compustat in years – 1, 0 [$N = 208$]				
A.1. Continuous compounding	7.18	– 4.32	2.93	– 4.78
	8.61	– 1.82	3.60	– 1.84
	35.6	52.2	42.3	53.6
	26	71	96	238
A.2. Simple compounding	7.36	– 4.65	2.79	– 3.17
	9.29	– 1.12	4.56	– 0.89
	37.0	51.7	41.8	56.0
	26	71	96	238
Panel B. Firms on Compustat in years – 1, 0, + 1 [$N = 186$]				
B.1. Continuous compounding	6.00	– 6.00	0.11	– 8.74
	6.21	– 2.62	1.67	– 2.65
	38.2	55.2	45.2	54.0
	26	73	97	245
B.2. Simple compounding	6.04	– 6.04	– 0.25	– 6.97
	6.64	– 1.87	2.53	– 1.65
	39.2	54.6	44.6	56.7
	26	72	97	245

wealth effects for the subsamples based on Compustat data availability. For the purpose of sensitivity analysis, we report CARs estimated from both continuous and simple compounding.

Panel A of Table 5 reports the results for the 208 firms with Compustat data available in the year prior to and the year of contest initiation. Under both continuous compounding and simple compounding, the CAR averages 7%, which is one percentage point less than that for the full sample. Between contest initiation and resolution, the CAR is more negative than for the full sample. Hence, the CAR for the full-contest period is less than 3%, roughly half the magnitude of that for the full sample. The post-contest CAR for the sample of 208 firms is negative but less than two standard deviations from zero.

Panel B of Table 5 reports the results for the sample of 186 firms with Compustat data available in the year prior to, the year of, and the year following contest initiation. As one might expect, the performance of this subsample is measurably worse than for the full sample. The increase in shareholder wealth of 6% at contest initiation is matched by a comparable 6% decline between contest initiation and contest resolution. Hence, the CAR for the full-contest period is effectively zero. The CAR in the post-contest period is negative and large in absolute terms, with the CAR measured from continuous compounding being more than two standard deviations from zero.

These results confirm that minimum data requirements can affect the inferences taken from performance measurement. Because of the exclusion of a sizable number of firms acquired in the period proximate to the proxy contest, the Compustat subsamples experience a reversal in abnormal returns between contest initiation and contest resolution. Moreover, the Compustat subsamples, especially the subsample requiring data in the year following contest initiation, show evidence of a further post-contest decline in shareholder wealth.

This evidence may explain why we fail to find, in our full sample, the significant post-contest decline in shareholder wealth previously reported by Ikenberry and Lakonishok (1993). Because they also wished to analyze accounting performance surrounding proxy contests, Ikenberry and Lakonishok (1993, p. 408) imposed the requirement that 'Companies not followed by Compustat were removed from the sample'. At a minimum, this data requirement reduces the available sample size (as noted above, for the years in which we can compare samples, our sample size is more than twice as large as that of Ikenberry and Lakonishok). Further, at least for our sample, the effects of the reduction in sample size are nonrandom and disproportionately remove firms that are acquired in the period surrounding the proxy contest. Finally, the results in Table 5 suggests that the minimum data requirements have a measurable effect on the estimates of the performance of proxy contests.

4.3. Further analysis of post-contest wealth effects

As a further sensitivity check and to provide additional evidence on the effect of minimum data requirements, we estimate post-contest performance by employing a matched-firm, buy-and-hold analysis. Matching follows Barber and

Lyon (1997). The CRSP NYSE/Amex/Nasdaq tape is first scanned for every firm that is between 80% and 120% of each sample firm's equity value as of 40 days prior to each firm's event date. The market-to-book ratio of each of these potential matching firms is then taken from Compustat as of the year prior to the initiation of the contest. The actual match is the firm with the ratio closest to the sample firm.

The market-to-book ratio is measured as the ratio of market value of equity to book value of equity. When book equity for sample firms is missing from Compustat, values are taken from *Moody's Manuals* and *S&P Stock Reports* (when available). From the full sample of 270 contests, 11 firms cannot be included in the matched-firm analysis because seven have missing or non-positive book equity values and four do not trade in the post-contest period.

Estimates from the matched-firm, buy-and-hold analysis of the post-contest change in shareholder wealth are reported in Table 6. Panel A reports the results for all 259 firms having book equity data as well as returns data in the post-contest period. The abnormal wealth change is − 7.45%, although the estimate is less than two standard deviations from zero. These results resemble the estimates reported in Table 4 that employed conventional analyses of post-contest performance.

To assess the effect of Compustat data requirements on the analysis, Panel B of Table 6 partitions the results according to Compustat data availability in the year following the contest (i.e., the period being analyzed by the returns data). For the 181 firms with Compustat data available in the year following the contest, the abnormal wealth change is − 9.38% ($z = -1.70$). By comparison, the results for the firms without Compustat data available in the year following the contest are smaller in magnitude, with an abnormal wealth change of − 2.99% ($z = -0.53$).

Although neither estimate in Panel B is more than two standard deviations from zero, the results resemble those reported in Table 5; the requirement that the firms be listed on Compustat imparts a downward bias on the estimation of shareholder wealth effects, arguably because of the exclusion of acquired firms. In the particular implementation of matched-firm analysis that employs book equity values, these results indicate that the researcher should take care to supplement data from Compustat with data available in sources such as *Moody's* and *Standard & Poor's*, or else the analysis can exclude firms acquired in the period surrounding the event under question. More generally, these results further point to successful acquisitions as a source of wealth gains in proxy contests, an issue to which we now turn.

5. Sources of wealth changes in proxy contests

In this section, we look for the sources of value creation in proxy contests. We analyze subsamples of the 270 proxy contests according to whether the

Table 6
Post-contest shareholder wealth effects: matched-firm, buy-and-hold analysis

This table reports a matched-firm, buy-and-hold analysis of the shareholder wealth effects of a sample of proxy contests in the one year following contest resolution. Matched firms are found by first identifying all firms with a market equity value between 80% and 120% of the sample firm and then choosing from these potential matches the firm with the closest market-to-book ratio in the year prior to the contest. When book equity is missing from Compustat, values are taken from Moody's Manuals and S&P Stock Reports. From the full sample of 270 contests, 11 firms cannot be included in the matched-firm analysis because seven have missing or nonpositive book equity values and four do not trade in the post-contest period. Panel A reports results for the 259 sample firms with available data. Panel B reports results for subsamples based on whether the firm had nonzero asset value data on Compustat in the year prior to, the year of, and the year following the contest. z-Statistics are computed from standardized prediction errors. Each cell also reports the fraction of negative CARs and the average number of days in the event window.

Mean CAR (%), z-Statistic, % negative, average days in window

Sample [# contests]	Post-contest (1 y post resolution)
Panel A. Complete Sample of 259 Firms	
	– 7.45 – 1.78 52.1 226
Panel B. Subsamples based on Compustat data availability in year -1, 0, + 1	
B.1. Compustat in years – 1,0, + 1 [N = 181]	– 9.38 – 1.70 51.9 247
B.2. No Compustat in years – 1,0, + 1 [N = 78]	– 2.99 – 0.53 52.6 177

firm is a takeover target, whether dissidents attain seats, and whether the senior officer of the target firm is replaced. This analysis addresses whether the positive wealth effects in proxy contests reported in Section 4 emanate from all types of contests or instead are driven by contests that facilitate major changes such as an acquisition or a change in leadership. For comparisons across particular subsamples, such as acquired versus nonacquired takeover targets, the null hypothesis of equal mean CARs is tested with conventional t-tests.

In the cross-sectional analysis, we report results that employ simple compounding with the CRSP equally weighted index as the market index.

Alternative estimation procedures such as continuous compounding or size-based portfolio indexes provide similar results and are not reported in the text. For proxy contests in which a takeover bid commences prior to the initiation of an actual contest, we reestimate results using the takeover announcement as the initiation date; because the results from this procedure do not differ materially from our basic specification, they are not reported in the text.

5.1. Wealth effects for the contests with an accompanying takeover bid

Panel A of Table 7 reports evidence on the wealth effects of the 116 proxy contests accompanied by a takeover bid. The shareholder wealth gain at contest announcement is 9.93% ($z = 10.7$). There is an insignificant decline of 1.39% ($z = 1.02$) in the period between contest initiation and resolution. Hence, the wealth appreciation for the full-contest period is positive and significant, averaging 8.71% ($z = 7.54$). In the year following the contest, the average abnormal return for the takeover subsample is less than two standard deviations from zero.

Partitioning the data according to whether the acquisition attempt was successful reveals interesting, albeit understandable, differences in shareholder wealth gains. For the 63 firms that are acquired, the abnormal returns both at contest initiation and in the post-initiation period are positive and significant, resulting in an abnormal return of 20.1% ($z = 9.49$) for the full-contest period. The abnormal return in the year following the resolution of the contest is 12.4% ($z = 1.83$).

For the 53 firms for which the acquisition attempt is not completed, the abnormal return at contest initiation is positive and significant. However, the nonacquired targets experience an abnormal return of − 10.81% ($z = -2.37$) in the post-initiation period, which is significantly less than the abnormal return for the acquired firms over the same event window ($t = 3.30$). Hence, the nonacquired firms have an insignificant abnormal return for the full-contest period. The nonacquired takeover targets suffer a further decline of 23.7% ($z = -4.18$) in the year following the resolution of the contest, which again is significantly less than the post-contest return of the acquired firms ($t = 2.96$). The contrasting results for the acquired and nonacquired firms in the takeover-bid subsample resemble prior research on proxy contests by DeAngelo and DeAngelo (1989) as well as research on tender offers by Bradley et al. (1983). (See also Choi, 1991; Malatesta and Thompson, 1985; Marais et al., 1989; Ruback, 1988.)

5.2. Wealth effects for contests with no accompanying takeover bid

Panel B of Table 7 reports the shareholder wealth effects for the 154 contests not accompanied by a takeover bid. There is a positive and significant increase

Table 7
Cross-sectional analysis of shareholder wealth effects

This table reports cumulative abnormal returns (CARs) for subsamples of proxy contests based on whether the firm was the object of a takeover bid, whether dissidents attain seats, and whether senior management is replaced. Information on the classification of contests is provided in the Appendix. Definition of the event windows is provided in Table 4. CARs are determined from simple compounding using the CRSP equally weighted index as the market index. z-Statistics are computed from standardized prediction errors.

Sample [# contests]	Mean CAR (%), z-Statistic, % negative, average days in window			
	Initiation (−20, +5)	Post-initiation (+6,resolution)	Full contest (−20,resolution)	Post-contest (1 y post resolution)
Panel A. Contests with a takeover bid				
Firms with an accom-	9.93	−1.39	8.71	−4.66
panying takeover bid	10.7	1.02	7.54	−1.54
	31.0	46.0	37.1	52.7
[N = 116]	26	68	92	200
Target is acquired	13.5	6.65	20.1	12.4
	10.5	3.58	9.49	1.83
[N = 63]	23.8	34.4	27.0	49.1
	26	56	80	161
Target is not acquired	5.66	−10.81	−4.88	−23.7
	4.42	−2.37	0.83	−4.18
[N = 53]	39.6	59.6	49.0	56.6
	26	82	106	243
Equality of means: t-test of acquired vs. not acquired	1.87	3.30	3.56	2.96
Panel B. Contests with no takeover bid				
Firms with no accom-	7.28	−4.11	3.27	0.54
panying takeover bid	6.14	−0.98	2.77	0.24
	39.0	54.3	42.2	55.1
[N = 154]	26	65	90	243
Dissidents win seats	7.99	−3.24	4.88	−1.66
	5.16	−0.36	2.60	−0.72
[N = 85]	36.5	52.4	36.5	60.0
	26	66	89	240
Dissidents do not win seats	6.42	−5.14	1.28	3.25
	3.44	−1.06	1.25	1.15
[N = 69]	42.0	56.5	49.3	49.3
	26	65	91	247

Table 7. Continued.

Sample [# contests]	Mean CAR (%), z-Statistic, % negative, average days in window			
	Initiation (– 20, + 5)	Post-initiation (+ 6,resolution)	Full contest (– 20,resolution)	Post-contest (1 y post resolution)
Equality of means: t-test of seats vs. no seats	0.50	0.37	0.59	0.38
Panel C. The interaction of management turnover and obtaining seats in contests with no takeover bid				
C.1. Dissidents win seats				
Management turnover	7.62	1.93	9.56	2.55
	4.67	1.02	3.69	0.34
[N = 68]	35.3	48.5	30.9	55.9
	26	61	85	239
No management turnover	9.43	– 24.6	– 13.8	– 18.5
	2.20	– 2.91	– 1.56	– 2.29
[N = 17]	41.2	68.7	58.8	76.5
	26	86	107	243
Equality of means: t-test of turnover vs. no turnover	0.35	2.98	2.46	1.09
C.2. Dissidents do not win seats				
Management turnover	9.12	– 4.04	5.07	31.3
	2.32	– 1.34	0.67	2.88
[N = 25]	32.0	60.0	48.0	36.0
	26	45	71	248
No management turnover	4.89	– 5.76	– 0.87	– 12.7
	2.56	– 0.32	1.06	– 0.72
[N = 44]	47.7	54.5	50.0	56.8
	26	76	102	246
Equality of means: t-test of turnover vs. no turnover	0.88	0.23	0.61	2.06

of 7.28% ($z = 5.79$) at contest initiation. For the full-contest period, the wealth change is also positive and significant; the CAR is 3.27% ($z = 2.77$). In the year following the contest, the abnormal return is effectively zero.

A noticeable aspect of the results for the subsample without an accompanying takeover bid is that the shareholder wealth gains are not greater when dissidents attain seats. As reported in the last row of Panel B, the CARs for the 85 contests in which dissidents attain seats and the 69 contests in which dissidents do not attain seats are not significantly different in any of the four event windows. Although possibly surprising, the result that shareholder wealth gains are not distinguished by whether dissidents attain seats has been reported in prior research by Dodd and Warner (1983). These results suggest that the success of a proxy contest is not determined by the mere results of the voting but instead by whether the target firm undergoes specific changes such as the replacement of the senior officer.

To pursue the importance of management turnover, Panel C of Table 7 more closely studies the wealth effects of the 154 proxy contests not accompanied by a takeover bid. In particular, Panel C details the interaction between whether dissidents attain seats and whether the senior officer is replaced within three years of the contest.

Of the 85 contests in which dissidents win seats, reported in Panel C.1 of Table 7, management is replaced in 68 cases and is not replaced in 17 cases. For both sets of firms, the market responds favorably to the initiation of the contest. But following contest initiation, the changes in shareholder wealth differ between the two subsamples: the set of firms in which management is replaced experiences a sustained increase in shareholder wealth while the set of firms that retain incumbent management suffers a significant decline in shareholder wealth. This evidence indicates that investors anticipate that contests in which dissidents win seats will be followed by management turnover. In the minority of cases in which this expectation is not fulfilled, investors later revise their estimates of firm value downward.

Similar inferences can be taken from the 69 contests in which dissidents do not win seats, reported in Panel C.2 of Table 7. Through the full-contest period, there is no significant difference between the shareholder wealth gains of the firms that ultimately replace senior management and the firms in which incumbent management is retained. But in the one year following the contest, the 25 firms that replace senior management experience an average shareholder wealth increase of 31.3% ($z = 2.88$) that is significantly greater than the wealth decline of 12.7% ($z = -0.72$) of the 44 firms that do not replace senior management.

These results clarify some puzzling findings of post-contest stock return reversals reported in period research. Borstadt and Zwirlein (1992) report wealth declines following contests in which dissidents win seats, but the authors do not condition their findings on whether senior management is replaced. Our results indicate that accounting for management turnover is integral to understanding the post-contest changes in shareholder wealth. Ikenberry and Lakonishok (1993) report a wealth decline when dissidents attain seats but note that the result is driven by contests with no management turnover. However, possibly due to a small subsample size, these authors do not find any appreciation in shareholder wealth for the contests in which the incumbent board weathers the proxy contest but the senior officer is later replaced. Hence, they fail to observe that, whether or not dissidents gain seats, wealth changes following proxy contests are greater when the senior officer is deposed.

5.3. Summary of the wealth effects of proxy contests

Our cross sectional analysis of proxy contests reveals a straightforward chain of events. The initiation of a proxy contest is viewed favorably by the market. When the target firm is acquired, the firm experiences sustained wealth appreciation. By contrast, firms that repel a takeover bid experience a post-contest decline in value. For proxy contests not accompanied by a takeover bid, the key measure of success is whether the senior officer is replaced. In particular, regardless of whether dissidents attain seats, shareholder wealth appreciation is measurably greater when senior management is replaced. As a whole, the results indicate that proxy contests that induce corporate change are a source of gains to shareholders.

To summarize the source of wealth gains, we partition the data in a 2×2 framework according to whether the firm is acquired and whether senior management is replaced. For each of the four possible categories, we report CARs for the full sample of contests for the period from 20 days prior to contest initiation to contest resolution and for the one year following the contest. CARs are estimated using simple compounding and the CRSP equally weighted index, although similar results obtain using other estimation procedures.

The results of this analysis are presented in Table 8. The data indicate that corporate acquisitions are the driving force behind shareholder wealth gains in proxy contests. As reported in Panel A, regardless of whether senior management is replaced, the 63 contests that induce an acquisition of the target firm are associated with a large positive increase in shareholder wealth during the full contest period. As reported in Panel B, this gain is sustained following the contest with a nonnegative post-contest change in shareholder wealth for the firms that are acquired.

For the 197 firms that are not acquired, the change in shareholder wealth is a function of whether or not senior management is replaced. As reported in Panel A of Table 8, the 122 firms that are not acquired but that replace senior management experience an abnormal wealth increase of 6.96% ($z = 3.57$) in the full-contest period. By contrast, the firms that retain senior management experience a negative, insignificant change in shareholder wealth over the full-contest period. As reported in Panel B of Table 8, the firms with management

Table 8
Summary of shareholder wealth effects

This table reports data on CARs for the full-contest period from 20 days prior to contest initiation through contest resolution and for the post-contest period of one year following the contest. The 270 proxy contests are partitioned by whether the firm is acquired and by whether the senior officer is replaced. Information on the classification of contests is provided in the Appendix. CARs are estimated using simple compounding and the CRSP equally weighted index. z-Statistics are computed from standardized prediction errors.

	Mean CAR (%), z-Statistic, % negative, average days in window	
	Management turnover	No turnover
Panel A. The full-contest period [– 20, *resolution*], Full sample [N = 270]		
Firm acquired	18.7	23.3
	7.67	5.57
	27.9	25.0
	84	70
	[N = 43]	[N = 20]
Firm not acquired	6.96	– 6.96
	3.57	0.12
	37.2	53.5
	86	105
	[N = 122]	[N = 85]
Panel B. The post-contest period [1 *y post resolution*], Full sample [N = 270]		
Firm acquired	9.63	17.9
	1.53	1.05
	46.1	55.0
	157	170
	[N = 43]	[N = 20]
Firm not acquired	4.61	– 20.1
	0.35	– 3.38
	50.4	62.8
	241	246
	[N = 122]	[N = 85]

turnover have an insignificant wealth change in the year following the contest. By contrast, the firms that do not replace management experience a negative and significant wealth change of – 20.1% (z = – 3.38) in the post-contest period.

To determine the robustness of our findings, we repeat the analysis for three different time periods: 1979–1983, 1984–1989, and 1990–1994. As reported earlier in Table 3, the primary distinguishing feature across these time periods is the rate of accompanying takeover bids, which varies from 29% in the 1979–1983 period to 52% in the 1984–1989 period.

The results of this subperiod analysis are reported in Table 9. The CARs are for the period from 20 days prior to contest initiation through one year following the contest. In all sub-periods, the qualitative ordering across the partitions resembles that of the full sample. The bulk of shareholder wealth gains stems from the target firms that are acquired. Moreover, the worst performance obtains in the firms that are neither acquired nor replace senior management.

As a whole, these results support the view that proxy contests play an active role in monitoring the performance of US corporations by complementing outright takeover bids and by removing poorly performing managers. The following section further develops the role of proxy contests by examining why management turnover is an important outcome.

6. The interaction of management turnover and corporate restructuring

The analysis of shareholder wealth confirms the inferences of DeAngelo and DeAngelo (1989) that replacement of senior management is an important feature of proxy contests. To further pursue why management turnover is an important outcome, we gather information on the restructuring activity in the three years following the contest of the sample of 207 firms that were not acquired in the period proximate to the proxy contest and cross-tabulate the restructuring results with management turnover. To measure corporate restructuring, we assess whether the firm liquidates, sells a major division(s), sells assets representing 10% or more of asset value, or otherwise downsizes as evidenced by plant closings or a substantial write-down of assets. The classification of corporate restructuring relies on information from a variety of sources including annual reports (especially the president's letter), stories in the *Wall Street Journal* and other financial media, and *Moody's* and *Standard & Poor's* publications.

The results of the analysis of the interaction between management turnover and corporate restructuring are presented in Table 10. As reported in Panel A for the full sample, there is a direct relation between management turnover and corporate restructuring. Seventy-one percent of the 122 firms with management turnover engage in corporate restructuring, compared to only 45% of the 85 firms that do not replace senior management. A chi-square test rejects the null of no association between management turnover and corporate restructuring.

Our results on the interaction of management turnover and corporate restructuring are consistent with Boot's (1992) model in which the replacement of management enforces optimal divestiture decisions. The results also support

Table 9
Shareholder wealth effects by subperiod

This table reports results on shareholder wealth effects for three time periods: 1979–1983, 1984–1989, and 1990–1994. CARs are for 20 d prior to contest initiation through one year following the contest. In each subperiod, proxy contests are partitioned by whether the firm is acquired and by whether the senior officer is replaced. Information on the classification of contests is provided in the Appendix. CARs are estimated using simple compounding and the CRSP equally weighted index. z-Statistics are computed from standardized prediction errors.

	Mean CAR (%), z-Statistic, % negative, average days in window	
	Management turnover	No turnover
A. 1979–1983 [N = 59]		
Firm acquired	57.1	23.6
	3.75	1.31
	12.5	66.7
	229	289
	[N = 8]	[N = 3]
Firm not acquired	13.6	3.01
	1.68	0.47
	39.3	45.0
	328	344
	[N = 28]	[N = 20]
B. 1984–1989 [N = 133]		
Firm acquired	15.6	27.9
	4.81	2.19
	33.3	22.2
	227	196
	[N = 27]	[N = 9]
Firm not acquired	10.3	− 48.8
	1.42	− 3.69
	41.1	56.1
	332	363
	[N = 57]	[N = 40]
C. 1990–1994 [N = 78]		
Firm not acquired	37.4	62.8
	3.01	3.58
	37.5	37.5
	222	272
	[N = 8]	[N = 8]
Firm not acquired	12.0	− 10.7
	0.52	− 1.36
	48.6	60.0
	318	339
	[N = 37]	[N = 25]

Note: 20 d prior to initiation through one year following resolution.

Table 10
Interaction of management turnover and corporate restructuring

This table reports the interaction between management turnover and corporate restructuring for the 207 sample firms not acquired proximate to the proxy contest and for three subsamples based on time period. The determination of management turnover is defined in the Appendix. Corporate restructuring is defined as complete liquidation, sale of a major division(s), sale of assets representing 10% or more of asset value, or other downsizing as evidenced by plant closings or a substantial write-down of assets. The chi-square statistic tests the null of no association between management turnover and corporate restructuring (*p*-values are in parentheses).

		Restructuring			Chi-square
		No	Yes	% Restructuring	
Panel A. Full Sample (N = 207 firms not acquired)					
Management turnover	No	47	38	45%	14.82 (0.000)
	Yes	35	87	71%	
Panel B. Subperiod Analysis					
B.1. 1979–1983 (*N = 48 firms not acquired*)					
Management turnover	No	14	6	30%	11.32 (0.001)
	Yes	6	22	79%	
B.2. 1984–1989 (*N = 97 firms not acquired*)					
Management turnover	No	19	21	53%	2.53 (0.112)
	Yes	18	39	68%	
B.3. 1990–1994 (*N = 62 firms not acquired*)					
Management turnover	No	14	11	44%	4.28 (0.039)
	Yes	11	26	70%	

a generalization in the strategy literature that 'a precondition for almost all successful turnarounds is the replacement of the current top management of the business in question' Hofer (1980, p. 25).

The results are also consistent with related research that more generally analyzes the causes and effects of management turnover. Studying the later divestitures following a series of acquisitions made in the 1971–1982 period, Weisbach (1995) finds that the probability of divesting poorly performing assets increases after a management change. Studying the subsequent behavior of firms experiencing management turnover in the 1984–1989 period, Denis and Denis (1995, Table 7) document a substantial amount of restructuring activity. Similarly, in analysis of the 1983–1989 period, Denis and Serrano (1996) find that a significant number of firms that repel the raider in a hostile takeover contest still experience a change in senior management and also engage in post-contest asset restructuring.

To examine whether the relation between management turnover and corporate restructuring varies over time, Panel B of Table 10 reports the cross-tabulation results for three time periods: 1979–1983, 1984–1989, and 1990–1994. Consistent with the results for the full sample, management turnover is associated with a greater likelihood of restructuring in each of the three subperiods.

One noticeable difference across subperiods, however, is the rate of restructuring in the 1984–1989 period for the firms not experiencing management turnover. In this period, which is marked by the greatest rate of outright takeover bids, over half of the firms without management turnover still engage in corporate restructuring. These results resemble findings of Mikkelson and Partch (1997) showing that the market for managers faced more discipline during the high takeover activity of the 1984–1988 period compared to the relatively lower takeover activity of the 1989–1993 period.

7. Summary and implications

Proxy contests for board seats have long been a part of the market for corporate control in the US. Due to their widespread use, proxy contests have also been the focus of substantial theoretical and empirical research. The theory of the firm (e.g., Alchian and Demsetz, 1972; Manne, 1965) depicts the proxy contest as an integral component of the control devices disciplining management. Motivated by this theory, a number of papers have studied the causes and effects of proxy contests. Consistent with the theory of the firm, prior research has found that proxy contests occur at poorly performing firms and that the announcement of a proxy contest is associated with a significant increase in shareholder wealth. However, prior research has also documented shareholder wealth declines following proxy contests, with the greatest post-contest wealth decline occurring in contests in which dissidents attain seats.

We resolve many of the ambiguous findings of the prior research. Our results indicate that, on average, proxy contests create value. The bulk of the shareholder wealth gains arise from firms that are acquired in the period surrounding the contest. In related findings, we show that the requirement that a firm be listed on Compustat in the period proximate to the proxy contest imparts a downward bias on the estimated performance effects of proxy contests because such a requirement excludes a sizable fraction of the firms acquired during the proxy contest. For firms that are not acquired, we show that the occurrence of management turnover has a significant, positive effect on shareholder wealth relative to the firms that do not replace senior management. We further show that one reason that management turnover is an important outcome is that firms replacing management are more likely to engage in restructuring following the contest.

Our results on the important complementary role between proxy contests and outright takeover bids can be viewed as one realization of Roe's (1993, p. 393) prediction of the use of 'a new technology to overcome the [growing trend in] antitakeover laws'. In effect, proxy contests can turn a hostile tender offer into a friendly deal by removing incumbent management who might otherwise use the terms of poison pills or the provisions in state laws to block an acquisition. The ability of proxy contests to facilitate tender offers suggests one reason for Comment and Schwert's (1995) finding that the growing occurrence of hurdles to tender offers did not systematically deter corporate control transactions in the 1980s.

In addition to contributing to the policy debate on the corporate control market, our results also have implications for the broader study of the performance effects of corporate events. Consistent with recent analysis by Barber and Lyon (1997) and Kothari and Warner (1997), we show that sampling procedure is quite important in the study of proxy contests. In particular, the requirement that a firm be listed on Compustat in the year before through the year after a proxy contest imparts a significant downward bias in the estimation of the shareholder wealth effects of proxy contests. This negative effect of the Compustat requirement is the opposite of the normal positive bias for sample survivors because the firms in our sample that are the Compustat 'survivors' are much less likely to be acquired in the period proximate to the proxy contest. Related research of the long-term shareholder wealth effects of corporate spinoffs (Cusatis et al., 1993) and open market share repurchases (Ikenberry et al., 1995) also document that wealth changes are greater for firms that are acquired following the event. As a whole, the interaction of takeovers with other corporate events suggests that care must be taken by researchers who wish to study both equity and accounting performance surrounding the event.

Appendix A. Sample formation and variable definition

Our sample comprises 270 proxy contests for board seats in the 1979–1994 period. Our sample selection proceeds at two different stages. We initially gather information on proxy contests in the 1979–1989 period and later extend this analysis by gathering information on proxy contests in the 1990–1994 period. The source from which we derive the sample contests differs across these two time periods. For the 1979–1989 period, we employ the list of proxy solicitations (Schedule 14b) filed at the US Securities and Exchange Commission (SEC). For the 1990–1994 period, we use the Securities Data Company's Proxy Fight

Database (SDC). While we have no a priori reason to believe that the different sources for sample formation would affect our results, we separately report information on the contests in the 1990–1994 period.

For each of these sample sources, we exclude firms not having stock returns on the NYSE/Amex or Nasdaq CRSP data files. We also drop observations in the original databases for which the proxy solicitation was not for board seats or where the occurrence of the contest could not be verified in the *Wall Street Journal* or on the *Dow Jones News Retrieval Service*.

For the 1979–1989 period, we begin with roughly 500 Schedule 14b solicitations. The requirement of available CRSP data reduces the number of contests to 371. We then drop all firms for which we can find no listing at all in the *Wall Street Journal* or on the *Dow Jones News Retrieval Service* in the year of the contest, leaving 313 observations. Finally, we check each remaining firm's *WSJ Index* and *DJ News Retrieval* stories for evidence that a proxy contest for board seats occurred and arrive at 192 contests in the 1979–1989 period.

For the 1990–1994 period, we begin with 198 proxy fights listed in the SDC database. We delete 32 firms not listed on CRSP, 58 firms with no mention of a proxy fight in the *Wall Street Journal*, 24 contests for which the *Wall Street Journal* indicated the contest was not for board seats, and six contests with incomplete or inconsistent records in the SDC database. The 1990–1994 period thereby comprises 78 proxy contests for board seats.

We consult multiple sources for information on each of the 270 contests in our sample, including (i) annual reports, proxy filings by incumbents and dissidents, and other SEC documents, (ii) material reported quarterly in *Standard & Poor's Stock Reports* and material reported annually in *Moody's Manuals*, and (iii) stories in the *Wall Street Journal*, the *Dow Jones News Retrieval Service*, the *New York Times*, and other financial publications. Below, we note the primary source for each variable.

(1) *Steady dividend*. As a measure of pre-contest performance, we analyze the dividend record of the sample firms in the period before and during the proxy contest. We create four mutually exclusive categories according to whether the firm (i) paid no dividend at all in the three years prior to the contest through two years following the contest, (ii) reduced or omitted a dividend in the three years prior to the contest, (iii) reduced or omitted a dividend in the two years following the contest, or (iv) paid a steady or increasing dividend from three years prior to the contest through two years following the contest. Firms in the latter category are classified as paying a steady dividend. Our main source of information for this variable is the *Wall Street Journal Index*, with supplementary information taken from *Standard & Poor's Stock Reports* and *Moody's Manuals*.

(2) *Dissident stake*. This variable measures the fraction of common stock held by the dissident group at the time of the contest. Dissident ownership is

commonly reported in the *Wall Street Journal*. We supplement such reports with information from proxy filings.

(3) *Type of contest*. As is common in the analysis of proxy contests, we classify the sample contests according to whether they are for full or partial control. A full-control contest is defined as one in which dissidents seek at least a majority of total board seats, although in most cases a full-control contest entails an attempt by dissidents to attain all board seats. A partial control contest is defined as one in which dissidents seek less than a majority of the total number of board seats, with most partial-control contests occurring at firms with a staggered election of directors or with cumulative voting. Information for this variable comes from proxy filings and from stories in the *Wall Street Journal*.

(4) *Accompanying takeover bid*; *Acquisition of target firms*. For each contest, we determine whether the target firm is also the object of an ongoing tender offer, merger, or leveraged buyout bid by either the dissident or a third party in the period from 20 d prior to the initiation of the proxy contest through one year following the resolution of the proxy contest. For those firms that are the object of a takeover bid, we then determine whether the firm is actually acquired. Information about takeover attempts and actual acquisitions is taken primarily from stories in the *Wall Street Journal* and in other financial publications.

(5) *Poison pill*. For each sample firm, we examine whether the firm has a poison pill in place at the time of the proxy contest. The primary source for this variable is *Moody's Manuals*, which reports firms with shareholder rights plans, preferred stock purchase rights, and other poison pills discussed in Ryngaert (1988). We also obtain information on poison pills from the *Wall Street Journal* and from *Standard & Poor's Stock Reports*.

(6) *Dissidents win seats*. We classify each contest according to whether dissidents attain seats. A contest is classified as one in which dissidents attain seats if at least one dissident representative attains a place on the board. Information for this variable comes primarily from proxy filings and from stories in the *Wall Street Journal*, with some additional information taken from *Moody's Manuals*.

(7) *Management turnover*. For each sample firm, we determine whether the senior officer of the target company is replaced within the three years following the proxy contest. The standard of three years follows prior research, although most of the cases of management turnover occur within one year of the contest. In cases involving acquired firms, we follow Martin and McConnell (1991) in registering management turnover only when we find an explicit reference to the replacement of senior management; for example, if the manager remains as head of the acquiring firm's new subsidiary, we classify the contest as not having management turnover. The *Wall Street Journal* is the primary source used to classify management turnover, but we also consult proxy filings, annual reports,

Moody's Manuals, and the *Standard & Poor's Directory of Corporations and Directors*.

References

Alchian, A., Demsetz, H., 1972. Production, information costs and economic organization. American Economic Review 62, 777–795. Reprinted in Alchian, A., 1977. Economic Forces at Work. Liberty Press, Indianapolis, pp. 73–110.

Barber, B., Lyon, J., 1997. Detecting long-run abnormal stock returns: the empirical power and specification of test statistics. Journal of Financial Economics 43, 341–372.

Boot, A., 1992. Why hang on to losers? Divestitures and takeovers. Journal of Finance 47, 1401–1423.

Borstadt, L., Zwirlein, T., 1992. The efficient monitoring role of proxy contests: an empirical analysis of post-contest control changes and firm performance. Financial Management 21, 22–34.

Bradley, M., Desai, A., Kim, E.H., 1983. The rationale behind interfirm tender offers: information or synergy. Journal of Financial Economics 11, 183–206.

Choi, D., 1991. Toehold acquisitions, shareholder wealth, and the market for corporate control. Journal of Financial and Quantitative Analysis 26, 391–407.

Comment, R., Schwert, G.W., 1995. Poison or placebo? Evidence on the deterrence and wealth effects of modern antitakeover measures. Journal of Financial Economics 39, 3–43.

Cusatis, P., Miles, J., Woolridge, J.R., 1993. Restructuring through spinoffs: the stock market evidence. Journal of Financial Economics 33, 293–311.

DeAngelo, L., 1988. Managerial competition, information costs, and corporate governance: the use of accounting measures in proxy contests. Journal of Accounting and Economics 10, 3–36.

DeAngelo, H., DeAngelo, L., 1989. Proxy contests and the governance of publicly held corporations. Journal of Financial Economics 23, 29–59.

DeAngelo, H., DeAngelo, L., 1990. Dividend policy and financial distress: an empirical investigation of troubled NYSE firms. Journal of Finance 45, 1415–1431.

Denis, D., Denis, D., 1995. Performance changes following top management dismissals. Journal of Finance 50, 1029–1057.

Denis, D., Serrano, J., 1996. Active investors and management turnover following unsuccessful control contests. Journal of Financial Economics 40, 239–266.

Dimson, E., Marsh, P., 1986. Event study methodology and the size effect: the case of UK press recommendations. Journal of Financial Economics 17, 113–142.

Dodd, P., Warner, J., 1983. On corporate governance: a study of proxy contests. Journal of Financial Economics 11, 401–438.

Duvall, R., Austin, D., 1965. Predicting the results of proxy contests. Journal of Finance 20, 464–471.

Hofer, C., 1980. Turnaround strategies. Journal of Business Strategy 1, 19–31.

Ikenberry, D., Lakonishok, J., 1993. Corporate governance through the proxy contest: evidence and implications. Journal of Business 66, 405–435.

Ikenberry, D., Lakonishok, J., Vermaelen, T., 1995. Market underreaction to open market share repurchases. Journal of Financial Economics 39, 181–208.

Jarrell, G., 1987. Financial innovation and corporate mergers. In: Browne, L., Rosengren, E. (Eds.), The Merger Boom. Federal Reserve Bank of Boston, Boston, pp. 52–73.

Kothari, S.P., Warner, J., 1997. Measuring long-horizon security price performance. Journal of Financial Economics 43, 301–339.

Malatesta, P., Thompson, R., 1985. Partially anticipated events: a model of stock price reactions with an application to corporate acquisitions. Journal of Financial Economics 14, 237–250.

Manne, H., 1965. Mergers and the market for corporate control. Journal of Political Economy 73, 110–120.

Marais, L., Schipper, K., Smith, A., 1989. Wealth effects of going private for senior securities. Journal of Financial Economics 23, 155–191.

Martin, K., McConnell, J., 1991. Corporate performance, corporate takeovers, and management turnover. Journal of Finance 46, 671–687.

Mikkelson, W., Partch, M., 1997. The decline of takeovers and disciplinary managerial turnover. Journal of Financial Economics 44, 205–228.

Mukherjee, T., Varela, O., 1993. Corporate operating performance around the proxy contest. Journal of Business Finance and Accounting 20. 417–425.

Pound, J., 1992. Beyond takeovers: politics comes to corporate control. Harvard Business Review 70, 83–93.

Roe, M., 1993. Takeover politics. In: Blair, M. (Ed.), The Deal Decade: What Takeovers and Leveraged Buyouts Mean for Corporate Governance. The Brookings Institution, Washington, D.C., pp. 321–353.

Ruback, R., 1988. Do target shareholders lose in unsuccessful control contests? In: Auerbach, A. (Ed.), Corporate Takeovers: Causes and Consequences. University of Chicago Press, Chicago, pp. 137–152.

Ryngaert, M., 1988. The effect of poison pill securities on shareholder wealth. Journal of Financial Economics 20, 377–417.

Seyhun, H.N., 1993. Biases from continuously compounded returns: an application to bidder firm performance. Unpublished working paper. University of Michigan.

Sharara, N., Hoke-Witherspoon, A., 1993. The evolution of the 1992 shareholder communication proxy rules and their impact on corporate governance. The Business Lawyer 49, 327–358.

Sridharan, U., Reinganum, M., 1995. Determinants of the choice of the hostile takeover mechanism: an empirical analysis of tender offers and proxy contests. Financial Management 24, 57–67.

Weisbach, M., 1995. CEO turnover and the firm's investment decisions. Journal of Financial Economics 37, 159–188.

[16]

ELSEVIER Journal of Financial Economics 52 (1999) 79–117

JOURNAL OF Financial ECONOMICS

Deregulation and the adaptation of governance structure: the case of the U.S. airline industry☆

Stacey R. Kole[a,]*, Kenneth M. Lehn[b]

[a]William E. Simon Graduate School of Business Administration, University of Rochester, Rochester, NY 14627, USA

[b]Katz Graduate School of Business, University of Pittsburgh, Pittsburgh PA 15260, USA

Received 12 September 1996; received in revised form 20 May 1998

Abstract

Deregulation provides a natural experiment for examining how governance adapts to structural changes in the business environment. We investigate the evolution of governance structure, characterized by ownership concentration, compensation policy, and board composition, in the U.S. airline industry during a 22-year period surrounding the Airline Deregulation Act of 1978. Consistent with theory, we find that after deregulation (i) equity ownership is more concentrated, (ii) CEO pay increases, (iii) stock option grants to CEOs increase, and (iv) board size decreases. Airlines' governance structures gravitate toward the system of governance mechanisms used by unregulated firms. The adaptation process is gradual, however, suggesting that it is costly to alter organizational capital. We also present evidence on the relation between governance structure and firm survival. © 1999 Elsevier Science S.A. All rights reserved.

JEL classification: G32; G38; J33; L93

Keywords: Corporate Governance; Regulation; Airlines

* Corresponding author. Tel.: + 1-716-2753869; fax: + 1-716-2731140.

☆The authors thank seminar participants at the University of Chicago, Columbia University, Cornell University, the University of Kansas, Michigan University, Notre Dame University, the University of Oregon, Pennsylvania State University, the University of Rochester, UCLA, and Washington University, and Karen Wruck (the referee) and Bill Schwert (the editor) for helpful input. Po-Hung Fan, Tomas Jandik, and Tom Bates provided excellent research assistance. Kole acknowledges the financial support of the Olin and Bradley Foundations.

PII: S0304-405X(99)00005-7

1. Introduction

Despite a large and growing literature on corporate governance, our understanding of the dynamics of governance is quite limited. We know little about how the governance structures of firms adapt to structural change in their business environment. To this point, economics has had little to say about how change unfolds within an organization, or the path that organizations take from one equilibrium to another.

The ability of an organization to effect change is critical to its survival. However, it is common for researchers to presume that firms that survive in competitive markets have optimal governance structures, either by luck or design. As a firm's business environment changes, the firm either adapts its governance structure appropriately, or suffers extinction via takeover or bankruptcy.

In this paper, we build on the comparative static predictions in the literature on corporate governance, and empirically document the evolution of ownership structure, management compensation, and board size and composition of airlines following industry deregulation. Most theory in the area involves comparative static predictions linking the attributes of a firm's environment to various governance dimensions, including ownership structure, executive compensation plans, and board structure (see, e.g., Demsetz, 1983; Hölmstrom, 1979; Hermalin and Weisbach, 1989). Empirical work on governance generally focuses on testing these static predictions, or examining cross-sectional relations between governance structure and firm performance (see, e.g., Demsetz and Lehn, 1985; Smith and Watts, 1992; Weisbach, 1988). Less attention has been paid to questions concerning the dynamics of governance. How stable are governance structures? Do they adapt to sudden changes in the business environment? If so, do they adapt in ways predicted by static theory? How quickly do they adapt? Is firm survival related to adaptation of governance structure? Our knowledge of these topics is quite limited.

We address these questions by examining the governance structures of U.S. airlines during the period 1971–1992. This period spans the Airline Deregulation Act of 1978, which removed price and entry restrictions in the industry. Viewing deregulation as a shock that radically changes the nature of competition, and thus increases the sensitivity of firm value to managerial decisions, we use this event as an experiment to examine several issues related to the evolution of corporate governance structures. Specifically, we examine how the governance structures of airlines adapt to deregulation, the speed with which they adapt, and whether changes in governance are associated with firm survival.

We find that, relative to two benchmark samples, the governance structures of airlines change significantly after deregulation. Equity ownership becomes more concentrated, board size contracts, and increases are observed in the level of chief executive officer (CEO) pay, the use of stock-based forms of CEO compensation, and CEO turnover. Two elements of governance structure, insider holdings and cash compensation, do not change significantly after deregulation. We find that changes in governance structure occur gradually, rather than immediately after deregulation, and that survivors adapt their compensation policies more rapidly than nonsurvivors. Controlling for firm size, the internal governance mechanisms of incumbent airlines, such as compensation and board structure, differ significantly from those of firms that enter the industry after deregulation. New entrants have smaller boards with greater representation by outsiders, and more equity-based pay than do formerly regulated carriers.

We draw several inferences from the results. First, the observed changes in ownership structure and management compensation are consistent with comparative static predictions. The documented reduction in board size concurs with our expectation and suggests, as does some recent literature (see, e.g., Gertner and Kaplan, 1996; Yermack, 1996), that more consideration be given to the role played by board size. Second, governance changes, especially internal governance changes, are costly since they occur gradually and because new entrants adopt different governance structures than incumbent airlines. Third, adaptation of governance structure is related to firm survival.

Section 2 provides some background information on airline deregulation, and a brief discussion of how deregulation affected the management of airlines. We discuss sample selection and construction of the database in Section 3. Sections 4 and 5 present the static and dynamic predictions, respectively, along with corresponding results. Section 6 contains concluding comments.

2. Implications of deregulation for the management of airlines

2.1. Background on deregulation

During most of the forty years beginning with the creation of the Civil Aeronautics Board (CAB) in 1938, through the Airline Deregulation Act of 1978, prices and entry in the U.S. interstate airline industry were tightly regulated. The Civil Aeronautics Act (CAA) of 1938, which created the CAB, stated that an objective of this regulation was 'to … foster sound economic conditions' in the industry (U.S. Statutes at Large 52 : 973 (1938), 101(b)). Price and entry regulation in the airline industry was deliberately designed to promote the financial stability of airlines.

Scholars of the political economy of airline regulation generally agree that during most of its history the CAB used its regulatory authority to maintain the financial solvency of incumbent interstate airlines. For example, Behrman (1980, 86) states that the CAB 'refused to allow new airlines to enter the industry or existing carriers to enter each other's routes when it appeared that entry would harm the financial interests of an existing carrier'. Similarly, Caves (1962, 154) notes 'the [Civil Aeronautic] Board's fear of any action that might, even indirectly, yield low rates of returns for the carriers'.

The CAB's unabashed protection of incumbent airlines in the early 1970s led to the formation of a coalition of liberal and market-oriented politicians that advocated deregulation of the airline industry. Dissatisfied with rising airfares, consumer groups joined free-market supporters in their call for less government intervention in the private sector. They argued for an end to CAB policies that insulate carriers from competition by would-be entrants on new and existing routes, and shielded the airlines from factor price shocks by approving large fare increases and capacity limitation agreements.

Increased Congressional support for airline deregulation and several 'pro-deregulation' appointments to the CAB shifted CAB policy toward deregulation. In 1977, the CAB facilitated entry by low-fare airlines, such as World Airlines and Laker Airways, approved innovative discount fares on a limited basis, and canceled existing capacity limitation agreements. However, the CAB's statutory authority constrained the degree to which it could deregulate the industry. In October 1978 Congress passed, and President Carter signed, the Airline Deregulation Act of 1978, which eliminated both price and entry regulation in the airline industry, and called for the gradual abolition of the CAB.

2.2. Implications for airline management

The types of decisions that airline managers had to make, and the consequences of the decisions for firms' values, changed substantially in the deregulated environment. Meyer and Oster (1984), (p. 3) describe the entrepreneurial role of airline managers after deregulation:

> Regulation, to understate the case, was not conducive to entrepreneurship, at least of the classic Schumpeterian type concerned with capitalistic innovations … To the extent there was any tendency toward entrepreneurship under regulation, it was usually a pale imitation stressing 'service' or 'quality' difference … Experimentation with new combinations of services and fares was particularly rare. With deregulation, however, airline managers have had far greater freedom, and the result has been a rebirth of true economic or Schumpeterian entrepreneurship in the industry.

The shift from nonprice to price competition that accompanied deregulation encouraged airlines to lower costs. Five areas of managerial decisions became critical to firms' success in the deregulated environment.

Fare structure. The abolition of price regulation by the CAB dramatically changed the pricing of airline services. Competition among incumbent airlines and 'no-frills' entrants precipitated a decline in average fares and an increase in the number of fares offered per route as airlines priced service characteristics, such as departure time, advance booking, or nonstop service. To foster customer loyalty, frequent flier programs were created. In 1981, a senior vice-president of marketing at United Airlines stated that 'pricing had gone from being a nonfactor to being one of the keys to an airline's success' (Curley, 1981).

Route structure. CAB regulation of entry resulted in fragmented, point-to-point route systems. Following deregulation, route structures were redesigned as 'hub and spoke' systems which funnel flights through central hub airports. Major trunk airlines also exited from many short-haul routes, which were more efficiently served by new entrants with smaller aircraft.

Fleet composition. Under CAB regulation, airlines favored wide-bodied aircraft, largely because the size and comfort of these planes provided a means of nonprice competition. After deregulation, many trunk airlines shifted to smaller aircraft to increase load factors, reduce fuel costs, and better conform their fleets to their hub and spoke route structures. Because of the joint determination of fleet composition with route structure, the cost of aircraft, and the long lead time required to purchase aircraft, decisions concerning fleet composition became a major determinant of performance in the deregulated environment. Vietor (1990), (p. 86) writes that under regulation,

> fleet composition and route structure ... had become artifacts of public policy. Moreover, most other aspects of the business ... were shaped to fit the routes and fleet. Managers who realized this, and who could implement effective changes quickly, had an immense competitive advantage.

Labor costs. Organized labor benefited greatly from CAB regulation, as indicated by labor's strong opposition to airline deregulation. The lower fares that emerged after deregulation required airlines to reduce labor costs substantially. Most airlines engaged in acrimonious negotiations with flight attendants, pilots, machinists, and teamsters, on issues like wage reductions, elimination of restrictive work rules, and compensation of flight crews for nonflight time. Some airlines also adopted novel ways of reducing labor costs, including two-tier wage systems and Chapter 11 bankruptcy filings (Weiss and Wruck, 1998). Other carriers, such as US Airways, continue to struggle with high labor costs (Kole and Lehn, 1997).

Distribution channels. The proliferation of new fares and routing options after deregulation increased information costs for air passengers, who relied increasingly on travel agencies for fare and route information. Vietor (1990), (p. 86) notes that 'under regulation, distribution channels were unimportant and unsophisticated ... with the transition to competition, customer access and control suddenly became critical for sellers'. American Airlines and United Airlines invested heavily in developing computerized reservation systems that travel agents access for information on routes, fares, and reservations. By 1988, these two airlines serviced 70% of the travel agency sales.

In summary, these five areas illustrate important ways in which deregulation changed the managerial function in the airline industry. In addition to calling for a different set of managerial skills, deregulation increased the importance of the managerial function in airlines. To the extent that the equity values of airlines became more sensitive to managerial decisions, we expect changes in the governance structures of airlines to align managers' behavior more closely with the interests of shareholders.

2.3. *Implications for resource reallocation and airlines' survival*

Deregulation resulted in a substantial reallocation of resources in the airline industry, as organizations with different management teams and governance structures competed for the right to manage assets in the new business environment. Shortly after deregulation, the industry was characterized by excess capacity, making it necessary for some airlines to exit. In addition, the skills required to effectively manage airlines changed with deregulation. Before deregulation, there was more demand for managers skilled in managing the regulatory process, while after deregulation there was greater demand for managers skilled in managing in competitive environments. The two principal

Table 1
Exit from the airline industry

Value and number of firms dropped from the Center for Research in Security Prices (CRSP) database for selected industries between 1963–1993. Amounts are calculated for two time periods, pre- and post-airline deregulation, 1963–1977 and 1979–1993. Firms are typically delisted when taken over by another company, or when they file for bankruptcy. For comparison, delistings of airline, regulated electric utility, and unregulated manufacturing firms are shown. Value amounts are in billions of current U.S. dollars.

	Airlines	Electric utilities	Manufacturing
Panel A: 1963–1977			
1963 Aggregate equity value	$1.9	$45.0	$256.3
Value of delistings	$0.1	$0.7	$24.1
% of industry	2%	2%	9%
Number of delistings	4	4	488
% of industry	19%	4%	41%
Panel B: 1979–1993			
1979 Aggregate equity value	$5.2	$73.1	$550.2
Value of delistings	$3.1	$11.4	$128.6
% of industry	59%	16%	23%
Number of delistings	17	30	620
% of industry	65%	21%	52%

mechanisms for effecting the required reallocation of resources were the market for corporate control and the bankruptcy process.

As Table 1 reveals, there was an unusually high level of takeover and bankruptcy activity in the airline industry after deregulation. Mitchell and Mulherin's (1996) study of industry-level patterns in takeover and restructuring activity during 1982–1989 affirms this characterization of the airline industry. As reported in Panel B of Table 1, 59% of the aggregate asset value of publicly traded airlines in 1979 were ultimately deleted from the Center for Research in Security Prices (CRSP) tapes because of a takeover or bankruptcy filing during 1979–1993. This proportion is substantially higher than the corresponding percentages for regulated electric utilities, at 16%, and firms in unregulated industries, at 23%. Panel A of Table 1 shows that, over a comparable period during airline regulation, 1963–1977, only 2% of the aggregate asset value of publicly traded airlines is accounted for by firms deleted from the CRSP tapes, on par with the utilities industry, at 2%, and less than that for unregulated firms, at 9%. Similarly, Table 2 lists the status as of year-end 1992 of 21 formerly

Table 2
Status of 21 regulation-era airlines as of year-end 1992

The status of air carriers regulated prior to the Airline Deregulation Act of 1978 is reported. The status of each airline was ascertained by consulting annual editions of the Wall Street Journal index for each year, 1978–1992.

Airline	Status
Alaska	Independent
Aloha	Acquired by AQ Group (1987)
American	Independent, target of takeover attempt (1989)
Braniff	Chapter 11 (1982, 1989)
Continental	Acquired by Texas Air (1982), Chapter 11 (1983)
Delta	Independent
Eastern	Acquired by Texas Air (1986), Chapter 11 (1989), Liquidated (1991)
Frontier	Acquired by People Express (1985) which later merged with Texas Air (1986)
Hawaiian	Acquired by Ueberroth Group (1989)
Northwest	Acquired by Checchi Group (1989)
Ozark	Acquired by TWA (1986)
PSA	Sold airline assets to USAir Group (1986)
Pan Am	Chapter 11 (1991), Liquidated (1992)
Piedmont	Acquired by USAir (1987)
Republic	Acquired by Northwest (1986)
Southwest	Independent
Texas	Changed name to Continental Airlines (1990), Chapter 11 (1990)
TWA	Acquired by Icahn (1985), Chapter 11 (1992)
United	Independent, target of several takeover attempts (1987, 1989)
USAir	Independent, target of takeover attempt (1987)
Western	Acquired by Delta Airlines (1986)

regulated airlines examined in this paper. Eleven airlines are taken over after deregulation, six file for Chapter 11 bankruptcy, and only six continue to provide passenger air travel as independent carriers.

The substantial reallocation of corporate assets that followed airline deregulation is consistent with the experiences of other industries encountering industry-level economic shocks. The timing of the resource reallocation, however, suggests that the loosening of antitrust restrictions during the Reagan Administration, which facilitated mergers more generally, may have encouraged the consolidation of airline assets in the late 1980s. Regardless of the reason, it is striking that so few of the formerly regulated airlines survive as independent carriers after deregulation. Later in the paper, we examine whether the choice of mechanisms airlines employ to monitor and motivate managers is related to firm survival.

3. Sample selection and methodology

Our sample consists of 21 U.S. airlines that were publicly traded for at least six years before and six years after passage of the Airline Deregulation Act of 1978. For each firm, we collect annual data on governance attributes, stock returns, and financial characteristics from the CRSP and Compustat databases, and from corporate proxy statements for the 22-year period spanning 1971–1992. The sample airlines are publicly traded in 365 of the potential 462 firm-years. Proxy statements, the source of the governance data, are available for 359, or 98%, of the 365 observations.

To disentangle the effect of airline deregulation on measures of corporate governance from possible secular trends in these variables, we create two benchmark samples, one drawn from a regulated industry and the other from unregulated industries. We intentionally refer to these samples as benchmarks rather than controls. Our benchmark firms do not control for all relevant yet unobservable characteristics that could impact firms' governance mechanisms. Rather, they offer a yardstick against which to compare airlines as they transition from a regulated to an unregulated operating environment. In addition to controlling for secular trends, the benchmark samples allow us to see whether the governance structures of airlines increasingly resemble those of unregulated firms after deregulation.

For each airline, we select two benchmark firms, one from each of the two benchmark samples. Each airline is matched with a regulated electric utility, a firm in Standard Industrial Classification (SIC) Code 4911 or 4931, and an unregulated manufacturing firm in SIC codes 2000–3999, closest in market value of common equity at year-end 1978 to the respective airline. We match on an equity-based measure of firm size because of documented correlations of both ownership structure and management compensation with firm equity-value. We recognize that this match does not control for capital structure differences across firms. For each benchmark firm, we collect data on governance attributes, stock returns, and financial variables for the subset of the 462 firm-years during which the benchmark firms trade. For the benchmark samples, there are 455 regulated firm-years, for which we locate 433, or 95%, of the proxy statements, and 437 possible firm-years in the case of the unregulated sample, for which we locate 419, or 96%, of the proxies. A list of each airline and its two corresponding benchmark firms is contained in Table 3.

We define the period of 1971–1977 as the regulation period, and 1979–1992 as the deregulation period. As discussed later, for some tests we decompose the deregulation period into two subperiods, 1979–1985 and 1986–1992, to ascertain the speed with which governance variables change in response to deregulation.

To test hypotheses about the relation between deregulation and governance structures, we examine relative changes in governance variables from the regulation to deregulation periods for airlines relative to firms in the two benchmark samples. We use ordinary least squares regression analysis with fixed effects on the assumption that differences in governance measures across firms can be captured in the constant term. This methodology allows us to emphasize the time-series, or dynamic dimension, of the data. A cost of this technique is that standard goodness-of-fit measures are uninformative. We report adjusted R^2 values to provide information on the relative fit of variants of a single model.

4. Static predictions and results

In Section 2, we describe various ways in which deregulation expands the managerial function in the airline industry. As the role of managers becomes more important, we expect the governance structures of airlines to change to mitigate new potential agency problems in the deregulated environment. In this section, we discuss several comparative static predictions, and present our empirical findings from the airline industry. In the next section, we present predictions and results on the time pattern of governance changes.

4.1. Ownership structure

We expect deregulation to increase the concentration of equity ownership (see Demsetz and Lehn, 1985). By increasing both the importance of the managerial role and the costs of observing managerial performance, deregulation increases the costs of monitoring managers. This change has two reinforcing effects that lead to greater ownership concentration. First, an outside shareholder engages in monitoring only if his private benefits, which are proportional to his equity stake, exceed the costs of monitoring. To make it privately rational for an

Table 3
Airlines and matched regulated and unregulated benchmark firms

Airline sample includes 21 U.S. airlines that were publicly traded for at least six years before and six years after the Airline Deregulation Act of 1978. Each firm in the sample is matched with two other firms drawn from benchmark samples, comprised of regulated electric utility firms and unregulated manufacturing firms, based on market equity value in 1978. Information is taken from the Center for Research in Security Prices (CRSP) and Compustat databases. All values shown are in millions of current U.S. dollars as of 1978.

Airline	Value	Matched benchmark firms			
		Electric Utility	Value	Manufacturing	Value
Alaska	$20.5	Green Mountain Power	$21.9	Plenum Publishing	$20.5
Aloha	10.0	Maine Public Services	11.7	White hall	9.7
American (AMR)	380.0	Southwestern Public Service	353.4	Whitman	379.2
Braniff International	255.2	Idaho Power	254.5	Betz Laboratories	254.7
Continental	49.9	Central Vermont Public Service	41.7	Standard Register	49.6
Delta	830.0	Houston Industries	851.1	General Dynamics	839.5
Eastern	211.1	Kansas Gas & Electric	200.4	Amfac	210.5
Frontier	70.5	Eastern Utilities Association	68.9	Computervision	71.1
Hawaiian (HAL)	8.9	Southwestern Electric Service	8.6	Ply-Gem Industries	8.9
Northwest (NWA)	616.3	Utah Power & Light	609.3	Reynolds Metals	612.7
Ozark	33.5	TNP Enterprises	34.9	General Shale Products	33.4
Pacific Southwest (PSA)	169.8	Central Maine Power	175.6	Holly Farms	167.7
Pan Am	470.4	Duquesne Light	468.3	Quantum Chemical	479.1
Piedmont Aviation	25.7	Bangor-Hydro Electric	25.1	Huffy	25.7
Republic	88.1	Nevada Power	108.9	Loral	88.5
Southwest	58.9	Empire District Electric	53.5	Binks Manufacturing	58.9
Texas International	84.2	Madison Gas & Electric	85.0	Houghton Mifflin	84.3
Trans World	260.2	Boston Edison	275.4	Trinova	264.3
United (UAL)	764.4	Ohio Edison	775.3	PPG	765.3
USAir	71.8	Otter Tail Power	69.2	Russell	71.8
Western	107.3	El Paso Electric	117.5	Chiquita Brands	107.5

outside shareholder, or group of shareholders, to incur the higher monitoring costs induced by deregulation, ownership concentration must increase. Second, to internalize the agency problems associated with higher monitoring costs, managers themselves may own larger stakes so that they bear a larger proportion of the wealth consequences associated with their decisions (see Hölmstrom, 1979). This consequence also increases ownership concentration.

Hence, comparative static analysis predicts an increase in ownership concentration by both outside shareholders and managers after deregulation. The theory is less clear, however, on whether deregulation is likely to induce a greater consolidation of shares by outside investors or managers. The primary advantage of higher managerial stockholdings is that it avoids monitoring costs that would be incurred by outside investors are avoided. There are two major disadvantages of higher stockholdings by managers versus outside investors. First, managers may not have the personal wealth to own large stakes in their respective companies, and second, managers may become excessively risk averse, since higher stockholdings tie up more of their wealth in the fortunes of the firm. The effect of deregulation on the consolidation of blocks by outside investors versus managers rests on the magnitude of these countervailing forces.

To test the relation between deregulation and the concentration of equity ownership, we examine changes in two groups of owners: (i) officers and directors and (ii) outside blockholders, defined as parties unaffiliated with the board. Fig. 1 presents annual averages on the percentage of equity held by the two groups during the sample period.

Two noteworthy findings are revealed by the officer and director data (see Fig. 1a). First, mean levels of managerial ownership vary significantly across the three samples, but vary little within each group. Throughout the sample period, beneficial ownership hovers around 20%, 14%, and 1%, respectively, for the managers of unregulated, airline, and regulated firms. Second, though considerable stability characterizes airline managements' holdings over the entire sample period, wide swings in annual averages, measuring as large as ten percentage points between 1985–1986, are observed. This variation is symptomatic of the high degree of control activity in the industry. These findings are mirrored in median officer and director holdings, which are not reported.

Results from fixed effects regressions, reported in Columns 1 and 2 of Table 4, confirm the inferences drawn from annual averages of beneficial ownership by officers and directors. Controlling for firm size, we find no evidence of a change in the level of officer and director holdings from 1971–1977 to 1979–1992 that is attributable to deregulation.

A greater post-deregulation consolidation of ownership interests is evident in the patterns of outside blockholder stakes. Fig. 1b reveals that outside stakes in airlines grow at an increasing rate through the sample period. In the regulation years, outside stakes are flat and resemble the regulated benchmark. In the early years of deregulation, they mimic the level and rate of change experienced by the

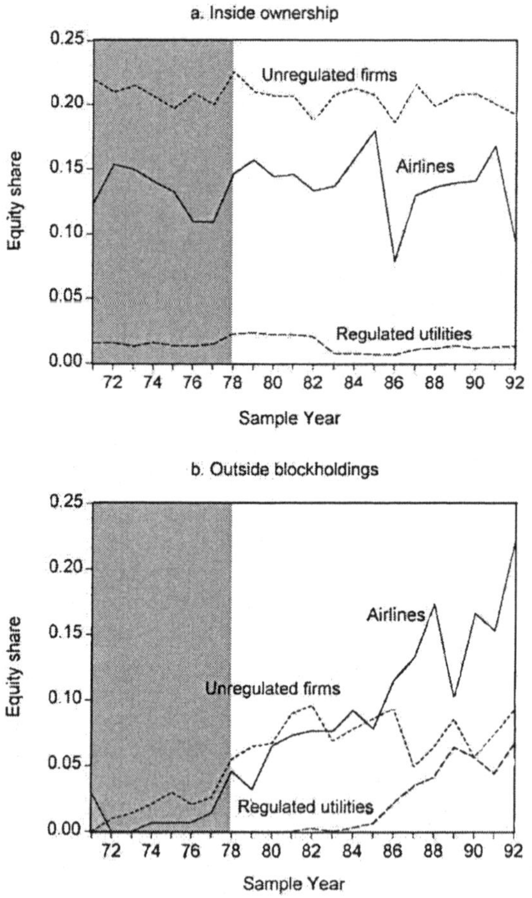

Fig. 1. Line graphs showing mean annual values of equity ownership by insiders (panel a) and outside blockholders (panel b) for 21 airlines and two similarly-sized benchmark samples (21 regulated utilities and 21 unregulated firms.) Data are drawn from corporate proxy statements for the 1971–1992 sample period. The shaded region covers the sample period prior to the Airline Deregulation Act, 1971–1978, when carriers providing interstate passenger air service were regulated by the Civil Aeronautics Board. The ownership series for airlines are represented by solid lines, the series for regulated utilities with long dashes, and unregulated firms with short dashes.

unregulated sample, and, after 1986 they diverge from the unregulated benchmark group.

Regression results on outside blockholdings are reported in the remaining columns of Table 4. As shown in Column 3, the cumulative stake of outside owners reported in company filings increases significantly during 1979–1992 by three percentage points for regulated firms, seven percentage points for unregulated firms, and nine percentage points for airlines. The OLS regressions used throughout the paper are structured so that the deregulation dummy variables capture the time trend as defined by the regulated firms. Subsample dummies for the airlines and unregulated firms similarly estimate the incremental effect of time on these subsamples. Hence, the full effect of deregulation on airlines is determined by the sum of the coefficient estimates on the deregulation and airline dummies, and the full effect of deregulation on unregulated firms is determined by the sum of the coefficient estimates on the deregulation and unregulated dummy variables. Column 4 reveals that the increase in ownership concentration for airlines is especially large towards the end of the deregulation period.

However, changes in the SEC's disclosure requirements pertaining to beneficial ownership suggest that the results in Columns 3 and 4 of Table 4 overstate the impact of deregulation on outside ownership. Before 1979, the SEC required companies to disclose security ownership for officers, directors, and owners of 10% or more of a company's shares. In 1979, the SEC altered the rules governing disclosure by (1) expanding the definition of beneficial ownership to include all securities, such as options, exercisable within 60 days and (2) lowering the threshold for disclosure of outside blocks, from 10% to 5% of a company's outstanding shares. Hence, all things being equal, we expect to observe a jump in 1979 in measures of ownership by both officers and directors and outside block holdings as reported in proxy statements. Left unadjusted, this reporting change obscures the impact of deregulation on the ownership structure of airlines. This change in reporting of governance data is a good illustration of the type of data consistency problems that can arise in the construction of time series spanning our sample period.

In Columns 5 and 6 of Table 4, we report regression results on outside interests calculated according to pre-1979 SEC reporting criterion as the sum of outside blocks of 10% or more. Use of this shadow variable limits the confounding influence of the change in reporting rules on our assessment of the impact of airline deregulation on firms' ownership structures. While we do have the data necessary to add securities excersisable in 60 days into pre-1979 officer and director ownership, we have no reason to believe that this reporting change distorts the ownership data differently for airlines versus the unregulated benchmark firms. This assessment is based on the fact that throughout the regulatory period, the airlines and the unregulated firms exhibit comparable patterns of stock option grants to managers. Over the entire 1979–1992 period, the airlines experience a significant increase in the concentration of outside ownership interests of 10% or more, though not significantly different from the increase experienced by regulated firms. Column 6 shows, however, that there is a significant consolidation of ownership that is unique to the airlines in the later years of the deregulation period. Overall, the results are consistent with the hypothesis

Table 4
Effect of airline deregulation on ownership structure

Ordinary least squares regressions with fixed effects of two ownership variables, the percent of outstanding shares held by officers and directors and outside (non-management, non-ESOP) blocks, on market value of firm equity, post-deregulation dummy variables (full for 1979–1992, early for 1979–1985, and late for 1986–1992), and interactions of the post-deregulation dummy variables with airline and unregulated dummies. The airline dummy variable takes the value of one if the sample firm is an airline and zero otherwise and the unregulated dummy variable equals one if the sample firm is an unregulated benchmark firm and zero otherwise. The blockholder variable is constructed both with all data reported in proxy statements and aggregating only 10% owners to reflect changes in reporting criterion during the sample period. Ownership data is taken from proxy statements and equity values from Compustat. Sample consists of 21 airlines and 42 benchmark firms during the period 1971–1992. Firm years are excluded if data is missing. *t*-statistics appear in parentheses.

Independent variables:	Ownership by:					
	Officers & directors (as a group)		Outside blockholders (as reported in proxy)		Outside blockholders (10% or more owners)	
	(1)	(2)	(3)	(4)	(5)	(6)
Real market value of equity (β_1)	– 1.97E-8	– 1.54E-8	– 7.47E-9	– 2.58E-8	– 6.43E-9	– 1.18E-8
	(– 3.46)	(– 2.53)	(– 1.49)	(– 5.07)	(– 1.70)	(– 2.99)
Deregulation-full or early (γ_1)	0.00	0.00	0.03	0.00	0.00	0.00
	(0.24)	(0.19)	(3.79)	(0.54)	(0.54)	(0.14)
Deregulation-late (γ_2)		0.00		0.05		0.01
		(0.04)		(7.23)		(0.16)
Interaction of airlines and deregulation-full or early (δ_1)	– 0.00	0.00	0.06	0.05	0.02	0.01
	(– 0.39)	(0.07)	(5.89)	(5.28)	(2.90)	(0.89)
Interaction of airlines and deregulation-late (δ_2)		– 0.02		0.11		0.06
		(– 1.29)		(8.52)		(6.69)

Interaction of unregulated and deregulation-full or early (ζ_1)	− 0.01 (− 0.75)	− 0.00 (− 0.25)	0.04 (3.92)	0.06 (5.68)	0.01 (1.40)	0.02 (2.78)
Interaction of unregulated and deregulation-late (ζ_2)		− 0.02 (− 1.23)		0.02 (1.99)		− 0.00 (− 0.37)
p-values on F-tests:						
$\gamma_1 + \delta_1 = 0$	0.7629	0.7760	0.0001	0.0001	0.0001	0.1654
$\gamma_2 + \delta_2 = 0$		0.1306		0.0001		0.0001
$\gamma_1 + \zeta_2 = 0$	0.4266	0.8683	0.0001	0.0001	0.0154	0.0001
$\gamma_2 + \delta_2 = 0$		0.1156		0.0001		0.5554
$\delta_1 = \zeta_1 = 0$	0.7396	0.7494	0.0371	0.1204	0.1251	0.0629
$\delta_2 = \zeta_2$		0.8037		0.0001		0.0001
Sample size	1,207	1,207	1,208	1,208	1,208	1,208
Adjusted R^2	0.8696	0.8698	0.5017	0.5526	0.2729	0.3153

that airline deregulation encouraged a more concentrated ownership structure of airlines.

4.2. Compensation

Management remuneration can take a variety of forms, including guaranteed salary, payments contingent on performance, appreciation of stockholdings in the employer firm, and continued employment. Each of these mechanisms influences managerial behavior. In this section, we consider the level of incentives provided to the CEO by cash and stock option awards, as well as the mix of these two forms of pay and the incentives provided by stock price appreciation and the threat of job loss.

4.2.1. Level of executive compensation

Section 2.2 delineates new areas of managerial influence that arise in airlines operating in an deregulated environment. The enlarged, more complex job of managing an airline suggests, as argued by Smith and Watts (1992), that the value of managerial skills is higher in deregulated environments. Hubbard and Palia (1995) offer another rationale for the prediction of increased pay in the post-deregulation period. They argue that increased product market competition necessitates greater managerial talent, and, in order to attract higher-quality managers, compensation will rise. Whether the complexity of the task or the labor market drives the change in pay, we expect the level of compensation of airline executives to increase in response to deregulation.

To test this prediction, we define the level of real compensation in 1982–1984 dollars to include cash remuneration, usually offered as salary and bonus awards, and the value of stock option grants. To value stock option awards, we follow Jensen and Murphy (1990) and others and use the Black-Scholes (1973) option pricing valuation with continuously paid dividends. The dollar value of the options is calculated as $N[{*}\Phi(Z) - \mathrm{P}e^{-rT}\Phi(Z - \sigma(T^{1/2}))]$ where $* = S - De^{-rT}$ and $Z = [\ln(*/P) + (r + \sigma^2/2)T]/\sigma(T^{1/2})$. The number of options awarded (N), the exercise price (P), and the maturity of the grant (T) were taken

Fig. 2. Line graphs showing mean annual levels of real CEO compensation (panel a) and component cash remuneration (panel b) and stock option awards (panel c) for 21 airlines and two similarly-sized benchmark samples (21 regulated utilities and 21 unregulated firms.) Data are reported in 1982–1984 constant dollars and are drawn from corporate proxy statements for the 1971–1992 sample period. Stock option grants are valued using the Black-Scholes option pricing formula with standard deviations calculated with stock price data, drawn from CRSP, for the year prior to the year of the grant. The shaded region covers the sample period prior to the Airline Deregulation Act, 1971–1978, when carriers providing interstate passenger air service were regulated by the Civil Aeronautics Board. United Airlines' 1988 and 1991 observations are excluded from the airline series in panels a and c. The airlines' compensation series are represented by solid lines, the series for regulated utilities with long dashes, and unregulated firms with short dashes.

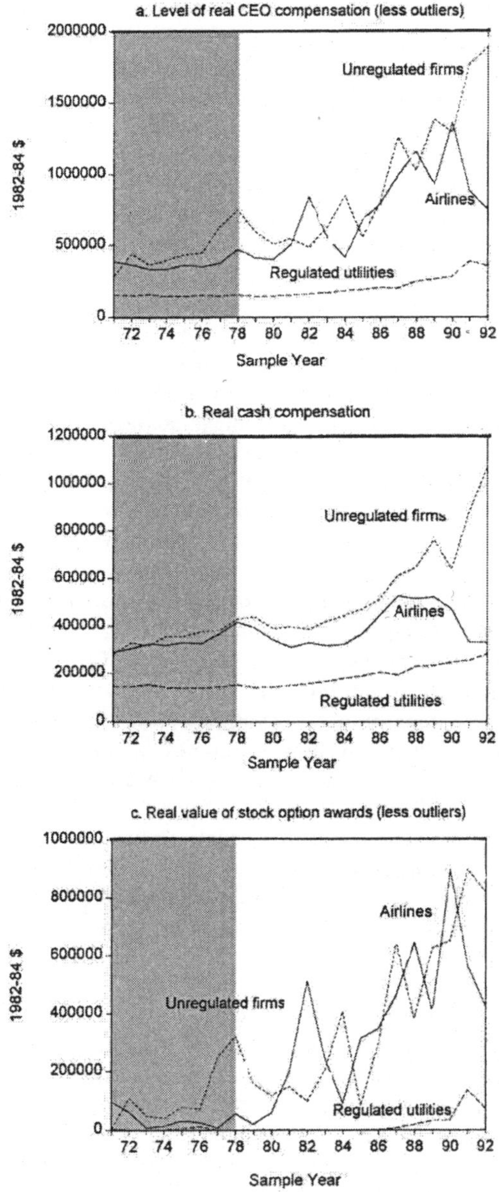
a. Level of real CEO compensation (less outliers)
2000000
1500000
1000000
500000
0
1982-84 $
Unregulated firms
Airlines
Regulated utilities
72 74 76 78 80 82 84 86 88 90 92
Sample Year
b. Real cash compensation
1200000
1000000
800000
600000
400000
200000
0
1982-84 $
Unregulated firms
Airlines
Regulated utilities
72 74 76 78 80 82 84 86 88 90 92
Sample Year
c. Real value of stock option awards (less outliers)
1000000
800000
600000
400000
200000
0
1982-84 $
Airlines
Unregulated firms
Regulated utilities
72 74 76 78 80 82 84 86 88 90 92
Sample Year

from proxy statements; the stock price (S), company dividend information (D), and the interest rate on constant maturity ten-year Treasury bonds (r) were drawn from CRSP. The cumulative standard normal distribution function is denoted by $\Phi(\cdot)$. Estimates of the standard deviation of the underlying stock, σ, were derived using stock price data for the year prior to the grant. In seven cases where options were awarded but no exercise price is available, we assume the exercise price equals the year-end stock price.

Fig. 2 shows the time paths of the annual sample averages of real CEO compensation (Fig. 2a) and its cash and option components (Fig. 2b and c, respectively). These plots omit two outlier observations, United Airlines (UAL) in 1988 and 1991. We discuss this omission below. The plot of the level of compensation reveals little change in the mean value of CEO pay throughout the regulation years, much like the series for the regulated benchmark sample. With deregulation, we observe an increase in both the level of pay and its rate of change. Indeed, each sample experiences an increase in top management remuneration that is indicative of the secular trend in executive compensation that has captivated the popular press. Although not reported here, these patterns are mirrored in median values of real compensation.

Table 5 reports regression results of the effect of airline deregulation and the level of CEO pay. Using the full sample, we observe a significant increase in the level of airline CEO pay following deregulation that is comparable to the trend toward higher pay among unregulated firms in the 1986–1992 period. However, the estimated impact of deregulation on the level of CEO pay is sensitive to two extreme observations. In 1988 and 1991, the CEO of UAL received large grants of stock options, contemporaneously valued at \$18.7 and \$14.2 million, respectively. These awards dwarf the compensation of other executives in our sample, and lie 15 and 10 standard deviations above the mean option grant in the airline sample. As shown in Columns 3 and 4 of Table 5, omitting these observations does not change the basic result that airline deregulation is accompanied by a significant jump in the level of real compensation for CEOs. It does, however, significantly alter the magnitude of the estimated effect of deregulation on airline CEO pay in the post-deregulation period.

4.2.2. Form of compensation

The structure of executive compensation is also predicted to change in response to deregulation. Specifically, the sensitivity of management compensation to firm performance is expected to rise. Varied explanations are offered for this prediction. First, Smith and Watts (1992, 276) argue that 'regulation restricts [a firm's] investment opportunity set and makes observation of the manager's actions easier'. Since managers seek to utilize the most informative performance measures available, reliance on accounting-based criterion for managerial performance evaluation is expected during regulation, and reliance on stock-based measures is expected following deregulation. Joskow et al. (1993)

Table 5
Effect of airline deregulation on the level of CEO compensation

Ordinary least squares regressions with fixed effects of the level of chief executive officer (CEO) real compensation on market value of firm equity in 1982–1984 dollars, post-deregulation dummy variables (full for 1979–1992, early for 1979–1985, and late for 1986–1992), and interactions of the post-deregulation variable(s) with airline and unregulated dummies. CEO real compensation is reported in 1982–1984 dollars and includes cash remuneration and the value of stock option grants. Compensation data is drawn from proxy statements and supplemented by CRSP data to calculate option values. Stock option grants are valued using the Black-Scholes formula with standard deviations calculated using stock price data for the year prior to year of the grant. Equity values are taken from Compustat. Sample consists of 21 airlines and 42 benchmark firms during the period 1971–1992. Firm years are excluded if data is missing. *t*-statistics appear in parentheses.

Independent variables	Full sample		Full sample less two outliers[a]	
	(1)	(2)	(3)	(4)
Real market value of equity (β_1)	0.56 (9.42)	0.44 (6.94)	0.48 (10.33)	0.39 (8.01)
Deregulation-full or early (γ_1)	− 37,928 (− 0.48)	− 14,560 (− 0.16)	− 21,641 (− 0.36)	− 11,526 (− 0.17)
Deregulation-late (γ_2)		− 13,240 (− 0.14)		2,311 (0.03)
Interaction of airlines and deregulation full or early (δ_1)	330,656 (2.84)	176,307 (1.38)	223,272 (2.49)	172,281 (1.75)
Interaction of airlines and deregulation late (δ_2)		749,880 (4.83)		374,439 (3.12)
Interaction of unregulated and deregulation-full or early (ζ_1)	296,911 (2.65)	97,540 (0.77)	308,051 (3.57)	102,640 (1.05)
Interaction of unregulated and deregulation-late (ζ_2)		583,796 (4.44)		593,004 (5.86)
p-values on F-tests:				
$\gamma_1 + \delta_1 = 0$	0.0007	0.0761	0.0026	0.0218
$\gamma_2 + \delta_2 = 0$		0.0001		0.0002
$\gamma_1 + \zeta_1 = 0$	0.0016	0.3567	0.0001	0.1880
$\gamma_1 + \zeta_2 = 0$		0.0001		0.0001
$\delta_1 = \zeta_1$	0.7739	0.5379	0.3495	0.4785
$\delta_2 = \zeta_2$		0.2916		0.0729
Sample size	1,208	1,208	1,206	1,206
Adjusted R^2	0.4934	0.5099	0.5916	0.6068

[a]In 1988 and 1991, United Airlines' CEO received grants of 250,000 and 225,000 stock options, valued at $15,873,943 and $10,489,031 in 1982–1984 dollars, respectively.These observations are more than 10 standard deviations above the airline sample mean of $195,998, and at least twice as large as the next largest grant in the 1208 firm-year sample.

Table 6
Effect of airline deregulation on the form of CEO compensation

Ordinary least squares regressions with fixed effects of the form of chief executive officer (CEO) real compensation on market value of firm equity in 1982–1984 dollars, post-deregulation dummy variables (full for 1979–1992, early for 1979–1985, and late for 1986–1992), and interactions of the post-deregulation variables with airline and unregulated dummies. CEO real compensation is reported in 1982–1984 dollars and includes cash remuneration and the value of stock option grants.Compensation data is drawn from proxy statements and supplemented by CRSP data to calculate option values. Stock option grants are valued using the Black-Scholes formula with standard deviations calculated using stock price data for the year prior to year of the grant. Equity values are taken from Compustat. Sample consists of 21 airlines and 42 benchmark firms during the period 1971–1992. Firm years are excluded if data is missing. *t*-statistics appear in parentheses.

Independent variables	Dependent variable					
	Cash compensation		Stock option grants ($) (full sample)		Stock option grants ($) (less two outliers[a])	
	(1)	(2)	(3)	(4)	(5)	(6)
Real market value of equity (β_1)	0.14 (7.59)	0.09 (4.94)	0.43 (7.86)	0.35 (5.98)	0.34 (8.84)	0.30 (7.27)
Deregulation-full or early (γ_1)	25,184 (1.06)	9,056 (0.34)	− 63,112 (− 0.88)	− 23,616 (− 0.29)	− 46,457 (− 0.92)	− 20,496 (− 0.36)
Deregulation-late (γ_2)		58,757 (2.15)		− 71,997 (− 0.85)		− 56,008 (− 0.94)
Interaction of airlines and deregulation-full or early (δ_1)	− 1,334 (− 0.04)	5,031 (0.13)	331,990 (3.14)	171,276 (1.47)	227,710 (3.01)	167,166 (2.04)
Interaction of airlines and deregulation-late (δ_2)		22,124 (0.48)		727,756 (5.12)		345,327 (3.44)

Interaction of unregulated and deregulation-full or early (ζ_1)	117,414 (3.49)	37,291 (0.99)	179,497 (1.76)	60,249 (0.52)	190,889 (2.68)	65,493 (0.80)
Interaction of unregulated and deregulation-late (ζ_2)		236,296 (6.07)		347,499 (2.89)		356,968 (4.22)
p-values on F-tests:						
$\gamma_1 + \delta_1 = 0$	0.3591	0.6015	0.0006	0.0767	0.0014	0.0124
$\gamma_2 + \delta_2 = 0$		0.0362		0.0001		0.0006
$\gamma_1 + \zeta_1 = 0$	0.0001	0.0821	0.1182	0.6564	0.0057	0.4368
$\gamma_2 + \zeta_2 = 0$		0.0001		0.0027		0.0001
$\delta_1 = \zeta_1$	0.0008	0.3940	0.1530	0.3425	0.6708	0.2161
$\delta_2 = \zeta_2$		0.0001		0.0084		0.9090
Sample Size	1,208	1,208	1,208	1,208	1,206	1,206
Adjusted R^2	0.7399	0.7554	0.2683	0.2818	0.3650	0.3738

[a] In 1988 and 1991, United Airlines' CEO received grants of 250,000 and 225,000 stock options, valued at $15,873,943 and $10,489,031 in 1982–1984 dollars, respectively. These observations are more than 10 standard deviations above the airline sample mean of $195,998, and at least twice as large as the next largest grant in the 1208 firm-year sample.

argue that political pressure can shape CEO compensation. To make managers more responsive to consumers, regulators may tie compensation to service rather than profitability, or shy away from the use of value-sensitive forms of pay, such as options, to avoid 'politically unpopular large lump-sum payments' (ibid., 4). Lastly, if deregulation leads to an increase in managerial stakeholdings, as we argue in Section 4.1, stock options can be used to counteract heightened risk aversion by managers.

In Table 6, we decompose the level of real compensation into cash and stock option grants.[1] Regression analysis shows that, controlling for firm size and compensation trends among the regulated benchmark firms, cash compensation does not change for airline CEOs in response to deregulation. These results serve to caution researchers of the importance of controlling for secular trends when attempting to attribute time series variation in compensation to deregulation (see Hubbard and Palia, 1995). Indeed, the source of the significant increase in the level of pay for airline executives is attributable to stock-based remuneration. The value of stock option grants is estimated to have risen approximately $260,000 in the 1979–1992 period (see Column 3). Results in Column 4 of Table 6 show that the impact of deregulation on this form of CEO compensation grows over time. In the 1986–1992 period, the value of stock option grants to airline CEOs increased nearly $400,000 more than for CEOs in the unregulated benchmark firms. Once again, note that both the magnitude of the 1986–1992 coefficient estimate, and the statistical significance of the difference between airlines and the unregulated benchmark, are inflated by the inclusion of two outliers observations (see Columns 5 and 6). Notwithstanding, the finding that stock-based rewards account for the jump in CEO pay, post-deregulation, is unchanged.

4.2.3. Equity ownership by the CEO

Managerial ownership of the firm's equity aligns shareholder and management interests, and places voting power in the hands of corporate decision makers. Because our understanding of how stockholdings are amassed is quite limited, it is unclear how deregulation will affect the level of managerial stockholdings. For example, if managerial ownership results from restrictions on company-awarded equity, either restricted stock per se or option awards with restrictions on exercise, increased reliance on equity-based pay in the deregulation period would increase CEO stockholdings. However, an individual manager can counteract the use of equity-based pay by selling unrestricted equity shares, or short-selling his company's stock, so as to minimize his exposure to firm-specific risk. Alternatively, if equity stakes are accumulated largely through

[1] Changes in reporting rules governing the disclosure of executive pay during the sample period prevents us from exploring finer categories of pay, such as bonuses.

open market purchases, managers may increase their fractional holdings during deregulation, either by purchasing stock on personal account or repurchasing stock using company funds, in an effort to increase their voting power. Frank Lorenzo's beneficial ownership in Texas International illustrates this case. Lorenzo's personal stake in Texas International rose from 1% of all outstanding equity in 1972 to 14% by 1979.

Whether we consider airline CEO stockholdings in percentage terms, in real dollar value, or in relation to annual cash compensation as a proxy for wealth, there is no evidence that managerial ownership varies as a result of industry deregulation. Table 7 reports mean, standard deviation, and median values of fractional ownership by the CEO (Panel A), the real value of CEO stockholdings in 1982–1984 dollars (Panel B), and the value of CEO stockholdings as a fraction of annual cash compensation (Panel C).

Table 7
Descriptive statistics on CEO ownership variables

Mean, standard deviation, and median values of ownership variables are shown for three industry samples. CEO ownership is presented as the percentage of all outstanding common equity held by the CEO (panel A), in 1982–1984 dollar terms (panel B reported in thousands) and as a fraction of the CEO's cash compensation (panel C). Statistics are shown for two periods, regulation (1971–1977) and deregulation (1979–1992).The airline sample includes 21 formerly regulated carriers for which proxies are available for six years before and six years after 1978. The electric utility and manufacturing samples include 21 firms each, matched on the 1978 equity value of the sample airline firms. *p*-values testing for the equivalence of means across periods are shown.

Statistic	Airlines		Electric Utilities		Manufacturing	
	1971–1977	1979–1992	1971–1977	1979–1992	1971–1977	1979–1992
Panel A: Fraction of outstanding common equity held by CEO (%)						
Mean	2.67	3.05	0.19	0.14	5.47	5.60
Median	0.39	0.34	0.05	0.05	1.05	0.85
Standard Deviation	7.66	10.29	0.47	0.41	8.06	9.46
p-value	0.70		0.26		0.89	
Panel B: CEO equity ownership, at year-end (in thousands of 1982–1984 $)						
Mean	1376	3479	161	201	3733	14022
Median	305	670	99	113	1364	3867
Standard Deviation	2166	6043	193	257	5683	35222
p-value	0.01		0.08		0.01	
Panel C: CEO equity as a fraction of annual cash compensation (%)						
Mean	75.04	74.45	6.90	5.83	116.82	156.62
Median	28.51	15.94	2.98	2.96	31.71	28.47
Standard Deviation	141.64	153.80	11.14	11.13	166.47	437.63
p-value	0.97		0.36		0.20	

Panel A of Table 7 shows unsurprising variation across samples in the mean and median values of fractional ownership by CEOs, with the strongest link between ownership and firm value in the unregulated firms, but no significant within-sample temporal variation. A pooled OLS regression with fixed effects of fractional ownership on firm size, such as market value, and dummy variables for samples, like airlines and regulated firms, deregulation, and interactions of those dummy variables shows a post-deregulation increase in fractional ownership by airline CEOs. Specifically, the coefficient estimate on the interaction between airlines and the second phase of deregulation, 1986–1992, is positive and statistically significant, revealing a trend among CEOs of airlines toward larger equity stakes. That the real value of CEO ownership rises over the sample period is clear in Panel B of Table 7. For both the airline and unregulated samples, median CEO stockholdings roughly triple between 1971–1977 and 1979–1992. The comparable increase for regulated firms is less than 15%. Using regression analysis described above, we find that airlines do not share uniformly in this appreciation. Decomposing the airline sample into surviving carriers and airlines that do not remain independent through 1992 shows that the value of CEO stockholdings among surviving firms increases significantly after 1978. That is, if one removes the effect of declining stock prices for exiting airlines, surviving airlines mimic the secular trend toward increasingly valuable CEO ownership claims.

Last, we consider CEO equity ownership as a fraction of the CEO's annual cash compensation to gauge whether the value of that equity is growing disproportionately with a crude proxy for managerial wealth. Panel C of Table 7 shows little within-sample variation in this variable, and more substantial variation across samples. Regression analysis shows no incremental effect of airline deregulation and the importance of stock ownership on CEO wealth. We conclude that, on average, deregulation did not alter the relation between managerial ownership and CEO remuneration.

4.2.4. *Threat of dismissal*

Several studies (e.g., Warner et al., 1988; Weisbach, 1988) document an inverse relation between a company's stock returns and the likelihood that its CEO is replaced. The relation suggests that the threat of dismissal for poor performance is a pertinent form of CEO pay (see Jensen and Murphy, 1990). We expect the likelihood of dismissal to increase after deregulation for at least two reasons. First, the immediate change from regulation to deregulation is likely to highlight differences in managerial abilities across firms. As less capable managers are revealed, they are likely to be replaced either through takeover, bankruptcy, or dismissal by the board. Second, the sensitivity of management turnover for a given level of poor performance is likely to be higher in the deregulated environment, where the sensitivity of firm value to managerial input is greater.

Table 8 reports the likelihood that an incumbent chief executive officer is in his final year as CEO for each of the three samples in the regulation and deregulation periods. Consistent with theory, the incidence of CEO departures increases significantly among airline firms in the 1979–1992 period. Within the deregulation period, the rate of departures remains flat at roughly 10% until 1984, when 10 of 19 CEOs serve their final year. Following 1984, the annual rate of airline CEO departures is 19%. This pattern of turnover rates contrasts with the benchmark samples, where no significant change is observed during the sample period.

We searched annual indexes of the Wall Street Journal to find the stated reasons for the departure of airline CEOs. In 22 of the 59 departures, or 40%, between 1971 and 1992 appear to be related to an orderly transition of managers. Of these 22 departures, 17 firms cite retirement as the reason for a CEO's exit, and the remaining 5 mention promoting the outgoing CEO to chairman or vice-chairman of the board, with the incoming CEO reporting to his predecessor. Where the CEOs were retiring, the age of the CEO in his last year of employment was 64 or older in 15 of the 17 cases. The remaining two cases have CEOs retiring at age 58, raising the question of whether these were forced, rather than the voluntary, departures. An additional 22% of turnover cases, or 13 cases, of the 59 we observe, is attributable to control changes, virtually all of which occur in the mid-1980s. While poor performance is never mentioned explicitly, rumors of performance-related firings are found in 6 cases, and departures coincident with bankruptcy filings account for an additional 4 cases. Of the remaining 14 CEO departures, 4 executives left for positions at other airlines, boardroom battles and personal reasons were noted in 2 cases each, and in 6 cases, no explanation for the CEO's departure was offered. Overall, these data parallel the press reports of CEO departures documented by Weisbach (1988).

We estimate logistic regressions predicting the probability of CEO departure as a function of firms' stock price performance to ascertain whether poor

Table 8
Chief executive officer departures

Mean rates of CEO departure for airlines, and regulated and unregulated benchmark samples during 1971–1992. A test of the significance of the difference between CEO turnover across the 1971–1977 and 1979–1992 period is reported, with *p*-values denoting level of statistical significance. CEO departures are identified from proxy reports and verified in the Wall Street Journal. Sample consists of 21 airlines and 42 benchmark firms during the period 1971–1992. Firm years are excluded if data is missing.

	1971–1977	1979–1992	*t*-stat	*p*-value
Airlines	10.09	18.88	− 2.15	0.03
Regulated electric utilities	12.40	11.87	0.15	0.88
Unregulated manufacturing	8.73	12.84	− 1.25	0.21

performance, per se, or increased risk of job loss explains the airline data. We interpret poor performance to include CEO departures that are coincident with takeovers. Following Jensen and Murphy (1990), we estimate restricted ($b_2 = 0$, $c_2 = 0$) and unrestricted versions of the following relation for the airlines:

$$\ln[\text{prob(departure)}/(1 - \text{prob(departure)})] = a_0 + a_1 D + b_1(R_{\text{net-of-mkt}}) + b_2(D*R_{\text{net-of-mkt}}) + c_1(\text{lagged } R_{\text{net-of-mkt}}) + c_2(D*(\text{lagged } R_{\text{net-of-mkt}})), \tag{1}$$

where D denotes a dummy variable that equals one for years after 1977, and zero otherwise. We omit observations for 1978. Lack of stock price data reduces the number of CEO departures considered by this test, from 59 to 46 cases. Consistent with the results in Table 8, Table 9 shows that a_1 is estimated to be positive and significant. For the unrestricted regression, shown in Column 2 of Table 9, the coefficient estimates on the net-of-market return variables are all negative and insignificant at conventional levels, suggesting no change in the sensitivity of dismissal to stock price performance after deregulation. These

Table 9
Likelihood of CEO departure among airlines

Logistic regression results estimating the relation of stock price performance to the likelihood that an airline CEO is in his final year of tenure. Explanatory variables include a dummy variable for the deregulation period, 1979–1992, the current or contemporaneous net-of-market return, lagged net-of-market returns and interactions between the deregulation and two net-of-market return variables. The sample covers 21 formerly regulated airlines during the period 1971–1992. Asymptotic t-statistics are reported in parentheses.

	(1)	(2)
Intercept	− 2.18	− 2.19
Deregulation dummy (D)	0.70	0.70
	(1.88)	(1.86)
Current net-of-market return	− 0.32	− 0.43
	(− 0.64)	(− 0.45)
$D*$(Current net-of-market return)		0.13
		(0.11)
Lagged net-of-market return	(− 0.85)	− 0.45
	(− 1.71)	(− 0.48)
$D*$(Lagged net-of-market return)		− 0.55
		(− 0.50)
Sample size	305	305
Number of departures	46	46
Significance of model	0.0479	0.1471

results are insensitive to the use of equal-or value-weighted market returns. Thus, poor performance, rather than a heightened probability of dismissal, explains the observed increase in CEO departures following airline deregulation.

4.3. Board structure

4.3.1. Size of boards

Little is known, theoretically or empirically, about the optimal size of boards. We take the perspective that the value-maximizing size of a company's board is governed by a tradeoff between the incremental costs and benefits associated with additional board members. We conjecture that the principal benefit of additional board members is the incremental expertise they bring to the board, while the principal cost is the incremental increase in the cost of decision-making, including the longer time it takes to make decisions with larger boards, and free-riding induced by larger boards. If value-maximization prevails, of course, firms will select board sizes that equate the incremental benefits and costs of the marginal board member.

As a theoretical matter, the effect of deregulation on optimal board size is ambiguous. Since deregulation changes the role of managers, we expect the monitoring function of boards to change after deregulation. This could result in an increase in board size, since additional board members bring information that facilitates the monitoring of managers. Alternatively, deregulation might result in a contraction of board size, since the costs of sluggish decision-making and free-riding are higher in a less-regulated environment.

While the theoretical effect of deregulation on board size is ambiguous, there is some basis for expecting a reduction in the size of airlines' boards after deregulation. During the regulatory period of 1971–1977, the average size of airline boards is 13.8, versus 10.7 and 10.6, for the unregulated and regulated benchmark samples, respectively. An emerging literature on board size suggests that boards as large as those in the airline industry during the period of regulation are ineffective as monitors. For example, Jensen (1993, 865) conjectures that 'keeping boards small can help improve their performance. When boards get beyond seven or eight people they are less likely to function effectively …'. Lipton and Lorsch (1992, 65) argue that "[w]hen a board has more than ten members, it becomes more difficult for them all to express their ideas and opinions". Gertner and Kaplan (1996) document that the average board size of firms doing reverse leverage buyouts (LBOs) is 8.2. They infer that reverse LBOs are likely to have optimal board sizes, given the incentive of the LBO sponsor to maximize value. If board sizes of ten or fewer are more effective in monitoring managers, we expect the size of airline boards to contract after deregulation.

Fig. 3a shows the size of boards over time for the three samples. As noted above, during the regulatory period, airline boards were typically 30–40% larger

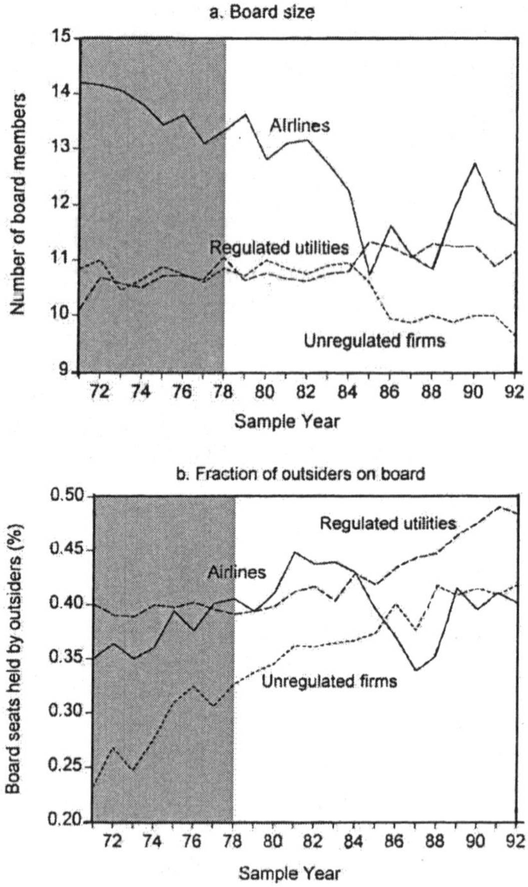

Fig. 3. Line graphs showing mean annual values of board size (panel a) and the fraction of board seats held by outsiders (panel b) for 21 airlines and two similarly-sized benchmark samples (21 regulated utilities and 21 unregulated firms.) Data are drawn from corporate proxy statements for the 1971–1992 sample period. The shaded region covers the sample period prior to the Airline Deregulation Act, 1971–1978, when carriers providing interstate passenger air service were regulated by the Civil Aeronautics Board. The series on board size and composition for airlines are represented by solid lines, the series for regulated utilities with long dashes, and unregulated firms with short dashes.

than those of the benchmark firms. There is a marked contraction of board size evident in the period prior to 1985, when corporate control activity in the airline industry increases. Table 10 reports the effect of airline deregulation on board size, controlling for firm size (see columns 1 and 2). Airlines counter the

Table 10
Effect of airline deregulation on board structure

Ordinary least squares regressions with fixed effects of the size and composition of the board of directors, post-deregulation dummy variables (full for 1979–1992, early for 1979–1985, and late for 1986–1992), and interactions of the post-deregulation variables with airline and unregulated dummies.The airline dummy variable takes the value of one if the sample firm is an airline and zero otherwise and the unregulated dummy variable equals one if the sample firm is an unregulated benchmark firm and zero otherwise. Data on board structure is extracted from proxy statements. Sample consists of 21 airlines and 42 benchmark firms during the period 1971–1992.Firm years are excluded if data is missing. *t*-statistics appear in parentheses.

Independent variables	Dependent variables:			
	Number of board members		Fraction of board members classified as outsiders[a]	
	(1)	(2)	(3)	(4)
Fraction of outstanding equity held by board (β_1)	− 1.48 (− 2.32)	− 1.61 (− 2.55)	− 0.19 (− 5.25)	− 0.18 (− 5.04)
Deregulation-full or early (γ_1)	0.31 (1.72)	0.08 (0.38)	0.04 (4.01)	0.02 (1.29)
Deregulation-late (γ_2)		0.55 (2.62)		0.07 (5.76)
Interaction of airlines and deregulation-full or early (δ_1)	− 1.33 (− 4.94)	− 0.98 (− 3.29)	− 0.00 (− 0.32)	0.03 (1.64)
Interaction of airlines and deregulation-late (δ_2)		− 1.86 (− 5.21)		− 0.05 (− 2.40)
Interaction of unregulated and deregulation-full or early (ζ_1)	− 0.60 (− 2.31)	0.05 (0.17)	0.05 (3.67)	0.05 (3.30)
Interaction of unregulated and deregulation-late (ζ_2)		− 1.37 (− 4.45)		0.06 (3.42)
p-values on F-tests:				
$\gamma_1 + \delta_1 = 0$	0.0001	0.0001	0.0011	0.0004
$\gamma_2 + \delta_2 = 0$		0.0001		0.2113
$\gamma_1 + \zeta_1 = 0$	0.1218	0.5346	0.0001	0.0001
$\gamma_2 + \zeta_2 = 0$		0.0003		0.0001
$\delta_1 = \zeta_1$	0.0073	0.0006	0.0001	0.1004
$\delta_2 = \zeta_2$		0.1733		0.0001
Sample Size	1,211	1,211	1,211	1,211
Adjusted R^2	0.9764	0.9768	0.9431	0.9450

[a]Outsiders are defined as board members who are not, and have not been, either employed by or provided contractual service for the sample firm.

deregulation period trend among regulated firms toward increased board size, contracting their boards by an estimated one member during 1979–1985 and an additional 1.8 members over 1986–1992. Overall, airline boards contract more rapidly than the boards of benchmark firms in the years immediately following deregulation, and then mirror the trend among unregulated firms toward smaller boards.

4.3.2. Composition of boards

Several studies find evidence consistent with the argument that outside directors monitor managerial performance. Weisbach (1988) finds that the sensitivity of CEO turnover to firm performance is greater when outside directors constitute a majority of the board. Hermalin and Weisbach (1989) find that outside directors are more likely to be added to a firm's board following poor performance, suggesting that outside directors play more than a perfunctory role.

If outside directors play a substantive monitoring role, the value of outside directors is likely to be higher in a deregulated environment. Holding changes in other governance mechanisms constant, we expect to observe an increase in the proportion of outsiders on airlines' boards of directors following deregulation of the industry.

Over the sample period, the regulated benchmark firms systematically increase the representation of outside directors on their boards. We define outsiders to include board members who are not employees, former employees, or representatives of firms that have or have had contractual relations, like investment bankers, with the sample firm. As shown in Fig. 3b, airlines follow this trend into the early 1980s, and then reduce the fraction of board seats held by outsiders. Determinants of the fraction of board members classified as outsiders are examined in Columns 3 and 4 of Table 10. Regression results reveal that, although the representation of outsiders among airlines' directors increases after deregulation, the increase from 37% to 41% in the average fraction of board seats held by outsiders reflects a systematic trend in board composition across industries, and is not attributable to deregulation.

5. Dynamic predictions and results

In the previous section, we document that the governance structures of airlines changed after deregulation, generally in ways consistent with comparative static predictions. In this section, we discuss the dynamics of governance changes, a topic that is largely undeveloped in the governance literature. We first offer some predictions and results on the speed with which internal versus external governance mechanisms are likely to adapt, and then discuss the relation between the speed of adaptation and firm survival.

5.1. Internal versus external governance mechanisms

Some governance mechanisms involve decisions made by parties outside the firm, such as investors who act to consolidate a firm's ownership structure, or launch a takeover bid for the firm. Other governance mechanisms, such as compensation plans and board structure, involve decisions made by parties inside the firm. For purposes of this discussion, we refer to the former as external and the latter as internal governance mechanisms.

The distinction between external and internal mechanisms has been noted previously in the literature. Jensen (1993), (p. 852), for example, argues that capital markets and the market for corporate control are considerably more effective in disciplining managers than internal control systems, which 'seldom respond in the absence of a crisis'. Similarly, Gilson (1996) argues that internal mechanisms are less likely than external mechanisms to adapt swiftly to changes in the business environment. Gilson notes that the recent wave of corporate restructuring began much earlier in the U.S. than it did in Germany and Japan, countries that rely less on external governance mechanisms than does the U.S.

We suggest two reasons why internal mechanisms are likely to respond more sluggishly to environmental changes. First, it is difficult to quickly change organizational 'rules of the game' that firms develop to govern employee behavior. These rules include the structure of compensation, operating procedures, and social norms, which collectively define a firm's corporate culture. Employees acclimate their behavior to the incentives embodied in these rules, which by design are not malleable. On average, firms presumably select cultures that are appropriate for their respective business environments. As a firm's environment changes, its original culture becomes less appropriate. However, the costs of reorienting employees to a new set of rules can lead to the perpetuation of the original culture. For this reason, internal mechanisms are likely to exhibit a higher degree of inertia than external mechanisms.

Second, changes in internal governance can involve wealth transfers among the stakeholders of a firm, which can impede a quick adjustment to a new set of rules. For example, consider employees who, perhaps due to specialized training, wield some measure of hold-up power. If these employees stand to lose under a new incentive or monitoring system, they are likely to exercise their hold-up power to slow the pace of change, by engaging in strikes, for example. Thus, resolution of these wealth transfers can prevent rapid movement from one set of internal mechanisms to another.

External mechanisms, such as changes in ownership by outside investors, do not suffer from these problems. Ownership changes involve costs of their own, including the transaction costs of buying or selling large blocks, and the costs of complying with regulations. If these costs are less than the costs of changing internal governance mechanisms, then, as a firm's business environment changes, we expect its ownership structure to adapt more quickly than its internal governance mechanisms. In the case of airlines, we expect the changes in ownership structure to occur more rapidly than changes in executive compensation plans and board structure.

In Section 4, we document how the governance structures of airlines changed after deregulation, and noted whether the changes occurred during the earlier or later years of deregulation. For all of the variables, including ownership structure, the changes during the later years were greater than the changes during the earlier years, suggesting that governance changes occur somewhat sluggishly. However, consistent with our expectations, ownership structure exhibits more substantial change during the early years of deregulation than do other governance mechanisms. Column 4 of Table 4 shows a statistically significant increase in the fraction of equity held by outside blockholders that raised mean outside ownership from below one, to more than five, percentage points during 1979–1985. Note that this increase may be partially attributable to a change in reporting of beneficial ownership stakes from 10% to 5% in 1979. Among the internal governance variables, only board size changed significantly for airlines during the 1979–1985 period, contracting by one board member or 7% during this period, versus 1.8 members, or 15%, during the 1986–1992 period. The level of compensation rose significantly also, reflecting higher valued stock option grants, which may reflect increased stock prices for successful firms, rather than policy changes.

As a robustness check on these results, we also investigate the governance mechanisms adopted by new airlines that enter the industry after deregulation. Since these airlines were starting from scratch, they were not laden with regulation-era internal governance structures. If internal governance structures are more costly to change than external governance mechanisms, there should be a larger difference in the internal versus external governance mechanisms of new versus incumbent airlines.

We identify six publicly traded airlines, with SIC 451, established after 1977 for which corporate proxy statements are available through Q-files for the years 1984 and 1985. These six airlines are American West, Atlantic Southeast, Jet America, Mid Pacific, Muse Air, and People Express. We selected these firms from a list of 96 CRSP airline securities that traded between 1972 and 1994. We eliminate 22 securities, which correspond to sample firms studied in Section 4 and 24 firms which did not trade in the deregulation period, 1979–1992. Of the remaining 50 observations, 23 new entrant firms traded in 1984 and 1985, when the number of airline stocks peaked. Annual proxy statements for 1984 and 1985, for 15 of these 23 firms, but only six of the 15 airlines were established after 1977.

Table 11 reports the evidence on the governance structures of existing airlines ($n = 19$) and new entrants ($n = 6$). Controlling for firm size, measured either as the market value of equity or the book value of assets, we find that only governance mechanisms determined within the firm differ significantly between

Table 11
Cost of adjusting governance structures: evidence from new entrants

Ordinary least square regressions of measures of corporate governance mechanisms on firm size and firm status as a post-deregulation entrant or a regulatory-survivor for a sample of 25 firms, of which six are new entrant airlines, for the years 1983–1984. New entrant denotes a dummy variable that takes the value of one if the airline did not provide service prior to 1977 and zero otherwise.

Dependent variables	Independent variables			Adj. R^2
	Intercept	Firm size	New Entrant	
Ownership structure:				
Officer & directors	0.24	− 1.78E-7	− 0.06	0.2069
	(6.88)	(− 3.87)	(− 1.08)	
Outside blocks	0.08	6.34E-9	0.04	− 0.0188
	(3.51)	(0.21)	(1.03)	
Real compensation:				
Level	199,895	0.21	− 79,068	0.6318
	(10.77)	(8.15)	(− 2.52)	
Cash	200,983	0.20	− 106,114	0.6527
	(10.98)	(7.95)	(− 3.41)	
Option grants	− 2,062	0.004	28,865	0.1916
	(− 0.46)	(0.71)	(3.78)	
Board structure:				
Members	11.59	1.77E-6	− 4.74	0.3226
	(15.35)	(1.76)	(− 3.87)	
Fraction outsiders	0.20	− 1.25E-8	0.19	0.2710
	(7.09)	(0.33)	(4.14)	

new entrant and formerly regulated airlines. Specifically, for 1984–1985, new entrant firms have boards that are smaller by nearly 50%, with twice the representation by outsiders and lower real compensation, than those of established airlines. The form of pay differs across the two groups of airlines as well. New entrants have significantly more compensation in the form of stock option grants, and less in cash. There is no difference, however, in measures of ownership structure across the groups of firms. As a whole, we interpret these results as supporting the argument that internal governance mechanisms evolve slowly, perhaps because of the wealth effects of destroying existing organizational capital, or because of the difficulty initiating change in organizations.

5.2. Adaptation and survival

The Darwinian view of organizations supposes that firms that fail to adapt their governance structures appropriately are less likely to survive in competitive markets. Two mechanisms exist by which inefficient firms become extinct: liquidation bankruptcy and takeover.[2] Despite the predominance of the Darwinian view, little is known about the relation between adaptation and survival. Two recent studies examine the relation between firm characteristics and survival in the trucking industry after trucking deregulation (see Zingales, 1998; Silverman et al., 1997). Weiner (1994) notes that little is known empirically about adaptation and survival in the natural sciences as well. In this section, we investigate whether airlines that maintain their independence through 1992, or those firms not subject to bankruptcy or takeover, adapt their governance structures differently from firms that do not survive the period.

We presume that surviving airlines create more value than airlines that do not survive the deregulation period. This presumption seems reasonable, but we recognize that an alternative view exists. Since target firms receive large premiums in takeovers, firms that exit through takeover might actually create more value than firms not taken over. Also, some firms that exit due to bankruptcy may have enhanced their values previously by taking on large amounts of debt that increased the likelihood of bankruptcy. Ultimately, it is an empirical issue as to whether surviving airlines create more or less value than airlines that exit via takeover or bankruptcy.

To examine whether surviving or nonsurviving airlines create more value for shareholders, we examine buy-and-hold returns for each airline from January 1978 through either December 29, 1992, or the last date on which the airline's stock traded publicly, whichever is earlier. Surviving airlines are defined as airlines that survive the entire period without being taken over or filing for bankruptcy. This group includes Alaska, American, Delta, Southwest, United and USAir. For each nonsurviving airline, we compare its buy-and-hold return, using monthly data, with the corresponding return for the portfolio of six surviving airlines from January 1978 through the nonsurviving airline's last trade date. Table 12 contains these results, which show that the returns of the survivors are significantly higher than nonsurvivor returns. Of the 15 nonsurvivors, 12 had returns that were lower than those of surviving airlines over the deregulation period. Braniff and Pan Am, which liquidated, have buy-and-hold returns of − 0.95 and − 0.99, respectively. The corresponding returns on the portfolio of surviving airlines are 1.70 and 7.48. Of the remaining 13 nonsurvivors that exited due to takeover, 10 had returns that were lower than the survivors' returns. Some of the nonsurvivors that were taken over later filed for bankruptcy. Hence, notwithstanding the large premiums paid in takeovers, airlines that were taken over created significantly less shareholder value than the six surviving airlines. The average difference between the buy-and-hold returns

[2] Note that our assertion is not that all takeovers are motivated by inefficient adaptation by target firms, but rather, that some are.

Table 12
Buy-and-hold returns for surviving (independent) and nonsurviving firms

Comparison of buy-and-hold returns for airlines that do not remain independent due to bankruptcy or takeover, and the portfolio of six airlines that remain independent through December 1992. The returns are calculated using monthly stock price returns for the period January 1978 through the last trade data or December 29, 1992, whichever is earlier. The surviving firms and their respective buy-and-hold return as of December 29, 1992 include: Alaska, 8.847; American, 5.780; Delta, 2.588; Southwest, 42.031; United, 5.960; and USAir, 2.575. *Date of last trade* corresponds to the last date during the sample period ending December 29, 1992. Some 'exiting firms' de re-emerge as publicly traded firms post-1992. For the purpose of our anlaysis, Braniff, Continental and Texas International exited following bankruptcy filings, while Hawaiian experienced a control change that left its stock trading on the American Stock Exchange

Exiting firm	Date of last trade	Exiting firm's return	Independent's return	Difference
Braniff	May 26, 1982	– 0.945	1.702	– 2.647
Continental	October 28, 1982	– 0.0306	3.382	– 3.689
Frontier	November 21, 1985	2.237	5.781	– 3.544
Republic	August 12, 1986	2.757	5.272	– 2.514
Ozark	September 15, 1986	5.857	5.809	0.048
Eastern	November 25, 1986	0.549	6.346	– 5.797
Western	December 18, 1986	0.878	6.144	– 5.268
Aloha	December 26, 1986	5.885	6.186	– 0.301
TWA	March 31, 1987	7.686	6.861	0.824
PSA	April 30, 1987	5.120	6.315	– 1.195
Piedmont	November 4, 1987	8.410	4.593	3.817
Northwest	July 26, 1989	5.558	9.905	– 4.347
Hawaiian	December 29, 1989	4.406	7.778	– 3.373
Pan Am	September 25, 1991	– 0.988	7.481	– 8.469
Texas	March 20, 1992	– 0.677	9.876	– 10.554
Mean				– 3.134
(t-statistic)				(– 3.35)

of nonsurvivors and survivors is – 3.13, which is significantly different from zero at the 0.01 level.

To test whether surviving airlines adapted their governance structures differently from other firms, we extend the fixed effects regression methodology used to generate results reported in Tables 4–6 and 10. We replicate these regressions, replacing the airline dummy variable with two separate dummy variables designed to capture survivorship. The first is a deregulation dummy that is interacted with a dummy variable (SURV) equal to one for Alaska, American, Delta, Southwest, United and USAir, and zero for other airlines, and the second is interacts a deregulation dummy with a dummy variable (NSURV) equal to one if SURV equals zero, and zero elsewhere. The coefficient estimates on these interaction terms enable us to detect differences in the

Table 13
Evolution of governance structure and survivor airlines

Ordinary least squares regressions with fixed effects on measures of corporate governance on a post-deregulation dummy variable, interactions of the dummy variables with group dummy variables (e.g., all airlines, airlines that remain autonomous through 1992, and unregulated firms), and control variables (e.g., real market value of equity or board ownership). The sample consists of 21 airlines and 42 benchmark firms during the period 1971–1992. Firm years are excluded if data is missing. Corporate governance data is taken from proxy statements and equity values from Compustat. *t*-statistics appear in parentheses.

Independent variable	Dependent variables						
	Ownership (% of shares)		Real compensation (in 1982–84 $)			Board structure	
	O&D (1)	Outsiders (2)	Level (3)	Cash (4)	Options (5)	Size (6)	Outsiders (%) (7)
Real market value of equity (β_1)	− 1.59E-8	− 5.87E-9	0.48	0.13	0.34		
	(− 2.78)	(− 1.15)	(10.19)	(7.31)	(8.85)		
Fraction of equity held by board (β_2)						− 1.58	− 0.20
						(− 2.46)	(− 5.56)
Deregulation dummy (γ)	0.01	0.03	− 21,250	25,897	− 46,796	0.45	0.05
	(1.03)	(4.77)	(− 0.35)	(1.09)	(− 0.93)	(2.31)	(4.76)
Interaction of surviving airlines and deregulation (δ)	− 0.04	0.01	253,747	151,959	196,288	− 1.05	− 0.04
	(3.81)	(0.94)	(1.96)	(1.04)	(1.84)	(− 4.01)	(− 2.59)
Interaction of nonsurviving airlines and deregulation (ε)	0.01	0.05	207,479	− 129,202	236,402	− 1.46	− 0.01
	(0.71)	(4.36)	(2.04)	(− 0.74)	(2.81)	(− 4.69)	(− 0.31)
Interaction of unregulated firms and deregulation (ζ)	− 0.01	0.03	308,318	117,902	190,657	− 0.48	0.05
	(− 0.57)	(2.83)	(3.57)	(3.51)	(2.67)	(− 1.94)	(3.75)
p-value on F-tests:							
$\delta = \varepsilon$	0.0003	0.0009	0.7431	0.1390	0.7310	0.2279	0.0800
Sample Size	1,207	1,207	1,206	1,208	1,206	1,211	1,211
Adjusted R^2	0.8716	0.4947	0.5913	0.7401	0.3645	0.9765	0.9434

adaptation of surviving airlines and airlines that ceased to operate as independent carriers.

The results are reported in Table 13. As reported in Column 1, insider holdings of equity decline for surviving airlines during the deregulation period. Nonsurviving airlines show no change in insider holdings for the deregulation period as a whole, though subsample estimates not reported here indicate a significant rise in officer and director holdings during 1979–1985. This increase may reflect the increased stakes taken by top managers in firms struggling to remain autonomous. The statistically significant difference in the concentration of outside blocks (Column 2) between surviving and nonsurviving airlines is also likely to be due to takeover activity.

For the entire 1979–1992 period, compensation policy differs little between surviving and nonsurviving airlines. Cash compensation is estimated to be $280,000 lower for carriers that lose their independence, though the statistical significance of the difference is weak (p-value = 0.1390.) The real value of stock-based pay and the corresponding level of real compensation, though significantly above the trend in pay for regulated firms, are not different across the airline subgroups (Columns 5 and 3, respectively.) However, this result masks a large, statistically significant positive differential between the value of stock option grants, and hence the level of real compensation, awarded to the CEOs of nonsurviving carriers during 1986–1992.

The evidence on board structure suggests that board composition, rather than size, is related to survivorship. Results presented in Column 6 of Table 13 reveal that airlines, both survivors and nonsurvivors, significantly reduced the size of their boards following deregulation. Contrary to the trend toward greater representation of outsiders in the regulated benchmark, surviving airlines decrease the fraction of the board represented by outsiders during deregulation, while nonsurviving carriers show no significant change for the entire deregulation period (Column 7). It is worth noting that this result hides a statistically significant increase of 3.4 percentage points in the fraction of outside representation on the boards of nonsurviving carriers during 1979–1985, followed by a 3.8 percentage point decrease in outside representation in the 1986–1992 period.

6. Conclusions

This paper sheds light on how firms adapt their governance structures to economic shocks by examining the U.S. airline industry before and after deregulation. We find that governance structures generally adapt in ways predicted by static theory, but the changes occur more gradually than one might presume, indicating that it is costly to abruptly change organizational capital. Surviving airlines adapt differently and more quickly than do their nonsurviving counterparts, suggesting that governance structures influence firm performance.

In addition, we document secular trends in governance variables for firms outside the airline industry, including significant increases in block ownership, the real level of CEO pay, especially in the 1986–1992 period, the value of stock option grants for CEOs, and the fraction of board seats held by outside directors.

The paper suggests several avenues for future research. First, the fact that some dimensions of governance change in predictable ways while others, like insider stockholdings or outsider representation on boards, do not, suggests differences in the advantages and disadvantages of alternative governance features. Existing theory provides little guidance in predicting which of several governance features are likely to change in response to a shock, suggesting that more theoretical work is needed on comparative governance features. Second, comparative static predictions generally focus on individual governance features, but little is known about the interaction of governance features, or systems of governance. Third, the cost of changing organizational capital appears to be large, but we know little about the magnitude or determinants of these costs. Greater knowledge of these costs is necessary to understand the dynamics of organizational change. Finally, while we document a relation between firm survival and corporate governance, causality remains an open question. Whether surviving firms maintain their independence because of their success at adapting their governance structure, or because of underlying firm characteristics that lead to endogenously determined compensation policy, along with ownership and board structures, is an important question that is not resolved in this paper.

References

Behrman, B., 1980. Civil aeronautics board. In: Wilson, J.Q. (Ed.), The Politics of Regulation. Basic Books, New York, 75–120.

Caves, R.E., 1962. Air Transportation and its Regulators. Harvard University Press, Cambridge, MA.

Curley, J., 1981. Decontrol of airline shifts pricing from a cost to a competition basis. Wall Street Journal.

Demsetz, H., 1983. The structure of ownership and the theory of the firm. Journal of Law and Economics 26 (1), 375–390.

Demsetz, H., Lehn, K., 1985. The structure of corporate ownership: causes and consequences. Journal of Political Economy 93, 1155–1177.

Gertner, R., Kaplan, S.N., 1996. The value-maximizing board. Unpublished Manuscript. Graduate School of Business Administration, University of Chicago.

Gilson, R.J., 1996. Corporate governance and economic efficiency: When do institutions matter? Washington University Law Quarterly 74, 327–345.

Hermalin, B.E., Weisbach, M.S., 1989. The determinants of board composition. Rand Journal of Economics 19, 95–112.

Hölmstrom, B., 1979. Moral hazard and observability. Bell Journal of Economics 10, 74–91.

Hubbard, R.G., Palia, D., 1995. Executive pay and performance: evidence from the U.S. banking industry. Journal of Financial Economics 38, 105–130.

Jensen, M.C., 1993. Presidential address: The modern industrial revolution, exit, and the failure of internal control systems. Journal of Finance 48, 831–880.

Jensen, M.C., Murphy, K.J., 1990. Performance pay and top-management incentives. Journal of Political Economy 98, 225–264.

Joskow, P., Rose, N., Shepard, A., 1993. Regulatory constraints on CEO Compensation. Brookings Papers on Economic Activity: Microeconomics 1993, 1–58.

Kole, S., Lehn, K., 1997. Workforce integration and the dissipation of firm value in mergers: The case of USAir's acquisition of Piedmont Aviation. Presented at NBER Conference Volume on Mergers and Productivity (January 1997, Islamorada Florida).

Lipton, M., Lorsch, J.W., 1992. A modest proposal for improved corporate governance. Business Lawyer 48, 59–77.

Meyer, J.R., Oster Jr., C.V., 1984. Deregulation and the New Airline Entrepreneurs. MIT Press, Cambridge, MA.

Mitchell, M.L., Mulherin, J.H., 1996. The impact of industry shocks on takeover and restructuring activity. Journal of Financial Economics 41, 193–229.

Silverman, B.S., Nickerson, J.A., Freeman, J., 1997. Profitability, transactional alignment, and organizational mortality in the U.S. trucking industry. Strategic Management Journal 18, 31–52.

Smith Jr., C.W., Watts, R.L., 1992. The investment opportunity set and corporate financing dividend, and compensation policies. Journal of Financial Economics 32, 263–292.

Vietor, R.H.K., 1990. Contrived competition: Airline regulation and deregulation, 1925–88. Business History Review 64, 61–108.

Warner, J.B., Watts, R.L., Wruck, K.H., 1988. Stock prices and top management changes. Journal of Financial Economics 20, 461–492.

Weiner, J., 1994. The Beak of the Finch. Vintage, New York.

Weisbach, M.S., 1988. Outside directors, and CEO turnover. Journal of Financial Economics 20, 431–460.

Weiss, L.A., Wruck, K.H., 1998. Informational problems, conflicts of interest and asset-stripping: Chapter 11's failure in the case of Eastern Airlines. Journal of Financial Economics 48, 55–97.

Yermack, D., 1996. Higher market valuation of companies with a small board of directors. Journal of Financial Economics 40, 185–211.

Zingales, L., 1998. Survival of the fittest or the fattest? Exit and financing in the trucking industry. Journal of Finance 53, 905–938.

Name Index

Denis, D. 452